HILTON HHONORS

go.

see.

Feel the Hamptonality

laugh.

drive.

let us be a part of your journey.

With free hot breakfast, free high-speed internet access and our clean and fresh Hampton bed™ with duvets washed fresh for every guest, Hampton helps to make your trip easier, so you can focus on the more important things. To book AAA rates,* call your AAA agent, visit **hampton.com** or call 1-800-HAMPTON.

AAA **CAA**
Show Your Card & Save

Hampton

Feel the Hamptonality™

Maine, New Hampshire & Vermont

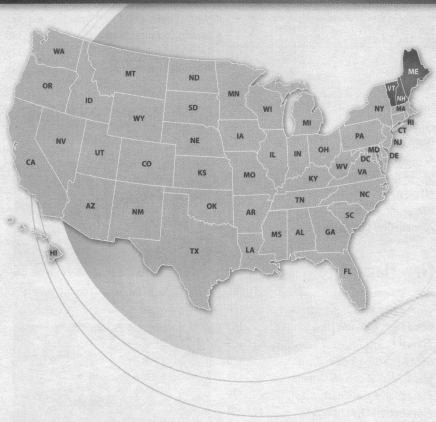

Published by AAA Publishing
1000 AAA Drive, Heathrow, FL 32746-5063
Copyright AAA 2013, All rights reserved

Advertising Rate and Circulation Information: (407) 444-8280

Printed in the USA by Quad/Graphics

This book is printed on paper certified by third-party standards for sustainably managed forestry and production.

Printed on recyclable paper.
Please recycle whenever possible.

Stock #4615

CONTENTS

Attractions, hotels, restaurants and other travel experience information are all grouped under the alphabetical listing of the city in which those experiences are physically located—or the nearest recognized city.

Featured Information

Using Your Guide 5
Just For Members 11
Ⓐ Offices 326
Metric Equivalents Chart 327
Driving Distances Map 328
Border Information 329
Points of Interest Index 333

Maine

Historic Timeline 20
What To Pack 20
Good Facts To Know 21
Annual Events 22
GEM Attraction Index 24
Maps: Atlas Section & Orientation 26
Recreation Areas Chart 36
Alphabetical City Listings 38-163

New Hampshire

Historic Timeline 166
What To Pack 166
Good Facts To Know 167
Annual Events 168
GEM Attraction Index 170
Maps: Atlas Section & Orientation 171
Recreation Areas Chart 175
Alphabetical City Listings 177-254

Vermont

Historic Timeline 258
What To Pack 258
Good Facts To Know 259
Annual Events 260
GEM Attraction Index 262
Maps: Atlas Section & Orientation 263
Recreation Areas Chart 268
Alphabetical City Listings 270-323

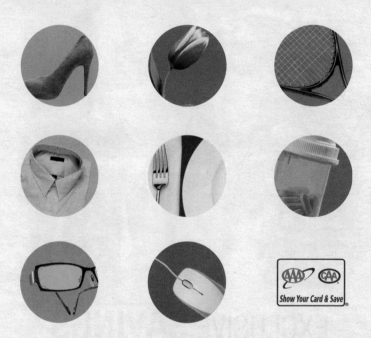

Highlights

Enjoy the trimmer, more colorful, reorganized
TourBook® format introduced to make the
series richer and easier to use.

Plus, find even more of the visuals,
expert recommendations and special
extras you value most for reliable travel
planning and decision making.

Colorful visuals
- More attraction photos
- *New!* Destination area maps
  for seven national parks

Travel recommendations
- More *Must Do: AAA Editor's
  Picks* and *1-Day Itineraries*
- *New! Top Picks for Kids*
  for 19 destination cities

Special extras
- Mass transit information for six
  metropolitan areas
- *New!* Electric vehicle charging
  station locations

See for yourself. Travel better
with AAA TourBook® guides.

A to Z City Listings

Cities and places are listed alphabetically within each state or province. Attractions, hotels and restaurants are listed once — under the city in which they are physically located.

Cities that are considered part of a larger destination city or area have an expanded city header. The header identifies the larger region and cross-references pages that contain shared trip planning resources:

- Destination map – outline map of the cities that comprise a destination city or area
- Attraction spotting map – regional street map marked with attraction locations
- Hotel/restaurant spotting map and index – regional street map numbered with hotel and restaurant locations identified in an accompanying index

Cities that are not considered part of a larger destination city or area but have a significant number of listings may have these resources within the individual city section:

- Attraction spotting map
- Hotel/restaurant spotting map and index

About Listed Establishments

AAA/CAA Approved attractions, hotels and restaurants are listed on the basis of merit alone after careful evaluation and approval by full-time, professionally trained AAA/CAA inspectors. An establishment's decision to advertise in the TourBook guide has no bearing on its evaluation or rating; nor does inclusion of advertising imply AAA endorsement of products and services.

Information in this guide was believed accurate at the time of publication. However, since changes inevitably occur between annual editions, please contact your AAA travel professional or visit AAA.com to confirm prices and schedules.

Location Abbreviations

Directions are from the center of town unless otherwise specified, using these highway abbreviations:

Bus. Rte.=business route
CR=county road
FM=farm to market

FR=forest road
Hwy.=Canadian highway
I=interstate highway
LR=legislative route
R.R.=rural route
SR/PR=state or provincial route
US=federal highway

Atlas Section

The Atlas Section provides navigable road maps from the AAA Road Atlas series. The overview map displays the entire coverage area. Corresponding, numbered detail maps offer a closer view for route planning and navigation.

Mobile Tags

Look for Microsoft Tags or QR codes throughout the TourBook guide and scan them with your smartphone to access special online offers, menus, videos and more.

To scan Microsoft Tags or QR codes:

- Download AAA's recommended scanning app to your smartphone at http://gettag.mobi.
- Start scanning Tags or QR codes.
- Link to featured content.

Some advertisers may use bar codes other than Microsoft Tags or QR codes. In those cases, please note any accompanying text that indicates where to download the required reader.

Attraction Listings

 ATTRACTION NAME, 3 mi. n. off SR 20A (Main Ave.), consists of 250 acres with Olmsted-designed gardens, a 205-foot marble and coquina bell tower and a Mediterranean-style mansion. One of the state's oldest attractions, the tower and gardens were dedicated to the American people in 1929 by President Calvin Coolidge on behalf of their founder, a Dutch immigrant.

Other features include daily concerts from the 60-bell carillon, a nature observatory and Nature Preserve Trail. The visitor center presents art exhibits, an orientation film and exhibits about the family legacy, the carillon and endangered plants and animals found on the property.

Hours: Gardens daily 8-6. Last admission 1 hour before closing. Visitor center daily 9-5. Estate tours are given at noon and 2. Carillon concerts are given at 1 and 3. Phone ahead to confirm schedule. **Cost:** $10; $3 (ages 5-12). Gardens and estate $16; $8 (ages 5-12). **Phone:** (555) 555-5555.
Dupont Circle, 13

AAA/CAA inspectors may designate an attraction of exceptional interest and quality as a AAA GEM — a *Great Experience for Members®*. See GEM Attraction Index (listed on CONTENTS page) for complete list of locations.

Adventure Travel

Activities such as air tours, hiking, skiing and white-water rafting are listed to provide member information and do not imply AAA/CAA endorsement. For your safety, be aware of inherent risks and adhere to all safety instructions.

Cost

Prices are quoted without sales tax in the local currency (U.S. or Canadian dollars). Children under the lowest age specified are admitted free when accompanied by an adult. Most establishments accept credit cards, but a small number require cash, so please call ahead to verify.

Icons

SAVE Show Your Card & Save® member discount

Electric vehicle charging station on premises. Station locations are provided by Department of Energy.

Camping facilities

Food on premises

Recreational activities

Pets on leash allowed

Picnicking allowed

In select cities only:

Mass transit station within 1 mile. Icon is followed by station name and AAA/CAA designated station number within listing.

Information-Only Attraction Listings

Bulleted listings, which include the following categories, are listed for informational purposes as a service to members:

- **Gambling establishments** (even if located in a AAA/CAA Approved hotel)
- **Guided food tours**
- **Participatory recreational activities** (those requiring physical exertion or special skills)
- **Wineries that offer tours and tastings**

Hotel and Restaurant Listings

1 Diamond Rating – AAA/CAA Approved hotels and restaurants are assigned a rating of one to five Diamonds. Red Diamonds distinguish establishments that participate in the AAA/CAA logo licensing program. For details, see p. 11 or AAA.com/Diamonds.

fyi indicates hotels and restaurants that are not AAA/CAA Approved and Diamond Rated but are listed to provide additional choices for members:

- **Hotels** may be unrated if they are: too new to rate, under construction, under major renovation, not evaluated, do not meet all AAA requirements. Hotels that do not meet all AAA requirements may be included if they offer member value or are the only option; details are noted in the listing.
- **Restaurants** may be unrated if they have not yet been evaluated by AAA.

2 Classification or Cuisine Type – Noted after the Diamond Rating.

- **Hotel Classifications** indicate the style of operation, overall concept and service level. Subclassifications may also be added. (See p. 12 list.)
- **Restaurant Cuisine Types** identify the food concept from more than 100 categories. If applicable, a classification may also be added. (See p. 13 list.)

3 Dollar Amounts – Quoted without sales tax in the local currency (U.S. or Canadian dollars), rounded up to the nearest dollar. Most establishments accept credit cards, but a small number require cash, so please call ahead to verify.

- **Hotel Rates** indicate the publicly available two-person rate or rate range for a standard room, applicable all year.
- **Restaurant Prices** represent the minimum and maximum entrée cost per person. Exceptions may include one-of-a-kind or special market priced items.

4 Spotting Symbol – Ovals containing numbers correspond with numbered location markings on hotel and restaurant spotting maps.

5 Parking – Unless otherwise noted, parking is free, on-site self parking.

6 Hotel Value Nationwide – Blue boxes highlight member benefits available at all AAA/CAA Approved locations across a hotel chain. (See Just For Members section for details.)

7 Hotel Unit Limited Availability – Unit types, amenities and room features preceded by "some" are available on a limited basis, potentially as few as one.

8 Hotel Terms – Cancellation and minimum stay policies are listed. Unless otherwise noted, most properties offer a full deposit refund with cancellations received at least 48 hours before standard check-in. Properties that require advance payment may not refund the difference for early departures. "Resort fee" indicates a charge may apply above and beyond the quoted room rate.

9 Hotel Check-in/Check-out – Unless otherwise noted, check-in is after 3 p.m. and check-out is before 10 a.m.

10 Restaurant Dress Code – Unless otherwise noted, dress is casual or dressy casual.

11 Restaurant Menu – Where indicated, menus may be viewed in a secure online environment at AAA.com or, if a mobile tag is provided, via the restaurant's website.

12 Hotel Icons – May be preceded by CALL, FEE and/or SOME UNITS.

Member Information:

SAVE Rate guarantee: discounted standard room rate or lowest public rate available at time of booking for dates of stay.

ECO Eco-certified by government or private organization. Visit AAA.com/eco for details.

⬚ Electric vehicle charging station on premises. Station locations are provided by Department of Energy.

⊠ Smoke-free premises

In select cities only:

🚇 Mass transit station within 1 mile. Icon is followed by station name and AAA/CAA designated station number within listing.

Services:

📶 Wireless Internet service on premises

✈ Airport transportation

🐾 Pets allowed (Call property for restrictions and fees.)

HOTEL LISTING

HOTEL NAME   (555)555-5555 50   4

⬥⬥⬥⬥⬥
Hotel
$109-$199

LOGO **AAA Benefit:** Members save a minimum 5% off the best available rate.   6

Address: 300 Main St 55555 **Location:** I-275 exit 31 southbound; exit 30 northbound. 1.6 mi w on SR 688 (Oak Rd). Dupont Circle, 13. **Facility:** 149 units, some efficiencies. 3 stories, interior corridors. **Parking:** on-site (fee). **Terms:** check-in 4 pm, cancellation fee imposed, resort fee. **Amenities:** video games. **Pool(s):** heated outdoor. **Activities:** whirlpool, exercise room. **Guest Services:** valet and coin laundry. **Free Special Amenities:** newspaper and expanded continental breakfast.

1 2 3 5 9 12 7 8

RESTAURANT LISTING

RESTAURANT NAME   555/555-5555

⬥⬥⬥⬥⬥
Continental
Steak Seafood
Fine Dining
$15-$35

AAA Inspector Notes: *Historic.* A romantic aura punctuates the modern and casual dining room, which is accented with floral arrangements and dramatic, freshly cut branches. The seasonal menu centers on Tuscan-American cuisine. The pastry chef's decadent creations are popular. Semi-formal attire. **Bar:** full bar. **Address:** 26 N Main St 55555 **Location:** SR A1A southbound, 2.7 mi s of jct SR 520. Dupont Circle, 13. *Menu on AAA.com* ECO ⚡ L D

1 2 3 11 10 13

Restaurant on premises

Restaurant off premises

Room service for 2 or more meals

Full bar

Child care

BIZ Business services

Accessible features (Call property for available services and amenities.)

Activities:

Full-service casino

Pool

Health club on premises

Health club off premises

In-Room Amenities:

Pay movies

Refrigerator

Microwave

Coffee maker

No air conditioning

No TV

No telephones

13 Restaurant Icons

SAVE Show Your Card & Save® member discount

ECO Eco-certified by government or private organization. Visit AAA.com/eco for details.

Electric vehicle charging station on premises. Station locations are provided by Department of Energy.

No air conditioning

Accessible features (Call property for available services and amenities.)

Designated smoking section

B Breakfast

L Lunch

D Dinner

24 Open 24 hours

LATE Open after 11 p.m.

In select cities only:

Mass transit station within 1 mile. Icon is followed by station name and AAA/CAA designated station number within listing.

Just For Members

Understanding the Diamond Ratings

Hotel and restaurant evaluations are unscheduled to ensure our professionally trained inspectors encounter the same experience members do.

- When an establishment is Diamond Rated, it means members can expect a good fit with their needs. The inspector assigns a rating that indicates the type of experience to expect.

- While establishments at high levels must offer increasingly complex personalized services, establishments at every level are subject to the same basic requirements for cleanliness, comfort and hospitality. Learn more at AAA.com/Diamonds.

Hotels

Budget-oriented, offering basic comfort and hospitality.

Affordable, with modestly enhanced facilities, décor and amenities.

Distinguished, multi-faceted with enhanced physical attributes, amenities and guest comforts.

Refined, stylish with upscale physical attributes, extensive amenities and high degree of hospitality, service and attention to detail.

Ultimate luxury, sophistication and comfort with extraordinary physical attributes, meticulous personalized service, extensive amenities and impeccable standards of excellence.

What's the difference?

Red Diamonds mark establishments that participate in the AAA/CAA logo licensing program for increased visibility to members.

Black Diamonds identify all other AAA/CAA Approved and Diamond Rated establishments.

Restaurants

Simple, familiar specialty food at an economical price. Often self-service, basic surroundings.

Familiar, family-oriented experience. Home-style foods and family favorites, often cooked to order, modestly enhanced and reasonably priced. Relaxed service, casual surroundings.

Fine dining, often adult-oriented. Latest cooking trends and/or traditional cuisine, expanded beverage offerings. Professional service staff and comfortable, well-coordinated ambience.

Distinctive fine-dining, typically expensive. Highly creative chefs, imaginative presentations and fresh, top-quality ingredients. Proficient service staff, upscale surroundings. Wine steward may offer menu-specific knowledge.

Luxurious and consistently world-class. Highly acclaimed chefs, artistic and imaginative menu selections using the finest ingredients. Maitre d' and unobtrusive, expert service staff.

Hotel Classifications

Quality and comfort are usually consistent across each Diamond Rating level, but décor, facilities and service levels vary by classification.

1884 Paxton House Inn
Thomasville, GA

Bed & Breakfast – Typically small-scale, emphasizing personal touches. Individually decorated units may not include televisions, telephones or private bathrooms. Usually a common room and continental or full, hot breakfast.

Barkwells
Mills River, NC

Cabin – Vacation-oriented, typically small-scale, free-standing units with simple construction and basic décor. Often in wooded, rural or waterfront location. Cleaning supplies, utensils and bath linens provided. Check-in may be off site.

Camelot by the Sea
Myrtle Beach, SC

Condominium – Vacation-oriented, commonly for extended stays. Routinely rented through a management company. Generally one or more bedrooms, living room, full kitchen and eating area. Studio units combine sleeping and living areas. Cleaning supplies, utensils and linens provided. Check-in may be off site.

The Dunes on the Waterfront
Ogunquit, ME

Cottage – Vacation-oriented, typically small-scale, freestanding units with homey design and décor. Often in wooded, rural or waterfront location. Cleaning supplies, utensils and linens provided. Check-in may be off site.

The Lodge at Moosehead
Lake, Greenville, ME

Country Inn – Similar to bed and breakfasts but larger scale with spacious public areas and dining facility that serves, at a minimum, breakfast and dinner.

The Grand America Hotel
Salt Lake City, UT

Hotel – Commonly multistory with interior room entrances. Unit styles vary. Public areas determined by overall theme, location and service level, but may include restaurant, shops, fitness center, spa, business center and meeting rooms.

Best Western Plus Sea Island
Inn, Beaufort, SC

Motel – Commonly one- or two-story with exterior room entrances and drive-up parking. Typically one bedroom with bathroom. Limited public areas and facilities.

Lost Valley Ranch
Deckers, CO

Ranch – Typically a working ranch with rustic, Western theme, equestrian activities and various unit styles.

Indian Creek-Alexander
Holiday Homes
Kissimmee, FL

Vacation Rental House – Commonly for extended stays. Typically large scale, freestanding and of varying design. Routinely rented through a management company. Often two or more bedrooms, living room, full kitchen, dining room and multiple bathrooms. Cleaning supplies, utensils and linens supplied. Check-in may be off site.

Hotel Subclassifications

These additional descriptives may be added to the classification for more information:

- **Boutique** – Often thematic and informal, highly personalized experience. May have fashionable, luxurious or quirky style.
- **Casino** – (Identified by listing icon) Extensive gambling facilities such as blackjack, craps, keno and slot machines.
- **Classic** – Landmark property, older than 50 years, renowned style and ambience.
- **Contemporary** – Design and theme reflective of current mainstream tastes and style.
- **Extended Stay** – Predominantly long-term units with full-service kitchens.
- **Historic** – Typically 75 years or older with historic architecture, design, furnishings, public record or acclaim and at least one of the following: maintains integrity of the historical nature, listed on the National Register of Historic Places, designated a National Historic Landmark or located in a National Register Historic District.
- **Resort** – Recreation-oriented, geared to a specific destination experience. Typically offer travel packages, meal plans, themed entertainment and social and recreational programs. Extensive recreational facilities may include spa treatments, golf, tennis,

skiing, fishing or water sports. Larger resorts may offer a variety of unit types.

- **Retro** – Contemporary design and theme that reinterpret styles of a bygone era.
- **Vacation Rental** – Typically a house, condo, cottage or cabin offering space, value and conveniences such as full kitchens and washers/dryers. Located in a resort or popular destination area near major points of interest. May require reservations and off-site check-in. Limited housekeeping services.
- **Vintage** – Design and theme reflective of a bygone era.

Restaurant Classifications

If applicable, in addition to the cuisine type noted under the Diamond Rating, restaurant listings may also include one or both classifications:

- **Classic** – Renowned and landmark operation in business for 25 plus years; unique style and ambience.
- **Historic** – Meets one of the following: Listed on National Register of Historic Places, designated a National Historic Landmark or located in a National Register Historic District.

Service Animals

Under the Americans with Disabilities Act (ADA), U.S. businesses that serve the public must allow people with disabilities to bring their service animals into all areas of the facility where customers are normally allowed to go.

Businesses may ask if an animal is a service animal and what tasks the animal has been trained to perform. Businesses may not ask about the person's disability, require special identification for the animal or request removal of the animal from the premises except in limited cases that require alternate assistance. Businesses may not charge extra fees for service animals, including standard pet fees, but may charge for damage caused by service animals if guests are normally charged for damage they cause.

Call the U.S. Department of Justice ADA Information Line: (800) 514-0301 or TTY (800) 514-0383, or visit ada.gov. Regulations may differ in Canada.

AAA/CAA Approved Hotels

For members, AAA/CAA Approved means quality assured.

- Only properties that meet basic requirements for cleanliness, comfort and hospitality pass inspection.
- Approved hotels receive a Diamond Rating that tells members the type of experience to expect.

Guest Safety

Inspectors view a sampling of rooms during evaluations and, therefore, AAA/CAA cannot guarantee the presence of working locks and operational fire safety equipment in every guest unit.

Member Rates

AAA/CAA members can generally expect to pay no more than the maximum TourBook listed rate for a standard room. Member discounts apply to rates quoted within the rate range and are applicable at the time of booking. Listed rates are usually based on last standard room availability. Within the range, rates may vary by season and room type. Obtain current AAA/CAA member rates and make reservations at AAA.com.

Exceptions

- Rates for properties operating as concessionaires for the U.S. National Park Service are not guaranteed due to governing regulations.
- Special advertised rates and short-term promotional rates below the rate range are not subject to additional member discounts.
- During special events, hotels may temporarily increase room rates, not recognize discounts or modify pricing policies. Special events may include Mardi Gras, the Kentucky Derby (including pre-Derby events), college football games, holidays, holiday periods and state fairs. Although some special events are listed in the TourBook guides and on AAA.com, it's always wise to check in advance with AAA travel professionals for specific dates.

If you are charged more than the maximum TourBook listed rate, question the additional charge. If an exception is not in effect and management refuses to adhere to the published rate, pay for the room and contact AAA/CAA. The amount paid above the stated maximum will be refunded if our investigation indicates an unjustified charge.

Reservations and Cancellations

When making your reservation, identify yourself as a AAA/CAA member and request written confirmation of your room type, rate, dates of stay, and cancellation and refund policies. At registration, show your membership card.

To cancel, contact the hotel or your AAA/CAA club office, depending on how you booked your reservation. Request a cancellation number or proof of cancellation.

If your room is not as specified and you have written confirmation of your reservation for a specific room type, you should be given the option of choosing a different room or receiving a refund. If management refuses to issue a refund, contact AAA/CAA.

Contacting AAA/CAA About Approved Properties

If your visit to a AAA/CAA Approved attraction, hotel or restaurant doesn't meet your expectations, please tell us about it — *during your visit or within 30 days*. Be sure to save your receipts and other documentation for reference.

Use the easy online form at AAA.com/TourBookComments to send us the details.

Alternatively, you can email your comments to: memberrelations@national.aaa.com or submit them via postal mail to: AAA Member Comments, 1000 AAA Dr., Box 61, Heathrow, FL 32746.

AAA/CAA Preferred Hotels

All AAA/CAA Approved hotels are committed to providing quality, value and member service. In addition, those designated as AAA/CAA Preferred Hotels also offer these extra values at Approved locations nationwide. Valid AAA/CAA membership required.

- **Best AAA/CAA member rates for your dates of stay.**
- **Seasonal promotions and special member offers.** Visit AAA.com to view current offers.
- **Member benefit.** Look for the blue boxes in the TourBook listings to find values offered at AAA/CAA Approved locations nationwide. Chains and offers valid at time of publication may change without notice.

- **Total satisfaction guarantee.** If you book your stay with AAA/CAA Travel and your stay fails to meet your expectations, you can apply for a full refund. Bring the complaint to the hotel's attention during the stay and request resolution; if the complaint is not resolved by the hotel, ask your AAA/CAA travel agent to request resolution through the AAA/CAA Assured Stay program.

Show Your Card & Save

Preferred Hotels

Total Satisfaction Guarantee

Best Western, Best Western Plus and Best Western Premier

Conrad Hotels & Resorts, DoubleTree by Hilton, Embassy Suites, Hampton Inns & Suites, Hilton Hotels & Resorts, Hilton Garden Inns, Hilton Grand Vacations, Home2 Suites, Homewood Suites, and Waldorf Astoria

ANdAZ, Grand Hyatt, Hyatt Hotels & Resorts, Hyatt House, Hyatt Place, Hyatt Regency and Park Hyatt

Autograph Collection, Courtyard, EDITION, Fairfield Inn & Suites, JW Marriott, Marriott Hotels & Resorts, Renaissance Hotels, Residence Inn, The Ritz-Carlton, SpringHill Suites and TownePlace Suites

starwood
Hotels and Resorts

Aloft, Element, Four Points, Le Meridien, Sheraton, St. Regis Hotels & Resorts, The Luxury Collection, Westin and W Hotels

Show Your Card & Save® Member Discounts

Visit AAA.com/Discounts to find local Show Your Card & Save discounts. Your AAA/CAA club may offer even greater discounts on theme park tickets. Amtrak, Gray Line and theme park discounts may be used for up to six tickets; restaurant savings may be used for up to six patrons. Other restrictions may apply. All offers subject to change. For complete restrictions visit your AAA office or AAA.com/restrictions.

ATTRACTIONS

SeaWorld, Busch Gardens, Sesame Place

- Save on admission at the gate, participating AAA/CAA offices or AAA.com/SeaWorld.
- Save 10% on up-close dining; visit Guest Relations for details.

Six Flags

- Save on admission at the gate, participating AAA/CAA offices or AAA.com/SixFlags.
- Save 10% on merchandise of $15 or more at in-park stores.

Universal Orlando Resort and Universal Studios Hollywood

- Save on admission at the gate, participating AAA/CAA offices or AAA.com/Universal.
- Save at select food and merchandise venues in-park and at Universal CityWalk®.

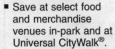

The Entertainment Capital of L.A.®

DINING & SHOPPING

Hard Rock Cafe

- Save 10% on food, nonalcoholic beverages and merchandise at all U.S., Canadian and select international locations.

Landry's Seafood House, The Crab House, Chart House, Oceanaire, Saltgrass Steak House, Muer Seafood Restaurants and Aquarium Restaurants

- Save 10% on food and nonalcoholic beverages at all of the above restaurants.
- Save 10% on merchandise at Aquarium and Downtown Aquarium restaurants.
- Location information: AAA.com/Discounts.

Tanger Outlet Centers

- Save up to 20% on total purchase at select merchants with FREE coupon booklet available with registration at AAA/CAA customer service desk.
- Location information: tangeroutlet.com.

TRANSPORTATION & TOURS

Amtrak

- Save 10% on rail fare booked at least 3 days in advance of travel date at AAA.com/Amtrak.

Gray Line

- Save 10% on sightseeing tours of 1 day or less worldwide at AAA.com/GrayLine.

Hertz

- Save on daily, weekend, weekly and monthly rentals at AAA.com/hertz or 1-800-654-3080.

Portland Head Light, Cape Elizabeth

Maine

Historic Timeline 20
What To Pack 20
Good Facts To Know 21
Annual Events 22
GEM Attraction Index 24
Maps: Atlas Section & Orientation 26
Recreation Areas Chart 36
Alphabetical City Listings 38

Maine is a love affair between earth and water. Here, the two meet in an embrace to create some of the most beautiful coastal scenery in America. And like any relationship, the encounter between unlike partners can be stormy; whipped by marine winds and pounded by white-capped breakers, the rugged shore is a sight to behold.

No visit to Maine would be complete without an excursion to the crown jewel of its scenic coast: Acadia National Park. Consisting mostly of Mount Desert Island, Acadia is the second most visited national park in the country. The reason? An array of stunning landscapes range from sandy beaches—a rare sight along Maine's rocky northern coast—to Cadillac Mountain, the highest point on the eastern coastline of North America.

From a distance, the rounded granite humps of Acadia's mountains seem to materialize out of the ocean. Two of the island's

The picturesque village of Bar Harbor

top draws: Thunder Hole, a cleft in the Otter Cliffs that produces a rumbling boom when the surf crashes through it, and Bar Harbor, a resort village of fine mansions, quaint inns and fishing wharves.

Think of Maine and you'll likely picture a lighthouse looming over a rock-strewn, wave-washed shore. There's a reason: More than 60 towers dot the coast here, including Pemaquid Point Lighthouse, one of the state's most picturesque. During storms, raging surf often engulfs the lighthouse's base, which is 79 feet above water. In Portland's Fort Williams Park stands the Portland Head Light, one of the nation's most historic; it was constructed in 1791 under the authorization of George Washington.

More than 90 percent of Maine's land area is forested, hence its official nickname: The "Pine Tree State." Vast areas of virtually uninhabited woodland offer plenty of room for vacationers to get away from it all. And there's no better time to make your escape than during Maine's fall foliage season, when the hills catch fire with autumn hues.

The Appalachian Trail is always a good bet for gorgeous alpine scenery; the footpath follows the crest of the Appalachian Mountains from Mount Springer in Georgia to the foot of Mount Katahdin. A huge granite monolith rising 5,268 feet, this peak—Maine's highest—is just a stone's throw away from Moosehead Lake, an outdoor recreation magnet attracting campers, boaters and water skiers.

Authors and Artists

For more than a century artists of all kinds

have sought refuge and inspiration along the state's craggy shores and wooded hillsides.

One of the first to do so was poet Henry Wadsworth Longfellow, who referred to his childhood home of Portland as "the beautiful town that is seated by the sea." To explore the town, stop by the brick 1786 Longfellow House, where the poet lived as a boy; to experience the sea, hop aboard one of the tour boats that cruise into Casco Bay among the picturesque Calendar Islands.

Maine has recharged the creative batteries of other authors as well. Harriet Beecher Stowe penned Uncle Tom's Cabin while living in Brunswick. Edna St. Vincent Millay was born in Rockland and began her career in Camden, where she is honored by a statue at the harbor's head. And various state locations have served as backdrops in the horror novels of Bangor resident Stephen King.

The dramatic, wind-swept coastline and hardy Down East fishermen kept painter Winslow Homer busy for many years of his career, while the town of Cushing inspired several of Andrew Wyeth's paintings.

Recreation

Warm weather brings a migration of visitors to the powder-soft sand of southern Maine's shoreline. Despite the summer crowds, there still are some quiet beaches where you can enjoy the rush of water between your toes. But getting wet isn't necessary to enjoy the water; windjammer cruises in Penobscot Bay pass by historic lighthouses and nature preserves filled with dolphins, seals and bald eagles.

Swimmers will find the water somewhat warm July through August. Ogunquit, a historic seaside village, was named after the Abenaki Indian word for "the beautiful place by the sea." Its beach is a wide sandbar between the Ogunquit River and the Atlantic.

Old Orchard Beach, with its amusement park, pier and arcades, is a center for summer fun. As a result, the beach around the pier can be a bit crowded late June through Labor Day. Try heading north up the shore if you need room for sand castles or sunning.

Other water adventures lead you inland. The Forks—where two churning rivers meet to form the Kennebec—offers a 12-mile rafting run through a deep, tree-lined gorge. High water combines with few obstacles, creating raging foam and class IV drops. The rafting season starts with the spring run-off and continues through October.

Acadia National Park, Maine's premier outdoor destination, is a breathtaking combination of cobblestone beaches and glacier-carved mountains. More than 115 miles of hiking trails range from short beach walks to the steep Precipice Trail. Forty-five miles of broken-stone carriage roads are populated with hikers and cyclists in summer; they are groomed for cross-country skiers and snowshoers soon after the first snowfall.

Nearly all of Acadia is contained on Mount Desert Island. Park Loop Road, which passes jagged bluffs, glassy lakes and Cadillac Mountain, is wide enough to offer a safe, scenic route for cyclists. In summer the road is full, but you'll have the island practically to yourself during the spring and fall.

Baxter State Park in north-central Maine is the northern terminus of the Appalachian Trail. Maine's highest peak, Mount Katahdin, is the main attraction here.

Downhill skiing takes on a new twist at Camden Snow Bowl. There's nowhere else in the East where you can sail down slopes while enjoying spectacular views of the Atlantic Ocean. The Snow Bowl also has Maine's only public toboggan chute. Other major ski areas include Sunday River, renowned for its snowmaking ability, and Sugarloaf/USA.

Longfellow Square, Portland

Historic Timeline

1604	Samuel de Champlain sights Mount Desert Island, now the location of Acadia National Park.
1628	A trading post is begun by the Plymouth Colony at the present-day site of Augusta.
1775	The first naval battle of the Revolutionary War is fought in Machias Bay.
1820	Maine enters the Union as a free state as part of the Missouri Compromise.
1827	Augusta is named state capital.
1842	Maine's northeastern boundary with New Brunswick is finally settled by the Webster-Ashburton Treaty.
1868	The University of Maine opens with 12 students and two teachers.
1947	The first Maine Lobster Fest is held in Rockland, known as the "Lobster Capital of the World."
1962	The main ground station for the nation's first communications satellite is installed in Andover.
1968	Maine native Edmund Muskie is the Democratic nominee for vice president of the United States.
1997	Senator William Cohen is chosen by President Clinton to be Secretary of Defense.

What To Pack

Temperature Averages Maximum/Minimum	JANUARY	FEBRUARY	MARCH	APRIL	MAY	JUNE	JULY	AUGUST	SEPTEMBER	OCTOBER	NOVEMBER	DECEMBER
Augusta	28/10	32/14	41/24	53/34	66/45	75/54	80/60	79/58	70/50	58/39	46/30	34/17
Bangor	28/8	31/12	40/22	53/33	65/44	74/53	80/59	78/57	69/49	57/38	45/29	33/16
Bar Harbor	32/10	34/14	42/22	53/32	65/42	74/51	80/57	78/56	69/48	58/38	47/29	37/17
Caribou	19/0	23/3	34/15	47/29	63/41	72/50	76/55	74/53	64/44	51/34	37/24	25/8
Greenville	21/-2	25/-1	34/11	46/26	61/37	70/48	75/54	73/51	64/43	52/33	39/23	26/7
Portland	31/12	34/16	42/25	53/35	63/44	73/53	79/59	77/57	69/49	58/37	47/30	36/19

From the records of The Weather Channel Interactive, Inc.

Good Facts To Know

ABOUT THE STATE

POPULATION: 1,328,361.

AREA: 33,215 square miles; ranks 39th.

CAPITAL: Augusta.

HIGHEST POINT: 5,268 ft., Mount Katahdin.

LOWEST POINT: Sea level, Atlantic Ocean.

TIME ZONE(S): Eastern. DST.

GAMBLING

MINIMUM AGE FOR GAMBLING: 21.

REGULATIONS

TEEN DRIVING LAWS: No passengers other than family members are permitted for 270 days after a driver's license is obtained unless supervised by a licensed driver with 2 consecutive years of full licensure. Driving is not permitted midnight-5 a.m. The minimum age for an unrestricted driver's license is 16 years and 9 months. For more information about Maine driver's license regulations phone (207) 624-9000.

SEAT BELT/CHILD RESTRAINT LAWS: Seat belts are required for driver and all passengers ages 18 and over. Children ages 8-18 and at least 57 inches tall are required to use a seat belt. Booster seats are required for children under age 8 and weighing 40-80 pounds; child safety seats are required for those under 40 pounds. Children under age 12 and less than 100 pounds are required to be in the rear seat, if available.

CELL PHONE RESTRICTIONS: Text messaging is prohibited for all drivers. Learner's permit holders, intermediate license holders and persons under 18 are banned from using cell phones while driving. State law also prohibits distracted driving, defined as any activity unrelated to the actual operation of a motor vehicle and interfering with the vehicle's safe operation.

HELMETS FOR MOTORCYCLISTS: Required for drivers under 18, drivers with a learner's permit, drivers in their first year of licensure, and all passengers if the driver is required to wear one.

RADAR DETECTORS: Permitted.

MOVE OVER LAW: Driver is required to slow down and vacate the lane nearest stopped police, fire and rescue vehicles using audible or flashing signals. Law also requires driver to move over for tow truck drivers assisting motorists.

FIREARMS LAWS: Vary by state and/or county. Contact Maine State Police Gaming and Weapons Unit, State House Station #164, Augusta, ME 04333; phone (207) 624-7210.

HOLIDAYS

HOLIDAYS: Jan. 1 ▪ Martin Luther King Jr. Day, Jan. (3rd Mon.) ▪ Washington's Birthday/Presidents Day, Feb. (3rd Mon.) ▪ Patriot's Day, Apr. (3rd Mon.) ▪ Memorial Day, May (4th Mon.) ▪ July 4 ▪ Labor Day, Sept. (1st Mon.) ▪ Columbus Day, Oct. (2nd Mon.) ▪ Veterans Day, Nov. 11 ▪ Thanksgiving, Nov. (4th Thurs.) ▪ Christmas, Dec. 25.

MONEY

TAXES: Maine's general sales tax is 5 percent. There is a 7 percent tax for lodging and prepared food and a 10 percent tax for short-term automobile rentals.

VISITOR INFORMATION

INFORMATION CENTERS: State welcome centers are at 499 US 1 in Kittery, (207) 439-1319 ▪ at I-295 exit 17 and 1100 US 1 in Yarmouth, (207) 846-0833 ▪ at 97 Main St. in Fryeburg, (207) 935-3639 ▪ at 39 Union St., Suite B in Calais, (207) 454-2211 ▪ in Hampden North at Milepost 175 on I-95N, (207) 862-6628 ▪ in Hampden South at Milepost 179 on I-95S, (207) 862-6638 ▪ and at 28 Ludlow Rd. in Houlton, (207) 532-6346. The Hampden North, Hampden South, Calais, Kittery, Yarmouth and Houlton offices are open daily 8-6, Memorial Day-Columbus Day, and daily 9-5, rest of year. The Fryeburg office is open Wed.-Mon. 8-6, mid-July through Labor Day, and Wed.-Mon. 9-5, rest of year. The Kittery office is closed Thanksgiving and Christmas, and the Hampden offices are closed Jan. 1, Easter, Thanksgiving and Christmas.

FURTHER INFORMATION FOR VISITORS:
Maine Office of Tourism
59 State House Station
Augusta, ME 04333-0059
(888) 624-6345
Maine Tourism Association
327 Water St.
Hallowell, ME 04347
(207) 623-0363
(800) 767-8709

FISHING AND HUNTING REGULATIONS:
Department of Inland Fisheries and Wildlife
41 State House Station
Augusta, ME 04333-0041
(207) 287-8000

Maine Annual Events

Please call ahead to confirm event details.

JANUARY

- Maine Lakes Mushers' Bowl and Winter Carnival
  Bridgton
  207-647-3472
- Camden Winterfest
  Camden
  207-236-9656
- Snodeo / Rangeley
  207-864-7336

FEBRUARY

- Winter Carnival
  Old Orchard Beach
  207-281-2114
- MooseStompers Weekend
  Houlton
  207-532-6593, ext. 11
- U.S. National Toboggan
  Championships / Camden
  207-236-3438

MARCH

- Bath Blarney Days / Bath
  207-442-7291
- Can-Am Crown Dog Sled
  Race / Fort Kent
  207-834-5626
- Portland Flower Show
  Portland
  207-775-4403

APRIL

- Patriots Day Weekend
  Celebration / Ogunquit
  207-646-2939
- Wabanaki Arts Festival
  Brunswick
  207-725-3375
- Fishermen's Festival
  Boothbay Harbor
  207-633-2353

MAY

- Owls Head Spring Antique
  Auto and Aeroplane Show
  Owls Head
  207-594-4418
- Moose Mainea / Greenville
  207-695-2702
- May Day Festival
  Kennebunk
  207-967-0857

JUNE

- The Whatever Family
  Festival / Augusta
  207-623-4559
- Windjammer Days
  Boothbay Harbor
  207-633-2353
- Greek Heritage Festival
  Portland
  207-774-0281

JULY

- Bath Heritage Days / Bath
  207-442-7291
- Yarmouth Clam Festival
  Yarmouth
  207-846-3984
- Old Home Week 4th of July
  Celebration / Eastport
  207-853-2930

AUGUST

- American Folk Festival
  Bangor
  207-992-2630
- Skowhegan State Fair
  Skowhegan
  207-474-2947
- Maine Lobster Festival
  Rockland
  207-596-0376

SEPTEMBER

- Harvest Fest and Chowdah
  Cook-Off / Bethel
  207-824-2282
- Eastport Salmon Festival
  Eastport
  207-853-4644
- Capriccio / Ogunquit
  207-646-6170

OCTOBER

- North American Wife
  Carrying Championship
  Newry
  207-824-3000
- York Harvestfest and
  Kidsfest / York
  207-363-4422
- Fling Into Fall Celebration
  Searsport
  207-548-6372

NOVEMBER

- Country Christmas in Bethel
  Bethel
  207-824-2282
- Rockland Festival of Lights
  Celebration / Rockland
  207-593-6093
- Holiday Light Parade
  Houlton
  207-532-4216

DECEMBER

- Holiday Stroll / Skowhegan
  207-612-2571
- Christmas Prelude
  Kennebunkport
  207-967-0857
- Freeport Sparkle Weekend
  Freeport
  207-865-1212

Sailing Penobscot Bay

Coastal Maine Botanical
Gardens, Boothbay

Shop signs of
Kennebunkport

Maine Lighthouse Museum, Rockland

Quoddy Head State Park, Lubec

Index: Great Experience for Members

AAA editor's picks of exceptional note

Maine Maritime
Museum

Portland Museum of
Art

Maine State Museum

Ogunquit Museum of
American Art

Acadia National Park (I-6)
Acadia National Park *(See p. 38.)*

Augusta (I-4)
Maine State Museum *(See p. 42.)*

Bangor (H-5)
Cole Land Transportation Museum
(See p. 44.)

Bath (J-4)
Maine Maritime Museum *(See p. 63.)*

Boothbay (J-4)
Coastal Maine Botanical Gardens
(See p. 67.)

Lubec (H-8)
Roosevelt Campobello International Park
(See p. 110.)

Ogunquit (L-2)
Ogunquit Museum of American Art
(See p. 116.)

Portland (K-3)
Longfellow House *(See p. 127.)*
Portland Museum of Art *(See p. 129.)*
Victoria Mansion *(See p. 130.)*

Wiscasset (J-4)
Musical Wonder House
(See p. 158.)

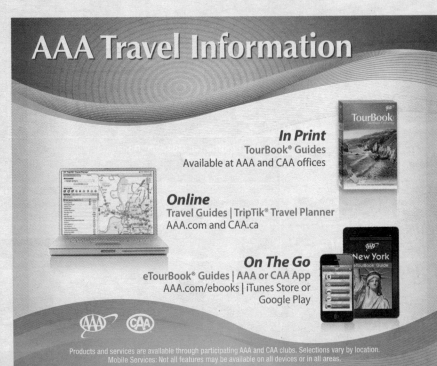

AAA Travel Information

In Print
TourBook® Guides
Available at AAA and CAA offices

Online
Travel Guides | TripTik® Travel Planner
AAA.com and CAA.ca

On The Go
eTourBook® Guides | AAA or CAA App
AAA.com/ebooks | iTunes Store or
Google Play

Make the Most of Your Trip
with AAA eTourBook® Guides

Maximize your travel experience when you take along AAA eTourBook guides for your ereader or smartphone. Each of the more than 100 available digital titles is packed with:

- Destination details
- AAA Approved and Diamond Rated hotel and restaurant listings
- Attraction and event information
- Preplanned itineraries
- Editor's don't-miss picks

Download now at
AAA.com/ebooks

Maine

Atlas Section

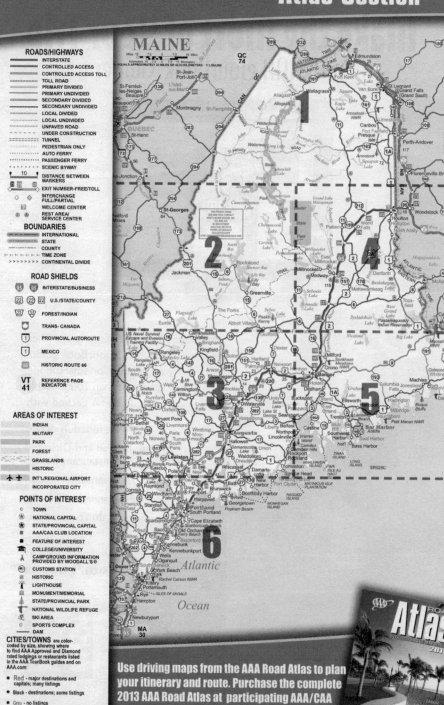

ROADS/HIGHWAYS
- INTERSTATE
- CONTROLLED ACCESS
- CONTROLLED ACCESS TOLL
- TOLL ROAD
- PRIMARY DIVIDED
- PRIMARY UNDIVIDED
- SECONDARY DIVIDED
- SECONDARY UNDIVIDED
- LOCAL DIVIDED
- LOCAL UNDIVIDED
- UNPAVED ROAD
- UNDER CONSTRUCTION
- TUNNEL
- PEDESTRIAN ONLY
- AUTO FERRY
- PASSENGER FERRY
- SCENIC BYWAY
- DISTANCE BETWEEN MARKERS
- EXIT NUMBER-FREE/TOLL
- INTERCHANGE FULL/PARTIAL
- WELCOME CENTER
- REST AREA/ SERVICE CENTER

BOUNDARIES
- INTERNATIONAL
- STATE
- COUNTY
- TIME ZONE
- CONTINENTAL DIVIDE

ROAD SHIELDS
- INTERSTATE/BUSINESS
- U.S./STATE/COUNTY
- FOREST/INDIAN
- TRANS- CANADA
- PROVINCIAL AUTOROUTE
- MEXICO
- HISTORIC ROUTE 66
- **VT 41** REFERENCE PAGE INDICATOR

AREAS OF INTEREST
- INDIAN
- MILITARY
- PARK
- FOREST
- GRASSLANDS
- HISTORIC
- INT'L/REGIONAL AIRPORT
- INCORPORATED CITY

POINTS OF INTEREST
- TOWN
- NATIONAL CAPITAL
- STATE/PROVINCIAL CAPITAL
- AAA/CAA CLUB LOCATION
- FEATURE OF INTEREST
- COLLEGE/UNIVERSITY
- CAMPGROUND INFORMATION PROVIDED BY WOODALL'S®
- CUSTOMS STATION
- HISTORIC
- LIGHTHOUSE
- MONUMENT/MEMORIAL
- STATE/PROVINCIAL PARK
- NATIONAL WILDLIFE REFUGE
- SKI AREA
- SPORTS COMPLEX
- DAM

CITIES/TOWNS are color-coded by size, showing where to find AAA Approved and Diamond rated lodgings or restaurants listed in the AAA TourBook guides and on AAA.com:
- ● Red - major destinations and capitals; many listings
- ■ Black - destinations; some listings
- Grey - no listings

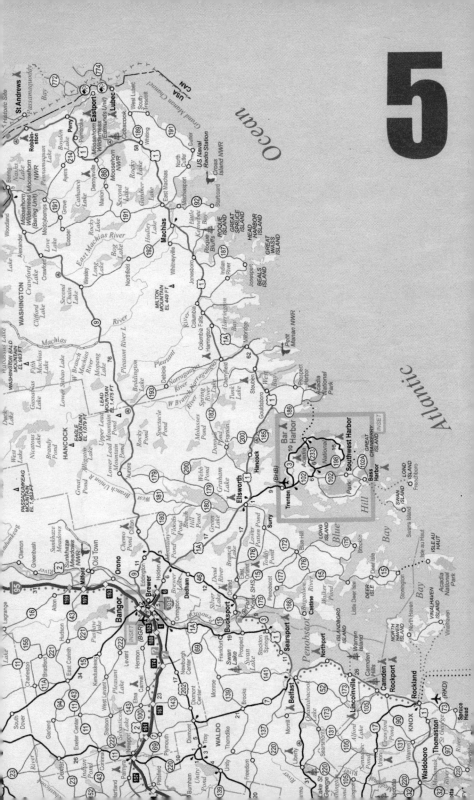

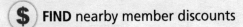

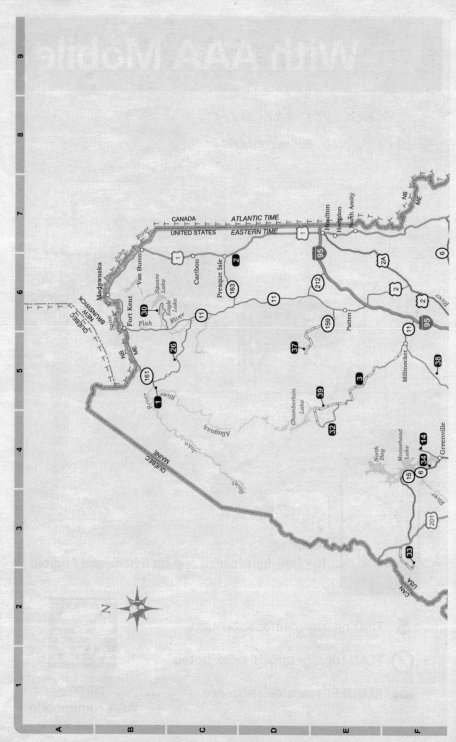

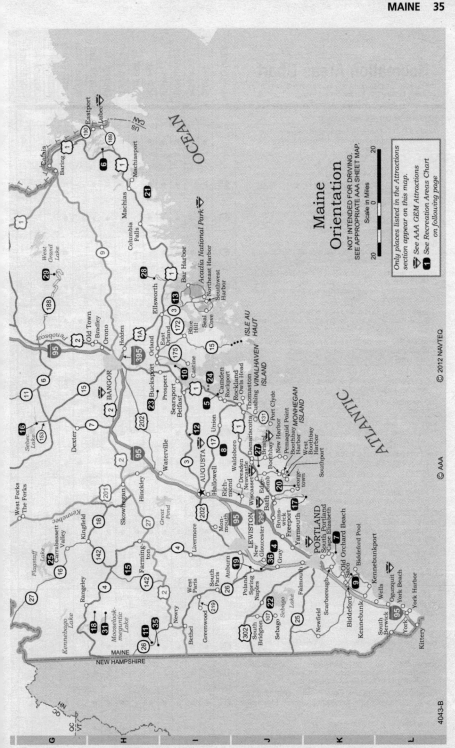

Maine
Orientation

NOT INTENDED FOR DRIVING.
SEE APPROPRIATE AAA SHEET MAP.

Scale in Miles

20   0   20

*Only places listed in the Attractions
section appear on this map.*

See AAA GEM Attractions

See Recreation Areas Chart
on following page

© 2012 NAVTEQ

© AAA

4043-B

Recreation Areas Chart

The map location numerals in column 2 show an area's location on the preceding map.

	MAP LOCATION	CAMPING	PICNICKING	HIKING TRAILS	BOATING	BOAT RAMP	BOAT RENTAL	FISHING	SWIMMING	PETS ON LEASH	BICYCLE TRAILS	WINTER SPORTS	VISITOR CENTER	LODGE/CABINS	FOOD SERVICE
NATIONAL PARKS (See place listings.)															
Acadia (I-6) 47,748 acres. Bird-watching, cross-country skiing, horseback riding, ice fishing, mountain climbing, snowmobiling, snowshoeing, whale watching.		•	•	•	•	•		•	•	•	•	•	•		•
STATE															
Allagash Wilderness Waterway (B-5) River and lakes in northwestern Maine. Canoeing, cross-country skiing, hunting, ice fishing, snowmobiling, snowshoeing.	**1**	•		•	•	•		•	•	•		•			
Aroostook (C-6) 800 acres 4 mi. s. of Presque Isle on US 1, then w. and s. via a park road. Scenic. Bird-watching, canoeing, cross-country skiing, snowmobiling, snowshoeing; nature trails, playground. (See Presque Isle p. 140.)	**2**	•	•	•	•			•	•	•		•			
Baxter (E-5) 209,501 acres (10 separate areas) n. of Millinocket and w. of Patten in north-central Maine off SR 159. Canoeing, primitive camping, rock-climbing, snowmobiling.	**3**	•	•	•	•		•					•	•		
Bradbury Mountain (J-3) 800 acres w. of Freeport off US 95 on SR 136, then n. on SR 9. Bird-watching, cross-country skiing, horseback riding, hunting, snowmobiling, snowshoeing; nature trails, playground.	**4**		•	•						•	•	•	•		
Camden Hills (I-5) 5,474 acres 2 mi. n. of Camden on US 1. Scenic. Bird-watching, cross-country skiing, horseback riding, hunting, snowmobiling, snowshoeing. (See Camden p. 75.)	**5**	•	•	•						•	•	•			
Cobscook Bay (H-8) 888 acres 2 mi. s.e. of Dennysville off US 1. Beachcombing, bird-watching, canoeing, kayaking; nature trails, playground.	**6**	•	•		•	•				•					
Crescent Beach (K-3) 243 acres 8 mi. s. of Portland off CR 77 in Cape Elizabeth. Beachcombing, bird-watching, cross-country skiing, sea kayaking. (See Cape Elizabeth p. 78.)	**7**		•	•					•	•		•			•
Damariscotta Lake (I-4) 17 acres in Jefferson off SR 32. Canoeing; beach.	**8**		•						•	•					
Ferry Beach (K-2) 117 acres in Saco on SR 9. Beachcombing; beach, nature trails. Note: Seasonal restrictions apply to leashed pets. (See Saco p. 145.)	**9**		•	•					•	•	•				
Fort Point (I-5) 120 acres 7 mi. n.e. of Searsport off US 1. Historic. Bird-watching, cross-country skiing; fort ruins, lighthouse, pier.	**10**		•	•	•			•		•		•	•		
Grafton Notch (H-2) 3,000 acres 14 mi. n. of Bethel on SR 26 between Upton and Newry. Bird-watching, cross-country skiing, hunting, snowmobiling, snowshoeing, wildlife viewing. (See Bethel p. 65.)	**11**		•	•	•			•		•		•			
Lake St. George (I-4) 1,017 acres 2 mi. w. of Liberty on SR 3. Canoeing, cross-country skiing, hunting, snowmobiling; playground.	**12**	•	•	•	•	•	•	•	•	•		•			
Lamoine (I-6) 55 acres 6.5 mi. s.e. of Ellsworth on SR 184. Cross-country skiing, hunting, sea kayaking. (See Ellsworth p. 83.)	**13**	•	•	•	•			•		•		•			
Lily Bay (F-4) 925 acres 8 mi. n.e. of Greenville on Lily Bay Rd. Bird-watching, canoeing, cross-country skiing, hunting, ice fishing, kayaking, snowmobiling, snowshoeing; playground.	**14**	•	•	•	•	•	•	•	•	•		•			
Mt. Blue (H-3) 8,000 acres (two areas) n. of Weld on a gravel road. Bird-watching, canoeing, cross-country skiing, horseback riding, hunting, snowmobiling, snowshoeing; motorized-vehicle trails, nature center, playground.	**15**	•	•	•	•	•		•	•	•		•	•		
Peaks-Kenny (G-4) 839 acres 6 mi. n. of Dover-Foxcroft on SR 153. Canoeing, hunting; beach.	**16**	•	•	•	•			•	•	•					
Popham Beach (J-3) 529 acres w. of Popham Beach via SR 209. Beachcombing, bird-watching, hunting, sea kayaking, surfing, windsurfing. Note: Seasonal pet restrictions apply.	**17**		•						•	•	•				
Rangeley Lake (H-2) 869 acres s.w. of Rangeley via SR 17 on the s. shore of Rangeley Lake. Bird-watching, canoeing, snowmobiling; playground.	**18**	•	•	•	•	•	•	•	•			•			
Range Ponds (J-3) 750 acres in Poland off SR 122. Canoeing, hunting, kayaking, windsurfing; nature trails, playground.	**19**		•	•	•	•		•	•	•					

Recreation Areas Chart

The map location numerals in column 2 show an area's location on the preceding map.

	MAP LOCATION	CAMPING	PICNICKING	HIKING TRAILS	BOATING	BOAT RAMP	BOAT RENTAL	FISHING	SWIMMING	PETS ON LEASH	BICYCLE TRAILS	WINTER SPORTS	VISITOR CENTER	LODGE/CABINS	FOOD SERVICE
Reid (J-4) 768 acres 2 mi. e. of Georgetown on SR 127. Beachcombing, bird-watching, cross-country skiing.	20		•	•				•	•	•		•			•
Roque Bluffs (H-7) 275 acres 7 mi. s. of Machias off US 1 on Roque Bluffs Rd. Bird-watching, canoeing, cross-country skiing, sea kayaking, snowshoeing; beach. *(See Machias p. 111.)*	21		•	•	•	•		•	•	•		•			
Sebago Lake (J-2) 1,300 acres 3 mi. s. of Naples off US 302. Nature programs. Canoeing, cross-country skiing, snowshoeing; beach, playground. *(See Sebago p. 148.)*	22	•	•	•	•	•		•	•			•			•
Swan Lake (H-5) 67 acres n. of Swanville off SR 141. Canoeing, hunting; beach, playground.	23		•			•		•	•						
Warren Island (I-5) 70 acres in Penobscot Bay. Accessible by private boat only. Bird-watching, kayaking.	24	•	•	•				•							
OTHER															
Bigelow Preserve (G-3) 36,000 acres n. of New Portland off SR 27. Bird-watching, canoeing, cross-country skiing, hunting, kayaking, snowmobiling, snowshoeing.	25	•	•	•				•	•	•	•	•			
Deboullie (C-5) 21,871 acres 41 mi. s.w. of Fort Kent. Canoeing, cross-country skiing, hunting, snowmobiling, snowshoeing.	26	•		•				•				•			
Dodge Point (J-4) 521 acres 3.5 mi. s.w. of Newcastle off River Road. Scenic. Beachcombing, cross-country skiing, hunting; interpretive trails. *(See Newcastle p. 114.)*	27		•	•				•				•			
Donnell Pond (H-6) 14,000 acres 15 mi. n.e. of Ellsworth off SR 182 and Donnell Pond Road. Scenic. Canoeing, cross-country skiing, hunting, snowshoeing.	28	•	•	•				•				•			
Duck Lake (G-6) 27,000 acres 59 mi. n.e. of Old Town. Canoeing, cross-country skiing, hunting, snowmobiling, snowshoeing; all-terrain vehicle trails.	29	•		•	•			•				•			
Eagle Lake (B-6) 23,000 acres 16 mi. s. of Fort Kent off CR 11. Cross-country skiing, hunting, snowmobiling, snowshoeing; all-terrain vehicle trails.	30	•	•	•				•				•			
Four Ponds (H-2) 6,000 acres 20 mi. s.w. of Rangeley off SR 17. Canoeing, cross-country skiing, hunting, snowmobiling, snowshoeing.	31			•				•							
Gero Island (E-4) 3,845 acres n.w. of Millinocket off SR 11. Canoeing, hunting, wildlife viewing.	32	•	•	•				•	•						
Holeb (F-3) 20,000 acres 44 mi. n.w. of The Forks off US 201 and Holeb Road. Canoeing, hunting.	33	•	•	•	•			•	•						
Little Moose (F-4) 15,000 acres 7.5 mi. w. of Greenville. Birdwatching, canoeing, cross-country skiing, hunting, snowmobiling, snowshoeing; all-terrain vehicle trails.	34	•		•				•				•	•		
Mahoosuc (H-2) 27,000 acres near Bethel off SR 26. Cross-country skiing, hunting, snowmobiling, snowshoeing, wildlife viewing; ATV trails.	35	•	•			•	•			•		•			
Outlet Beach (J-3) on Outlet Rd. 1 mi. e. of SR 26 on shore of Sabbathday Lake near Poland Spring. Canoeing, kayaking, paddleboating. *(See Poland Spring p. 125.)*	36		•		•	•	•	•							•
Scraggly Lake (D-5) 9,092 acres off Grand Lake Rd. n.w. of Mount Chase. Bird-watching, cross-country skiing, hunting, snowmobiling, snowshoeing.	37	•	•	•				•	•	•		•			
Seboeis Lake (F-5) 15,628 acres 20 mi. s.w. of Millinocket off SR 11. Canoeing, hunting, snowmobiling; all-terrain vehicle trails.	38	•	•		•	•		•	•				•		
Telos Lake (F-5) 23,000 acres 48 mi. n.w. of Millinocket off Telos Road. Canoeing, cross-country skiing, hunting, snowmobiling, snowshoeing.	39	•	•		•	•		•				•			

Learn about inspections and Diamond
Ratings at AAA.com/Diamonds

ACADIA NATIONAL PARK (I-6)
• **Attractions map p. 39**

Elevations in the park range from sea level at Sand Beach to 1,530 ft. at Cadillac Mountain. Refer to AAA maps for additional elevation information.

Southeast of Bangor, Acadia National Park possesses an unusual combination of ocean and mountain scenery. The park includes more than 54 square miles of Mount Desert Island, the largest rock-based island on the Atlantic coast.

Dominating the park are the ancient, rounded peaks of the Mount Desert Mountains, worn down by countless centuries of erosion. Great granite cliffs, undermined by the pounding surf at their bases, rise from the ocean. Nowhere along the Atlantic seaboard is the "stern and rockbound coast" more picturesque.

More than 15 peaks, mostly bare at their summits, are forested with spruce, fir, pine and northern hardwood trees. Some 500 types of wildflowers, including many Arctic species, grow in the park, and the area is a sanctuary for a variety of birds and other animals.

Samuel de Champlain sighted Mount Desert Island in 1604 and named it "L'Isle des Monts Deserts," which means island of bare mountains. It was the site of a short-lived settlement by French Jesuits in 1613, and for many years was part of the French province of Acadia, from which the park derives its name.

General Information and Activities

The park is accessible all year. However, except for a 2-mile section along the ocean, the 27-mile Park Loop Road is typically closed early December to mid-April by snow, sleet or ice; state and town roads are kept open. Cadillac Mountain Road extends to the summit of 1,530-foot Cadillac Mountain (see attraction listing), offering a spectacular view of the coast.

More than 125 miles of hiking trails reach every mountain summit and valley; maps are available. There also are 45 miles of graded carriage roads suitable for walking tours, bicycling, cross-country skiing and jogging. See Recreation Areas Chart.

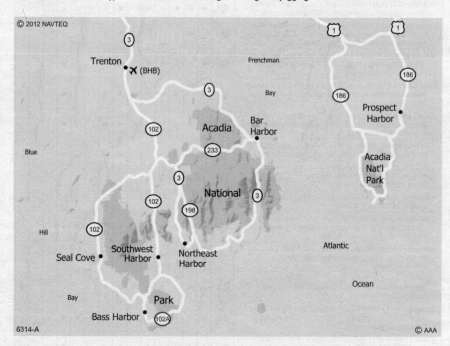

This map shows cities in Acadia National Park where you will find attractions, hotels and restaurants. Cities are listed alphabetically in this book on the following pages.

Bar Harbor 46
Bass Harbor 62
Northeast Harbor 115
Seal Cove 147
Southwest Harbor 151

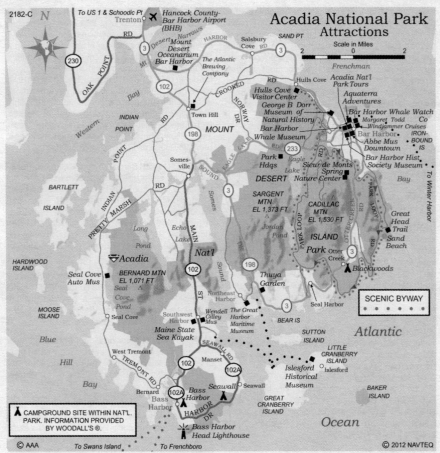

2182-C N

To US 1 & Schoodic Pt
Trenton

Hancock County-
Bar Harbor Airport
(BHB)

Acadia National Park
Attractions

Scale in Miles

Desert Narrows
Mount
Desert
Oceanarium
Bar Harbor

The Atlantic
Brewing
Company

Salsbury
Cove

Frenchman

Hulls Cove

Acadia Nat'l
Park Tours

Aquaterra
Adventures

Hulls Cove
Visitor Center

George B Dorr
Museum of
Natural History

Bar Harbor
Whale Museum

Bar Harbor Whale Watch
Margaret Todd   Co
Windjammer Cruises

Bar Harbor
Abbe Mus
Downtown

IRON-
BOUND
IS

Bar Harbor Hist
Society Museum

Town Hill

MOUNT

Somesville

Park
Hdqs

Eagle
Lake

Sieur de Monts
Spring

DESERT   Nature Center

To Winter Harbor

INDIAN
POINT

BARTLETT
ISLAND

SARGENT
MTN
EL 1,373 FT

CADILLAC
MTN
EL 1,530 FT

Bay

Great
Head
Trail

Jordan
Pond

ISLAND

Long
Pond

Echo
Lake

Nat'l

Park

Otter
Creek

Sand
Beach

HARDWOOD
ISLAND

Acadia

Seal Cove
Auto Mus

BERNARD MTN
EL 1,071 FT

Seal
Cove
Pond

Blackwoods

Thuya
Garden

MOOSE
ISLAND

Seal Cove

Northeast
Harbor

Seal Harbor

SCENIC BYWAY

Blue

West Tremont

Southwest
Harbor

Wendell
Gilley
Mus

The Great
Harbor
Maritime
Museum

BEAR IS

SUTTON
ISLAND

Atlantic

Maine State
Sea Kayak

Hill

Bay

Manset

Seawall

Seawall

Islesford
Historical
Museum

Islesford

LITTLE
CRANBERRY
ISLAND

BAKER
ISLAND

Bernard

Bass
Harbor

Bass
Harbor

GREAT
CRANBERRY
ISLAND

Ocean

CAMPGROUND SITE WITHIN NAT'L.
PARK. INFORMATION PROVIDED
BY WOODALL'S ®.

Bass Harbor
Head Lighthouse

© AAA   To Swans Island   To Frenchboro

© 2012 NAVTEQ

Park ranger programs are usually offered late May through Columbus Day. Programs include mountain hikes, campground programs and natural history walks. Check the park's program schedule for details. Park rangers also explain the area's geology, history, marine life and wildlife on four cruises around Frenchman Bay and the Cranberry Islands. Check at the visitor center for a current listing of programs.

Park information may be obtained year-round at the winter visitor center located on SR 233, 3 miles west of Bar Harbor. The center is open Mon.-Fri. 8-4:30; closed Jan. 1, Thanksgiving, Christmas Eve and Christmas. Information also is available at the Hulls Cove Visitor Center (see attraction listing), which is open daily 8-6, July-Aug.; 8-4:30, Apr. 15-June 30 and Sept.-Oct.

Private operators are available during the season to conduct daily sightseeing, deep-sea fishing, whale-watching and lobster-fishing cruises from Bar Harbor as well as from Northeast, Southwest and Bass harbors.

Tape Tours, available at the Hulls Cove Visitor Center through Eastern National Bookstore, describe the geological origin, ecology and history of

the park and contain instructions for making the drive around Acadia, beginning at Hulls Cove; phone (207) 288-4988 for the bookstore.

ADMISSION to the park is by 7-day pass, which costs $20 per private vehicle, late June-early Oct.; $10, May 1-late June and early Oct.-Oct. 31; free, rest of year. Admission per person arriving on foot, bicycle or motorcycle is $5, May-Oct.; free, rest of year. Annual passes cost $40. A camping fee is charged. **Cards:** AX, DS, MC, VI.

PETS are permitted in the park if they are attended and physically restricted at all times; leashes may be up to 6 feet in length. Pets are not permitted on the swimming beaches or the ladder hiking trails on mountain cliffs.

ADDRESS inquiries to Acadia National Park Information, P.O. Box 177, Bar Harbor, ME 04609; phone (207) 288-3338 or TTY (207) 288-8800.

CADILLAC MOUNTAIN is accessible by way of 3.5-mi. Cadillac Mountain Rd., which is off Park Loop Rd. about 1 mi. s. of the park's Cadillac Mountain entrance. Visitors can drive all the way to the rocky summit of 1,530-foot Cadillac Mountain, the highest point on the U.S. Atlantic seaboard. From a .4-mile loop trail at the top, the panorama encompasses Bar Harbor, almost the whole of Mount Desert Island and the wooded islands in Frenchman Bay. Hikers also can reach the summit via the strenuous 3.7-mi. (one way) Cadillac Mountain South Ridge Trail from Blackwoods Campground. **Note:** Cadillac Mountain Road is closed in winter (typically Dec. 1-Apr. 14).

Cost: Included in Acadia National Park admission (valid for 7 days). Park admission per private vehicle $20, late June-early Oct.; $10, May 1-late June and early Oct.-Oct. 31; free, rest of year. Park admission per person arriving on foot, bicycle or motorcycle $5, May-Oct.; free, rest of year. **Phone:** (207) 288-3338 or TTY (207) 288-8800.

CARRIAGES OF ACADIA, departing from Wildwood Stables, off SR 3 at Acadia National Park's Stanley Brook entrance, offers horse-drawn carriage rides along the carriage roads. Tour options include the 1-hour Day Mountain Tour, the 2-hour Mr. Rockefeller's Bridge Tour, the 2-hour Jordan Pond House–Tea & Popover Ride and the 2-hour Day Mountain Summit ride.

Hours: Day Mountain Tour departs daily at 9 and 1, June-Oct. Mr. Rockefeller's Bridge Tour departs daily at 10 and 2:15, June-Oct. Jordan Pond House–Tea & Popover Ride departs daily at 1:15, June-Oct. Day Mountain Summit ride departs daily at 4:30, June-Oct. Tour times may vary late Sept.-Oct.; phone ahead to confirm schedule. **Cost:** $18-$24.50; $9-$10 (ages 6-12); $5-$7 (ages 2-5). Reservations are recommended. **Phone:** (207) 276-5721 or (877) 276-3622.

GREAT HEAD TRAIL is accessible from the Sand Beach parking lot off Park Loop Rd., 4 mi. s. of Bar Harbor. The 1.5-mile loop trail atop the sea cliffs of the Great Head Peninsula offers wonderful views of the ocean, Sand Beach, Otter Point and a steep granite hill known as the Beehive. Because the route from the beach is steep, this trail is considered moderately difficult. **Phone:** (207) 288-3338 or TTY (207) 288-8800.

HULLS COVE VISITOR CENTER is 2.75 mi. n. of Bar Harbor on SR 3 at Hulls Cove. A 15-minute film about the island is shown on the half-hour. **Hours:** Daily 8-6, July-Aug.; 8-4:30, Apr. 15-June 30 and Sept.-Oct. **Cost:** Free. **Phone:** (207) 288-3338.

ISLESFORD HISTORICAL MUSEUM is accessible via mail boat or tour boat from Northeast or Southwest Harbor to Little Cranberry Island. The exhibits focus on 19th-century living on the Cranberry Islands and include tools, harpoon guns and ship clocks. **Time:** Allow 30 minutes minimum. **Hours:** Daily 10-noon and 12:30-4:30, mid-June through Sept. 30. Phone ahead to confirm schedule. **Cost:** Free. **Phone:** (207) 244-9224.

PARK LOOP ROAD begins near the Hulls Cove Visitor Center and runs s. in a loop, connecting Mount Desert Island's mountains and seashore. It provides access to a number of interesting features: Sand Beach, partially formed of shell fragments; Great Head, one of the highest sheer Atlantic headlands in the United States; Thunder Hole, a wave-cut chasm producing loud reverberations when waves and tide are right; Otter Cliffs, with a dense forest that extends to the edge of the sea; and Cadillac Mountain, with its stunning views. **Time:** Allow 3 hours, 30 minutes minimum. **Phone:** (207) 288-3338 or TTY (207) 288-8800.

SCHOODIC POINT is at the tip of Schoodic Peninsula on the eastern side of Frenchman Bay—about an hour's drive from Bar Harbor. Beside the point, Schoodic Head rises more than 400 feet, commanding a sweeping view eastward toward the Bay of Fundy and westward toward the Mount Desert Mountains. A park road from SR 186 follows the coast of the peninsula. **Phone:** (207) 288-3338 or TTY (207) 288-8800.

SIEUR DE MONTS SPRING, near Bar Harbor, is a memorial to George B. Dorr, a co-founder of Acadia National Park. The area includes the Abbe Museum at Sieur de Monts Spring, the Nature Center and the Wild Gardens of Acadia.

Abbe Museum at Sieur de Monts Spring, off Sieur de Monts near the spring, contains regional artifacts of American Indian culture. **Hours:** Daily 10-5, late May to mid-Oct. **Cost:** $3; $1 (ages 6-15). **Phone:** (207) 288-3519.

Nature Center, near Sieur de Monts Spring, includes several natural history exhibits. The Wild Gardens of Acadia, a living field guide to flowers and trees found within the park, is next to the center. **Hours:** Nature center daily 9-5, June-Aug.; 9-4, Sept. 1 to mid-Oct.; Sat.-Sun. 9-5 with varying hours, in May. Gardens daily 24 hours, year-round. **Cost:** Free. **Phone:** (207) 288-3338 or TTY (207) 288-8800.

ARUNDEL
• Hotels & Restaurants map & index p. 98

BLUE MOON CLASSY DINER	207/985-6666 (20)

▼▼ American. Family Dining. $4-$22 **AAA Inspector Notes:** The dining room has a 1940s and '50s feel, with jukeboxes and posters from the era. Made-to-order American comfort food is served in large portions. **Bar:** full bar. **Address:** 1132 Portland Rd 04046 **Location:** On US 1; center. L D

SEAFOOD CENTER	207/985-7391 (19)

▼ Seafood. Quick Serve. $8-$28 **AAA Inspector Notes:** Open all year, the restaurant enables guests to savor traditional lobster pound offerings without going to the ocean's edge. **Address:** 1181 Portland Rd 04046 **Location:** On US 1; center.

L D 🗶

Visit AAA.com/Travel or
CAA.ca/Travel for complete
trip planning and reservations

AUBURN (J-3) pop. 23,055, elev. 183'

Auburn and its more populous neighbor Lewiston *(see place listing p. 108)* flank the Androscoggin River 30 miles inland from its mouth. With a rich heritage of textile and shoe production and the more recent additions of electronics, plastics and other manufacturers, the two cities constitute what is often termed the "industrial heart" of Maine.

During the early 1840s the exploitation of water-power potential spurred swift manufacturing development in Auburn. The shoe industry, which had begun in the 1830s, grew despite the laborious hand methods of the time. Then, about 1850, the factory system and the first laborsaving machinery were introduced. By the 1870s two million pairs of shoes were leaving Auburn factories each year.

Although shoe production has declined significantly, new technological and entrepreneurial enterprises have combined with the growth of a large service and retail industry and have successfully revitalized the city.

Opportunities exist for play as well as for work. Lake Auburn, 3 miles north, offers fishing at selected sites.

ANDROSCOGGIN HISTORICAL SOCIETY MUSEUM,
at 2 Turner St. in the County Building, presents exhibits tracing the history of the state and county. Displays include a bird collection, American Indian artifacts, Civil War memorabilia, military items, postcards, photographs, clothing, and farm and domestic tools. A library containing local, county and state history is available for research purposes. **Time:** Allow 30 minutes minimum. **Hours:** Wed.-Thurs. 1-4:30, Fri. 1-4. Closed major holidays. **Cost:** Donations. **Phone:** (207) 784-0586 or (207) 786-2129.

RECREATIONAL ACTIVITIES
Skiing (Cross-country)
• **Lost Valley Ski Area** is off Youngs Corner Rd. **Hours:** Daily, Dec. 17-Mar. 13. **Phone:** (207) 784-1561.

FIRESIDE INN & SUITES   207/777-1777
Hotel $80-$120 **Address:** 1777 Washington St 04210 **Location:** I-95 exit 75, 0.5 mi s on US 202, SR 4 and 100. **Facility:** 100 units, some efficiencies. 2 stories (no elevator), interior/exterior corridors. **Terms:** cancellation fee imposed. **Pool(s):** outdoor. **Activities:** limited exercise equipment. **Guest Services:** coin laundry.

HILTON GARDEN INN AUBURN RIVERWATCH
                                              (207)784-4433

| | Hilton Garden Inn | **AAA Benefit:** Unparalleled hospitality at a special Member rate. |
| Hotel $119-$329 | | |

Address: 14 Great Falls Plaza 04210 **Location:** SR 4, just e on Hampshire St; center. **Facility:** 138 units. 6 stories, interior corridors. **Terms:** 1-7 night minimum stay, cancellation fee imposed. **Amenities:** high-speed Internet. **Dining:** entertainment. **Pool(s):** heated indoor. **Activities:** whirlpool, exercise room. **Guest Services:** valet and coin laundry. **Free Special Amenities:** local telephone calls and newspaper.

RESIDENCE INN BY MARRIOTT AUBURN   (207)777-3400
Extended Stay Hotel $119-$309 **Address:** 670 Turner St 04210 **Location:** I-95 exit 80 southbound; exit 75 northbound; from SR 100, just w. **Facility:** 100 units, some two bedrooms, efficiencies and kitchens. 4 stories, interior corridors. **Amenities:** high-speed Internet, safes. **Pool(s):** heated indoor. **Activities:** whirlpool, sports court, exercise room. **Guest Services:** valet and coin laundry.

AAA Benefit: AAA hotel discounts of 5% or more.

SLEEPY TIME MOTEL   207/783-1435
Motel $89-$99 **Address:** 46 Danville Corner Rd 04210 **Location:** I-95 exit 75, 0.5 mi ne on US 202, then just e. **Facility:** 6 units. 1 story, exterior corridors. **Amenities:** high-speed Internet. **Activities:** hiking trails.

WHERE TO EAT

MAC'S GRILL   207/783-6885
American. Casual Dining. $8-$23 **AAA Inspector Notes:** Rustic decor, including a moose head wall mount, enhances the genuine log cabin. The restaurant's lively and casual atmosphere makes it a popular destination for locals and visitors alike. Although Black Angus steak is the main attraction, chicken and seafood also are available. Various sauces and ribs have hearty flavors. **Bar:** full bar. **Address:** 1052 Minot Ave 04210 **Location:** Jct US 202, 2 mi on SR 121.

ROLANDEAU'S   207/784-2110
American. Casual Dining. $8-$24 **AAA Inspector Notes:** The varied menu includes a good variety of French-style dishes as well as prime rib, rack of lamb, veal, fresh lobster and dessert, including cheesecake terrine and peach Melba. This fine restaurant has been serving guests in a comfortable, country setting for some 30 years. **Bar:** full bar. **Reservations:** suggested. **Address:** 775 Washington St 04210 **Location:** I-95 exit 75, e on US 202 to town; 2.5 mi w on US 202 and SR 4, follow signs.

AUGUSTA (I-4) pop. 19,136, elev. 47'
• Hotels p. 42 • Restaurants p. 43

A trading post was founded in 1628 by the Plymouth Colony. John Alden and Capt. Miles Standish, immortalized by Henry Wadsworth Longfellow, were among the original settlers. In 1754 Fort Western was erected on the east bank of the Kennebec River. In 1797 the community chose Augusta as its name, presumably to honor the daughter of Gen. Henry Dearborn.

Capital of the state since 1827, Augusta is at the head of navigation on the Kennebec River. The city differs from most Maine communities that occupy both sides of a river in that it did not grow into twin cities. Augusta is the seat of many of Maine's governmental agencies and offices.

Kennebec Valley Chamber of Commerce: 21 University Dr., P.O. Box 676, Augusta, ME 04332. **Phone:** (207) 623-4559.

CAPITOL PARK, between the State House and the Kennebec River, contains 72 species of indigenous trees and 23 species of exotic trees as well as varieties of shrubs and ferns. The 20-acre park also is the site of the Maine Vietnam Veterans Memorial, a unique triangular piece of art, and the Enoch Lincoln Monument, a granite obelisk marking the grave of the former governor who played an important role in designating Augusta as the state capitol. **Hours:** Daily dawn-dusk. **Cost:** Free. **Phone:** (207) 287-1615.

CHILDREN'S DISCOVERY MUSEUM is at 171 Capitol St., Suite 2. In a variety of hands-on exhibits, the museum encourages experimentation, exploration and role-playing. Children may participate in such simulated settings as a bank, grocery store, rainforest, restaurant and theater. Other highlights include a construction area with a life-size skid steer, a tree house and a touch tank with local marine life.

Exhibits are most appropriate for children through grade five; parents are encouraged to play along. **Hours:** Tues.-Thurs. 10-4, Fri.-Sat. 10-5, Sun. 11-4. **Cost:** $5.50 (ages 1-13); $4.50 (adults). **Phone:** (207) 622-2209.

MAINE STATE HOUSE, State and Capitol sts., was originally designed by Charles Bulfinch. Although many additions and changes have been made, the graceful portico has been left undisturbed. The 1832 building contains many portraits, an exhibit of battle flags and four wildlife dioramas. Guided tours are available by reservation. **Time:** Allow 30 minutes minimum. **Hours:** Tours Mon.-Fri. 9-1. Closed major holidays. **Cost:** Free. **Phone:** (207) 287-2301 for tour information.

MAINE STATE MUSEUM, in the Library-Museum-Archives Building in the State House Complex, contains exhibits depicting Maine's natural environment, prehistory, social history and manufacturing heritage. Back to Nature features five natural history scenes and a display of gems and minerals found in Maine, while 12,000 Years in Maine presents an extensive view of the state's prehistoric cultures and archeologically recovered materials.

At Home in Maine depicts life in the state throughout the centuries. Made In Maine is the museum's exhibit of 19th-century manufacturing technologies and products. Other exhibits examine various aspects of natural science, history and art.

Time: Allow 1 hour minimum. **Hours:** Tues.-Fri. 9-5, Sat. 10-4. Closed major holidays. **Cost:** $2; $1 (ages 6-18 and 62+); $6 (family, two adults and all accompanying children ages 6-18). **Phone:** (207) 287-2301.

OLD FORT WESTERN, 16 Cony St., is said to be America's oldest surviving wooden fort. Costumed interpreters guide visitors through the fort's military, storekeeping and residential past spanning the years from the 1750s to the early 1800s. **Time:** Allow 1 hour minimum. **Hours:** Daily 1-4, Memorial Day-Labor Day; Sat.-Sun. 1-4, day after Labor Day-Columbus Day. **Cost:** $6; $4 (ages 6-16). **Phone:** (207) 626-2385.

▼ See AAA listing this page ▼

BEST WESTERN PLUS CIVIC CENTER INN
(207)622-4751

Hotel
$89-$189

Best Western PLUS

AAA Benefit: Members save 10% or more with Best Western.

Address: 110 Community Dr 04330 **Location:** I-95 exit 112A northbound; exit 112 southbound, just s on SR 8, 11 and 27. Adjacent to Augusta Civic Center. **Facility:** 100 units. 2 stories, interior corridors. **Pool(s):** outdoor. **Activities:** exercise room. **Guest Services:** valet and coin laundry. **Free Special Amenities: expanded continental breakfast and high-speed Internet.**

COMFORT INN
(207)623-1000

Hotel $89-$149 **Address:** 281 Civic Center Dr 04330 **Location:** I-95 exit 112B northbound; exit 112 southbound. **Facility:** 99 units. 3 stories, interior corridors. **Terms:** 3 day cancellation notice-fee imposed. **Pool(s):** heated indoor. **Activities:** whirlpool, exercise room. **Guest Services:** valet laundry.

FAIRFIELD INN & SUITES BY MARRIOTT AUGUSTA
(207)623-2200

Hotel $179-$259 **Address:** 14 Anthony Ave 04330 **Location:** I-95 exit 112B, s to Belgrade Rd, then left on Darin Dr. **Facility:** 81 units. 3 stories, interior corridors. **Amenities:** high-speed Internet. **Pool(s):** heated indoor. **Activities:** whirlpool, exercise room. **Guest Services:** valet and coin laundry.

AAA Benefit: AAA hotel discounts of 5% or more.

HAMPTON INN AUGUSTA
207/622-4077

[fyi] Hotel. Rates not provided. Too new to rate. **Address:** 388 Western Ave 04330 **Location:** On US 202. **Amenities:** 80 units, coffeemakers, microwaves, refrigerators, pool, exercise facility.

AAA Benefit: Members save up to 10%!

SENATOR INN & SPA
(207)622-5804

Hotel $80-$229 **Address:** 284 Western Ave 04330 **Location:** I-95 exit 109 northbound; exit 109A southbound, on US 202, SR 11 and 100. **Facility:** 124 units. 2 stories, interior/exterior corridors. **Terms:** cancellation fee imposed. **Amenities:** Some: high-speed Internet. **Dining:** Cloud 9, see separate listing. **Pool(s):** heated outdoor, heated indoor. **Activities:** saunas, whirlpool, steamroom, exercise room, spa. **Guest Services:** valet laundry.

WHERE TO EAT

CLOUD 9
207/622-0320

American Casual Dining $7-$24

AAA Inspector Notes: Do not let the formal décor fool you into thinking the atmosphere is stuffy—diners wear everything from jeans to business suits here. The menu features fresh Maine seafood as well as pasta, vegetarian items and Yankee dinners. Be sure to ask for the dessert cart as it looks good enough to add calories at a glance. **Bar:** full bar. **Address:** 284 Western Ave 04330 **Location:** I-95 exit 109 northbound; exit 109A southbound, on US 202, SR 11 and 100; in Senator Inn & Spa. [B] [L] [D]

RIVERFRONT BARBEQUE & GRILL
207/622-8899

Barbecue. Casual Dining. $9-$23 **AAA Inspector Notes:** Popular with locals and tourists alike, the restaurant serves Memphis-style barbecue, which is made on the premises. Guests also can sample such dishes as jambalaya, shrimp Louisianne and Santa Fe chicken. **Bar:** full bar. **Address:** 300 Water St 04330 **Location:** Downtown. **Parking:** street only. [L] [D]

BAILEY ISLAND

LOG CABIN AN ISLAND INN
207/833-5546

Country Inn $139-$349 **Address:** 5 Log Cabin Ln 04003 **Location:** Cross Bailey Island Bridge, 0.5 mi s on SR 24. **Facility:** The inn overlooks Casco Bay and has an upscale log cabin ambience throughout. Guest rooms feature contemporary décor; most have a private deck. 9 units, some kitchens. 2 stories (no elevator), interior/exterior corridors. **Terms:** closed 10/31-3/31, 21 day cancellation notice-fee imposed. **Pool(s):** heated outdoor.

WHERE TO EAT

COOK'S LOBSTER HOUSE
207/833-2818

Seafood. Family Dining. $7-$28 **AAA Inspector Notes:** In business since 1955, the focus at this must-see eatery remains constant in both the fresh seafood (often fried) and the location (surrounded by Merriconeag Sound). Diners can motor up by car or boat. **Bar:** full bar. **Address:** 68 Garrison Cove Rd 04003 **Location:** Cross Bailey Island Bridge, 0.5 mi s on SR 24. [L] [D] CALL

BANGOR (H-5) pop. 33,039, elev. 21'
• Hotels p. 44 • Restaurants p. 45

Bangor, at the head of tidewater and navigation on the Penobscot River, is the principal retail, cultural and commercial center for eastern and northern Maine. Bangor area industries are based on papermaking, timber products, electronics, shoes and tourism. Several notable public and private colleges and universities are located here.

Bangor's survival was threatened by the War of 1812; blockade running and privateering became essential to maintain solvency. A resurgence in the timber trade following the war tripled Bangor's population during the 1830s. Within a few decades, the city became the leading lumber port of the world. Bangor's harbor became known as the Devil's Half-Acre due to the proliferation of drinking and gambling.

Of interest is the Paul Bunyan statue on Main Street, which is an appropriate 31 feet high and weighs about 1.5 tons. The Bangor Museum and Center for History, in the Thomas A. Hill House at 159 Union St., contains antiques, artifacts and pictures from the 19th century. Various walking tours also are offered; phone (207) 942-5766 or (207) 942-1900.

Blackbeard's Family Fun Park at 339 Odlin Rd. offers miniature golf courses, bumper boats, a ropes obstacle course, waterslides, laser tag, a go-cart track and a 10-cage batting facility; phone (207) 945-0233. The Hollywood Casino Hotel & Raceway, in Bass Park at 500 Main St., features live harness racing May through November; phone (207) 561-6068.

Note: Policies concerning admittance of children to pari-mutuel betting facilities vary. Phone ahead for information.

At downtown's 🏵 American Folk Festival in late August, there's music aplenty; genres include bluegrass, gospel, jazz and polka; phone (207) 992-2630.

Bangor Region Chamber of Commerce: 208 Maine Ave., Bangor, ME 04401. **Phone:** (207) 947-0307.

Self-guiding tours: Aspects of the city's history can be experienced through a self-guiding walking tour; maps are available from the Bangor Historical Society at 159 Union St.; phone (207) 942-1900.

COLE LAND TRANSPORTATION MU-SEUM, off I-95 exit 182A following signs to the War Memorials at 405 Perry Rd., includes a 72-foot 1840s covered bridge and more than 200 vehicles illustrating the evolution of land transportation from wagons to automobiles to 18-wheelers. Among the items exhibited are antique recreational vehicles, motorcycles, a locomotive, a railroad station, farm equipment, horse-drawn logging sleds, farm and logging trucks, snowplows and more than 2,000 enlarged and captioned photographs of early life in Maine.

Also featured are hundreds of military artifacts from the Civil War to World War II, including uniforms, insignias, weapons and armored vehicles. The museum also is home to the Maine World War II Veterans Memorial, the Maine Vietnam Veterans Memorial, the Maine Korean Veterans Memorial and the Maine Military Order of the Purple Heart Memorial. **Time:** Allow 1 hour minimum. **Hours:** Daily 9-5, May 1-Nov. 11. **Cost:** $7; $5 (ages 62+); free (ages 0-18). **Phone:** (207) 990-3600.

MAINE DISCOVERY MUSEUM is at 74 Main St. This museum comprises three floors of hands-on exhibits and activities for children including Nature Trails and Turtle Alley; Booktown, featuring classic Maine children's books; Fit for Fun; Body Journey; Artscape; Trade Winds; and Sounds Abound, which features a karaoke studio.

Time: Allow 1 hour minimum. **Hours:** Tues.-Sat. 10-5, Sun. noon-5, with extended hours in summer. Closed Easter, July 4, Labor Day week, Thanksgiving, Christmas Eve and Christmas. **Cost:** $7.50; free (ages 0-12 months). **Phone:** (207) 262-7200.

GAMBLING ESTABLISHMENTS

• **Hollywood Casino Hotel & Raceway** is .2 mi. s.e. on Union St., then .7 mi. s. on Main St./US 1A/US 202/SR 9 to 500 Main St. **Hours:** Daily 8 a.m.-3 a.m. **Phone:** (877) 779-7771.

BANGOR MOTOR INN (207)947-0355

Hotel
$72-$149

Address: 701 Hogan Rd 04401 **Location:** I-95 exit 187 (Hogan Rd), 0.3 mi w. Adjacent to a mall. **Facility:** 103 units. 2 stories (no elevator), interior corridors. **Guest Services:** valet laundry, area transportation-mall, hospital & bus station. **Free Special Amenities: continental breakfast and high-speed Internet.**

BEST WESTERN WHITE HOUSE (207)862-3737

Hotel
$112-$290

AAA Benefit: Members save 10% or more with Best Western.

Address: 155 Littlefield Ave 04401 **Location:** I-95 exit 180 (Coldbrook Rd), 5.5 mi s of downtown. Located by a truck stop. **Facility:** 77 units, some efficiencies. 3 stories, interior/exterior corridors. **Parking:** winter plug-ins. **Amenities:** *Some:* high-speed Internet. **Pool(s):** heated outdoor. **Activities:** whirlpool, exercise room. *Fee:* game room. **Guest Services:** valet and coin laundry. **Free Special Amenities: continental breakfast and high-speed Internet.**

COMFORT INN 207/990-0888

Hotel. Rates not provided. **Address:** 10 Bangor Mall Blvd 04401 **Location:** I-95 exit 187 (Hogan Rd). **Facility:** 115 units. 3 stories, interior corridors. **Activities:** exercise room. **Guest Services:** valet and coin laundry, area transportation-within town.

COURTYARD BY MARRIOTT BANGOR (207)262-0070

Hotel $159-$209 **Address:** 236 Sylvan Rd 04401 **Location:** I-95 exit 187 (Hogan Rd), just se, then 0.5 mi sw; in Sylvan Business Park. **Facility:** 92 units. 4 stories, interior corridors. **Amenities:** high-speed Internet. **Pool(s):** heated indoor. **Activities:** whirlpool, exercise room. **Guest Services:** valet and coin laundry.

AAA Benefit: AAA hotel discounts of 5% or more.

DAYS INN BANGOR (207)942-8272

Hotel $75-$105 **Address:** 250 Odlin Rd 04401 **Location:** I-95 exit 182B, just e on US 2 and SR 100. Located in a commercial area. **Facility:** 101 units. 2 stories (no elevator), interior corridors. **Amenities:** safes. **Pool(s):** heated indoor. **Guest Services:** valet and coin laundry.

ECONO LODGE INN & SUITES (207)945-0111

Motel $75-$175 **Address:** 327 Odlin Rd 04401 **Location:** I-95 exit 182B, just e on US 2 and SR 100. Adjacent to a theme park. **Facility:** 116 units. 4 stories, interior corridors. **Parking:** winter plug-ins. **Terms:** cancellation fee imposed. **Pool(s):** heated indoor. **Guest Services:** valet and coin laundry.

FAIRFIELD INN BY MARRIOTT BANGOR (207)990-0001

Hotel
$129-$199

AAA Benefit: AAA hotel discounts of 5% or more.

Address: 300 Odlin Rd 04401 **Location:** I-95 exit 182B, just e on US 2 and SR 100. Located in a commercial area. **Facility:** 153 units. 3 stories, interior corridors. **Pool(s):** heated indoor. **Activities:** whirlpool, exercise room. **Guest Services:** valet and coin laundry. **Free Special Amenities: local telephone calls and high-speed Internet.**

FIRESIDE INN & SUITES (207)942-1234

Hotel $89-$189 **Address:** 570 Main St 04401 **Location:** I-395 exit 3B. **Facility:** 51 units, some two bedrooms and kitchens. 2 stories (no elevator), interior corridors. **Terms:** 7 day cancellation notice-fee imposed. **Guest Services:** valet laundry.

FOUR POINTS BY SHERATON BANGOR   (207)947-6721

Hotel
$125-$199

FOUR POINTS
BY SHERATON

AAA Benefit: Members get up to 20% off, plus Starwood Preferred Guest® bonuses.

Address: 308 Godfrey Blvd 04401 **Location:** At Bangor International Airport. **Facility:** 111 units. 9 stories, interior corridors. **Dining:** Godfrey's Grille & Lounge, see separate listing. **Pool(s):** heated indoor. **Activities:** exercise room. **Guest Services:** valet laundry. **Free Special Amenities: local telephone calls and newspaper.**

HAMPTON INN BANGOR   (207)990-4400

 **Hotel** $149-$179 **Address:** 261 Haskell Rd 04401 **Location:** I-95 exit 187, just ne. **Facility:** 115 units. 4 stories, interior corridors. **Terms:** 1-7 night minimum stay, cancellation fee imposed. **Amenities:** *Some:* high-speed Internet. **Pool(s):** heated indoor. **Activities:** whirlpool, exercise room. **Guest Services:** valet and coin laundry, area transportation-within 4 mi.

AAA Benefit: Members save up to 10%!

HILTON GARDEN INN BANGOR   (207)262-0099

Hotel $149-$209 **Address:** 250 Haskell Rd 04401 **Location:** I-95 exit 187 (Hoban Rd), just se, then 0.5 mi ne. **Facility:** 141 units. 5 stories, interior corridors. **Terms:** 1-7 night minimum stay, cancellation fee imposed. **Amenities:** high-speed Internet. **Pool(s):** heated indoor. **Activities:** whirlpool, exercise room. **Guest Services:** valet and coin laundry, area transportation-within 5 mi.

AAA Benefit: Unparalleled hospitality at a special Member rate.

HOLIDAY INN-BANGOR   207/947-0101

Hotel. Rates not provided. **Address:** 404 Odlin Rd 04401 **Location:** I-95 exit 182B; jct Odlin Rd and I-395. **Facility:** 208 units. 3 stories, interior corridors. **Terms:** check-in 4 pm. **Amenities:** *Some:* video games (fee). **Pool(s):** heated indoor. **Activities:** whirlpool, exercise room. **Guest Services:** valet and coin laundry, area transportation-Bangor Mall.

HOLLYWOOD CASINO HOTEL & RACEWAY   (207)974-3500

Hotel
$109-$249

Address: 500 Main St 04401 **Location:** I-395 exit 3B, just n. **Facility:** 152 units. 7 stories, interior corridors. **Amenities:** high-speed Internet, safes. **Dining:** Epic Buffet, see separate listing. **Activities:** exercise room. **Guest Services:** valet and coin laundry. **Free Special Amenities: local telephone calls and high-speed Internet.**

HOWARD JOHNSON INN   (207)942-5251

Hotel
$55-$122

Address: 336 Odlin Rd 04401 **Location:** I-95 exit 182B; jct Odlin Rd and I-395. Located in a commercial area. **Facility:** 58 units. 2 stories (no elevator), interior corridors. **Amenities:** safes. **Pool(s):** heated outdoor. **Free Special Amenities: local telephone calls and newspaper.**

QUALITY INN BANGOR   (207)942-7899

Hotel $69-$139 **Address:** 750 Hogan Rd 04401 **Location:** I-95 exit 187 (Hogan Rd), 0.5 mi nw. Adjacent to shopping mall. **Facility:** 96 units. 2 stories, interior corridors. **Parking:** winter plug-ins. **Amenities:** video games (fee), safes. **Activities:** game room, exercise room. **Guest Services:** valet laundry.

RAMADA   (207)947-6961

Hotel $89-$129 **Address:** 357 Odlin Rd 04401 **Location:** I-95 exit 182B; jct Odlin Rd and I-395. **Facility:** 118 units. 2 stories (no elevator), interior corridors. **Pool(s):** heated indoor. **Activities:** exercise room. **Guest Services:** valet laundry, area transportation-within 10 mi & Bangor Mall.

RIVERSIDE INN   207/973-4100

Hotel $99-$159 **Address:** 495 State St 04401 **Location:** Adjacent to Eastern Maine Medical Center. **Facility:** 56 units. 5 stories, interior corridors. **Terms:** 7 day cancellation notice. **Guest Services:** valet and coin laundry.

SUPER 8   (207)945-5681

Hotel
$51-$79

Address: 462 Odlin Rd 04401 **Location:** I-95 exit 182A or B, 0.5 mi w on Hammond St. **Facility:** 77 units. 2 stories (no elevator), interior corridors. **Guest Services:** valet laundry. **Free Special Amenities: expanded continental breakfast and local telephone calls.**

WHERE TO EAT

CAPTAIN NICK'S   207/942-6444

Seafood. Family Dining. $8-$21 **AAA Inspector Notes:** This family-style restaurant across from the Bangor International Airport has several dining areas, including a railroad dining car. Service is very casual. **Bar:** full bar. **Reservations:** suggested, weekends. **Address:** 1165 Union St 04401 **Location:** Corner of Griffin Rd.

DYSART'S RESTAURANT & TRUCK STOP   207/942-4878

American. Family Dining. $7-$18 **AAA Inspector Notes:** A city tradition since 1967, the truck-stop restaurant never closes. Representative of home-style cooking are soups, fresh salads, sandwiches, subs, burgers, seafood, pot roast, spaghetti and stew. Two favorites are lobster stew and homemade raspberry pie. **Address:** 530 Coldbrook Rd 04401 **Location:** I-95 exit 180 (Coldbrook Rd).

EPIC BUFFET   207/974-3500

American
Casual Dining
$10-$14

AAA Inspector Notes: Casino goers and locals alike appreciate this fine buffet, which covers the full spectrum of food choices. You'll find the items to be very well prepared and nicely presented behind glass partitions. Don't fill up too much because you'll want to leave room for an excellent homemade dessert. **Bar:** full bar. **Address:** 500 Main St 04401 **Location:** I-395 exit 3B, just n; in Hollywood Casino Hotel & Raceway. **Parking:** on-site (fee).

GODFREY'S GRILLE & LOUNGE   207/947-6721

American. Casual Dining. $10-$24 **AAA Inspector Notes:** Whether waiting for a plane or just arriving, this spot is a nice place to unwind while enjoying a favorite beverage or sampling one of their well-prepared entrées in comfortable seats. The menu includes a selection of finger foods, soups, chowders, salads, burgers, crab cakes, fish and chips and steak. **Bar:** full bar. **Address:** 308 Godfrey Blvd 04401 **Location:** At Bangor International Airport; in Four Points by Sheraton Bangor. **Parking:** on-site (fee).

GOVERNOR'S RESTAURANT & BAKERY   207/947-3113

▼▼ ▼▼ American. Family Dining. $7-$17 AAA Inspector Notes: At this casual spot, diners can flip through pages of wonderful seafood and varied Italian dishes, in addition to such choices as homemade meatloaf, steaks, burgers and sandwiches. Breakfast dishes also can be ordered at any time of the day. Weekends stay bustling with families filing in the casual spot to indulge in the daily-made bakery treats and desserts. Bar: beer & wine. Address: 643 Broadway St 04401 Location: I-95 exit 185, just n.

[B] [L] [D]

ICHIBAN JAPANESE RESTAURANT   207/262-9308

▼▼ ▼▼ Japanese. Casual Dining. $6-$16 AAA Inspector Notes: The casual, family-friendly restaurant features fresh sushi selections, tempura, teriyaki and combination lunches and dinners, plus other traditional dishes. Bar: beer & wine. Address: 226 Union St 04401 Location: Jct US 2/SR 100 and 222. [L] [D]

MASSIMO'S CUCINA ITALIANA   207/945-5600

▼▼▼▼ Italian. Casual Dining. $14-$25 AAA Inspector Notes: Serving traditional Italian fare, the family owned and operated upscale trattoria offers excellent quality food and service in a relaxed, friendly atmosphere. Bar: full bar. Address: 96 Hammond St 04401 Location: Center; at Court St. Parking: street only. [D]

MIGUEL'S MEXICAN RESTAURANT   207/942-3002

▼▼ ▼▼ Mexican. Casual Dining. $11-$22 AAA Inspector Notes: This spacious restaurant offers a fine array of Mexican fare in an upbeat atmosphere. From various fajitas, tacos and burritos to ribs, steaks, chicken and salmon, there is sure to be something for everyone. Portions are ample. Bar: full bar. Address: 697 Hogan Rd 04401 Location: I-95 exit 187 (Hogan Rd), 0.5 mi n.

[L] [D]

ORIENTAL JADE RESTAURANT   207/947-6969

▼▼ ▼▼ Chinese. Casual Dining. $8-$23 AAA Inspector Notes: The splendid buffet at this restaurant features Polynesian, Cantonese and Szechuan specialties, as well as several American dishes. Four different dining rooms display a contemporary Oriental décor. Bar: full bar. Address: 555 Stillwater Ave 04401 Location: I-95 exit 187 (Hogan Rd), 0.3 mi w; behind cinemas near Bangor Mall.

[L] [D]

PEPINO'S MEXICAN RESTAURANT   207/947-1233

▼▼ ▼▼ Mexican. Casual Dining. $8-$17 AAA Inspector Notes: You'll enjoy the open and airy dining room at this restaurant where a plentiful menu selection is offered. The restaurant also features a fine cocktail and beer list as well as several Mexican beers and a wine list with by-the-glass offerings. Service is friendly. Bar: full bar. Address: 570 Stillwater Ave 04401 Location: I-95 exit 186 (Stillwater Ave), just n. [L] [D]

SEA DOG BREWING CO   207/947-8009

▼▼ ▼▼ American. Casual Dining. $7-$28 AAA Inspector Notes: A bustling atmosphere and good food draw patrons to this nautically-decorated spacious restaurant/microbrewery. Enjoy a wonderful view of the Penobscot River from inside or on the spacious deck. Bar: full bar. Address: 26 Front St 04401 Location: Center; between US 1 alternate route and May St. [L] [D] [LATE]

THISTLES RESTAURANT   207/945-5480

▼▼▼▼ International. Casual Dining. $11-$27 AAA Inspector Notes: Located in a business center, the restaurant offers a pleasant ambience with fine piano music and a friendly staff. The menu features various seafood, meat and pasta dishes. The delicious desserts are prepared on the premises. Bar: full bar. Reservations: suggested. Address: 175 Exchange St 04401 Location: Center; in Maliseet Plaza. [L] [D]

ZEN ASIAN BISTRO & LOUNGE   207/947-3030

▼▼ Fusion. Casual Dining. $10-$20 AAA Inspector Notes: Zen is an attractive Asian fusion restaurant where patrons can sample creatively presented Japanese, Vietnamese or Thai delights in an upbeat friendly atmosphere. The various seating arrangements on two levels include a Japanese-style sunken area with comfy cushions on the floor. Bar: full bar. Address: 128 Main St 04401 Location: Between Water and Union sts; downtown. Parking: street only. [L] [D]

BAR HARBOR (I-6) pop. 2,552, elev. 240'

- Hotels p. 53 • Restaurants p. 60
- Attractions map p. 39
- Hotels & Restaurants map & index p. 49, 51
- Part of Acadia National Park area — see map p. 38

Bar Harbor lies at the entrance to Acadia National Park on Mount Desert Island. The beauty of sea, mountain, lake and forest have made this region well-known as a resort. By the turn of the 20th century Bar Harbor had become the summer playground for America's wealthy; millionaires J.P. Morgan, Joseph Pulitzer and John D. Rockefeller were among those who owned "cottages."

However, newly instituted income taxes, World War I and the Great Depression nearly removed the leisure class from Bar Harbor by the 1930s. Many of the abandoned cottages, like their owners, succumbed to disaster and bad luck. Then a fire swept through Bar Harbor in 1947, ravaging 237 homes, including most of the estates, destroying more than 17,000 acres and leaving $23 million in charred ruins. The history of Bar Harbor can be seen in a collection of photographs and artifacts at the Bar Harbor Historical Society Museum, 33 Ledgelawn Ave.; phone (207) 288-0000.

A network of motor highways, carriage roads and mountain trails preserves the striking scenery for visitors. The Great Meadow Loop Trail connects downtown Bar Harbor with Acadia National Park.

One of the best ways to explore the area is to hop on the Island Explorer, a free shuttle bus operating late June through Columbus Day. Rides to Northeast Harbor, Southwest Harbor, Acadia National Park, beaches, campgrounds and other destinations originate at the Bar Harbor Village Green. Rides to Brown Mountain are offered June through August. Shuttle passengers going to Acadia National Park should purchase a park entry permit at the Village Green prior to departing; phone (207) 288-4573.

Whale-watching cruises, sailing charters and working lobster boat excursions depart from Bar Harbor May through October.

Jackson Laboratory, 1.5 miles south on SR 3, is a national genetics research center. Tours are offered June through September; phone (207) 288-6051 for reservations.

Bar Harbor Chamber of Commerce / Acadia Welcome Center: 1201 Bar Harbor Rd., Trenton, ME 04605. **Phone:** (207) 288-5103 or (800) 345-4617.

ABBE MUSEUM DOWNTOWN is downtown at 26 Mount Desert St. Permanent and changing exhibits devoted to Maine's American Indian heritage grace the galleries. Exhibits focus on the cultures, history and archeology of the Wabanaki people—members of the Passamaquoddy, Penobscot, Micmac and Maliseet tribes—who live in Maine today. **Time:** Allow 1 hour minimum. **Hours:** Daily 10-5, Memorial Day weekend-Nov. 1; Thurs.-Sat. 10-4, rest of year. **Cost:** $6; $2 (ages 6-15). **Phone:** (207) 288-3519.

(See maps & indexes p. 49, 51.)

ACADIA NATIONAL PARK TOURS, 53 Main St., offers narrated 2.5-hour bus tours of Bar Harbor and Acadia National Park. The tour includes the mansions of Bar Harbor, Sieur de Monts Spring, Thunder Hole and Cadillac Mountain. **Hours:** Tours depart daily at 10 and 2, mid-May to late Oct. **Cost:** $27.50; $15 (ages 0-12). **Phone:** (207) 288-0300.

THE ATLANTIC BREWING COMPANY, 6 mi. w. on Mt. Desert St./SR 3 (becomes Eagle Lake Rd./SR 233), 1.3 mi. w. on Sound Dr./SR 3/SR 198, 2 mi. n. on Main St./SR 102/SR 198, then .1 mi. n. to 15 Knox Rd., offers 30-minute tours during which visitors observe the entire brewing process, from fermentation to bottling. The brewery produces 60 kegs per day; samples of its ales, as well as its root beer, are available.

Time: Allow 1 hour minimum. **Hours:** Tours depart daily at 2, 3 and 4, Memorial Day-Columbus Day. Tastings are offered on the half-hour. **Cost:** Free. **Phone:** (207) 288-2337. ⟨📆⟩

BAR HARBOR WHALE MUSEUM is .2 mi. n. on Main St., then .1 mi. w. to 52 West St. The museum's exhibits focus on the biology, history and habits of all whales, particularly finbacks, humpbacks, minkes and other varieties seen in the Gulf of Maine. Interactive displays, games and videos allow visitors to distinguish whale types; a puzzle of minke whale bones may be assembled. A life-size replica of a 50-million-year-old whale and skeletons of whales and other marine mammals are displayed.

Note: The museum is currently closed; reopening is scheduled for early 2014 at a new location. **Time:** Allow 30 minutes minimum. **Hours:** Daily 9-9, July-Aug.; 10-8 in June and Sept.-Oct.; by appointment rest of year. **Cost:** Donations. **Phone:** (207) 288-0288.

BAR HARBOR WHALE WATCH CO. departs from the Harbor Place at 1 West St. The company offers narrated, 3-hour whale-watching or 3.5-hour combination whale- and puffin-watching excursions aboard a 112-foot high-speed catamaran. The catamaran offers three decks for viewing. A nature/sightseeing cruise, lobster fishing excursion, seal-watching cruise and the Baker Island tour are offered aboard other craft. The 2.5-hour Historical Lighthouse Tour travels to five offshore island lighthouses.

Note: Warm clothing is recommended. **Hours:** Whale-watching trips daily at 8:30 and 1, late June-early Oct. (also at 4:30, mid-July to early Sept.); at noon, early Oct.-late Oct. Combination whale- and puffin-watching trips daily at noon, late May to mid-June; at 8:30, mid-June to late Aug. Nature/sightseeing cruise daily at 10 and 1:15, mid-May to late Oct. (also at 3:30 and 6:30, in July; and at 4 in June and late Aug.-early Oct.). Historical Lighthouse Tour daily at 1:30, late May-late Oct. Phone ahead to confirm schedule.

Cost: Whale-watching and combination whale- and puffin-watching trips each $59; $33 (ages 6-14); $9 (ages 0-5). Baker Island tour $46; $27 (ages 6-14); $9 (ages 0-5). Historical Lighthouse Tour $45; $27 (ages 6-14); $9 (ages 0-5). Nature/sightseeing cruise $29; $19 (ages 6-14); $9 (ages 0-5). Lobster fishing or seal-watching cruise $29; $18 (ages 6-14). Fares may vary; phone ahead. **Phone:** (207) 288-2386 or (800) 942-5374. ⟨📆⟩

GEORGE B. DORR MUSEUM OF NATURAL HISTORY is at 105 Eden St. on the College of the Atlantic campus. The museum displays mounted

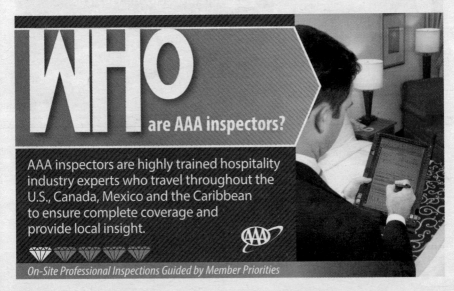

(See maps & indexes p. 49, 51.)

mammals and birds in lifelike scenes. Other exhibits depict natural aspects of maritime Maine, including a tide pool. A changing interpretive program is offered daily July 1 through Labor Day. **Time:** Allow 30 minutes minimum. **Hours:** Tues.-Sat. 10-5. **Cost:** Donations. **Phone:** (207) 288-5395.

MARGARET TODD WINDJAMMER CRUISES depart from the Bar Harbor Inn Pier. Three cruises of Frenchman's Bay are available on the 151-foot-long, four-masted schooner. Bald eagles, porpoises and seals may be seen during a morning sail; on the afternoon narrated sail, passengers may picnic and help hoist the sails. The sunset sail offers live music.

Note: Passengers are advised to bring a warm jacket or sweater, particularly during cooler months. Tickets may be purchased at the ticket office at 27 Main St. **Time:** Allow 2 hours minimum. **Hours:** Cruises depart daily at 10, 2 and dusk, May 15-Oct. 15. Phone ahead to confirm schedule. **Cost:** $37.50; $35 (ages 65+); $27.50 (ages 6-11); $5 (ages 2-5). **Phone:** (207) 288-4585, (207) 546-2927 during winter, or (207) 288-2373 during summer. 🏠 🅰

**Download
eTourBook®
Guides**

AAA.com/ebooks

MOUNT DESERT OCEANARIUM BAR HARBOR, 8.5 mi. w. to 1351 SR 3, includes the Maine Lobster Museum and the Oceanarium Lobster Hatchery. The museum features net-making demonstrations and a visit aboard a lobster boat; a licensed Maine lobsterman is on site to answer questions. At the hatchery, visitors can examine fry via a microscope linked to a television monitor. The Discovery Pool is a touch tank containing local marine life. A 45-minute marsh walk is offered.

Guided tours are available late May to late October. **Time:** Allow 2 hours minimum. **Hours:** Mon.-Sat. 9-5, mid-May to late Oct. Phone ahead to confirm schedule. **Cost:** Including marsh walk $16; $10 (ages 4-12). Excluding marsh walk $13.50; $8.50 (ages 4-12). **Phone:** (207) 288-5005.

RECREATIONAL ACTIVITIES

Kayaking

- **Aquaterra Adventures** departs the Harbor Place Building, 1 West St. The company offers a variety of sea kayaking tours in the waters off Mount Desert Island. **Hours:** Daily, mid-May to late Oct. **Phone:** (207) 288-0007 or (877) 386-4124.
- **Coastal Kayaking Tours** departs from 48 Cottage St. Visitors can choose from a variety of sea kayaking tours including harbor, sunset and half-day trips. **Hours:** Daily, mid-May to late Oct. **Phone:** (207) 288-9605 or (800) 526-8615.
- **National Park Sea Kayak Tours** departs from 39 Cottage St. Among the options are half-day tours into Western Bay, Blue Hill Bay or Somes Sound. **Hours:** Daily, late May-early Oct. **Phone:** (800) 347-0940.

▼ See AAA listing p. 110 ▼

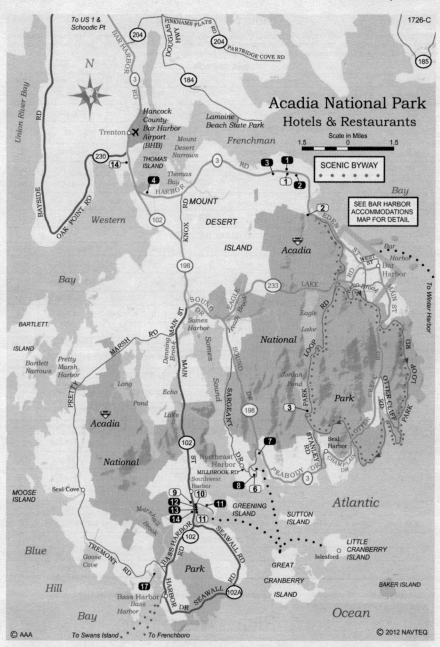

Acadia National Park
Hotels & Restaurants

SCENIC BYWAY

SEE BAR HARBOR
ACCOMMODATIONS
MAP FOR DETAIL

Acadia National Park

This index helps you "spot" where approved hotels and restaurants are located on the corresponding detailed maps. Hotel daily rate range is for comparison only. Restaurant price range is a combination of lunch and/or dinner. Turn to the listing page for more detailed rate and price information and consult display ads for special promotions.

BAR HARBOR

Map Page	Hotels	Diamond Rated	Rate Range	Page
1 p. 49	High Seas Motel	▽▽	$55-$145	59
2 p. 49	Hutchins Mountain View Cottages	▽▽	$74-$98	59
3 p. 49	BEST WESTERN Acadia Park Inn *(See ad p. 84.)*	▽▽	$99-$189 SAVE	58
4 p. 49	Acadia Sunnyside Motel & Cottages	▽▽	$55-$145	53

Map Page	Restaurants	Diamond Rated	Cuisine	Price Range	Page
① p. 49	Log Cabin Restaurant	▽▽	American	$7-$18	61
② p. 49	**The Chart Room**	▽▽	American	$13-$28	60
③ p. 49	Jordan Pond House	▽▽	American	$9-$25	61

NORTHEAST HARBOR

Map Page	Hotels	Diamond Rated	Rate Range	Page
7 p. 49	Asticou Inn	▽▽	$175-$380	115
8 p. 49	**Kimball Terrace Inn**	▽▽	$75-$225 SAVE	115

Map Page	Restaurant	Diamond Rated	Cuisine	Price Range	Page
⑥ p. 49	Watermark Restaurant & Lounge	▽▽	American	$8-$21	115

SOUTHWEST HARBOR

Map Page	Hotels	Diamond Rated	Rate Range	Page
11 p. 49	Clark Point Inn	▽▽▽	$139-$239	152
12 p. 49	The Inn at Southwest	▽▽▽	$125-$200	152
13 p. 49	The Kingsleigh Inn	▽▽▽	$140-$315	152
14 p. 49	Acadia Cottages	▽▽	$115-$150	152

Map Page	Restaurants	Diamond Rated	Cuisine	Price Range	Page
⑨ p. 49	Cafe 2/Eat-a-Pita	▽▽	American	$13-$26	152
⑩ p. 49	Cafe Dry Dock	▽▽	American	$8-$24	152
⑪ p. 49	Fiddler's Green Restaurant	▽▽▽	American	$18-$28	152

BASS HARBOR

Map Page	Hotel	Diamond Rated	Rate Range	Page
17 p. 49	**Ann's Point Inn**	▽▽▽▽	$270-$350 SAVE	62

TRENTON

Map Page	Restaurant	Diamond Rated	Cuisine	Price Range	Page
⑭ p. 49	Trenton Bridge Lobster Pound	▽	Seafood	$9-$18	153

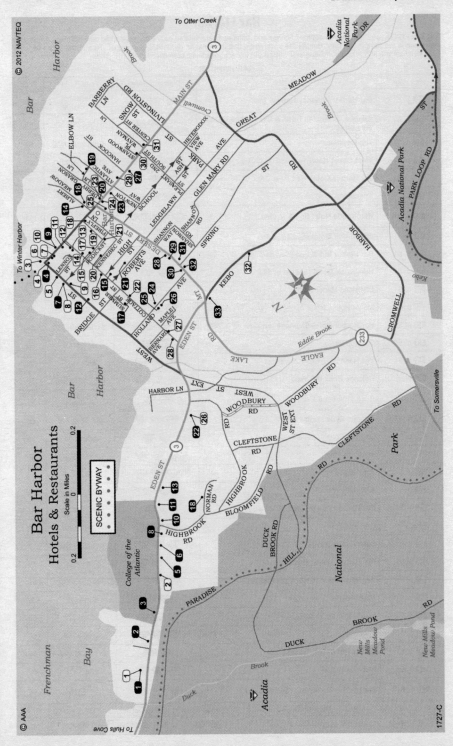

© 2012 NAVTEQ

Bar Harbor
Hotels & Restaurants

Scale in Miles

SCENIC BYWAY

© AAA

1727-C

Bar Harbor

This index helps you "spot" where approved hotels and restaurants are located on the corresponding detailed maps. Hotel daily rate range is for comparison only. Restaurant price range is a combination of lunch and/or dinner. Turn to the listing page for more detailed rate and price information and consult display ads for special promotions.

BAR HARBOR

Map Page	Hotels	Diamond Rated	Rate Range	Page
1 p. 51	**Bar Harbor Regency Holiday Inn**	◆◆◆	Rates not provided [SAVE]	56
2 p. 51	**Atlantic Oceanside Hotel & Conference Center** *(See ad p. 54.)*	◆◆◆	$119-$399 [SAVE]	55
3 p. 51	**The Bayview**	◆◆◆	$185-$520 [SAVE]	57
4 p. 51	**West Street Hotel**	◆◆◆◆	$139-$1200 [SAVE]	60
5 p. 51	**Bar Harbor Motel** *(See ad p. 54.)*	◆◆◆	$89-$155 [SAVE]	55
6 p. 51	**Acadia Inn** *(See ad p. 54.)*	◆◆◆	$79-$189 [SAVE]	53
7 p. 51	**Harborside Hotel Spa & Marina**	◆◆◆◆	Rates not provided [SAVE]	58
8 p. 51	**Edenbrook Motel** *(See ad p. 58.)*	◆	$45-$120 [SAVE]	58
9 p. 51	**Bar Harbor Inn & Spa** *(See ad p. 54.)*	◆◆◆	$89-$389 [SAVE]	55
10 p. 51	**Highbrook Motel** *(See ad p. 59.)*	◆◆	$59-$179 [SAVE]	59
11 p. 51	Cleftstone Manor	◆◆◆	$120-$215	58
12 p. 51	Manor House Inn	◆◆◆	$90-$275	59
13 p. 51	**Bar Harbor Hotel-Bluenose Inn** *(See ad p. 56.)*	◆◆◆◆	$119-$539 [SAVE]	55
14 p. 51	Seacroft Inn	◆◆	$79-$149	60
15 p. 51	The Hearthside Bed & Breakfast	◆◆◆	$85-$185	59
16 p. 51	**Balance Rock Inn 1903**	◆◆◆	$155-$635 [SAVE]	55
17 p. 51	Black Friar Inn & Pub	◆◆	Rates not provided	58
18 p. 51	**Atlantic Eyrie Lodge**	◆◆◆	$85-$249 [SAVE]	55
19 p. 51	Moseley Cottage Inn & Town Motel	◆◆	$89-$300	60
20 p. 51	**Ivy Manor Inn**	◆◆◆	$99-$275 [SAVE]	59
21 p. 51	The Maples Inn	◆◆◆	$120-$215	59
22 p. 51	**A Wonder View Inn**	◆◆	$99-$269 [SAVE]	55
23 p. 51	**Bar Harbor Villager Motel** *(See ad p. 54.)*	◆◆	$89-$179 [SAVE]	57
24 p. 51	Graycote Inn	◆◆◆	$98-$198	58
25 p. 51	**Castlemaine Inn**	◆◆◆	$79-$289 [SAVE]	58
26 p. 51	**Bar Harbor Manor** *(See ad p. 57.)*	◆◆◆	$65-$195 [SAVE]	55
27 p. 51	**Bar Harbor Grand Hotel** *(See ad p. 54.)*	◆◆◆	$89-$235 [SAVE]	55
28 p. 51	Anne's White Columns Inn	◆◆	$85-$175	53
29 p. 51	Mira Monte Inn & Suites	◆◆◆	$101-$272	60
30 p. 51	Primrose Inn Bed and Breakfast	◆◆◆	$134-$289	60
31 p. 51	**Aurora Inn** *(See ad p. 54.)*	◆◆	$79-$189 [SAVE]	55
32 p. 51	Holbrook House	◆◆◆	$89-$289	59
33 p. 51	**Bar Harbor Quality Inn** *(See ad p. 54.)*	◆◆◆	Rates not provided [SAVE]	56

Map Page	Restaurants	Diamond Rated	Cuisine	Price Range	Page
1 p. 51	Stewman's Lobster Pound	◆◆	Seafood	$8-$30	62

Map Page	Restaurants (cont'd)	Diamond Rated	Cuisine	Price Range	Page
② p. 51	Jack Russell's Steakhouse & Brewery	♦♦	American	$17-$28	61
③ p. 51	Fish House Grill & Oyster Bar	♦♦	Seafood	$12-$34	60
④ p. 51	**Paddy's Irish Pub**	♦♦♦	Irish	$10-$26	61
⑤ p. 51	Stewman's Downtown	♦♦	Seafood	$8-$22	62
⑥ p. 51	Galyn's Restaurant	♦♦♦	American	$8-$31	60
⑦ p. 51	Geddy's Pub	♦♦	American	$8-$26	61
⑧ p. 51	**La Bella Vita Ristorante**	♦♦♦	Italian	$11-$27	61
⑨ p. 51	West Street Cafe	♦♦	American	$8-$28	62
⑩ p. 51	**The Reading Room Restaurant at the Bar Harbor Inn & Spa**	♦♦♦	American	$24-$38	62
⑪ p. 51	**Testa's Restaurant**	♦♦	American	$8-$30	62
⑫ p. 51	Jeannie's Great Maine Breakfast	♦♦	Breakfast	$7-$12	61
⑬ p. 51	Route 66 Restaurant	♦♦	American	$9-$23	62
⑭ p. 51	Portside Grill Fresh Seafood	♦♦	Seafood	$7-$21	62
⑮ p. 51	Siam Orchid Thai Restaurant	♦♦	Thai	$9-$18	62
⑯ p. 51	Cottage Street Bakery & Deli	♦♦	Breads/Pastries	$7-$14	60
⑰ p. 51	Lompoc Cafe	♦♦	American	$8-$21	61
⑱ p. 51	Rupununi-An American Bar & Grill	♦♦	American	$9-$26	62
⑲ p. 51	The Dog and Pony Tavern	♦	American	$7-$15	62
⑳ p. 51	Mama DiMatteo's	♦♦	Italian	$16-$27	61
㉑ p. 51	Side Street Cafe	♦♦	American	$10-$20	62
㉒ p. 51	Jordan's Restaurant	♦♦	American	$5-$14	61
㉓ p. 51	Michelle's Fine Dining	♦♦♦	French	$25-$38	61
㉔ p. 51	Cherrystones	♦♦	American	$10-$29	60
㉕ p. 51	Cafe This Way	♦♦♦	American	$15-$25	60
㉖ p. 51	The Looking Glass Restaurant *(See ad p. 56.)*	♦♦♦	American	$12-$37	61
㉗ p. 51	2 Cats Bed & Breakfast	♦♦	Breakfast	$8-$14	60
㉘ p. 51	Mache Bistro	♦♦♦	French	$16-$25	61
㉙ p. 51	McKay's Public House	♦♦♦	American	$12-$28	61
㉚ p. 51	Poor Boys Gourmet Restaurant	♦♦	American	$12-$24	61
㉛ p. 51	**Havana Restaurant**	♦♦♦	Latin American	$19-$34	61
㉜ p. 51	**Acadia Cafe**	♦♦	American	$7-$15	60

ACADIA INN (207)288-3500 **6**

♦♦♦♦
Hotel
$79-$189

Address: 98 Eden St 04609 **Location:** 1 mi w on SR 3. **Facility:** 95 units. 3 stories, interior corridors. **Terms:** closed 11/12-4/9, cancellation fee imposed. **Amenities:** safes. **Pool(s):** heated outdoor. **Activities:** whirlpool, hiking trails, playground. **Guest Services:** coin laundry. **Free Special Amenities: continental breakfast and local telephone calls.** *(See ad p. 54.)*

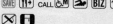

ACADIA SUNNYSIDE MOTEL & COTTAGES
207/288-3602 **4**

♦♦ Cottage $55-$145 **Address:** 1441 State Hwy 3 04609 **Location:** On SR 3, 9 mi w. **Facility:** 20 units, some cottages. 1 story, exterior corridors. **Terms:** closed 10/21-4/30, cancellation fee imposed. **Pool(s):** outdoor. **Guest Services:** coin laundry.

ANNE'S WHITE COLUMNS INN 207/288-5357 **28**

♦♦♦ Bed & Breakfast $85-$175 **Address:** 57 Mt Desert St 04609 **Location:** Just s of Holland Ave; center. **Facility:** 10 units. 2 stories (no elevator), interior corridors. **Terms:** closed 12/1-5/31, 14 day cancellation notice-fee imposed.

(See maps & indexes p. 49, 51.)

ATLANTIC EYRIE LODGE   207/288-9786 **18**

Hotel
$85-$249

Address: 6 Norman Rd 04609 **Location:** 1 mi w on SR 3 to Highbrook Rd. **Facility:** 58 units, some efficiencies. 4 stories, exterior corridors. **Terms:** closed 10/21-5/9, check-in 4 pm, 7 day cancellation notice-fee imposed. **Pool(s):** heated outdoor. **Activities:** playground. **Guest Services:** coin laundry. **Free Special Amenities: expanded continental breakfast and high-speed Internet.**

SAVE ∏↦ CALL &M ➘ BIZ 🛜 ✕ 🖃 🖼️ 🖵
/SOME UNITS FEE 🐾

ATLANTIC OCEANSIDE HOTEL & CONFERENCE CENTER   (207)288-5801 **2**

Hotel
$119-$399

Address: 119 Eden St 04609 **Location:** Oceanfront. 1.8 mi w on SR 3. Adjacent to ferry landing. **Facility:** 153 units, some two bedrooms, efficiencies, kitchens and houses. 2-4 stories, interior/exterior corridors. **Terms:** 7 day cancellation notice-fee imposed. **Amenities:** safes. Some: high-speed Internet. **Pool(s):** heated outdoor, heated indoor. **Activities:** whirlpools, boat dock, exercise room. Fee: fishing, charter fishing. **Guest Services:** coin laundry. **Free Special Amenities: local telephone calls.** (See ad p. 54.)

SAVE ECO ∏↦ ➘ BIZ 🛜 ✕ 🖃 🖼️ 🖵
/SOME UNITS FEE 🐾

AURORA INN   (207)288-3771 **31**

Motel
$79-$189

Address: 68 Mt Desert St 04609 **Location:** At Holland Ave. **Facility:** 22 units. 1 story, exterior corridors. **Terms:** closed 10/29-4/14, 3 day cancellation notice. **Amenities:** safes. **Free Special Amenities: local telephone calls and newspaper.** (See ad p. 54.)

SAVE ECO ∏↦ 🛜 ✕ 🖃 🖼️
🖵

A WONDER VIEW INN   (207)288-3358 **22**

Hotel
$99-$269

Address: 50 Eden St 04609 **Location:** 0.5 mi w on SR 3. Located in a quiet secluded area. **Facility:** 72 units, some two bedrooms. 1-2 stories (no elevator), exterior corridors. **Terms:** closed 11/4-5/9, 3 day cancellation notice-fee imposed. **Dining:** The Looking Glass Restaurant, see separate listing. **Pool(s):** heated outdoor. **Activities:** volleyball. **Guest Services:** coin laundry. **Free Special Amenities: newspaper and high-speed Internet.**

SAVE ∏ ➘ 🛜 ✕ 🖃 /SOME UNITS FEE 🐾 🖼️ 🖵

BALANCE ROCK INN 1903   207/288-2610 **16**

Historic Bed
& Breakfast
$155-$635

Address: 21 Albert Meadow 04609 **Location:** Oceanfront. Just s of Main St; center. Located in a residential area. **Facility:** This turn-of-the-20th-century oceanfront mansion borders a shore path. Many rooms feature decks, fireplaces and whirlpool baths. 24 units, some kitchens. 3 stories, interior/exterior corridors. **Terms:** closed 10/27-5/16, 14 day cancellation notice-fee imposed. **Pool(s):** heated outdoor. **Activities:** exercise room. **Free Special Amenities: full breakfast and local telephone calls.**

SAVE Y ➘ 🖃 🛜 ✕ 📷
/SOME UNITS FEE 🐾 🖃 🖼️ 🖵

BAR HARBOR GRAND HOTEL   207/288-5226 **27**

Hotel
$89-$235

Address: 269 Main St 04609 **Location:** Between Newton Way and Hancock St. **Facility:** 70 units, some two bedrooms. 4 stories, interior corridors. **Terms:** closed 11/11-4/4, cancellation fee imposed. **Amenities:** high-speed Internet, safes. **Pool(s):** heated outdoor. **Activities:** whirlpool, exercise room. **Guest Services:** coin laundry. **Free Special Amenities: continental breakfast and local telephone calls.** (See ad p. 54.)

SAVE ECO ∏↦ ➘ 🛜 ✕ 📷 🖃 🖵

BAR HARBOR HOTEL-BLUENOSE INN   (207)288-3348 **13**

Hotel
$119-$539

Address: 90 Eden St 04609 **Location:** 1 mi w on SR 3. **Facility:** On an elevated site overlooking Frenchman's Bay, this inn offers spacious suites and guest rooms in two buildings. Many rooms afford lovely bay views. 97 units. 3-4 stories, interior/exterior corridors. **Terms:** closed 11/4-4/25, 10 day cancellation notice-fee imposed. **Amenities:** high-speed Internet, safes. **Dining:** entertainment. **Pool(s):** heated indoor. **Activities:** whirlpool, steamroom, exercise room, spa. **Guest Services:** coin laundry, area transportation. **Free Special Amenities: local telephone calls and high-speed internet.** (See ad p. 56.)

SAVE ECO ∏↦ 🛏 🛜 ✕
🖃 CALL &M ➘ BIZ 🛜 ✕
🖃 🖵 /SOME UNITS 🖼️

BAR HARBOR INN & SPA   (207)288-3351 **9**

Hotel
$89-$389

Address: Newport Dr 04609 **Location:** Oceanfront. At Main St; center. Located on waterfront by town pier. **Facility:** 153 units, some two bedrooms. 2 stories, interior/exterior corridors. **Terms:** closed 11/26-3/14, 10 day cancellation notice-fee imposed. **Amenities:** safes. **Dining:** The Reading Room Restaurant at the Bar Harbor Inn & Spa, see separate listing. **Pool(s):** heated outdoor. **Activities:** saunas, whirlpool, playground, exercise room, spa. **Guest Services:** valet laundry. **Free Special Amenities: expanded continental breakfast and local telephone calls.** (See ad p. 54.)

SAVE ∏ Y ➘ BIZ 🛜 ✕ 📷 🖃 🖵

BAR HARBOR MANOR   (207)288-3829 **26**

Hotel
$65-$195

Address: 47 Holland Ave 04609 **Location:** Between Cottage and Mt Desert sts; center. **Facility:** 24 units, some two bedrooms and kitchens. 1-2 stories (no elevator), exterior corridors. **Terms:** closed 10/25-5/1, 10 day cancellation notice-fee imposed. **Free Special Amenities: local telephone calls and high-speed Internet.** (See ad p. 57.)

SAVE ∏↦ 🛜 ✕ 🖃 🖵
/SOME UNITS 🖼️

BAR HARBOR MOTEL   207/288-3453 **5**

Hotel
$89-$155

Address: 100 Eden St 04609 **Location:** 1.8 mi n on SR 3. **Facility:** 86 units, some two bedrooms. 1 story, exterior corridors. **Terms:** closed 10/28-5/1, 3 day cancellation notice-fee imposed. **Pool(s):** heated outdoor. **Activities:** hiking trails, playground. **Guest Services:** coin laundry. (See ad p. 54.)

SAVE ∏↦ ➘ BIZ 🛜 ✕ 🖃 🖵

(See maps & indexes p. 49, 51.)

BAR HARBOR QUALITY INN   207/288-5403 **33**

Hotel
Rates not provided

Address: 40 Kebo St 04609 **Location:** Jct SR 3 and 233; center. **Facility:** 77 units, some two bedrooms and efficiencies. 2 stories (no elevator), exterior corridors. **Amenities:** safes. **Pool(s):** heated outdoor. **Activities:** whirlpool. **Guest Services:** coin laundry. **Free Special Amenities:** local telephone calls and newspaper. *(See ad p. 54.)*

BAR HARBOR REGENCY HOLIDAY INN

207/288-9723 **1**

Hotel
Rates not provided

Address: 123 Eden St 04609 **Location:** Oceanfront. 1 mi w on SR 3. **Facility:** 280 units. 3-4 stories, interior corridors. **Terms:** check-in 4 pm. **Amenities:** safes. **Dining:** Stewman's Lobster Pound, see separate listing. **Pool(s):** heated outdoor. **Activities:** sauna, putting green, 2 lighted tennis courts, exercise room. *Fee:* boat dock. **Guest Services:** coin laundry. **Free Special Amenities:** local telephone calls and high-speed Internet.

THE BLUENOSE
A Classic Bar Harbor Hotel

AAA Four Diamond Award

Sitting dramatically atop a granite, terraced hillside just minutes from Acadia National Park, the Bluenose Inn offers the ultimate escape from the every day. With luxurious amenities and a casually elegant atmosphere, a visit with us is the perfect way to experience the best of Bar Harbor.

- Dine high above Bar Harbor at *The Looking Glass Restaurant*, named a *Wine Spectator* **2012 Award of Excellence Winner.**
- Indulge yourself with one of our exquisite spa treatments at *The Eden Spa.*
- Heated Indoor and Outdoor Pools, Fitness Room, Whirlpool Tub, and Steam Room - *no resort fees.*
- Magnificent *Great Room Piano Lounge* featuring light fare & seasonal live entertainment.
- Convenient location - close to town, Acadia National Park, and to a complimentary Island Explorer pick-up.

ENVIRONMENTAL LEADER   *We are a Certified Green Hotel by the State of Maine.*

For Reservations Call: 1-800-445-4077
90 Eden Street | Bar Harbor, ME 04609 | (207) 288-3348
visitus@barharborhotel.com • www.barharborhotel.com

Be a better driver. Keep your mind on the road.

(See maps & indexes p. 49, 51.)

BAR HARBOR VILLAGER MOTEL (207)288-3211

 Motel $89-$179

Address: 207 Main St 04609 **Location:** On SR 3, at Atlantic Ave; center. **Facility:** 52 units. 2 stories (no elevator), exterior corridors. **Terms:** closed 10/27-5/9, cancellation fee imposed. **Pool(s):** heated outdoor. (See ad p. 54.)

THE BAYVIEW (207)288-5861

 Hotel $185-$520

Address: 111 Eden St 04609 **Location:** Oceanfront. 1 mi w on SR 3. **Facility:** 32 units, some two bedrooms, three bedrooms and kitchens. 2-3 stories (no elevator), interior corridors. **Terms:** closed 10/18-5/17, 10 day cancellation notice-fee imposed. **Pool(s):** heated outdoor. **Guest Services:** valet laundry. **Free Special Amenities:** expanded continental breakfast and high-speed Internet.

▼ See AAA listing p. 55 ▼

Keep seasonal vehicles travel-ready with a AAA/CAA Battery Tender®

(See maps & indexes p. 49, 51.)

BEST WESTERN ACADIA PARK INN

(207)288-5823   **3**

Hotel
$99-$189

AAA Benefit: Members save 10% or more with Best Western.

Address: 452 State Hwy 3 04609 **Location:** 4.8 mi w. Located in a rural area. **Facility:** 94 units. 1 story, exterior corridors. **Terms:** closed 10/28-4/25. **Pool(s):** heated outdoor. **Guest Services:** coin laundry. **Free Special Amenities: expanded continental breakfast and local telephone calls.** *(See ad p. 84.)*

SAVE 🚲 BIZ 🛜 ✖ 💻

/ SOME UNITS 🛗

BLACK FRIAR INN & PUB

207/288-5091   **17**

🔻🔻 **Country Inn.** Rates not provided. **Address:** 10 Summer St 04609 **Location:** Jct Cottage St; downtown. **Facility:** 6 units. 3 stories (no elevator), interior corridors. **Terms:** check-in 4 pm, age restrictions may apply. 🍴 🍷 🛜 ✖ 🎦

CASTLEMAINE INN

(207)288-4563   **25**

🔻🔻🔻
Historic Bed
& Breakfast
$79-$289

Address: 39 Holland Ave 04609 **Location:** Just s of Cottage St; center. Located in a quiet residential area. **Facility:** Rooms are tastefully decorated and vary in style and shape at the elegantly appointed, renovated 1886 home. In a quiet residential area, the inn was once the summer residence of an Austro-Hungarian ambassador. 17 units. 3 stories (no elevator), interior/exterior corridors. **Terms:** closed 10/31-4/30, 2 night minimum stay - weekends, 15 day cancellation notice-fee imposed. **Free Special Amenities: full breakfast and local telephone calls.**

SAVE 🍴 BIZ 🛜 ✖ 🎦 🎦 / SOME UNITS 🛗

Get more from your membership
with an upgrade to Plus or Premier

CLEFTSTONE MANOR

207/288-8086   **11**

🔻🔻🔻🔻 **Historic Bed & Breakfast** $120-$215 **Address:** 92 Eden St 04609 **Location:** 1 mi w on SR 3. **Facility:** This 19th-century Victorian-style country mansion includes some antique furnishings and features some guest rooms with a fireplace. 16 units. 3 stories (no elevator), interior corridors. **Terms:** 2 night minimum stay - seasonal, 14 day cancellation notice-fee imposed.

🍴 🛜 ✖ / SOME UNITS 🎦

EDENBROOK MOTEL

207/288-4975   **8**

Motel
$45-$120

Address: 96 Eden St 04609 **Location:** 1 mi w on SR 3. **Facility:** 47 units, some two bedrooms. 1-2 stories (no elevator), exterior corridors. **Terms:** closed 10/14-5/18, 3 day cancellation notice. **Free Special Amenities: local telephone calls and preferred room (subject to availability with advance reservations).** *(See ad this page.)*

SAVE 🛜 ✖ 💻 / SOME UNITS 🛗

GRAYCOTE INN

207/288-3044   **24**

🔻🔻 **Historic Bed & Breakfast** $98-$198 **Address:** 40 Holland Ave 04609 **Location:** Between Cottage and Mt Desert sts; center. **Facility:** This 19th-century Victorian home, previously owned by the first Vicar of Bar Harbor, has been restored to encompass all of the style and charm of the Victorian era. 12 units, some two bedrooms. 2-3 stories (no elevator), interior/exterior corridors. **Terms:** 2 night minimum stay - seasonal, 14 day cancellation notice-fee imposed. ECO 🍴 🛜 ✖ 🎦 / SOME UNITS 🅿

HARBORSIDE HOTEL SPA & MARINA

207/288-5033   **7**

🔻🔻🔻🔻 Hotel
Rates not provided

Address: 55 West St 04609 **Location:** Oceanfront. Center. **Facility:** In the heart of downtown, the hotel sits on the edge of Frenchman Bay; the property's nearby Bar Harbor Club has been lovingly restored. 187 units, some two bedrooms, three bedrooms and efficiencies. 3 stories, interior corridors. **Terms:** check-in 4 pm. **Amenities:** safes. *Some:* high-speed Internet. **Dining:** La Bella Vita Ristorante, see separate listing. **Pool(s):** 2 heated outdoor. **Activities:** whirlpools, boat dock, recreation programs, exercise room, spa. **Guest Services:** complimentary laundry.

SAVE ECO 🍴 🍷 🚲 BIZ 🛜 ✖ 💻 / SOME UNITS 🛗 🍽

▼ See AAA listing this page ▼

(See maps & indexes p. 49, 51.)

THE HEARTHSIDE BED & BREAKFAST 207/288-4533 **15**
▼▼▼ Bed & Breakfast $85-$185 **Address:** 7 High St 04609
Location: Center. Located in a residential area. **Facility:** This turn-of-the-20th-century home is on a quiet residential street and offers comfortable guest rooms decorated in bold and vibrant colors. 9 units. 3 stories (no elevator), interior corridors. **Terms:** closed 11/1-4/30, 2 night minimum stay - seasonal, 14 day cancellation notice-fee imposed. 🍴 📶 ✕ 🅆 🔒

HIGHBROOK MOTEL 207/288-3591 **10**
▼▼▼
Motel
$59-$179

Address: 94 Eden St 04609 **Location:** 1 mi w on SR 3. **Facility:** 26 units. 1 story, exterior corridors. **Terms:** closed 10/23-5/16, 3 day cancellation notice-fee imposed. **Free Special Amenities:** continental breakfast and high-speed Internet. *(See ad this page.)* SAVE 📶 ✕ 🔒 📺

HIGH SEAS MOTEL 207/288-5836 **1**
▼▼ Motel $55-$145 **Address:** 339 State Hwy 3 04609 **Location:** 4 mi w. **Facility:** 39 units. 1 story, exterior corridors. **Terms:** closed 10/15-5/22, 3 day cancellation notice-fee imposed. **Pool(s):** heated outdoor. **Activities:** playground. **Guest Services:** coin laundry. 🍴 CALL 🄼 📶 🔒

HOLBROOK HOUSE 207/288-4970 **32**
▼▼▼ Historic Bed & Breakfast $89-$289 **Address:** 74 Mt Desert St 04609 **Location:** At Spring St; center. Located in historic corridor. **Facility:** A large front porch with comfortable seating accents this handsome 1876 Victorian home, which also offers a bright and airy sunroom. Guest rooms are individually decorated and furnished with antiques. 13 units, some two bedrooms. 2 stories (no elevator), interior/exterior corridors. **Terms:** closed 10/30-5/10, 2 night minimum stay - seasonal, 14 day cancellation notice-fee imposed. 🍴 BIZ 📶 ✕ 🅉 / SOME UNITS 🅆

HUTCHINS MOUNTAIN VIEW COTTAGES 207/288-4833 **2**
▼▼ Cottage $74-$98 **Address:** 286 State Rt 3 04609 **Location:** On SR 3, 4 mi w. **Facility:** 16 cottages. 1 story, exterior corridors. *Bath:* shower only. **Terms:** closed 10/14-6/13, 14 day cancellation notice-fee imposed. **Pool(s):** heated outdoor. ECO 🛏 📶 ✕ 🄼 🅉 🔒 🔒 📺 / SOME UNITS 🐾

IVY MANOR INN (207)288-2138 **20**
▼▼▼
Country Inn
$99-$275

Address: 194 Main St 04609 **Location:** At Derby Ln; center. **Facility:** This 1940 Tudor is in town, close to restaurants and shops. Antiques furnish the guest rooms, which vary in size and include some fireplaces. 8 units, some two bedrooms. 2 stories (no elevator), interior corridors. **Terms:** 14 day cancellation notice-fee imposed. **Dining:** Michelle's Fine Dining, see separate listing. **Free Special Amenities:** full breakfast and local telephone calls. SAVE 🍴 🍸 CALL 🄼 BIZ 📶 ✕

MANOR HOUSE INN 207/288-3759 **12**
▼▼▼ Historic Bed & Breakfast $90-$275 **Address:** 106 West St 04609 **Location:** Just s of Rodick St; center. Located in a commercial area. **Facility:** Tastefully decorated guest rooms are offered at this 1887 Victorian inn and carriage house. Also available are a few deluxe cottages and spacious suites, some with a double whirlpool bath and fireplace. 18 units, some two bedrooms and cottages. 1-3 stories (no elevator), interior/exterior corridors. **Terms:** closed 10/21-4/12, 14 day cancellation notice-fee imposed. 🍴 📶 ✕ 🅉 / SOME UNITS 🅆 🔒

THE MAPLES INN 207/288-3443 **21**
▼▼▼ Historic Bed & Breakfast $120-$215 **Address:** 16 Roberts Ave 04609 **Location:** Center. Located in residential area. **Facility:** This is a quaint 1903 Victorian home with varied-size guest rooms that are tastefully decorated. A few offer a private deck. 6 units. 3 stories (no elevator), interior corridors. *Bath:* shower only. **Terms:** closed 10/25-5/31, 14 day cancellation notice-fee imposed. 🍴 📶 ✕ 🅆 🅉

AAA/CAA travel information:
Available in print, online and on the go!

▼ See AAA listing this page ▼

(See maps & indexes p. 49, 51.)

MIRA MONTE INN & SUITES   (207)288-4263 **29**

▼▼▼ **Historic Bed & Breakfast** $101-$272 **Address:** 69 Mt Desert St 04609 **Location:** On SR 3, just e of Holland Ave. **Facility:** Manicured grounds enhance this lovely 1864 mansion. Guest rooms vary in size; some are equipped with a private deck, balcony or fireplace. 20 units, some two bedrooms, efficiencies and kitchens. 2 stories (no elevator), interior corridors. **Terms:** closed 10/31-5/12, 2 night minimum stay - seasonal and/or weekends, 10 day cancellation notice-fee imposed. **Amenities:** high-speed Internet.

[ECO] [¶+] [BIZ] [📶] [✕] [🎥] / SOME UNITS [🖥] [🖨] [🖳]

MOSELEY COTTAGE INN & TOWN MOTEL
207/288-5548 **19**

▼▼ **Hotel** $89-$300 **Address:** 12 Atlantic Ave 04609 **Location:** Just n of Main St; center. Located in a residential area. **Facility:** 18 units. 1-3 stories (no elevator), interior/exterior corridors. **Terms:** closed 10/25-4/14, 2 night minimum stay - seasonal and/or weekends, 20 day cancellation notice-fee imposed. **Activities:** limited beach access.

[¶+] [BIZ] [📶] [✕] [🖥] / SOME UNITS [📼] [🖳]

PRIMROSE INN BED AND BREAKFAST   (207)288-4031 **30**

▼▼▼ **Historic Bed & Breakfast** $134-$289 **Address:** 73 Mt Desert St 04609 **Location:** Corner of Holland Ave. **Facility:** A striking Victorian inn offering tastefully decorated guest rooms furnished with period antiques or fine reproductions. Some of the rooms feature a fireplace, balcony or whirlpool bath. 15 units. 2 stories (no elevator), interior corridors. **Terms:** closed 10/21-5/9, check-in 4 pm, 2 night minimum stay - seasonal, 14 day cancellation notice.

[ECO] [¶+] [📶] [✕] [🎥]

SEACROFT INN   207/288-4669 **14**

▼▼ **Bed & Breakfast** $79-$149 **Address:** Just e of Main St; center. **Facility:** 7 units, some two bedrooms and efficiencies. 2 stories (no elevator), interior/exterior corridors. **Terms:** closed 11/1-5/10, 2 night minimum stay - seasonal and/or weekends, 30 day cancellation notice-fee imposed.

[¶+] [📶] [✕] [🖥] [📼]

WEST STREET HOTEL   (207)288-0825 **4**

▼▼▼▼ **Hotel** $139-$1200

Address: 50 West St 04609 **Location:** Jct Main St. **Facility:** Guests will find delightfully modern guest rooms that are spacious. Each has a nautical theme and a balcony overlooking the harbor or town. 82 units, some two bedrooms. 4 stories, interior corridors. *Bath:* shower only. **Terms:** closed 10/24-5/24, check-in 4 pm, 3 day cancellation notice-fee imposed, resort fee. **Amenities:** high-speed Internet, safes. *Dining:* Paddy's Irish Pub, see separate listing. **Pool(s):** heated outdoor. **Activities:** exercise room. *Fee:* massage. **Guest Services:** complimentary laundry. **Free Special Amenities:** local telephone calls and high-speed Internet.

[SAVE] [¶] [🎿] [🍴] CALL [📞M] [🏊] [BIZ] [📶] [✕] [🎥]

[🖥] [🖳] / SOME UNITS FEE [🐾]

WHERE TO EAT

2 CATS BED & BREAKFAST   207/288-2808 **27**

▼▼ Breakfast. Casual Dining. $8-$14 **AAA Inspector Notes:** This place specializes in gourmet breakfasts served until 1 pm. The menu includes lobster eggs Benedict and various creative omelets, tasty blueberry pancakes and generous fruit plates, fresh squeezed juices and fair-trade coffee. Dine in the quaint dining rooms or on the porch overlooking the gardens. **Address:** 130 Cottage St 04609 **Location:** Between Eden St and Maple Ave. **Parking:** street only.

[B]

ACADIA CAFE   207/288-5003 **32**

▼▼ American Casual Dining $7-$15

AAA Inspector Notes: This spacious restaurant serves home-style breakfast meals including ham and eggs, omelets and blueberry pancakes. A take-out lunch menu also is available for a day in the park. **Address:** 39 Kebo St 04609 **Location:** Jct SR 3 and 233; opposite Bar Harbor Quality Inn. [B]

CAFE THIS WAY   207/288-4483 **25**

▼▼▼ American. Casual Dining. $15-$25 **AAA Inspector Notes:** Guests are invited to follow the footsteps to this pleasant restaurant just off the beaten path. The cafe serves hearty breakfasts and well-prepared dinners, with options ranging from fresh local seafood to chicken, pork and steaks. The desserts are excellent. Both indoor and outdoor seats are available. **Bar:** full bar. **Address:** 14 1/2 Mt Desert St 04609 **Location:** Between School and Main sts.

[B] [D] [AC]

THE CHART ROOM   207/288-9740 **2**

▼▼▼ American Casual Dining $13-$28

AAA Inspector Notes: Located at the entrance to Acadia National Park, the restaurant serves only the freshest seafood and certified Angus beef, with over 35 entrees featured on the menu. The pleasant seaside setting and seasonal patio dining provide a relaxed atmosphere. **Bar:** full bar. **Reservations:** suggested. **Address:** 585 Eden St 04609 **Location:** On SR 3, 2.5 mi w at Hulls Cove.

[L] [D]

CHERRYSTONES   207/801-2290 **24**

▼▼▼ American. Casual Dining. $10-$29 **AAA Inspector Notes:** This is an ideal location for people-watching as it is located on a busy corner across from the village green. The atmosphere can be bustling during peak meal times, however, service remains attentive. The menu features a fine array of fresh local seafood and meat entrées. **Bar:** full bar. **Reservations:** suggested, for dinner. **Address:** 185 Main St 04609 **Location:** Jct Mt Desert St. **Parking:** street only.

[L] [D] [AC]

COTTAGE STREET BAKERY & DELI   207/288-3010 **16**

▼▼ Breads/Pastries. Casual Dining. $7-$14 **AAA Inspector Notes:** Offering various breakfast dishes to a fine selection of burgers, sandwiches, salads and excellent desserts, pastries and delicious homemade jam and jelly. The staff will also prepare a full picnic lunch for you. Patio dining in season. **Address:** 59 Cottage St 04609 **Location:** Center. **Parking:** street only. [B] [L] [D]

THE DOG AND PONY TAVERN   207/288-0900 **19**

▼ American. Casual Dining. $7-$15 **AAA Inspector Notes:** A locally popular tavern with an outdoor terrace-style tiki bar with plenty of seating. An excellent variety of bottled and draft beers are featured along with a fine menu of primarily traditional bar food. **Bar:** full bar. **Address:** 4 Rodick Pl 04609 **Location:** Between Main and Rodick sts; downtown. **Parking:** street only. [L] [D]

FISH HOUSE GRILL & OYSTER BAR   207/288-3070 **3**

▼▼ Seafood. Casual Dining. $12-$34 **AAA Inspector Notes:** From a waterfront location overlooking the harbor, the eatery sports one of the state's largest oyster bars. Guests can sit indoors or out to savor fresh seafood and a few offerings of land fare. **Bar:** full bar. **Address:** 1 West St 04609 **Location:** Center; at Town Pier. **Parking:** street only. [L] [D] [AC]

GALYN'S RESTAURANT   207/288-9706 **6**

▼▼▼ American. Casual Dining. $8-$31 **AAA Inspector Notes:** Flavorful fresh fish and slow-roasted prime rib are the house specialties. All desserts, including the chocolate truffle mousse cake, are made from scratch on the premises. Antique-style, 1880s decor includes the original pressed-tin ceilings. **Bar:** full bar. **Address:** 17 Main St 04609 **Location:** Just s of West St; center; opposite Agamont Park. **Parking:** street only. [L] [D]

(See maps & indexes p. 49, 51.)

GEDDY'S PUB 207/288-5077 ⑦

American. Casual Dining. $8-$26 **AAA Inspector Notes:** Diners can enjoy heaping portions off a varied menu at this long-standing local favorite. The spacious, upbeat, bustling pub employs a prompt, friendly staff. **Bar:** full bar. **Address:** 19 Main St 04609 **Location:** Just s of West St; center. **Parking:** street only. L D

HAVANA RESTAURANT 207/288-2822 ㉛

Latin American
Fine Dining
$19-$34

AAA Inspector Notes: Patrons appreciate the restaurant's creativity of cuisine, which is peppered with Latin touches, as well as the festive, relaxed atmosphere. Innovative dishes center on fresh local seafood and prime steak, all of which pair nicely with choices from the large and eclectic wine list. Desserts are delightful. The seasonal terrace is popular in summer. **Bar:** full bar. **Address:** 318 Main St 04609 **Location:** Center. **Parking:** street only. D

JACK RUSSELL'S STEAKHOUSE & BREWERY 207/288-5214 ②

American. Casual Dining. $17-$28 **AAA Inspector Notes:** Named after the meanest Jack Russell terrier that ever lived, this brewpub offers beer made on the premises. The brewery can be toured. The menu has an emphasis on steaks, with a number of seafood items also offered. Patrons can unwind in the pub, dining room or on the patio in season. This place is dog-friendly. **Bar:** full bar. **Address:** 102 Eden St 04609 **Location:** 1.8 mi w on SR 3. D 𝒦

JEANNIE'S GREAT MAINE BREAKFAST 207/288-4166 ⑫

Breakfast. Casual Dining. $7-$12 **AAA Inspector Notes:** The restaurant specializes in breakfast dishes, including various pancake and egg creations. Some gluten-free and vegetarian options are offered. Be sure to sample their strawberry-rhubarb fruit spread. **Address:** 15 Cottage St 04609 **Location:** Just w of Main St. **Parking:** street only. B L

JORDAN POND HOUSE 207/276-3316 ③

American. Casual Dining. $9-$25 **AAA Inspector Notes:** The restaurant occupies an idyllic setting overlooking lovely Jordan Pond and the hills known as the Bubbles. If the weather permits, guests may opt to dine outside on the lawn, which affords a calming breeze off the pond. Folks come for the popovers and homemade jams but should also sample the fresh Maine seafood, poultry and beef selections as well as homemade ice cream. **Bar:** full bar. **Reservations:** suggested. **Address:** Acadia National Park 04609 **Location:** On Park Loop Rd, 1.8 mi n of jct SR 3; in Acadia National Park, Stanley Brook entrance. L D 𝒦

JORDAN'S RESTAURANT 207/288-3586 ㉒

American. Casual Dining. $5-$14 **AAA Inspector Notes:** A local favorite since 1976, this has been the place for anything blueberry and preferably with Maine maple syrup. Great breakfasts served hot off the grill all day share menu space with an ample variety of comfort foods for lunch. Bubbly, good-natured servers wend through the casual diner setting. **Address:** 80 Cottage St 04609 **Location:** At High St; center. **Parking:** street only. B L

LA BELLA VITA RISTORANTE 207/288-5033 ⑧

Italian
Casual Dining
$11-$27

AAA Inspector Notes: In the heart of town this ristorante is very attractive with patio dining overlooking the pool and harbor. The menu features a fine selection of Italian dishes using fresh local ingredients, including gourmet brick-oven pizza. **Bar:** full bar. **Reservations:** suggested. **Address:** 55 West St 04609 **Location:** Center; in Harborside Hotel Spa & Marina. *Menu on AAA.com*

B L D CALL ⎷M

LOG CABIN RESTAURANT 207/288-3910 ①

American. Family Dining. $7-$18 **AAA Inspector Notes:** Enjoy attentive table service at this country-style restaurant with its high post-beam construction, comfortable booth and table seating, plus the convenience of a 100-space parking area. Menu selection is vast with portions to match. Seafood is fried or broiled. If meat is your choice they have prime rib and New York Angus steak. **Bar:** full bar. **Address:** 336 Bar Harbor Rd 04609 **Location:** 4 mi w on SR 3.

B L D CALL ⎷M

LOMPOC CAFE 207/288-9392 ⑰

American. Casual Dining. $8-$21 **AAA Inspector Notes:** The cafe has an eclectic menu with seafood and vegetarian creations as well as a variety of microbrewed beers. Dining is available in the shady courtyard where one can enjoy a game of bocce ball. Live entertainment is featured on the weekends. **Bar:** full bar. **Address:** 36 Rodick St 04609 **Location:** Just s of Cottage St; center. **Parking:** street only. D 𝒦

THE LOOKING GLASS RESTAURANT 207/288-5663 ㉖

American. Casual Dining. $12-$37 **AAA Inspector Notes:** Named after famous mystery author Mary Roberts Rinehart, the restaurant is located high atop a hill on her former estate. Guests will enjoy the fantastic views of Frenchman's Bay and Bar Harbor with an option to dine on the seasonal outdoor deck around the open fire pit. A full breakfast menu is available in the morning. The dinner menu includes steak, roast prime rib, chicken, seafood, lobster and vegetarian selections. **Bar:** full bar. **Address:** 50 Eden St 04609 **Location:** 0.5 mi w on SR 3; in A Wonder View Inn & Suites. *(See ad p. 56.)* B D

MACHE BISTRO 207/288-0447 ㉘

French. Casual Dining. $16-$25 **AAA Inspector Notes:** This quaint restaurant specializes in rustic French cuisine made from local Maine seafood, meats and produce. The menu changes regularly depending on the local supply. Service is friendly and casual. **Bar:** full bar. **Reservations:** suggested. **Address:** 135 Cottage St 04609 **Location:** Just n of Eden St. **Parking:** street only. D

MAMA DIMATTEO'S 207/288-3666 ⑳

Italian. Casual Dining. $16-$27 **AAA Inspector Notes:** This quaint eatery has a rustic décor and a menu that emphasizes a fine selection of pasta, pizza, steak and seafood. The staff is very friendly. **Bar:** full bar. **Address:** 34 Kennebec Pl 04609 **Location:** Center; at top of Rodick St. **Parking:** street only. D

MCKAY'S PUBLIC HOUSE 207/288-2002 ㉙

American. Casual Dining. $12-$28 **AAA Inspector Notes:** In the former home of a Prohibition-era bootlegger, the restaurant provides casual pub fare and a more substantial dining room menu of dishes that use organic and fresh local ingredients. Patio seating is available seasonally amid perennial beds at the front of the property. **Bar:** full bar. **Address:** 231 Main St 04609 **Location:** Just s of Newton Way; center. **Parking:** street only. D

MICHELLE'S FINE DINING 207/288-0038 ㉓

French. Fine Dining. $25-$38 **AAA Inspector Notes:** Exquisite dining rooms enhance the intimate atmosphere. Fresh local and some imported ingredients go into New England-influenced preparations of traditional French cuisine. The appearances of marvelous and flavorful desserts show a creative flair. The wine list is extensive. A chef's table is available several nights a week; call ahead for information and reservations. **Bar:** full bar. **Reservations:** suggested. **Address:** 194 Main St 04609 **Location:** At Derby Ln; center; in Ivy Manor Inn. B L D

PADDY'S IRISH PUB 207/288-0825 ④

Irish
Gastropub
$10-$26

AAA Inspector Notes: Ideally located across from the harbor. Paddy's is an upbeat and friendly place offering indoor and outdoor dining. The vast menu includes selections of local fresh seafood, steaks and items cooked on the popular open rotisserie, which guests can view through the glass. **Bar:** full bar. **Address:** 50 West St 04609 **Location:** Jct Main St; in West Street Hotel. **Parking:** on-site (fee).

B L D CALL ⎷M

POOR BOYS GOURMET RESTAURANT 207/288-4148 ㉚

American. Casual Dining. $12-$24 **AAA Inspector Notes:** In a two-story house, the popular restaurant offers seating in the lounge and on the patio and enclosed verandah. The varied menu lists fresh seafood and pasta dishes, which are served in heaping portions and accompanied by selections from a good wine list. Included in the extensive choice of desserts made on the premises is sugar-free cheesecake. Service is attentive. The on-site parking is limited. **Bar:** full bar. **Reservations:** suggested. **Address:** 300 Main St 04609 **Location:** Downtown. D

(See maps & indexes p. 49, 51.)

PORTSIDE GRILL FRESH SEAFOOD   207/288-4086   (14)

▼▼▼ Seafood. Casual Dining. $7-$21 **AAA Inspector Notes:** This centrally located casual restaurant offers a wide range of seafood, including seafood crêpes and lobster served many different ways. Some meat items available. **Bar:** full bar. **Reservations:** suggested. **Address:** 38 Cottage St 04609 **Location:** Just w of Main St; center. **Parking:** street only. (L) (D)

THE READING ROOM RESTAURANT AT THE BAR HARBOR INN & SPA   207/288-3351   (10)

▼▼▼▼ American Fine Dining $24-$38   **AAA Inspector Notes:** The popular and busy restaurant used to be an 1887 social club. The lovely oceanfront setting and outdoor terrace afford splendid harbor views. On the menu are flavorful fresh seafood and pasta dishes, which match with a good wine list. Blueberry pie is excellent. **Bar:** full bar. **Reservations:** suggested. **Address:** Newport Dr 04609 **Location:** At Main St; center; in Bar Harbor Inn & Spa. *Menu on AAA.com* (B) (D)

ROUTE 66 RESTAURANT   207/288-3708   (13)

▼▼ American. Casual Dining. $9-$23 **AAA Inspector Notes:** The varied menu features a wide variety of meat and tasty fresh seafood dishes served in a lively and upbeat atmosphere that has a great nostalgic theme from the '50s and includes two levels filled with memorabilia. **Bar:** full bar. **Address:** 21 Cottage St 04609 **Location:** Center. **Parking:** street only. (L) (D)

RUPUNUNI-AN AMERICAN BAR & GRILL   207/288-2886   (18)

▼▼ American. Casual Dining. $9-$26 **AAA Inspector Notes:** This upbeat restaurant features a varied menu ranging from fresh local seafood to Choice steaks and spare ribs. Offering an excellent selection of fine liquor, wine and local and imported beer on tap. The pleasant staff will cater to all needs while guests enjoy inside or outdoor dining on the patio. **Bar:** full bar. **Address:** 119 Main St 04609 **Location:** Center; at Village Green. **Parking:** street only. (L) (D) (AC)

SIAM ORCHID THAI RESTAURANT   207/288-9669   (15)

▼▼ Thai. Casual Dining. $9-$18 **AAA Inspector Notes:** This is the place for authentic Thai cuisine that can be made as hot as you like it. The flavorful meat, seafood and vegetarian dishes are made to order. A sushi menu also is available. **Bar:** beer & wine. **Address:** 30 Rodick St 04609 **Location:** Just s of Cottage St. **Parking:** street only. (L) (D)

SIDE STREET CAFE   207/801-2591   (21)

▼▼ American. Casual Dining. $10-$20 **AAA Inspector Notes:** Guests can take a seat indoors or out on the patio at this popular café. An eclectic menu features local seafood including lobster rolls, seafood quesadilla and crab cakes, as well as burgers and build-your-own sandwiches. A well-stocked bar offers several beers on tap. Service is relaxed and friendly. **Bar:** full bar. **Address:** 49 Rodick St 04609 **Location:** Just s of Cottage St. **Parking:** street only. (L) (D)

STEWMAN'S DOWNTOWN   207/288-0346   (5)

▼▼ Seafood. Casual Dining. $8-$22 **AAA Inspector Notes:** In the town proper, this spot is spacious and has the feel of a traditional lobster pound. Enjoy the atmosphere from indoor or outdoor dining on the spacious decks. Some steak and chicken dishes complement mostly tried-and-true favorites. **Bar:** full bar. **Address:** 35 West St 04609 **Location:** Just w of Main St; center. **Parking:** street only. (L) (D) CALL (&M) (AC)

STEWMAN'S LOBSTER POUND   207/288-9723   (1)

▼▼ Seafood. Casual Dining. $8-$30 **AAA Inspector Notes:** One of two waterfront lobster pounds in the town proper, this place has the feel of a traditional lobster pound. Some steak and chicken dishes complement mostly tried-and-true favorites. **Bar:** beer & wine. **Address:** 123 Eden St 04609 **Location:** 1 mi w on SR 3; in Bar Harbor Regency Holiday Inn. (L) (D) (AC)

TESTA'S RESTAURANT   207/288-3327   (11)

▼▼▼ American Casual Dining $8-$30   **AAA Inspector Notes:** Testa's is a popular dining spot featuring seafood, steak, veal, chicken and Italian specialties, plus sandwiches, salad, soup, fresh dessert and berry pie, cappuccino and espresso. The casual pub-style environment displays antiques and memorabilia. **Bar:** full bar. **Reservations:** suggested. **Address:** 53 Main St 04609 **Location:** Center; in Bayside Landing. **Parking:** street only. (L) (D)

WEST STREET CAFE   207/288-5242   (9)

▼▼ American. Casual Dining. $8-$28 **AAA Inspector Notes:** If you crave lobster it's very likely this family-style restaurant will fulfill your needs with lobster prepared many ways. The menu includes basic comfort foods from burgers, sandwiches and pasta dishes to steaks and a variety of fresh seafood. **Bar:** full bar. **Address:** 76 West St 04609 **Location:** Jct Rodick St. **Parking:** street only. (L) (D)

BARING (G-8) elev. 89'

MOOSEHORN NATIONAL WILDLIFE REFUGE is 3 mi. s. of US 1, following signs to the refuge headquarters off Charlotte Rd. at 103 Headquarters Rd. This migratory bird haven is divided into two sites: the Baring Unit and the Edmunds Unit. Encompassing 17,200 acres, the Baring Unit contains nature and hiking trails as well as a 4,700-acre wilderness area featuring 160 acres of the state's oldest white pines.

The 7,200-acre Edmunds Unit, at Cobscook Bay State Park *(see Recreation Areas Chart),* includes a 2,782-acre wilderness area offering nature trails and fishing and snowshoeing opportunities. **Note:** Refuge roads are closed to private vehicles. **Time:** Allow 1 hour minimum. **Hours:** Daily dawn-dusk. **Cost:** Free. **Phone:** (207) 454-7161.

BASS HARBOR

- Hotels & Restaurants map & index p. 49
- Part of Acadia National Park area — see map p. 38

ANN'S POINT INN   207/244-9595   (17)

▼▼▼▼ Bed & Breakfast $270-$350   **Address:** 79 Ann's Point Rd 04653 **Location:** Oceanfront. Jct SR 102 and 102A, 0.7 mi w on SR 102. **Facility:** Nestled at the end of a small peninsula this oceanfront property offers spacious, tastefully decorated guest rooms, all with water views and king-size beds, some with patio or deck. 4 units. 1 story, interior/exterior corridors. **Terms:** closed 10/22-6/14, check-in 3:30 pm, 2 night minimum stay, age restrictions may apply, 14 day cancellation notice-fee imposed. **Amenities:** high-speed Internet. **Pool(s):** heated indoor. **Activities:** sauna, whirlpool. **Free Special Amenities:** full breakfast and high-speed Internet.

BATH (J-4) pop. 8,514, elev. 7'

Bath, on the west bank of the Kennebec River, has been an active center of shipbuilding since the early 1600s. Nuclear naval vessels and large merchant ships are now built at Bath Iron Works. Residential sections have a number of old mansions dating from Bath's days as a major port. The Chocolate Church Arts Center, 804 Washington St., offers year-round cultural events; phone (207) 442-8455.

In the town of Woolwich, one mile east of Bath, visitors can tour the Woolwich Historical Society Rural Museum, which is housed in an early 19th-century home and features quilts, rugs, fabrics, home furnishings, farm equipment and tools from the 19th and early 20th centuries; phone (207) 443-4833 during the summer, or (207) 443-5684 during the off-season.

MAINE MARITIME MUSEUM, 243 Washington St., is on a 20-acre site of a 19th-century shipyard where large wooden sailing ships were constructed and launched. In five original shipyard buildings, visitors learn about the process of building a wooden schooner. The Maritime History Building contains paintings, ship models, displays of ship artifacts, photographs and audiovisual presentations. The lobstering exhibit describes the development of one of the state's leading economic activities.

At the dock in summer, visitors may explore the 142-foot schooner *Sherman Zwicker* while learning about its history and use as a fishing boat. In season, visitors can take a trolley tour of Bath Iron Works to see modern U.S. Navy destroyers under construction, glimpse up to 10 lighthouses on a boat cruise from the Long Reach area of the Kennebec River, or peek into the Victorian-era life of the Bath family at the William T. Donnell House.

Note: Cameras are not permitted on the Bath Iron Works tour. **Tours:** Guided tours are available. **Time:** Allow 2 hours minimum. **Hours:** Daily 9:30-5. Bath Iron Works tour daily at 12:30 (also at 2:30, July-Aug.), Memorial Day-Columbus Day. Closed Jan. 1, Thanksgiving and Christmas. **Cost:** $15; $12 (ages 65+ and students with ID); $10 (ages 6-18). Bath Iron Works tour $33. Reservations are required for Bath Iron Works tour. **Phone:** (207) 443-1316.

THE GALEN C MOSES HOUSE   (207)442-8771

Bed & Breakfast
$129-$269

Address: 1009 Washington St 04530 **Location:** US 1 exit historic district, 0.5 mi n; downtown. **Facility:** Original molding and beautifully restored wood-work can be found throughout this striking 1874 converted Victorian mansion. 5 units, some two bedrooms. 2 stories (no elevator), interior/exterior corridors. **Terms:** 2 night minimum stay - seasonal and/or weekends, age restrictions may apply, 7 day cancellation notice-fee imposed. **Free Special Amenities: full breakfast and high-speed Internet.**

HAMPTON INN BATH BRUNSWICK   (207)386-1310

AAA Benefit: Members save up to 10%!

Address: 140 Commercial St 04530 **Location:** Center. **Facility:** 94 units. 4 stories, interior corridors. **Terms:** 1-7 night minimum stay, cancellation fee imposed. **Amenities:** high-speed Internet. **Pool(s):** heated indoor. **Activities:** whirlpool, exercise room. **Guest Services:** valet and coin laundry. **Free Special Amenities: full breakfast and high-speed Internet.**

HOLIDAY INN BATH/BRUNSWICK   (207)443-9741

Hotel
$79-$199

Address: 139 Richardson St 04530 **Location:** 0.3 mi s on US 1. **Facility:** 141 units. 4 stories (no elevator), interior corridors. **Pool(s):** heated outdoor. **Activities:** exercise room. **Guest Services:** valet and coin laundry. **Free Special Amenities: newspaper and high-speed Internet.**

WHERE TO EAT

BEALE STREET BARBEQUE   207/442-9514

Barbecue. Family Dining. $8-$19 **AAA Inspector Notes:** Popular with locals and tourists alike, the restaurant makes Memphis-style barbecue on the premises. Patrons also can sample such dishes as jambalaya, shrimp Louisiane and Santa Fe chicken. **Bar:** full bar. **Address:** 215 Water St 04530 **Location:** Center. **Parking:** street only.

J. R. MAXWELL'S & CO.   207/443-2014

American. Casual Dining. $6-$25 **AAA Inspector Notes:** An eclectic and varied menu of seafood, steaks and poultry sure to appeal to many. Some popular items include the lobster roll served in a grilled hot dog roll, fried haddock and chicken Maxwell. Salad dressings and soups are from scratch. **Bar:** full bar. **Address:** 122 Front St 04530 **Location:** Just n of US 1. **Parking:** street only.

KENNEBEC TAVERN & MARINA   207/442-9636

American. Casual Dining. $9-$26 **AAA Inspector Notes:** Patrons will find fresh local ingredients, with an emphasis on Maine seafood, at this restaurant featuring views of the river and marina. In addition to seafood, pasta, prime rib and vegetarian fare are featured on the menu. Don't miss out on the homemade desserts. **Bar:** full bar. **Address:** 119 Commercial St 04530 **Location:** Center.

MAE'S CAFE & BAKERY   207/442-8577

Breads/Pastries Sandwiches. Casual Dining. $8-$15 **AAA Inspector Notes:** A local favorite, diners to this spot are greeted by a mouthwatering pastry cabinet and a friendly staff. The menu is nicely balanced to include eggs Benedict and omelet varieties, pancakes, burgers and creative deli sandwiches. Carry-out also is an option for a hike or a picnic at the beach. **Address:** 160 Centre St 04530 **Location:** At SR 209. **Parking:** street only.

BELFAST (I-5) pop. 6,668, elev. 103'
• Hotels p. 64 • Restaurants p. 64

Formerly a prosperous shipbuilding center, Belfast is a community resplendent with restored Federal and early Victorian homes built by former sea merchants. The city, located on Penobscot Bay, is becoming a cultural center with artists, writers and craftspeople adding to the economic revival of Waldo County.

The Belfast Maskers, a local theater group, offers productions year-round; phone (207) 338-9668. Local cruise and aviation companies offer summer tours.

Belfast Area Chamber of Commerce-Belfast: 12 Main St., P.O. Box 58, Belfast, ME 04915. **Phone:** (207) 338-5900.

Self-guiding tours: Walking tour brochures are available from the chamber of commerce.

BELFAST BAY INN   207/338-5600

Boutique Hotel
$198-$388

Address: 72 Main St 04915 **Location:** Just e of High St; downtown. **Facility:** Located in the historic heart of town, this intimate boutique-style hotel offers splendid spacious suites with lovely furnishings and upscale artwork, a few with balconies and gas fireplaces. 8 units. 3 stories, interior corridors. **Terms:** 15 day cancellation notice-fee imposed. **Amenities:** high-speed Internet, safes. **Guest Services:** complimentary laundry. **Free Special Amenities:** full breakfast and high-speed Internet.

BELFAST HARBOR INN   (207)338-2740

Hotel
$64-$169

Address: 91 Searsport Ave (Rt 1) 04915 **Location:** Oceanfront. On US 1, 1.2 mi n from jct SR 3. **Facility:** 61 units. 2 stories (no elevator), interior/exterior corridors. **Terms:** cancellation fee imposed. **Pool(s):** heated outdoor. **Guest Services:** coin laundry. **Free Special Amenities:** expanded continental breakfast and high-speed Internet.

 Located on seven oceanfront acres overlooking beautiful Belfast Bay.

FIRESIDE INN & SUITES, OCEAN'S EDGE   (207)338-2090

Hotel $85-$329 **Address:** 159 Searsport Ave 04915 **Location:** Oceanfront. On US 1, 2 mi n from jct SR 3. **Facility:** 83 units, some efficiencies. 3 stories, interior corridors. **Amenities:** Some: high-speed Internet. **Dining:** Ocean's Edge Restaurant & Lounge, see separate listing. **Pool(s):** heated indoor. **Activities:** sauna, whirlpool. *Fee:* game room. **Guest Services:** coin laundry.

GULL MOTEL   (207)338-4030

Motel $59-$159 **Address:** 196 Searsport Ave 04915 **Location:** On US 1, 3 mi n from jct SR 3. **Terms:** 3 day cancellation notice-fee imposed, exterior corridors.

THE JEWELED TURRET INN   (207)338-2304

Historic Bed & Breakfast $130-$179 **Address:** 40 Pearl St 04915 **Location:** Center; corner of Church St. **Facility:** Afternoon refreshments are served to guests of this 1898 Victorian home, which is enhanced by a large veranda. Lovely stained-glass windows provide the basis for the inn's name. 7 units. 2 stories (no elevator), interior corridors. **Terms:** 2 night minimum stay - seasonal and/or weekends, 14 day cancellation notice-fee imposed.

SEASCAPE MOTEL & COTTAGES   (207)338-2130

Motel $69-$199 **Address:** 202 Searsport Ave 04915 **Location:** US 1, 3 mi n from jct SR 3. **Facility:** 15 units, some cottages. 1 story, exterior corridors. **Terms:** closed 10/20-4/25, 3 day cancellation notice-fee imposed. **Pool(s):** heated outdoor. **Activities:** whirlpool.

YANKEE CLIPPER MOTEL   (207)338-2353

Motel
$69-$139

Address: 50 Searsport Ave 04915 **Location:** On US 1, 1 mi n from jct SR 3. **Facility:** 24 units. 1 story, exterior corridors. **Terms:** closed 10/13-6/13, cancellation fee imposed. **Guest Services:** coin laundry. **Free Special Amenities:** high-speed Internet.

 1950's Vintage Motel. All rooms newly remodeled featuring modern decor & amenities.

WHERE TO EAT

DARBY'S RESTAURANT & PUB   207/338-2339

International. Casual Dining. $7-$20 **AAA Inspector Notes:** A bar or restaurant has been at this location since it was built in 1865. Patrons will appreciate the antique bar, tin ceiling and colorful décor. The cuisine is an eclectic mix that includes a bit of everything from Grandma Dublinsky's potato latkes to enchiladas, pad thai, spare ribs and BLTs. **Bar:** full bar. **Reservations:** suggested. **Address:** 155 High St 04915 **Location:** Center; just n of Main St. **Parking:** street only. L D

DOCKSIDE FAMILY RESTAURANT   207/338-6889

American. Family Dining. $7-$20 **AAA Inspector Notes:** This popular eatery offers a vast array of comfort foods from local fresh seafood and steaks to pasta, burgers and homemade desserts. Comfortable padded booths are offered, as is table seating with a view of Belfast Harbor. Enjoy seasonal outdoor dining on the spacious deck. **Bar:** full bar. **Address:** 30 Main St 04915 **Location:** At Cross St; downtown. L D

OCEAN'S EDGE RESTAURANT & LOUNGE   207/338-2090

American. Casual Dining. $9-$22 **AAA Inspector Notes:** This casual restaurant offers a wide variety of menu options and daily specials from basic comfort foods like burgers, fish and chips and pizza to fresh seafood and steaks. Patio dining, available in season, provides guests with splendid views of Penobscot Bay. **Bar:** full bar. **Address:** 159 Searsport Ave 04915 **Location:** On US 1, 2 mi n from jct SR 3; in Comfort Inn Ocean's Edge. D

PAPA J'S & THE LOBSTER BAR   207/338-6464

American. Casual Dining. $14-$24 **AAA Inspector Notes:** A classic, eclectic downeaster establishment would best describe Papa J's. Patrons will find the atmosphere most relaxing with friendly, accommodating staff. One section offers a view of the bay. Serving fresh lobster, steaks, burgers, chicken and deep-fried corn on-the-cob, there is likely something for everyone. **Bar:** full bar. **Address:** 193 Searsport Ave 04915 **Location:** US 1, 3 mi n from jct SR 3. D

SENG THAI RESTAURANT   207/338-0010

Thai. Casual Dining. $8-$18 **AAA Inspector Notes:** Enjoy authentic Thai cuisine while taking in the splendid view of Belfast Bay. The presentation is creative, and the menu selection is vast with wonderful soups, salads, fresh seafood, various curry dishes and some vegetarian options. **Bar:** full bar. **Address:** 139 Searsport Ave 04915 **Location:** US 1, 1.5 mi n from jct SR 3. L D

WEATHERVANE SEAFOOD RESTAURANT   207/338-1774

▼▼ Seafood. Family Dining. $7-$24 **AAA Inspector Notes:** The popular, family-oriented restaurant presents a large menu with lobster, fried clams and crisp Cape Cod apple-cranberry cobbler. Flavorful dishes are served in large portions. A fish market is on the premises. **Bar:** full bar. **Address:** 3 Main St 04915 **Location:** At public landing; center. L D CALL 🅜

YOUNG'S LOBSTER POUND   207/338-1160

▼ Seafood. Quick Serve. $12-$27 **AAA Inspector Notes:** The authentic lobster pound is on a working dock overlooking Penobscot Bay. Patrons can dine inside on the upper deck or outside on the dock. The menu lines up shore dinners, lobster rolls, chowders, freshly caught lobster, scallops, mussels, clams and crabs. Guests can pick their own lobster from the aquarium. **Address:** 2 Fairview St 04915 **Location:** Jct SR 3, 1.5 mi n on US 1, just e on Mitchell Ave, follow signs. L D 🅐🅒

BETHEL (I-2) elev. 643'
• Restaurants p. 66

Bethel sits along a quiet stretch of the Androscoggin River adjacent to the Mahoosuc mountain range that lies in the northeast corner of the White Mountains. Settled in 1774 as Sudbury Canada, it is one of the oldest towns in northwestern Maine. The Revolutionary War so slowed growth that in 1781, when the town experienced the last New England raid by Indians from Canada, it had only 10 families.

Bethel, as the community was rechristened in 1796, grew into an important farming and lumbering center. Once the railroad linked it with Portland and Montréal, assuring its position in commerce, Bethel became a favorite spot for visitors to the White Mountains. Founded in 1836, Gould Academy on Church Street is one of the state's leading preparatory schools. A well-known resident was Dr. John Gehring, a neurologist for whom a ward of the New York Neurological Institute is named.

Swimming, camping, hiking, bicycling, canoeing, kayaking, fishing and rockhounding are favorite summer activities.

Grafton Notch State Park *(see Recreation Areas Chart),* 14 miles north on SR 26, is at the end of the Mahoosuc Range between Newry and Upton. The park, which is open daily from mid-May to mid-October, contains such scenic points as Screw Auger Falls, Spruce Meadow, Mother Walker Falls, Old Spec Mountain and Moose Cave; phone (207) 824-2912.

Bethel Area Chamber of Commerce: 8 Station Pl., P.O. Box 1247, Bethel, ME 04217. **Phone:** (207) 824-2282 or (800) 442-5826.

Self-guiding tours: A self-guiding walking tour of the Broad Street Historic District and Bethel Hill Village is available at the Bethel Historical Society Regional History Center *(see attraction listing)* and the chamber of commerce. Information about scenic driving tours also is available from the chamber of commerce.

BETHEL HISTORICAL SOCIETY REGIONAL HISTORY CENTER, 10 Broad St., features the restored 1813 Federal-style home of Dr. Moses Mason, physician and U.S. congressman. The home contains nine rooms and is furnished in period. Of special interest

are the Rufus Porter School murals depicting seascapes and foliage. A research library is available; an exhibit hall contains changing exhibits. The O'Neil Robinson House, built in 1821, has changing exhibits.

Time: Allow 30 minutes minimum. **Hours:** Robinson House Tues.-Fri. 10-4 (also Sat. 1-4, July-Aug. and by appointment). Research library and exhibit hall Thurs.-Fri. 1-4, June-Oct.; by appointment rest of year. Mason House museum Tues.-Sat. 1-4, July-Aug.; by appointment rest of year. **Cost:** Mason House museum $3; $1.50 (ages 6-12). Donations are accepted for the Robinson House, the exhibit hall and use of the research library. **Phone:** (207) 824-2908 or (800) 824-2910.

BRIAR LEA INN AT THE JOLLY DRAYMAN ENGLISH PUB
(207)824-4717

▼▼▼ **Historic Country Inn** $85-$140 **Address:** 150 Mayville Rd (US 2) 04217 **Location:** 1 mi n of jct US 2, SR 5 and 26. **Facility:** Situated close to Sunday River Ski Resort and Mount Abrams, this renovated 1850s farmhouse is decorated with eclectic antique décor. Guest rooms feature up-to-date amenities for your comfort. 6 units. 3 stories (no elevator), interior corridors. **Terms:** check-in 4 pm, 14 day cancellation notice. **Dining:** The Jolly Drayman English Pub at the Briar Lea Inn, see separate listing. **Activities:** cross country skiing, snowmobiling, hiking trails, game room.

🍽 📶 ✕ 🎿 ▣

THE INN AT THE ROSTAY   207/824-3111

▼▼ **Motel** $68-$140 **Address:** 186 Mayville Rd (US 2) 04217 **Location:** On US 2, 2 mi e. **Facility:** 18 units. 1 story, exterior corridors. **Terms:** 2-3 night minimum stay - seasonal and/or weekends, 14 day cancellation notice-fee imposed. **Pool(s):** outdoor. **Activities:** whirlpool. **Guest Services:** coin laundry.

🏊 BIZ 📶 ✕ 📶 ▣ / SOME UNITS FEE 🐾

JORDAN GRAND RESORT HOTEL & CONFERENCE CENTER
(207)824-5000

▼▼▼ **Hotel** $139-$259 **Address:** 27 Grand Ave 04217 **Location:** US 2 to Sunday River Rd, just n, follow signs. **Facility:** 186 units, some two bedrooms, three bedrooms and kitchens. 3 stories, interior corridors. **Parking:** on-site and valet. **Terms:** check-in 4:30 pm, 2 night minimum stay - seasonal and/or weekends, 15 day cancellation notice-fee imposed, resort fee. **Dining:** 2 restaurants. **Pool(s):** heated outdoor. **Activities:** sauna, whirlpools, steamroom, recreation programs in season, hiking trails, playground, spa. *Fee:* downhill skiing, game room. **Guest Services:** coin laundry.

ECO 🍽 🚶 CALL 🅜 🏊 📶 BIZ 📶 ✕ ▣ / SOME UNITS 📶 📶

NORSEMAN MOTEL   (207)824-2002

▼▼ **Motel** $78-$168 **Address:** 134 Mayville Rd 04217 **Location:** On US 2, 2 mi e. **Facility:** 22 units. 2 stories (no elevator), interior/exterior corridors. **Terms:** 7 day cancellation notice-fee imposed. **Activities:** cross country skiing, hiking trails, game room. **Guest Services:** coin laundry. BIZ 📶 ✕ 📶 ▣

WHERE TO EAT

THE JOLLY DRAYMAN ENGLISH PUB AT THE BRIAR LEA INN   207/824-4717

English
Casual Dining
$9-$20

AAA Inspector Notes: *Classic.* This pub, which occupies a fully renovated 1850s farmhouse with a distinctive pub décor, offers a memorable dining and drinking experience. The menu offers classic pub fare along with British specialties (fish and chips, bangers and mash and shepherd's pie) and Indian specialties (korma, tikka masala, vindaloo). There is a good selection of draft and bottled beers. A children's menu is available. Located near the Sunday River Ski/Golf Facility. **Bar:** full bar. **Address:** 150 Mayville St 04217 **Location:** 1 mi n of jct US 2, SR 5 and 26; in Briar Lea Inn at the Jolly Drayman English Pub. *Menu on AAA.com* [D]

Pull up a pint & a stool - Meet friends new & old

PHOENIX HOUSE & WELL   207-824-2222

▼▼▼ American. Casual Dining. $9-$25 **AAA Inspector Notes:** Opposite the Sunday River base lodge, the restaurant offers casual dining in the pleasant lower lounge and a more upscale setting in the upstairs room, which affords a view of the mountains. Menu preparations center on quality meats and fresh seafood. **Bar:** full bar. **Address:** Sunday River Rd 04217 **Location:** Jct US 2, 3.5 mi n. [L] [D] [🍴]

ROOSTER'S ROADHOUSE   207-824-0309

▼▼ American. Casual Dining. $7-$29 **AAA Inspector Notes:** In a barnlike setting, this is a great place to take the family for a casual dinner. The menu reflects American cuisine including fresh seafood, chops and steaks. A children's menu is available. Casual fare such as wraps and burgers are served in the pub. Dine on the deck seasonally, and enjoy free Wi-Fi throughout the establishment. **Bar:** full bar. **Address:** 159 Mayville Rd (US 2) 04217 **Location:** 1.1 mi n of jct US 52, SR 5 and 26. [L] [D]

BIDDEFORD (K-2) pop. 21,277, elev. 75'
• Hotels & Restaurants map & index p. 98

In 1662 one of the region's first sawmills was erected in Biddeford. The lure of waterpower gradually built the city into an important manufacturing center. Biddeford's diverse economic base relies on boatbuilding and the production of plastic, machinery, electronics and baked goods.

Biddeford is closely bound economically and culturally to Saco *(see place listing p. 145)*, its sister city across the river. This interdependency is evident in the cooperative efforts shown in the restoration of the 1895 opera house; the acoustically perfect City Theater, (207) 282-0849, is an outstanding example of late 19th-century ornamental architecture.

Both cities take advantage of the educational and cultural opportunities offered by the University College at Saco and the University of New England, 4 miles east on Pool Road overlooking the sea.

AMERICAS BEST VALUE INN   (207)284-2440 **36**

Motel
$43-$139

Address: 2 Pomerleau St 04005 **Location:** I-95 exit 32 (SR 111), 0.5 mi w. **Facility:** 19 units. 2 stories (no elevator), exterior corridors. **Terms:** cancellation fee imposed. **Free Special Amenities:** local telephone calls and high-speed Internet.

BIDDEFORD POOL (K-3) elev. 20'

EAST POINT SANCTUARY, 5 mi. s. on US 208 on Lester B. Orcutt Blvd. to end, encompasses 30 acres of rocky coastal headland considered to be one of the best sites for bird-watching in southern Maine. A shoreline trail offers views of such marine birds as gannets, red-throated loons, sea ducks and terns. Two rocky islands visible from the trail support large bird colonies. **Hours:** Daily dawn-dusk. **Cost:** Free. **Phone:** (207) 781-2330.

BLUE HILL (I-6) pop. 943, elev. 40'

Since its 19th-century halcyon days as a ship-building, seafaring and lumbering town, Blue Hill has become a popular summer vacation and crafts center. It is especially noted for wheel-thrown pottery, some of which is produced from local clays. Rackliffe Pottery on Ellsworth Road, phone (207) 374-2297 or (888) 631-3321, and Lowell Hill Pottery on Union Street, phone (207) 951-8229, welcome visitors. A number of art galleries are in the area.

Craftsmanship is not new; in the early 1800s, Parson Jonathan Fisher designed and built his own house, made the paint that adorned it and created most of his furniture, paintings and woodcuts. Having invented machines to saw wood, split straws and dig stones, he then built a windmill to power them. The life of this unusual man was chronicled by Mary Ellen Chase, a novelist born in Blue Hill in 1887. The Jonathan Fisher House still stands on SR 15 at 44 Mines Rd.; phone (207) 374-2459.

The village is the namesake of a 934-foot hill that overlooks the town, situated at the head of Blue Hill Bay. The hill's blue appearance from a distance no doubt inspired the name. From its summit the view extends eastward to Mount Desert Island and Acadia National Park *(see place listing p. 38)* and westward to Camden Hills State Park *(see Recreation Areas Chart)*.

An extensive and eclectic collection of sheet music is housed in Blue Hill's Bagaduce Music Lending Library. Organized according to the instrument for which each piece was written, the library's more than 250,000 scores include many rare items that might be difficult to find anywhere else; phone (207) 374-5454. Throughout the summer the Kneisel Hall Chamber Music Festival's concerts and recitals showcase the talents of young performers; phone (207) 374-2203.

BOOTHBAY (J-4) elev. 127'

BOOTHBAY RAILWAY VILLAGE, 3.5 mi. n. on SR 27 to 586 Wiscasset Rd., depicts a turn-of-the-20th-century Maine village containing railroad memorabilia, antique cars and trucks and a general store as well as the 1847 Boothbay Town Hall and the Spruce Point Chapel. Visitors can ride on a narrow-gauge, coal-fired steam engine. A Halloween train runs in late October.

Time: Allow 2 hours minimum. **Hours:** Daily 9:30-5, early June to mid-Oct. Trains depart hourly 10-4. Phone ahead to confirm schedule. **Cost:** $9; $5 (ages 3-16). **Phone:** (207) 633-4727.

COASTAL MAINE BOTANICAL GARDENS is, from Rte. 1, 9.3 mi. s. on SR 27, .25 mi. w. on Corey Ln., then 1 mi. w. on Barters Island Rd. to 132 Botanical Gardens Dr. The 250-acre botanical garden contains some 80,000 plants representing more than 1,350 species. Waterfalls, sculptures and stonework are featured, and 2 miles of trails are in waterfront and woodland settings.

Water-spraying whale sculptures welcome visitors to the 2-acre Bibby and Harold Alfond Children's Garden, which celebrates the works of E.B. White, Robert McCloskey, Barbara Cooney and other children's authors with ties to the state. Kids can listen to a storyteller, curl up with a good book in the Story Barn, explore a tree house, maneuver their way through a maze and sit in a rowboat.

In the Lerner Garden of the Five Senses visitors stimulate their bodies and minds by walking barefoot on a stone labyrinth, admiring and smelling blooming lavender, sampling fresh herbs, touching a fuzzy lamb's ear leaf and trying out a "sound stone."

Little ones will have a ball designing and constructing homes for imaginary forest dwellers in two Fairy House Villages. Sustainability is the theme of the LEED-certified Bosarge Family Education Center. Other must-sees include the Rhododendron, Rose, Kitchen, Hillside, Meditation and Forest Pond gardens. The site hosts workshops, art shows, concerts and events throughout the year.

Food is available seasonally. **Tours:** Guided tours are available. **Time:** Allow 2 hours minimum. **Hours:** Gardens daily 9-5. Visitor center and Bosarge Family Education Center daily 9-5, Apr.-Oct.; Mon.-Fri. 9-5, rest of year. Closed Thanksgiving and Christmas. **Cost:** $14; $12 (ages 65+); $6 (ages 3-17); $34 (family, two adults and two children); free (in Nov.). **Phone:** (207) 633-4333.

KENNETH E. STODDARD SHELL MUSEUM, 4.5 mi. n. on SR 27 past the lighthouse parking lot, displays thousands of shells in wood-and-glass cases housed in a building inside a covered bridge. The mainly Pacific shells range in size from specimens smaller than a finger to large conch shells. Sand dollars and lobster claws also are exhibited. **Time:** Allow 1 hour minimum. **Hours:** Daily 10-10, May 1-Sept. 15; by appointment rest of year. **Cost:** Donations. **Phone:** (207) 633-4828, or (207) 633-2601 in the off-season.

WHITE ANCHOR INN   207/633-3788
Motel. Rates not provided. **Address:** 609 Wiscasset Rd 04537 **Location:** US 1 to SR 27, 7.5 mi s. **Facility:** 23 units. 1-2 stories (no elevator), interior/exterior corridors.

BOOTHBAY HARBOR (J-4) pop. 1,086, elev. 20'
• Restaurants p. 70

A picturesque seaport, Boothbay Harbor retains the atmosphere of an old New England village. Fishing craft lie alongside wharves that follow the quaint, winding village streets. Yachtsmen and artists began vacationing in the area in the early 1900s. Word soon spread of the region's natural beauty, and Boothbay Harbor began the slow transition from shipping center to resort area.

The Boothbay Harbor region's waterfront offers visitors a glimpse into seafaring history and an array of nautical activities on the Maine coast. With a strong shipbuilding and fishing heritage, the harbor shelters a wide variety of boats.

River cruises, ocean cruises, whale watches, sailing and deep-sea fishing trips leave local piers daily and vary in length from 1 hour to an entire day. The *Balmy Days II* makes day trips to Monhegan Island *(see place listing p. 113)* early June to late September; phone (207) 633-2284 or (800) 298-2284.

In late June antique boats and a parade are part of the 2-day Windjammer Days celebration. The Fall Foliage Festival, featuring craft displays and train rides, is held early to mid-October.

Boothbay Harbor Region Chamber of Commerce: 192 Townsend Ave., P.O. Box 356, Boothbay Harbor, ME 04538. **Phone:** (207) 633-2353.

CAP'N FISH'S WHALE WATCH AND SCENIC NATURE CRUISES, downtown on the waterfront at Pier 1, offers a variety of sightseeing cruises along the Maine coast, including the Puffin Nature, Whale- and Seal-Watching, Damariscove Harbor, Kennebec River-Bath and Pemaquid Point Lighthouse cruises.

Hours: Cruises depart daily at 1 and 3:30, June 1 to mid-Oct. (also at 10, June 1-Labor Day). Ticket office opens at 8. Phone ahead to confirm schedule. **Cost:** $19-$48; $10-$22 (ages 0-11). Fares may vary; phone ahead. Reservations are recommended. **Phone:** (207) 633-3244 or (800) 636-3244.

ATLANTIC ARK INN   (207)633-5690
Bed & Breakfast $130-$220 **Address:** 62 Atlantic Ave 04538 **Location:** 0.3 mi se of SR 27; east side of town. **Facility:** This inn is characterized by a simple elegance and offers well-appointed rooms. It's designed to be peaceful and stress free with simplistic surroundings. 6 units. 3 stories (no elevator), interior/exterior corridors. **Terms:** closed 10/23-5/17, 2 night minimum stay - seasonal and/or weekends, 14 day cancellation notice-fee imposed.

BEACH COVE WATERFRONT INN   207/633-0353
Motel. Rates not provided. **Address:** 48 Lakeview Rd 04538 **Location:** Waterfront. Off SR 27. **Facility:** 35 units. 2 stories (no elevator), exterior corridors. **Pool(s):** heated outdoor.

BLUE HERON SEASIDE INN 207/633-7020

▼▼▼ **Bed & Breakfast** $175-$275 **Address:** 65 Townsend Ave 04538 **Location:** Waterfront. Center. **Facility:** This downtown, 19th-century renovated home features rooms with Victorian, Colonial and nautical-style themes as well as decks boasting harbor views. 6 units, some two bedrooms. 3 stories (no elevator), interior/exterior corridors. **Terms:** closed 10/27-5/23, 2-3 night minimum stay - seasonal and/or weekends, 30 day cancellation notice-fee imposed. **Activities:** boat dock.

BOOTHBAY HARBOR INN 207/633-6302

▼▼ **Hotel** $99-$249 **Address:** 31 Atlantic Ave 04538 **Location:** Waterfront. 0.3 mi e of SR 27; on east side of Boothbay Harbor. **Facility:** 59 units. 2 stories (no elevator), interior/exterior corridors. **Terms:** closed 10/20-5/16, 2 night minimum stay - seasonal and/or weekends, 3 day cancellation notice-fee imposed.

BROWN'S WHARF INN 207/633-5440

▼▼▼
Hotel
$89-$209

Address: 121 Atlantic Ave 04538 **Location:** Waterfront. East side of town. **Facility:** 72 units, some kitchens. 3 stories, exterior corridors. **Terms:** closed 10/14-5/10, 2 night minimum stay - weekends, 3 day cancellation notice-fee imposed. **Amenities:** safes. **Dining:** Brown's Wharf Restaurant, see separate listing. **Activities:** fishing. *Fee:* marina. **Guest Services:** coin laundry. **Free Special Amenities:** local telephone calls and high-speed Internet. *(See ad p. 69.)*

CAP'N FISH'S WATERFRONT INN 207/633-6605

▼▼ **Hotel** $75-$175 **Address:** 65 Atlantic Ave 04538 **Location:** Waterfront. 0.3 mi se of SR 27; on east side of Boothbay Harbor. **Facility:** 54 units, some efficiencies. 2 stories (no elevator), exterior corridors. **Terms:** closed 10/15-5/24, 2 night minimum stay - weekends, 7 day cancellation notice. **Activities:** *Fee:* marina.

FLAGSHIP INN (207)633-5094

▼▼▼ ◆
Motel
$74-$144

Address: 200 Townsend Ave 04538 **Location:** On SR 27, just n of jct SR 96. **Facility:** 82 units. 2 stories (no elevator), exterior corridors. **Terms:** 3 day cancellation notice-fee imposed. **Pool(s):** heated outdoor. **Activities:** whirlpool. **Free Special Amenities:** continental breakfast and high-speed Internet.

HARBORAGE INN ON THE OCEANFRONT 207/633-4640

▼▼▼ **Bed & Breakfast.** Rates not provided. **Address:** 75 Townsend Ave 04538 **Location:** Waterfront. Center. **Facility:** A private waterfront lawn enhances this 1875 Colonial inn that offers some rooms with a hot tub. A full continental breakfast is served. 11 units. 3 stories (no elevator), interior/exterior corridors. **Activities:** waterslide, boat dock.

Safety tip:
Keep a current AAA/CAA
Road Atlas in every vehicle

▼ See AAA listing p. 150 ▼

The Maine You Came For...

Ocean Gate Resort
ON THE WATERFRONT

Crossing the bridge makes all the difference...

Private, yet convenient, 45 acre Oceanfront Resort featuring COMPLIMENTARY Full Hot Breakfast, Canoes, Kayaks, Heated Pool, Hot Tub, Mini-Golf and Spectacular Ocean Views!

P.O. Box 673 • Boothbay Harbor, Maine 04538 • (800)221-5924 • (207)633-3321 • www.oceangateinn.com

▼ See AAA listing p. 68 ▼

TUGBOAT INN
(207)633-4434

Hotel
$85-$265

Address: 80 Commercial St 04538 **Location:** Waterfront. Center. **Facility:** 64 units, some two bedrooms and kitchens. 2-3 stories (no elevator), exterior corridors. **Terms:** closed 12/1-4/10, 2 night minimum stay - seasonal and/or weekends, 3 day cancellation notice-fee imposed. **Dining:** Tugboat Restaurant, see separate listing. **Activities:** Fee: marina. **Guest Services:** coin laundry. **Free Special Amenities: continental breakfast and local telephone calls.**

WHERE TO EAT

BOOTHBAY LOBSTER WHARF
207/633-4900

Seafood. Family Dining. $7-$22 **AAA Inspector Notes:** Guests can dine indoors or out at the dockside restaurant. Lobstermen dock nearby to unload their catch, which is on the menu shortly thereafter. **Bar:** full bar. **Address:** 97 Atlantic Ave 04538 **Location:** 0.4 mi e of SR 27; east side of town.

BROWN'S WHARF RESTAURANT
207/633-5440

Seafood
Casual Dining
$15-$28

AAA Inspector Notes: An area fixture since 1944, the family-owned restaurant provides a panoramic view of Boothbay Harbor. On the menu is a good selection of fresh seafood, steak, lamb and pasta dishes, plus prime rib on the weekends. **Bar:** full bar. **Reservations:** suggested. **Address:** 121 Atlantic Ave 04538 **Location:** East side of town; in Brown's Wharf Inn. *(See ad p. 69.)*

CHINA BY THE SEA
207/633-4449

Chinese
Casual Dining
$6-$19

AAA Inspector Notes: Traditional and quite tasty, the dishes here are made-to-order which obviously results in fresh flavors. Guests can stay connected with several, convenient computer stations. **Bar:** full bar. **Address:** 96 Townsend Ave 04538 **Location:** Center.

KALER'S CRAB AND LOBSTER HOUSE
207/633-5839

Regional
Seafood
Family Dining
$8-$22

AAA Inspector Notes: Located on the waterfront, the eatery is known for its fresh crab and lobster specialties. The menu also includes fresh salads, chowder, and fried, baked and broiled seafood as well as chicken, burgers, sandwiches and quesadillas. A children's menu is available. **Bar:** full bar. **Address:** 48 Commercial St 04538 **Location:** Center. **Parking:** street only. *Menu on AAA.com*

THE LOBSTER DOCK
207/633-7120

Regional Seafood. Quick Serve. $8-$25 **AAA Inspector Notes:** While the wonderful harbor views are enough to make the trip worthwhile, the restaurant's fresh, off-the-boat, local seafood makes a visit all the more appealing. Hot lobster rolls are a local favorite, along with slow-roasted prime rib, dry-aged steaks, from-scratch Maine-style chowders and crispy artichoke hearts. **Bar:** beer & wine. **Address:** 49 Atlantic Ave 04538 **Location:** 0.4 mi e of SR 27; east side of town.

MAMA D'S CAFE
207/633-3464

Breakfast Sandwiches. Casual Dining. $6-$9 **AAA Inspector Notes:** This spot is a local favorite and is open all year. A daily homemade soup, made-to-order sandwiches, cookies and pies are offered. Ask to have your order to go for a waterside excursion or beach picnic. **Bar:** beer & wine. **Address:** 50 Union St 04538 **Location:** Just e of SR 27.

TUGBOAT RESTAURANT
207/633-4434

Seafood. Casual Dining. $8-$23 **AAA Inspector Notes:** This popular restaurant lives up to its name—it's a converted tugboat! Its setting on the water gives a good view of the harbor. The menu features an excellent steak and lobster combination, wonderful seafood fettuccine and tugboat applejack crisp. **Bar:** full bar. **Address:** 80 Commercial St 04538 **Location:** Center; in Tugboat Inn.

BRADLEY (H-6)

LEONARD'S MILLS AND MAINE FOREST LOGGING MUSEUM, n. on SR 9, 4.5 mi. n. on SR 178, then 1.25 mi. e. to 686 Government Rd., allows visitors a glimpse into the area's forestry and logging history. Entered by crossing Blackman Stream through a covered bridge on foot, the site contains a sawmill powered by a water wheel as well as a blacksmith shop, a settler's house, a log cabin, a stone dam and nature trails. Site maps and information are available at the covered bridge. Special events are held April through October. **Hours:** Trails and museum daily dawn-dusk. **Cost:** Donations. A fee is charged for special events. **Phone:** (207) 974-6278.

BREWER pop. 9,482

MUDDY RUDDER
207/989-5389

Seafood. Casual Dining. $8-$21 **AAA Inspector Notes:** Soup, stew, salad, lobster pie, steak and seafood dinners are among choices at the warm and inviting restaurant, which affords good views of the Penobscot River and city skyline. The downeast clambake is also popular. Tables display area maps from the 1800s. **Bar:** full bar. **Address:** 5 S Main St 04412 **Location:** Corner of US 1A (Wilson St).

WEATHERVANE SEAFOOD RESTAURANT
207/989-4232

Seafood. Casual Dining. $7-$24 **AAA Inspector Notes:** The popular, family-oriented restaurant presents a large menu with lobster, fried clams and crisp Cape Cod apple-cranberry cobbler. Flavorful dishes are served in large portions. A fish market is on the premises. **Bar:** full bar. **Address:** 710 Wilson St 04412 **Location:** 2.5 mi e on US 1A (Wilson St).

BRIDGTON pop. 2,071

HIGHLAND LAKE RESORT
207/647-5301

Motel $75-$155 **Address:** 115 N High St 04009 **Location:** Waterfront. Jct US 302 and SR 117, 1.2 mi w on US 302. **Facility:** 22 units, some kitchens. 1 story, exterior corridors. **Terms:** 2 night minimum stay - seasonal, 8 day cancellation notice-fee imposed. **Activities:** sauna, whirlpool, limited beach access, boating, canoeing, paddleboats, boat dock, fishing, tennis court, cross country skiing, snowmobiling, playground, horseshoes, volleyball, exercise room. Fee: game room, massage. **Guest Services:** coin laundry.

WHERE TO EAT

THE BLACK HORSE TAVERN   207/647-5300
♥♥♥ American. Casual Dining. $5-$19 **AAA Inspector Notes:**
The tavern's motto is "casual dining in an equestrian atmosphere,"
which aptly describes the experience. The dining room resembles an
old stable, with riding gear on the walls and old saddles on the "stall"
walls between tables. On the menu are homemade soups, burgers,
pasta, seafood and chicken. Prime rib is a specialty. **Bar:** full bar. **Address:** 26 Portland St 04009 **Location:** On US 302; center.

[L] [D]

BRISTOL (J-4) elev. 73'

**COLONIAL PEMAQUID STATE HISTORIC SITE
AND FORT WILLIAM HENRY,** off SR 130 on Colonial Pemaquid Dr., is the site of an English settlement dating from the early 17th century. A museum
displays artifacts excavated from the area. The
original Fort Charles was replaced by Fort William
Henry in 1692; 4 years later the French captured
and destroyed it. Fort Frederick was erected on the
same site in 1729. A reproduction built on the
original foundation contains historical material.

Time: Allow 30 minutes minimum. **Hours:** Daily
9-6, Memorial Day-Labor Day. **Cost:** $3; $1 (ages
5-11 and 65+). **Phone:** (207) 677-2423, or (207)
624-6075 in the off-season.

BRUNSWICK (J-3) pop. 15,175, elev. 63'
• Hotels p. 72 • Restaurants p. 73

Industry, recreation and education are important
pursuits in Brunswick, the chief city of the eastern
Casco Bay area. Industry began in the 1620s when
an English trader's success with exporting sturgeon
and salmon from the falls of the lower Androscoggin
River induced his company to establish a post. From
that time until about 1730 the settlement of Pejepscot rose and fell as warring American Indians destroyed it in 1690 and again in 1722.

Between disasters, during 1714-15, a group
called the Pejepscot Proprietors bought the post,
built Fort George and planned the spacious grid pat-
tern of the streets. One thoroughfare was the Twelve
Rod Road, now Maine Street; measuring 198 feet
across, it is one of the widest streets in New England. By the late 1700s the settlement, renamed
Brunswick, was an important lumbering, milling and
shipbuilding center.

Bowdoin College, established in 1794, is the
home of the Maine State Music Theater, where a
professional cast performs Broadway musicals early
June to late August; phone (207) 725-8769. A
summer organ music series is presented on Tues-
days at noon in the summer at the First Parish
Church; phone (207) 729-7333. Free open-air concerts are held on the Mall on Wednesday evenings
late June through August.

Harriet Beecher Stowe's inspiration for "Uncle
Tom's Cabin" supposedly came from a sermon delivered at the First Parish Church on Maine Street,
open for worship since 1717. Another celebrated
local was Gov. Joshua Lawrence Chamberlain,
noted for his defense at Gettysburg and for being
the only Union general to receive a battlefield pro-
motion from Gen. Ulysses S. Grant.

Southern Midcoast Maine Chamber: Border Trust
Business Center, 2 Main St., Topsham, ME 04086.
Phone: (207) 725-8797 or (877) 725-8797.

BOWDOIN COLLEGE occupies a 110-acre campus
at Maine, Bath and College sts. In addition to Nathaniel Hawthorne and Henry Wadsworth Longfellow, alumni include Arctic explorers Robert Peary
and Donald MacMillan, and President Franklin
Pierce. Tours depart from the Burton-Little House
admissions office at 4 College St. **Time:** Allow 1
hour minimum. **Hours:** Campus tours Mon.-Fri. at
9:30, 11:30, 1:30 and 3:30; Sat. at 11:30. Closed
major holidays. Phone ahead to confirm schedule.
Cost: Free. **Phone:** (207) 725-3100.

Bowdoin College Museum of Art, in the Walker Art
Building, contains Colonial and Federal portraits, a
fine collection of classical antiquities, old masters'
drawings, a collection of more than 15,000 objects
featuring notable Assyrian reliefs, contemporary art,
works by European artists and changing exhibits.

Guided tours are available by reservation. **Time:**
Allow 1 hour minimum. **Hours:** Tues.-Sat. 10-5 (also
Thurs. 5-8:30), Sun. 1-5. Closed major holidays.
Cost: Free. **Phone:** (207) 725-3275.

Peary-MacMillan Arctic Museum, in Hubbard Hall,
has displays relating to the two explorers as well as
life and the environment in the Arctic region. The
collections include Arctic exploration gear, natural
history specimens, and artifacts and drawings created by Inuit and Indians of North America. **Time:**
Allow 30 minutes minimum. **Hours:** Tues.-Sat. 10-5,
Sun. 2-5. Closed major holidays. **Cost:** Donations.
Phone: (207) 725-3416.

JOSHUA LAWRENCE CHAMBERLAIN MUSEUM,
226 Maine St., is a partially restored Federal-style
house with Victorian Gothic additions. The house once
belonged to Joshua Lawrence Chamberlain, a Civil
War hero, president of Bowdoin College and governor
of Maine 1867-71. Guests Chamberlain entertained at
the house include Gen. Ulysses S. Grant, Helen Keller
and Henry Wadsworth Longfellow.

Hours: Tues.-Sat. 10-4, Sun. 1-4, Memorial Day-
Columbus Day. Guided tours depart on the hour.
Last admission 1 hour before closing. Closed major
holidays. **Cost:** $7.50; $2.50 (ages 6-16). Combina-
tion ticket with Pejepscot Museum/Skolfield-Whittier
House $13; $4 (ages 6-16). **Phone:** (207) 729-6606.

**PEJEPSCOT MUSEUM/SKOLFIELD-WHITTIER
HOUSE,** 159-161 Park Row, is a brick Italianate
semidetached house built by a shipmaster for his
two sons in 1858. The adjoining house contains
original furnishings and the personal belongings of

three generations of Skolfields and Whittiers left perfectly intact in 1925. The collections reflect the families' involvement in seafaring, shipping, medicine and education. The history museum features changing exhibits and research facilities.

Time: Allow 1 hour minimum. **Hours:** Museum Wed.-Sat. 10-4 (also Tues. 10-4, Columbus Day-Memorial Day). Guided tours of the Skolfield-Whittier House depart on the hour Wed.-Sat. 10-4, Memorial Day-Columbus Day. Closed major holidays. **Cost:** Museum free. Guided house tours $7.50; $2.50 (ages 6-16). Combination ticket with Joshua Lawrence Chamberlain Museum $13; $4 (ages 6-16). **Phone:** (207) 729-6606.

CAPTAIN DANIEL STONE INN, AN ASCEND COLLECTION HOTEL (207)373-1824

Historic Boutique Country Inn
$109-$289

Address: 10 Water St 04011 **Location:** Just n of US 1. **Facility:** Built in Federalist style during the early 1900s and over the years transformed into a country inn. Recently, new owners have beautifully restored the inn to reflect both historical charm and luxury. 24 units. 4 stories, interior corridors. **Terms:** 3 day cancellation notice-fee imposed. **Amenities:** safes. **Dining:** No. 10 Water, see separate listing. **Activities:** sauna, whirlpool, exercise room. **Guest Services:** valet laundry. *(See ad this page.)*

COMFORT INN (207)729-1129

Hotel $80-$160 **Address:** 199 Pleasant St 04011 **Location:** 1.3 mi s on US 1. **Facility:** 76 units. 2 stories, interior corridors. **Terms:** cancellation fee imposed. **Activities:** exercise room. **Guest Services:** valet laundry. BIZ 🛜 ✕ 🖥

FAIRFIELD INN & SUITES BY MARRIOTT (207)721-0300

Hotel
$109-$249

AAA Benefit: AAA hotel discounts of 5% or more.

Address: 36 Old Portland Rd 04011 **Location:** I-295 exit 28, just s on US 1. **Facility:** 81 units. 3 stories, interior corridors. **Amenities:** high-speed Internet. **Pool(s):** heated indoor. **Activities:** whirlpool, exercise room. **Guest Services:** valet and coin laundry. **Free Special Amenities:** expanded continental breakfast and high-speed Internet.

 / SOME UNITS

THE INN AT BRUNSWICK STATION (207)837-6565

Boutique Hotel
$129-$229

Address: 4 Noble St 04011 **Location:** Center. **Facility:** The local historical photographs hanging on the wall enhance the property's blend of contemporary and classic décor that's coupled with up-to-date amenities. 52 units. 3 stories, interior corridors. **Terms:** check-in 4 pm. **Guest Services:** valet laundry. **Free Special Amenities:** local telephone calls and high-speed Internet.

 / SOME UNITS FEE 🐕

KNIGHTS INN-BRUNSWICK (207)725-8761

Motel
$78-$120

Address: 133 Pleasant St 04011 **Location:** I-295 exit 28, 1 mi n on US 1. **Facility:** 52 units, some two bedrooms and efficiencies. 2 stories (no elevator), exterior corridors. **Pool(s):** outdoor. **Guest Services:** coin laundry. **Free Special Amenities:** continental breakfast and high-speed Internet.

TRAVELERS INN (207)729-3364

Motel
$55-$160

Address: 130 Pleasant St 04011 **Location:** I-295 exit 28, 1 mi n on US 1. **Facility:** 37 units, some two bedrooms. 2 stories (no elevator), exterior corridors. **Guest Services:** coin laundry. **Free Special Amenities:** continental breakfast and high-speed Internet.

▼ *See AAA listing this page* ▼

WHERE TO EAT

AMATO'S   207/729-5514

Deli. Quick Serve. $4-$14 **AAA Inspector Notes:** Known for their "Real Italian" sandwich, which was created over 100 years ago by an Italian immigrant who decided to place a little bit of meat, fresh vegetables, cheese, Greek olives, a zesty pickle and a specialty blended olive oil on a freshly made roll. This recipe has built up a loyal following of customers. Other menu choices include hot or cold sandwiches, calzones, specialty pizzas, pasta and freshly prepared salads. Diners may choose to eat in or take out. **Address:** 148 Pleasant St 04011 **Location:** I-295 exit 28, 1.5 mi n on US 1.

`L` `D`

BOMBAY MAHAL RESTAURANT   207/729-5260

Indian. Casual Dining. $8-$25 **AAA Inspector Notes:** You'll appreciate the wide variety of authentic and very well-prepared dishes at this restaurant, which has a pleasant storefront setting on the main street of this college town. The menu specializes in lamb, chicken, vegetarian delights and Thai dishes. **Reservations:** suggested, for dinner. **Address:** 99 Maine St 04011 **Location:** Center. **Parking:** street only. `L` `D`

EL CAMINO   207/725-8228

Mexican. Casual Dining. $12-$17 **AAA Inspector Notes:** A small but delicious selection of Mexican favorites are on the menu. Salsa and chips are made on the premises, and all entrees are made to order. **Bar:** full bar. **Address:** 15 Cushing St 04011 **Location:** Just n of US 1; center. `D`

GREAT IMPASTA   207/729-5858

Italian. Casual Dining. $7-$19 **AAA Inspector Notes:** This very popular restaurant is known for its garlic bread. The menu features a variety of nicely prepared pasta dishes combined with seafood, chicken and vegetables. The homemade desserts are worth a try. **Bar:** full bar. **Address:** 42 Maine St 04011 **Location:** Center.

`ECO` `L` `D`

HENRY & MARTY   207/721-9141

American. Casual Dining. $14-$29 **AAA Inspector Notes:** The lively downtown bistro is a local favorite. The menu features eclectic American cuisine centered on fresh, local produce and organic meats, whenever possible. **Bar:** full bar. **Reservations:** suggested. **Address:** 61 Maine St 04011 **Location:** Center. **Parking:** street only. `D`

NO. 10 WATER   207/373-9299

Regional American. Fine Dining. $10-$26 **AAA Inspector Notes:** This restaurant specializes in American and European cuisine with global influences and a focus on local purveyors, especially seafood and produce. Diners can settle into a comfortably clubby setting which includes an impressive fireplace and open kitchen. A lighter menu is offered in the warmer months. Lunch is sometimes offered in the warmer months. **Bar:** full bar. **Address:** 10 Water St 04011 **Location:** Just n of US 1; in Captain Daniel Stone Inn, an Ascend Collection hotel. `D` `CALL` `M`

PEDRO O'HARA'S   207/373-1300

Mexican. Casual Dining. $8-$17 **AAA Inspector Notes:** This charming restaurant combines Irish, Mexican and American favorites in a funky atmosphere. It is located in the basement of a Maine Street business which adds to the ambience. The ceiling is regaled with sports shirts and pennants. **Bar:** full bar. **Address:** One Center St 04011 **Location:** Center. **Parking:** street only. `L` `D`

RICHARD'S RESTAURANT   207/729-9673

German. Casual Dining. $10-$24 **AAA Inspector Notes:** This restaurant exudes an Old World ambience. The extensive menu lists German entrees, as well as a page of American dishes, such as black Angus steaks. **Bar:** full bar. **Address:** 115 Maine St 04011 **Location:** Center. `L` `D`

SCARLET BEGONIA'S   207/721-0403

American. Casual Dining. $5-$16 **AAA Inspector Notes:** The cuisine and service are tops at this bistro. Tucked around a corner or two from Bowdoin College, guests can find fantastic salads, pasta and pizza. Diners can choose from tables in the dining area or in the lively bar. **Bar:** full bar. **Address:** 16 Station Ave 04011 **Location:** Just e of SR 24. **Parking:** street only. `L` `D` `CALL` `M`

TAVERN AT BRUNSWICK STATION   207/837-6565

American. Casual Dining. $10-$30 **AAA Inspector Notes:** A new addition to the area, convenient to Bowdoin College and Maine Street. This casual eatery serves a variety of such creative comfort food as seafood risotto, roasted chicken, burgers, shepherd's pie and fish and chips. The menu changes seasonally, and outdoor dining is a nice option during the warmer months. **Bar:** full bar. **Reservations:** suggested. **Address:** 4 Noble St 04011 **Location:** Just w of SR 24; center. `B` `L` `D` `CALL` `M` `N`

WILD OATS BAKERY & CAFE   207/725-6287

Deli. Quick Serve. $6-$11 **AAA Inspector Notes:** Excellent range of specialty sandwiches, creative soups and salads, and delicious pastries and cakes. Don't be dissuaded by the casual chaos of this eatery, the dishes are well worth it. Everything is available to go. **Address:** 149 Maine St 04011 **Location:** Downtown; in Tontine Mall. B L

BRYANT POND

MOLLYOCKETT MOTEL & SWIM SPA   (207)674-2345

Motel $70-$99 **Address:** 1132 S Main St 04219 **Location:** 1.3 mi n on SR 26 from jct SR 219. **Facility:** 20 units, some efficiencies. 2 stories (no elevator), interior/exterior corridors. **Terms:** cancellation fee imposed. **Pool(s):** heated indoor. **Activities:** sauna, whirlpool, hiking trails, playground, horseshoes, volleyball.

BUCKSPORT   (H-5) pop. 2,885, elev. 43'

Bucksport was founded in the 1760s by Col. Jonathan Buck. The village lies east of Mount Waldo, the site of major granite quarries. Mount Waldo granite is found at nearby Fort Knox and in buildings in Boston, New York and Washington, D.C.

Bucksport Bay Area Chamber of Commerce: 52 Main St., P.O. Box 1676, Bucksport, ME 04416. **Phone:** (207) 469-6818.

NORTHEAST HISTORIC FILM, 85 Main St., is in a renovated 1916 cinema. An exhibit traces the history of northern New England moviegoing through films and movie artifacts. Every weekend, movie screenings are preceded by rare archival film clips at the Alamo Theatre. A study center with films, videos and books also is available for visitors.

Hours: Exhibit and study center Mon.-Fri. 9-4. Screenings Fri.-Sun. Phone ahead to confirm schedule. **Cost:** Exhibit and study center by donation. Screenings $7; $6 (ages 62+ and students with ID). Reservations are required. **Phone:** (207) 469-0924, (207) 469-6910 for screening information or (800) 639-1636.

BUCKSPORT MOTOR INN   (207)469-3111

Motel $69-$109 **Address:** 70 US Route 1 04416 **Location:** Center. **Facility:** 24 units. 1 story, exterior corridors. **Amenities:** Some: high-speed Internet.

FORT KNOX PARK INN   (207)469-3113

Hotel $80-$200 **Address:** 64 Main St 04416 **Location:** Waterfront. On SR 15; center. **Facility:** 40 units. 4 stories, interior corridors.

WHERE TO EAT

MACLEOD'S RESTAURANT   207/469-3963

American
Seafood
Casual Dining
$7-$21

AAA Inspector Notes: This casual restaurant offers a welcoming atmosphere for locals and visitors. The menu offers a wide variety of entrees, including great-tasting ribs, burgers, seafood, house-prepared coleslaw and tasty chocolate silk pie. **Bar:** full bar. **Reservations:** suggested. **Address:** 63 Main St 04416 **Location:** Corner of Main and Central sts; center. **Parking:** street only. L D

CALAIS   (G-8) pop. 3,123, elev. 19'

Calais (KAL-is) is on the west bank of Passamaquoddy Bay at the mouth of the St. Croix River, a U.S.-Canadian boundary. Connected by the International Bridge to St. Stephen, New Brunswick, the city enjoys the distinction of being Maine's only international city.

Timber, fertile soil and an abundance of fish and game attracted the first settlers to the area in 1604. The town became an important lumbering and shipbuilding center. In 1809 the Massachusetts legislature named the settlement for the port of Calais, France, in acknowledgment of that country's assistance during the American Revolution.

The section of US 1 between Calais and Bar Harbor is a scenic drive from which visitors might see nesting eagles.

St. Croix Valley Chamber of Commerce: 39 Union St., Calais, ME 04619. **Phone:** (207) 454-2308 or (888) 422-3112.

Shopping areas: A Duty Free Americas is at 40 Main St.; phone (207) 454-3476.

DR. HOLMES COTTAGE MUSEUM, 523 Main St., is a two-story, Cape Cod-style structure built about 1804 and restored to its appearance of the mid-1800s. The cottage housed the practices of several physicians, and it now displays medical equipment and period furnishings. **Time:** Allow 30 minutes minimum. **Hours:** Mon.-Sat. 1-4, July-Aug.; by appointment rest of year. **Cost:** Donations. **Phone:** (207) 454-2604, or (207) 454-3061 in the off-season.

ST. CROIX ISLAND INTERNATIONAL HISTORIC SITE is 8 mi. s. on US 1 to 84 St. Croix Dr. The site, on the mainland shore of the St. Croix River, offers a view of 6.5-acre St. Croix Island, settled by the French in 1604. Many in the French expedition died of scurvy that winter and were buried on the island; the survivors departed and founded Port Royal in present-day Nova Scotia. An interpretive trail leading to the viewpoint is adorned with bronze statues of French settlers and Passamaquoddy American Indians. A model depicting the settlement as it may have appeared in 1604 is displayed. The visitor center features interpretive panels, Native American baskets and replicas of artifacts excavated on the island. Ranger-led programs are offered daily.

Note: Visits to the island are discouraged due to the island's fragile nature. Picnicking is permitted on the mainland. **Time:** Allow 30 minutes minimum. **Hours:** Grounds daily dawn-dusk. Visitor center daily 8:30-6, July-Aug.; 9-5, Memorial Day-June 30 and Sept. 1-Columbus Day; by appointment rest of year. A park ranger is available daily, Memorial Day-Columbus Day. The bronze statues are covered during off-season and winter months to preserve them from inclement weather. **Cost:** Free. **Phone:** (207) 454-3871.

KING CHINA RESTAURANT   207/454-1111
💎💎 Chinese. Casual Dining. $8-$16 **AAA Inspector Notes:** This popular restaurant offers a wide variety of menu options as well as a large buffet. **Bar:** full bar. **Address:** 180 North St 04619 **Location:** Center. [L] [D]

CAMDEN (I-5) pop. 3,570, elev. 33'
• Restaurants p. 78

Camden's beauty has attracted many writers, painters and artisans, including Edna St. Vincent Millay, whose career began in this town. A statue at the head of the harbor honors the poet, and Millay memorabilia is housed in the Whitehall Inn at 52 High St. Shaded streets, white clapboard churches and flower gardens contribute to the tranquil atmosphere.

As a year-round resort the seaside town also is popular with sports enthusiasts. Bicycling is a favorite pastime and sailing, kayaking and canoeing, on either the ocean or one of many lakes, prevails in the summer; ice skating and cross-country and downhill skiing predominate in winter. The toboggan run at the Camden Snow Bowl is open to the public; phone (207) 236-3438. Windjammer cruises and lobstering provide summer recreation, and coastal cruising via scenic US 1 is rewarding year-round.

Cultural enthusiasts can attend performances at the Camden Opera House; phone (207) 236-7963. Summer highlights include a variety of events; schooner races, art shows, folk festivals, antique shows, church fairs and lobster festivals are all on the agenda. Occasional concerts as well as juried art shows in July and October are presented at Amphitheatre and Harbor Park, on Atlantic Avenue at the waterfront.

Camden Hills State Park *(see Recreation Areas Chart)* is 2 miles north on US 1. A 1-mile road that leads to the summit of Mount Battie offers scenic views of Camden village and harbor. On a clear day, Acadia National Park and Monhegan Island can be seen.

Penobscot Bay Regional Chamber of Commerce—Camden: 2 Public Landing, P.O. Box 919, Camden, ME 04843. **Phone:** (207) 236-4404, or (800) 223-5459 to request a visitors' guide.

Self-guiding tours: Brochures and maps are available from the chamber of commerce, which is on the public landing.

MERRYSPRING NATURE CENTER is at 30 Conway Rd. The 66-acre nature park and education center includes herb, rose and perennial gardens; the Kitty Todd Arboretum; a greenhouse; walking trails; and the Ross Center, which houses a library and visitor facilities. **Time:** Allow 1 hour, 30 minutes minimum. **Hours:** Park open daily dawn-dusk. Ross Center open Tues.-Fri. 9-2. **Cost:** Free. **Phone:** (207) 236-2239.

ABIGAIL'S BED & BREAKFAST INN   207/236-2501
💎💎💎 Historic Bed & Breakfast $125-$225 **Address:** 8 High St 04843 **Location:** Just n on US 1; downtown. Located in a residential area. **Facility:** Close to the center of town, this attractive Federal-style 1847 home has spacious rooms and well-manicured grounds. Three guest rooms include a gas fireplace. 4 units, some two bedrooms. 2 stories (no elevator), interior/exterior corridors. **Terms:** 2 night minimum stay - weekends, 14 day cancellation notice.

BELMONT INN   (207)236-8053
💎💎💎 Historic Bed & Breakfast $149-$229 **Address:** 6 Belmont Ave 04843 **Location:** US 1, just s via School St. Located in a residential area. **Facility:** This attractive 1892 Edwardian-style inn offers a pleasant sunporch, seasonal gardens and varied rooms. Some guest rooms have gas-fire stoves. 6 units. 3 stories (no elevator), interior corridors. **Terms:** 2 night minimum stay - seasonal, 15 day cancellation notice-fee imposed.

BIRCHWOOD SUSTAINABLE LODGING   (207)236-4204
💎💎 Motel $80-$150 **Address:** 530 Belfast Rd 04843 **Location:** 3 mi n on US 1. **Facility:** 16 units, some cottages. 1 story, exterior corridors. **Terms:** closed 11/2-5/1, 3 day cancellation notice-fee imposed. **Free Special Amenities: continental breakfast and high-speed Internet.**

BLUE HARBOR HOUSE, A VILLAGE INN   (207)236-3196
💎💎💎 Bed & Breakfast $99-$215 **Address:** 67 Elm St 04843 **Location:** On US 1; center. **Facility:** English-style gardens and a New England country décor adorn this 1810 inn; rooms are individually decorated with great care and comfort in mind. 11 units. 2 stories (no elevator), interior/exterior corridors. **Terms:** 2 night minimum stay - seasonal and/or weekends, 14 day cancellation notice-fee imposed. **Free Special Amenities: full breakfast and high-speed Internet.**

CAMDEN HARBOUR INN   (207)236-4200
💎💎💎💎 Country Inn $225-$1195 **Address:** 83 Bayview St 04843 **Location:** Off US 1, 0.3 mi e. **Facility:** All rooms at this Camden landmark, built in 1874, are tastefully decorated with a modern theme; some rooms offer a fireplace. Guests enjoy fine views of Penobscot Bay or of the town and surrounding hills. 20 units. 3 stories (no elevator), interior corridors. **Terms:** 2 night minimum stay - seasonal and/or weekends, 14 day cancellation notice-fee imposed. **Dining:** Natalie's, see separate listing. **Activities:** Fee: massage. **Guest Services:** valet laundry. **Free Special Amenities: full breakfast and high-speed Internet.**

CAMDEN RIVERHOUSE HOTEL   (207)236-0500
💎💎💎 Hotel $109-$250 **Address:** 11 Tannery Ln 04843 **Location:** Center; just e of Washington St. Located in a commercial area. **Facility:** 42 units, some kitchens and cottages. 1-4 stories, interior corridors. **Terms:** 2 night minimum stay - seasonal and/or weekends, 14 day cancellation notice-fee imposed. **Pool(s):** heated indoor. **Activities:** whirlpool, horseshoes, exercise room. **Guest Services:** coin laundry. **Free Special Amenities: expanded continental breakfast and high-speed Internet.**

THE CAMDEN WINDWARD HOUSE   207/236-9656
💎💎💎 Historic Bed & Breakfast. Rates not provided. **Address:** 6 High St 04843 **Location:** Center. **Facility:** Formerly the home of a shipbuilder, this 1854 house offers a spacious and well-landscaped backyard and well-decorated guest rooms. 8 units, some two bedrooms. 3 stories (no elevator), interior corridors.

CAPTAIN SWIFT INN
207/236-8113

Historic Bed & Breakfast
$99-$305

Address: 72 Elm St 04843 **Location:** Center. **Facility:** This Federal-style, 1810 home has been restored and offers rooms of varying size and decor; colorful gardens, which bloom in season, surround the inn. 8 units. 2 stories (no elevator), interior/exterior corridors. **Terms:** 2 night minimum stay - seasonal and/or weekends, 14 day cancellation notice-fee imposed. **Free Special Amenities:** full breakfast and high-speed Internet.

CEDAR CREST INN
(207)236-4839

Hotel
$84-$149

Address: 115 Elm St 04843 **Location:** 0.8 mi s on US 1. **Facility:** 37 units. 2 stories (no elevator), exterior corridors. **Terms:** closed 10/20-5/9, cancellation fee imposed. **Pool(s):** heated outdoor. **Activities:** playground. **Guest Services:** coin laundry. **Free Special Amenities:** local telephone calls and high-speed Internet.

Quality, affordable accommodations since 1929.

GRAND HARBOR INN
(207)230-7177

Boutique Hotel
$159-$549

Address: 14 Bay View Landing 04843 **Location:** Waterfront. Center; just e of Main St. **Facility:** Located in the heart of Camden, these splendid spacious rooms and suites are on the second floor overlooking the harbor and marina. All rooms offer balconies and jetted tubs with separate showers. 11 units. 2 stories, interior corridors. **Terms:** closed 2/25-4/4, cancellation fee imposed. **Amenities:** high-speed Internet. **Free Special Amenities:** expanded continental breakfast and high-speed Internet.

Camden's only waterfront inn, private balconies, complimentary in-suite breakfast, high speed Wi-Fi.

GRAND HARBOR INN

HARTSTONE INN & HIDEAWAY
(207)236-4259

Country Inn
$105-$295

Address: 41 Elm St 04843 **Location:** US 1, just s of Washington St; center. **Facility:** Nestled in the heart of town on landscaped grounds, this inn offers tastefully decorated guest rooms and spacious suites in three separate buildings. Each unit has elegant beds and soft seating. 21 units, some two bedrooms. 2-3 stories (no elevator), interior/exterior corridors. **Terms:** 2 night minimum stay - seasonal and/or weekends, 14 day cancellation notice-fee imposed. **Activities:** *Fee:* massage. **Free Special Amenities:** full breakfast and high-speed Internet. **Dining:** Hartstone Inn, see separate listing.

▼ See AAA listing p. 109 ▼

HAWTHORN INN   207/236-8842

 Historic Bed & Breakfast $130-$295 **Address:** 9 High St 04843 **Location:** 0.3 mi n on US 1. Located in a residential area. **Facility:** Some of the rooms at this restored 1894 Queen Anne home and carriage house offer harbor views; a few feature decks and gas fireplaces. 10 units. 3 stories (no elevator), interior corridors. **Terms:** 2 night minimum stay - seasonal and/or weekends, 14 day cancellation notice-fee imposed.

INNS AT BLACKBERRY COMMON   (207)236-6060

 Bed & Breakfast $125-$285 **Address:** 82 Elm St 04843 **Location:** On US 1; center. **Facility:** Built in 1849, Blackberry Inn is an Italianate-style painted lady with fireplaces and lovely perennial gardens, including a blackberry patch. 18 units, some two bedrooms. 2-3 stories (no elevator), interior/exterior corridors. **Terms:** 2 night minimum stay - weekends, 14 day cancellation notice-fee imposed.

Plan complete trip routings with the TripTik®
Travel Planner on AAA.com/CAA.ca

LORD CAMDEN INN   (207)236-4325

Hotel
$99-$349

Address: 24 Main St 04843 **Location:** Just n of Washington St; center. **Facility:** 36 units. 4 stories, interior corridors. **Terms:** cancellation fee imposed. **Free Special Amenities:** full breakfast and high-speed Internet.

Affordable elegance in downtown Camden. Private balconies, full buffet breakfast & free Wi-Fi.

▼ *See AAA listing p. 115* ▼

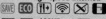

WHITEHALL INN
(207)236-3391

▼▼▼ **Historic Country Inn** $129-$224 **Address:** 52 High St 04843 **Location:** US 1, 0.4 mi n of SR 52. **Facility:** Built in 1834 and then expanded in 1901 and again in 1910, the inn features manicured grounds, extensive common areas and excellent beds in all the guest rooms. 40 units, some two bedrooms. 3 stories (no elevator), interior corridors. **Bath:** some shared. **Terms:** closed 10/22-5/14, 10 day cancellation notice-fee imposed. **Activities:** shuffleboard.

❙❘ Ⓣ BIZ 🛜 ✕

WHERE TO EAT

ATLANTICA RESTAURANT
207/236-6011

▼▼▼ Regional Seafood. Casual Dining. $18-$29 **AAA Inspector Notes:** Upscale contemporary American cuisine shows an emphasis on seafood. The harborside restaurant offers dishes that are made to order; fresh, locally grown ingredients are used whenever possible. **Bar:** full bar. **Reservations:** suggested. **Address:** 1 Bayview Landing 04843 **Location:** On harborfront; center. Ⓓ Ⓐ𝗖

CAMDEN DELI
207/236-8343

♦ Deli. Quick Serve. $5-$9 **AAA Inspector Notes:** Diners can eat in or take out; both are options at the popular delicatessen in the center of town. **Bar:** beer & wine. **Address:** 37 Main St 04843 **Location:** On US 1; center. **Parking:** street only.

Ⓑ Ⓛ Ⓓ Ⓐ𝗖

CAPPY'S CHOWDER HOUSE
207/236-2254

♦
Seafood
Family Dining
$9-$18

AAA Inspector Notes: Since 1979 this lively restaurant has been a local favorite with a pub-style atmosphere and a menu that focuses on fresh seafood, but also includes a selection of meat entrées such as burgers and steak. A bakery and coffee bar is on the lower floor, with a pleasant garden terrace in back. **Bar:** full bar. **Address:** 1 Main St 04843 **Location:** Corner of Bay View St. **Parking:** street only.

Menu on AAA.com Ⓛ Ⓓ Ⓐ𝗖

FRANCINE BISTRO
207/230-0083

▼▼ Regional American. Casual Dining. $19-$26 **AAA Inspector Notes:** This quaint popular bistro offers a casual bustling atmosphere. Daily changing menus list dishes made from fresh local ingredients. All items, including bread and desserts, are made on the premises. Patio seating is available seasonally. **Bar:** full bar. **Reservations:** suggested. **Address:** 55 Chestnut St 04843 **Location:** Just s of Elm St; center. **Parking:** street only. Ⓓ

FRESH
207/236-7005

▼▼▼
American
Casual Dining
$12-$26

AAA Inspector Notes: Located in the heart of Camden, this quaint bistro offers well-prepared fresh local seafood, excellent meats and organic vegetables. Desserts are homemade and portions are ample. The small street-side patio is perfect for people watching. **Bar:** full bar.

Address: 1 Bay View Landing 04843 **Location:** Just s of Elm and Main sts; center. **Parking:** street only. Ⓛ Ⓓ

HARTSTONE INN
207/236-4259

▼▼▼▼ American. Fine Dining. $25-$49 **AAA Inspector Notes:** A memorable dining experience awaits at this fine inn. A two-course light supper menu is featured at 6 pm, and the signature five-course dinner has only one seating at 7 pm. Guests can savor the culinary delights of chef Michael Salmon's five-course prix-fixe menu, which changes nightly. An extensive wine and cocktail list is assured to complement the courses. **Bar:** full bar. **Reservations:** required. **Address:** 41 Elm St 04843 **Location:** US 1, just s of Washington St; center; in Hartstone Inn & Hideaway. Ⓓ

LOTUS ASIAN GOURMET CHINESE RESTAURANT
207/236-2133

▼▼ Chinese. Casual Dining. $8-$18 **AAA Inspector Notes:** This popular restaurant has ample variety on its menu of traditional Szechuan cuisine, seafood specials, tasty soups and egg rolls. A daily buffet is offered for lunch. Service is prompt, pleasant and friendly. Patrons are seated at either booths or regular tables. **Bar:** full bar. **Address:** 133 Elm St 04843 **Location:** 0.9 mi s on US 1.

Ⓛ Ⓓ

NATALIE'S
207/236-7008

▼▼▼
American
Fine Dining
$26-$44

AAA Inspector Notes: Located within a local inn, the eatery offers an upscale dining experience. A tasting menu is available nightly, as is an a la carte menu. The dining room affords a lovely view of Camden and a marina. Reservations are strongly recommended. **Bar:** full bar.

Reservations: suggested. **Address:** 83 Bayview St 04843 **Location:** Off US 1, 0.3 mi e; in Camden Harbour Inn. Ⓓ

PETER OTT'S STEAKHOUSE & TAVERN
207/236-4032

▼▼ American. Casual Dining. $20-$26 **AAA Inspector Notes:** The spacious restaurant has a casual pub atmosphere and offers a fine selection of meats and seafood entrees. Works from local artists adorn the walls. **Bar:** full bar. **Address:** 16 Bayview St 04843 **Location:** Just s of Main St; center. **Parking:** street only. Ⓓ

THE WATERFRONT RESTAURANT
207/236-3747

▼▼ American. Casual Dining. $9-$26 **AAA Inspector Notes:** Bordering Camden Harbor, the pleasant restaurant is decorated with a nautical theme. Some sections offer a nice harbor view and patio seating is available in season. The menu varies from burgers to fresh seafood to steak, and food is plated in ample portions. Raw bar items are served daily in the bar from 2:30 to 5 pm. **Bar:** full bar. **Address:** 40 Bayview St 04843 **Location:** Center; on the harborfront.

Ⓛ Ⓓ Ⓐ𝗖

CAPE ELIZABETH (K-3) elev. 27'

Cape Elizabeth was named by Capt. John Smith in 1615 for Princess Elizabeth, sister of Charles I of England. Early settlers managed to exist by fishing and farming, despite repeated raids by American Indians and pirates. Closely associated with Portland (then Falmouth) in its earliest days, the settlement was recognized as a separate district in 1765 and finally granted status as an incorporated town during the Revolutionary unrest of 1775.

Few farms remain, as "the Cape" has become primarily a residential center for the Greater Portland area. The diverse coastal landscape includes sandy beaches, craggy cliffs and saltwater marshes and is accessible through two state parks as well as one town-owned park.

Two Lights State Park, 3 miles south on SR 77, features walking areas, scenic views from a rocky headland and picnic facilities. The park is next to Two Lights Lighthouse, which marks the entrance to Casco Bay. Crescent Beach State Park, 1 mile south on SR 77, offers recreational opportunities, picnic facilities and views of Richmond Island *(see Recreation Areas Chart).*

PORTLAND HEAD LIGHT is at 1000 Shore Rd. in Fort Williams Park. First operated in 1791 under the authorization of President George Washington, it was the first light completed after the founding of the United States and is one of the oldest lighthouses in continuous use in the country. Highlights include a museum, several walking paths, an arboretum and views of Casco Bay.

Hours: Park open daily dawn-dusk. Museum open daily 10-4, late May to mid-Oct.; Sat.-Sun. 10-4, mid-Apr. to late May and mid-Oct. to mid-Dec. **Cost:** Park free. Museum $2; $1 (ages 6-18). **Phone:** (207) 799-2661. 🎟

INN BY THE SEA (207)799-3134

Hotel
$199-$1799

Address: 40 Bowery Beach Rd (SR 77) 04107 **Location:** Oceanfront. On SR 77, 7 mi s. **Facility:** Lovely ocean views greet you at this shingle-style inn located at Crescent Beach. The inn has meticulously landscaped grounds and gardens that beckon you to explore. 61 efficiencies, some two bedrooms and kitchens. 2 stories, interior/exterior corridors. **Parking:** on-site and valet. **Terms:** check-in 4 pm, 2 night minimum stay - seasonal and/or weekends, 14 day cancellation notice-fee imposed, resort fee. **Amenities:** *Some:* high-speed Internet. **Pool(s):** heated outdoor. **Activities:** limited beach access, jogging, volleyball, exercise room, spa. **Guest Services:** valet laundry.

[SAVE] [ECO] [icons] CALL [icons] [icons] BIZ [icons] [icons]

WHERE TO EAT

THE GOOD TABLE RESTAURANT 207/799-4663

Regional American. Casual Dining. $7-$24 **AAA Inspector Notes:** The charming beach road spot is set in a shingled cottage and offers a screened dining porch strung with colorful lights. Such traditional Maine fare as clam rolls, chowders and blueberry pie are favorites, and guests will also find foods influenced by the owner's Greek heritage, like gyros, spanakopita and a local haddock baked in tomato sauce. **Bar:** full bar. **Address:** 527 Ocean House Rd 04107 **Location:** On SR 77, 6 mi s. [B] [L] [D] CALL[icons]

TWO LIGHTS LOBSTER SHACK RESTAURANT 207/799-1677

Seafood. Quick Serve. $6-$25 **AAA Inspector Notes:** Popular with locals and tourists alike, the oceanfront lobster house offers excellent seafood and great views of the lighthouse. Specialties include clam chowder and lobster stew as well as lobster dinners. Desserts are made on the premises. **Address:** 225 Two Lights Rd 04107 **Location:** On SR 77, 2 mi e. [L] [D] [icon]

CARIBOU (C-6) pop. 8,189, elev. 400'

Caribou is a business center for Aroostook County, source of 90 percent of the state's potato crop and one of the largest potato-shipping areas in the world. The Aroostook and Little Madawaska rivers, which offer excellent trout and salmon fishing, flow through town. The city offers a variety of recreational opportunities, including canoeing, fishing, camping, autumn foliage drives and winter sports.

Caribou was settled by soldiers who had been sent to the frontier during the 1838-39 Aroostook War and then stayed to log or farm. Development was slow, primarily because the town lacked the means to transport goods to market. The potato crop was unable to realize its commercial potential until the Bangor and Aroostook Railroad arrived in the early 1890s. As a major junction point, Caribou flourished.

The Nylander Museum of Natural History, 657 Main St., contains the extensive collections of rocks, minerals, fossils, shells, marine specimens and Native American artifacts of Swedish-born naturalist Olof Nylander. Nylander spent his life amassing and classifying—an effort which gained him an honorary Master of Science degree from the University of Maine. Other features of the museum include an herb garden, wildflowers and mounted regional animals; phone (207) 498-6156.

Northwest of Caribou along SR 161, communities with such names as Sweden, New Sweden, Jemtland and Stockholm reveal the origins of those who settled the region in the 1870s.

Caribou Area Chamber of Commerce: 657 Main St., Suite 1, Caribou, ME 04736. **Phone:** (207) 498-6156 or (800) 722-7648.

CARIBOU INN & CONVENTION CENTER (207)498-3733

Hotel
$98-$146

Address: 19 Main St 04736 **Location:** 3 mi s on US 1. **Facility:** 73 units, some efficiencies. 2 stories (no elevator), interior corridors. **Terms:** cancellation fee imposed. **Dining:** The Greenhouse Restaurant, see separate listing. **Pool(s):** heated indoor. **Activities:** sauna, whirlpool. **Guest Services:** coin laundry. **Free Special Amenities:** local telephone calls and high-speed Internet.

[SAVE] [icons] BIZ [icons] [icons] / SOME UNITS FEE [icons]

CROWN PARK INN 207/493-3311

Hotel. Rates not provided. **Address:** 30 Access Hwy 04736 **Location:** On SR 80, 0.4 mi e of jct US 1. **Facility:** 58 units, some efficiencies. 2 stories (no elevator), interior corridors. **Activities:** whirlpool, game room, exercise room. **Guest Services:** coin laundry. [BIZ] [icons] / SOME UNITS [icons]

WHERE TO EAT

THE GREENHOUSE RESTAURANT 207/498-3733

American Casual Dining
$7-$24

AAA Inspector Notes: The menu at this spot features different meat and seafood entrées each night along with a large variety of desserts. Guests especially enjoy the warm, cozy environment with a bright and airy feeling. This place is suitable for all occasions. **Bar:** full bar. **Address:** 19 Main St 04736 **Location:** 3 mi s on US 1; in Caribou Inn & Convention Center. [B] [L] [D]

JADE PALACE RESTAURANT 207/498-3648

Chinese. Casual Dining. $7-$16 **AAA Inspector Notes:** Unpretentious décor characterizes the spacious restaurant, a popular spot for well-prepared Hunan, Szechuan and Peking-style cuisine, as well as American entrées, all served in ample portions. **Bar:** full bar. **Address:** Skyway Plaza 04736 **Location:** US 1 at jct SR 89; in Skyway Plaza. [L] [D]

THE PAR & GRILL 207/492-0988

American. Casual Dining. $6-$16 **AAA Inspector Notes:** The distinctive sports bar features a golf simulator, dartboards and TVs to keep patrons up to speed on their favorite game. The menu offers homemade pizza, soup and salad, as well as sandwiches, burgers and steaks. **Bar:** full bar. **Address:** 118 Bennett Dr 04736 **Location:** Just n of jct US 1 and SR 89; in Caribou Shopping Center. [L] [D]

CARRABASSETT VALLEY (G-3)
• Hotels p. 80

RECREATIONAL ACTIVITIES
Skiing

• **Sugarloaf/USA Ski and Golf Resort** is off SR 27 at 5092 Access Rd. Other activities are offered. **Hours:** Daily year-round. Ski season mid-Nov. through Apr. 30 (weather permitting). **Phone:** (207) 237-2000 or (800) 843-5623.

THE SUGARLOAF MOUNTAIN HOTEL   207/237-2222

▼▼▼▼ Hotel $179-$350 Address: 5091 Access Rd 04947 Location: Off SR 27, 1.8 mi w up Sugarloaf Mountain access road. Facility: 119 units, some two bedrooms, three bedrooms, efficiencies and kitchens. 6 stories, interior/exterior corridors. Terms: check-in 4 pm, 2 night minimum stay - seasonal and/or weekends, 21 day cancellation notice-fee imposed. Pool(s): heated indoor. Activities: sauna, whirlpools, steamroom, ice skating, recreation programs, playground, exercise room, spa. Fee: golf-18 holes, downhill & cross country skiing. Guest Services: coin laundry.

[ECO] [❍] [Y] [➤] [BIZ] [📶] [✕] [🖥] [❐]
/ SOME UNITS [🍳]

CASCO pop. 587

ALYSSAS MOTEL ON THOMAS POND   207/655-2223

▼▼ Motel $75-$169 Address: 11 Roosevelt Tr 04015 Location: Waterfront. On US 302 at the Casco/Raymond line. Facility: 9 units, some two bedrooms. 1 story, exterior corridors. Terms: 2 night minimum stay - seasonal and/or weekends, 30 day cancellation notice-fee imposed. Activities: canoeing, boat dock, fishing.

[📶] [✕] [🗲] [❐] / SOME UNITS FEE [🍳] [🖥] [🍳]

CASTINE (I-5) pop. 1,029

Coveted by world powers for its strategic port, Castine endured 2 centuries of disputes among the American Indians, French, British, Dutch and Americans. The French erected a fort in 1613, but the first permanent settlement was made by England in 1760. The British occupied the town during the Revolution, after handing the American Navy its most humiliating and devastating defeat in the largest amphibious operation of the Revolutionary War.

Although severely outnumbered, a handful of British sloops-of-war pummeled a Colonial fleet of some 40 ships sent to defend the harbor, which was used as a base for hit-and-run missions against His Majesty's navy. After securing the town the British built Fort George in 1779; it passed into American possession in 1783. Fort Madison was built in 1811. The British occupied both forts during the War of 1812.

Fort Madison was rebuilt during the Civil War; the earthworks and protective moat are still visible. Fort George, partially restored, is maintained as a memorial. Castine also is home to Maine Maritime Academy; founded in 1941, it prepares its students for careers in nautical and ocean sciences, engineering and management.

The town boasts towering elms, 18th- and early 19th-century homes and more than 100 historical landmarks.

THE T.S. STATE OF MAINE, berthed at the Maine Maritime Academy waterfront, is a 499-foot training ship for academy students. The ship, the former USNS Tanner, originally served as a Navy oceanographic research vessel. Note: Valid government-issued photo ID is required. All bags may be searched. Hours: Guided 30-minute tours are given daily on the hour 10-3, July 1-late Aug.; Sat.-Sun. on the hour 10-3, late Aug.-late Apr. Closed major holidays and during college breaks. Phone ahead to confirm schedule. Cost: Free. Phone: (207) 326-4311 or (207) 326-2420.

WILSON MUSEUM is at 120 Perkins St. Exhibits include prehistoric artifacts from North and South America, Europe and Africa; ship models; rocks and minerals; 19th-century carpenter's tools; and farm and home equipment. Also featured is the John Perkins House, a pre-Revolutionary War structure restored and furnished with period antiques. Living history demonstrations, workshops and lectures are scheduled throughout the summer.

Tours: Guided tours are available. Time: Allow 1 hour minimum. Hours: Museum Mon.-Fri. 10-5, Sat.-Sun. 2-5, May 27-Sept. 30. John Perkins House and blacksmith shop Wed. and Sun. 2-5, July-Aug. Cost: Free. John Perkins House $5. Phone: (207) 326-9247.

THE CASTINE INN   207/326-4365

▼▼ Historic Bed & Breakfast $125-$235 Address: 33 Main St 04421 Location: Center. Facility: Operating since 1898, the inn has lovely landscaped gardens and features a variety of room types: from standard rooms to superior quality units, some with a harbor or garden view. 19 units. 3 stories (no elevator), interior corridors. Terms: closed 10/22-6/1, 14 day cancellation notice-fee imposed. Activities: sauna. [❍] [📶] [✕] [🎿] [🏊] [🗲]

PENTAGOET INN   207/326-8616

▼▼▼ Historic Country Inn. Rates not provided. Address: 26 Main St 04421 Location: Center. Facility: An 1894 Victorian inn and an adjacent Federal-style building house the guest rooms at this lovely property located in the center of town. A small gift shop also is featured. 16 units. 3 stories (no elevator), interior corridors. Parking: street only. Dining: Pentagoet Inn Dining Room, see separate listing. Activities: bicycles.

[❍] [BIZ] [📶] [✕] [🎿] [🗲] / SOME UNITS FEE [🍳] [🏊]

WHERE TO EAT

DENNETT'S WHARF   207/326-9045

▼▼ Seafood. Casual Dining. $9-$27 AAA Inspector Notes: This nautical-themed casual restaurant offers great views of Castine Harbor. On nice days they have a large covered patio available for guests as well as limited bar seating. A wide variety of entrées are available such as seafood, steak and ribs. Bar: full bar. Address: 15 Sea St 04421 Location: Center; on SR 166 at Castine Harbor.

[L] [D]

PENTAGOET INN DINING ROOM   207/326-8616

▼▼▼ Seafood. Fine Dining. $15-$30 AAA Inspector Notes: In the center of the charming seaside town, this restaurant occupies an 1894 Victorian inn. A romantic ambience pervades the candlelit dining room, where diners sit down to seasonally changing dishes that incorporate fresh local ingredients and a New England sensibility. Bar: full bar. Reservations: suggested. Address: 26 Main St 04421 Location: Center; in Pentagoet Inn. Parking: street only. [D] [🎿]

COLUMBIA FALLS (H-7) elev. 30'

Columbia Falls was established around 1780 on the banks of the Pleasant River, which the Downeast Salmon Federation stocks with Atlantic salmon each year. The town's early successes in lumbering and shipbuilding resulted in the construction of elegant homes for its prominent businessmen; a number of these structures still stand. Over time the town began to focus on agricultural pursuits, and today the blueberry industry is one of the primary drivers of the local economy.

RUGGLES HOUSE, .5 mi. off US 1 on Main St., was built 1818-20 for Judge Thomas Ruggles, a wealthy lumber dealer, merchant, postmaster and militia captain. The Adamesque-style house is noted for its flying staircase that rises without lateral support and for its delicate interior and exterior woodcarvings. Many of the period furnishings are original and much of the art in the house was created by Ruggles' granddaughters.

Tours: Guided tours are available. **Hours:** Mon.-Sat. 9:30-4:30, Sun. noon-4:30, June 1-Oct. 15. Closed July 4 and Labor Day. **Cost:** $5; $2 (ages 6-12). **Phone:** (207) 483-4637, or (207) 546-7903 in the off-season.

CUSHING (J-5) elev. 43'

OLSON HOUSE, 384 Hathorne Point Rd., is a late-1700s saltwater farmhouse best known for its depiction in Andrew Wyeth's painting "Christina's World," completed on the property in 1948. Guided tours take visitors around the home to see where Wyeth worked and stayed for many summers. Some of Wyeth's completed works are now housed in the Farnsworth Art Museum and the Wyeth Center in Rockland.

Cameras are not permitted inside the house. **Time:** Allow 1 hour, 30 minutes minimum. **Hours:** Tours Tues.-Sun. on the hour 11-5, July 1-early Oct.; Wed.-Sun. on the hour noon-4, late May-June 30. **Cost:** Grounds free. House $10; $8 (ages 65+ and students ages 17+ with ID); free (ages 0-16). Combination ticket with Farnsworth Art Museum and the Wyeth Center $17; $15 (ages 65+ and students ages 17+ with ID); free (ages 0-16). **Phone:** (207) 596-6457.

DAMARISCOTTA (J-4) pop. 1,142

Although John Brown—recipient in 1625 of the first deed tendered within the present borders of Maine—lived in this area in the mid-1600s, permanent settlement did not take place until 1730. In that year, three Boston families sailed up the Damariscotta River to take up grants along its shore. Their village prospered with an economy based on lumbering, agriculture, shipping and brick making.

Its position at the head of navigation and the ready supply of timber made Damariscotta a natural place for shipbuilding. Among several noted vessels built in this town was the 1849 *Excelsior,* the first three-decked ship constructed in Maine.

Damariscotta is now a shopping and financial center for the nearby resort area that extends south to Christmas Cove and the Pemaquids. Much of the character of the Main Street business district stems from the brick structures erected after a fire in 1845. Houses dating from the Colonial and Federal periods are scattered throughout the community and south along SR 129/130.

Damariscotta Region Chamber of Commerce: 15 Courtyard St., Suite 2, P.O. Box 13, Damariscotta, ME 04543. **Phone:** (207) 563-8340.

SALT BAY CAFE   207/563-3302

▼▼ American. Casual Dining. $7-$24 **AAA Inspector Notes:** With decor reminiscent of a library, the local favorite offers a good selection of seafood and meat entrees, as well as an extensive list of vegetarian items. Among homemade desserts is a superb strawberry shortcake. The staff is friendly and attentive. **Bar:** full bar. **Address:** 88 Main St 04543 **Location:** Center. [B] [L] [D]

SCHOONER LANDING RESTAURANT & MARINA
                                                        207/563-7447

▼▼ Regional Seafood. Casual Dining. $8-$21 **AAA Inspector Notes:** Although the emphasis is on fresh seafood, the menu also lists chicken and beef dishes, wraps and quesadillas. The dining room overlooks the water, and boaters often sail up and come in. The dining patio opens seasonally. **Bar:** full bar. **Address:** 40 Main St 04543 **Location:** Center; on the waterfront. [L] [D] [🅰🅒]

DEDHAM

THE LUCERNE INN DINING ROOM   207/843-5123

▼▼▼ American. Fine Dining. $16-$38 **AAA Inspector Notes:** Pleasant dining rooms in the grand old mansion afford terrific views of Phillips Lake. Sunday brunch is popular, as are such specialties as roast duckling and Atlantic salmon. Daily specials and homemade desserts are offered. **Bar:** full bar. **Reservations:** suggested. **Address:** 2517 Main Rd 04429 **Location:** On US 1A; in The Lucerne Inn. [D]

DEXTER (G-4) pop. 2,158, elev. 429'

DEXTER HISTORICAL SOCIETY'S GRIST MILL CAMPUS, downtown at 3 Water St., features an 1854 gristmill that was operational until 1965, a restored one-room schoolhouse used 1845-1944 and the 1825 Miller's House. Exhibits include an old-fashioned kitchen and parlor, farm implements and World War I memorabilia. The Abbott Museum, 12 Church St. in the 1836 Town Hall, contains a genealogy and research library.

Hours: Campus Mon.-Fri. 10-4, Sat. 1-4, mid-June through Sept. 30. Abbott Museum Mon.-Fri. 10-4, Sat. 1-4, mid-June to early Oct.; Sat. 1-4, rest of year. Research archives open year-round; phone for schedule. Phone ahead to confirm schedule. **Cost:** Donations. **Phone:** (207) 924-5721.

DRESDEN (J-4)

POWNALBOROUGH COURTHOUSE is w. on SR 128. The only pre-Revolutionary War courthouse remaining in the state, this three-story 1761 structure includes a furnished courtroom, judges' chambers, bedrooms, kitchen, tavern and parlor. Before he became president, John Adams once tried a case at the courthouse. Displays of antique tools and machinery chronicle the area's history. A Revolutionary-era cemetery is on the grounds.

Guided tours and nature trails are available. **Time:** Allow 30 minutes minimum. **Hours:** Tues.-Sat. 10-4, Sun. noon-4, July-Aug.; Sat. 10-4, Sun. noon-4, Memorial Day-June 30 and Sept. 1-Columbus Day. **Cost:** $4; free (ages 0-16). **Phone:** (207) 882-6817. [🅰]

DURHAM

ROYALSBOROUGH INN AT THE BAGLEY HOUSE
207/353-6372

▼▼ **Historic Bed & Breakfast.** Rates not provided. **Address:** 1290 Royalsborough Rd 04222 **Location:** I-295 exit 22, 6 mi n on SR 136. **Facility:** Elegant simplicity characterizes the décor of this 1722 farmhouse, and the new carriage house offers modern conveniences and country décor. Expect fine hospitality in a restful setting. 7 units. 2 stories (no elevator), interior corridors.

🛜 ⊠ ✍ / SOME UNITS ⓚ ⓦ

EAGLE LAKE pop. 625

OVERLOOK MOTEL & LAKESIDE CABINS 207/444-4535

▼▼ **Motel** $78 **Address:** 3232 Aroostook Rd 04739 **Location:** On SR 11; center. **Facility:** 18 units, some two bedrooms, three bedrooms, kitchens and cabins. 1-2 stories (no elevator), interior/exterior corridors. **Parking:** winter plug-ins. **Activities:** canoeing, paddleboats. **Guest Services:** coin laundry.

🛜 ⊠ 🖥 📠 💻 / SOME UNITS FEE 🐾 ⓚ

EAST BOOTHBAY

FIVE GABLES INN (207)633-4551

▼▼▼ **Historic Bed & Breakfast** $145-$245 **Address:** 107 Murray Hill Rd 04544 **Location:** Jct SR 27 and 96, 2.1 mi e. Located in a semi-residential area. **Facility:** Built in 1886, the inn is located on the side of a hill overlooking Linekin Bay. Individually decorated, all guest rooms sport a seaside theme; many afford lovely ocean views. 16 units. 3 stories (no elevator), interior corridors. **Terms:** closed 10/14-5/23, age restrictions may apply, 10 day cancellation notice.

BIZ 🛜 ⊠ ⓚ ⓦ

OCEAN POINT INN & RESORT 207/633-4200

▼▼ **Hotel** $79-$249 **Address:** 191 Shore Rd 04544 **Location:** Oceanfront. Jct SR 27, 4.2 mi s on SR 96, 0.6 mi w on Middle Rd. **Facility:** 61 units, some two bedrooms, kitchens and cottages. 1-2 stories (no elevator), interior/exterior corridors. **Terms:** closed 10/14-5/14, 14 day cancellation notice-fee imposed. **Pool(s):** heated outdoor. **Activities:** whirlpool, fishing.

🍽 🍸 ⛵ 🛜 ⊠ 🖥 / SOME UNITS 📠 💻

WHERE TO EAT

LOBSTERMAN'S WHARF RESTAURANT 207/633-3443

▼▼ Regional Seafood. Casual Dining. $9-$27 **AAA Inspector Notes:** Beside a boatyard, the restaurant offers waterside tables, nautical decor and lots of seafood, such as lobster stew and crab cakes. Also on the menu are burgers, pasta and good wines. Popular with locals, this place is ideal for escaping the crowds. **Bar:** full bar. **Address:** 224 Ocean Point Rd 04544 **Location:** Jct SR 27 and 96, 2.5 mi e. Ⓛ Ⓓ ⓚ

EAST ORLAND (H-5)

The Great Pond Mountain Wildlands, a 4,300-acre wilderness area with more than 15 miles of scenic trails, offers visitors opportunities for hiking, bicycling, horseback riding, cross-country skiing and snowmobiling. The main gate is located on US 1 just south of the SR 176 intersection. Some vehicle traffic is permitted on weekends, June through October.

CRAIG BROOK NATIONAL FISH HATCHERY, 1.3 mi. n. of US 1 on Hatchery Rd., is dedicated to the replenishment of the wild Atlantic salmon in Maine's waters. More than 4 million eggs are hatched here annually. A visitor center contains educational displays, and a display pool and a nature trail are on the grounds. The Craig Brook Atlantic Salmon Museum also is featured.

Hours: Visitor center daily 8-4. Museum Thurs. and Sat.-Sun. noon-3, mid-June through Labor Day; by appointment rest of year. **Cost:** Free. **Phone:** (207) 469-6701, (207) 469-7300 or TTY (800) 877-8339. 🅣

EASTPORT (H-8) pop. 1,331, elev. 41'

Eastport, on Moose Island in Passamaquoddy Bay, was first settled about 1780. In a roundabout way, the capture of Eastport by the British in 1814 put Gen. Andrew Jackson in the White House 15 years later. News of Eastport's fall during the War of 1812 halted peace negotiations and prolonged the fighting so that Jackson won the decisive Battle of New Orleans. It was the general's victory that ultimately led him to the presidency in 1829.

In Eastport, fishing, scallop harvesting and lumber shipping are principal concerns. A deepwater commercial port and a large aquaculture industry that specializes in raising trout and salmon characterize the waterfront.

The moor-like wilderness of Washington County, which is larger in area than Rhode Island and Delaware combined, yields some of the state's richest blueberry and cranberry harvests. The record tidal variation on the east coast of the United States is registered in the vicinity, with a rise and fall as great as 26 feet during some seasons.

Old Sow, which is said to be the second largest whirlpool in the world, can be seen 2 hours before high tide from Dog Island, reached by way of Water Street. Boat charters are available to view the region's scenic areas, whales and other marine life and such native birds as eagles and ospreys.

Eastport Area Chamber of Commerce: 64 Water St., P.O. Box 254, Eastport, ME 04631. **Phone:** (207) 853-4644.

THE MOTEL EAST (207)853-4747

▼▼ **Motel** $75-$150 **Address:** 23A Water St 04631 **Location:** Oceanfront. Center. **Facility:** 14 units. 2 stories (no elevator), exterior corridors. 🛗 🛜 ⓚ 🖥 📠 / SOME UNITS FEE 🐾

WHERE TO EAT

EASTPORT CHOWDER HOUSE 207/853-4700

▼▼ Seafood. Casual Dining. $10-$25 **AAA Inspector Notes:** Occupying a lovely location in a converted cannery overlooking the harbor and islands, the chowder house is a spacious, family-style eatery specializing in fresh lobster, various seafood entrees and chowders. Some meat entrees and comfort foods are also available. Pleasant outdoor dining is available in season. **Bar:** full bar. **Address:** 169 Water St 04631 **Location:** At ferry terminal; center.
Ⓛ Ⓓ ⓚ

HAPPY CRAB RESTAURANT 207/853-9400
 American. Casual Dining. $7-$18 **AAA Inspector Notes:** In the heart of town, this place has several dining sections, including a seasonal patio overlooking the harbor. The menu lists fresh seafood, steaks, burgers and great chowders. **Bar:** full bar. **Address:** 35 Water St 04631 **Location:** Center. **Parking:** street only.

L D 🅐

EDGECOMB (J-4)

FORT EDGECOMB STATE HISTORIC SITE occupies 3 acres on the s. end of Davis Island, just s. off US 1. An 1808-09 octagonal wooden blockhouse built of hand-hewn timbers for the War of 1812 is one of the best-preserved of its kind in North America and offers a skillfully made example of the construction methods of the period. Living-history encampments featuring demonstrations of cooking, sewing and Colonial games take place June through August. Informational panels are available.

Tours: Guided tours are available. **Time:** Allow 30 minutes minimum. **Hours:** Daily 9-5, Memorial Day-Labor Day. **Cost:** $3; $1 (ages 5-11 and 65+). **Phone:** (207) 882-7777, or (207) 624-6080 in the off-season. 🅰

SHEEPSCOT HARBOUR VILLAGE & RESORT
(207)882-6343

Hotel
$119-$369

Address: 306 Eddy Rd 04556 **Location:** 1 mi w on US 1; on east side of Davies Bridge; 1 mi e of Wiscasset. **Facility:** 65 units, some two bedrooms, kitchens, houses, cottages and condominiums. 1-2 stories (no elevator), interior/exterior corridors. **Terms:** 14 day cancellation notice-fee imposed. **Pool(s):** heated indoor. **Activities:** whirlpool, bicycles. **Free Special Amenities:** continental breakfast and high-speed Internet.

SAVE ECO 🛋 BIZ 🛜 ✕ 🅱 🖥
/SOME UNITS FEE 🐾 🅐 🖥

ELLSWORTH (I-6) pop. 7,741, elev. 112'
• Restaurants p. 85

Ellsworth began as a lumbering and shipbuilding center in 1763 and moved into the industrial era via waterpower from the Union River. Today the city is a bustling service center for the region. Lamoine State Park *(see Recreation Areas Chart)*, 6.5 miles southeast of the southern terminus of SR 184, offers scenic views of Frenchman Bay and Mount Desert Island. Visitors can see eagles, ospreys, harbor seals and other wildlife at Ellsworth Marine Waterfront Park off Water Street.

Ellsworth also is surrounded by several lakes and streams that offer opportunities for boating, canoeing and fishing.

Ellsworth Area Chamber of Commerce: 163 High St., P.O. Box 267, Ellsworth, ME 04605. **Phone:** (207) 667-5584.

DOWNEAST SCENIC RAILROAD, departing from Cadillac Mountain Sports, 32 High St., offers a scenic 10-mile round-trip excursion on the historical Calais Branch line. From railcars pulled by a 1948 diesel-powered locomotive, passengers view forests, wetlands and lakes and often spot such wildlife as beavers, deer, moose, herons and osprey. The

trip lasts about 90 minutes. **Hours:** Trips depart Sat.-Sun (also Labor Day and Columbus Day) at 10:30 and 1:30. **Cost:** $16; $8 (ages 3-12). Reservations are recommended. **Phone:** (866) 449-7245.

STANWOOD HOMESTEAD MUSEUM AND WILDLIFE SANCTUARY (BIRDSACRE), on SR 3 just s. of US 1, is the former home of Cordelia Stanwood, Maine's pioneer ornithologist and photographer. The museum, built in 1850, houses original furnishings. Also on exhibit at the Richmond Nature Center are collections of mounted birds, nests, eggs, paintings and prints. Birdsacre, a 200-acre wildlife preserve with nature trails and picnic facilities, is a sanctuary for more than 100 bird species.

Time: Allow 1 hour minimum. **Hours:** Sanctuary daily dawn-dusk. Museum daily 10-4, June 1 to mid-Oct. Museum hours may vary; phone ahead. **Cost:** Donations. **Phone:** (207) 667-8460. 🅰

WOODLAWN MUSEUM/BLACK HOUSE is on SR 172 off US 1. On a self-guiding audio tour visitors explore this Federal-style house built in the 1820s for Col. John Black, who played a major role in developing Maine's lumber industry. With elegant woodwork and an elliptical flying staircase, the home is as it appeared during occupation by three generations of the Black family. Period furnishings reflect a privileged lifestyle. On the 180-acre grounds are gardens, hiking trails, a carriage house and what is said to be the state's largest croquet court.

Time: Allow 30 minutes minimum. **Hours:** Grounds daily dawn-dusk. House Tues.-Sat. 10-5, Sun. 1-4, June-Sept.; Tues.-Sun 1-4 in May and Oct. **Cost:** Grounds free. House $10; $3 (ages 6-18). **Phone:** (207) 667-8671. 🅰

ACADIA BIRCHES KNIGHTS INN 207/667-3621

Motel
$95-$145

Address: 19 Thorsen Rd 04605 **Location:** US 1, 1.5 mi n of SR 3. **Facility:** 65 units, some efficiencies. 1 story, exterior corridors. **Terms:** closed 10/23-5/19. **Free Special Amenities:** continental breakfast and local telephone calls. *(See ad p. 84.)*

SAVE 🛜 🖥 /SOME UNITS FEE 🐾 🅱 🖥

COMFORT INN (207)667-1345

Hotel
$109-$159

Address: 130 High St 04605 **Location:** Center on US 1 and SR 3. Located in a commercial area. **Facility:** 63 units. 2 stories (no elevator), interior corridors. **Terms:** cancellation fee imposed. **Activities:** exercise room. **Guest Services:** coin laundry. **Free Special Amenities:** expanded continental breakfast and high-speed Internet. *(See ad p. 84.)*

SAVE 🍴 CALL &M BIZ 🛜 ✕ 🖥
/SOME UNITS FEE 🐾 🅱 🖥

THE EAGLE'S LODGE   (207)667-3311
Motel $70-$130 **Address:** 278 High St 04605 **Location:** Jct US 1 and 1A, 1.3 mi se on SR 3. **Facility:** 44 units, some efficiencies. 2 stories (no elevator), interior corridors. **Pool(s):** heated outdoor.

ELLSWORTH RAMADA   (207)667-9341

Hotel
$119-$189

Address: 215 High St 04605 **Location:** Jct US 1, 1A and SR 3. Next to shopping plaza. **Facility:** 103 units. 2 stories (no elevator), interior corridors. **Pool(s):** heated indoor. **Activities:** sauna, whirlpool, 2 indoor tennis courts, exercise room. **Guest Services:** coin laundry. **Free Special Amenities:** expanded continental breakfast and high-speed Internet. *(See ad this page.)*

Contact us about AAA/CAA
Approved properties at
AAA.com/TourBookComments

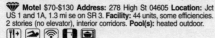

HAMPTON INN (207)667-2688

WWW
Hotel
$129-$199

 AAA Benefit: Members save up to 10%!

Address: 6 Downeast Hwy 04605 **Location:** Jct US 1 and SR 3. Opposite Maine Coast Mall. **Facility:** 85 units. 3 stories, interior corridors. **Terms:** 1-7 night minimum stay, cancellation fee imposed. **Amenities:** high-speed Internet, safes. **Pool(s):** heated indoor. **Activities:** whirlpool, exercise room. **Guest Services:** coin laundry. **Free Special Amenities: expanded continental breakfast and high-speed Internet.** (See ad p. 84.)

SAVE ⟨Ψ⟩ CALL ⟨&M⟩ ⟨≈⟩ BIZ ⟨≈⟩ ⟨✕⟩ ⟨🖵⟩ / SOME UNITS ⟨🗄⟩ ⟨🖃⟩

SUNSET MOTEL 207/667-8390

WWW
Cabin
$65-$78

Address: 210 Twin Hill Rd 04605 **Location:** 6 mi s on US 1 and SR 3. **Facility:** 6 cabins, some two bedrooms. 1 story, exterior corridors. **Terms:** closed 10/21-5/29. **Guest Services:** coin laundry.

SAVE ⟨≈⟩ ⟨✕⟩ ⟨🎞⟩ ⟨🗄⟩ ⟨🖃⟩ ⟨🖵⟩ / SOME UNITS FEE ⟨🐾⟩

TWILITE MOTEL (207)667-8165

WWW
Motel
$54-$126

Address: 147 Bucksport Rd 04605 **Location:** Jct US 1A, 1.5 mi w on US 1 and SR 3. **Facility:** 22 units. 1 story, exterior corridors. **Terms:** cancellation fee imposed. **Activities:** playground, horseshoes. **Guest Services:** coin laundry. **Free Special Amenities: continental breakfast and use of on-premises laundry facilities.**

SAVE BIZ ⟨≈⟩ ⟨✕⟩ ⟨🖵⟩ / SOME UNITS FEE ⟨🐾⟩ ⟨🗄⟩

WHERE TO EAT

THE BANGKOK RESTAURANT 207/667-1324

WWW Thai. Casual Dining. $9-$19 **AAA Inspector Notes:** This spacious restaurant with a relaxed atmosphere offers a very fine selection of made-to-order Thai and sushi dishes. The vast menu includes various curry, noodle and rice dishes with chicken, beef, duck, pork and fresh seafood along with some vegetarian specialties. **Bar:** full bar. **Address:** 78 Downeast Hwy 04605 **Location:** 0.6 mi n on US 1. ⟨L⟩ ⟨D⟩

CHINA HILL 207/667-5308

WWW Chinese. Casual Dining. $7-$18 **AAA Inspector Notes:** This spacious restaurant has four dining areas. The vast menu features Szechuan, Cantonese and Mandarin cuisine, with many combination plates served in ample portions. The serving staff is pleasant and attentive. **Bar:** full bar. **Address:** 301 High St 04605 **Location:** 1.3 mi se on SR 3. ⟨L⟩ ⟨D⟩

HELEN'S RESTAURANT 207/667-2433

WWW American. Family Dining. $6-$16 **AAA Inspector Notes:** Memorabilia from the '30s decorates this country-style family restaurant. On the menu is a variety of entrees--from fried or broiled seafood to steak, chicken and burgers. Boiled lobster is a favorite, as are the homemade desserts that satisfy a sweet tooth. **Bar:** beer & wine. **Address:** 55 Downeast Hwy 04605 **Location:** 0.5 mi n on US 1. ⟨L⟩ ⟨D⟩

JORDAN'S SNACK BAR 207/667-2174

W American. Quick Serve. $5-$14 **AAA Inspector Notes:** A bit off the beaten path but worth the cruise, the drive-in offers not only good quality food but also fun entertainment, including a large playground, video arcade, various dining areas, a screened pavilion, a large enclosed banquet room and picnic tables among the trees. All portions are ample, and the lobster rolls are splendid. **Address:** Hancock Rd 04605 **Location:** 1 mi n on US 1. ⟨L⟩ ⟨D⟩

THE MEX 207/667-4494

WW WW Mexican. Casual Dining. $12-$22 **AAA Inspector Notes:** The menu features Mexican cuisine with a Maine twist: seafood. Offerings are made to order and desserts are made on the premises. **Bar:** full bar. **Address:** 191 Main St 04605 **Location:** On US 1; center. **Parking:** street only. ⟨L⟩ ⟨D⟩

THE RIVERSIDE CAFE 207/667-7220

WW American. Family Dining. $6-$16 **AAA Inspector Notes:** A variety of simple but flavorful lunch dishes are served at this restaurant. Breakfast is available all day. On the menu are omelets, breakfast burritos, pancakes, sandwiches and fresh salads, all of which are made to order. On Fridays and Saturdays, dinner, accompanied by live music, is offered. **Address:** 151 Main St 04605 **Location:** Center; at Franklin St. ⟨B⟩ ⟨L⟩

UNION RIVER LOBSTER POT 207/667-5077

WW WW Seafood. Casual Dining. $8-$26 **AAA Inspector Notes:** In a pleasant location bordering Union River, the spacious restaurant specializes in fresh seafood and also serves a number of meat options. Service is friendly, portions are ample and guests may dine inside or out on a large, screened deck that's heated in cooler weather. **Bar:** beer & wine. **Address:** 8 South St 04605 **Location:** Off Main St, center; just s of bridge. ⟨D⟩

FALMOUTH (J-3) pop. 1,855, elev. 48'
- Restaurants p. 86
- Hotels & Restaurants map & index p. 131

Originally part of Portland, Falmouth became a separate community in 1786. Farming and fishing, the town's traditional industries, have enabled Falmouth to retain much of its rural charm. The Foreside area along SR 88 is the location of several waterfront estates as well as the Portland Yacht Club.

GILSLAND FARM AUDUBON CENTER, 1.9 mi. n. off I-295N exit 9 on US 1 following signs to 20 Gilsland Farm Rd., encompasses 65 acres of coastal lowlands along the Presumpscot River and features more than 2 miles of trails winding along a pond and through woods, meadow, orchard and salt marsh. Other highlights include an Environmental Center and Children's Discovery Room. The farm is a habitat for bald eagles, red-tailed hawks, finches, red fox, weasels, deer and black woodchucks.

Hours: Grounds and trails daily dawn-dusk. Buildings Mon.-Sat. 9-5, Sun. and some holidays noon-4. Closed major holidays. **Cost:** Free. **Phone:** (207) 781-2330.

FALMOUTH INN 207/781-2120 **16**

W
Motel
$69-$156

Address: 209 US 1 04105 **Location:** I-295 exit 10, just e on Buckman Rd, then just s. **Facility:** 33 units. 1 story, exterior corridors. **Guest Services:** coin laundry. **Free Special Amenities: local telephone calls and high-speed Internet.**

SAVE ⟨Ψ⟩ ⟨≈⟩ / SOME UNITS FEE ⟨🐾⟩ ⟨🗄⟩

(See map & index p. 131.)

WHERE TO EAT

FORESIDE TAVERN & SIDE BAR   207/347-4205 ⑩

♦♦ American. Casual Dining. $9-$24 **AAA Inspector Notes:** Patrons can enjoy a casual meal in the sports bar or main dining room. The menu lists choices from full entrees to lighter fare. **Bar:** full bar. **Address:** 270 US Rt 1 04105 **Location:** I-295 exit 10; center.

[L] [D]

LOTUS CHINESE RESTAURANT   207/781-3453 ⑫

♦♦ Chinese. Casual Dining. $8-$22 **AAA Inspector Notes:** Locals are loyal to this spot for its prepared-to-order dishes featuring quality ingredients. Dine-in or takeout options are available. **Bar:** full bar. **Address:** 251 US 1 04105 **Location:** Center.

[L] [D] CALL [&M]

RICETTA'S BRICK OVEN PIZZERIA   207/781-3100 ⑪

♦♦ Pizza. Casual Dining. $9-$19 **AAA Inspector Notes:** A great place to bring the kids for a meal, this eatery is known for its creative, award-winning pizzas. Patrons can watch them being made at the open area with a brick oven. Also on the menu are original pasta dishes and calzones, and lunch features an all-you-can-eat buffet. **Bar:** full bar. **Address:** 240 US Rt 1 04105 **Location:** Center. [L] [D] CALL [&M]

FARMINGTON (H-3) pop. 4,288, elev. 365'

Farmington is the shire town and a major commercial center for Franklin County, which ranges from rolling farms and apple orchards in the south to lakes and forested mountains in the north. The first settlers were recipients of land grants for service in the Revolutionary War in the area of Farmington Falls, a few miles down the Sandy River; soon families were scattered all along the valley.

With the opening of its first school in a log cabin home in 1788, Farmington began a long association with education. In 1841 the Abbott family opened a boys' school that gained fame as the "Little Blue School." Additionally, Jacob Abbott was author of the "Rollo" stories, children's sermons laced with history and science. The tradition continues: The University of Maine at Farmington is an outgrowth of the Farmington Academy, founded in the late 1860s.

Recreational opportunities include boat and canoe rentals at Clearwater Lake, 4 miles east on SR 43. Cross-country skiing and snowmobiling are favorite winter activities.

Franklin County Chamber of Commerce: 248 Wilton Rd., Suite 1, Farmington, ME 04938. **Phone:** (207) 778-4215.

ART GALLERY AT THE UNIVERSITY OF MAINE-FARMINGTON, 246 Main St., displays works by Maine artists. Rotating exhibits represent a variety of media. **Hours:** Tues.-Sun. noon-4 and by appointment; closed holidays and university breaks. **Cost:** Free. **Phone:** (207) 778-7001 or TTY (207) 778-7000.

NORDICA HOMESTEAD MUSEUM, 1.5 mi. n. on SR 4, then .5 mi. e. on Holly Rd. to 116 Nordica Ln., is the birthplace of opera singer Lillian Nordica, whose pure, strong voice brought her world renown.

Displays present her costumes, stage jewelry, career mementos and original 19th-century furnishings. A library also is available. **Time:** Allow 30 minutes minimum. **Hours:** Tues.-Sun. 1-5, June 1-Sept. 15; by appointment, Sept. 16-Oct. 15. **Cost:** $2; $1 (ages 0-12). **Phone:** (207) 778-2042. ⊞

THE HOMESTEAD KITCHEN-BAR-BAKERY   207/778-6162

♦♦ American. Casual Dining. $6-$23 **AAA Inspector Notes:** The popular restaurant features unpretentious decor and hearty portions of down-home cooking. A bakery on the premises lines up a fine selection of desserts. **Bar:** full bar. **Address:** 186 Broadway St 04938 **Location:** Just w of N Main St; center. **Parking:** street only.

[B] [L] [D]

FORT KENT (B-6) pop. 2,488, elev. 522'

Separated from Canada by the St. John River, Fort Kent was settled by French Acadians deported from Nova Scotia by the British in 1755. Incorporated in the 1820s, the territory became the issue of a boundary dispute between Great Britain and the United States. Troops were called in and a fort was built, but the Webster-Ashburton Treaty of 1842 averted bloodshed.

Fort Kent is the starting point of US 1, which runs along the eastern coast to Key West, Fla.; it also is the northern terminus for a scenic section of SR 11, which stretches south to Portage, as well as for the Allagash Wilderness Waterway and canoe trips down the St. John River.

Greater Fort Kent Area Chamber of Commerce: 291 W. Main St., P.O. Box 430, Fort Kent, ME 04743-0430. **Phone:** (207) 834-5354.

FORT KENT STATE HISTORIC SITE, off US 1, features a blockhouse of hand-hewn timber. The fort was built in 1839 for defense during the bloodless Aroostook War. **Time:** Allow 30 minutes minimum. **Hours:** Daily 9-dusk, Memorial Day-Labor Day. **Cost:** $3; $1 (ages 5-11 and 65+). **Phone:** (207) 768-8341. ⊞

FREEPORT (J-3) pop. 1,485, elev. 126'
• Restaurants p. 91

Founded in 1789, the town is best known as the home of the L.L. Bean sporting goods store, which is open daily 24 hours, 365 days a year. More than 170 other retail shops and name-brand outlets surround the village.

In addition to retail outlet merchandising, chief contributors to the economy are tourism, crabbing and crabmeat packing. The 40-foot Big Indian statue, 1 mile north of I-295 exit 17, is a frequently photographed local landmark.

Wolfe's Neck Woods State Park, 426 Wolfe's Neck Rd., offers several self-guiding nature trails that include views of Casco Bay and the Harraseeket River. The park, which is open April through October, also presents educational and interpretive programs.

Freeport Historical Society's Harrington House, 45 Main St., features changing exhibits relating to the history of Freeport dating from the late 18th century to the present. Pettengill Farm & Gardens, 1.5 miles east of downtown Freeport, is a 19th-century saltwater farm that includes an 1810 saltbox house and 140 acres of gardens, fields and woods; phone (207) 865-3170 for both attractions.

Freeport U.S.A.: 23 Depot St., P.O. Box 452, Freeport, ME 04032. **Phone:** (207) 865-1212, or (800) 865-1994 for the automated request line.

ATLANTIC SEAL CRUISES departs from a point off Garrison Cove Rd. on Bailey Island (Tues. and Fri.), and from Freeport Town Wharf (Wed.-Thurs. and Sat.-Mon.). Three-hour sightseeing excursions take passengers to Eagle Island State Park, where they can visit the Robert E. Peary State Memorial, explore wooded island trails and comb the beaches.

The 6-hour Atlantic Seal Cruise includes a 2.5-hour stop at Seguin Island for a lighthouse and museum tour. Also offered are 3-hour fall foliage trips along the coast, where seal and eagle sightings are common.

Hours: Sightseeing trips depart daily at 9:30 and 1:30, Memorial Day weekend to mid-Sept. Atlantic Seal Cruise departs Thurs. at 10, July-Aug. Fall foliage trips depart daily at 1:30 (also Sat.-Sun. at 9:30), mid-Sept. through Oct. 31 (weather permitting). **Cost:** Sightseeing and fall foliage trips each $35; $25 (ages 5-12); $20 (ages 1-5). Atlantic Seal Cruise (includes lighthouse and museum admission) $55; $40 (ages 0-10). Reservations are recommended. **Phone:** (207) 865-6112.

DESERT OF MAINE, I-295 exit 20 (Desert Rd.), then 2 mi. w. to 95 Desert Rd., is an area of sand dunes that has grown since the early 1900s. What was once the Tuttle Farm is now an area of moving sand dunes, some more than 90 feet high and covering trees and a small building. In 1897 the topsoil began to erode, exposing the ancient glacial plain. The barn is all that remains of the farm.

Guided coach and walking tours, nature trails, a butterfly observatory and a museum are available. **Time:** Allow 30 minutes minimum. **Hours:** Daily 9-5, early May to mid-Oct. **Cost:** $10.50; $7.75 (ages 13-16); $6.75 (ages 4-12). **Phone:** (207) 865-6962.

MAST LANDING SANCTUARY is 1 mi. e. on Bow St., then n. on Upper Mast Landing Rd. to entrance. Situated at the tideway on the Harraseeket River, the site once served as a delivery point for Maine timbers. The sanctuary now encompasses 140 acres of open fields, apple orchards, alder lowlands and mature pine and hemlock forest. Porcupines, minks, deer and the ruins of a historic mill can be seen along 2.5 miles of marked trails. **Hours:** Daily dawn-dusk. **Cost:** Free. **Phone:** (207) 781-2330.

▼ *See AAA listing this page* ▼

BREWSTER HOUSE BED & BREAKFAST (207)865-4121

▼▼▼ **Historic Bed & Breakfast** $169-$259 **Address:** 180 Main St 04032 **Location:** Just n. **Facility:** Tin ceilings, carved moldings and large guest rooms furnished with antiques set the stage at this restored Queen Anne home, which dates from 1888. 7 units. 3 stories (no elevator), interior corridors. **Terms:** 2 night minimum stay - seasonal and/or weekends, 7 day cancellation notice-fee imposed.

BIZ 🛜 ✕ 🖨 / SOME UNITS 🛏 📺 💻

CAPTAIN BRIGGS HOUSE B & B 207/865-1868

▼▼▼ **Bed & Breakfast** $105-$235 **Address:** 8 Maple Ave 04032 **Location:** Just n of downtown, then just w. **Facility:** This charming Federal-style home offers a variety of accommodations and is convenient to shopping and restaurants. 6 units, some two bedrooms. 2 stories (no elevator), interior corridors. **Terms:** 5 day cancellation notice-fee imposed.

🛜 ✕ 🖨 / SOME UNITS FEE 🛏 ⧖ ☐

CASCO BAY INN 207/865-4925

▼▼▼
Hotel
Rates not provided

Address: 107 US Rt 1 04032 **Location:** I-295 exit 17 northbound, 1 mi n; exit 20 southbound, 1.5 mi s. **Facility:** 48 units. 2 stories (no elevator), interior corridors. **Guest Services:** coin laundry. **Free Special Amenities: expanded continental breakfast and high-speed Internet.** *(See ad this page.)*

SAVE BIZ 🛜 ✕ 📺 💻 / SOME UNITS 🖨

COMFORT SUITES (207)865-9300

▼▼▼
Hotel
$100-$170

Address: 500 US 1 04032 **Location:** I-295 exit 20, just s. **Facility:** 78 units. 3 stories, interior corridors. **Terms:** cancellation fee imposed. **Pool(s):** heated indoor. **Activities:** whirlpool, exercise room. **Guest Services:** valet laundry. **Free Special Amenities: continental breakfast and local telephone calls.**

SAVE CALL 🛜M 🚐 BIZ 🛜 ✕ 🖨 📺 💻

ECONO LODGE (207)865-3777

▼▼▼
Motel
$75-$160

Address: 537 US Rt 1 04032 **Location:** I-295 exit 20, 0.3 mi s. **Facility:** 62 units. 2 stories (no elevator), exterior corridors. **Terms:** cancellation fee imposed. **Free Special Amenities: continental breakfast and high-speed Internet.**

SAVE BIZ 🛜 💻 / SOME UNITS FEE 🛏 🖨 🖼

HAMPTON INN (207)865-1400

▼▼▼ **Hotel** $99-$259 **Address:** 194 Lower Main St 04032 **Location:** I-295 exit 20, just n on US 1. **Facility:** 77 units. 3 stories, interior corridors. **Terms:** 1-7 night minimum stay, cancellation fee imposed. **Amenities:** video games (fee). *Some:* high-speed Internet. **Pool(s):** heated indoor. **Activities:** exercise room. **Guest Services:** valet and coin laundry.

AAA Benefit:
Members save up to 10%!

CALL 🛜M 🚐 BIZ 🛜 ☂ 🖨 🖼 💻

HARRASEEKET INN (207)865-9377

▼▼▼
Classic
Country Inn
$135-$305

Address: 162 Main St 04032 **Location:** I-295 exit 22, 0.5 mi e. **Facility:** Located just north of the center of town within easy walking distance of outlet shops, the inn is decorated in a Colonial style. Many of the rooms have a whirlpool tub and/or a fireplace. 84 units. 4 stories, interior corridors. **Terms:** 3 day cancellation notice. **Dining:** Broad Arrow Tavern, see separate listing. **Pool(s):** heated indoor. **Activities:** exercise room. **Guest Services:** valet laundry. **Free Special Amenities: full breakfast and high-speed Internet.** *(See ad p. 90.)*

SAVE ECO 🍴 ▥ ☂ CALL 🛜M 🚐 BIZ 🛜 ✕ 🖨 💻 / SOME UNITS FEE 🛏

Trust your vehicle to AAA/CAA
Approved Auto Repair facilities

HILTON GARDEN INN FREEPORT DOWNTOWN

(207)865-1433

▼▼▼▼ **Hotel** $98-$359 **Address:** 5 Park St 04032 **Location:** Just e of US 1 via Bow St. **Facility:** 99 units. 3 stories, interior corridors. **Terms:** 1-7 night minimum stay, cancellation fee imposed. **Amenities:** video games (fee), high-speed Internet. **Pool(s):** heated indoor. **Activities:** whirlpool, exercise room. **Guest Services:** valet and coin laundry.

AAA Benefit: Unparalleled hospitality at a special Member rate.

ECO ❙❙ ✈ ▨ CALL &M 🏊 BIZ 🛜 🎥 🔌 🖥 📠

HOLIDAY INN EXPRESS HOTEL & SUITES

(207)865-9020

▼▼▼▼ **Hotel** $99-$299 **Address:** 450 US 1 04032 **Location:** I-295 exit 20, just s. **Facility:** 78 units. 3 stories, interior corridors. **Amenities:** high-speed Internet. **Pool(s):** heated indoor. **Activities:** whirlpool, exercise room. **Guest Services:** valet and coin laundry.

CALL &M 🏊 BIZ 🛜 ✖ 🔌 🖥 📠 / SOME UNITS 📠

THE JAMES PLACE INN

207/865-4486

▼▼▼▼ **Bed & Breakfast** $135-$195 **Address:** 11 Holbrook St 04032 **Location:** Just off US 1, s of L.L. Bean; center. **Facility:** Located in a quiet setting but close to Freeport shopping, this cottage-style inn is an attractive residential B&B. Some rooms have a fireplace and a whirlpool tub. A full breakfast is served. 7 units, some efficiencies. 2 stories (no elevator), interior corridors. **Terms:** 3 day cancellation notice-fee imposed. **Guest Services:** complimentary laundry.

ECO ♿ 🛜 ✖ ☎ / SOME UNITS 🔌 🖥 📠

KENDALL TAVERN BED & BREAKFAST

(207)865-1338

▼▼▼▼ **Historic Bed & Breakfast** $140-$180 **Address:** 213 Main St 04032 **Location:** I-295 exit 22, 0.5 mi e, then just n on US 1. **Facility:** Dating from the 1800s, the B&B offers comfortable common areas and well-appointed guest rooms. 7 units. 3 stories (no elevator), interior corridors. *Bath:* shower only. **Terms:** 5 day cancellation notice-fee imposed. 🛜 ✖ ▨ ☎

WHITE CEDAR INN

207/865-9099

▼▼▼▼ **Historic Bed & Breakfast** $145-$250 **Address:** 178 Main St 04032 **Location:** I-295 exit 22, 0.5 mi e, then just n on US 1. **Facility:** A century-old converted Victorian, this inn is within walking distance of outlet shops and is decorated with antiques. Some rooms have a fireplace. A full breakfast is served each morning. 7 units. 2 stories (no elevator), interior/exterior corridors. *Bath:* shower only. **Terms:** 7 day cancellation notice-fee imposed.

ECO BIZ 🛜 ✖ ☎ / SOME UNITS ▨

Learn the
local driving laws at
DrivingLaws.AAA.com

▼ See AAA listing p. 159 ▼

AAA.com/
TourBook
Comments

Tell Us How We're Doing

If your visit to a TourBook-listed property doesn't meet your expectations, tell us about it.

AAA.com/TourBookComments

▼ See AAA listing p. 88 ▼

AZURE ITALIAN CAFE   207/865-1237

Italian. Casual Dining. $10-$32 **AAA Inspector Notes:** The cafe's patio is the place to be to watch the happenings on Main Street. The intimate dining room has a colorful bistro feel and includes a Gulf of Maine fish tank. The menu features authentic Italian cuisine. **Bar:** full bar. **Reservations:** suggested. **Address:** 123 Main St 04032 **Location:** On US 1; center. L D

BROAD ARROW TAVERN   207/865-9377

Regional
American
Casual Dining
$11-$30

AAA Inspector Notes: *Classic.* This popular restaurant, with a moose head and canoe on the walls, has a definite Maine backwoods hunting lodge feel, right down to the colorful Christmas lights border. The wood-fired oven and grill produce all the menu favorites, with local organic ingredients, from pizza to filet mignon. Dining is casual and portions are hearty. **Bar:** full bar. **Address:** 162 Main St 04032 **Location:** I-295 exit 22, 0.5 mi e; in Harraseeket Inn. *(See ad p. 90.)*

L D CALL M

2 blocks N. of LL Bean, garden patio with stone firepit

BUCK'S NAKED BBQ   207/865-0600

Barbecue. Family Dining. $8-$32 **AAA Inspector Notes:** While spices are rubbed onto the meat, sauces are on the side, which is why the barbecue is considered "naked." The dining room has the feel of a traditional roadhouse and is complemented by a variety of pig-themed art. Portions are generous, and kids have their own menu. **Bar:** full bar. **Address:** 568 US Rt 1 04032 **Location:** I-295 exit 17 northbound; exit 20 southbound. L D

CONUNDRUM   207/865-0303

American. Casual Dining. $9-$16 **AAA Inspector Notes:** This local favorite has an extensive list of martinis and wines by the glass. On the menu you'll have the choice of a number of cheeses, appetizers and salads, as well as several plates to complement your beverage selection. **Bar:** full bar. **Address:** 117 US Rt 1 04032 **Location:** I-295 exit 17 northbound, 1 mi n; exit 20 southbound, 1.5 mi s. D

THE CORSICAN RESTAURANT   207/865-9421

American. Family Dining. $8-$18 **AAA Inspector Notes:** In business since 1986, the casual eatery offers customers a choice of pizza, pasta, soups, sandwiches and vegetarian and seafood entrees. Breads and desserts are homemade. **Bar:** beer & wine. **Address:** 9 Mechanic St 04032 **Location:** Just e of US 1. **Parking:** street only. L D

GRITTY MCDUFF'S BREW PUB & RESTAURANT
    207/865-4321

American. Casual Dining. $9-$15 **AAA Inspector Notes:** The lively restaurant and bar attracts a younger crowd. Good American fare along the lines of burgers and pizza goes down easy with terrific and flavorful microbrews. This place is convenient to L.L. Bean. **Bar:** full bar. **Address:** 187 US 1 04032 **Location:** I-295 exit 20, just n. L D

JAMESON TAVERN   207/865-4196

Steak. Casual Dining. $10-$40 **AAA Inspector Notes:** *Historic.* In the heart of the downtown outlet district, the restaurant was built in 1779 as a private residence. The menu features American fare, including fresh seafood and steaks. A lighter all-day pub menu is presented in the dining room at lunch. **Bar:** full bar. **Reservations:** suggested. **Address:** 115 Main St 04032 **Location:** Center. L D

THE LOBSTER COOKER RESTAURANT   207/865-4349

Seafood. Quick Serve. $7-$18 **AAA Inspector Notes:** In the heart of the downtown outlet district, this casual restaurant is located in an 1860 barn boasting simple decor and a lovely garden patio that is available seasonally. The menu features award-winning chowder as well as fresh seafood, sandwiches and salads. Counter service is fast and friendly. Be sure to try a delicious lobster roll. **Bar:** beer & wine. **Address:** 39 Main St 04032 **Location:** Center. L D M

OLD WORLD GOURMET DELI & WINE SHOP   207/865-4477

Deli. Quick Serve. $5-$8 **AAA Inspector Notes:** A popular lunch spot, this delicatessen is a showcase for the products of local producers. Sandwiches, soups, salads, pastries and fresh breads are just some of the items on the menu. Desserts are made from scratch on the premises. Take-out dinners also are available. Hours vary seasonally. **Bar:** wine only. **Address:** 117 US Rt 1 S 04032 **Location:** I-295 exit 17 northbound, 1 mi n; exit 20 southbound, 1.5 mi s. L

PETRILLO'S   207/865-6055

Italian. Casual Dining. $8-$19 **AAA Inspector Notes:** This cozy and casual eatery serves up traditional American-Italian fare including homemade pizza, spaghetti and meatballs and traditional lasagna. **Bar:** full bar. **Address:** 15 Depot St 04032 **Location:** Just s of US 1. L D

THAI GARDEN RESTAURANT   207/865-6005

Thai. Casual Dining. $7-$16 **AAA Inspector Notes:** The menu reflects authentic Thai cuisine including salads served at room temperature, chicken seafood, noodles, stir-fry and curries. The dining room has a casual ambience. **Bar:** beer & wine. **Address:** 491 US Rt 1 04032 **Location:** I-295 exit 20, just s. L D

FRYEBURG pop. 1,631

MAIN STREET BED & BREAKFAST   207/935-7171

Bed & Breakfast $119-$240 **Address:** 660 Main St 04037 **Location:** US 302, just e of jct SR 113; center of village. **Facility:** Wonderful views of the mountains can be found at the rear of this B&B. 4 units. 2 stories (no elevator), interior corridors. **Terms:** check-in 4 pm, 2 night minimum stay - seasonal and/or weekends, 14 day cancellation notice-fee imposed. **Activities:** cross country skiing, snowmobiling.

THE OXFORD HOUSE INN   207/935-3442

Historic Country Inn $129-$195 **Address:** 548 Main St 04037 **Location:** US 302, just w of jct SR 113; center of village. **Facility:** Fine woodwork distinguishes this Edwardian-style house, which offers nicely appointed guest rooms and is convenient to the fairgrounds. 4 units. 2 stories (no elevator), interior corridors. **Terms:** 14 day cancellation notice-fee imposed. **Dining:** restaurant, see separate listing. **Activities:** cross country skiing.

ECO

THE OXFORD HOUSE INN   207/935-3442

American. Fine Dining. $12-$31 **AAA Inspector Notes:** *Classic.* This restaurant, which is very popular with locals and visitors alike, is in a handsome Edwardian-period inn offering wonderful mountain views. The very creative menu features contemporary country cuisine using fresh Maine products. **Bar:** full bar. **Reservations:** suggested. **Address:** 548 Main St 04037 **Location:** US 302, just w of jct SR 113; center of village. D

GEORGETOWN (J-4)

JOSEPHINE NEWMAN SANCTUARY is 9 mi. s. of jct. US 1 and SR 127. Owned and managed by Maine Audubon, the sanctuary incorporates various habitats rich in animal life within its 119 acres, including tidal mud flats, marshes and forest. The sanctuary's 2 miles of walking trails meander through stands of hemlock, pine, oak and spruce. **Note:** Visitors are warned that the area harbors an abundance of mosquitoes and ticks. **Hours:** Daily dawn-dusk. **Cost:** Free. **Phone:** (207) 781-2330.

COVESIDE BED & BREAKFAST   207/371-2807

Bed & Breakfast
$150-$225

Address: 6 Gotts Cove Ln 04548 **Location:** Waterfront. US 1 from Bath, 13 mi s on SR 127, follow signs. Located in a quiet area. **Facility:** Wide water views and an open-concept floor plan enhance this renovated B&B. Its 5-acre grounds extend to the cove and river. A full, hot, gourmet breakfast is served family-style each morning. 7 units. 2 stories (no elevator), interior/exterior corridors. **Terms:** closed 10/14-5/24, 2 night minimum stay - weekends, age restrictions may apply, 14 day cancellation notice-fee imposed. **Activities:** canoeing, boat dock, bicycles, limited exercise equipment. **Free Special Amenities:** full breakfast and high-speed Internet.

THE MOORING B&B   207/371-2790

 Bed & Breakfast $140-$210 **Address:** 132 Seguinland Rd 04548 **Location:** 13 mi s of US 1; in Reid State Park. **Facility:** 5 units. 2 stories (no elevator), interior corridors. **Bath:** shower only. **Terms:** closed 10/16-5/7, 2 night minimum stay - seasonal and/or weekends, 14 day cancellation notice-fee imposed.

GORHAM pop. 6,882

PINECREST BED & BREAKFAST INN   207/839-5843

 Bed & Breakfast. Rates not provided. **Address:** 91 South St 04038 **Location:** Jct SR 25, 0.5 mi s on SR 114. Located in a residential area. **Facility:** Built on the foundation of a 1753 building, the 1825 inn is ensconced in a residential area not far from the University of Southern Maine. 9 units. 3 stories (no elevator), interior corridors. **Terms:** check-in 4 pm.

WHERE TO EAT

AMATO'S   207/839-2511

Deli. Quick Serve. $4-$14 **AAA Inspector Notes:** Known for their "Real Italian" sandwich, which was created over 100 years ago by an Italian immigrant who decided to place a little bit of meat, fresh vegetables, cheese, Greek olives, a zesty pickle and a specialty blended olive oil on a freshly made roll. This recipe has built up a loyal following of customers. Other menu choices include hot or cold sandwiches, calzones, specialty pizzas, pasta and freshly prepared salads. Diners may choose to eat in or take out. **Bar:** beer & wine. **Address:** 3 Main St 04038 **Location:** On US 202, jct SR 114.

L   D

SEBAGO BREWING COMPANY   207/839-2337

American. Gastropub. $9-$23 **AAA Inspector Notes:** The stylish brewpub sustains a friendly, informal atmosphere. Self-described "American pub" cuisine includes delicious pasta, chicken, seafood and steak entrées as well as tasty salads, burgers and sandwiches; the latter are available all day. The resident pastry chef prepares desserts on the premises each day. **Bar:** full bar. **Address:** 29 Elm St 04038 **Location:** Just e of US 202/SR 25; center.

L   D

GRAY (J-3) pop. 884, elev. 300'

Needing land upon which to raise their families, the original settlers of the area known as New Boston petitioned the General Court of Boston for the grant of a township. Although the pioneers were blessed with abundant stands of white pine and oak, American Indian raids caused repeated desertions of the buildings and land.

Incorporated as the town of Gray in 1778, the settlement prospered when several mills, including what is said to be the first machine-powered woolen mill in the United States, were erected. Within its boundaries Gray boasts four freshwater bodies and other natural resources that offer residents and visitors many outdoor recreational opportunities. Five major routes pass through the village, which is known as the "Crossroads of Maine."

MAINE WILDLIFE PARK, e. off I-95 exit 63 following signs, then 3.5 mi. n. on SR 26 (Shaker Rd.), houses wildlife native to Maine, including moose, deer and bears. Most of the animals cared for at the park had been injured or orphaned or had become dependent upon man because they were raised in captivity. The visitor center has interactive displays about Maine's wildlife resources. Several nature trails and wildlife gardens are available.

Guided tours are available by appointment. **Time:** Allow 1 hour minimum. **Hours:** Daily 9:30-6, mid-Apr. through Nov. 11 (weather permitting). Last admission is at 4:30. **Cost:** $7; $5 (ages 4-12 and 61+). **Phone:** (207) 657-4977.

COLE FARMS   207/657-4714

American. Family Dining. $2-$14 **AAA Inspector Notes:** In business since 1952, the family restaurant prepares made-to-order home-style dishes. **Address:** 64 Lewiston Rd 04039 **Location:** I-95 exit 63, 1.3 mi e on US 202. B   L   D   CALL

GREENVILLE (F-4) pop. 1,257, elev. 1,034'

Greenville, at the south end of Moosehead Lake, is in an area noted for a variety of year-round recreational activities. Swimming, fishing, canoeing, hiking, mountain climbing, horseback riding, seaplane tours and white-water rafting are pursued in summer. Hunting for deer, bears and partridges is available in the fall; cross-country and alpine skiing and snowmobiling are enjoyed in winter.

Several cruises and a shuttle service are available to Mount Kineo, a historic American Indian gathering place in Moosehead Lake. Visitors to the peninsula can enjoy hiking trails and a pebble beach.

Moosehead Lake Region Chamber of Commerce: 480 Moosehead Lake Rd., P.O. Box 581, Greenville, ME 04441. **Phone:** (207) 695-2702 or (888) 876-2778.

KATAHDIN, 12 Lily Bay Rd. at the center of town, is a restored 1914 lake steamboat. The vessel makes 3-hour narrated sightseeing voyages on Moosehead

Lake as well as 4.5-hour cruises to Mount Kineo; a galley is on board. Seasonal themed cruises also are available. **Time:** Allow 3 hours minimum. **Hours:** Sightseeing cruise departs Tues.-Sat. at 12:30, late June-early Oct. Mount Kineo cruise departs every other Wed. at 12:30. Phone ahead to confirm schedule. **Cost:** Sightseeing cruise $33; $29 (ages 62+); $18 (ages 11-16); $3 (ages 0-10). Mount Kineo cruise $38; $34 (ages 62+); $21 (ages 11-16); $5 (ages 0-10). **Phone:** (207) 695-2716.

Moosehead Marine Museum, 12 Lily Bay Rd., comprises two rooms of area memorabilia, including a map collection and items pertaining to lake transportation and logging history. **Time:** Allow 30 minutes minimum. **Hours:** Daily 10-2, mid-June to early Oct. **Cost:** Donations. **Phone:** (207) 695-2716.

BLAIR HILL INN   207/695-0224

Historic
Country Inn
$300-$495

Address: 351 Lily Bay Rd 04441 **Location:** 2 mi n. **Facility:** This is a very lovely restored 1897 mansion. Many of the guest units offer a splendid view of Moosehead Lake, and four have a wood-burning fireplace. 8 units, some two bedrooms. 3 stories (no elevator), interior corridors. **Terms:** closed 11/1-5/15, 2 night minimum stay - weekends, age restrictions may apply, 21 day cancellation notice-fee imposed. **Activities:** hiking trails. **Free Special Amenities: full breakfast and high-speed Internet.**

CHALET MOOSEHEAD LAKEFRONT MOTEL   (207)695-2950

 Motel $79-$165 **Address:** 12 N Birch St 04442 **Location:** Waterfront. 1.5 mi w on SR 15. **Facility:** 27 units, some two bedrooms and efficiencies. 2 stories (no elevator), exterior corridors. **Terms:** closed 11/3-5/14, 7 day cancellation notice-fee imposed. **Activities:** canoeing, paddleboats, boat dock.

EVERGREEN LODGE AT MOOSEHEAD   (207)695-3241

Bed & Breakfast $120-$160 **Address:** 182 Greenville Rd 04441 **Location:** 5.5 mi s on SR 15. Located in a quiet rural area. **Facility:** A casual ambience characterizes this property, which offers some guest rooms with fireplaces and others with balconies overlooking gardens. The property is in a rural area set back from the highway. 6 units. 2 stories (no elevator), interior corridors. **Terms:** closed 10/31-5/16, 2 night minimum stay - seasonal and/or weekends, 21 day cancellation notice-fee imposed.

INDIAN HILL MOTEL   207/695-2623

Motel $80-$100 **Address:** 127 Moosehead Lake Rd 04442 **Location:** 0.5 mi s on SR 15. **Facility:** 15 units. 1 story, exterior corridors. **Terms:** 3 day cancellation notice-fee imposed.

KINEO VIEW MOTOR LODGE   207/695-4470

Motel
$79-$199

Address: 50 Overlook Dr 04441 **Location:** 2.5 mi s on SR 15; gravel access road from highway. **Facility:** 13 units, some two bedrooms and kitchens. 2 stories (no elevator), interior corridors. **Activities:** whirlpool. **Free Special Amenities: early check-in/late check-out and preferred room (subject to availability with advance reservations).**

THE LODGE AT MOOSEHEAD LAKE   (207)695-4400

Country Inn
$250-$695

Address: 368 Lily Bay Rd 04441 **Location:** 2.5 mi n. **Facility:** Set on a hill overlooking Moosehead Lake the lodge presents splendid views of both the lake and mountains. The guest rooms are tastefully decorated in Maine themes and feature fabulous beds. 9 units, some two bedrooms and kitchens. 2 stories (no elevator), interior corridors. **Terms:** closed 4/1-4/30 & 11/1-11/30, 2 night minimum stay - seasonal and/or weekends, age restrictions may apply, 21 day cancellation notice-fee imposed. **Activities:** game room. Fee: massage. **Guest Services:** valet laundry. **Free Special Amenities: full breakfast and high-speed Internet.**

WHERE TO EAT

THE BLACK FROG   207/695-1100

American. Casual Dining. $7-$25 **AAA Inspector Notes:** On the shores of Moosehead Lake, this spacious restaurant is a scenic spot in which to enjoy selections of mostly seafood and cooked-to-order steak. For the best views, diners should try to reserve a window table. Outdoor dining on a floating dock is available in season. **Bar:** full bar. **Address:** 17 Pritham Ave 04441 **Location:** On SR 15; center. **Parking:** street only. L D

GREENVILLE INN DINING ROOM   207/695-2206

American. Fine Dining. $21-$38 **AAA Inspector Notes:** Some of the cozy restaurant's tastefully decorated dining areas overlook Moosehead Lake. The menu features fresh seafood, steak and some game meat, all creatively prepared and well matched with selections from the fine wine list. The homemade desserts are wonderful. **Bar:** full bar. **Reservations:** required. **Address:** 40 Norris St 04441 **Location:** 0.3 mi s; in Greenville Inn at Moosehead Lake. D AC

KELLY'S LANDING   207/695-4438

American. Family Dining. $7-$23 **AAA Inspector Notes:** Kelly's Landing offers a delightful view of Moosehead Lake; the deck is right on the water. The menu filled with home-style cooking features prime rib, seafood, chicken, pork, beef and veal entrees as well as sandwiches, soup and homemade dessert. **Bar:** full bar. **Address:** Rt 15 04442 **Location:** 1.5 mi w on SR 6 and 15. B L D

STRESS FREE MOOSE PUB & CAFE   207/695-3100

American. Casual Dining. $7-$15 **AAA Inspector Notes:** As the name would imply, this is a wonderful spot to relax over your favorite beverage and sample an enormous sandwich or wrap with a bowl of their famous chili. Upstairs, guests will find a lounge area with board games. A patio section is available seasonally. **Bar:** full bar. **Address:** 65 Pritham Ave 04441 **Location:** On SR 15; center. L D

GREENWOOD (I-2)

RECREATIONAL ACTIVITIES
Skiing
- **Mt. Abram Ski Resort** is 1.5 mi. w. of SR 26 on Howe Hill Rd. **Hours:** Thurs.-Sun. and holidays 9-4, mid-Dec. to early Apr. **Phone:** (207) 875-5000.

HALLOWELL pop. 2,381, elev. 53'

MAPLE HILL FARM INN AND CONFERENCE CENTER
(207)622-2708

▼▼▼▼ **Historic Bed & Breakfast** $105-$210 **Address:** 11 Inn Rd 04347 **Location:** I-95 exit 109 northbound; exit 109A southbound, on SR 202 W, then s on Whitten Rd (immediate left), then 1.4 mi nw to Winthrop St (right turn), then just left onto Town Farm Rd, follow signs. Located in a quiet rural area. **Facility:** Built circa 1890, the inn is on a 62-acre working farm that houses a variety of animals, including llamas. 8 units. 2 stories (no elevator), interior corridors. **Terms:** 1-2 night minimum stay - seasonal and/or weekends, 14 day cancellation notice. **Activities:** sauna, whirlpool, cross country skiing, hiking trails. (ECO) ⊤ CALL (&M) (BIZ) 🛜 (✕)

WHERE TO EAT

HATTIE'S CHOWDER HOUSE 207/621-4114

▼▼ **Seafood. Family Dining.** $7-$24 **AAA Inspector Notes:** The popular family restaurant is known for its homemade lobster stew, but patrons also have the choice of chowders, pastas, salads, chicken, burgers and sandwiches, as well as beef and seafood. The brownies are to-die-for. **Bar:** full bar. **Address:** 103 Water St 04347 **Location:** Corner of Winthrop St. **Parking:** street only.

(L) (D)

THE LIBERAL CUP 207/623-2739

▼▼ **English. Casual Dining.** $7-$15 **AAA Inspector Notes:** Not far from the state capitol, the eatery lets patrons match English-style pub fare with the hand-crafted beers made on the premises. **Bar:** full bar. **Address:** 115 Water St 04347 **Location:** Center. **Parking:** street only. (L) (D)

HANCOCK

LE DOMAINE INN 207/422-3395

▼▼▼▼ **Country Inn.** Rates not provided. **Address:** 1513 US Rt 1 04640 **Location:** On US 1, 9 mi e of Ellsworth; center. **Facility:** This charming French-style inn is offers lovely gardens and guest rooms decorated with a taste of Provence, fireplaces and a deck. 4 units. 2 stories (no elevator), exterior corridors. **Dining:** Le Domaine Restaurant Francais, see separate listing.

(¶) 🛜 (✕) (⋈) (🖵) / SOME UNITS FEE (🐕)

WHERE TO EAT

LE DOMAINE RESTAURANT FRANCAIS 207/422-3395

▼▼▼▼ **Regional French. Fine Dining.** $22-$33 **AAA Inspector Notes:** The charming restaurant offers a delightful French country theme and a large, open-hearth fireplace reflecting on polished wooden floors. Patrons can relax with a beverage in the lounge before savoring the owner/chef's creative delights. Specialties include French-cut hanger steaks pan seared with green peppercorn demi-glace sauce, quail roasted with juniper berries and grilled veal with mushrooms. Desserts are exquisite. The vast wine list comprises more than 5,000 bottles. **Bar:** full bar. **Reservations:** suggested. **Address:** 1513 US Rt 1 04640 **Location:** On US 1, 9 mi e of Ellsworth; center; in Le Domaine Inn. (D)

HARPSWELL

DOLPHIN MARINA & RESTAURANT 207/833-6000

▼▼ **Seafood. Family Dining.** $8-$29 **AAA Inspector Notes:** Owned by the same family for 37 years, the restaurant is known for its clam chowder and lobster stew. Patrons can come by land, by sea or sometimes by air to enjoy fresh local seafood and water views. **Bar:** beer & wine. **Address:** 515 Basin Point Rd 04079 **Location:** From Brunswick, jct SR 24, 12 mi s on SR 123, follow signs 2.5 mi.

(L) (D)

HINCKLEY (H-4) elev. 135'

L.C. BATES MUSEUM, 5 mi. n. of I-95 exit 133 on US 201, is housed in a three-story Romanesque building constructed in 1903. Exhibits relate to Maine's natural history, archeology and ethnology. Additional highlights include a children's room and a turn-of-the-19th-century classroom. The grounds feature an arboretum and walking trails.

Guided nature walks and children's workshops are offered weekly. **Hours:** Wed.-Sat. and holidays 10-4:30, Sun. 1-4:30, Apr. 1 to mid-Nov.; by appointment rest of year. **Cost:** $3; $1 (ages 0-17 and students with ID). **Phone:** (207) 238-4250. (🏛)

HODGDON (E-7) elev. 427'

LT. GORDON MANUEL WILDLIFE MANAGEMENT AREA, 63 Station Hill Rd., is a recreation area offering more than 6,400 acres of woodlands and wetlands ideal for fishing, canoeing, hiking, bird-watching and cross-country skiing. Two small boat launches on the Meduxnekeag River are available.

Camping is not permitted. In winter snowmobile trails are available. Roads are not plowed Dec.-Mar. and are closed during mud season, Apr.-May. **Hours:** Daily 24 hours (weather permitting). **Cost:** Free. **Phone:** (207) 435-3231, ext. 1. (✕)

HOLDEN (H-5) elev. 180'

FIELDS POND AUDUBON CENTER is at 216 Fields Pond Rd. Well-marked trails and a 300-foot boardwalk allow for wildlife viewing and exploration of the 192-acre sanctuary, which includes meadows, woodlands, wetlands and a small beach area at Fields Pond. Bears, foxes, deer, moose and a variety of birds may be seen. Nature programs and exhibits are available from the nature center. **Tours:** Guided tours are available. **Time:** Allow 2 hours minimum. **Hours:** Grounds daily dawn-dusk. Nature center Thurs.-Sat. 10-4. **Cost:** Free. **Phone:** (207) 989-2591.

HOULTON (E-7) pop. 4,856, elev. 357'

On the Meduxnekeag River, Houlton is the seat and one of the oldest communities of 6,453-square-mile Aroostook County, largest in the state and greater in area than Rhode Island and Connecticut combined. Houlton first prospered from lumber, but now the Aroostook potato dominates its economy, along with various light industries and technological and educational ventures. As the shipping point for the products of this agriculturally rich region, Houlton is sometimes referred to as the "Garden of Maine."

The Aroostook County Historical and Art Museum in the White Building, 109 Main St., displays tools, vintage clothing, historical artifacts and local archival materials. The museum is open Memorial Day-Labor Day; phone (207) 532-6687. In Pierce Park is a drinking fountain with an interesting 1916 cast-iron statue, "The Boy with the Leaking Boot." The sculptor is unknown; one theory is that the boy is bringing water to a wounded soldier.

Greater Houlton Chamber of Commerce: 109 Main St., Houlton, ME 04730. **Phone:** (207) 532-4216.

ELM TREE DINER   207/532-3777

▼▼ ◆ American. Casual Dining. $6-$15 **AAA Inspector Notes:** A spacious, modern diner offering a wide variety of home-style dishes served in ample portions. Also on the menu are various burgers, sandwiches, homemade soups, salads and excellent desserts. **Bar:** full bar. **Address:** 146 Bangor St 04730 **Location:** 1 mi w on US 2A; at Hogan St. B L D CALL ♿M

TANG'S CHINESE CUISINE   207/532-9981

▼▼ Chinese. Casual Dining. $7-$14 **AAA Inspector Notes:** The popular restaurant offers a wide variety of well-prepared Asian dishes, which are served by the friendly, laid-back staff. The large, open dining room works well for families, couples or individuals. **Bar:** full bar. **Address:** 60 North St 04730 **Location:** I-95 exit 302, 0.7 mi s. L D

JACKMAN

BISHOP'S COUNTRY INN MOTEL   (207)668-3231

▼▼ Motel $65-$100 **Address:** 461 Main St 04945 **Location:** On US 201; center. **Facility:** 22 units. 2 stories (no elevator), exterior corridors. **Parking:** winter plug-ins. **Terms:** cancellation fee imposed. **Amenities:** high-speed Internet. **Guest Services:** coin laundry.

[†] CALL ♿M BIZ 📶 ✕ 🛏 🍴 💻 / SOME UNITS FEE 🐾

WHERE TO EAT

FOUR SEASONS RESTAURANT   207/668-7778

▼ American. Family Dining. $6-$15 **AAA Inspector Notes:** Decorated with coffee mugs from around the world, the restaurant provides a comfortable, yet worldly, atmosphere. Featuring popular comfort foods, the menu includes burgers, pork chops, meat loaf, steaks, fish and, on weekends, prime rib. The house-prepared coconut cream pie is a great way to wrap up a meal. **Bar:** full bar. **Address:** 417 Main St 04945 **Location:** On US 201; center.

B L D

KENNEBUNK (K-2) pop. 5,214, elev. 51'
• Hotels & Restaurants map & index p. 98

The Kennebunks—Kennebunk, Kennebunkport *(see place listing)* and Kennebunk Beach—constitute one of Maine's most popular coastal resort areas. Kennebunk developed between the Mousam and Kennebunk rivers about 1650 and was originally part of the town of Wells *(see place listing p. 155)*. By 1730 there were shipyards along the Mousam; these and a brisk West Indies trade supported Kennebunk until the Revolution, after which water-powered industries assumed economic leadership.

In the first half of the 19th century Kennebunk, like Kennebunkport and nearly every other tidewater Maine settlement, caught shipbuilding fever. Between 1800 and 1850 more than 1,000 wooden schooners, clippers and cargo vessels emerged from the area's 50-odd shipyards.

Legacies of this period's wealth and skill are the beautifully detailed Colonial, Federal, Greek Revival

and Victorian houses that grace Kennebunk's national historic district, which includes upper Main Street, Summer Street and a portion of US 1. First Parish Church on Main Street has a bell cast by Paul Revere's foundry in its Christopher Wren steeple.

Kennebunk-Kennebunkport-Arundel Chamber of Commerce: 17 Western Ave. (SR 9), P.O. Box 740, Kennebunk, ME 04043. **Phone:** (207) 967-0857.

THE BRICK STORE MUSEUM, 117 Main St., occupies an early 19th-century commercial block in the heart of Kennebunk's National Register Historic District. Changing exhibitions showcase fine and decorative arts and artifacts pertaining to regional history. Architectural walking tours are available seasonally. **Time:** Allow 2 hours minimum. **Hours:** Tues.-Fri. 10-4:30, Sat. 10-1. Archives by appointment. Closed major holidays. **Cost:** $5. **Phone:** (207) 985-4802.

TURNPIKE MOTEL   207/985-4404 ㉟

▼▼ Motel Rates not provided **Address:** 77 Old Alewive Rd 04043 **Location:** I-95 exit 25, just e on SR 35, then just n. **Facility:** 24 units. 2 stories (no elevator), interior/exterior corridors.

SAVE 📶 🛏 / SOME UNITS FEE 🐾

WALDO EMERSON INN   (207)985-4250 ㊵

▼▼▼ Historic Bed & Breakfast $115-$195 **Address:** 108 Summer St 04043 **Location:** Jct US 1/SR 35, 1.2 mi e. Adjacent to Wedding Cake House. **Facility:** Located relatively close to the shore and within close proximity of shops and restaurants, this beautifully restored circa 1753 inn boasts very pleasant public spaces and handsome guest rooms. 4 units. 3 stories (no elevator), interior corridors. **Terms:** age restrictions may apply, 10 day cancellation notice-fee imposed. **Activities:** bicycles. **Free Special Amenities:** full breakfast and manager's reception.

SAVE BIZ 📶 ✕ Ⓩ / SOME UNITS W

WHERE TO EAT

ACADEME AT THE KENNEBUNK INN   207/985-3351 ⑮

▼▼▼ Regional American Fine Dining $9-$38 **AAA Inspector Notes:** *Historic.* Guests can enjoy the romantic ambience at the 1799 inn while savoring American bistro fare made from fresh local ingredients. The casual Grill Room Pub, which opens for lunch and dinner, serves lighter fare in addition to the dining room offerings. In season, consider dining al fresco on the patio. **Bar:** full bar. **Reservations:** suggested. **Address:** 45 Main St 04043 **Location:** On US 1; center of village. L D

ON THE MARSH BISTRO   207/967-2299 ⑯

▼▼▼ Continental. Fine Dining. $21-$39 **AAA Inspector Notes:** The lovely setting overlooks the salt marshes and colorful perennial gardens. In an 1800 converted barn, the restaurant features a romantic ambience, upscale rustic decor and attractive table settings. The menu centers on European classic country cuisine with excellent flavors. Guests can enjoy sushi on the balcony. The wine list is award-winning. **Bar:** full bar. **Reservations:** suggested. **Address:** 46 Western Ave 04043 **Location:** Jct US 1, 5 mi e on SR 9. D CALL ♿M

(See map & index p. 98.)

SEBAGO BREWING COMPANY   207/985-9855

▼▼ American. Gastropub. $9-$23 **AAA Inspector Notes:** This stylish brewpub has an informal, friendly atmosphere. The self-described "American pub" cuisine includes delicious pasta, chicken, seafood and steak entrées as well as tasty salads, burgers and sandwiches. The latter are available all day. Desserts are prepared on the premises each day by their pastry chef. **Bar:** full bar. **Address:** 65 Portland Rd 04043 **Location:** On US 1; at Shops at Long Bank.

[L] [D] CALL [&M]

KENNEBUNK BEACH
• Hotels & Restaurants map & index p. 98

THE BEACH HOUSE INN   (207)967-3850   **61**

▼▼ **Historic Bed & Breakfast** $109-$850 **Address:** 211 Beach Ave 04043 **Location:** Oceanfront. Jct SR 9 and Beach Ave, 1.6 mi se. **Facility:** Nestled across from the ocean, many rooms offer full water views while others afford partial views. This property has a lovely garden area. A continental breakfast is served each morning. 34 units. 4 stories, interior corridors. **Terms:** 2-3 night minimum stay - seasonal and/or weekends, 30 day cancellation notice-fee imposed. **Activities:** canoeing, bicycles. *Fee:* massage. **Guest Services:** valet laundry. [📶] [✕]

THE GRAND HOTEL   207/967-0355   **58**

▼▼ **Boutique Hotel.** Rates not provided. **Address:** 1 Chase Hill Rd 04043 **Location:** Jct SR 35 and 9; just sw of Dock Square. **Facility:** Mixing plush comforts and modernity, this new addition to the Kennebunk Beach area is a refreshing option. Walk to the village area or bike to the beach. 17 units. 2 stories, interior corridors. *Bath:* shower only. **Activities:** bicycles, spa.

CALL [&M] [BIZ] [📶] [✕] [▭]

KING'S PORT INN   (207)967-4340   **59**

▼▼▼ **Hotel** $79-$349 **Address:** 18 Western Ave 04043 **Location:** Jct SR 35 and 9; just sw of Dock Square. **Facility:** 34 units. 2-3 stories (no elevator), interior/exterior corridors. **Terms:** 2 night minimum stay - seasonal and/or weekends, 14 day cancellation notice-fee imposed. [🍴] [Ⅰ] [BIZ] [📶] [✕] [📱]

THE WHITE BARN INN & SPA   (207)967-2321   **60**

▼▼▼ ▼▼
Historic
Country Inn
$465-$1700

Address: 37 Beach Ave 04043 **Location:** I-95 exit 25, 5.6 mi se on SR 35. **Facility:** This handsome 19th-century country inn features well-designed public rooms and lodgings as well as elegant cottages. 28 units, some cottages. 1-3 stories (no elevator), interior/exterior corridors. **Parking:** valet only. **Terms:** 2 night minimum stay - seasonal and/or weekends, age restrictions may apply, 30 day cancellation notice-fee imposed. **Dining:** The White Barn Inn Restaurant, see separate listing. **Pool(s):** heated outdoor. **Activities:** canoeing, bicycles, spa. *Fee:* charter fishing. **Guest Services:** valet laundry. **Free Special Amenities:** expanded continental breakfast and high-speed Internet. *(See ad p. 105.)* [SAVE] [🍴] [🛎] [♿] [🛥] [🚣] [📶] [✕]

WHERE TO EAT

FEDERAL JACK'S RESTAURANT & BREWPUB
          207/967-4322   **36**

▼▼ American. Casual Dining. $10-$20 **AAA Inspector Notes:** On the site of a former shipyard, the restaurant affords wonderful views of the Kennebunk River. Diners can tour the brewery or sample one of the many hand-crafted beers. The menu includes a variety of salads, sandwiches, wraps and burgers as well as pasta, seafood, lamb, steak and chicken entrées. Seafood paella is outstanding. **Bar:** full bar. **Address:** 8 Western Ave 04043 **Location:** On SR 9, 0.5 mi w of Dock Square. [L] [D]

GRISSINI ITALIAN BISTRO   207/967-2211   **38**

▼▼▼▼ Italian. Casual Dining. $14-$32 **AAA Inspector Notes:** This elegant bistro features a flavorful array of dishes such as osso buco, linguine Bolognese, wood-grilled pizza and baked chicken stuffed with herb cream cheese. The very good staff can help you choose from their fine selection of wines. The décor is refined yet has a rustic Italian feel with wood floors and a two-story centerpiece stone fireplace. **Bar:** full bar. **Reservations:** suggested. **Address:** 27 Western Ave, Lower Village 04043 **Location:** US 1, 4 mi e on SR 35 and 9A. [D] CALL [&M]

MEKHONG THAI RESTAURANT   207/967-8827

▼▼▼ Thai. Casual Dining. $8-$17 **AAA Inspector Notes:** On the menu is a good variety of well-prepared seafood, chicken, stir-fry, curry and ginger dishes. Contemporary decor lends to a warm atmosphere. The staff is friendly, prompt and knowledgeable. **Bar:** full bar. **Address:** 37 Western Ave, Suite 8 04043 **Location:** Just w of jct SR 9 and 35, 0.5 mi w of Dock Square; in Lower Village Shopping Center. [L] [D]

RYAN'S CORNER HOUSE IRISH PUB & RESTAURANT
          207/967-3564   **37**

▼▼▼ Irish. Casual Dining. $8-$28 **AAA Inspector Notes:** The lively local favorite serves tasty Irish fare like Guinness stew, corned beef and cabbage, burgers and more. Weather permitting, outdoor dining is a treat overlooking bustling Kennebunkport. It typically closes for a bit of a winter break after Christmas Prelude and reopens the weekend before St. Patrick's Day. **Bar:** full bar. **Address:** 17 Western Ave 04043 **Location:** On SR 9A; just before bridge to Dock Square in Kennebunkport. [L] [D] CALL [&M]

THE WHITE BARN INN RESTAURANT
          207/967-2321   **39**

▼▼▼▼ ▼▼
American
Fine Dining
$106-$160

AAA Inspector Notes: Rustic, elegant country décor is found in a beautifully renovated barn. The menu, which varies weekly, features outstanding American cuisine with an emphasis on New England. While the atmosphere is formal — jackets are required for gentlemen — it still is relaxed. Floor-length table linens, formally-attired staff and a grand piano contrast wonderfully with the rustic nature of the barn, the memorabilia in the hayloft, old silverware table sculptures and the shiny copper bar top. Semiformal attire. **Bar:** full bar. **Reservations:** suggested. **Address:** 37 Beach Ave 04043 **Location:** I-95 exit 25, 5.6 mi se on SR 35; in The White Barn Inn & Spa. **Parking:** valet only. *(See ad p. 105.)* [D]

KENNEBUNKPORT (K-2) pop. 1,238, elev. 5'
• Hotels p. 105 • Restaurants p. 106
• Hotels & Restaurants map & index p. 98

A popular summer resort, Kennebunkport has long been a favorite among artists and writers who have found both its history and quaint setting conducive to creativity. Novelist Kenneth Roberts, born in Kennebunk, used the Kennebunkport area as a setting for his "Chronicles of Arundel," and author Booth Tarkington wrote at dockside in his schooner *Regina.* Many galleries and craft shops attest to Kennebunkport's continuing affinity with the arts.

Dock Square has restored structures housing boutiques and galleries. Parson's Way, a scenic public walkway, begins at Dock Square and continues past Walker's Point. Along the docks several boats offer chartered deep-sea fishing, sailing, whale-watching or lobstering excursions. Sightseeing cruises of the Kennebunk River and coastal islands also are available.

(See map & index p. 98.)

Beyond the village Ocean Avenue follows the rocky shore of Cape Arundel to Cape Porpoise, a year-round fishing village. From Cape Porpoise pier it is possible to view the lighthouse on Goat Island. This scenic drive is lined with fine old mansions that are now restaurants or lodgings.

A waterspout, produced by water forced by the incoming tide through such formations as the spouting rock and the blowing cave, can be seen at Cape Arundel near Walker's Point—summer home of former President George H.W. Bush. Parking is not permitted along Ocean Avenue, but it is available at nearby Womby Beach. Farther "down east" via SR 9 is picturesque Goose Rocks Beach.

The Kennebunkport Historical Society offers guided walking tours of the historic village; phone (207) 967-2751 for schedule. Tours depart from the Nott House *(see attraction listing)*.

Self-guiding tours: Guide books for a self-guiding walking tour of Kennebunkport are available at The Nott House *(see attraction listing)*.

THE KENNEBUNKPORT HISTORICAL SOCIETY oversees a complex of five historical buildings at 125-135 North St. The Henry H. Pasco Exhibit Center offers exhibits about Kennebunkport's past. The Town House School, home to a research center, evokes the nostalgia of a typical New England one-room schoolhouse. A shipwright's office and blacksmith shop also provide glimpses into Victorian-era life. Jail cells from the colonial period also are on view.

Hours: Exhibit center Tues.-Fri. 10-4. Schoolhouse Wed. and Fri. 10-1. Blacksmith shop Wed. and Fri. 1-4, mid-June to mid-Sept.; by appointment rest of year. Jail cells and shipwright's office by appointment. **Cost:** Donations. **Phone:** (207) 967-2751.

THE NOTT HOUSE is at 8 Maine St. Guided tours take visitors through this 1853 Greek Revival-style house containing original Victorian furnishings, pictures and personal belongings from four generations of Perkins and Nott families. Displays offer insight into the town's history. The garden offers a peaceful park-like setting. One-hour guided walking tours of historic downtown also are offered.

Time: Allow 1 hour minimum. **Hours:** House tours Thurs.-Sat. 11:15-2:15, July-Aug. Downtown walking tours depart Thurs.-Sat. at 11, July-Aug. Closed major holidays. Phone ahead to confirm schedule. **Cost:** House or downtown walking tour $10; free (ages 0-12). Combination house and downtown walking tour $15; free (ages 0-12). Guide books for self-guiding tours $4. **Phone:** (207) 967-2751.

SEASHORE TROLLEY MUSEUM, off I-95 Kennebunk exit to US 1N to Log Cabin Rd., has one of the world's largest collections of antique electric streetcars—more than 250. Visitors have an opportunity to experience public transportation from a bygone era by embarking on a 3-mile trolley ride.

Time: Allow 2 hours minimum. **Hours:** Daily 10-5, Memorial Day weekend-Columbus Day; Sat.-Sun. 10-5 in early May and late Oct. Last tour departs 45 minutes before closing. **Cost:** $10; $8 (ages 60+); $7.50 (ages 6-16). **Phone:** (207) 967-2712 or (207) 967-2800.

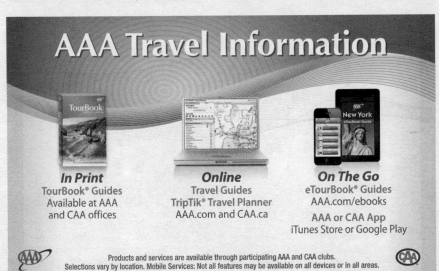

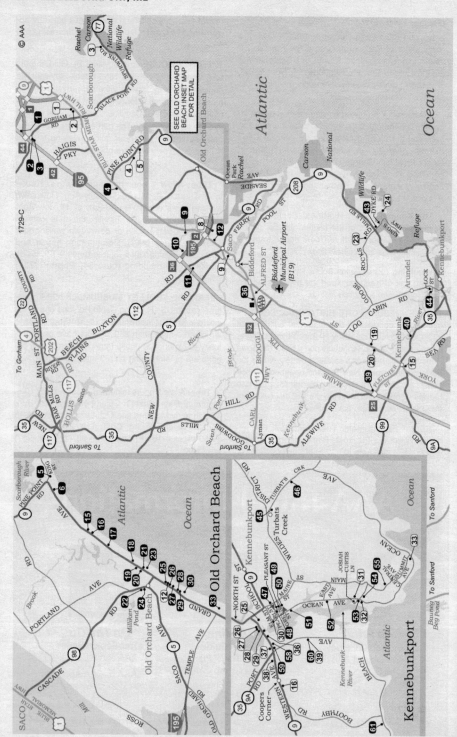

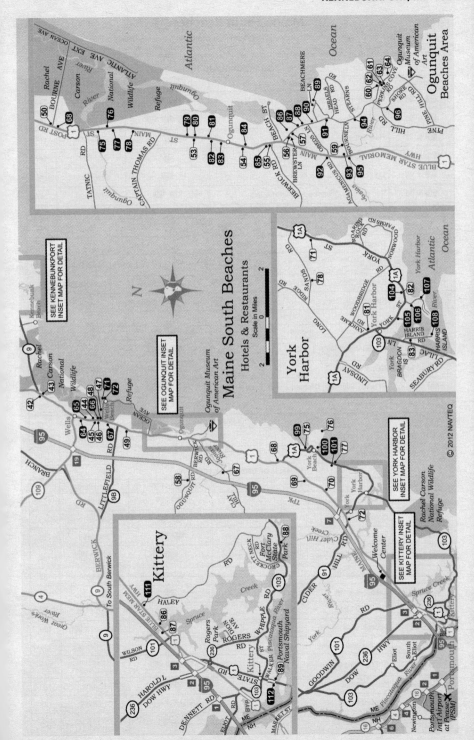

Maine South Beaches
Hotels & Restaurants

Scale in Miles

© 2012 NAVTEQ

Ogunquit Beaches Area

York Harbor

Kittery

Portsmouth

SEE KENNEBUNKPORT INSET MAP FOR DETAIL

SEE OGUNQUIT INSET MAP FOR DETAIL

SEE YORK HARBOR INSET MAP FOR DETAIL

SEE KITTERY INSET MAP FOR DETAIL

Ogunquit Museum of American Art

Rachel Carson National Wildlife Refuge

Welcome Center

Portsmouth Int'l Airport at Pease (PSM)

Maine South Beaches

This index helps you "spot" where approved hotels and restaurants are located on the corresponding detailed maps. Hotel daily rate range is for comparison only. Restaurant price range is a combination of lunch and/or dinner. Turn to the listing page for more detailed rate and price information and consult display ads for special promotions.

SCARBOROUGH

Map Page	Hotels	Diamond Rated	Rate Range	Page
1 p. 98	Fairfield Inn by Marriott Portland Maine Mall	◆◆	$129-$329	146
2 p. 98	TownePlace Suites by Marriott	◆◆◆	$99-$259	147
3 p. 98	Residence Inn by Marriott	◆◆◆	$139-$329	147
4 p. 98	Pride Motel & Cottages	◆	$65-$225	147
5 p. 98	Lighthouse Inn at Pine Point	◆	$155-$255	146
6 p. 98	Sea-ward on Oceanfront Guest House	◆◆	$88-$193	147

Map Page	Restaurants	Diamond Rated	Cuisine	Price Range	Page
1 p. 98	The Egg & I	◆◆	American	$5-$9	147
2 p. 98	Dimitri's Restaurant	◆◆	Greek	$5-$14	147
3 p. 98	Uncle Don's Spurwink Country Kitchen	◆◆	New American	$8-$24	147
4 p. 98	Bayley's Seafood Restaurant	◆	Seafood	$10-$25	147
5 p. 98	Ken's Place	◆	Seafood	$5-$24	147

SACO

Map Page	Hotels	Diamond Rated	Rate Range	Page
9 p. 98	Wagon Wheel Motel	◆◆	Rates not provided	146
10 p. 98	Hampton Inn	◆◆◆	$99-$259 [SAVE]	146
11 p. 98	Ramada Saco Old Orchard Beach Area	◆◆◆	$80-$230 [SAVE]	146
12 p. 98	Saco Motel	◆	$50-$90 [SAVE]	146

Map Page	Restaurants	Diamond Rated	Cuisine	Price Range	Page
8 p. 98	The Lobster Claw	◆	Seafood	$7-$20	146
9 p. 98	Traditions	◆◆	Italian	$5-$21	146

OLD ORCHARD BEACH

Map Page	Hotels	Diamond Rated	Rate Range	Page
15 p. 98	Royal Anchor Resort	◆◆	$78-$225	123
16 p. 98	Ocean Walk Hotel	◆◆	$80-$310	123
17 p. 98	Friendship Oceanfront Suites	◆◆	$69-$259	123
18 p. 98	Beachfront Condotels	◆	Rates not provided	122
19 p. 98	Beau Rivage Motel	◆◆	$69-$299	122
20 p. 98	Executive Motel	◆	$85-$185	123
21 p. 98	The Crest Motel	◆	$100-$329	122
22 p. 98	Atlantic Birches Inn	◆◆◆	$101-$220 [SAVE]	122
23 p. 98	The Aquarius Motel	◆	$59-$139 [SAVE]	122
24 p. 98	Old Orchard Beach Inn	◆◆◆	Rates not provided [SAVE]	123
25 p. 98	Kebek 3 Motel	◆◆	$90-$195	123
26 p. 98	The Edgewater	◆◆◆	$79-$289	122
27 p. 98	Sea View Inn	◆◆	Rates not provided [SAVE]	123

OLD ORCHARD BEACH (cont'd)

Map Page	Hotels (cont'd)	Diamond Rated	Rate Range	Page
28 p. 98	Waves Oceanfront Resort	◆◆	$60-$260	123
29 p. 98	The Gull Motel	◆◆	$75-$200	123
30 p. 98	White Cap Village	◆◆	$75-$375	123

Map Page	Restaurant	Diamond Rated	Cuisine	Price Range	Page
12 p. 98	Joseph's By the Sea	◆◆◆	Continental	$19-$33	123

OCEAN PARK

Map Page	Hotel	Diamond Rated	Rate Range	Page
33 p. 98	BillowHouse Oceanfront Motel & Guesthouse	◆◆	$115-$300	116

BIDDEFORD

Map Page	Hotel	Diamond Rated	Rate Range	Page
36 p. 98	Americas Best Value Inn	◆◆	$43-$139 SAVE	66

KENNEBUNK

Map Page	Hotels	Diamond Rated	Rate Range	Page
39 p. 98	**Turnpike Motel**	◆◆	Rates not provided SAVE	95
40 p. 98	**Waldo Emerson Inn**	◆◆◆	$115-$195 SAVE	95

Map Page	Restaurants	Diamond Rated	Cuisine	Price Range	Page
15 p. 98	**Academe at The Kennebunk Inn**	◆◆◆	Regional American	$9-$38	95
16 p. 98	On the Marsh Bistro	◆◆◆	Continental	$21-$39	95

KENNEBUNKPORT

Map Page	Hotels	Diamond Rated	Rate Range	Page
43 p. 98	Ocean Woods Resort	◆◆	Rates not provided	106
44 p. 98	**1802 House Bed & Breakfast Inn**	◆◆◆	$169-$369 SAVE	105
45 p. 98	Lodge At Turbat's Creek	◆◆	$69-$179	106
46 p. 98	Rhumb Line Resort	◆◆	$69-$209	106
47 p. 98	**Maine Stay Inn & Cottages**	◆◆◆	$129-$379 SAVE	106
48 p. 98	The Captain Jefferds Inn	◆◆◆	$149-$399	105
49 p. 98	**Captain Lord Mansion**	◆◆◆◆	$179-$549 SAVE	105
50 p. 98	**Captain Fairfield Inn**	◆◆◆	$159-$439 SAVE	105
51 p. 98	The Yachtsman Lodge & Marina	◆◆◆	$129-$399	106
52 p. 98	The Nonantum Resort	◆◆◆	$109-$449	106
53 p. 98	The Breakwater Inn & Spa	◆◆◆	$149-$799	105
54 p. 98	**The Colony Hotel**	◆◆◆	$134-$294 SAVE	105
55 p. 98	Old Fort Inn & Resort	◆◆◆	Rates not provided	106

Map Page	Restaurants	Diamond Rated	Cuisine	Price Range	Page
23 p. 98	Earth	◆◆◆◆	New American	$18-$38	106
24 p. 98	Tides Beach Club	◆◆◆	Regional American	$18-$38	107
25 p. 98	Bandaloop	◆◆◆	International	$17-$29	106
27 p. 98	Alisson's Restaurant	◆◆	Seafood	$8-$24	106
28 p. 98	**Hurricane Restaurant**	◆◆◆	American	$10-$39	106
29 p. 98	The Clam Shack	◆	Seafood	$4-$25	106

Map Page	Restaurants (cont'd)	Diamond Rated	Cuisine	Price Range	Page
③⓪ p. 98	**Arundel Wharf Restaurant**	▽▽▽	Seafood	$8-$30	106
③① p. 98	Mabel's Lobster Claw	▽▽	Seafood	$5-$35	107
③② p. 98	Stripers Restaurant	▽▽▽	Seafood	$19-$38	107
③③ p. 98	Cape Arundel Inn	▽▽▽	New England	$27-$40	106

KENNEBUNK BEACH

Map Page	Hotels	Diamond Rated	Rate Range	Page
⑤⑧ p. 98	The Grand Hotel	▽▽▽	Rates not provided	96
⑤⑨ p. 98	King's Port Inn	▽▽▽	$79-$349	96
⑥⓪ p. 98	**The White Barn Inn & Spa** (See ad p. 105.)	▽▽▽▽	$465-$1700 SAVE	96
⑥① p. 98	The Beach House Inn	▽▽▽	$109-$850	96

Map Page	Restaurants	Diamond Rated	Cuisine	Price Range	Page
③⑥ p. 98	Federal Jack's Restaurant & Brewpub	▽▽	American	$10-$20	96
③⑦ p. 98	Ryan's Corner House Irish Pub & Restaurant	▽▽	Irish	$8-$28	96
③⑧ p. 98	Grissini Italian Bistro	▽▽▽	Italian	$14-$32	96
③⑨ p. 98	**The White Barn Inn Restaurant** (See ad p. 105.)	▽▽▽▽▽	American	$106-$160	96

WELLS

Map Page	Hotels	Diamond Rated	Rate Range	Page
⑥④ p. 98	Carriage House Motel, Cottages & Suites	▽▽	$59-$175	156
⑥⑤ p. 98	**Elmwood Resort Hotel**	▽▽▽	$79-$459 SAVE	156
⑥⑥ p. 98	Garrison Suites Motel & Cottages	▽▽▽	$69-$229	156
⑥⑦ p. 98	**Hampton Inn & Suites**	▽▽▽	$89-$299 SAVE	156
⑥⑧ p. 98	Wells-Moody Motel	▽	$49-$149	156

Map Page	Restaurants	Diamond Rated	Cuisine	Price Range	Page
④② p. 98	Bull & Claw	▽▽	Regional American	$6-$26	156
④③ p. 98	**Maine Diner**	▽▽	American	$6-$30	157
④④ p. 98	The Steakhouse	▽▽	Steak	$15-$27	157
④⑤ p. 98	**Mike's Clam Shack**	▽▽	Seafood	$8-$24	157
④⑥ p. 98	**Congdon's Donuts & Family Restaurant**	▽▽	American	$3-$12	156
④⑦ p. 98	Billy's Chowder House	▽▽	American	$12-$26	156
④⑧ p. 98	Varano's Italian Restaurant	▽▽	Italian	$14-$30	157
④⑨ p. 98	**Mainiax Restaurant**	▽▽	American	$8-$25	157
⑤⓪ p. 98	Jake's Seafood Restaurant	▽	Seafood	$5-$20	156

WELLS BEACH

Map Page	Hotels	Diamond Rated	Rate Range	Page
⑦① p. 98	Atlantic Oceanfront Motel	▽▽	$69-$309	157
⑦② p. 98	Lafayette's Ocean Front Resort At Wells Beach	▽▽	$49-$500	157

OGUNQUIT

Map Page	Hotels	Diamond Rated	Rate Range	Page
⑦⑤ p. 98	**Towne Lyne Motel**	▽▽	$45-$179 SAVE	121
⑦⑥ p. 98	Mariner Resort Motel	▽▽	$59-$249	120

OGUNQUIT (cont'd)

Map Page	Hotels (cont'd)	Diamond Rated	Rate Range	Page
77 p. 98	Ogunquit Resort Motel	◈◈◈	$54-$399	120
78 p. 98	**The Milestone** *(See ad p. 120.)*	◈◈◈	$59-$239 [SAVE]	120
79 p. 98	**Colonial Village Resort**	◈◈	$69-$292 [SAVE]	117
80 p. 98	**The Dunes on the Waterfront**	◈◈◈	$105-$510 [SAVE]	117
81 p. 98	Stage Run By The Sea	◈◈	$49-$209	121
82 p. 98	**Gorges Grant Hotel** *(See ad p. 118.)*	◈◈◈	$99-$289 [SAVE]	117
83 p. 98	Sea View Motel	◈◈	Rates not provided	120
84 p. 98	**Juniper Hill Inn** *(See ad p. 117.)*	◈◈◈	$92-$274 [SAVE]	118
85 p. 98	Studio East Motor Inn	◈◈	Rates not provided	121
86 p. 98	**Terrace by the Sea**	◈◈	$69-$300 [SAVE]	121
87 p. 98	Sea Chambers	◈◈	$74-$269	120
88 p. 98	**Sparhawk Oceanfront Resort**	◈◈◈	$120-$330 [SAVE]	121
89 p. 98	**The Beachmere Inn**	◈◈◈	$95-$425 [SAVE]	117
90 p. 98	The Anchorage by the Sea	◈◈◈	$89-$359	116
91 p. 98	Pink Blossoms Family Resort	◈◈◈	$60-$419	120
92 p. 98	Admiral's Inn	◈◈◈	$59-$279	116
93 p. 98	**Meadowmere Resort** *(See ad p. 119.)*	◈◈◈	$89-$499 [SAVE]	120
94 p. 98	The Grand Hotel	◈◈◈	$69-$299	118
95 p. 98	Seafarer Motel	◈◈	Rates not provided	120
96 p. 98	Yardarm Village Inn	◈◈	$100-$170	121

Map Page	Restaurants	Diamond Rated	Cuisine	Price Range	Page
53 p. 98	The Egg & I	◈	American	$4-$15	121
54 p. 98	Bintliff's Ogunquit	◈◈◈	American	$9-$39	121
55 p. 98	The Old Village Inn	◈◈	American	$9-$28	122
56 p. 98	Gypsy Sweethearts Restaurant	◈◈◈	Seafood	$18-$32	121
57 p. 98	Five-O	◈◈◈	Regional American	$19-$33	121
58 p. 98	Arrows Restaurant	◈◈◈◈	Regional American	$85-$135	121
59 p. 98	**Jonathan's Restaurant**	◈◈◈	Continental	$20-$34	121
60 p. 98	Jackie's Too	◈◈	Seafood	$7-$25	121
61 p. 98	Oarweed Restaurant & Lobster Pound	◈◈	Seafood	$7-$28	122
62 p. 98	Barnacle Billy's Etc.	◈◈	American	$8-$31	121
63 p. 98	Barnacle Billy's	◈	American	$5-$25	121
64 p. 98	MC Perkins Cove	◈◈◈	American	$9-$27	122

YORK BEACH

Map Page	Hotels	Diamond Rated	Rate Range	Page
99 p. 98	The Union Bluff Hotel	◈◈◈	$79-$399	161
100 p. 98	Lighthouse Inn & Carriage House	◈◈	$85-$185	161
101 p. 98	The Anchorage Inn	◈◈◈	$70-$585	161

Map Page	Restaurants	Diamond Rated	Cuisine	Price Range	Page
(75) p. 98	Union Bluff Pub & Grill	◆◆	American	$7-$28	161
(76) p. 98	Fox's Lobster House	◆◆	Seafood	$14-$39	161
(77) p. 98	Sun & Surf	◆◆	American	$8-$30	161
(78) p. 98	Chef Mimmo's	◆◆	Italian	$21-$28	161

YORK HARBOR

Map Page	Hotels	Diamond Rated	Rate Range	Page
(104) p. 98	York Harbor Inn	◆◆◆	$109-$349	163
(105) p. 98	Inn at Harmon Park	◆◆◆	$99-$139	162
(106) p. 98	Edwards Harborside Inn	◆◆◆	$90-$290	162
(107) p. 98	Stage Neck Inn *(See ad p. 162.)*	◆◆◆	$182-$444 SAVE	163
(108) p. 98	Dockside Guest Quarters	◆◆◆	$140-$345	162

Map Page	Restaurants	Diamond Rated	Cuisine	Price Range	Page
(81) p. 98	Foster's Restaurant and Foster's Downeast Clambake	◆	Regional Seafood	$6-$30	163
(82) p. 98	The York Harbor Inn & Ship's Cellar Pub	◆◆◆	Regional American	$7-$29	163
(83) p. 98	Dockside Restaurant on York Harbor	◆◆◆	Seafood	$9-$29	163

KITTERY

Map Page	Hotels	Diamond Rated	Rate Range	Page
(111) p. 98	**The Coachman Inn**	◆◆	$69-$209 SAVE	108
(112) p. 98	Portsmouth Harbor Inn & Spa	◆◆◆	$145-$245	108

Map Page	Restaurants	Diamond Rated	Cuisine	Price Range	Page
(86) p. 98	Robert's Maine Grill	◆◆	Seafood	$10-$30	108
(87) p. 98	Bob's Clam Hut	◆	Regional Seafood	$4-$24	108
(89) p. 98	**Warren's Lobster House**	◆◆	Seafood	$8-$22	108

ARUNDEL

Map Page	Restaurants	Diamond Rated	Cuisine	Price Range	Page
(19) p. 98	Seafood Center	◆	Seafood	$8-$28	40
(20) p. 98	Blue Moon Classy Diner	◆◆	American	$4-$22	40

YORK

Map Page	Restaurants	Diamond Rated	Cuisine	Price Range	Page
(67) p. 98	Clay Hill Farm	◆◆◆	American	$24-$29	161
(68) p. 98	**Cape Neddick Inn Restaurant and Tavern**	◆◆◆	American	$10-$32	161
(69) p. 98	Lobster Barn	◆◆	Seafood	$7-$35	161
(70) p. 98	Wild Willy's Burgers	◆	Burgers	$7-$9	161
(71) p. 98	Lobster Cove	◆◆	Seafood	$8-$28	161
(72) p. 98	Ruby's Genuine Brick Oven	◆◆	American	$7-$19	161

(See map & index p. 98.)

1802 HOUSE BED & BREAKFAST INN

(207)967-5632 **44**

Historic Bed & Breakfast
$169-$369

Address: 15 Locke St 04046 **Location:** From Dock Square, just ne to Maine St, 0.4 mi n, then just w. **Facility:** Attractive common areas and well-furnished accommodations characterize this intimate, circa 1800s inn. 6 units. 2 stories (no elevator), interior corridors. **Terms:** 2 night minimum stay - seasonal and/or weekends, age restrictions may apply, 14 day cancellation notice-fee imposed. **Free Special Amenities: full breakfast.**

THE BREAKWATER INN & SPA

(207)967-5333 **53**

Historic Boutique Hotel $149-$799 **Address:** 127 and 133 Ocean Ave 04046 **Location:** From Dock Square, 1 mi e; close to the mouth of Kennebunk River. **Facility:** Many rooms are offered—two have a balcony—at this property overlooking the Kennebunk River and Atlantic Ocean. 37 units. 3-4 stories (no elevator), interior corridors. **Parking:** on-site and valet. **Terms:** 2-3 night minimum stay - seasonal and/or weekends, 30 day cancellation notice-fee imposed. **Dining:** Stripers Restaurant, see separate listing. **Activities:** steamrooms, canoeing, bicycles, exercise room, spa. *Fee:* marina. **Guest Services:** valet laundry.

CAPTAIN FAIRFIELD INN

(207)967-4454 **50**

Historic Boutique Bed & Breakfast
$159-$439

Address: 8 Pleasant St 04046 **Location:** From Dock Square, 0.3 mi s on Ocean Ave, just ne; corner of Green and Pleasant sts. Located in a quiet area. **Facility:** A three-course breakfast is served at this 1813 former sea captain's home, which is set in a quiet area and furnished with an eclectic mix of modern furnishings and art. 9 units. 2 stories (no elevator), interior corridors. **Terms:** 2 night minimum stay - seasonal and/or weekends, 14 day cancellation notice-fee imposed. **Free Special Amenities: full breakfast and high-speed Internet.**

THE CAPTAIN JEFFERDS INN

(207)967-2311 **48**

Historic Bed & Breakfast $149-$399 **Address:** 5 Pearl St 04046 **Location:** From Dock Square, 0.3 mi s on Ocean Ave, then just ne; corner of Pearl and Pleasant sts. **Facility:** This circa 1804 Federal-style mansion offers inviting parlor rooms, fresh flowers in each room and Katie, a friendly dog on the premises. 15 units. 3 stories (no elevator), interior/exterior corridors. **Terms:** 2 night minimum stay - seasonal and/or weekends, 14 day cancellation notice-fee imposed. **Activities:** bicycles.

CAPTAIN LORD MANSION

(207)967-3141 **49**

Historic Bed & Breakfast
$179-$549

Address: 6 Pleasant St 04046 **Location:** From Dock Square, 0.3 mi s on Ocean Ave, then just ne on Greene St. **Facility:** Guest rooms in this beautifully restored 1814 Federalist-style home feature fine furnishings and décor that is plush yet enhances the feel of the period. 16 units. 3 stories (no elevator), interior corridors. **Terms:** 2 night minimum stay - weekends, 15 day cancellation notice-fee imposed. **Activities:** bicycles. *Fee:* massage. **Guest Services:** complimentary and valet laundry. **Free Special Amenities: full breakfast and high-speed Internet.**

THE COLONY HOTEL

(207)967-3331 **54**

Classic Historic Hotel
$134-$294

Address: 140 Ocean Ave 04046 **Location:** From Dock Square, 1 mi s. **Facility:** Exquisite grounds surround this impressive turn-of-the-century destination overlooking the ocean. Guests have access to a private beach. 125 units, some two and three bedrooms. 2-3 stories, interior corridors. **Terms:** closed 10/28-5/24, check-in 4 pm, 2-3 night minimum stay - seasonal and/or weekends, 7 day cancellation notice-fee imposed. **Amenities:** safes. *Some:* high-speed Internet. **Dining:** 2 restaurants. **Pool(s):** heated outdoor. **Activities:** limited beach access, putting green, recreation programs, shuffleboard. *Fee:* bicycles.

▼ See AAA listing p. 96 ▼

Download eTourBook guides for top destinations at AAA.com/ebooks

(See map & index p. 98.)

LODGE AT TURBAT'S CREEK (207)967-8700 45

▼▼ Motel $69-$179 **Address:** 7 Turbats Creek Rd 04046 **Location:** From Dock Square, 0.5 mi se on Maine St, 0.6 mi ne on Wildes District Rd, then just se. **Facility:** 27 units. 2 stories (no elevator), interior corridors. **Terms:** closed 12/8-5/31, 2 night minimum stay - seasonal and/or weekends, 14 day cancellation notice-fee imposed. **Pool(s):** heated outdoor.

CALL ⓖⓜ 🏊 📶 ✕ 🖥 / SOME UNITS FEE 🐾

MAINE STAY INN & COTTAGES 207/967-2117 47

▼▼▼
Bed & Breakfast
$129-$379

Address: 34 Maine St 04046 **Location:** From Dock Square, just e on SR 9 to Maine St, then just s. **Facility:** Select from a variety of individually decorated rooms and suites at this updated 1860s property. If you're traveling with the kids, you'll need to reserve a cottage. 17 units, some two bedrooms, kitchens and cottages. 2 stories (no elevator), interior/exterior corridors. **Terms:** 2-3 night minimum stay - seasonal and/or weekends, 14 day cancellation notice-fee imposed. **Activities:** volleyball. **Free Special Amenities: full breakfast and high-speed Internet.**

SAVE 🍴+ BIZ 📶 ✕ 🌊 / SOME UNITS 🖥 🖼 🖥

THE NONANTUM RESORT (207)967-4050 52

▼▼/▼▼▼ **Historic Resort Hotel** $109-$449 **Address:** 95 Ocean Ave 04046 **Location:** Waterfront. From Dock Square, 0.7 mi s. **Facility:** Reflecting an antique charm, this 19th-century inn and modern motel-style building are on the Kennebunk River. 109 units, some two bedrooms. 3-4 stories, interior corridors. **Terms:** closed 12/15-5/1, 2 night minimum stay - seasonal and/or weekends, 7 day cancellation notice-fee imposed. **Pool(s):** heated outdoor. **Activities:** fishing, recreation programs. *Fee:* bicycles.

ECO 🍴 🍸 🏊 BIZ 📶 ✕
/ SOME UNITS 🖥 🖼 🖥

OCEAN WOODS RESORT 207/967-1928 43

▼▼ **Hotel.** Rates not provided. **Address:** 71 Dyke Rd 04046 **Location:** I-95 exit 25, 5 mi se on SR 35 to SR 9, 4.8 mi ne to Dyke Rd, then just se. **Facility:** 32 units. 2 stories (no elevator), interior corridors. **Pool(s):** outdoor. **Activities:** whirlpool, playground, basketball, horseshoes, shuffleboard.

🍴 🍸 🏊 BIZ 📶 ✕ 🖥 🖥 / SOME UNITS 🖼

OLD FORT INN & RESORT 207/967-5353 55

▼▼▼ **Historic Boutique Resort Hotel.** Rates not provided. **Address:** 8 Old Fort Ave 04046 **Location:** From Dock Square, 1 mi s on Ocean Ave, 0.3 mi se via Kings Hwy, then just s on S Maine St. Located in a quiet area. **Facility:** Located off the beaten path, this renovated 1900s carriage house provides a bit of seclusion. Luxurious décor and original gallery-style artwork add a touch of elegance throughout. 16 units, some two bedrooms. 2 stories (no elevator), interior corridors. **Terms:** age restrictions may apply. **Pool(s):** heated outdoor. **Activities:** bicycles.

🍸 🏊 BIZ 📶 ✕ 🖥 🖼 🖥

RHUMB LINE RESORT (207)967-5457 46

▼▼ Hotel $69-$209 **Address:** 41 Turbats Creek Rd 04046 **Location:** From Dock Square, 0.5 mi se on Maine St, 0.6 mi ne on Wildes District Rd, then 0.4 mi se. Located in a residential area. **Facility:** 59 units, some efficiencies and kitchens. 2 stories (no elevator), interior/exterior corridors. **Terms:** closed 12/31-2/2, 2 night minimum stay - seasonal and/or weekends, 7 day cancellation notice-fee imposed, resort fee. **Pool(s):** heated outdoor, heated indoor. **Activities:** whirlpools, exercise room.

🏊 BIZ 📶 🖥 🖥 / SOME UNITS

THE YACHTSMAN LODGE & MARINA (207)967-2511 51

▼▼▼ Motel $129-$399 **Address:** 57 Ocean Ave 04046 **Location:** Waterfront. From Dock Square, just s. **Facility:** 30 units. 1 story, exterior corridors. **Terms:** closed 12/4-4/12, 30 day cancellation notice-fee imposed. **Activities:** canoeing, bicycles. *Fee:* marina.

🍴+ 🚲 📶 ✕ 🖥 🖥 / SOME UNITS FEE 🐾

ALISSON'S RESTAURANT 207/967-4841 27

▼▼ Seafood. Casual Dining. $8-$24 **AAA Inspector Notes:** A favorite with both residents and visitors, Alisson's Restaurant is the place to see and be seen in Kennebunkport. The casual family-friendly restaurant specializes in seafood, but the menu also includes other selections such as burgers, sandwiches, pasta, chicken and steak. There are two can't misses, the delicious lobster rolls and the flavorful chowder. **Bar:** full bar. **Address:** 11 Dock Square 04046 **Location:** Center. **Parking:** street only. L D

ARUNDEL WHARF RESTAURANT 207/967-3444 30

▼▼▼
Seafood
Family Dining
$8-$30

AAA Inspector Notes: This attractive harborfront restaurant serves well-prepared fresh local seafood. Lighter fare is offered at lunch. The nautical-themed dining room feels casual and relaxed. If the weather is nice, ask for a table on the deck. **Bar:** full bar. **Reservations:** suggested. **Address:** 43 Ocean Ave 04046 **Location:** From Dock Square, just e. *Menu on AAA.com* L D

BANDALOOP 207/967-4994 25

▼▼▼ International. Casual Dining. $17-$29 **AAA Inspector Notes:** Named after a tribe who knew the secret of eternal life in a Tom Robbins novel, the restaurant's owners believe in serving food that is free of pesticides and hormones. Ingredients are all natural, organic and from local Maine farmers whenever possible. A variety of sauces, some of them vegan, are listed on the menu and can be matched to any entree. Entrees include fish, pasta and free-range chicken. The atmosphere is lively and child-friendly. **Bar:** full bar. **Reservations:** suggested. **Address:** 2 Dock Square 04046 **Location:** On Dock Square. **Parking:** street only. D

CAPE ARUNDEL INN 207/967-2125 33

▼▼▼ New England. Fine Dining. $27-$40 **AAA Inspector Notes:** This shingle-style, cottage-turned-country inn features lovely ocean views of the rocky Maine Coast as well as Walker's Point (summer home of former President George H. Bush). The menu features American cuisine including seafood, beef and game along with desserts made on the premises. The professional service staff will make an evening at the inn a memorable one. **Bar:** full bar. **Reservations:** suggested. **Address:** 208 Ocean Ave 04046 **Location:** From Dock Square, 2 mi e; corner of Ocean and Summit aves. D 🎿

THE CLAM SHACK 207/967-2560 29

▼ Seafood. Quick Serve. $4-$25 **AAA Inspector Notes:** Located in the Lower Village, the Clam Shack, a local institution, is just across the bridge from Dock Square. Order fresh seafood at the window and sit on a bench and watch the activity on the river while you eat. Cash is the only form of payment accepted. **Address:** 2 Western Ave 04043 **Location:** On SR 9; across the bridge from Dock Square; in Lower Village. L 🎿

EARTH 207/967-6550 23

▼▼▼▼ New American. Fine Dining. $18-$38 **AAA Inspector Notes:** Located in a wooded setting within a rustic yet chic barn. Tree trunks that once stood in the restaurant's footprint were recycled and used to create the interesting woven wall paneling. A preserved cherry tree with sparkling white lights hangs upside down from the vaulted ceiling, and a two-story bar and stone fireplace add drama. Guests also can dine on the screened-in porch or large, well-tended garden, both of which afford wonderful views of the pond and nightly bonfire. **Bar:** full bar. **Reservations:** suggested. **Address:** 354 Goose Rocks Rd 04046 **Location:** Jct SR 9, 0.5 mi nw; in Hidden Pond Resort. D 🎿

HURRICANE RESTAURANT 207/967-9111 28

▼▼▼
American
Casual Dining
$10-$39

AAA Inspector Notes: Offering lovely water views, the restaurant serves fresh seafood, including lobster and oysters. Steaks and vegetarian options are also available, as is an extensive wine list. **Bar:** full bar. **Reservations:** suggested. **Address:** 29 Dock Square 04046 **Location:** Center. **Parking:** on-site (fee). *Menu on AAA.com*

L D

(See map & index p. 98.)

MABEL'S LOBSTER CLAW   207/967-2562   (31)

▼▼▼ Seafood. Casual Dining. $5-$35 **AAA Inspector Notes:** *Classic.* Since 1953, this popular restaurant has been serving up excellent local seafood, lobster, chowder and freshly-made pies such as blueberry and peanut butter ice cream pie. Located close to the water, the décor features knotty-pine walls and local artwork on display. Couples like this place. Free car bumper stickers are provided if you heart the place. Seasonal covered sidewalk seating available in summer. **Bar:** full bar. **Reservations:** suggested. **Address:** 124 Ocean Ave 04046 **Location:** From Dock Square, 1 mi e on Ocean Ave; close to mouth of Kennebunk River. **Parking:** street only.

[L] [D]

STRIPERS RESTAURANT   207/967-5333   (32)

▼▼▼ Seafood. Fine Dining. $19-$38 **AAA Inspector Notes:** Fresh seafood, simply prepared can be found at this restaurant. Fish and chips has proved to be a popular choice with regulars, who also enjoy wonderful views of the Kennebunk River and ocean from French doors that open up onto the manicured lawn. Contemporary nautical décor with saltwater fish aquariums complete the look. Servers are knowledgeable and attentive. **Bar:** full bar. **Reservations:** suggested. **Address:** 131 Ocean Ave 04046 **Location:** From Dock Square, 1 mi e; close to the mouth of Kennebunk River; in The Breakwater Inn & Spa. **Parking:** on-site and valet. [L] [D]

TIDES BEACH CLUB   207/967-3757   (24)

▼▼▼ Regional American. Casual Dining. $18-$38 **AAA Inspector Notes:** *Historic.* The innovative menu at this restaurant features excellent seafood, grass-fed beef and farm-fresh vegetables along with sumptuous homemade desserts and an exceptional cocktail and wine list. The chic coastal interior with its beige toned walls, lots of mirrors, clear-glass bar stools and dark-wood floors will have guests second guessing what state they are in—the owner/designer spends his winters in South Beach Miami. Request a table with a view of Goose Rocks Beach from across the street. **Bar:** full bar. **Reservations:** suggested. **Address:** 254 Kings Hwy 04046 **Location:** I-95 exit 25, just e on SR 35 to SR 9; through Dock Square, 5.5 mi e to Dyke Rd, just e to end, then 0.3 mi n along Beachfront Rd.

[L] [D]

KINGFIELD (H-3) elev. 570'

Surrounded by the Longfellow Mountains (the name, a tribute to the renowned Maine-born poet, actually refers to *all* mountains in the state), scenic Kingfield is where SRs 16, 27 and 42; the Carrabassett and West Branch rivers; and those who can't get enough of the great outdoors converge.

For avid snowmobilers, the mostly wooded town is home to a segment of the Black Fly Loop trail. For those heading north with their skis and poles, it's the gateway to Carrabassett Valley's popular Sugarloaf/USA Ski and Golf Resort *(see attraction listing p. 79).* And for those looking to snap some stunning shots, it's a glistening white paradise captured beautifully with a camera.

Kingfield is chiefly a winter town, but it's a spring, summer and fall town, too. The area allures travelers with its canoeing, kayaking, hiking, biking and hunting opportunities and good fishing spots like Day Pond, Pinnacle Pond and the Carrabassett River reservoir. If you visit Kingfield between September and November, expect to be entranced by glorious hues of red, orange and yellow—Maine's western regions are known for their spectacular autumn scenes.

Not the outdoorsy type? Unwind in a lovely B&B, treat yourself to a belt-loosening experience at a local restaurant or explore downtown's specialty shops and art galleries. For a glimpse of local history, check out the 1890 Kingfield Historical House at 45 High St., open late spring to early October. Featuring 10 rooms, three porches and an attached two-story barn, the Victorian home is filled with fascinating artifacts; phone (207) 265-4032.

SKI MUSEUM OF MAINE is at 256 Main St. in the Sugarloaf Sports Outlet. The museum, home to the Maine Ski Hall of Fame, details the evolution of skiing in the state. Historically significant documents, Olympic ski uniforms and other memorabilia are displayed. Skiing artifacts, including a ski believed to be handmade in the early 20th century, are collected in the museum's archive. **Time:** Allow 30 minutes minimum. **Hours:** Daily 9-5, Sept.-Apr.; Thurs.-Mon. 9-5, July-Aug. Phone ahead to confirm schedule. **Cost:** Free. **Phone:** (207) 265-2023.

THE STANLEY MUSEUM, 40 School St., is a tribute to the creative efforts of the Stanley family, best known for the Stanley Steamer automobile. Photography by Chansonetta Stanley and other family artworks depict turn-of-the-20th-century rural Maine life. Other items created by family members also are displayed. In addition, the museum exhibits three steam-powered cars from 1905, 1910 and 1916.

Time: Allow 1 hour minimum. **Hours:** Tues.-Sun. 1-4, June-Oct.; Tues.-Fri. 1-4, rest of year. **Cost:** $4; $3 (ages 65+); $2 (ages 5-12). **Phone:** (207) 265-2729.

LONGFELLOW'S   207/265-4394

▼▼ American. Casual Dining. $6-$18 **AAA Inspector Notes:** Great for budget-conscious patrons, the popular restaurant offers a good view of the Carrabassett River. The 19th-century building setting features a pub, open-beam dining room and upstairs area with an outdoor deck. Good soups, crepes and sandwiches contribute to the menu. **Bar:** full bar. **Address:** 247 Main St 04947 **Location:** Center. [L] [D]

KITTERY (L-2) pop. 4,562, elev. 34'
- Hotels p. 108 • Restaurants p. 108
- Hotels & Restaurants map & index p. 98, 239

Settled in the early 1600s, Kittery was an important shipbuilding, shipping and lumbering center. One of the oldest shipyards in the nation and among the first owned by the federal government, the Portsmouth Naval Shipyard on Seavey's Island was established in 1800. The *Ranger,* the first ship to fly the Stars and Stripes, was launched at Kittery under the command of John Paul Jones on May 10, 1777. In 1917 the first American submarine, the USS *L-8,* was launched from the Portsmouth Navy Yard.

Kittery is noted for its historic sites, rocky beaches and thriving outlet trade on US 1. Fort Foster, constructed soon after the Civil War, is situated on Gerrish Island in a park setting. The remains of the fort are open to the public Memorial Day to Labor Day, and visitors can enjoy views of Portsmouth Harbor, picnicking and nature trails.

Shopping areas: More than 120 outlet shops can be found at Kittery Outlets, off N. US 1, including

(See maps & indexes p. 98, 239.)

 Tanger Outlet Center, Calvin Klein, Banana Republic, Coach and Reebok.

FORT McCLARY STATE HISTORIC SITE covers

27 acres about 2 mi. e. on SR 103. The initial fortifications were erected in the early 18th century; the current blockhouse was built about 1844 and modified in the 1860s. **Time:** Allow 30 minutes minimum. **Hours:** Daily 10-8, Memorial Day-Labor Day; 9-5, day after Labor Day-Columbus Day; most Sat.-Sun. 9-5, in Nov. (weather permitting). **Cost:** $3; $1 (ages 5-11 and 65+). **Phone:** (207) 384-5160, or (207) 490-4079 in the off-season.

KITTERY HISTORICAL AND NAVAL MUSEUM is

off I-95 exit 2 to SR 236S. At the traffic circle follow signs to US 1N, then make the first right after the traffic circle onto Rogers Rd. Exhibits portray more than 350 years of Kittery's maritime and cultural heritage. Included are early shipbuilding tools; navigational instruments; ship models; a 14-foot replica of John Paul Jones' ship, the *Ranger*; photographs; and the lens from the Boon Island Lighthouse. A reconstructed garrison house from the early 18th century is on display.

Time: Allow 1 hour minimum. **Hours:** Tues.-Sat. 10-4, June 1-Columbus Day; Wed. and Sat. 10-4, day after Columbus Day-Thanksgiving; by appointment rest of year. Closed major holidays. **Cost:** $5; $3 (ages 7-15); $10 (family). **Phone:** (207) 439-3080.

THE COACHMAN INN (207)439-4434 **111**

Motel
$69-$209

Address: 380 US Rt 1 03904 **Location:** I-95 exit 2, 1 mi n. **Facility:** 43 units, some two bedrooms. 2 stories (no elevator), interior/exterior corridors. **Terms:** cancellation fee imposed. **Pool(s):** heated outdoor. **Free Special Amenities: continental breakfast and local telephone calls.**

SAVE CALL &M [BIZ] ⊠
/SOME UNITS FEE 🐾 🔲 🔳

PORTSMOUTH HARBOR INN & SPA 207/439-4040 **112**

Bed & Breakfast $145-$245 **Address:** 6 Water St 03904 **Location:** I-95 exit 2, 0.3 mi se on SR 236 to Kittery Traffic Circle, then just s on US 1; at base of Memorial Bridge. **Facility:** The house is close to the Memorial Bridge leading into downtown Portsmouth and is convenient to the Kittery outlets. Attractively landscaped grounds with perennial gardens surround the home. 5 units. 3 stories (no elevator), interior corridors. **Terms:** check-in 4 pm, 2 night minimum stay - seasonal and/or weekends, age restrictions may apply, 15 day cancellation notice-fee imposed. **Activities:** whirlpool, spa. 🛜 ⊠ 🎿

WHERE TO EAT

BOB'S CLAM HUT 207/439-4233 **87**
Regional Seafood. Quick Serve. $4-$24 **AAA Inspector Notes:** Originating in 1956 as a typical roadside clam shack, this place now continues the tradition but with a few modern changes. An inside all-weather dining room was added, and Ben & Jerry's famous ice cream joined the ranks of menu offerings. Fried clams are outstanding. Guests should be prepared to wait during peak meal times, but it is worth every minute. **Address:** 315 US 1 03904 **Location:** I-95 exit 2, 0.6 mi n. L D 🅰🅲

ROBERT'S MAINE GRILL 207/439-0300 **86**
Seafood. Casual Dining. $10-$30 **AAA Inspector Notes:** Robert's Maine Grill is the more upscale cousin of sister restaurant Bob's Clam Hut. At this location you'll see a definite gourmet twist to its fresh fish entrées. Dine in a setting that's both warm and lively, with nautical color tones and views of the marsh. The staff is exceptional and eager to assist you with recommendations. **Bar:** full bar. **Address:** 326 US Rt 1 03904 **Location:** I-95 exit 2, 0.6 mi n. L D CALL &M

WARREN'S LOBSTER HOUSE 207/439-1630 **89**

Seafood
Casual Dining
$8-$22

AAA Inspector Notes: Overlooking the Piscataqua River, this landmark from the 1940s has a varied menu offering several beef dishes and plenty of seafood. The salad bar has more than 50 selections. The specialty is lobster which is priced daily. **Bar:** full bar. **Address:** 11 Water St 03904 **Location:** I-95 exit 2, 0.3 mi e on SR 236 to Kittery Traffic Circle, just s on US 1; at base of Memorial Bridge. *Menu on AAA.com* L D CALL &M

WEATHERVANE SEAFOOD RESTAURANT 207/439-0330
Seafood. Family Dining. $8-$24 **AAA Inspector Notes:** The popular, family-oriented restaurant presents a large menu with lobster, fried clams and crisp Cape Cod apple-cranberry cobbler. Flavorful dishes are served in large portions. A fish market is on the premises. **Bar:** full bar. **Address:** 306 US 1 03904 **Location:** I-95 exit 2, 0.5 mi n. L D CALL &M

LEWISTON (J-3) pop. 36,592, elev. 200'

The larger of the "Twin Cities of the Androscoggin" and the second largest city in the state, Lewiston occupies the river's east bank, across from Auburn *(see place listing p. 41)*. Lewiston's early years gave little hint of what it would become. The first settler erected a log cabin within the present city limits in 1770, but subsequent growth was slow.

Although a woolen mill began operation in 1819, it was not until the waterpower of the Androscoggin River was harnessed about 1850 that Lewiston began developing into a major textile center. By the 1870s cottons and woolens were issuing from the mills of several large companies.

At the same time many French Canadians were recruited to work in the mills, leaving Lewiston with a rich Franco-American heritage. The city now is experiencing economic diversification, with strong service, retail and innovative technology sectors.

Another Lewiston tradition is Bates College, founded in 1864. A highlight of the 75-acre campus is rocky 340-foot Mount David. The view from its summit encompasses Lewiston, Auburn and the Androscoggin Valley and extends 50 miles west to the Presidential Range in New Hampshire. Lewiston Falls and Dam, which provided the city's industrial impetus, is best seen from Longley Bridge on US 202.

The Franco-American Heritage Center, 46 Cedar St., was built in 1907 as St. Mary's Parish. The converted church features stained-glass windows and hosts dance and musical performances; phone (207) 783-1585.

Androscoggin County Chamber of Commerce— Lewiston: 415 Lisbon St., P.O. Box 59, Lewiston, ME 04243-0059. **Phone:** (207) 783-2249.

BATES COLLEGE MUSEUM OF ART is 2 blks. e. of US 202 (Main St.) at 75 Russell St. in the Olin Arts Center located on the Bates College campus. The museum displays changing exhibits of 18th-, 19th- and 20th-century prints, contemporary art, watercolors and drawings, and works by Marsden Hartley, a Lewiston native and prominent 20th-century artist. **Time:** Allow 1 hour minimum. **Hours:** Tues.-Sat. 10-5 (also Wed. 5-7, Sept.-May). Closed major holidays. **Cost:** Free. **Phone:** (207) 786-6158.

THORNCRAG NATURE SANCTUARY, .1 mi. e. at jct. Montello St. and Highland Spring Rd., encompasses 372 acres of forest, fields and ponds. The sanctuary is a habitat for a wide variety of birds native to northern New England. There are 4 miles of marked hiking trails; maps are available at the gate. Hiking, cross-country skiing and snowshoeing are permitted. **Hours:** Daily dawn-dusk. **Cost:** Free. **Phone:** (207) 782-5238. 🏞

RAMADA CONFERENCE CENTER   (207)784-2331
▼▼ **Hotel** $99-$160 **Address:** 490 Pleasant St 04240 **Location:** I-95 exit 80, right turn on Foch St, follow signs. **Facility:** 117 units. 2 stories (no elevator), interior corridors. **Amenities:** high-speed Internet. **Pool(s):** heated indoor. **Activities:** sauna, whirlpool, exercise room. **Guest Services:** valet and coin laundry.
📶 🅿 🏊 ⓑⓘⓩ 📶 ✕ 🎬 🛎 ▯ / SOME UNITS 🖥

WHERE TO EAT

DAVINCI'S   207/782-2088
▼▼ Italian. Casual Dining. $8-$22 **AAA Inspector Notes:** The locally popular dining room features such original features of the mill as the brick walls. The menu features Italian favorites. **Bar:** full bar. **Address:** 150 Mill St 04240 **Location:** Center; in Bates Mill Complex. ⓁⒹ

GOVERNOR'S RESTAURANT & BAKERY   207/753-0173
▼▼ American. Family Dining. $8-$24 **AAA Inspector Notes:** Diners flip through a dozen pages of wonderful seafood and varied Italian dishes, in addition to choices such as homemade meatloaf, steaks, burgers and sandwiches, on Governor's Restaurant's diverse menu. Breakfast dishes also can be ordered at any time of the day. Weekends stay bustling with families filing in to the casual spot to indulge in the daily made bakery treats and desserts. **Bar:** beer & wine. **Address:** 1185 Lisbon St 04240 **Location:** I-95 exit 80, just n.
ⒷⓁⒹ

LINCOLNVILLE
• Restaurants p. 110

• Restaurants p. 110

CEDARHOLM GARDEN BAY INN   207/236-3886
▼▼▼▼ Cottage $250-$495 **Address:** 2159 Atlantic Hwy 04849 **Location:** Oceanfront. On US 1, 1.6 mi s of jct SR 173. **Facility:** Cottages with well-tended perennial gardens offer nice ocean views; an expanded Continental breakfast is served daily. Check-in is available 3-7 pm. 6 cottages. 1 story, exterior corridors. **Terms:** closed 11/16-4/30, 2 night minimum stay - weekends, 30 day cancellation notice-fee imposed.
📶 ✕ 🛎 ▯ / SOME UNITS 🅺 ☎ 🖥

THE INN AT OCEANS EDGE   (207)236-0945
▼▼▼▼ **Address:** 24 Stonecoast Rd 04849 **Location:** Oceanfront. On US 1, 1 mi s of jct SR 173. **Facility:** Picturesque gardens and ocean breezes give this property a retreat-like ambience. Rooms are well appointed and have gas fireplaces. 32 units. 3 stories (no elevator), interior corridors. **Terms:** closed 11/1-5/10, 2 night minimum stay - seasonal and/or weekends, 14 day cancellation notice-fee imposed. **Pool(s):** heated outdoor. **Activities:** sauna, whirlpool, limited exercise equipment. *Fee:* massage. **Free Special Amenities: full breakfast and newspaper.**
Bed & Breakfast $175-$475
SAVE ECO CALL 🅛Ⓜ 🏊 📶 ✕ / SOME UNITS 🛎 🖥

THE INN AT SUNRISE POINT   207/236-7716
▼▼▼▼ **Address:** 55 Sunrise Point Rd 04849 **Location:** Oceanfront. On US 1, 1.6 mi s of jct SR 173. Located in a quiet area. **Facility:** Nestled along the shores of the Penobscot Bay, this secluded inn has large picture windows overlooking the bay. Some guest units have a whirlpool tub, a private deck and a natural wood-burning fireplace. 9 units. 1-2 stories (no elevator), interior/exterior corridors. **Terms:** closed 11/17-4/19, 15 day cancellation notice-fee imposed. **Amenities:** safes. **Activities:** *Fee:* massage. **Free Special Amenities: full breakfast and newspaper.**
Bed & Breakfast $320-$650
SAVE 👬 📶 ✕ 🛎 🖥 / SOME UNITS 🖥

MOUNT BATTIE MOTEL   (207)236-3870
▼▼▼ Motel $156-$176 **Address:** 2158 Atlantic Hwy 04849 **Location:** On US 1, 1.6 mi s of jct SR 173. **Facility:** 21 units, some two bedrooms. 1 story, exterior corridors. **Terms:** closed 10/25-5/3, 7 day cancellation notice-fee imposed. **Free Special Amenities: expanded continental breakfast and local telephone calls.** *(See ad p. 76.)*

SAVE 📶 ✕ 🛎 🖥 / SOME UNITS 🖥

(See ad p. 76.)

VICTORIAN BY THE SEA   (207)236-3785
▼▼▼ Historic Bed & Breakfast $149-$269 **Address:** 33 Seaview Dr 04849 **Location:** Oceanfront. On US 1, 1.2 mi s of jct SR 173. **Facility:** A pleasant porch dresses the front of this Victorian home dating from 1889. Six guest rooms feature fireplaces and some have water views. 7 units. 3 stories (no elevator), interior corridors. **Terms:** closed 11/1-4/15, 2 night minimum stay - seasonal and/or weekends, 10 day cancellation notice-fee imposed.
📶 ✕ 🅺 📺 ☎ / SOME UNITS FEE 🐾

YOUNGTOWN INN & RESTAURANT   207/763-4290
▼▼▼ Historic Country Inn. Rates not provided. **Address:** 581 Youngtown Rd 04849 **Location:** 2 mi s on SR 52; 4 mi n of Camden. Located in a quiet rural area. **Facility:** A large dining room and cozy guest rooms, including two with fireplaces, are featured at this Federal-style farmhouse dating from 1810. 6 units. 3 stories (no elevator), interior/exterior corridors. **Dining:** restaurant, see separate listing. 🍴 🍷 📶 ✕

WHERE TO EAT

LOBSTER POUND RESTAURANT 207/789-5550

Seafood
Family Dining
$9-$30

AAA Inspector Notes: This ever-popular place is a mecca for lobster lovers. The menu also offers other seafood, clams, roast turkey, ham, steak and chicken. This is a family-style restaurant and has picnic tables near a sandy beach and a take-out window. **Bar:** full bar. **Address:** 2521 Atlantic Ave 04849 **Location:** On US 1, just n of jct SR 173. *Menu on AAA.com*

L D CALL M

YOUNGTOWN INN & RESTAURANT 207/763-4290

French. Casual Dining. $22-$30 **AAA Inspector Notes:** *Historic.* Fireplaces warm the casually elegant dining rooms, and the French chef/owner creates a selection of well-prepared entrees and excellent homemade desserts. Veal chops, rack of lamb, souffles and salmon en croute are a few choices. Expect a fine wine list. **Bar:** full bar. **Reservations:** suggested. **Address:** 581 Youngtown Rd 04849 **Location:** 2 mi s on SR 52; 4 mi n of Camden. D

LIVERMORE (I-3) elev. 344'

With a lake at its north edge and 1,207-foot Bear Mountain to the west, Livermore enjoys a pleasant setting. The community is a trading center for the farming, dairying and lumbering interests in the area. Washburn-Norlands Living History Center, 290 Norlands Rd., is a working farm and museum. The former estate of the Washburn family, the center now operates as an educational facility offering a glimpse into 19th-century life in rural Maine. The 445-acre estate includes a one-room schoolhouse, a stone library, a Universalist meeting house, the Washburn family mansion and a farmer's cottage. Tours are available by appointment; phone (207) 897-4366.

LUBEC (H-8) pop. 349, elev. 10'

Settled in 1780, Lubec is in the easternmost area of Maine. It holds the distinction of being the first spot where the sun rises in the continental United States. Situated on a peninsula, the community offers scenic ocean vistas and many opportunities to explore Maine's rugged coastline.

Tours of Lubec and Cobscook provides self-guiding audio tours, including an inside look at a working organic farm, an intertidal zone shore walk, a nature walk through an Arctic bog, and a walk along historic Water Street; phone (207) 733-2997 or (888) 347-9302.

Boats may be chartered to view the coastal scenery as well as whales, seals and birds. Machias Seal Island, one of only three islands in Maine that serve as home to the Atlantic puffin, also is accessible by boat. Some of the highest tides in the United States occur at Johnson Bay.

West Quoddy Head Light Keepers Association and Visitor Center: in Quoddy Head State Park at 973 S. Lubec Rd., P.O. Box 378, Lubec, ME 04652. **Phone:** (207) 733-2180.

CAMPOBELLO ISLAND, in New Brunswick, Canada, lies across Lubec Narrows and is connected to Lubec by the Franklin D. Roosevelt Memorial Bridge. From 1767 to 1881 the island belonged to the Owen family. The 1835 home of Adm. William F. Owen, who so loved the sea that he reputedly built a quarterdeck on which to pace, is preserved at Deer Point.

James Roosevelt went to Campobello in 1883, when his son Franklin was 1 year old. From then until 1921, FDR spent most of his summers on the island. **Phone:** (877) 851-6663.

Roosevelt Campobello International Park, on Campobello Island in New Brunswick, Canada, is connected to Lubec by the Franklin D. Roosevelt Memorial Bridge. The centerpiece of the 2,802-acre memorial is a 34-room "cottage" occupied 1905-21 by the soon-to-be president and his family. The house contains original furniture, photographs, toys and other items belonging to the Roosevelts.

The visitor center has one exhibit about the Roosevelts' history and another about the friendship between the U.S. and Canada. A 15-minute film tells the story of the Roosevelts' lives on Campobello Island. The park's natural areas feature scenic drives and walking trails along coves, bogs, beaches and cliffs.

Self-guided audio tours are available. **Note:** The park is in the Atlantic time zone, 1 hour ahead of the Eastern time zone. Hours listed here are in Eastern daylight time. **Hours:** Grounds, nature areas and trails daily dawn-dusk, year-round. Visitor center daily 9-5, Memorial Day weekend-Columbus Day; 9-4, day after Columbus Day-Oct. 31. Cottage daily 9-5, Memorial Day weekend-Columbus Day. Last admission 15 minutes before closing. **Cost:** Donations. **Phone:** (506) 752-2922 or (877) 851-6663. *(See ad p. 48.)*

QUODDY HEAD STATE PARK, s. of Lubec, consists of more than 500 acres. The West Quoddy Head Light, on West Quoddy Point, was built in 1808 and rebuilt in 1858. The lighthouse is closed to the public. The park features 5 miles of hiking trails, extensive forests, two bogs and diverse habitat for rare plants. A visitor center/museum in the lighthouse keeper's house is available.

Time: Allow 1 hour minimum. **Hours:** Park daily 9-dusk, May 15-Oct. 15. Visitor center/museum daily 10-4, Memorial Day weekend-Oct. 15. **Cost:** $3; $1 (ages 5-11); free (ages 65+). **Phone:** (207) 733-0911 or (207) 941-4014.

BETSY ROSS LODGING 207/733-8942

Motel $85-$115 **Address:** 61 Water St 04652 **Location:** SR 189, just s on Washington St, then just e; center. **Facility:** 4 units. 3 stories (no elevator), interior corridors. **Terms:** closed 11/1-4/30, 14 day cancellation notice-fee imposed.

CALL M

THE EASTLAND MOTEL   207/733-5501
Motel $70-$85 **Address:** 385 County Rd 04652 **Location:** Jct US 1 and SR 189, 8.4 mi e on SR 189. **Facility:** 20 units. 1 story, interior/exterior corridors.

THE HOME PORT BED & BREAKFAST   207/733-2077
Historic Bed & Breakfast $95-$125 **Address:** 45 Main St 04652 **Location:** Center. **Facility:** This Colonial-style home, which dates from 1880, offers quaint guest rooms and a homey parlor with a large fireplace. The bathrooms vary in size from compact to spacious. 7 units. 2 stories (no elevator), interior corridors. **Terms:** closed 11/1-4/30, 14 day cancellation notice-fee imposed.

THE INN ON THE WHARF   207/733-4400
Country Inn $100-$150 **Address:** 69 Johnson St 04652 **Location:** Oceanfront. Just n of Main St. **Facility:** Offered is spacious rooms and fully equipped suites with kitchens, each with a wonderful ocean view and some with a balcony. 18 units, some two bedrooms and kitchens. 1 story, interior corridors. **Terms:** closed 10/15-5/26, 14 day cancellation notice. **Dining:** Fisherman's Wharf Restaurant & Seafood, see separate listing. **Activities:** boat dock, rental bicycles. *Fee:* charter fishing, massage. **Guest Services:** coin laundry.

PEACOCK HOUSE   207/733-2403
Historic Bed & Breakfast $98-$140 **Address:** 27 Summer St 04652 **Location:** At Church St; center. **Facility:** A very pleasant Victorian home built in 1860 offering well-appointed common areas and comfortable accommodations. 7 units. 3 stories (no elevator), interior corridors. **Parking:** street only. **Terms:** closed 11/1-4/30, 14 day cancellation notice-fee imposed.

WHERE TO EAT

FISHERMAN'S WHARF RESTAURANT & SEAFOOD
                                      207/733-4400
Seafood. Casual Dining. $10-$28 **AAA Inspector Notes:** This seaside restaurant is located in a circa 1900 sardine factory. Guest can enjoy lovely bay views from all of the tables or dine outside on the seasonal deck. Lobster and daily fresh seafood are served in ample portions with French fries or hand-cut potato chips. **Bar:** full bar. **Address:** 69 Johnson St 04652 **Location:** Just n of Main St; in The Inn on The Wharf.

FRANK'S DOCKSIDE RESTAURANT & TAKE OUT
                                      207/733-4484
American. Casual Dining. $7-$18 **AAA Inspector Notes:** Overlooking the harbor and Campobello Island, this casual eatery offers indoor and outdoor dining on a deck overlooking the harbor. Patrons can expect great chowders, fresh seafood, burgers, sandwiches and homemade desserts. **Address:** 20 Water St 04652 **Location:** Center; at harborfront.

UNCLE KIPPY'S RESTAURANT   207/733-2400
American. Casual Dining. $6-$19 **AAA Inspector Notes:** The restaurant is known for its home-style cooking, including such selections as fresh seafood, steaks and comfort foods from burgers to soups and sandwiches. **Bar:** beer & wine. **Address:** 170 Main St 04652 **Location:** Jct US 1 and SR 189, 10 mi e on SR 189.

MACHIAS (H-7) pop. 1,274, elev. 20'

Founded in 1763, Machias (ma-CHY-us) is Maine's oldest town east of the Penobscot River. The name means "bad little falls," in reference to the Machias River's plunge through a deep gorge that lies just behind Main Street. Machias is the center of commerce and government for Washington County; industries include blueberry processing, seafood harvesting and processing, and lumber and wood products. It also is a starting point for hunting and fishing trips into the interior lake country.

As the Revolution became inevitable, patriotic enthusiasm engulfed the citizens of Machias, especially the group who frequented Job Burnham's tavern. In June 1775, after learning that a British warship would arrive to requisition lumber for British barracks, Capt. Jeremiah O'Brien and his cohorts convened at the tavern to plan a Colonial response. The battle resulting from that meeting took place off Machiasport *(see place listing p. 112)* on June 12, 1775—5 days before Bunker Hill.

Roque Bluffs State Park, 7 miles south off US 1 on Roque Bluffs Road, contains Maine's easternmost sandy beach. *See Recreation Areas Chart.*

Machias Bay Area Chamber of Commerce: 85 Main St., Suite 2; P.O. Box 606, Machias, ME 04654. **Phone:** (207) 255-4402.

BURNHAM TAVERN MUSEUM, Colonial Way (SR 192) and Free St., contains articles from the Revolutionary period. Built in 1770, it is one of the oldest structures in eastern Maine and served as the meeting place where plans were formulated for the first naval battle of the Revolutionary War, which resulted in the capture of the British-armed vessel *Margaretta.* Photographs, paintings, antique furniture and Civil War relics also are on display.

Time: Allow 1 hour minimum. **Hours:** Mon.-Fri. 9:30-3:30, mid-June through Sept. 30. **Cost:** $5; $2 (high-school students); $1 (elementary-school students). **Phone:** (207) 255-6930, or (207) 733-4577 in the off-season.

THE BLUEBIRD MOTEL   (207)255-3332
Motel $75-$85 **Address:** 231 Dublin St 04654 **Location:** On US 1, 1 mi s. Located in a rural area. **Facility:** 40 units. 1 story, exterior corridors. **Terms:** 7 day cancellation notice. **Amenities:** high-speed Internet. **Free Special Amenities:** local telephone calls and high-speed Internet.

MACHIAS MOTOR INN   207/255-4861
Motel $84-$124 **Address:** 103 Main St 04654 **Location:** 0.5 mi e on US 1. **Facility:** 38 units, some two bedrooms and kitchens. 2 stories (no elevator), exterior corridors. **Free Special Amenities:** local telephone calls and high-speed Internet.

WHERE TO EAT

THE BLUEBIRD RANCH RESTAURANT   207/255-3351
American. Family Dining. $7-$19 **AAA Inspector Notes:** The large and casual family-style restaurant centers its menu on hearty home-style cooking, including daily specials. Tasty pastries are freshly baked. Service is friendly. **Bar:** full bar. **Address:** 3 E Main St 04654 **Location:** On US 1; center.

HELEN'S RESTAURANT   207/255-8423
◇◇ ◇ American. Family Dining. $7-$18 **AAA Inspector Notes:**
Since 1950, this family restaurant has featured generous servings
and a wide choice of seafood, meat entrées, salad, fish stews, sandwiches, deep-fried items and down-home country cooking. Their specialty is homemade pie made with real whipped cream, including
strawberry and banana cream. **Bar:** full bar. **Address:** 28 E Main St
04654 **Location:** 0.5 mi e on US 1. [B] [L] [D]

HING GARDEN RESTAURANT   207/255-8881
◇◇ ◇ Chinese. Casual Dining. $7-$17 **AAA Inspector Notes:** In
the heart of town, the restaurant presents a menu of well-prepared
Chinese and Polynesian cuisine. Numerous combination plates and
a lunch buffet are available Sunday through Thursday. **Bar:** full bar.
Address: 15 Main St 04654 **Location:** On US 1; downtown.
[L] [D]

MACHIASPORT (H-8)

The first naval engagement of the American
Revolution was fought in Machias Bay on June 12,
1775, when Capt. Jeremiah O'Brien and 40 ill-
armed colonists aboard the small sloop *Unity* captured the English warship *Margaretta.* Among the
casualties was the *Margaretta's* commander, who
died in Machias the next day. The incident gave
weight to the Revolutionary leaders' arguments for
the establishment of a U.S. Navy.

Soon after the beginning of the Revolutionary
War, Fort Machias was built on the bluffs overlooking the Machias River. Strengthened in 1777,
the fort stood until 1814 when the British destroyed
it. The present earthworks, which overlook Machias
Bay, are the remnants of a fort erected on the spot
in 1863; Fort O'Brien is now a state park and historic
site that is open daily dawn to dusk, Memorial Day
through Labor Day.

Quieter now, Machiasport concentrates on such
daily concerns as fishing, boatbuilding and pleasing
its many summer visitors. Rockhounds can while
away the hours seeking jasper pebbles at Jasper
Beach, south on SR 92 near Bucks Harbor.

GATES HOUSE, on SR 92, is an 1810 Federal-style
house. The Marine Room houses an extensive collection of photographs of sea captains, vessels and
sardine carriers. Exhibits include ship models,
caulking tools, a stick barometer and other navigational tools. Several rooms are furnished in period.
Visitors may utilize the genealogical library. **Time:**
Allow 1 hour minimum. **Hours:** Tues.-Fri. 12:30-
4:30, July-Aug.; by appointment rest of year. Phone
ahead to confirm schedule. **Cost:** Donations.
Phone: (207) 255-8461, or (207) 255-8860 in the
off-season.

Cooper House, on SR 92 next to the Gates House,
includes a replica of an 1820s schoolroom and a
post office. The schoolroom contains a collection of
1800s reading materials and textbooks. Antique
tools from the 1800s and old post office artifacts are
displayed. **Time:** Allow 1 hour minimum. **Hours:**
Tues.-Fri. 12:30-4:30, July-Aug.; by appointment
rest of year. Phone ahead to confirm schedule.
Cost: Donations. **Phone:** (207) 255-8461, or (207)
255-8860 in the off-season.

MADAWASKA (B-6) pop. 2,967, elev. 500'

Madawaska, a Malecite Indian word meaning "por-
cupine," was settled by Acadian refugees from Nova
Scotia in 1785. The Acadian Cross Historic Shrine off
US 1 commemorates the first Acadian landing in the
St. John Valley. On the site of the shrine is the Tante
Blanche Museum, which depicts the Acadians and the
founding of the St. John Valley.

Greater Madawaska Chamber of Commerce: 356
Main St., Suite 101, P.O. Box 144, Madawaska, ME
04756. **Phone:** (207) 728-7000.

TWIN RIVERS PAPERS, on Bridge Ave., makes
paper from pulp produced across the river in Ed-
mundston, New Brunswick, and sent by pipeline to
Madawaska. Guided 30- to 40-minute tours allow
visitors to explore the mill, which produces a variety
of papers on five paper machines and is one of the
world's largest producers of specialty papers.

Note: Ages 0-11, cameras and open-toed shoes
are not permitted. **Hours:** Tours Mon., Wed. and Fri.
at 10 and 1. **Cost:** Free. Reservations are required
24 hours in advance. **Phone:** (207) 728-8200 for
tour reservations.

MEDWAY

KATAHDIN SHADOWS MOTEL   207/746-5162
◇ Motel. Rates not provided. **Address:** 2166 Medway Rd 04460
Location: I-95 exit 244, 1.5 mi w on SR 157. **Facility:** 10 units. 1
story, exterior corridors. *Bath:* shower only. **Pool(s):** outdoor. **Activities:** boat dock, fishing, snowmobiling.
[⊹] [◄] [🖵] [▤]

MILFORD

MILFORD MOTEL ON THE RIVER   (207)827-3200
◇   **Address:** 174 Main Rd 04461 **Loca-**
Motel   **tion:** 0.5 mi n on US 2. **Facility:** 22
$72-$135   units, some two bedrooms, efficiencies
            and kitchens. 2 stories (no elevator),
            interior/exterior corridors. **Terms:** 3 day
cancellation notice-fee imposed. **Guest Services:** coin laundry.
Free Special Amenities: high-speed Internet and use of on-
premises laundry facilities.
[SAVE] [◄] [▤] [🖵] [▤] / SOME UNITS [🐾]

MILLINOCKET (F-5) pop. 4,466, elev. 359'

RECREATIONAL ACTIVITIES
White-water Rafting

• **New England Outdoor Center** is at 30 Twin
  Pines Rd. Other activities are offered. **Hours:**
  Daily year-round. **Phone:** (207) 723-5438 or (800)
  766-7238. [⊹]

5 LAKES LODGE   207/723-5045
◇◇◇ **Bed & Breakfast.** Rates not provided. **Address:** Marina
Dr (Fire Rd #4) 04462 **Location:** Waterfront. On SR 11, 7 mi s of
center. Located on South Twin Lake. **Facility:** The delightful rooms at
this spacious lodge feature upscale appointments, and each guest-
room offers lovely views of Mt. Katahdin across the lake. 5 units. 2
stories (no elevator), interior corridors. **Terms:** age restrictions may
apply. **Activities:** sauna, canoeing, boat dock, exercise room. *Fee:*
boats, snowmobiling. [◄] [✕] [✦] [▤] [🖵]

BAXTER PARK INN   (207)723-9777

▼▼ ▼▼ **Hotel** $79-$119 **Address:** 935 Central St 04462 **Location:** 0.8 mi e on SR 11 and 157. Located in a commercial area. **Facility:** 48 units. 2 stories (no elevator), interior corridors. **Terms:** cancellation fee imposed. **Pool(s):** heated indoor. **Activities:** whirlpools, limited exercise equipment. **Guest Services:** coin laundry.

[icons] FEE 🐕 FEE 🔲 FEE 🖼

WHERE TO EAT

CHANTERELLE'S AT THE RIVER DRIVERS PUB
                                                                 207/723-5523

▼▼▼ ▼ Regional American. Casual Dining. $12-$26 **AAA Inspector Notes:** In the New England Outdoor Center, this restaurant has a casual atmosphere and rustic décor bordering Millinocket Lake with a lovely view of Mt. Katahdin. The often-changing menu lists fish, chicken, meat and vegetarian entrées. All dishes are made to order with fresh local ingredients. **Bar:** full bar. **Reservations:** suggested. **Address:** Black Cat Rd 04462 **Location:** I-95 exit 244, 8 mi n on SR 157; in Twin Pines Camps Cabins. [L] [D]

SCOOTIC IN RESTAURANT   207/723-4566

▼▼ ▼▼ American. Casual Dining. $6-$22 **AAA Inspector Notes:** In the heart of town, this spacious restaurant with large booths and table seating serves ample portions of home-style fare, from burgers and pizzas to steaks and seafood, in a sports bar-theme setting. **Bar:** full bar. **Address:** 70 Penobscot Ave 04462 **Location:** Corner of Poplar St. [L] [D]

MONHEGAN ISLAND (J-5)

Tiny Monhegan Island, 9 miles off the Maine coast, has the highest cliffs on the New England shore. Artists who flocked to the 1.5-mile-long island during the late 19th century are credited with popularizing it. Many working studios are open to the public.

Lobster and fishing boats, as well as pleasure craft, keep the harbor busy all year. A 1-day excursion from Boothbay Harbor *(see place listing p. 67)* and New Harbor *(see place listing p. 114)* also visits the island. Contrasting with the bustle of Monhegan's port is a wildlife sanctuary containing more than 600 varieties of wildflowers and some 200 kinds of birds, such as peregrine falcons, ospreys and marsh hawks.

Other peaceful retreats on the island include Cathedral Woods and the 160-foot cliffs Black Head and White Head. Nine miles of hiking trails lead to scenic points on the island; comfortable shoes are recommended, as some trails are fairly rugged. Maritime exhibits and flora, fauna and marine life collections are displayed at a museum on Lighthouse Hill. The lighthouse was built in 1824.

Regular passenger service between Monhegan Island and Port Clyde aboard the *Laura B.* and the *Elizabeth Ann* is offered daily, May through October; the boats run Monday, Wednesday and Friday, rest of year. Cars are not permitted on the ferries. Round-trip fare $32; $18 (ages 2-12); $5 (pets). One-way fare $20; $18 (ages 2-12); $5 (pets). Reservations are recommended. Contact Monhegan Boat Line, P.O. Box 238, Port Clyde, ME 04855; phone (207) 372-8848.

A ferry service between Monhegan Island and New Harbor departs daily, mid-June through Sept. 28; Wed., Sat. and Sun., mid-May to mid-June and early Oct. to mid-Oct., with additional departures

Memorial Day and Columbus Day weekends. Round-trip fare $33; $18 (ages 3-11). One-way fare $16.50; $9 (ages 3-11). Reservations are required. Contact Hardy Boat Cruises, P.O. Box 326, 132 SR 32, New Harbor, ME 04554; phone (207) 677-2026 or (800) 278-3346. Other cruise options are offered *(see p. 114).*

MONMOUTH (I-3) elev. 265'

The Cochnewagon Indians were the first inhabitants of the Monmouth area, though by the 1800s they were virtually wiped out by the arrival of white settlers, disease and war. Incorporated in 1792, the town was named after the Battle of Monmouth, N.J., which involved one of its first citizens, Gen. Henry Dearborn.

Cumston Hall, on Main Street, is a beautiful Victorian opera house ornamented with frescoes and murals. It is home to the Theater at Monmouth, a professional repertory company that performs Shakespeare plays and other classics July through September with special performances in May, June and October through December; phone (207) 933-9999.

MONMOUTH MUSEUM, in the center of town at 751 Main St., is a complex of five buildings that recreates various aspects of 19th-century rural Maine. The structures include a stencil shop, blacksmith shop, carriage house and freight shed containing farm equipment and other artifacts. The five-room Blossom House is estimated to have been built in 1802. Also on site are genealogical records.

Children must be accompanied by an adult. **Hours:** Guided tours Wed.-Sun. 1-4, Memorial Day-Labor Day; by appointment rest of year. **Cost:** $5; $1 (children). **Phone:** (207) 933-2287.

NAPLES (J-2) pop. 428, elev. 276'
• Hotels p. 114

On the northwestern edge of Sebago Lake, Naples is the location of the Songo Lock, opened in 1830 for transportation along the 42-mile canal system to Portland. The lock now links the north end of Long Lake and Sebago Lake. The hand-operated gate is the only remnant of the old lock system connecting western Maine with the coast.

Such recreational opportunities as boating, windsurfing, seaplane rides and mail boat runs are popular in Naples, an area characterized by rolling hills and crystal-blue lakes. The causeway offers the opportunity for striking views of Mount Washington in the White Mountains of New Hampshire.

The old-fashioned riverboat *Songo River Queen II,* berthed at the causeway in the center of town on US 302, offers sightseeing cruises early May to mid-October; phone (207) 693-6861.

Sebago Lakes Region Chamber of Commerce: 747 Roosevelt Tr., P.O. Box 1015, Windham, ME 04062. **Phone:** (207) 693-3285 or (207) 892-8265.

AUGUSTUS BOVE HOUSE   (207)693-6365
▼▼▼ **Historic Bed & Breakfast** $125-$250 **Address:** 11 Sebago Rd 04055 **Location:** Corner of US 302 and SR 114. **Facility:** Built in 1830, the inn was one of the first summer lodgings in the area. Across the street from Long Lake, the inn offers rooms decorated in a mix of antiques and Victorian-style reproductions. 10 units. 3 stories (no elevator), interior corridors. *Bath:* shower only. **Terms:** age restrictions may apply, 45 day cancellation notice-fee imposed.

📶 ✕ / SOME UNITS FEE 🐕 🛏 💻

NEWCASTLE (J-4) pop. 667, elev. 91'

DODGE POINT PUBLIC RESERVED LAND, 3.5 mi. s. on River Rd. to Fire Lane A31, preserves 521 acres of habitat along the Damariscotta River. An interpretive trail relates educational information about the local environment.

This is a day-use area only; camping is not permitted. Swimming, fishing and ice skating are permitted. Hiking and cross-country skiing trails wind through the property. **Note:** Exercise caution; hunting is permitted on the property, yet hunters are not allowed to fire a weapon within 300 feet of a marked trail. *See Recreation Areas Chart.*. **Hours:** Preserve open daily dawn-dusk. **Cost:** Free. **Phone:** (207) 778-8231. ✕

ST. PATRICK'S CHURCH is 2.5 mi. n. of US 1 on Academy Hill Rd. Although the cemetery dates from 1760, the church itself was built in 1808 and is said to be the oldest active Catholic church in New England. A larger sanctuary space now adjoins the original structure. **Hours:** Daily 9-3. Phone ahead to confirm schedule. **Cost:** Donations. **Phone:** (207) 563-3240.

NEWCASTLE INN   207/563-5685
▼▼▼ **Historic Bed & Breakfast** $155-$275 **Address:** 60 River Rd 04553 **Location:** Jct US 1 and River Rd, 0.5 mi nw. **Facility:** This property dates from 1840 and has been in operation as an inn since 1920. All rooms feature elegant bedding and soft seating. 14 units. 3 stories (no elevator), interior/exterior corridors. **Terms:** 2 night minimum stay - seasonal and/or weekends, 14 day cancellation notice, 21 day 8/1-8/31-fee imposed.

🍽 📶 ✕ ☎ / SOME UNITS FEE 🐕 ⓦ

WHERE TO EAT

NEWCASTLE PUBLICK HOUSE   207/563-3434
▼▼ American. Casual Dining. $8-$24 **AAA Inspector Notes:** New to the area, this eatery serves tasty pub fare of burgers, baked macaroni and cheese, bangers and mash, and fish and chips. The decor is attractive, with old-fashioned, wide-board wood floors and a mural depicting the local shore of Newcastle. Outdoor seating is available. **Bar:** full bar. **Address:** 52 Main St 04553 **Location:** 0.5 mi e of US 1. Ⓛ Ⓓ

NEWFIELD (K-2)

Apple orchards, farms and summer cottages adorn the gently rolling, pond-dotted terrain around Newfield. The township was settled in 1778 and known as Washington Plantation until its incorporation in 1794. The village flourished in the 19th century; many of the buildings from that time are incorporated in the 19th Century Willowbrook Village *(see attraction listing)* restoration.

19TH CENTURY WILLOWBROOK VILLAGE, off SR 11 at 70 Elm St., is a 25-structure complex depicting 19th-century rural New England life. Visitors may tour two historic houses and their barns, view 60 restored carriages and sleighs and a working 1894 Armitage Herschell carousel. A Saturday farmer and artisan market is held May through November.

Time: Allow 3 hours minimum. **Hours:** Thurs.-Mon. 10-5, Memorial Day weekend-Columbus Day. **Cost:** $10; $7.50 (ages 65+); $5 (ages 6-18). **Phone:** (207) 793-2784. 🍴

NEW GLOUCESTER (J-3)

SABBATHDAY LAKE SHAKER VILLAGE, 8 mi. n. off I-95 exit 63 on SR 26, is said to be the last active Shaker village; it dates from 1782. Most of the late 18th- and early 19th-century buildings are of singular Shaker design and contain Shaker furniture, ingenious inventions, handicrafts and workshops. Special events are held throughout the season. Shaker Sunday meetings also are open to visitors.

Tours: Guided tours are available. **Time:** Allow 2 hours minimum. **Hours:** Mon.-Sat. 10-4:30, Memorial Day-Columbus Day. Tours are given at 10:30, 11:30, 12:30, 1:30, 2:30 and 3:15. **Cost:** Free. Guided tour $7; $2 (ages 6-12). **Phone:** (207) 926-4597.

NEW HARBOR (J-4)

HARDY BOAT CRUISES depart from Shaw's Wharf at 132 SR 32 for tours of the area's picturesque coastal waters. Offered are 1.5-hour puffin-watching cruises with a National Audubon Society naturalist to Eastern Egg Rock, 1-hour narrated seal-watching cruises, 1-hour lighthouse cruises to Pemaquid Point and 1.5-hour fall coastal cruises. Ferry service to Monhegan Island is available.

Hours: Puffin watches depart daily at 5:30 p.m., early June-late Aug.; Wed. and Sat.-Sun. at 5:30 p.m., late May-early June. Seal watches depart Tues.-Wed. and Fri.-Sun. at noon, mid-June through Labor Day; Sat.-Sun. at noon, late May to mid-June and day after Labor Day-Columbus Day. Lighthouse cruises depart Mon. and Thurs. at noon, mid-June through Labor Day. Fall coastal cruises depart Tues., Thurs. and Sat. at 4:45, Labor Day-Columbus Day. Monhegan Island ferry departs from New Harbor daily at 9 and 2 and departs from the island at 10:15 and 3:15, early June-late Sept.; departure times vary late May-early June and in Oct.

Cost: Puffin watch $25; $15 (ages 3-11). Seal watch and lighthouse cruise each $15; $10 (ages 3-11). Fall coastal cruise $18; $12 (ages 3-11). Monhegan Island ferry round-trip fare $33; $18 (ages 3-11). Reservations are recommended. **Parking:** $3 (cash only). **Phone:** (207) 677-2026 or (800) 278-3346. 🐕

SHAW'S FISH & LOBSTER WHARF RESTAURANT   207/677-2200

◆ Seafood. Quick Serve. $6-$22 **AAA Inspector Notes:** You'll be right on top of a working harbor at this popular, picturesque dockside restaurant that serves lobster (of course), steamed clams, scallops and shrimp as well as meatloaf, fish cakes, stews, roast turkey and sandwiches. Outdoor deck dining is also available. **Bar:** full bar. **Address:** 129 SR 32 04554 **Location:** Jct SR 130 and 32, 0.5 mi ne. [L] [D] [✕]

NEWRY (I-2) elev. 642'

In October thousands flock to the Sunday River Ski Resort for the 🏃 North American Wife Carrying Championship. Teams comprised of one male and one female (usually a husband and wife) race—with one teammate carrying the other—through a 278-yard course. The winning team goes home with a supply of beer equal to the woman's weight and a wad of cash valued at five times her weight.

RECREATIONAL ACTIVITIES
Skiing

- **Sunday River Ski Resort** is off US 2 at 15 South Ridge Rd. Other activities are offered. **Hours:** Daily, Nov.-Apr. **Phone:** (207) 824-3000.

NORTH AMITY (E-7) elev. 656'

A.E. HOWELL WILDLIFE CONSERVATION CENTER AND SPRUCE ACRES REFUGE, 101 Lycette Rd., consists of more than 64 acres featuring 5.5 miles of marked walking trails. On guided tours visitors may see a variety of wild animals, including hawks, owls, moose, deer, wolves and coyotes. The refuge also is home to Baxter, a 618-pound black bear; Dolly the cougar; and Bell, reputedly the oldest living captive bald eagle in Maine.

A wildlife collection by Bill Silliker Jr., a renowned Maine photographer dubbed the Mooseman of Baxter Park, is on display. An environmental learning center and a library are available. **Time:** Allow 1 hour minimum. **Hours:** Tours Mon.-Sat. 10-4 by appointment, May 15-Oct. 31. Additional hours may be available. Phone ahead to confirm schedule. **Cost:** $10; free (ages 0-15). Reservations are required 24 hours in advance to enter the center and refuge. **Phone:** (207) 532-6880. [🏕]

NORTHEAST HARBOR (I-6)
- **Hotels & Restaurants map & index p. 49**
- **Part of Acadia National Park area — see map p. 38**

Located on the southern end of Mount Desert Island at the mouth of Somes Sound, this bustling village is a major yachting center and popular summer vacation spot. The Great Harbor Maritime Museum, 124 Main St., features boat models, photographs and changing exhibits relating to the region's seafaring history; phone (207) 276-5262.

THUYA GARDEN is accessed via the Asticou Terraces gravel parking area, 1 mi. w. on Harborside

Rd. to jct. SR 198, then 1 mi. s. on SR 3. The .25-mile Terrace Trail affords beautiful views of Northeast Harbor from several terraces and lookout points along the granite hillside. At the top, semiformal English gardens, indigenous eastern Maine woodlands, winding paths and a reflecting pool comprise Thuya Garden.

The Asticou Terraces trail is fairly steep and includes stairs. Comfortable walking shoes are recommended. A handicap accessible parking lot can be reached via Thuya Drive. **Time:** Allow 1 hour, 30 minutes minimum. **Hours:** Daily dawn-dusk, May-Oct. **Cost:** $5. **Phone:** (207) 276-3727.

ASTICOU INN   (207)276-3344   [7]

◆◆ Hotel $175-$380 **Address:** 15 Peabody Dr 04662 **Location:** Jct SR 3 and Peabody Dr; center. **Facility:** 48 units, some two bedrooms and efficiencies. 2-4 stories, interior corridors. **Terms:** closed 10/13-5/23, 2 night minimum stay - weekends, 31 day cancellation notice-fee imposed, resort fee. **Pool(s):** heated outdoor. **Activities:** tennis court, rental bicycles. **Guest Services:** valet laundry.
[🍽] [🍸] [🏊] [📶] [✕] / SOME UNITS [✕] [W] [⊞]

KIMBALL TERRACE INN   (207)276-3383   [8]

◆◆ Hotel $75-$225
Address: 10 Huntington Rd 04662 **Location:** Overlooking Municipal Pier. **Facility:** 70 units. 2-3 stories, exterior corridors. **Terms:** closed 10/28-5/13, 7 day cancellation notice-fee imposed.
Dining: Watermark Restaurant & Lounge, see separate listing. **Pool(s):** outdoor. **Free Special Amenities:** high-speed Internet. [SAVE] [🍽] [🍸] [🏊] [📶] [✕]

▬▬▬ **WHERE TO EAT** ▬▬▬

WATERMARK RESTAURANT & LOUNGE   207/276-5857   [6]

◆◆ American. Family Dining. $8-$21 **AAA Inspector Notes:** The Watermark offers family dining in an open and spacious room overlooking the splendid marina, harbor and hills. In season, choose the patio for a terrific view. The menu's seafood, beef and some Italian dishes are prepared with creativity and skill. **Bar:** full bar. **Address:** 10 Huntington Rd 04662 **Location:** Overlooking Municipal Pier; in Kimball Terrace Inn. [B] [L] [D]

NORTHPORT
- **Restaurants p. 116**

POINT LOOKOUT RESORT & CONFERENCE CENTER
(207)789-2000

◆◆◆ Resort Cottage $129-$449
Address: 67 Atlantic Hwy 04849 **Location:** 4 mi s on US 1; at Lincolnville town line. **Facility:** These well-appointed one-, two- and three-bedroom pine cottages sit in a mature forest setting on the side of a mountain. 106 cabins. 1 story, exterior corridors. **Bath:** shower only. **Terms:** check-in 4 pm, 3 day cancellation notice-fee imposed. **Dining:** 2 restaurants. **Activities:** 2 tennis courts, hiking trails, playground, sports court, basketball, exercise room. **Fee:** game room, massage. **Guest Services:** coin laundry. (See ad p. 77.)
[SAVE] [ECO] [🍽] [🍸] [BIZ] [📶] [✕] [📶] [⊞] [☐] / SOME UNITS [FEE] [🛏]

WHERE TO EAT

DOS AMIGOS MEXICAN RESTAURANT & CANTINA
207/338-5775

▼▼ ▼▼ Mexican. Casual Dining. $10-$20 **AAA Inspector Notes:** The restaurant has colorful dining rooms and a pleasant seasonal patio that reflect a Baja Mexican theme. On the menu are many preparations of fresh seafood. **Bar:** full bar. **Address:** 144 Bayside Rd 04849 **Location:** On US 1, 3.6 mi s of jct US 3.

L D

OCEAN PARK
• Hotels & Restaurants map & index p. 98

BILLOWHOUSE OCEANFRONT MOTEL & GUESTHOUSE **33**

▼▼♦ Historic Hotel $115-$300 **Address:** 2 Temple Ave 04064 **Location:** Oceanfront. Jct SR 9 (E Grand Ave), just se. **Facility:** Located in Ocean Park, a small summer community established in 1881, this oceanfront property includes a Victorian-era inn as well as a motel. 13 units, some efficiencies and kitchens. 4 stories (no elevator), interior/exterior corridors. **Terms:** closed 1/1-6/15, 7 night minimum stay - seasonal, 30 day cancellation notice-fee imposed. **Activities:** limited beach access. **Guest Services:** complimentary laundry. 📶 ✕ 📶 📶 💻

OGUNQUIT   (L-2) elev. 20'
• Restaurants p. 121
• Hotels & Restaurants map & index p. 98

Ogunquit was called "beautiful place by the sea" by the Abenaki Indians, who were early inhabitants of this region. The town is 15 miles north of the New Hampshire border, with a 3-mile sandy beach stretching northward and more than a mile of picturesque rocky shore to the south. The Ogunquit River, a 2-mile tidewater river, parallels the beach and is separated from it by sand dunes.

Shore Road leads to Perkins Cove, a quaint working harbor with a footbridge spanning its entrance. Perkins Cove offers specialty shops, waterfront restaurants and art galleries as well as fishing, lobstering and whale-watching opportunities. The "Marginal Way" is a mile-long scenic footpath along the granite shoreline leading from Perkins Cove to Ogunquit's village and beach.

Ogunquit is a popular summer resort, especially among artists. The Village Center has shops, theaters and parks lining its streets. The Ogunquit Playhouse, a half-mile south of town on US 1, has presented exceptional summer theater since the 1930s; phone (207) 646-5511. Art exhibits are held throughout the summer months at the Ogunquit Museum of American Art *(see attraction listing)* and the Barn Gallery. Trolleys offer transportation around town from June to October.

Ogunquit Chamber of Commerce: 36 Main St., P.O. Box 2289, Ogunquit, ME 03907. **Phone:** (207) 646-2939 or (207) 646-1279.

FINESTKIND SCENIC CRUISES depart from Barnacle Billy's Dock in Perkins Cove at 75 Perkins Cove Rd. A number of cruises are offered, including a lobster boat trip with a narrated lobstering demonstration, 1.5-hour lighthouse sightseeing trips and sailing cruises. Breakfast and evening cocktail cruises are offered in season.

Time: Allow 1 hour minimum. **Hours:** Lobstering cruises depart about every hour Mon.-Sat. 9:30-3, July 1-Labor Day; daily at 10, 11, 1 and 2, May-June and day after Labor Day to mid-Oct. Lighthouse trips depart daily at 10, noon, 2 and 4, May 1 to mid-Oct. Sailing cruises depart daily at 11, 2 and 4, May 1 to mid-Oct. Breakfast cruise departs daily at 9, July 1-Labor Day. Cocktail cruises depart daily at 5:45, 7 and 8:15, July 1-Labor Day; at 5:45, May-June and day after Labor Day to mid-Oct. Departure times may vary due to weather; phone ahead.

Cost: Lobstering cruise $16; $8 (ages 4-11). Lighthouse trip $24; $12 (ages 4-11). Sailing cruise $30. Breakfast cruise $24; $12 (ages 4-11). Cocktail cruise $16; $8 (ages 4-11). Fares may vary; phone ahead. **Phone:** (207) 646-5227.

🔷 **OGUNQUIT MUSEUM OF AMERICAN ART** is s.e. of Perkins Cove at 543 Shore Rd. The museum showcases some 1,800 works of such renowned American artists as Charles Burchfield, Marsden Hartley, Robert Henri, Rockwell Kent, Walt Kuhn, Gaston Lachaise, Reginald Marsh and William Zorach.

Highlights include a comprehensive American Modernism collection featuring pieces by artists who were part of the Ogunquit Art Colony, which was established in the 1890s. Changing special exhibits spotlight other nationally known American artists. The main gallery's glass wall offers stunning views of the Atlantic Ocean. Lush gardens, alluring coastline, a reflection pond, sculptures and sheltered benches allow visitors an opportunity to unwind on the 3-acre grounds. **Time:** Allow 1 hour minimum. **Hours:** Daily 10-5, May-Oct. Phone ahead to confirm schedule. **Cost:** $10; $9 (ages 60+ and students with ID); free (ages 0-11). **Phone:** (207) 646-4909.

THE *SILVERLINING* departs from Perkins Cove, 1 mi. s. on Shore Rd. The 42-foot yacht, a 1939 Hinckley sloop, takes visitors on 1.5- and 2-hour excursions along the Ogunquit coastline. **Time:** Allow 1 hour, 30 minutes minimum. **Hours:** Departures daily at 9:30, 11:30, 2 and 4:30, Memorial Day weekend-early Oct. (also at 6:30 p.m., Memorial Day weekend-Labor Day). **Cost:** The 1.5-hour cruise $35. The 2-hour cruise $40. Reservations are recommended. **Phone:** (207) 646-9800.

ADMIRAL'S INN   (207)646-7093 **92**

▼▼▼ Hotel $59-$279 **Address:** 87 Main St 03907 **Location:** Just s on US 1. **Facility:** 52 units, some kitchens. 2 stories, interior/exterior corridors. **Terms:** 14 day cancellation notice-fee imposed. **Amenities:** high-speed Internet. **Pool(s):** 2 heated outdoor. **Activities:** sauna, whirlpools, exercise room. **Fee:** massage. **Guest Services:** coin laundry.

ECO 🛏 BIZ 📶 ✕ 📶 💻 / SOME UNITS 📶

THE ANCHORAGE BY THE SEA   207/646-9384 **90**

▼▼▼ Hotel $89-$359 **Address:** 125 Shore Rd 03907 **Location:** Oceanfront. 0.5 mi s of US 1. **Facility:** 241 units, some condominiums. 2-3 stories, interior/exterior corridors. **Terms:** 2-5 night minimum stay - seasonal and/or weekends, 14 day cancellation notice-fee imposed. **Amenities:** safes. **Pool(s):** heated outdoor, heated indoor. **Activities:** sauna, whirlpool.

🍽 🍸 🛏 ♿ BIZ 📶 ✕ 📶 / SOME UNITS 📶 💻

(See map & index p. 98.)

THE BEACHMERE INN   (207)646-2021

Hotel
$95-$425

Address: 62 Beachmere Pl 03907 **Location:** Jct US 1, just se on Shore Rd, then just e. **Facility:** 73 units, some efficiencies and houses. 1-3 stories, interior/exterior corridors. **Terms:** 3-7 night minimum stay - seasonal and/or weekends, 21 day cancellation notice-fee imposed. **Activities:** sauna, limited beach access, fishing, exercise room. *Fee:* massage. **Guest Services:** coin laundry.

COLONIAL VILLAGE RESORT   (207)646-2794 79

Hotel
$69-$292

Address: 548 Main St 03907 **Location:** 0.8 mi n on US 1. **Facility:** 70 units, some two bedrooms, three bedrooms, efficiencies, kitchens and cottages. 2 stories (no elevator), exterior corridors. **Terms:** closed 11/1-3/31, 7 day cancellation notice-fee imposed. **Pool(s):** outdoor, heated indoor. **Activities:** whirlpools, boating, tennis court, limited exercise equipment. *Fee:* game room. **Guest Services:** coin laundry. **Free Special Amenities:** continental breakfast and use of on-premises laundry facilities.

THE DUNES ON THE WATERFRONT   (207)646-2612 80

Cottage
$105-$510

Address: 518 Main St 03907 **Location:** Waterfront. 0.8 mi n on US 1. **Facility:** Attractive guest rooms and New England-style cottages border the Ogunquit Tidal River, offering nice water views. The gorgeous grounds offer a peaceful setting. 36 units, some two bedrooms and cottages. 1-2 stories (no elevator), exterior corridors. **Terms:** closed 10/29-4/25, check-in 4 pm, 3-14 night minimum stay - seasonal and/or weekends, 21 day cancellation notice-fee imposed. **Amenities:** high-speed Internet (fee). **Pool(s):** heated outdoor. **Activities:** boating, boat dock, playground, sports court, shuffleboard.

New England style cottages and guestrooms, most with great views of the river, dunes & the ocean.

GORGES GRANT HOTEL   (207)646-7003 82

Hotel
$99-$289

Address: 449 Main St 03907 **Location:** 0.3 mi n on US 1. **Facility:** 81 units. 2 stories (no elevator), interior corridors. **Pool(s):** heated outdoor, heated indoor. **Activities:** whirlpool, exercise room. **Guest Services:** coin laundry. **Free Special Amenities:** newspaper and high-speed Internet. *(See ad p. 118.)*

▼ See AAA listing p. 118 ▼

(See map & index p. 98.)

THE GRAND HOTEL (207)646-1231 **94**
▼▼▼ Hotel $69-$299 **Address:** 276 Shore Rd 03907 **Location:** Jct US 1, 0.7 mi se. **Facility:** 28 units. 3 stories, interior corridors. **Terms:** closed 11/16-3/31, 2-3 night minimum stay - seasonal and/or weekends, 14 day cancellation notice-fee imposed. **Pool(s):** heated indoor. **Activities:** whirlpool.

JUNIPER HILL INN (207)646-4501 **84**
▼▼▼▼

Hotel
$92-$274

Address: 336 Main St 03907 **Location:** 0.3 mi n on US 1. **Facility:** 101 units. 2 stories (no elevator), interior/exterior corridors. **Pool(s):** 2 heated outdoor, heated indoor. **Activities:** whirlpools, exercise room. *Fee:* game room. **Guest Services:** coin laundry. **Free Special Amenities: continental breakfast and high-speed Internet.** *(See ad p. 117.)*

(See map & index p. 98.)

Plan. Map. Go.
TripTik® Travel Planner

Where premier mapping technology meets complete travel information.
Only on AAA.com and CAA.ca.

(See map & index p. 98.)

MARINER RESORT MOTEL (207)646-5931 **76**
▽▽ **Hotel** $59-$249 **Address:** 734 Main St 03907 **Location:** 1.3 mi n on US 1. **Facility:** 55 units. 2 stories (no elevator), exterior corridors. **Terms:** closed 10/22-4/26, 2-3 night minimum stay - seasonal and/or weekends, 7 day cancellation notice-fee imposed. **Pool(s):** outdoor, heated indoor. **Activities:** whirlpool, volleyball, exercise room.

MEADOWMERE RESORT (207)646-9661 **93**
▽▽▽ Hotel $89-$499

Address: 74 Main St 03907 **Location:** 0.5 mi s on US 1. **Facility:** 145 units, some two bedrooms, efficiencies and kitchens. 3 stories, interior/exterior corridors. **Terms:** 2-3 night minimum stay - seasonal and/or weekends, 7 day cancellation notice-fee imposed. **Pool(s):** outdoor, heated indoor. **Activities:** saunas, whirlpools, steamrooms. *Fee:* game room, massage. **Guest Services:** coin laundry. **Free Special Amenities: continental breakfast and high-speed Internet.** *(See ad p. 119.)*

THE MILESTONE (207)646-4562 **78**
▽▽▽ Hotel $59-$239

Address: 687 Main St 03907 **Location:** On US 1, 1 mi n. **Facility:** 70 units. 1-2 stories (no elevator), exterior corridors. **Terms:** closed 10/28-4/10. **Pool(s):** heated outdoor. **Activities:** whirlpool, shuffleboard, exercise room. **Guest Services:** coin laundry. **Free Special Amenities:** continental breakfast and high-speed Internet. *(See ad this page.)*

OGUNQUIT RESORT MOTEL 207/646-8336 **77**
▽▽▽ **Hotel** $54-$399 **Address:** 719 Main St 03907 **Location:** 1.3 mi n on US 1. **Facility:** 95 units, some two bedrooms. 2 stories (no elevator), interior/exterior corridors. **Terms:** 2 night minimum stay - seasonal and/or weekends, 7 day cancellation notice-fee imposed. **Amenities:** *Some:* safes. **Pool(s):** heated outdoor. **Activities:** whirlpool, exercise room. *Fee:* game room. **Guest Services:** coin laundry.

PINK BLOSSOMS FAMILY RESORT (207)646-7397 **91**
▽▽▽ **Hotel** $60-$419 **Address:** 154 Shore Rd 03907 **Location:** Jct US 1, 0.6 mi se. **Facility:** 30 units, some kitchens. 2-3 stories (no elevator), interior/exterior corridors. **Terms:** closed 10/28-4/15, 3-7 night minimum stay - seasonal and/or weekends, 30 day cancellation notice-fee imposed. **Pool(s):** heated outdoor. **Activities:** whirlpool, tennis court, playground.

SEA CHAMBERS 207/646-9311 **87**
▽▽ **Hotel** $74-$269 **Address:** 67 Shore Rd 03907 **Location:** Oceanfront. Jct US 1, just se. **Facility:** 46 units, some efficiencies and kitchens. 2 stories (no elevator), exterior corridors. **Terms:** closed 12/16-3/25, 3-4 night minimum stay - seasonal and/or weekends, 14 day cancellation notice-fee imposed. **Pool(s):** heated outdoor. **Activities:** fishing. **Guest Services:** coin laundry.

SEAFARER MOTEL 207/646-4040 **95**
▽▽ **Motel.** Rates not provided. **Address:** 35 Main St 03907 **Location:** 0.5 mi s on US 1. **Facility:** 80 units, some efficiencies. 2 stories (no elevator), exterior corridors. **Pool(s):** outdoor, heated indoor. **Guest Services:** coin laundry.

SEA VIEW MOTEL 207/646-7064 **83**
▽▽ **Motel.** Rates not provided. **Address:** 417 Main St 03907 **Location:** 0.3 mi n on US 1. **Facility:** 43 units, some houses. 3 stories (no elevator), exterior corridors. **Pool(s):** heated outdoor. **Activities:** whirlpool.

▼ *See AAA listing this page* ▼

(See map & index p. 98.)

SPARHAWK OCEANFRONT RESORT

207/646-5562 **88**

Hotel
$120-$330

Address: 85 Shore Rd 03907 **Location:** Oceanfront. Jct US 1, just se. **Facility:** 88 units, some two bedrooms, efficiencies and cottages. 2-3 stories (no elevator), interior/exterior corridors. **Terms:** closed 10/29-4/10, 2-7 night minimum stay - seasonal and/or weekends, 14 day cancellation notice-fee imposed. **Pool(s):** heated outdoor. **Activities:** tennis court. **Free Special Amenities: expanded continental breakfast and high-speed Internet.** SAVE

STAGE RUN BY THE SEA

207/646-4823 **81**

Motel $49-$209 **Address:** 2 Kingfield Ave 03907 **Location:** US 1, 0.6 mi n of center of village. **Facility:** 24 units. 2 stories (no elevator), exterior corridors. **Terms:** closed 10/27-4/3, 10 day cancellation notice-fee imposed. **Pool(s):** heated outdoor.

STUDIO EAST MOTOR INN

207/646-7297 **85**

Motel. Rates not provided. **Address:** 267 Main St 03907 **Location:** On US 1; center. **Facility:** 45 units, some efficiencies. 2 stories (no elevator), exterior corridors. **Activities:** whirlpool.

BIZ   /SOME UNITS FEE

TERRACE BY THE SEA

207/646-3232 **86**

Hotel
$69-$300

Address: 23 Wharf Ln 03907 **Location:** Oceanfront. Jct US 1, just se on Shore Rd, then just e. **Facility:** 61 units, some two bedrooms, efficiencies and kitchens. 2 stories (no elevator), interior/exterior corridors. **Terms:** closed 12/15-3/28, 2-4 night minimum stay - seasonal and/or weekends, 14 day cancellation notice-fee imposed. **Pool(s):** heated outdoor. **Free Special Amenities: expanded continental breakfast and high-speed Internet.** SAVE

TOWNE LYNE MOTEL

207/646-2955 **75**

Motel
$45-$179

Address: 747 Main St 03907 **Location:** 1.2 mi n on US 1. **Facility:** 20 units, some efficiencies. 1 story, exterior corridors. **Terms:** 2 night minimum stay - weekends, 14 day cancellation notice-fee imposed. **Free Special Amenities:** preferred room (subject to availability with advance reservations) and high-speed Internet. SAVE

YARDARM VILLAGE INN

207/646-7006 **96**

Bed & Breakfast $100-$170 **Address:** 406 Shore Rd 03907 **Location:** 1.1 mi s on Shore Rd, then just s of entrance to Perkins Cove; center of village. **Facility:** 10 units. 3 stories (no elevator), interior corridors. **Terms:** closed 10/27-5/9, 2-3 night minimum stay - weekends, 14 day cancellation notice-fee imposed. **Amenities:** high-speed Internet.

BIZ

WHERE TO EAT

ARROWS RESTAURANT

207/361-1100 **58**

Regional American. Fine Dining. $85-$135 AAA Inspector Notes: *Historic.* Once a private residence, this 18th-century country home now serves as the memorable setting for a meal where you can enjoy items off an incredible changing menu. Unusual, always freshly prepared delectables include Alaskan king salmon, grilled venison loin and sautéed Maryland soft-shelled crabs. Attentive, friendly servers are eager to assist with entrée and wine selections and may recommend a dessert. The homemade pastries are a sweet and satisfying end to a delicious meal. Semiformal attire. **Bar:** full bar. **Reservations:** suggested. **Address:** 41 Berwick Rd 03907 **Location:** 1.8 mi w of jct US 1. D

BARNACLE BILLY'S

207/646-5575 **63**

American. Quick Serve. $5-$25 AAA Inspector Notes: The deck at this eatery gives a great view of Perkins Cove, and the stone fireplace offers a cozy, comfortable ambience. Fresh boiled lobster, steamed clams, grilled chicken, chowder and salad are a few of the selections on the varied menu. **Bar:** full bar. **Address:** 50-70 Perkins Cove Rd 03907 **Location:** Jct US 1 and Shore Rd, 1 mi se on Shore Rd; in Perkins Cove. L D

BARNACLE BILLY'S ETC.

207/646-4711 **62**

American. Casual Dining. $8-$31 AAA Inspector Notes: The outdoor deck overlooks the harbor and the garden is at the water's edge at this popular restaurant, which has been in business since 1961. "Luxury" lobster is among the top menu choices. When the weather cools, the fireplaces crackle. **Bar:** full bar. **Address:** 50 Perkins Cove Rd 03907 **Location:** Jct US 1 and Shore Rd, 1 mi se on Shore Rd; in Perkins Cove. **Parking:** valet only. L D

BINTLIFF'S OGUNQUIT

207/646-3111 **54**

American. Casual Dining. $9-$39 AAA Inspector Notes: The popular bistro-style restaurant serves an impressive brunch menu daily. The dinner menu offers traditional chicken, seafood and steak favorites. **Bar:** full bar. **Address:** 335 Main St 03907 **Location:** Just n of center on US 1. B L D

THE EGG & I

207/646-8777 **53**

American. Family Dining. $4-$15 AAA Inspector Notes: This place is a great spot for breakfast and lunch, offering an impressive variety of eggs benedicts, burgers and more. All the dishes are sure to satisfy comfort food cravings. Service is both efficient and pleasant. Take note that it's cash only at this eatery, but an ATM is conveniently located on site. **Address:** 501 Main St 03907 **Location:** On US 1. B L

FIVE-O

207/646-5001 **57**

Regional American. Fine Dining. $19-$33 AAA Inspector Notes: Among the American-inspired specialties are gingered salmon, filet mignon and onion-encrusted, pan-seared haddock. A lighter-fare lounge menu offering sandwiches and burgers is available as well. **Bar:** full bar. **Reservations:** suggested. **Address:** 50 Shore Rd 03907 **Location:** Jct US 1, just se. D

GYPSY SWEETHEARTS RESTAURANT

207/646-7021 **56**

Seafood. Casual Dining. $18-$32 AAA Inspector Notes: Chef/owner Judy Clayton's menu specialties include East Coast crab cakes, fresh raspberry salad, shrimp margarita, Cuban adobo pork and shelled native lobster. Patrons are treated to a fine-dining experience in a charming old house with a porch overlooking Shore Road. Seating is also offered on the deck and the seasonal garden patio. The wine list is wonderful. **Bar:** full bar. **Reservations:** suggested. **Address:** 30 Shore Rd 03907 **Location:** Jct US 1, just se. D

JACKIE'S TOO

207/646-4444 **60**

Seafood. Casual Dining. $7-$25 AAA Inspector Notes: On the water's edge on Perkins Cove, the popular eatery affords lovely ocean views from large windows in the dining area. Although the menu emphasizes seafood, it also lists sandwiches, salads and pasta dishes. Deck seating is a seasonal option. **Bar:** full bar. **Address:** 91 Perkins Cove Rd 03907 **Location:** Jct US 1, 1 mi s via Shore Rd; in Perkins Cove. L D

JONATHAN'S RESTAURANT

207/646-4777 **59**

Continental
Fine Dining
$20-$34

AAA Inspector Notes: Specialties include caramelized, pan-seared salmon dusted with sugar and dill and lobster ravioli, each presented in attractive surroundings. Ask to see the "lighter side of Jonathan's" menu. Contributing to the atmosphere are a fine collection of American paintings and pretty gardens. **Bar:** full bar. **Reservations:** suggested. **Address:** 92 Bourne Ln 03907 **Location:** 0.5 mi s on US 1, just e. *Menu on AAA.com* D

(See map & index p. 98.)

MC PERKINS COVE   207/646-6263   64

▼▼▼▼ American. Fine Dining. $9-$27 **AAA Inspector Notes:** The must-stop destination boasts fabulous food and a primo location. You'll gaze out at Maine's rocky, wave-lashed coast from the dining room, a beautiful spot in which to enjoy richly flavored, made-from-scratch cuisine. The owner-chefs, of Arrow's fame, use only the freshest ingredients. And while the menu offers excellent meats and vegetables, it's the amazing local fish and shellfish that are worth writing home about. It's important to note that hours and days open vary by season. **Bar:** full bar. **Address:** 111 Perkins Cove Rd 03907 **Location:** At Perkins Cove. **Parking:** on-site (fee). [L] [D]

OARWEED RESTAURANT & LOBSTER POUND
                                   207/646-4022   61

▼▼ Seafood. Casual Dining. $7-$28 **AAA Inspector Notes:** Nothing is fried at this eatery which is a pleasant surprise when most casual eateries are riddled with fried seafood. This seasonal spot (open May through October) affords a panoramic view of the Atlantic Ocean. Another added bonus—valet parking allows guests to dine and then walk though Perkins Cove at their leisure. **Bar:** full bar. **Address:** 65 Perkins Cove Rd 03907 **Location:** At Perkins Cove. **Parking:** valet only. [L] [D] [AC]

THE OLD VILLAGE INN   207/646-7088   55

▼▼▼ American. Casual Dining. $9-$28 **AAA Inspector Notes:** *Historic.* This charming, Victorian-style restaurant is home to an English pub-style bar. Paintings by local artists enhance the warm, nautical-style decor. Helpful, uniformed servers will assist in selections of both wine and cuisine off a menu featuring nicely prepared regional dishes. While pasta, stir-fries, rack of lamb, filet mignon and great seafood selections are all prepared with local ingredients, the lobster is a standout, as is the huge selection of desserts. **Bar:** full bar. **Reservations:** suggested. **Address:** 250 Main St 03907 **Location:** On US 1; center of village. [D]

OLD ORCHARD BEACH (K-3) pop. 8,624, elev. 15'
• Hotels & Restaurants map & index p. 98

Old Orchard Beach, one of the oldest seashore resorts in Maine, boasts a 7-mile strip of white sand coastline. The low surf makes the area a favorite spot for swimming. Recreational pastimes include golf, tennis and deep-sea fishing. There are amusement parks and arcades in town. Automobile races take place May through September at nearby Beech Ridge Motor Speedway; phone (207) 885-5800. In summer there's harness racing at Scarborough Downs, 7 miles north of town; phone (207) 883-4331.

Note: Policies concerning admittance of children to pari-mutuel betting facilities vary. Phone for information.

Old Orchard Beach Chamber of Commerce: 11 First St., P.O. Box 600, Old Orchard Beach, ME 04064. **Phone:** (207) 934-2500.

PALACE PLAYLAND AMUSEMENT PARK is at 1 Old Orchard St. Established in 1902, the 4-acre oceanfront park offers 28 rides and a 24,000-square-foot arcade featuring more than 200 electronic games. Among the rides are two roller coasters, the Galaxi and the Orient Express; the Chance Menagerie carousel; the Electra Wheel, a Ferris wheel more than 70 feet tall; and many rides for children, including Dizzy Dragon and Winky the Whale. Games of skill and free entertainment are available.

Note: Height restrictions apply to certain rides. **Time:** Allow 1 hour minimum. **Hours:** Rides open Mon.-Fri. at noon, Sat.-Sun. at 11, mid-June through

Labor Day; closing times vary. Arcade open mid-Apr. through Columbus Day; phone for days and hours. Ride and arcade schedules vary; phone ahead. Fireworks display Thurs. at 9:45, mid-June to late Aug. **Cost:** Park free. Single tickets $1.25 (two to four tickets required per ride). Twenty tickets $23. Fifty tickets $53. One-day unlimited rides pass $30.95; $22.95 (for two-ticket rides, under 42 inches tall). Prices may vary; phone ahead. A two-day unlimited rides pass also is available. **Phone:** (207) 934-2001. [🍴]

THE AQUARIUS MOTEL   207/934-2626   23

▼▼▼
Motel
$59-$139
Address: 1 Brown St 04064 **Location:** Oceanfront. Just e on SR 9 (E Grand Ave). **Facility:** 16 units, some efficiencies. 2 stories (no elevator), exterior corridors. **Terms:** closed 10/18-5/31, 1-3 night minimum stay - seasonal and/or weekends, 21 day cancellation notice-fee imposed. **Activities:** limited beach access. **Free Special Amenities:** local telephone calls and newspaper.

[SAVE] [🍴+] [📶] [✕] [🔌] [🖥]

ATLANTIC BIRCHES INN   (207)934-5295   22

▼▼▼▼
Bed & Breakfast
$101-$220
Address: 20 Portland Ave (SR 98) 04064 **Location:** Jct SR 5 and 98, just n. Located in a residential area. **Facility:** This Victorian inn is close to the beach yet it sits in a residential setting. 10 units, some efficiencies. 3 stories (no elevator), interior/exterior corridors. **Terms:** 2 night minimum stay - seasonal and/or weekends, 21 day cancellation notice-fee imposed. **Amenities:** *Some:* high-speed Internet. **Pool(s):** heated outdoor. **Free Special Amenities:** expanded continental breakfast and high-speed Internet.

[SAVE] [🛶] [📶] [✕] /SOME UNITS [📺] [🔌] [🖥] [📋]

BEACHFRONT CONDOTELS   207/934-7434   18

▼ Motel. Rates not provided. **Address:** 1 Walnut St 04064 **Location:** Oceanfront. 0.4 mi ne on SR 9 (E Grand Ave), just se. **Facility:** 24 units, some two bedrooms, efficiencies and kitchens. 2 stories (no elevator), exterior corridors. *Bath:* shower only. **Guest Services:** coin laundry. [📶] [✕] [🔌] [🖥]

BEAU RIVAGE MOTEL   (207)934-4668   19

▼▼ Motel $69-$299 **Address:** 54 E Grand Ave 04064 **Location:** Just ne of center. **Facility:** 60 units, some two bedrooms, efficiencies and kitchens. 2 stories (no elevator), exterior corridors. **Terms:** closed 10/16-5/31, 2-3 night minimum stay - seasonal and/or weekends, 14 day cancellation notice-fee imposed. **Pool(s):** heated outdoor. **Activities:** sauna, whirlpool. **Guest Services:** coin laundry.
[🍴+] [🛶] [BIZ] [📶] [✕] [🔌] [🖥]

THE CREST MOTEL   207/934-4060   21

▼ Motel $100-$329 **Address:** 35 E Grand Ave (SR 9) 04064 **Location:** Just ne of center. **Facility:** 26 units, some kitchens. 2 stories (no elevator), exterior corridors. **Terms:** closed 10/16-3/31, 2-3 night minimum stay - seasonal and/or weekends, 7 day cancellation notice-fee imposed. **Pool(s):** heated indoor/outdoor. **Activities:** sauna, whirlpool, limited beach access, playground. *Fee:* bicycles. **Guest Services:** coin laundry.
[🍴+] [🛶] [BIZ] [📶] [✕] [🔌] [🖥]

THE EDGEWATER   (207)934-2221   26

▼▼▼ Motel $79-$289 **Address:** 57 W Grand Ave (SR 9) 04064 **Location:** Oceanfront. 0.4 mi sw of center. **Facility:** 36 units, some two bedrooms and efficiencies. 2 stories (no elevator), exterior corridors. **Terms:** 3 night minimum stay - seasonal and/or weekends, 7 day cancellation notice-fee imposed. **Pool(s):** heated outdoor.

[ECO] [🍴+] [🛶] [📶] [✕] [🔌] [🖥]

(See map & index p. 98.)

EXECUTIVE MOTEL   207/934-4637   **20**
⬥ Motel $85-$185 **Address:** 38 E Grand Ave 04064 **Location:** On SR 9 (E Grand Ave), just e. **Facility:** 24 units. 1-2 stories (no elevator), exterior corridors. **Terms:** closed 9/8-5/14, 2-3 night minimum stay - seasonal and/or weekends, 3 day cancellation notice-fee imposed. **Pool(s):** heated outdoor. **Activities:** playground. ⬥⬥⬥⬥⬥⬥⬥⬥

FRIENDSHIP OCEANFRONT SUITES   207/934-4644   **17**
⬥⬥ Hotel $69-$259 **Address:** 167 E Grand Ave (SR 9) 04064 **Location:** Oceanfront. 0.8 mi ne of center. **Facility:** 71 units. 2 stories (no elevator), exterior corridors. **Bath:** shower only. **Terms:** closed 10/20-4/30, 3 night minimum stay - seasonal, 10 day cancellation notice-fee imposed. **Pool(s):** heated outdoor. **Activities:** limited beach access, fishing. **Guest Services:** coin laundry.
⬥⬥⬥⬥⬥⬥⬥

THE GULL MOTEL   207/934-4321   **29**
⬥⬥ Motel $75-$200 **Address:** 89 W Grand Ave 04064 **Location:** On SR 9 (W Grand Ave),0.5 mi sw of center. **Facility:** 21 efficiencies. 2 stories (no elevator), exterior corridors. **Terms:** closed 10/9-4/30, 3 night minimum stay - seasonal, 10 day cancellation notice-fee imposed. **Pool(s):** heated outdoor. **Activities:** beach access. ⬥⬥⬥⬥⬥

KEBEK 3 MOTEL   207/934-5253   **25**
⬥⬥ Motel $90-$195 **Address:** 53 W Grand Ave (SR 9) 04064 **Location:** Oceanfront. 0.5 mi e on SR 9 (W Grand Ave). **Facility:** 35 units, some efficiencies. 2 stories (no elevator), exterior corridors. **Terms:** closed 10/17-5/3, 3 night minimum stay - seasonal and/or weekends, 14 day cancellation notice-fee imposed.
⬥⬥⬥⬥⬥⬥⬥

OCEAN WALK HOTEL   207/934-1716   **16**
⬥⬥ Motel $80-$310 **Address:** 197 E Grand Ave (SR 9) 04064 **Location:** Oceanfront. 1.2 mi ne of center. **Facility:** 44 efficiencies. 2 stories (no elevator), exterior corridors. **Terms:** closed 10/16-4/11, 2-3 night minimum stay - seasonal and/or weekends, 10 day cancellation notice-fee imposed. **Pool(s):** heated indoor. **Guest Services:** coin laundry. ⬥⬥⬥⬥⬥⬥

OLD ORCHARD BEACH INN   207/934-5834   **24**
⬥⬥⬥
Historic Bed
& Breakfast
Rates not provided
Address: 6 Portland Ave (SR 98) 04064 **Location:** Jct SR 5 and 98, just n. Located in a residential area. **Facility:** Period antiques, patchwork quilts and original hardwood floors set the décor theme at this inn built in 1730. An expanded continental breakfast of fresh seasonal fruit, quick breads and cereals is served. 18 units. 3 stories (no elevator), interior corridors. **Free Special Amenities: expanded continental breakfast and local telephone calls.**
⬥⬥⬥

ROYAL ANCHOR RESORT   207/934-4521   **15**
⬥⬥ Motel $78-$225 **Address:** 203 E Grand Ave 04064 **Location:** Oceanfront. 1.3 mi e on SR 9 (E Grand Ave). Located in a quiet area. **Facility:** 40 units. 3 stories (no elevator), exterior corridors. **Terms:** closed 10/15-5/2, 3 night minimum stay - seasonal and/or weekends, 10 day cancellation notice-fee imposed. **Pool(s):** heated outdoor. **Activities:** fishing, tennis court, playground, sports court, shuffleboard, volleyball. **Guest Services:** coin laundry, area transportation-Amtrak station.
 ⬥⬥⬥⬥⬥⬥⬥/SOME UNITS⬥ FEE⬥

SEA VIEW INN   207/934-4180   **27**
⬥⬥⬥
Hotel
Rates not provided
Address: 65 W Grand Ave (SR 9) 04064 **Location:** Oceanfront. 0.5 mi w on SR 9 (W Grand Ave). **Facility:** 48 units, some two bedrooms and efficiencies. 3 stories (no elevator), exterior corridors. **Pool(s):** heated outdoor. **Activities:** exercise room. **Guest Services:** coin laundry. **Free Special Amenities: local telephone calls and high-speed Internet.**
 ⬥⬥⬥⬥⬥⬥⬥/SOME UNITS FEE⬥⬥

WAVES OCEANFRONT RESORT   (207)934-4949   **28**
⬥⬥ Hotel $60-$260 **Address:** 87 W Grand Ave (SR 9) 04064 **Location:** Oceanfront. 0.5 mi w on SR 9 (W Grand Ave). **Facility:** 169 units, some two bedrooms, efficiencies, kitchens and cottages. 1-2 stories (no elevator), exterior corridors. **Terms:** closed 11/1-5/11, 3-5 night minimum stay - seasonal and/or weekends, 7 day cancellation notice-fee imposed. **Pool(s):** heated outdoor. **Activities:** whirlpool, rental bicycles, exercise room. **Guest Services:** coin laundry.
⬥⬥⬥⬥⬥⬥/SOME UNITS⬥

WHITE CAP VILLAGE   207/934-2553   **30**
⬥⬥ Hotel $75-$375 **Address:** 5 Bay Ave 04064 **Location:** 0.6 mi w on SR 9 (W Grand Ave), just e. **Facility:** 24 units, some two bedrooms, three bedrooms, efficiencies and kitchens. 3 stories (no elevator), exterior corridors. **Terms:** closed 10/9-5/17, 2-7 night minimum stay - seasonal, 30 day cancellation notice-fee imposed. **Amenities:** high-speed Internet. **Pool(s):** heated outdoor. **Activities:** beach access, playground. ⬥⬥⬥⬥⬥

WHERE TO EAT

JOSEPH'S BY THE SEA   207/934-5044   **12**
⬥⬥⬥⬥ Continental. Fine Dining. $19-$33 **AAA Inspector Notes:** This popular oceanside restaurant is family-operated and has an airy décor. The skillfully prepared entrees include tasty baked stuffed lobster and pepper-crusted filet mignon. There's terrace dining in season. A 15% service charge is applied for dinner. **Bar:** full bar. **Address:** 55 W Grand Ave 04064 **Location:** 0.5 mi e on SR 9 (W Grand Ave). ⬥ ⬥

OLD TOWN (H-5) pop. 7,840, elev. 94'
• Restaurants p. 124

With the Penobscot River providing waterpower and transportation, Old Town grew into a busy saw-milling and iron-making center in the early 19th century. In 1836 it became the northern terminus of New England's first railroad—a 13-mile line between the Penobscot Ironworks and Bangor. The city spans several islands in the Penobscot River.

Diversified manufacturing continues to sustain the city; textiles, shoes, various wood products and metal goods are produced. The Old Town Canoe Co. makes canoes of fiberglass and other modern materials but is best known as one of the last remaining producers of traditional canvas and wooden canoes. An audiovisual presentation at the visitor center, 125 Gilman Falls Ave., details this process; phone (207) 827-1530.

The Penobscot Indian reservation occupies Indian Island at the north edge of the city and numerous uninhabited isles in the Penobscot River as far north as Mattawamkeag. Once the largest tribe of the Abenaki Confederacy, the Penobscots were excellent woodsmen and basket makers. A few Penobscot-made baskets can still be found in shops on the island.

OLD TOWN MUSEUM, at 353 Main St., offers rotating exhibits of historical objects in addition to displays depicting the lumber industry. Permanent exhibits include a birch bark canoe more than 200 years old, American Indian artifacts, a horse-drawn hearse mounted on runners used locally in the late 19th century and sculptures and paintings by Bernard Langlais, an Old Town native. **Time:** Allow 30 minutes minimum. **Hours:** Fri.-Sun. 1-4, June 1 to mid-Oct.; Sat.-Sun. 1-4, in May. **Cost:** Donations. **Phone:** (207) 827-7256.

GOVERNOR'S RESTAURANT & BAKERY   207/827-4277

▼▼ American. Family Dining. $7-$17 **AAA Inspector Notes:** Diners flip through a dozen pages of wonderful seafood and varied Italian dishes, in addition to choices such as homemade meatloaf, steaks, burgers and sandwiches, on Governor's Restaurant's diverse menu. Breakfast dishes also can be ordered at any time of the day. Weekends stay bustling with families filing in to the casual spot to indulge in the daily made bakery treats and desserts. **Bar:** beer & wine. **Address:** 963 Stillwater Ave 04468 **Location:** Just e of College Ave. Ⓑ ⓛ Ⓓ

ORLAND (H-5) elev. 190'

Traditional handcrafting became a major industry in Orland with the 1970 establishment of H.O.M.E. (Home-workers Organized for More Employment). The cooperative, which began as an outlet for locally made products, has since expanded to include a chapel, a museum, a lumber mill, pottery and weaving shops and an extensive rural education program.

Various craft demonstrations can be seen at the H.O.M.E. compound, which is at the corner of US 1 and School House Road; for further information phone (207) 469-7961.

The town's many lakes and streams as well as the Narramissic River are popular with swimmers, canoeists and kayakers.

ORONO (H-5) pop. 9,474, elev. 80'

Although small industries and farming contribute to Orono's economy, the main focus of this Penobscot Valley town is the University of Maine. Since its opening in 1868 with 12 students and two teachers, the land-grant institution, comprised of eight colleges, has grown to an enrollment of more than 11,000. The university is a center for teaching, research, public service and cultural activity.

The Collins Center for the Arts houses the 1,629-seat Hutchins Concert Hall; phone (207) 581-1755. The Maynard F. Jordan Planetarium and Observatory offers multimedia astronomy programs and views of the heavens; phone (207) 581-1341. Other university highlights are the ornamental gardens, anthropological museum, dairy and sheep barns, modern athletic facilities and the largest library in the state. Brochures for a self-guiding walking tour are available at the visitor center near the Munson Road entrance. Phone (207) 581-3740 for general information or (207) 521-1561 for university tour information.

HUDSON MUSEUM is at 5746 Flagstaff Rd. in the Collins Center for the Arts building on the University of Maine campus. Native American, African, Oceanic and pre-Columbian collections are featured in three galleries. Interactive exhibits are on display in the Minsky Culture Lab. **Time:** Allow 1 hour minimum. **Hours:** Mon.-Fri. 9-4, Sat. 11-4. Closed major holidays. **Cost:** Free. **Phone:** (207) 581-1901.

BLACK BEAR INN CONFERENCE CENTER & SUITES
(207)866-7120

▼▼ Hotel $99-$189 **Address:** 4 Godfrey Dr 04473 **Location:** I-95 exit 193 (Stillwater Ave). **Facility:** 68 units. 3 stories, interior corridors. **Terms:** 7 day cancellation notice-fee imposed. **Amenities:** Some: high-speed Internet. **Activities:** sauna, exercise room. **Guest Services:** coin laundry.

⍾ CALL ⌖Ⓜ BIZ 🛜 ✕ ▯ / SOME UNITS FEE 🐾 🛗 🖼

UNIVERSITY INN ACADEMIC SUITES   (207)866-4921

▼▼ Hotel $86-$149 **Address:** 5 College Ave 04473 **Location:** I-95 exit 191, 1.6 mi n on US 2; 8 mi n of Bangor. **Facility:** 48 units, some efficiencies. 2 stories (no elevator), interior corridors. **Terms:** cancellation fee imposed. **Pool(s):** heated outdoor. **Activities:** exercise room. **Guest Services:** area transportation-campus & village.

⍾⊹ ➴ BIZ 🛜 ✕ / SOME UNITS 🐾 🛗 🖼 ▯

WHERE TO EAT

WOODMAN'S BAR & GRILL   207/866-4040

▼▼ American. Casual Dining. $10-$20 **AAA Inspector Notes:** This popular bar and grill offers an upbeat atmosphere with live music on some nights. The pub's appetizer and entree portions are generously sized, with menu options ranging from fish and chips and hefty burgers to filet mignon, grilled salmon and glazed chicken. **Bar:** full bar. **Address:** 31 Main St 04473 **Location:** Corner of Forest Ave; center. Ⓓ

OWLS HEAD (J-5) elev. 65'

OWLS HEAD TRANSPORTATION MUSEUM, 117 Museum St., has antique aircraft, automobiles, motorcycles, bicycles and carriages—all in operating condition. The collection includes World War I fighter planes, Model Ts, limited-edition cars and pioneer vehicles. Demonstrations take place in the summer.

Time: Allow 1 hour minimum. **Hours:** Daily 10-5. Closed Jan. 1, Thanksgiving and Christmas. **Cost:** $10; $8 (ages 65+); free (ages 0-17). Special events admission $12-$15; free (ages 0-17). **Phone:** (207) 594-4418.

PATTEN (E-6) elev. 546'

Since the 1830s the Shin Pond Road (SR 159) through Patten has been a major artery for the lumber industry. In the early days, horses pulled supply-laden wagons along the rough trace to remote lumber camps. There loggers with axes and handsaws cut millions of board feet of pine and spruce, then hauled it out with ox teams or drove it down the Penobscot River to Bangor.

Patten developed as a trading, supply and business center for the lumber interests. Its primary industry is the manufacture of plywood and other wood products. The community also caters to hunters and anglers bound for the deep woods and recreationists who follow SR 159 to Baxter State Park *(see Recreation Areas Chart).*

PATTEN LUMBERMEN'S MUSEUM, .5 mi. w. on SR 159 to 61 Shin Pond Rd., at the n. entrance to Baxter State Park, has more than 4,000 exhibits in nine separate buildings—a legacy of the town's long-standing involvement with logging. Displays include carpenters', surveyors' and timber cruisers' tools; a blacksmith shop; a steam and a gas Lombard log hauler; pre-mechanized, horse-drawn equipment; photographs; and a full-scale replica of an 1820s lumber camp. **Hours:** Tues.-Sun. 10-4, July-Oct.; Fri.-Sun. 10-4, in June. **Cost:** $8; $7 (ages 65+); $3 (ages 4-11). **Phone:** (207) 528-2650. 🅰️

PEMAQUID POINT (J-4) elev. 72'

Pemaquid Point is at the end of a long peninsula jutting into the Atlantic. The first permanent settlement in Maine was made at the point 1625-26. The sea battle between the English brig *Boxer* and the American brig *Enterprise* was fought between the point and Monhegan Island in 1813. The 1827 Pemaquid Point Lighthouse *(see Lighthouse Park attraction listing)* is perched upon rugged granite ledges and is accessible by automobile.

LIGHTHOUSE PARK, s. on SR 130, covers 6 acres. A noteworthy feature of the park is the Pemaquid Point Lighthouse, commissioned by John Quincy Adams in 1827. Its 11,000-candlepower beam is visible up to 14 miles at sea. Visitors may climb stairs to the lantern room inside the lighthouse tower. Also on the premises are the Fishermen's Museum and the Pemaquid Art Gallery. **Hours:** Park daily 9-5, Mother's Day-Sun. after Columbus Day. Tower daily 10:30-5, Mother's Day-Sun. after Columbus Day. **Cost:** $2; free (ages 0-11). **Phone:** (207) 677-2494. 🐾 🅰️

Fishermen's Museum, on the grounds of Lighthouse Park in the Pemaquid Point lighthouse keeper's house, contains exhibits chronicling the history of the local fishing industry. Charts of lighthouses along the Maine coast, a bronze buoy bell with an iron chain and a Lyle gun for shooting a lifeline to ships in distress are displayed. Other exhibits include tools used in lobstering, gear for several different sea harvesting methods, and working models of fishing boats. **Hours:** Daily 9-5, Mother's Day-Sun. after Columbus Day (weather permitting). Phone ahead to confirm schedule. **Cost:** Included in Lighthouse Park admission of $2; free (ages 0-11). **Phone:** (207) 677-2494.

Pemaquid Art Gallery, on the grounds of Lighthouse Park, contains the works of local artists. **Hours:** Daily 10-5, mid-June through Columbus Day. **Cost:** Included in Lighthouse Park admission of $2; free (ages 0-11). **Phone:** (207) 677-2752.

PERRY

THE NEW FRIENDLY RESTAURANT   207/853-6610
💎💎 American. Family Dining. $6-$16 **AAA Inspector Notes:** The popular diner dishes up ample portions of basic comfort foods, including outstanding lobster rolls. Service is casual and friendly. **Bar:** beer & wine. **Address:** 855 Shore Rd 04667 **Location:** Just n on SR 190, on US 1. Ⓛ Ⓓ

POLAND SPRING (J-3) elev. 571'

Poland Spring is one of the oldest and best known resorts in the East. The spring, which flows from the solid ledge of one of the region's highest hills, is the source of Poland Spring water. The spring is owned by a commercial bottling company and is closed to visitors. A variety of water-oriented activities are available at nearby Outlet Beach *(see Recreation Areas Chart).*

MAINE STATE BUILDING AND ALL SOULS CHAPEL is at 37 Preservation Way. Originally built to represent Maine at the 1893 Columbian Exposition in Chicago, the Maine State building was dismantled and brought to Poland Spring. It was reconstructed as a library and an art gallery.

The solid granite chapel is a fine example of Victorian architecture with an oak ceiling and exquisite hand-painted windows. Exhibits relate to Poland Spring Resort and its renowned golf course; the Poland Spring water company; and Maine products. The Maine Golf Hall of Fame also is on the premises. **Hours:** Tues.-Sat. 9-4, Memorial Day-Columbus Day. **Cost:** Maine State Building $3. All Souls Chapel by donation. **Phone:** (207) 998-4142.

WOLF COVE INN   207/998-4976
💎💎💎 Bed & Breakfast $129-$169 **Address:** 5 Jordan Shore Dr 04274 **Location:** Waterfront. Just w of SR 11. **Facility:** Alongside Tripp Lake, this property was originally built in 1890 as a private home and has long since been hosting guests. A full breakfast is served each morning between 8 and 9 am. 10 units. 3 stories, interior corridors. *Bath:* some shared. **Terms:** 14 day cancellation notice-fee imposed. **Activities:** limited beach access, boating, canoeing.
📶 ❌ 📠 / SOME UNITS FEE 🐾 🚭

PORT CLYDE (J-4) elev. 65'

The Wyeth family of painters summered in Port Clyde for years; it was here that a teenage Andrew began exploring the medium of watercolor. The town's stunning coastal scenery inspired many of the polychrome land- and seascape paintings presented at his first solo exhibition, which drew a sellout crowd to a New York City gallery in 1937. Port Clyde also is the summer home of Chief Justice John Roberts.

Passenger service is available from Port Clyde to the getaway oasis of Monhegan Island *(see place listing p. 113)* courtesy of Monhegan Boat Line. The 10-mile excursion to the island passes a lighthouse and offers the possibility of whale sightings; the return trip provides a view of Seal Rock. For information and reservations phone (207) 372-8848.

MARSHALL POINT LIGHTHOUSE MUSEUM, off SR 131 at 179 Marshall Point Rd., is housed in the late 19th-century Colonial Revival keeper's house and displays exhibits about local history. You might recognize the 1858 Marshall Point Lighthouse as the landmark where Forrest ends the eastern segment of his cross-country run in the movie "Forrest Gump." A 1905 oil house also is on the grounds. **Note:** Pets are not permitted. **Hours:** Grounds daily dawn-dusk. Museum Sun.-Fri. 1-5, Sat. 10-5, Memorial Day-Columbus Day; Sat.-Sun. 1-5, May 1-day before Memorial Day. **Cost:** Donations. **Phone:** (207) 372-6450. 🅰🆃

PORTLAND (K-3) pop. 66,194, elev. 34'

• Hotels p. 135 • Restaurants p. 138
• Attractions map p. 127
• Hotels & Restaurants map & index p. 131

"The beautiful town that is seated by the sea," wrote poet Henry Wadsworth Longfellow of his birthplace, Portland. Longfellow's town has become the largest city in Maine and a major industrial and manufacturing center for northern New England. Attractively restored 19th-century buildings, tree-lined streets and a fringe of parks readily evoke the grace that inspired the poet's tribute.

The Old Port Exchange on the waterfront was the heart of Portland's busy 19th-century commercial activities. After fire leveled the heart of the city in 1866, the district was reconstructed in a classic Victorian style. The architecture, cobblestone streets and old gas street lamps recapture the flavor of the city's early seaport days. Many of the old warehouses, ship chandleries and merchant exchanges now serve as boutiques, restaurants, bars and bookshops. At the Maine State Pier on Commercial Street is the "Whaling Wall," a 950-foot mural depicting sea life found in the Gulf of Maine.

Culturally, Portland is Maine's showplace. Dozens of galleries and museums on Congress Street offer free admission during Art Walks, held the first Friday of every month from 5-8. The Portland Stage, 25A Forest Ave., was founded in 1974 and produces seven to nine shows each season; phone (207) 774-0465. Three centuries of art and architecture are on display at the Portland Museum of Art *(see attraction listing p. 129).* The Portland Symphony Orchestra, phone (207) 842-0800 or TTY (207) 842-0812, offers a wide spectrum of classical and contemporary music during its season; ballet, repertory opera and a variety of musical performances are held throughout the year.

The Calendar Islands, so called because of their number, 365, are east of Portland in Casco Bay. Capt. John Smith first visited these islands in 1614. Crescent Beach *(see Recreation Areas Chart)* and Two Lights state parks are nearby in Cape Elizabeth.

The city has a network of more than 30 trails for hiking, biking and cross-country skiing; phone (207) 775-2411. Excursions and charters for whale watching, deep-sea fishing, fall foliage viewing and

tours to lighthouses and the Casco Bay islands are available. For information contact AAA Northern New England, 68 Marginal Way, Portland, ME 04101; phone (207) 780-6800 or (800) 222-3760.

Convention and Visitors Bureau of Greater Portland: 14 Ocean Gateway Pier, Portland, ME 04101. **Phone:** (207) 772-5800.

Self-guiding tours: Brochures for a walking tour of the city's architectural highlights are available daily for $1.25 at the convention and visitors bureau. Each map outlines tours through the Old Port Exchange, Congress Street, State Street and the Western Promenade.

The Portland Freedom Trail walking tour identifies 16 former Underground Railroad sites; phone (207) 591-9980 for information.

Shopping areas: Gift shops and restaurants are housed in quaint 19th-century brick buildings in downtown's Old Port Exchange, between Congress and Commercial streets near Exchange Street. The Portland Farmers' Market is held on the Park Avenue side of Deering Oaks Park Sat. 7-noon and at Monument Square on Congress Street Wed. 7-2, May-Nov.; the market moves indoors to the Maine Irish Heritage Center on Gray and State streets Sat. 9-1, rest of year.

CASCO BAY LINES, on the waterfront at Commercial and Franklin sts., provides year-round ferry service to the Calendar Islands of Casco Bay. A lifeline to the islands, the ferries also offer passengers a scenic tour of the bay as they transport groceries, mail and residents to and from the islands. Lasting 5 hours, 45 minutes, the Bailey Island Day Cruise is among the other trips available.

Hours: Mail boat run departs daily at 10 and 2:15, mid-June through Labor Day; at 10 and 2:45, rest of year. Bailey Island Day Cruise departs daily at 10, late June-Labor Day; return trip departs Bailey Island at 2 and arrives in Portland at 3:45. **Cost:** Mail boat $15.50; $13.50 (ages 65+); $7.75 (ages 5-9). Bailey Island Day Cruise $25; $22 (ages 65+); $11.50 (ages 5-9). **Phone:** (207) 774-7871.

CHILDREN'S MUSEUM & THEATRE OF MAINE, 142 Free St., is housed in a historic brick building and contains interactive exhibits and programs designed to interest children and families. Displays include a lobster boat, a fire truck, a child-size grocery store, a farm exhibit, interactive science exhibits depicting the natural resources of Maine and a camera obscura demonstration. Theater performances and special events occur throughout the year.

Time: Allow 1 hour minimum. **Hours:** Tues.-Sat. 10-5, Sun. noon-5 (also Mon. 10-5, Memorial Day-Labor Day). Closed Jan. 1, Easter, July 4, Thanksgiving, Christmas Eve and Christmas. **Cost:** $9; free (ages 0-18 months). **Phone:** (207) 828-1234.

DOWNEAST DUCK ADVENTURES departs from 94 Commercial St. An amphibious vehicle transports visitors on a 1-hour narrated land and sea tour of

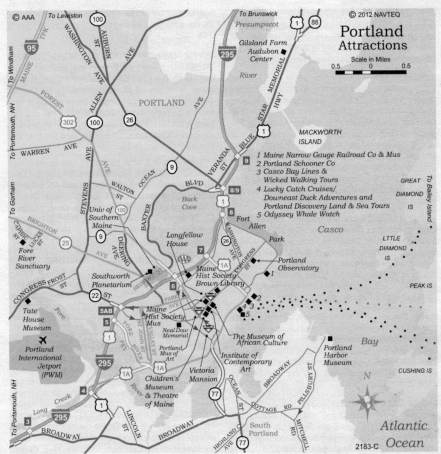

© AAA   To Lewiston   To Brunswick   © 2012 NAVTEQ

Portland Attractions

Scale in Miles
0.5 0 0.5

MACKWORTH ISLAND

1 Maine Narrow Gauge Railroad Co & Mus
2 Portland Schooner Co
3 Casco Bay Lines & Wicked Walking Tours
4 Lucky Catch Cruises/ Downeast Duck Adventures and Portland Discovery Land & Sea Tours
5 Odyssey Whale Watch

GREAT DIAMOND IS

Casco

LITTLE DIAMOND IS

PEAK IS

Bay

CUSHING IS

Atlantic Ocean

N

2183-C

(See map & index p. 131.)

Portland. The land cruise covers historical and scenic landmarks of the city. The sea cruise navigates the waters of Casco Bay with lighthouses, historic forts and the Calendar Islands on view.

Note: Visitors arriving in an RV may have difficulty finding a parking spot. **Time:** Allow 1 hour, 30 minutes minimum. **Hours:** Trips depart daily at 10, 11:30, 1:30 and 3, mid-May to mid-Oct. **Cost:** $26; $24 (ages 60+); $19 (ages 4-17). Reservations are recommended. **Phone:** (207) 774-3825.

FORE RIVER SANCTUARY, 1 mi. e. on Brighton Ave., then s. on Rowe Ave. to end, is an 85-acre preserve within the city of Portland that includes a 2.5-mile trail leading to the towpath of the historic Cumberland and Oxford Canal. The sanctuary includes salt marshes, forested ravines and Portland's only waterfall, Jewell Falls. Black ducks, cormorants and herring gulls nest in the area. **Hours:** Daily dawn-dusk. **Cost:** Free. **Phone:** (207) 775-2411.

INSTITUTE OF CONTEMPORARY ART is at 522 Congress St., on the Maine College of Art campus.

The institute features exhibitions and public programs that showcase new perspectives and trends in contemporary art. Guided tours are available by reservation. **Time:** Allow 30 minutes minimum. **Hours:** Wed.-Sun. 11-5 (also Thurs. 5-7 and first Fri. of the month 5-8). **Cost:** Free. **Phone:** (207) 699-5029.

LONGFELLOW HOUSE, 489 Congress St., was built 1785-86 by Gen. Peleg Wadsworth, maternal grandfather of Henry Wadsworth Longfellow. It was here that the curious blue-eyed boy turned celebrated poet spent his childhood years. Situated on about 1.5 acres on the back side of town, it was the first all-brick home in Portland, constructed in the neoclassical style with bricks barged from Philadelphia. The residence was originally a two-story structure; in 1815 a third story with seven rooms was added after an 1814 fire ruined the gable roof.

The brass knocker that greets you at the front door is the original. Upon crossing the threshold, you'll find a lovely blend of fixtures and décor from three different generations. An impressive collection

(See map & index p. 131.)

of furniture, including a circa 1805 leather side chair and an 1808 high-post bed; portraits; records; and other personal possessions of the Longfellow and Wadsworth families have been preserved.

The last family member to reside in the house was Anne Longfellow Pierce, who died in 1901 and deeded the property to the Maine Historical Society. During an extensive 2.5-year restoration project that concluded in 2002, experts analyzed family photographs and letters as well as paint shades and wallpaper scraps in an attempt to reproduce the woodwork hues, wall coverings, drapery, carpets and upholstery that adorned the interior in the 1850s. Today the Longfellow House is the one remaining private residence in the now urbanized eastern section of Congress Street.

Tours: Guided tours are available. **Time:** Allow 1 hour minimum. **Hours:** Mon.-Sat. 10-4, Sun. noon-4, May-Oct. Additional hours are available Nov.-Dec. Last tour departs 1 hour before closing. Closed major holidays. Phone ahead to confirm schedule. **Cost:** (includes Maine Historical Society Museum) $12; $10 (ages 65+ and students with ID); $3 (ages 6-17). **Phone:** (207) 774-1822.

Maine Historical Society Brown Library, at the rear of the Longfellow House grounds, is a research library containing a collection of more than 125,000 books and two million manuscript pages. **Hours:** Tues.-Sat. 10-4. Closed major holidays. **Cost:** First visit free. Subsequent visits $10 per day. **Phone:** (207) 774-1822.

LUCKY CATCH CRUISES is .3 mi. s.e. on Franklin Arterial/US 1A, then .2 mi. s.w. on Commercial St./US 1A to 170 Commercial St. (at Long Wharf). The intricacies of a lobster haul are demonstrated during 80- to 90-minute cruises on the 37-foot-long *Lucky Catch.* Willing passengers may don aprons and gloves and participate in setting an assortment of lobster traps. An overview of lobsters discusses their biology, conservation, humane treatment and a variety of methods for cooking.

Time: Allow 1 hour, 30 minutes minimum. **Hours:** Cruises depart Mon.-Sat. at 10:30, 12:15, 2 and 3:45, first weekend in May-Oct. 31 (also at 5:30, July-Aug.). Phone ahead to confirm schedule. **Cost:** $25; $22 (ages 63+); $20 (ages 13-18); $15 (ages 2-12). Reservations are recommended. **Phone:** (207) 761-0941.

MAINE HISTORICAL SOCIETY MUSEUM, 489 Congress St., displays changing exhibits about Maine's history; its extensive collection includes paintings, costumes, military items, political memorabilia, archeological materials and manuscripts.

Time: Allow 1 hour minimum. **Hours:** Mon.-Sat. 10-5 (also Sun. noon-5, May-Oct.). Closed holidays and between exhibitions. Phone ahead to confirm schedule. **Cost:** Museum $8; $7 (ages 65+ and students with ID); $2 (ages 6-17). Combination ticket

with Longfellow House $12; $10 (ages 65+ and students with ID); $3 (ages 6-17). **Phone:** (207) 774-1822.

MAINE NARROW GAUGE RAILROAD CO. AND MUSEUM, off I-295 exit 7, .8 mi. s.e. on Franklin St., then .3 mi. e. to 58 Fore St. following signs, is dedicated to preserving Maine's narrow gauge railroad equipment. Highlights of the museum include a two-foot gauge parlor car, coaches, locomotives and railroad artifacts. Thirty-minute train rides on two-foot gauge track run along Casco Bay and the Portland Waterfront.

Time: Allow 1 hour minimum. **Hours:** Museum daily 10-4, May-Oct. Trains depart daily on the hour 10-3, early May-late Oct. Steam trains are available on holiday weekends and during special events. Phone ahead to confirm schedule. **Cost:** Museum $3; $2 (ages 3-12 and 62+). Combination museum and train ride $10; $9 (ages 62+); $6 (ages 3-12). **Phone:** (207) 828-0814.

THE MUSEUM OF AFRICAN CULTURE is at 13 Brown St. The four-room museum features a 1,500-piece collection of sub-Saharan African tribal masks, textiles, art and artifacts. Educational programs are available. **Time:** Allow 30 minutes minimum. **Hours:** Tues.-Fri. 10:30-4, Sat. noon-4. **Cost:** $5. **Phone:** (207) 871-7188.

NEAL DOW MEMORIAL, 714 Congress St., is a Federal-style mansion built in 1829 for prominent Maine politician, abolitionist, women's rights advocate and prohibitionist Neal Dow, twice elected mayor of Portland. The family's original furniture, portraits, paintings and china are on display, as are memorabilia of Dow's military and political careers. There also is a library. Dow's death mask can be viewed upon special request. **Tours:** Guided tours are available. **Hours:** Tours Mon.-Fri. 11-4. Closed major holidays. Phone ahead to confirm schedule. **Cost:** $5; free (ages 0-5). **Phone:** (207) 773-7773.

ODYSSEY WHALE WATCH, departing from Long Wharf at 170 Commercial St. (US 1A), offers 4-hour narrated whale-watching cruises. Passengers might spot humpback, finback and minke whales as well as North Atlantic white-sided dolphins, basking sharks, ocean sunfish, sea turtles and seabirds.

Hours: Cruises depart daily, July-Oct.; phone for departure times. **Cost:** $48; $38 (ages 3-12); $9 (ages 0-2). Fares vary; phone ahead. Reservations are strongly recommended. **Phone:** (207) 775-0727.

PORTLAND DISCOVERY LAND & SEA TOURS, departing from Long Wharf at 170 Commercial St., offers a 90-minute narrated trolley tour of Portland, with a stop at Portland Head Light. A 90-minute harbor cruise affords passengers views of lighthouses, forts and wildlife. The combination Land & Sea tour includes the trolley tour and the harbor cruise. A sunset cruise also is available seasonally.

Hours: Trolley tour departs daily at 11:15, 1 and 2:45, mid-May to late May and mid-Oct. to late Oct.;

(See map & index p. 131.)

at 9:30, 11:15, 1 and 2:45, late May to mid-June and early Sept. to mid-Oct.; at 9:30, 11:15, 1, 2:45 and 4:30, mid-June to early Sept. Harbor cruise departs daily at 11:30 and 2:30, mid-May to late May and mid-Oct. to late Oct.; at 11:30, 1:30 and 3:30, late May to mid-Oct. Sunset cruise departs daily at 6:30, mid-June to mid-Aug.; daily at 6, mid-Aug. to early Sept.; Sat. at 5:30, early Sept.-late Sept. Phone ahead to confirm schedule.

Cost: Trolley tour or harbor cruise $22; $16 (ages 3-12). Land & Sea tour $40; $28 (ages 3-12). Sunset cruise $22; $16 (ages 3-12). **Phone:** (207) 774-0808.

PORTLAND HEAD LIGHT—see Cape Elizabeth p. 78.

PORTLAND MUSEUM OF ART, 7 Congress Sq., is housed in three architecturally significant buildings, including the award-winning Charles Shipman Payson Building designed by I.M. Pei & Partners, the L.D.M. Sweat Memorial Galleries and The McLellan House *(see attraction listing).*

The museum houses a collection of fine and decorative arts dating from the 18th century to the present. Displays include works by American artists Rockwell Kent, Winslow Homer and Andrew Wyeth. The museum's European collection includes works by Edgar Degas, Claude Monet and Pablo Picasso. Sculpture and decorative objects also are showcased.

The L.D.M. Sweat galleries, designed by prominent Maine architect John Calvin Stevens, opened in 1911 and house collections of 19th-century American art. Guided tours of the restored Winslow Homer Studio, where the renowned artist lived and worked from 1883

until his death in 1910, depart from the museum seasonally; reservations are required.

Time: Allow 1 hour minimum. **Hours:** Daily 10-5 (also Fri. 5-9), Memorial Day-Columbus Day; Tues.-Sun. 10-5 (also Fri. 5-9), rest of year. Winslow Homer Studio tour times vary; phone ahead to confirm schedule. Closed Jan. 1, Thanksgiving and Christmas. **Cost:** $12; $10 (ages 65+ and students with ID); $6 (ages 13-17); free (ages 0-12 and to all Fri. 5-9). Additional fees may be charged for special exhibitions. **Phone:** (207) 775-6148.

The McLellan House at the Portland Museum of Art reflects 19th-century architecture and design. Its interior is restored to the Federal period and includes vibrant wallpapers, carpeting and furniture. Featuring interactive computers, study centers provide detailed information pertaining to the social, economic, political and artistic history of the era and allow visitors to learn more about the house's former residents. **Time:** Allow 30 minutes minimum. **Hours:** Daily 10-5 (also Fri. 5-9), Memorial Day-Columbus Day; Tues.-Sun. 10-5 (also Fri. 5-9), rest of year. **Cost:** Included in Portland Museum of Art admission of $12; $10 (ages 65+ and students with ID); $6 (ages 6-17); free (ages 0-12 and to all Fri. 5-9). **Phone:** (207) 775-6148.

PORTLAND OBSERVATORY is off I-295 exit 7 to jct. Congress and Franklin sts., then n. to 138 Congress St. Exhibits detail the history, architecture and preservation of what is said to be the last remaining maritime signal tower in the United States. The observatory served Portland's bustling waterfront from 1807 to the early 20th century. Views of Portland, the White Mountains and Casco Bay are available from the 86-foot-high tower, reached by stairs.

Thirty-minute guided tours are available. **Time:** Allow 1 hour minimum. **Hours:** Tours depart daily 10-5, Memorial Day-Columbus Day. Sunset tours

(See map & index p. 131.)

depart Thurs. at 5, late July-late Aug. Last tour begins 30 minutes before closing. **Cost:** $8; $7 (ages 65+ and students with ID); $5 (ages 6-16); $25 (family, two adults and up to five children). **Phone:** (207) 774-5561.

PORTLAND SCHOONER CO. departs from Maine State Pier, 56 Commercial St., beyond Casco Bay Lines Gate 5. Launched in 1912 and 1924 respectively, the 88-foot and 72-foot wooden schooners *Wendameen* and *Bagheera* are elegantly decorated in period detail with mahogany trim and brass oil lamps. The 2-hour trip on Casco Bay affords visitors an opportunity to experience the sounds of the ocean and the sights along the Maine coast.

Time: Allow 2 hours minimum. **Hours:** Departures daily at 10:30, 1, 3:30 and 6, May 1-Labor Day; at noon, 2:30 and 5, day after Labor Day-Oct. 31. Phone ahead to confirm schedule. **Cost:** $39; $15 (ages 3-12). **Phone:** (207) 766-2500 or (877) 246-6637.

SOUTHWORTH PLANETARIUM is in the science building on the University of Southern Maine campus; take I-295 exit 6B, go 1 blk. w. on Forest Ave., then .5 blk. s. to 70 Falmouth St. Regularly changing astronomy shows, classes, movies and concerts are offered. Planetarium programs are projected onto a 30-foot dome. Seating capacity is 65. Featured in the exhibit area is Heaven on Earth, a permanent exhibit of the solar system.

Time: Allow 1 hour minimum. **Hours:** Astronomy shows Fri. at 7 and 8:30, Sat. at 3 (also Sun. at 3, Sept.-May). Phone ahead to confirm exhibit area schedule. **Cost:** One evening show $6.50; $6 (ages 5-17 and 65+). Sat. and Sun. matinee $6; $5.50 (ages 5-17 and 65+). Combination ticket for two evening shows $11; $10 (ages 5-17 and 65+). Exhibit area free. **Phone:** (207) 780-4249.

TATE HOUSE MUSEUM is 2 mi. w. on SR 22/9 at 1270 Westbrook St. in Stroudwater. In keeping with his importance as mast agent for the British Crown, George Tate built this Georgian Colonial house with indented gambrel roof in 1755. The house features 18th-century furnishings. Tour themes include 18th-century gardening techniques, architectural design and Colonial history.

Tours: Guided tours are available. **Time:** Allow 1 hour minimum. **Hours:** Wed.-Sat. 10-4, Sun. 1-4, early June-early Oct. Tours are given on the hour.

Last tour begins 1 hour before closing. Closed July 4 and Labor Day. **Cost:** $8; $6 (ages 62+); $3 (ages 6-12). **Phone:** (207) 774-6177.

VICTORIA MANSION, 109 Danforth St. between State and High sts., is a stunning Italianate-style house designed by distinguished New Haven architect Henry Austin. Built 1858-60 as an opulent summer home for hotelier Ruggles Sylvester Morse and his wife, the brownstone mansion boasts a four-story tower, several porches and such conveniences as running water, a gas lighting system and central heating.

An extensive collection of furniture by interior designer Gustave Herter complements the original painted *trompe l'oeil* walls and ceilings. Elaborate wood carvings and drapery; carpets; glassware; porcelain; and silver are some of the other treasures within. A whopping 90 percent of the home's original furnishings have been preserved.

The Turkish smoking room (believed to have been the first smoking room incorporated into a private American residence), the billiard room and the master bedroom's attached washroom are frills characteristic of mid-19th-century luxury hotels. Also noteworthy are the spectacular displays of stained glass, including the three-story stair hall's dazzling 6-by-25-foot skylight. From late December to early January holiday festivities showcase the house in Christmas splendor.

Tours: Guided tours are available. **Time:** Allow 1 hour minimum. **Hours:** Mon.-Sat. 10-4, Sun. 1-5, May-Oct. Additional hours are available day after Thanksgiving-first Sun. in Jan.; phone ahead to confirm schedule. Last tour begins 15 minutes before closing. Closed Jan. 1, Memorial Day, July 4, Labor Day and Christmas. **Cost:** $15; $13.50 (ages 62+); $5 (ages 6-17); $35 (family, two adults and up to five children in same household). **Phone:** (207) 772-4841.

WICKED WALKING TOURS depart from Bell Buoy Park, 72 Commercial St. On a walking tour through the Old Port, participants discover Portland's darker side as theatrical guides relate a blend of eerie legends, comedic tales and historical oddities. **Time:** Allow 1 hour minimum. **Hours:** Departures daily at 10:30 and 8. Phone ahead to confirm schedule. **Cost:** $16; $13 (ages 62+); $11 (ages 0-12). Reservations are required. **Phone:** (207) 730-0490 after hours, or (888) 718-4253 Mon.-Fri.

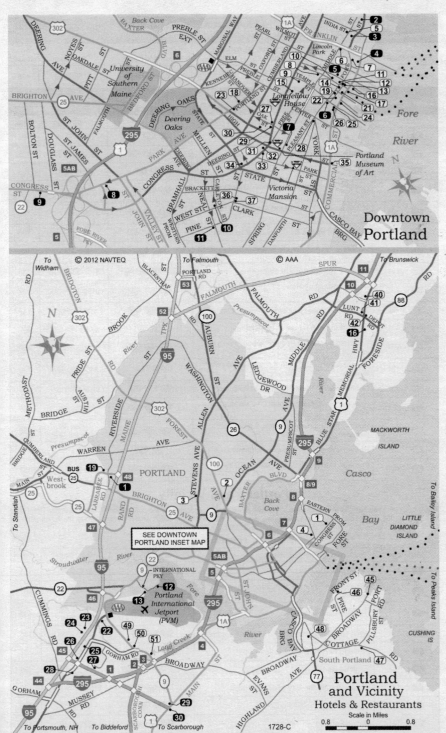

© 2012 NAVTEQ   © AAA

Downtown Portland

Fore River

Portland Museum of Art

Longfellow House

Victoria Mansion

University of Southern Maine

Deering Oaks

Portland and Vicinity
Hotels & Restaurants

Scale in Miles
0.8   0   0.8

To Widham
To Falmouth
To Brunswick
To Bailey Island
To Peaks Island
To Little Diamond Island

MACKWORTH ISLAND

Casco Bay

LITTLE DIAMOND ISLAND

CUSHING IS

Portland International Jetport (PVM)

South Portland

To Portsmouth, NH
To Biddeford
To Scarborough

1728-C

✈ Airport Accommodations

Map Page	MANCHESTER-BOSTON REGIONAL AIRPORT	Diamond Rated	Rate Range	Page
4 p. 131	Hilton Garden Inn Portland Downtown Waterfront, 7 mi ne of terminal	◆◆◆	$159-$339	135

✈ Airport Accommodations

Map Page	PORTLAND INTERNATIONAL JETPORT	Diamond Rated	Rate Range	Page
9 p. 131	Clarion Portland, 2.5 mi e of terminal	◆◆◆	$79-$239	135
12 p. 131	Embassy Suites Hotel, 0.3 mi w of terminal	◆◆◆	$109-$289 SAVE	135
1 p. 131	Fireside Inn & Suites, 3.7 mi n of terminal	◆◆	$110-$240	135
3 p. 131	Hampton Inn Portland Downtown - Waterfront, 7 mi ne of terminal	◆◆◆	Rates not provided	135
13 p. 131	Hilton Garden Inn Portland Airport, 0.3 mi n of terminal	◆◆◆	$129-$309 SAVE	135
7 p. 131	Holiday Inn by the Bay, 3 mi ne of terminal	◆◆◆	$152-$299 SAVE	136
8 p. 131	La Quinta Inn & Suites Portland, 2.5 mi e of terminal	◆◆	$87-$254	136
6 p. 131	Portland Harbor Hotel, 9 mi ne of terminal	◆◆◆◆	$189-$399 SAVE	136
5 p. 131	Portland Regency Hotel & Spa, 5 mi ne of terminal	◆◆◆	$139-$379 SAVE	137
2 p. 98	TownePlace Suites by Marriott, 4 mi s of terminal	◆◆◆	$99-$259	147
22 p. 131	Comfort Inn, 2.6 mi sw of terminal	◆◆	$74-$189 SAVE	150
28 p. 131	Courtyard by Marriott Portland Airport, 3 mi s of terminal	◆◆◆	$159-$359	150
26 p. 131	Days Inn Portland-South Portland, 2 mi sw of terminal	◆◆	$45-$350 SAVE	150
25 p. 131	DoubleTree by Hilton, 2.4 mi s of terminal	◆◆◆	$109-$349 SAVE	150
27 p. 131	Hampton Inn Portland Airport, 2 mi sw from terminal	◆◆◆	$99-$269	150
23 p. 131	Holiday Inn Express & Suites, 3 mi sw of terminal	◆◆◆	Rates not provided SAVE	150
29 p. 131	Howard Johnson Hotel, 3 mi se of terminal	◆◆	$70-$180	150
24 p. 131	Portland Marriott at Sable Oaks, 3 mi sw of terminal	◆◆◆	$129-$329 SAVE	151

Portland and Vicinity

This index helps you "spot" where approved hotels and restaurants are located on the corresponding detailed maps. Hotel daily rate range is for comparison only. Restaurant price range is a combination of lunch and/or dinner. Turn to the listing page for more detailed rate and price information and consult display ads for special promotions.

PORTLAND

Map Page	Hotels	Diamond Rated	Rate Range	Page
1 p. 131	Fireside Inn & Suites	◆◆	$110-$240	135
2 p. 131	Residence Inn by Marriott Portland Downtown/ Waterfront	◆◆◆	$139-$559	137
3 p. 131	Hampton Inn Portland Downtown - Waterfront	◆◆◆	Rates not provided	135
4 p. 131	Hilton Garden Inn Portland Downtown Waterfront	◆◆◆	$159-$339	135
5 p. 131	Portland Regency Hotel & Spa	◆◆◆	$139-$379 SAVE	137
6 p. 131	Portland Harbor Hotel (See ad p. 137.)	◆◆◆◆	$189-$399 SAVE	136
7 p. 131	Holiday Inn by the Bay (See ad p. 136.)	◆◆◆	$152-$299 SAVE	136
8 p. 131	La Quinta Inn & Suites Portland	◆◆	$87-$254	136
9 p. 131	Clarion Portland	◆◆◆	$79-$239	135

PORTLAND (cont'd)

Map Page	Hotels (cont'd)	Diamond Rated	Rate Range	Page
10 p. 131	Inn On Carleton	◆◆◆	$99-$210	136
11 p. 131	West End Inn	◆◆◆	Rates not provided	138
12 p. 131	**Embassy Suites Hotel**	◆◆◆	$109-$289 [SAVE]	135
13 p. 131	**Hilton Garden Inn Portland Airport**	◆◆◆	$129-$309 [SAVE]	135

Map Page	Restaurants	Diamond Rated	Cuisine	Price Range	Page
1 p. 131	The Front Room	◆◆	American	$8-$21	139
2 p. 131	**Sengchai Thai**	◆◆	Thai	$8-$12	140
3 p. 131	The Cafe at Pat's	◆◆◆	American	$10-$28	138
4 p. 131	Silly's	◆	American	$6-$19	140
5 p. 131	Ribollita	◆◆◆	Regional Italian	$13-$19	139
6 p. 131	**Hugo's Restaurant**	◆◆◆◆	Regional American	$50-$90	139
7 p. 131	Fore Street	◆◆◆◆	American	$20-$40	139
8 p. 131	Tandoor	◆◆	Indian	$8-$16	140
9 p. 131	Federal Spice	◆	Mediterranean	$5-$12	139
10 p. 131	Fuji	◆◆	Japanese	$9-$25	139
11 p. 131	Bull Feeney's	◆◆	American	$8-$23	138
12 p. 131	Old Port Sea Grill and Raw Bar	◆◆◆	Seafood	$10-$31	139
13 p. 131	The Old Port Tavern	◆◆	American	$6-$28	139
14 p. 131	Gritty McDuff's	◆◆	American	$9-$13	139
15 p. 131	**David's Restaurant**	◆◆◆	American	$8-$26	138
16 p. 131	Di'Millo's Floating Restaurant	◆◆	Seafood	$9-$30	138
17 p. 131	Portland Lobster Co	◆	Seafood	$8-$23	139
18 p. 131	**Back Bay Grill**	◆◆◆◆	Regional American	$18-$36	138
19 p. 131	Street & Company	◆◆◆	Mediterranean	$22-$30	140
21 p. 131	Vignola Cinque Terre	◆◆◆	Italian	$11-$34	140
22 p. 131	Cafe at Wharf Street & Wine Bar	◆◆	American	$8-$12	138
23 p. 131	Bintliff's American Cafe	◆◆	American	$6-$14	138
24 p. 131	Sapporo Restaurant	◆◆	Japanese	$7-$57	140
25 p. 131	Three Dollar Deweys	◆◆	American	$8-$18	140
26 p. 131	**the Salt Exchange**	◆◆◆◆	New American	$8-$26	140
27 p. 131	Emilitsa	◆◆◆	Greek	$21-$31	139
28 p. 131	Yosaku	◆◆	Japanese	$5-$25	140
29 p. 131	Five Fifty-Five	◆◆◆	American	$10-$38	139
30 p. 131	Bibo's Madd Apple Cafe	◆◆	American	$7-$20	138
31 p. 131	Local 188	◆◆	Spanish	$7-$21	139
32 p. 131	The Congress Bar & Grill	◆◆	American	$9-$22	138
33 p. 131	Mesa Verde	◆	Mexican	$6-$16	139
34 p. 131	Boda	◆◆◆	Thai	$11-$19	138

Map Page	Restaurants (cont'd)	Diamond Rated	Cuisine	Price Range	Page
㉟ p. 131	Becky's Diner	◆	American	$4-$20	138
㊱ p. 131	Caiola's	◆◆◆	Italian	$15-$26	138
㊲ p. 131	Aurora Provisions	◆◆	American	$6-$8	138

FALMOUTH

Map Page	Hotel	Diamond Rated	Rate Range	Page
⓰ p. 131	**Falmouth Inn**	◆	$69-$156 SAVE	85

Map Page	Restaurants	Diamond Rated	Cuisine	Price Range	Page
㊵ p. 131	Foreside Tavern & Side Bar	◆◆	American	$9-$24	86
㊶ p. 131	Ricetta's Brick Oven Pizzeria	◆◆	Pizza	$9-$19	86
㊷ p. 131	Lotus Chinese Restaurant	◆◆	Chinese	$8-$22	86

WESTBROOK

Map Page	Hotel	Diamond Rated	Rate Range	Page
⓳ p. 131	**Super 8**	◆◆	$58-$130 SAVE	157

SOUTH PORTLAND

Map Page	Hotels	Diamond Rated	Rate Range	Page
(22) p. 131	**Comfort Inn** *(See ad p. 135.)*	◆◆	$74-$189 SAVE	150
(23) p. 131	**Holiday Inn Express & Suites**	◆◆◆	Rates not provided SAVE	150
(24) p. 131	**Portland Marriott at Sable Oaks**	◆◆◆	$129-$329 SAVE	151
(25) p. 131	**DoubleTree by Hilton**	◆◆◆	$109-$349 SAVE	150
(26) p. 131	**Days Inn Portland-South Portland**	◆◆	$45-$350 SAVE	150
(27) p. 131	Hampton Inn Portland Airport	◆◆◆	$99-$269	150
(28) p. 131	Courtyard by Marriott Portland Airport	◆◆◆	$159-$359	150
(29) p. 131	Howard Johnson Hotel	◆◆	$70-$180	150
(30) p. 131	**BEST WESTERN Merry Manor Inn**	◆◆	$99-$209 SAVE	150

Map Page	Restaurants	Diamond Rated	Cuisine	Price Range	Page
㊺ p. 131	Joe's Boathouse	◆◆	American	$10-$27	151
㊻ p. 131	Saltwater Grille	◆◆◆	Regional Seafood	$12-$28	151
㊼ p. 131	Thai Taste Restaurant	◆◆	Thai	$8-$19	151
㊽ p. 131	Q Street Diner	◆	American	$4-$9	151
㊾ p. 131	Thai Pom's Restaurant	◆◆	Thai	$8-$19	151
㊿ p. 131	Sea Dog Brewing Co	◆◆	American	$8-$23	151
(51) p. 131	Wild Willy's Gourmet Burgers	◆	Burgers	$7-$12	151

(See map & index p. 131.)

CLARION PORTLAND   (207)774-5611 **9**

▼▼▼▼ Hotel $79-$239 **Address:** 1230 Congress St 04102 **Location:** I-295 exit 5, just w on SR 22. **Facility:** 149 units. 6 stories, interior corridors. **Terms:** cancellation fee imposed. **Amenities:** video games (fee). **Pool(s):** heated indoor. **Activities:** whirlpool, exercise room. **Guest Services:** valet and coin laundry, area transportation-hospitals, bus & train stations.

[icons] / SOME UNITS [icons]

EMBASSY SUITES HOTEL   (207)775-2200 **12**

▼▼▼▼
Hotel
$109-$289

E EMBASSY SUITES HOTELS

AAA Benefit: Members save 5% or more!

Address: 1050 Westbrook St 04102 **Location:** At Portland International Jetport. **Facility:** 119 units, some two bedrooms. 6 stories, interior corridors. **Terms:** 1-7 night minimum stay, cancellation fee imposed. **Pool(s):** heated indoor. **Activities:** saunas, whirlpool, exercise room. **Guest Services:** valet and coin laundry. **Free Special Amenities:** full breakfast and manager's reception.

SAVE [icons] / SOME UNITS FEE [icons]

FIRESIDE INN & SUITES   (207)774-5601 **1**

▼▼ Hotel $110-$240 **Address:** 81 Riverside St 04103 **Location:** I-95 exit 48. **Facility:** 196 units. 2 stories, interior corridors. **Amenities:** Some: high-speed Internet. **Dining:** name entertainment. **Pool(s):** heated outdoor, heated indoor. **Activities:** sauna, whirlpool, exercise room. **Guest Services:** valet and coin laundry, area transportation-Concord Trailways, Greyhound & Amtrak stations.

[icons] / SOME UNITS FEE [icons]

Get an insider view from AAA/CAA travel experts at AAATravelViews.com

HAMPTON INN PORTLAND DOWNTOWN - WATERFRONT
207/775-1454 **3**

▼▼▼▼ Hotel. Rates not provided. **Address:** 209 Fore St 04101 **Location:** In the Old Port; between Franklin and India sts. **Facility:** 122 units. 6 stories, interior corridors.

AAA Benefit: Members save up to 10%!

Terms: check-in 4 pm. **Amenities:** high-speed Internet. **Pool(s):** heated indoor. **Activities:** exercise room. **Guest Services:** valet and coin laundry, area transportation-within 2 mi.

[icons]

HILTON GARDEN INN PORTLAND AIRPORT
(207)828-1117 **13**

▼▼▼▼
Hotel
$129-$309

Hilton Garden Inn

AAA Benefit: Unparalleled hospitality at a special Member rate.

Address: 145 Jetport Blvd 04102 **Location:** At Portland International Jetport. **Facility:** 88 units. 3 stories, interior corridors. **Terms:** 1-7 night minimum stay, cancellation fee imposed. **Amenities:** high-speed Internet. **Pool(s):** heated indoor. **Activities:** whirlpool, exercise room. **Guest Services:** valet and coin laundry, area transportation-within 3 mi. **Free Special Amenities:** local transportation and airport transportation.

SAVE [icons] / SOME UNITS FEE [icons]

HILTON GARDEN INN PORTLAND DOWNTOWN WATERFRONT   (207)780-0780 **4**

▼▼▼▼ Hotel $159-$339 **Address:** 65 Commercial St 04101 **Location:** Waterfront. In the Old Port; across from Casco Bay ferry terminal. **Facility:** 120 units. 6 stories, interior corridors. **Parking:** valet only. **Terms:** check-in 4

AAA Benefit: Unparalleled hospitality at a special Member rate.

pm, 1-7 night minimum stay, cancellation fee imposed. **Amenities:** high-speed Internet. **Pool(s):** heated indoor. **Activities:** whirlpool, exercise room. **Guest Services:** valet and coin laundry.

[icons] / SOME UNITS FEE [icons]

▼ See AAA listing p. 150 ▼

(See map & index p. 131.)

HOLIDAY INN BY THE BAY (207)775-2311 **7**

Hotel
$152-$299

Address: 88 Spring St 04101 **Location:** Center. **Facility:** 239 units. 11 stories, interior corridors. **Terms:** check-in 4 pm. **Amenities:** safes. *Some:* high-speed Internet. **Pool(s):** heated indoor. **Activities:** saunas, exercise room. **Guest Services:** valet and coin laundry, area transportation-Amtrak station & Concord Trailways. **Free Special Amenities:** local telephone calls and high-speed Internet. *(See ad this page.)*

SAVE ⊞ ⊞ ⊞ ⊞ CALL ⊞ ⊞ ⊞ ⊞ ⊞ ⊞ ⊞

INN ON CARLETON 207/775-1910 **10**

▼▼▼ **Historic Bed & Breakfast** $99-$210 **Address:** 46 Carleton St 04102 **Location:** In the West End; just past Longfellow Monument, then just s. **Facility:** This restored 1869 Victorian townhouse is nestled in the historic Western Promenade Historic District, close to the Portland Museum of Art and the Maine Medical Center. 6 units. 3 stories (no elevator), interior corridors. **Terms:** 2 night minimum stay - seasonal and/or weekends, 14 day cancellation notice-fee imposed. ⊞ ⊞ ⊞ ⊞

LA QUINTA INN & SUITES PORTLAND (207)871-0611 **8**

▼▼ ▼▼ **Hotel** $87-$254 **Address:** 340 Park Ave 04102 **Location:** I-295 exit 5A southbound; exit 5 northbound, e on SR 22. **Facility:** 105 units. 4 stories, interior corridors. **Pool(s):** outdoor. **Activities:** limited exercise equipment. **Guest Services:** valet and coin laundry, area transportation-Amtrak station & Maine Medical Center.

⊞ CALL ⊞ ⊞ ⊞ ⊞ ⊞
/SOME UNITS ⊞ ⊞ ⊞

PORTLAND HARBOR HOTEL (207)775-9090 **6**

▼▼▼▼ ▼▼▼▼
Hotel
$189-$399

Address: 468 Fore St 04101 **Location:** In the Old Port. **Facility:** Look around the property and you'll feel as though you've been transported to the 19th century. The hotel's luxurious guest rooms and tons of amenities appeal to both business and leisure travelers. 101 units. 5 stories, interior corridors. **Parking:** valet only. **Terms:** check-in 4 pm, cancellation fee imposed. **Activities:** exercise room. **Fee:** massage. **Guest Services:** valet laundry, area transportation-Amtrak station & Concord Trailways. **Free Special Amenities:** newspaper and high-speed Internet. *(See ad p. 137.)*

SAVE ⊞ ⊞ ⊞ ⊞ CALL ⊞ ⊞ ⊞ ⊞
/SOME UNITS FEE ⊞ ⊞

▼ *See AAA listing this page* ▼

(See map & index p. 131.)

PORTLAND REGENCY HOTEL & SPA

(207)774-4200 **5**

Historic Hotel
$139-$379

Address: 20 Milk St 04101 **Location:** In the Old Port; between Market and Silver sts; downtown. **Facility:** The converted 19th-century armory (circa 1895) proudly sits on the National Registry of Historic Places. Guest rooms feature all the modern conveniences needed yet offer the feel of yesteryear. 95 units. 5 stories, interior corridors. **Parking:** valet only. **Terms:** cancellation fee imposed. **Activities:** saunas, whirlpool, steamrooms, spa. **Guest Services:** valet laundry, area transportation-Amtrak station & Concord Trailways. **Free Special Amenities:** high-speed Internet and airport transportation.

SAVE ECO 🛬 🍴 🛁 ⛲ 🏋 BIZ 📶 ✕ / SOME UNITS 🖥

RESIDENCE INN BY MARRIOTT PORTLAND DOWNTOWN/ WATERFRONT

(207)761-1660 **2**

Extended Stay **Contemporary Hotel** $139-$559 **Address:** 145 Fore St 04101 **Location:** Waterfront. In the Old Port; across from Casco Bay ferry terminal. **Facility:** 179 units, some two bedrooms, efficiencies and kitchens. 5 stories, interior corridors. **Parking:** on-site (fee). **Amenities:** high-speed Internet. **Pool(s):** heated indoor. **Activities:** whirlpool, exercise room. **Guest Services:** valet and coin laundry, area transportation-within 5 mi.

🛬 🛏 🍴 CALL 🦽 M 🚗 BIZ 📶 ✕ 🖥 📺 🖥 / SOME UNITS FEE 🐾

▼ See AAA listing p. 136 ▼

(See map & index p. 131.)

WEST END INN 207/772-1377 **11**

WWWW **Bed & Breakfast. Rates** not provided. **Address:** 146 Pine St 04102 **Location:** In the West End; just past Longfellow Monument, then just s. **Facility:** Nestled in the Western Promenade Historic District and offering comfortable rooms. Guests sit down to the full breakfast served each morning. It's a 20-minute walk to the Old Port. 6 units. 3 stories (no elevator), interior corridors. **Terms:** check-in 4 pm. 🛜 ✕ ☎

DIAMOND COVE 207/766-3005

fyi Not evaluated. **Location:** On Great Diamond Island; in Casco Bay; access by ferry. Facilities, services, and décor characterize a mid-scale property.

WHERE TO EAT

AMATO'S 207/773-1682

W **Deli. Quick Serve. $4-$14 AAA Inspector Notes:** Known for their "Real Italian" sandwich, which was created over 100 years ago by an Italian immigrant who decided to place a little bit of meat, fresh vegetables, cheese, Greek olives, a zesty pickle and a specialty blended olive oil on a freshly made roll. This recipe has built up a loyal following of customers. Other menu choices include hot or cold sandwiches, calzones, specialty pizzas, pasta and freshly prepared salads. Diners may choose to eat in or take out. **Bar:** beer & wine. **Address:** 71 India St 04101 **Location:** Between Middle and Newbury sts. **Parking:** street only. L D

AURORA PROVISIONS 207/871-9060 **37**

WW **American. Quick Serve. $6-$8 AAA Inspector Notes:** Gourmet sandwiches are prepared at this self-serve, bistro-style, specialty food store with a small café. You may also choose from their selection of cakes, cookies and other desserts, all made on site. Juices, soda, beer and wine also are offered. **Address:** 64 Pine St 04102 **Location:** Jct State St, just w. B L

BACK BAY GRILL 207/772-8833 **18**

WWWW
Regional
American
Fine Dining
$18-$36

AAA Inspector Notes: As seasons change so does this menu. The extensive wine list is spectacular, colorful murals add a lively feel and the crème brûlée is always special. You'll find this restaurant downtown near the main post office. **Bar:** full bar. **Reservations:** suggested. **Address:** 65 Portland St 04101 **Location:** I-295 exit 6A (Forest Ave), just e to Portland St, then just n. **Parking:** street only. D

BECKY'S DINER 207/773-7070 **35**

W **American. Family Dining. $4-$20 AAA Inspector Notes:** The long-standing tradition continues today, with the diner opening at 4 am and catering to the early-rising fishermen and lobstermen (and -women) before they venture out to sea. A bevy of egg dishes, omelet choices, pancakes and French toast are available. Lunch and dinner offerings include standard sandwiches, local seafood and New England comfort foods. **Address:** 390 Commercial St 04101 **Location:** In waterfront area. B L D

BIBO'S MADD APPLE CAFE 207/774-9698 **30**

WW **American. Casual Dining. $7-$20 AAA Inspector Notes:** Close to the Portland Performing Arts Center, this small and colorful cafe offers fresh ingredients and everything on the menu is made on the premises. **Bar:** beer & wine. **Reservations:** suggested. **Address:** 23 Forest Ave 04101 **Location:** In Arts District. **Parking:** street only. L D

BINTLIFF'S AMERICAN CAFE 207/774-0005 **23**

WW **American. Casual Dining. $6-$14 AAA Inspector Notes:** More than 110 items line the specialty brunch menu at the popular bistro-style restaurant, which occupies a Greek Revival building. **Bar:** full bar. **Address:** 98 Portland St 04101 **Location:** Jct Portland St and Forest Ave, just n; across from main post office. **Parking:** street only. B L

BODA 207/347-7557 **34**

WWW **Thai. Casual Dining. $11-$19 AAA Inspector Notes:** This amazing restaurant, serving imaginative Thai dishes, uses the freshest ingredients available. Organic tofu, fried rice with crab, stir-fried glass noodles and crispy duck along with impressive vegetarian and gluten-free options are just a sampling of what is available. There is convenient parking at Joe's Smokeshop. **Bar:** full bar. **Address:** 671 Congress St 04101 **Location:** Just w of State St. D

BULL FEENEY'S 207/773-7210 **11**

WW **American. Casual Dining. $8-$23 AAA Inspector Notes:** Sustaining the atmosphere of an Irish pub, this eatery offers lighter fare at lunch and in the pub. The dinner menu includes a number of seafood dishes, steaks, soups and salads, as well as such Irish favorites as shepherd's pie and bangers and colcannon. Do not miss the delicious Irish soda-bread biscuits. **Bar:** full bar. **Address:** 375 Fore St 04101 **Location:** In the Old Port; at Exchange St. **Parking:** street only. L D LATE

THE CAFE AT PAT'S 207/874-0706 **3**

WW **American. Casual Dining. $10-$28 AAA Inspector Notes:** On the second floor of a popular meat market, the chef-owned eatery serves excellent home-style dishes prepared with a creative twist. Standouts include pan-fried ravioli stuffed with exotic mushrooms and chevre and served with Roma tomato concasse; inside-out chicken cordon bleu, a backward version of the French favorite; and Guinness meatloaf with peppered demi-glace gravy. Butterscotch creme brulee is quite tasty. A beamed ceiling and wooden tables make for a cozy New England country setting. **Bar:** full bar. **Address:** 484 Stevens Ave 04103 **Location:** On SR 9, at Brentwood St. **Parking:** street only. D

CAFE AT WHARF STREET & WINE BAR 207/772-6976 **22**

WW **American. Casual Dining. $8-$12 AAA Inspector Notes:** On a cobblestone street, the restaurant and wine bar has a casual bistro atmosphere. The menu features fresh local seafood, choice meats and vegetarian dishes. A nice selection of wines complements dinner. **Bar:** full bar. **Address:** 38 Wharf St 04101 **Location:** In the Old Port. **Parking:** street only. D

CAIOLA'S 207/772-1110 **36**

WW **Italian. Fine Dining. $15-$26 AAA Inspector Notes:** If the weather is nice, grab a seat on the outdoor dining area or take a seat in the front dining room or through the bustling kitchen in the back dining area. Not a typical bistro, the chef/owner uses only the freshest ingredients. Soups are made from scratch, the salads are creative and an impressive selection of fish, chicken and beef appetizers and entrées will cover all dining desires. **Bar:** full bar. **Address:** 58 Pine St 04102 **Location:** West End; between Brackett and Clark sts. D

THE CONGRESS BAR & GRILL 207/828-9944 **32**

WW **American. Casual Dining. $9-$22 AAA Inspector Notes:** In the Arts District, the red brick dining room and bar is a lively spot in which to nibble items off a frequently changing tapas menu paired with a variety of locally brewed beers. The selection of fresh seafood is tempting as well. **Bar:** full bar. **Address:** 617 Congress St 04101 **Location:** Just s of jct Congress and State sts; center. **Parking:** street only. L D

DAVID'S RESTAURANT 207/773-4340 **15**

WWW
American
Casual Dining
$8-$26

AAA Inspector Notes: The restaurant serves such creative American cuisine as the signature pepper-crusted rare tuna, as well as more simply prepared items. The open kitchen, small tables, mosaic tile floors and long bar contribute to a casual, intimate atmosphere. Outside seating is a seasonal option. **Bar:** full bar. **Reservations:** suggested. **Address:** 22 Monument Square 04101 **Location:** In Arts District. **Parking:** no self-parking. L D CALL 🛗M

DI'MILLO'S FLOATING RESTAURANT 207/772-2216 **16**

WW **Seafood. Casual Dining. $9-$30 AAA Inspector Notes:** A former car ferry on the city's waterfront, the family-owned restaurant presents a menu of lobster, other seafood, steaks and Italian dishes. Tourists frequent this place for its views and nautical atmosphere, which includes mahogany paneling and brass railings. **Bar:** full bar. **Address:** 25 Long Wharf 04101 **Location:** Downtown. L D CALL 🛗M

(See map & index p. 131.)

EMILITSA
207/221-0245 27

▼▼▼▼ Greek. Fine Dining. $21-$31 **AAA Inspector Notes:** Memorable Greek cuisine prepared from scratch is what's on the menu at this upscale bistro. Not only are the dishes prepared with the freshest possible ingredients—including local items and those from Greece—but the setting is warm and inviting with soft lighting, brick walls and honey-toned wood floors. **Bar:** full bar. **Address:** 547 Congress St 04101 **Location:** At Oak St; downtown. **Parking:** no self-parking. [D]

FEDERAL SPICE
207/774-6404 9

▼ Mediterranean. Quick Serve. $5-$12 **AAA Inspector Notes:** Located in Monument Square, the restaurant has a variety of hot and cold wraps, soft tacos and quesadillas, all of which are homemade. Patrons can eat in or take out. **Bar:** beer & wine. **Address:** 225 Federal St 04101 **Location:** Just sw of Temple St; in Arts District. **Parking:** street only. [L] [D] [AC]

FIVE FIFTY-FIVE
207/761-0555 29

▼▼▼ American. Fine Dining. $10-$38 **AAA Inspector Notes:** Located in the Arts District, this upscale restaurant's name corresponds to its street number. The two-story dining room, with an open kitchen, has a sleek, modern feel. Fresh local ingredients enhance California-influenced cuisine. A daily cheese plate is offered. **Bar:** full bar. **Reservations:** suggested. **Address:** 555 Congress St 04101 **Location:** In Arts District. **Parking:** street only. [D]

FLATBREAD COMPANY
207/772-8777

▼ Pizza. Family Dining. $9-$19 **AAA Inspector Notes:** In a great waterfront location, the restaurant serves flatbread pizza made with organic, seasonal ingredients from local growers. All are cooked in a wood-fired clay oven open to the dining room. **Bar:** beer & wine. **Address:** 72 Commercial St 04101 **Location:** In the Old Port; waterfront area. **Parking:** street only. [L] [D] CALL ⑤M

FORE STREET
207/775-2717 7

▼▼▼▼ American. Fine Dining. $20-$40 **AAA Inspector Notes:** Housed in a converted factory building, this very popular downtown restaurant dishes up fantastic New England specialties. The wood-fired oven and rotisserie grill enhance the old brick and polished wood atmosphere. The friendly, attentive service is excellent. **Bar:** full bar. **Reservations:** suggested. **Address:** 288 Fore St 04101 **Location:** In the Old Port. [D]

THE FRONT ROOM
207/773-3366 1

▼▼▼ American. Casual Dining. $8-$21 **AAA Inspector Notes:** Located atop Munjoy Hill, this chef-owned bistro is a favorite among the East End locals. The attraction is the bevy of delicious, creative comfort foods. The cozy dining room includes an open kitchen, hanging pots and brick walls and features a bar on one end. **Bar:** full bar. **Address:** 73 Congress St 04101 **Location:** At Howard St. **Parking:** street only. [L] [D]

FUJI
207/773-2900 10

▼ Japanese. Casual Dining. $9-$25 **AAA Inspector Notes:** In the heart of the Old Port, the restaurant puts forth a menu of Japanese, Korean and Thai cuisines. The dining rooms include a sushi bar, hibachi tables and a traditional tatami room. Validated parking is available for the Fore Street garage. **Bar:** full bar. **Reservations:** suggested. **Address:** 29 Exchange St 04101 **Location:** In the Old Port; at Milk St. **Parking:** street only. [L] [D]

GRITTY MCDUFF'S
207/772-2739 14

▼▼▼ American. Casual Dining. $9-$13 **AAA Inspector Notes:** The Old Port favorite was the city's first brew pub since Prohibition. The on-premises brewery's English-style brewing process produces small batches of ales without preservatives or additives. The menu lists American and English pub fare. Patio seating is available seasonally. **Bar:** full bar. **Address:** 396 Fore St 04101 **Location:** In the Old Port. **Parking:** street only. [L] [D]

HUGO'S RESTAURANT
207/774-8538 6

▼▼▼▼ Regional American Fine Dining $50-$90 **AAA Inspector Notes:** Near the Old Port District, the small restaurant nurtures a warm, comfortable atmosphere. A frequently changing menu centers on France- and Italy-influenced food made from organic and fresh Maine and New England ingredients. The chef's tasting and prix fixe menus are outstanding. The cozy bar area is ideal for lighter meals. **Bar:** full bar. **Reservations:** suggested. **Address:** 88 Middle St 04101 **Location:** Just ne of Franklin St; close to the Old Port. [D]

LOCAL 188
207/761-7909 31

▼▼ Spanish. Casual Dining. $7-$21 **AAA Inspector Notes:** This is the only Spanish tapas restaurant in Portland. It is conveniently located near Maine Medical Center and has on-site parking in the back of the restaurant, a rarity in the city. **Bar:** full bar. **Address:** 685 Congress St 04101 **Location:** Just w of State St. [D]

MARGARITAS MEXICAN RESTAURANT
207/874-6444

▼▼ Mexican. Casual Dining. $8-$20 **AAA Inspector Notes:** Diners will feel as though they have just stepped south of the border at this fun Mexican cantina. Traditional music fills the air while warm terracotta colored walls accented by painted pottery and unique jeweled star lanterns surround you. Sip on a large margarita while enjoying the freshly prepared fajitas, burritos, enchiladas, or quesadillas. **Bar:** full bar. **Address:** 242 St. John St 04102 **Location:** On US 1, just s of jct SR 9. [D]

MEKHONG THAI RESTAURANT
207/773-8424

▼▼ Thai. Casual Dining. $8-$17 **AAA Inspector Notes:** On the menu is a good variety of well-prepared seafood, chicken, stir-fry, curry and ginger dishes. Contemporary decor lends to a warm atmosphere. The staff is friendly, prompt and knowledgeable. **Bar:** full bar. **Address:** 865 Forest Ave 04103 **Location:** I-295 exit 6B, 1.4 mi w on US 302. [L] [D]

MESA VERDE
207/774-6089 33

▼ Mexican. Casual Dining. $6-$16 **AAA Inspector Notes:** This restaurant is known for its food and for the variety of juices and smoothies available at the juice bar. **Bar:** full bar. **Address:** 618 Congress St 04101 **Location:** In Arts District. **Parking:** no self-parking. [L] [D] [AC]

OLD PORT SEA GRILL AND RAW BAR
207/879-6100 12

▼▼▼ Seafood. Casual Dining. $10-$31 **AAA Inspector Notes:** Stylish urban decor sets the scene for the dining experience. To ensure product quality, the restaurant obtains ingredients from local producers and fishermen. On the menu are wood-grilled seafood and meats, lobster, fried seafood, chicken and pork chops. **Bar:** full bar. **Address:** 93 Commercial St 04101 **Location:** In the Old Port. **Parking:** street only. [L] [D] CALL ⑤M

THE OLD PORT TAVERN
207/774-0444 13

▼▼▼ American. Casual Dining. $6-$28 **AAA Inspector Notes:** In business for more than 30 years, the restaurant is a favorite with locals and tourists alike. This place exudes the feel of its neighborhood, the historic district. While the menu has an emphasis on steak, it also lists seafood, chicken and such lighter pub choices as sandwiches, wraps and burgers. **Bar:** full bar. **Address:** 11 Moulton St 04101 **Location:** In the Old Port. **Parking:** street only. [L] [D]

PORTLAND LOBSTER CO
207/775-2112 17

▼ Seafood. Quick Serve. $8-$23 **AAA Inspector Notes:** Patrons can order any number of fresh seafood entrees and enjoy them either inside or outdoors on the waterfront dock. **Bar:** beer & wine. **Address:** 180 Commercial St 04101 **Location:** In the Old Port. **Parking:** no self-parking. [L] [D] [AC]

RIBOLLITA
207/774-2972 5

▼▼▼ Regional Italian. Casual Dining. $13-$19 **AAA Inspector Notes:** The menu centers on hearty country Italian cuisine, including pasta, seafood and vegetarian entrees. Cozy dining rooms are simply decorated, but nevertheless romantic. **Bar:** beer & wine. **Reservations:** suggested. **Address:** 41 Middle St 04101 **Location:** Just e of US 1A (Franklin Arterial). [D]

(See map & index p. 131.)

RI-RA IRISH PUB   207/761-4446

▼▼ ▼▼ Irish. Casual Dining. $10-$23 **AAA Inspector Notes:** The restaurant specializes in traditional Irish cuisine with a contemporary twist. Some examples include beef and Guinness pie and classic fish and chips. The noise level can be loud at times due to the pub's popularity and folk bands that regularly play. **Bar:** full bar. **Address:** 72 Commercial St 04101 **Location:** In the Old Port. **Parking:** street only. ⬜L ⬜D

THE SALT EXCHANGE   207/347-5687 ㉖

New
American
Fine Dining
$8-$26

AAA Inspector Notes: Chef Adam White focuses on using the freshest local ingredients, resulting in a creative menu and amazing cuisine. Small plates allow guests to choose two-to-four courses with such highlights as local oysters, pork belly, local cod and Maine lobster. **Bar:** full bar. **Reservations:** suggested. **Address:** 245 Commercial St 04101 **Location:** On US 1, between Cross and Union sts. **Parking:** street only.

⬜L ⬜D

SAPPORO RESTAURANT   207/772-1233 ㉔

▼▼ ▼▼ Japanese. Casual Dining. $7-$57 **AAA Inspector Notes:** This locally popular restaurant features sushi selections as well as tempura, teriyaki, combination lunches and dinners, and other traditional Japanese dishes. Presentations are attractive, and the serving staff is prompt, friendly and helpful. The dining room boasts a long sushi bar, wooden walls and a simple decor. **Bar:** full bar. **Reservations:** suggested, weekends. **Address:** 230 Commercial St 04101 **Location:** In the Old Port; in Union Wharf; on waterfront. **Parking:** street only. ⬜L ⬜D

SEBAGO BREWING COMPANY   207/775-2337

▼▼ ▼▼ American. Gastropub. $9-$23 **AAA Inspector Notes:** The stylish brew pub sustains a friendly, informal atmosphere. Self-described "American pub" cuisine includes delicious pasta, chicken, seafood and steak entrees, as well as tasty salads, burgers and sandwiches. The latter are available all day. The resident pastry chef prepares desserts on the premises each day. **Bar:** full bar. **Address:** 164 Middle St 04101 **Location:** In the Old Port. **Parking:** street only. ⬜L ⬜D

SENGCHAI THAI   207/773-1001 ②

Thai
Casual Dining
$8-$12

AAA Inspector Notes: One of the city's most popular restaurants, this place prepares dishes to order with fresh ingredients and no monosodium glutamate. **Bar:** beer & wine. **Address:** 803 Forest Ave 04103 **Location:** I-295 exit 6B, 1.3 mi w on US 302.

⬜L ⬜D

SILLY'S   207/772-0360 ④

▼▼ American. Casual Dining. $6-$19 **AAA Inspector Notes:** Indulge in tasty burgers, thick milk shakes and hand-cut french fries at this tiny eatery. It's all served up by no-nonsense staff with a smile. Cozy and lively define this local favorite that's swathed in colorful and eclectic décor. Parking is a challenge but worth the extra effort. **Bar:** beer & wine. **Address:** 40 Washington Ave 04101 **Location:** On SR 26; between Cumberland Ave and Oxford St. **Parking:** no self-parking. ⬜B ⬜L ⬜D

STREET & COMPANY   207/775-0887 ⑲

▼▼▼▼ Mediterranean. Casual Dining. $22-$30 **AAA Inspector Notes:** This small bistro, with an open kitchen, gives off a casual yet lively vibe. Fresh Mediterranean seafood is perfectly prepared, seasoned and presented in inventive ways. The Lobster Diablo is outstanding. **Bar:** full bar. **Reservations:** suggested. **Address:** 33 Wharf St 04101 **Location:** In the Old Port; between Dana and Union sts. **Parking:** no self-parking. ⬜D

TANDOOR   207/775-4259 ⑧

▼▼ ▼▼ Indian. Casual Dining. $8-$16 **AAA Inspector Notes:** Indian music, artwork and colorful walls enhance the atmosphere of this vibrant Indian restaurant. Guests can sample food cooked over charcoal in a traditional tandoor, a cylindrical clay oven. **Bar:** beer & wine. **Reservations:** suggested, weekends. **Address:** 88 Exchange St 04101 **Location:** In the Old Port. **Parking:** street only.

⬜L ⬜D

THREE DOLLAR DEWEYS   207/772-3310 ㉕

▼▼ ▼▼ American. Casual Dining. $8-$18 **AAA Inspector Notes:** Three kinds of wooden tables are casually set, and large, wall-mounted TVs airing sports events comprise this dining room. Diners have their choice of homemade soups and stews and excellent burgers. The beer selection is impressive. **Bar:** full bar. **Address:** 241 Commercial St 04101 **Location:** In the Old Port; at Union St. **Parking:** street only. ⬜L ⬜D

VIGNOLA CINQUE TERRE   207/772-1330 ㉑

▼▼▼▼ Italian. Casual Dining. $11-$34 **AAA Inspector Notes:** Settle into comfortable leather banquettes around the perimeter of the contemporary dining room and look around until the floor-to-ceiling wine cellar surrounded by glass catches your eye. The freshest available ingredients from local farmers and purveyors go into the chef-owner's food, and the impressive cheese menu spans from Maine to France to Spain. **Address:** 10 Dana St 04101 **Location:** In the Old Port. **Parking:** street only. ⬜L ⬜D

YOSAKU   207/780-0880 ㉘

▼▼ ▼▼ Japanese. Casual Dining. $5-$25 **AAA Inspector Notes:** The well-regarded restaurant has sushi, sashimi and maki sushi on the menu, as well as tempura, teppan, donburi, katsuretsu, and soba and udon noodles. Deck dining is offered in season. **Bar:** full bar. **Address:** 1 Danforth St 04101 **Location:** Jct Danforth and York sts; close to the Old Port. **Parking:** on-site and street. ⬜L ⬜D

EAST END CUPCAKES   207/228-3304

⬜fyi⬜ Not evaluated. A must stop for those wanting to taste a little piece of heaven. These buttercream-frosted cupcakes are flavorful, rich and yummy. **Address:** 426 Fore St 04101 **Location:** In the Old Port.

PRESQUE ISLE (C-6) pop. 9,692, elev. 445'

When Maxie Anderson, Ben Abruzzo and Larry Newman climbed into the gondola of the *Double Eagle II* on Aug. 11, 1978, they began an adventure momentous in the history of aviation. Six days later they landed in a field in France, having completed the first successful transatlantic hot air balloon flight. A replica of the balloon, at Double Eagle II Park on Spragueville Road just beyond Echo Lake, indicates the starting point of the flight.

For the most part, however, Presque Isle's interests are more down to earth. The city is the chief industrial and commercial center of Aroostook County. Nearby, the University of Maine's 375-acre experiment station explores improved methods of growing and marketing potatoes as well as other crops. The university's Reed Fine Art Gallery, at 181 Main Street, serves as a cultural resource for the community and features works by local and regional artists; phone (207) 768-9442.

Recreation is available year-round at Aroostook State Park *(see Recreation Areas Chart)*, 4 miles south on US 1, then west and south via a park road. In the winter snowmobile enthusiasts enjoy over 1,600 miles of groomed trails in the area.

Central Aroostook Chamber of Commerce: 3 Houlton Rd., Presque Isle, ME 04769. **Phone:** (207) 764-6561.

Shopping areas: The Aroostook Centre Mall, 830 Main St., offers some 30 stores, including JCPenney and Sears.

BUDGET TRAVELER INN & SUITES   207/769-0111

▼▼ **Motel.** Rates not provided. **Address:** 71 Main St 04769 **Location:** 1.3 mi s on US 1. **Facility:** 53 units. 2 stories (no elevator), interior corridors. **Guest Services:** coin laundry.

HAMPTON INN PRESQUE ISLE   (207)760-9292

▼▼▼▼ **Hotel** $109-$139 **Address:** 768 Main St 04769 **Location:** Jct Maysville Rd; center. **Facility:** 93 units. 4 stories, interior corridors. **Terms:** 1-7 night minimum stay, cancellation fee imposed. **Amenities:** high-speed Internet. **Pool(s):** heated indoor. **Activities:** exercise room. **Guest Services:** valet and coin laundry.

> **AAA Benefit:** Members save up to 10%!

PRESQUE ISLE INN & CONVENTION CENTER
(207)764-3321

◆◆ Hotel $88-$150   **Address:** 116 Main St 04769 **Location:** 1 mi s on US 1. **Facility:** 120 units, some kitchens. 3 stories (no elevator), interior corridors. **Terms:** cancellation fee imposed. **Dining:** Gram Russo's Italian Restaurant, see separate listing. **Pool(s):** heated indoor. **Activities:** whirlpool. **Guest Services:** coin laundry. **Free Special Amenities:** local telephone calls and high-speed Internet.

THE NORTHEASTLAND HOTEL   207/768-5321

[fyi] Not evaluated. **Address:** 436 Main St 04769 **Location:** On US 1; between State and Academy sts; center. Facilities, services, and décor characterize a mid-scale property.

WHERE TO EAT

THE CROW'S NEST RESTAURANT   207/540-1800

▼▼ **American. Casual Dining.** $8-$22 **AAA Inspector Notes:** The spacious restaurant has several dining sections, including a family dining area with a children's game room, private dining areas and a popular sports bar with large TVs. The diverse menu includes various steaks, cider house pork chops and prime rib. Guests will enjoy seafood dishes like lobster, as well as pasta and classic pub fare options like fish and chips, burgers and sandwiches. Gluten-free and vegetarian dishes are available. Portions are ample. **Bar:** full bar. **Address:** 150 Maysville St 04769 **Location:** Jct US 1, 1 mi e on SR 163; opposite Aroostook Centre Mall.

GOVERNOR'S RESTAURANT & BAKERY   207/769-2274

▼▼ **American. Family Dining.** $7-$17 **AAA Inspector Notes:** Diners flip through a dozen pages of wonderful seafood and varied Italian dishes, in addition to choices such as homemade meatloaf, steaks, burgers and sandwiches, on Governor's Restaurant's diverse menu. Breakfast dishes also can be ordered at any time of the day. Weekends stay bustling with families filing in to the casual spot to indulge in the daily made bakery treats and desserts. **Bar:** beer & wine. **Address:** 350 Main St 04769 **Location:** Center.

GRAM RUSSO'S ITALIAN RESTAURANT   207/764-3321

◆◆ Italian Casual Dining $6-$21   **AAA Inspector Notes:** The menu lists popular Italian dishes, as well as steak and seafood; portions are generous. The spacious dining room overlooks farm fields, providing an outdoor feel to its guests. **Bar:** full bar. **Address:** 116 Main St 04769 **Location:** 1 mi s on US 1; in Presque Isle Inn & Convention Center.

ORIENTAL PEARL RESTAURANT   207/762-3268

▼▼ **Chinese. Casual Dining.** $7-$16 **AAA Inspector Notes:** This spacious restaurant is decorated attractively with murals, plants and fountains. Although the buffet gets top billing, diners also can browse a full menu that includes sushi and many American dishes. **Bar:** full bar. **Address:** 745 Main St 04769 **Location:** On US 1; opposite Aroostook Centre Mall.

PROSPECT (I-5) elev. 95'

FORT KNOX STATE HISTORIC SITE is at 711 Fort Knox Rd. The pentagon-shaped fort was built on 125 acres overlooking the Penobscot River in the 1840s-60s as a deterrent to future British attempts to recapture Bangor and to control the river. The granite fort displays eight cannons and contains mounts for 64 cannons. Fort Knox garrisoned troops during the Civil and Spanish-American wars, yet the fort was never threatened. Such events as periodic Civil War musters and medieval tournaments occur on the grounds.

Tours: Guided tours are available. **Time:** Allow 1 hour minimum. **Hours:** Fort daily 9-dusk, May-Oct. Civil War reenactments most Sat.-Sun., July-Sept. **Cost:** $4.50; $1.50 (ages 65+); $1 (ages 5-11). Combination ticket with Penobscot Narrows Bridge & Observatory $7; $4 (ages 65+); $3 (ages 5-11). **Phone:** (207) 469-6553.

PENOBSCOT NARROWS BRIDGE & OBSERVATORY is at 711 Fort Knox Rd. To reach the observatory, visitors must enter Fort Knox State Historic Site. Perched 420 feet atop the south obelisk of the 2,120-foot-long Penobscot Narrows Bridge, the observatory offers a panoramic view encompassing adjacent Fort Knox, the town of Bucksport, the Penobscot River and Penobscot Bay and the surrounding, heavily forested hills and coastal islands of "Down East" Maine. Visitors enter the base of the tower at the river's edge and board an elevator that ascends to the three-floor, glass-walled observation area.

Admission is by timed ticket. **Time:** Allow 30 minutes minimum. **Hours:** Daily 9-6, July-Aug.; 9-5, May-June and Sept.-Oct. **Cost:** (Includes Fort Knox State Historic Site) $7; $4 (ages 65+); $3 (ages 5-11). **Phone:** (207) 469-6553 for Fort Knox State Historic Site.

RANGELEY (G-2)
• Hotels p. 142

HUNTER COVE WILDLIFE SANCTUARY, 2.5 mi. w. on SR 4, offers 3 miles of trails that pass through the cedar swamps, woodland meadows, alder thickets and mature pine, spruce-fir and poplar forests bordering Rangeley Lake. Bears, coyotes, bobcats, deer and moose dwell in the area. The visitor center in the Stony Batter building offers maps of conserved land and local scenic byways. **Hours:** Daily dawn-dusk. **Cost:** Free. **Phone:** (207) 864-7311.

THE WILHELM REICH MUSEUM, 3.5 mi. w. off SR 4 on Dodge Pond Rd., is an imposing stone building filled with exhibits that reflect the life and work of the natural scientist Wilhelm Reich. Guided tours of the museum begin with a biographical video presentation. The rooftop observatory affords visitors a panorama of the Rangeley Lakes Region. A nature program is offered in the summer. A hands-on discovery room for children is available.

Time: Allow 1 hour minimum. **Hours:** Wed.-Sun. 1-5, July-Aug.; Sat. 1-5, in Sept. Last tour begins 1 hour before closing. **Cost:** $6; free (ages 0-12). **Phone:** (207) 864-3443.

RECREATIONAL ACTIVITIES

Skiing

• **Saddleback Maine** is at 976 Saddleback Mountain Rd. Skiing and other activities are offered. **Hours:** Daily year-round. Ski season Dec.-Apr. (weather permitting). **Phone:** (207) 864-5671.

PLEASANT STREET INN BED & BREAKFAST   (207)864-5916
Bed & Breakfast $145-$165 **Address:** 104 Pleasant St 04970 **Location:** 0.5 mi ne from jct SR 4 and 16; center. **Facility:** This pristine village home has upscale, individually decorated guest rooms with excellent bedding, attractive furnishings, wireless Internet and satellite TV. 5 units. 2 stories (no elevator), interior corridors. **Parking:** winter plug-ins. **Terms:** check-in 4 pm, age restrictions may apply, 30 day cancellation notice-fee imposed. **Amenities:** high-speed Internet. **Activities:** canoeing, bicycles.

RANGELEY SADDLEBACK INN   207/864-3434
Hotel
$85-$250
Address: 2303 Main St 04970 **Location:** On SR 4, just s of village. **Facility:** 40 units. 2 stories (no elevator), exterior corridors. **Parking:** winter plug-ins. **Terms:** check-in 4 pm, 3 day cancellation notice-fee imposed. **Activities:** whirlpool, game room. **Free Special Amenities:** local telephone calls and high-speed Internet.

RAYMOND

THE GOOD LIFE MARKET   207/655-1196
Deli Specialty. Quick Serve. $5-$8 **AAA Inspector Notes:** Patrons come to carry out grilled panini and cold delicatessen sandwiches, fresh salads, soups and homemade desserts. Boxed lunches are a favorite, as are such kid-favorite sandwiches as peanut butter and jelly and grilled cheese. **Address:** 1297 Roosevelt Tr 04071 **Location:** Jct US 302 and SR 85.

RICHMOND (J-4) pop. 1,760, elev. 76'

Located on the Kennebec River about 16 miles north of Brunswick on SR 24, this area was first explored by Pierre de Gaust and Samuel de Champlain in 1604. Permanent settlement began in 1719 with the erection of a frontier trading house that became Fort Richmond. Shortly after the American Revolution, Richmond grew as a farming community.

Shipbuilding and merchant activity built the wealth of the town, and in the late 19th century, shoemaking and river ice harvesting resulted in another period of prosperity that lasted for several decades. Several historic homes attest to the area's prosperity and the skill of its builders, and one of the finest collections of temple-style Greek Revival houses can be found in Richmond's historic district.

In the 1950s and '60s the town experienced an influx of Slavic immigrants escaping the spread of communism. A church they established welcomes visitors today.

Town of Richmond: 26 Gardiner St., Richmond, ME 04357-0159. **Phone:** (207) 737-4305.

ROBBINSTON

REDCLYFFE SHORE MOTOR INN   207/454-3270

Hotel
$85-$95
Address: US Rt 1 04671 **Location:** Oceanfront. 12 mi s of Calais; center. **Facility:** 16 units. 1 story, interior/exterior corridors. **Terms:** closed 11/1-5/14, 14 day cancellation notice-fee imposed. **Dining:** Redclyffe Shore Dining Room, see separate listing. **Free Special Amenities:** local telephone calls and preferred room (subject to availability with advance reservations).

WHERE TO EAT

REDCLYFFE SHORE DINING ROOM   207/454-3270
American. Fine Dining. $14-$25 **AAA Inspector Notes:** The popular restaurant offers lovely views of the ocean and shoreline. On the menu are fresh local seafood dishes, varied beef and chicken entrées and homemade desserts. Service is friendly and attentive. **Bar:** full bar. **Reservations:** suggested. **Address:** 553 US Rt 1 04671 **Location:** 12 mi s of Calais; center; in Redclyffe Shore Motor Inn.

ROCKLAND (J-5) pop. 7,297, elev. 35'

Rockland, one of Maine's largest fishing ports, is known as the Lobster Capital of the World and the Schooner Capital of Maine—ferries to several nearby islands are available along with schooners for daily and weeklong cruises. Shipbuilding, commercial fishing, granite quarrying and limekilns have contributed to area history and economy. The poet Edna St. Vincent Millay was born in Rockland.

A granite breakwater, extending seven-eighths of a mile across Penobscot Bay, leads to the Rockland Breakwater Lighthouse at Jameson Point in Rockland Harbor, built around 1888. Tours are available on weekends from Memorial Day through Columbus Day. The town's historic Main Street district is now a shopping area. Owls Head Light, 5 miles southeast, offers outstanding views of Penobscot Bay.

In early August it's a true crustacean celebration at the Maine Lobster Festival, which features boat rides, crafts, cooking contests and the coronation of the Maine Sea Goddess. Come hungry— there's more than 10 tons of lobster to go around.

Penobscot Bay Regional Chamber of Commerce—Rockland: 1 Park Dr., P.O. Box 508, Rockland, ME 04841. **Phone:** (207) 596-0376 or (800) 562-2529.

FARNSWORTH ART MUSEUM AND THE WYETH CENTER, 16 Museum St., houses American art, with emphasis on artists with state ties: Winslow Homer; Fitz Henry Lane; John Marin; Louise Nevelson; and Andrew, James and N.C. Wyeth. Works by the Wyeth family are in a former church on Union Street across from the Farnsworth Homestead. Changing exhibits feature important artists, current trends or historical themes.

Time: Allow 1 hour, 30 minutes minimum. **Hours:** Daily 10-5 (also Wed. 5-8), May-Oct; Tues.-Sun. 10-5, Nov.-Dec. and Mar.-Apr., Wed.-Sun. 10-5, rest of year. Closed Jan. 1, Thanksgiving and Christmas. **Cost:** Combination ticket with Farnsworth Homestead $12; $10 (ages 65+ and students with ID); free (ages 0-16 and to all Wed. 5-8). **Phone:** (207) 596-6457.

Farnsworth Homestead, next to the Farnsworth Art Museum at 25 Elm St., is an example of a Victorian-era residence distinguished by its chaste Greek Revival exterior and elegant Victorian interior. Built in 1850, it contains many of the original family furnishings. **Note:** The home is currently closed for renovations, with plans to reopen in mid-2013; phone ahead to determine status. **Hours:** Daily 11-4, late May-early Nov. Phone ahead to confirm schedule. **Cost:** Combination ticket with Farnsworth Art Museum and the Wyeth Center $12; $10 (ages 65+ and students with ID); free (ages 0-16). **Phone:** (207) 596-6457.

MAINE LIGHTHOUSE MUSEUM is at 1 Park Dr. Also known as America's Lighthouse Museum, the facility contains a large collection of lighthouse artifacts as well as exhibits of U.S. Coast Guard relics, including working lights, horns, bells and lifesaving devices. Lighthouse models, Fresnel lenses, flags, uniforms and fog bells are displayed. A video explains the inner workings of the Fresnel lens. **Hours:** Mon.-Fri. 9-5, Sat. 10-4, June-Oct.; by appointment rest of year. Closed major holidays. **Cost:** $5; $4 (ages 60+); free (ages 0-12). **Phone:** (207) 594-3301.

PROJECT PUFFIN VISITOR CENTER is at 311 Main St. Interactive displays and exhibits provide information about the National Audubon Society's seabird restoration program. A 20-minute orientation film gives an overview of puffin conservation efforts on the coastal islands of Maine. Visitors can watch a live video feed from puffin nesting sites May through August. **Time:** Allow 30 minutes minimum. **Hours:** Daily 10-5 (also Wed. 5-7), June-Oct.; Wed.-Sun. 10-5, in May; Fri.-Sun. 10-4, Nov. 1 to mid-Dec. **Cost:** Donations. **Phone:** (207) 596-5566 or (877) 478-3346.

BERRY MANOR INN   207/596-7696

Historic Bed
& Breakfast
$125-$300

Address: 81 Talbot Ave 04841 **Location:** Just w of Union St; center. Located in a residential area. **Facility:** A lovely front porch, pleasant parlors and tastefully decorated guest rooms distinguish this 1898 Victorian mansion. All guest rooms feature a gas or wood-burning fireplace, and some have whirlpool tubs. 12 units. 3 stories (no elevator), interior corridors. **Terms:** 2 night minimum stay - seasonal and/or weekends, 10 day cancellation notice-fee imposed. **Amenities:** *Some:* high-speed Internet. **Free Special Amenities: full breakfast and high-speed Internet.**

SAVE ECO ♨ BIZ 🛜 ✕ 🐾

CAPTAIN LINDSEY HOUSE INN   (207)596-7950

Historic Bed
& Breakfast
$110-$218

Address: 5 Lindsey St 04841 **Location:** Between Main and Union sts. Located in the heart of town, this 1835 former sea captain's residence features a common parlor area that beckons guests to congregate and relax. 9 units. 3 stories (no elevator), interior corridors. **Terms:** 14 day cancellation notice-fee imposed. **Free Special Amenities: full breakfast and high-speed Internet.**

SAVE ECO ♨ BIZ 🛜 ✕

NAVIGATOR MOTOR INN   207/594-2131

Hotel
$79-$169

Address: 520 Main St 04841 **Location:** On US 1; between Talbot and Summer sts. **Facility:** 80 units. 4 stories, interior corridors. **Terms:** closed 10/16-5/31, cancellation fee imposed. **Guest Services:** coin laundry. **Free Special Amenities: continental breakfast and local telephone calls.**

SAVE ♨ ▽ 🛜 ✕ 🎧 / SOME UNITS FEE 🐾

TRADE WINDS MOTOR INN   207/596-6661

Hotel
$74-$234

Address: 2 Park Dr 04841 **Location:** On US 1; center. **Facility:** 138 units, some kitchens. 3-5 stories, interior/exterior corridors. **Terms:** cancellation fee imposed. **Pool(s):** heated indoor. **Activities:** sauna, whirlpool, exercise room. *Fee:* game room. **Guest Services:** coin laundry. **Free Special Amenities: expanded continental breakfast and high-speed Internet.**

SAVE ♨ ▽ 🏊 🛜 ✕
/ SOME UNITS FEE 🐾 🎧 🖥 🖥

WHERE TO EAT

AMALFI ON THE WATER   207/596-0012

▽▽ Mediterranean. Casual Dining. $14-$28 **AAA Inspector Notes:** Overlooking the harbor, this spacious modern restaurant has several dining sections and a raw bar. The emphasis is on fresh, local ingredients and Mediterranean flavors, especially those of Italy and Spain. Paella is the house specialty. In season, alfresco dining is available on the spacious patio. **Bar:** full bar. **Address:** 12 Water St, Suite 106 04841 **Location:** Corner of Water and Ocean sts; center.

L D

ATLANTIC BAKING COMPANY   207/596-0505

▽ Breads/Pastries. Quick Serve. $6-$12 **AAA Inspector Notes:** The fine baked goods and various hot and cold beverages will keep guests coming back. They also offer a selection of soups, salads and made-to-order sandwiches. **Address:** 351 Main St 04841 **Location:** Jct Winter St. **Parking:** street only. B L

THE BROWN BAG   207/596-6372

▽ Deli. Quick Serve. $4-$12 **AAA Inspector Notes:** This eatery and its attached bakery are popular. The owners pride themselves on offering wholesome homemade foods. Wireless Internet access is available. **Address:** 606 Main St 04841 **Location:** Center. **Parking:** street only. B L

CAFE MIRANDA   207/594-2034

▽▽ International. Casual Dining. $12-$29 **AAA Inspector Notes:** A diverse selection of entrees--from fresh pasta to seafood to Thai dishes--is available at this cozy, bistro-style restaurant. Well-prepared food is served in ample portions. The atmosphere is upbeat, and service is casual and friendly. **Bar:** beer & wine. **Reservations:** suggested. **Address:** 15 Oak St 04841 **Location:** Just w of Main St. L D

IN GOOD COMPANY   207/593-9110

▽▽▽ American. Casual Dining. $15-$23 **AAA Inspector Notes:** This popular wine bar features a cozy ambience. Couches and comfortable chairs provide a place for friends to meet and enjoy a glass of wine and any of a number of small plates and creative main dishes. **Bar:** full bar. **Address:** 415 Main St 04841 **Location:** On US 1; center. **Parking:** street only. D

PRIMO   207/596-0770

▽▽▽▽ American. Fine Dining. $28-$42 **AAA Inspector Notes:** Fresh local ingredients, many of which come from the eatery's own gardens and greenhouse, mingle in sophisticated preparations that reflect Mediterranean influences. Everything, including delicious breads made from the restaurant's own starter, is made in-house. Pizza and pasta selections appeal to those with lighter appetites. **Bar:** full bar. **Reservations:** suggested. **Address:** 2 Main St (Rt 73) 04841 **Location:** On SR 73, 1 mi s of US 1. D

ROCKLAND CAFE   207/596-7556

 American. Family Dining. $6-$21 **AAA Inspector Notes:** Popular with local residents, this family cafe presents a menu with a nice selection of shrimp and haddock platters as well as sublime carrot cake, lemon meringue pie and giant muffins, which are prepared on the premises. All-you-can-eat seafood is a draw. **Bar:** full bar. **Address:** 441 Main St 04841 **Location:** Just n of Limerick St; center. B L D

SUNFIRE MEXICAN GRILL   207/594-6196

 Mexican. Casual Dining. $7-$16 **AAA Inspector Notes:** In the center of town, this pleasant bistro prepares California-style Mexican cuisine in a relaxed atmosphere. Everything, including the salsa, is made on the premises. **Bar:** full bar. **Address:** 488 Main St 04841 **Location:** Corner of Lindsey St. **Parking:** street only.

L D

ROCKPORT (I-5)

Rockport was originally part of neighboring Camden; the towns officially split into two distinct communities in 1891. For many years Rockport was the summer sojourn of Andre, a harbor seal whose life was chronicled in the children's books "A Seal Called Andre" and "Andre."

The Vesper Hill Children's Chapel on Calderwood Lane offers views of Penobscot Bay and Rockport Harbor.

CENTER FOR MAINE CONTEMPORARY ART, 162 Russell Ave., offers changing exhibits of contemporary artwork by some of Maine's most talented artists. The gallery is housed in a large, renovated 19th-century livery stable. **Time:** Allow 1 hour minimum. **Hours:** Tues.-Sat. 10-5, Sun. 1-5, Memorial Day weekend to mid-Dec. **Cost:** Donations. **Phone:** (207) 236-2875.

CONWAY HOMESTEAD-CRAMER MUSEUM is at 7 Commercial St. The Conway Homestead is an 18th-century restored and fully furnished Cape Cod house built in 1770. The complex includes a museum, barn, blacksmith shop, 1820 maple sugar house, Victorian privy and herb garden. The Mary Meeker Cramer Museum exhibits ship models, quilts, period clothing and local memorabilia, including items from the USS *Conway*. Living-history days are scheduled weekly.

Time: Allow 1 hour minimum. **Hours:** Tues.-Fri. 11-3, July-Aug.; by appointment in June and Sept. **Cost:** $5; $4 (ages 60+); $2 (ages 7-18). **Phone:** (207) 236-2257.

ROCKPORT MARINE PARK is at 111 Pascal Ave. next to the harbor. Highlights include a statue of Andre the seal and three restored limekilns dating to the early 1800s. A set of drawings next to the kilns describes their former purpose and function. Another highlight is a replica of the locomotives that were used to transport lime to waiting ships in the harbor. A public boat launch is available. **Time:** Allow 30 minutes minimum. **Hours:** Daily dawn-dusk. **Cost:** Free. **Phone:** (207) 236-0676.

THE CLADDAGH MOTEL & SUITES   207/594-8479

Motel
$79-$169

Address: 1038 Commercial St 04856 **Location:** On US 1, 3.5 mi s of jct SR 90. **Facility:** 19 units, some two bedrooms, efficiencies and kitchens. 1-2 stories (no elevator), interior/exterior corridors. **Terms:** closed 11/14-4/30, 4 day cancellation notice-fee imposed. **Pool(s):** heated outdoor. **Free Special Amenities:** expanded continental breakfast and high-speed Internet.

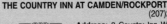 / SOME UNITS

GLEN COVE INN & SUITES   (207)594-4062

Motel
$69-$299

Address: 866 Commercial St 04856 **Location:** Jct SR 90, 3.0 mi on US 1. **Facility:** 34 units, some two bedrooms. 1 story, exterior corridors. **Terms:** closed 10/22-4/30, 2 night minimum stay - seasonal and/or weekends, 3 day cancellation notice-fee imposed. **Pool(s):** heated outdoor. **Activities:** playground. **Guest Services:** coin laundry. **Free Special Amenities:** continental breakfast and high-speed Internet.

 / SOME UNITS FEE

ISLAND VIEW INN   (207)596-0040

Motel
$79-$179

Address: 904 Commercial St 04856 **Location:** Oceanfront. On US 1, 3.4 mi s of jct SR 90. **Facility:** 15 units. 2 stories (no elevator), interior/exterior corridors. **Terms:** 3 day cancellation notice-fee imposed. **Pool(s):** heated outdoor. **Free Special Amenities:** local telephone calls and high-speed Internet.

 CALL

SAMOSET RESORT   (207)594-2511

Resort Hotel
$159-$1599

Address: 220 Warrenton St 04856 **Location:** Oceanfront. 3.5 mi s on US 1, then 0.5 mi e on Waldo Rd. **Facility:** The resort offers good recreational facilities and guest rooms with a patio or balcony. Many rooms overlook the ocean or a golf course. 182 units, some two bedrooms and cottages. 4 stories, interior corridors. **Parking:** on-site and valet. **Terms:** check-in 4 pm, 3 day cancellation notice-fee imposed, resort fee. **Amenities:** safes. **Dining:** 2 restaurants. **Pool(s):** heated outdoor, heated indoor. **Activities:** whirlpools, steamrooms, boat dock, 4 tennis courts, recreation programs, playground, basketball, horseshoes, volleyball, spa. *Fee:* golf-18 holes, game room. **Guest Services:** valet laundry. **Free Special Amenities:** high-speed Internet and children's activities.

 / SOME UNITS FEE

SCHOONER BAY MOTOR INN   207/236-2205

Motel
$81-$130

Address: 337 Commercial St 04856 **Location:** On US 1, 0.5 mi s of SR 90. **Facility:** 23 units. 2 stories (no elevator), exterior corridors. **Terms:** closed 11/1-4/30, 3 day cancellation notice. **Free Special Amenities: continental breakfast and high-speed Internet.** (SAVE) 🛜 ✕ / SOME UNITS 🛗

STRAWBERRY HILL SEASIDE INN   (207)594-5462

Motel
$79-$179

Address: 886 Commercial St 04856 **Location:** Jct SR 90, 3 mi s on US 1. **Facility:** 21 units, some kitchens. 3 stories (no elevator), exterior corridors. **Terms:** 3 day cancellation notice-fee imposed. **Pool(s):** heated outdoor. **Free Special Amenities: local telephone calls and high-speed Internet.**
(SAVE) 🏊 🛜 🛗

THE MARKET BASKET   207/236-4371

◇ Deli. Quick Serve. $4-$10 **AAA Inspector Notes:** Freshly baked bread, sandwiches, tea cakes, muffins, scones and luscious desserts can be carried out from the popular delicatessen. **Address:** 235 Commercial St 04856 **Location:** Jct US 1 and SR 90.
(B) (L) (D)

OFFSHORE RESTAURANT   207/596-6804

◇◇ American. Family Dining. $6-$22 **AAA Inspector Notes:** The expansive salad bar is an ever-popular choice at this place, as are offerings of fresh seafood and other Maine favorites. **Bar:** full bar. **Address:** 770 Commercial St 04856 **Location:** On US 1, 1.7 mi s of jct SR 90. (B) (L) (D)

SHEPHERD'S PIE   207/236-8500

◇◇◇ American. Gastropub. $14-$24 **AAA Inspector Notes:** An upbeat bustling atmosphere is what patrons will find at this popular pub. Creative dishes using local and regional ingredients are prepared in the open-style kitchen. The wonderful signature dish is shepherd's pie made with choice lamb and served on a piping-hot skillet. **Bar:** full bar. **Address:** 18 Central St 04856 **Location:** Just n of Rockport Marina. **Parking:** street only. (D)

ROUND POND

MUSCONGUS BAY LOBSTER CO   207/529-5528

◇ Seafood. Quick Serve. $10-$40 **AAA Inspector Notes:** Outstanding views of Muscongus Bay are among draws of this basic lobster pound. On the menu are cooked lobster, clams, oysters, lobster and crabmeat rolls, and corn on the cob. **Address:** 28 Landing Rd 04564 **Location:** SR 32, just e, follow signs. (L) (D) 🍴

SACO (K-2) pop. 18,482, elev. 75'
- **Hotels p. 146** • **Restaurants p. 146**
- **Hotels & Restaurants map & index p. 98**

Like its sister city Biddeford *(see place listing p. 66),* Saco (SAH-co) was settled in 1631 at a site first noted by Capt. John Smith in 1614; in 1762 the town was incorporated as Pepperellboro. Pepperellboro became Saco in 1805.

A few years later the first major industry, an ironworks, was established. Due to an abundance of readily available waterpower, Saco remained predominantly industrial until recently. The economy now has a broader base, with commerce taking the leading role.

Besides powering the city's industries, the Saco River provides opportunities for fishing, boating and swimming on its 4-mile run to the sea. Ferry Beach State Park *(see Recreation Areas Chart)* occupies 117 acres on the east bank; a stand of tupelo trees, rare at this northern latitude, grows in the park. Also nearby is one of the region's favorite seaside resorts, Old Orchard Beach *(see place listing p. 122).*

Biddeford-Saco Chamber of Commerce & Industry—Saco: 138 Main St., Suite 101, Saco, ME 04072. **Phone:** (207) 282-1567.

AQUABOGGAN WATER PARK, 4 mi. n. on US 1, offers a wave pool, go-carts, bumper boats, a miniature golf course, seven waterslides and a splash-and-play area for toddlers. **Hours:** Daily 10-6, late June-Labor Day (weather permitting). **Cost:** $20; $16 (under 48 inches tall); $10 (ages 60+); $5 (under 38 inches tall). Super Pass (includes unlimited miniature golf and bumper boat rides and two go-cart rides) $30. Rental tubes $5-$6. **Phone:** (207) 282-3112. 🍴 🎢

DYER LIBRARY AND SACO MUSEUM are in two buildings at 371 Main St. The Dyer Library, in the 19th-century Deering House, has changing exhibits and a circulating collection of more than 55,000 volumes. The Saco Museum, founded in 1866, contains changing exhibits of contemporary art and decorative arts such as silver, ceramics and textiles. The museum also has a large collection of portraits by American folk art painter John Brewster Jr.

Hours: Library Mon.-Fri. 9:30-5 (also Tues. and Thurs. 5-8), Sat. 9:30-12:30. Museum Tues.-Thurs. noon-4, Fri. noon-8, Sat. 10-4 (also Sun. noon-4, June 1-Dec. 15). **Cost:** Library free. Museum $5; $3 (ages 65+); $2 (ages 7-18 and students with ID); free (ages 0-6 and to all Fri. 4-8). **Phone:** (207) 283-3861.

FUNTOWN SPLASHTOWN USA, 1 mi. n. on US 1, comprises two parks and offers more than 45 rides, slides and pools. Included within the water park are Mammoth, Tornado, Mount Olympus and other water slides. Excalibur, reputedly northern New England's largest wooden roller coaster, is among the attractions featured in the amusement park. Dragon's Descent offers an accelerated drop from a 220-foot tower.

Hours: Amusement and water park open daily at 10, early June-Labor Day. Amusement park opens Sat.-Sun. at 11, mid-May to early June; at 10, in Sept. Closing times vary; phone ahead. **Cost:** Funtown ride pass $29; $21 (ages 60+ and 38-47 inches tall). Splashtown pass $25; $20 (ages 60+ and 38-47 inches tall). Combination pass $36; $27 (ages 60+ and 38-47 inches tall). Children 0-37 inches tall free. Ages 0-10 must be with a paying adult. **Phone:** (207) 284-5139.

RECREATIONAL ACTIVITIES
Kayaking
- **Bare Knee Point Kayak** is at 45 Camp Ellis Ave. **Hours:** Tours and rentals daily 9-dusk, May-Sept. **Phone:** (207) 283-4455.

(See map & index p. 98.)

HAMPTON INN   (207)282-7222   **10**

Hotel
$99-$259

Hampton

AAA Benefit: Members save up to 10%!

Address: 48 Industrial Park Rd 04072 **Location:** I-95 exit 36 (I-195) to exit 1 (Industrial Park Rd), just ne. **Facility:** 100 units. 5 stories, interior corridors. **Terms:** 1-7 night minimum stay, cancellation fee imposed. **Pool(s):** heated outdoor. **Activities:** exercise room. **Guest Services:** valet and coin laundry, area transportation-bus & train stations.

RAMADA SACO OLD ORCHARD BEACH AREA
(207)286-9600   **11**

Hotel
$80-$230

Address: 352 North St (SR 112) 04072 **Location:** I-95 exit 36 (I-195) to exit 1 (Industrial Park Rd), 0.6 mi sw to SR 112, then 0.4 mi nw. **Facility:** 88 units. 4 stories, interior corridors. **Terms:** 2 night minimum stay - seasonal and/or weekends, cancellation fee imposed. **Amenities:** high-speed Internet. **Pool(s):** heated outdoor. **Guest Services:** valet and coin laundry, area transportation-University of New England.

SACO MOTEL   207-284-6952   **12**

Motel
$50-$90

Address: 473 Main St 04072 **Location:** I-95 exit 36 (I-195) to exit 2A (US 1), just sw. **Facility:** 26 units. 1 story, exterior corridors. *Bath:* shower only. **Terms:** closed 10/26-4/30, 3 day cancellation notice. **Pool(s):** outdoor.

WAGON WHEEL MOTEL   207/283-3258   **9**

Motel. Rates not provided. **Address:** 726 Portland Rd (US 1) 04072 **Location:** I-95 exit 36 (I-195), 1.5 mi se to US 1, then 0.7 mi ne. **Facility:** 12 units. 2 stories (no elevator), exterior corridors. **Pool(s):** outdoor.

WHERE TO EAT

THE LOBSTER CLAW   207/282-0040   **8**

Seafood. Family Dining. $7-$20 **AAA Inspector Notes:** Decorated in the style of a waterfront lobster pound, the restaurant is known for its fresh lobster and other seafood. The menu also lists options for landlubbers, such as steak, chicken and spaghetti. **Bar:** full bar. **Address:** 41 Ocean Park Rd 04072 **Location:** US 1, just e on SR 5.   L   D

TRADITIONS   207/282-6661   **9**

Italian. Casual Dining. $5-$21 **AAA Inspector Notes:** This is a favorite spot among the locals and it always seems to be busy with folks getting together to catch up and enjoy some good food. The menu is traditional Italian fare of veal or chicken parmesan, lasagna, pasta primavera, and "open pit" charbroiled steaks and chickens. **Bar:** full bar. **Address:** 162 Main St 04072 **Location:** Jct Water St; downtown.   L   D

SANFORD pop. 9,761

SANFORD INN   207/324-4662

Motel. Rates not provided. **Address:** 1591 Main St (SR 109) 04073 **Location:** I-95 exit 19, 8.8 mi nw. **Facility:** 40 units, some efficiencies. 1 story, exterior corridors. **Pool(s):** outdoor.

SUPER 8   (207)324-8823

Hotel $52-$113 **Address:** 1892 Main St (Rt 109) 04073 **Location:** I-95 exit 19, 7 mi nw. Adjacent to Sanford Airport. **Facility:** 48 units. 2 stories (no elevator), interior corridors. **Guest Services:** coin laundry.

WHERE TO EAT

WEATHERVANE SEAFOOD RESTAURANT   207/324-0084

Seafood. Family Dining. $8-$25 **AAA Inspector Notes:** The popular, family-oriented restaurant presents a large menu with lobster, fried clams and crisp Cape Cod apple-cranberry cobbler. Flavorful dishes are served in large portions. A fish market is on the premises. **Bar:** full bar. **Address:** 1601 Main St 04073 **Location:** 1 mi s on SR 109; close to Sanford Airport.   L   D   CALL

SCARBOROUGH (K-3) pop. 4,403
• Hotels & Restaurants map & index p. 98, 131

SCARBOROUGH MARSH AUDUBON CENTER, .5 mi. e. of jct. US 1 and SR 9 at 135 Pine Point Rd., comprises more than 3,000 acres of tidal and fresh marsh, salt creeks and uplands. Wildlife can be observed along the Marsh Nature Trail. Interactive exhibits and nature programs are presented at the center. A bird-watching walk is offered weekly in summer for a fee.

Canoe tours and rentals are available. Full-moon canoe tours also are offered; phone for details. **Tours:** Guided canoe and walking tours are available. **Time:** Allow 1 hour, 30 minutes minimum. **Hours:** Daily 9:30-5:30, Memorial Day-Labor Day. **Cost:** Free. Tour prices vary. **Phone:** (207) 883-5100, or (207) 781-2330 in the off-season.

FAIRFIELD INN BY MARRIOTT PORTLAND MAINE MALL
(207)883-0300   **1**

Hotel $129-$329 **Address:** 2 Cummings Rd 04074 **Location:** I-95 exit 45, just s. **Facility:** 118 units. 3 stories, interior corridors. **Pool(s):** heated outdoor. **Guest Services:** valet laundry.

AAA Benefit: AAA hotel discounts of 5% or more.

HOMEWOOD SUITES PORTLAND   207/775-2700

Extended Stay Hotel
Rates not provided

HOMEWOOD SUITES BY HILTON

AAA Benefit: Contemporary luxury at a special Member rate.

Address: 200 Southborough Dr 04074 **Location:** I-95 exit 45, just s. **Facility:** 92 efficiencies, some two bedrooms. 4 stories, interior corridors. **Terms:** check-in 4 pm. **Amenities:** high-speed Internet. **Pool(s):** heated indoor. **Activities:** whirlpool, sports court, exercise room. **Guest Services:** valet and coin laundry.

LIGHTHOUSE INN AT PINE POINT   (207)883-3213   **5**

Motel $155-$255 **Address:** 3 King St 04074 **Location:** Oceanfront. I-95 exit 42, to US 1, 2 mi s to SR 9, then 3 mi e to Pine Point Beach. **Facility:** 22 units. 2 stories (no elevator), exterior corridors. **Terms:** closed 10/1-6/14, 2 night minimum stay - seasonal and/or weekends, 10 day cancellation notice-fee imposed.

(See maps & indexes p. 98, 131.)

PRIDE MOTEL & COTTAGES — 207/883-4816 [4]

◆ **Cottage** $65-$225 **Address:** 677 US Rt 1 04074 **Location:** I-95 exit 36, 0.5 mi e to US 1, then 4.5 mi n. **Facility:** 17 units, some efficiencies and cottages. 1 story, exterior corridors. **Terms:** 2-4 night minimum stay - seasonal - weekends, 7 day cancellation notice-fee imposed. **Pool(s):** heated outdoor. **Activities:** playground, volleyball. *Fee:* game room. **Guest Services:** coin laundry.

RESIDENCE INN BY MARRIOTT — (207)883-0400 [3]

◆◆◆ **Extended Stay Hotel** $139-$329 **Address:** 800 Roundwood Dr 04074 **Location:** I-95 exit 42, 1.5 mi n on Payne Rd. **Facility:** 78 units, some two bedrooms, efficiencies and kitchens. 3 stories, interior corridors. **Terms:** check-in 4 pm. **Amenities:** high-speed Internet. **Pool(s):** heated indoor. **Activities:** whirlpool, sports court, exercise room. **Guest Services:** valet and coin laundry.

AAA Benefit: AAA hotel discounts of 5% or more.

SEA-WARD ON OCEANFRONT GUEST HOUSE — 207/883-6666 [6]

◆◆ **Motel** $88-$193 **Address:** 7 Bliss St 04074 **Location:** Waterfront. I-95 exit 42, 1.5 mi to US 1, 1.5 mi s to SR 9, 3 mi e, just s on E Grand Ave, then just e. **Facility:** 9 units, some cottages. 2 stories (no elevator), interior/exterior corridors. *Bath:* shower only. **Terms:** closed 10/12-5/28, 14 day cancellation notice-fee imposed. **Activities:** beach access.

TOWNEPLACE SUITES BY MARRIOTT — (207)883-6800 [2]

◆◆◆ **Extended Stay Hotel** $99-$259 **Address:** 700 Roundwood Dr 04074 **Location:** I-95 exit 42, 1.5 mi n on Payne Rd. **Facility:** 95 kitchen units, some two bedrooms. 3 stories, interior corridors. **Amenities:** high-speed Internet. **Pool(s):** heated outdoor. **Activities:** exercise room. **Guest Services:** valet and coin laundry.

AAA Benefit: AAA hotel discounts of 5% or more.

WHERE TO EAT

AMATO'S — 207/883-2402

◆ Deli. Quick Serve. $4-$14 **AAA Inspector Notes:** Known for their "Real Italian" sandwich, which was created over 100 years ago by an Italian immigrant who decided to place a little bit of meat, fresh vegetables, cheese, Greek olives, a zesty pickle and a specialty blended olive oil on a freshly made roll. This recipe has built up a loyal following of customers. Other menu choices include hot or cold sandwiches, calzones, specialty pizzas, pasta and freshly prepared salads. Diners may choose to eat in or take out. **Bar:** beer & wine. **Address:** 234 US Rt 1 04074 **Location:** On US 1; jct SR 207.

BAYLEY'S SEAFOOD RESTAURANT — 207/885-9754 [4]

◆ Seafood. Quick Serve. $10-$25 **AAA Inspector Notes:** Diners order from a variety of fresh seafood items at the counter of this quick-service eatery. The ingredients are off-the-boat fresh. Favorite offerings include fried clams, fresh onion rings and homemade chowders. **Bar:** full bar. **Address:** 165 Pine Point Rd 04074 **Location:** Jct US 1, 1 mi e on SR 9.

DIMITRI'S RESTAURANT — 207/883-9800 [2]

◆◆ Greek. Casual Dining. $5-$14 **AAA Inspector Notes:** Traditional recipes are used to create the offerings at this restaurant, many of which are cooked in a brick oven. Greek music fills the light and airy dining room, whose walls are adorned with pictures of the Greek Isles. **Bar:** full bar. **Address:** 185 US Rt 1 04074 **Location:** Just n of SR 114.

THE EGG & I — 207/730-7215 [1]

◆◆◆ American. Family Dining. $5-$9 **AAA Inspector Notes:** This eatery serves much more than hearty breakfasts. The cooks prepare 'scratch-made' soups, creative salads and an array of made-to-order sandwiches prepared with fresh ingredients. **Address:** 183 US 1 04074 **Location:** On US 1.

KEN'S PLACE — 207/883-6611 [5]

◆ Seafood. Quick Serve. $5-$24 **AAA Inspector Notes:** A popular restaurant since 1929, this spot focuses its menu on fresh local seafood, including raw bar offerings. **Bar:** full bar. **Address:** 207 Pine Point Rd 04074 **Location:** Jct US 1, 1.8 mi e on SR 9.

SEBAGO BREWING COMPANY — 207/874-2337

◆◆◆ American. Gastropub. $9-$23 **AAA Inspector Notes:** The stylish brewpub sustains a friendly, informal atmosphere. Self-described "American pub" cuisine includes delicious pasta, chicken, seafood and steak entrées as well as tasty salads, burgers and sandwiches; the latter are available all day. The resident pastry chef prepares desserts on the premises each day. **Bar:** full bar. **Address:** 201 Southborough Dr 04074 **Location:** Near the Maine Mall.

UNCLE DON'S SPURWINK COUNTRY KITCHEN — 207/799-1177 [3]

◆◆ New American. Family Dining. $8-$24 **AAA Inspector Notes:** Amazing comfort food is offered in a casual setting. The lobster roll is super fresh and served in a grilled hot dog roll over a bit of shredded lettuce and a side of mayo—it is perfect. Other tasty items include meatloaf, fried seafood, burgers and sandwiches. Save room for dessert as their menu of homemade fruit pies and quick breads is impressive. **Address:** 150 Spurwink Rd 04074 **Location:** On SR 77.

BAYLEY'S LOBSTER POUND — 207/883-4571

[fyi] Not evaluated. Lobster and crab rolls are available for take-out at this simple lobster pound located near the beach. **Address:** 9 Avenue Six 04074 **Location:** Just n of SR 9 on Pine Point Rd.

SEAL COVE (I-6)

- Attractions map p. 39
- Part of Acadia National Park area — see map p. 38

SEAL COVE AUTO MUSEUM, 2.5 mi. n. on SR 102, houses more than 40 antique automobiles ranging from an 1899 De Dion Bouton to a 1927 Model T Ford. The museum's diverse collection includes rare models from the 1885-1918 "Brass Era." An assortment of antique motorcycles also is featured. **Time:** Allow 1 hour minimum. **Hours:** Daily 10-5, May-Oct. **Cost:** $5; $4.50 (ages 62+); $2 (ages 0-12). **Phone:** (207) 244-9242.

SEARSPORT (I-5) pop. 992, elev. 60'
- Restaurants p. 148

If shipping was the lifeblood of Maine from the late 1700s to the late 1800s, then Searsport was its heartbeat. During this time Searsport produced not only some 250 sailing vessels of substantial size but also more than 280 resident ship captains. In 1870 alone it was the home of 10 percent of the captains of the U.S. Merchant Marine.

Still a major Maine port, Searsport has since diversified. Its piers handle bulk cargoes for the manufacturing and agricultural industries throughout northern and eastern Maine.

A number of finely crafted mansions preside over the shaded streets of Searsport; some are part of the Penobscot Marine Museum *(see attraction listing)* and many have been turned into bed-and-breakfasts. A wealthy past carries into the present in the form of antiques; Searsport is one of the best known antique centers on Maine's mid-coast.

Those who prefer to experience seafaring on their own will find a municipal wharf and boat landing at their disposal. Just south of town off busy US 1, 183-acre Moose Point State Park offers picnic sites and an unobstructed view of Penobscot Bay. For exceptional sightseeing by car, the 46-mile drive on US 1 between Rockland and Verona runs through Searsport and along the ocean and bay.

PENOBSCOT MARINE MUSEUM is at 40 E. Main St. (US 1). Twelve buildings—including an early 19th-century captain's home and the original 1845 town hall—contain collections of traditional small craft, paintings, navigational instruments, builders' half-models, shipbuilders' tools, and Oriental Trade souvenirs and furnishings. Marine paintings by Thomas and James Buttersworth are on display. The museum also contains a research library.

Time: Allow 2 hours minimum. **Hours:** Mon.-Sat. 10-5, Sun. noon-5, late May-late Oct. **Cost:** $8; $3 (ages 7-15); $18 (family, two adults and all accompanying children). **Phone:** (207) 548-2529.

ANGLER'S FAMILY SEAFOOD RESTAURANT   207/548-2405
▼▼ Seafood. Family Dining. $6-$24 **AAA Inspector Notes:** This popular roadside diner is noted for fresh seafood, with a menu boasting chicken, steak, prime rib and roast pork. The restaurant caters to families. **Bar:** full bar. **Address:** 215 E Main St 04974 **Location:** 1.5 mi n on US 1. ⓛ ⓓ

SEBAGO (J-2) elev. 276'

The vacation village of Sebago lies among wooded hills a few miles from the west shore of Sebago Lake, Maine's second largest lake. Partly because of its proximity to Portland but mostly because of its lovely scenery and many recreational opportunities, the Sebago region is one of the most popular resort areas in the state.

There is fishing for trout and the indigenous landlocked salmon; local hatcheries keep lakes and streams supplied with both. Boating is especially good on Sebago Lake and the waterway that links it with Long Lake by way of the historic Songo Lock. Sebago Lake State Park *(see Recreation Areas Chart)*, off US 302 between Naples and South Casco, embraces 1,300 acres on the north shore.

SEBASCO ESTATES

SEBASCO HARBOR RESORT   207/389-1161
[fyi] Not evaluated. **Address:** Rt 217 04565 **Location:** Jct SR 209, 1.3 mi se on SR 217. Facilities, services, and décor characterize a mid-scale property.

Keep seasonal vehicles travel-ready
with a AAA/CAA Battery Tender®

SKOWHEGAN (H-4) pop. 6,297, elev. 175'

The Abenaki Indians called this island in the Kennebec River *skowhegan*—"a place to watch"—as they looked for salmon in the depths below the falls. One still watches: A 62-foot Indian sculpted in wood by Bernard Langlais rises above town in honor of those who first watched from this spot.

In 1771 the island's second settlers arrived, drawn by timber and the river's plenty. Their village was brushed by Revolutionary history in 1775, when Col. Benedict Arnold's expedition crossed the island en route to Québec; a granite boulder marks the site.

Although Skowhegan gradually evolved into a predominantly manufacturing city, the colorful history of log driving on the Kennebec did not end until 1976. A paper pulp mill with an 800-ton daily capacity, 7 miles south on US 201, is further evidence of the area's continued interest in lumbering.

Lakewood Theater, on Lake Wesserunsett 6 miles north of Skowhegan on US 201 to 76 Theatre Rd. in Madison, is Maine's state theater. Established in 1901, it is one of the oldest continuously operating summer stock theaters in the country. Matinee and evening performances run mid-May to mid-September; phone (207) 474-7176.

Skowhegan Area Chamber of Commerce: 23 Commercial St., Skowhegan, ME 04976. **Phone:** (207) 474-3621.

MARGARET CHASE SMITH LIBRARY, 56 Norridgewock Ave., offers displays about the life and career of Margaret Chase Smith, a prominent Maine politician who completed 32 years in the U.S. House of Representatives and Senate and ran for president in 1964.

Smith is known for her "Declaration of Conscience," delivered in the Senate in 1950, in which she stated her opposition to Senator Joseph McCarthy's anticommunist crusade. She was awarded the Presidential Medal of Freedom in 1989. **Hours:** Mon.-Fri. 10-4. Closed major holidays. **Cost:** Donations. **Phone:** (207) 474-7133.

SKOWHEGAN HISTORY HOUSE MUSEUM & RESEARCH CENTER, 66 Elm St., is a well-preserved 1839 brick cottage that includes antique furniture, clothing, kitchen tools, dolls and china. Early town records, genealogical accounts, maps, newspapers, Civil War items and artwork are on display in the attached museum. **Tours:** Guided tours are available. **Hours:** Tues.-Sat. 10-4, June 1-Oct. 8. **Cost:** Donations. **Phone:** (207) 474-6632.

BELMONT MOTEL   (207)474-8315

Motel
$85-$125
Address: 273 Madison Ave 04976 **Location:** 1 mi n on US 201. **Facility:** 36 units. 1 story, exterior corridors. **Parking:** winter plug-ins. **Amenities:** high-speed Internet. **Pool(s):** outdoor.

BREEZY ACRES MOTEL   207/474-2703

Classic Motel

$65-$78

Address: 315 Waterville Rd 04976 **Location:** 1.5 mi s on US 201. Located in a rural area. **Facility:** This classic, well-maintained 1940s roadside motel is situated on spacious grounds in a rural location. Guests will find a pleasant pool, large trout pond and game room located in the back. 13 units, some two bedrooms. 1 story, exterior corridors. **Terms:** closed 10/21-5/19. **Pool(s):** outdoor. **Activities:** paddleboats, fishing, horseshoes. **Free Special Amenities:** continental breakfast and local telephone calls.

     / SOME UNITS

WHERE TO EAT

HERITAGE HOUSE   207/474-5100

American. Casual Dining. $8-$25 **AAA Inspector Notes:** You'll enjoy the small and intimate Heritage House and its 18th-century renovated Victorian-home setting. The cuisine features seafood, steak, chicken and spirits. The chocolate mousse and almond cheesecake are two of their excellent desserts. **Bar:** full bar. **Address:** 182 Madison Ave 04976 **Location:** 0.5 mi n on US 201.

L   D

SOUTH BERWICK (L-2) elev. 97'

South Berwick grew up around some of the earliest lumbering efforts in Maine. The region's straight white pines were prized as masts for the ships of the British navy, and a sawmill was in operation before 1640. Later successes in milling and shipping also contributed to the town's present-day appearance—a charming New England community with many Colonial houses set on spacious lawns.

A combination of manufacturing and farming sustains South Berwick as well as the neighboring communities of Berwick and North Berwick.

HAMILTON HOUSE is reached via SR 236N off I-95, past jct. SR 91, w. on Brattle St., then s.w. on Vaughan's Ln. The Georgian mansion was built about 1785 by merchant Col. Jonathan Hamilton. He chose the site because of its commanding view of the Salmon Falls River. Later the house was the setting for Sarah Orne Jewett's book "The Tory Lover." It had lovely gardens, painted murals and an interesting collection of decorative arts and antique furnishings. Also featured is a garden cottage.

Tours: Guided tours are available. **Hours:** Grounds daily dawn-dusk, year-round. Tours are given on the hour Wed.-Sun. 11-5, June 1-Oct. 15. Last tour departs 1 hour before closing. **Cost:** $8; $7 (ages 65+); $4 (ages 6-12). **Phone:** (207) 384-2454.

SARAH ORNE JEWETT HOUSE, 5 Portland St., dates from 1774. From the early 19th century to the early 20th century, the stately Georgian residence was occupied by the Jewett family; author Sarah Orne Jewett was born in the house in 1849. The house museum is adorned with fine paneling, original 18th- and 19th-century wallpapers and period furnishings. Jewett's bedroom is arranged as she left it.

Tours: Guided tours are available. **Hours:** Tours are given on the hour Fri.-Sun. 11-5, June 1-Oct. 15. Last tour begins 1 hour before closing. **Cost:** $5; $4 (ages 65+); $2.50 (ages 6-12). **Phone:** (207) 384-2454.

VAUGHAN WOODS STATE PARK, off SR 236 to 28 Oldfields Rd. on the e. bank of Salmon Falls River, contains 250 wooded acres interspersed with 3.5 miles of marked foot trails. According to legend, the *Pied Cow* landed at Cow Cove in 1634, bringing the East Coast its first cows. Later that year the same ship brought the nation one of its first sawmills, which was erected nearby. **Hours:** Daily 9-dusk, Memorial Day-Sept. 30 (also some Sat.-Sun. in Oct.). **Cost:** $3; $1 (ages 5-11 and 65+). **Phone:** (207) 384-5160.

SOUTH BRIDGTON (J-2) elev. 659'

NARRAMISSIC is at 46 Narramissic Rd. Set on 25 acres with views of the White Mountains, Narramissic is a historic farmstead. On the premises are a restored Georgian-style house built in 1797 by the son of one of the area's first settlers, a barn and a blacksmith shop. Nature trails wind through the grounds. Traditional artisans and craftsmen periodically explain and demonstrate their trades.

Hours: Grounds daily dawn-dusk. House tours Fri.-Sat. 1-4, mid-June through Labor Day; by appointment rest of year. **Cost:** Free. Admission is charged for demonstrations. **Phone:** (207) 647-9954, or (207) 647-3699 in the off-season.

SOUTH FREEPORT

HARRASEEKET LUNCH & LOBSTER CO   207/865-4888

Seafood. Quick Serve. $9-$26 **AAA Inspector Notes:** At the town wharf, the restaurant affords views of the water and marina. Fresh seafood comes in off their own boats and their lobster pound. No credit cards are accepted, but an ATM is on the premises. **Address:** 36 Main St 04078 **Location:** At the town wharf.

L   D   AC

SOUTH PARIS (I-2) pop. 2,267, elev. 387'

HAMLIN MEMORIAL LIBRARY AND MUSEUM, off Paris Hill Rd. at 16 Hannibal Hamlin Dr., is in a converted 1822 Oxford County jail. The library has a collection of papers, paintings and artifacts circa 1850, including some belonging to Hannibal Hamlin, vice president under Abraham Lincoln, and Hamlin's family. Also noteworthy is an early 1800s map of the Rangeley Lakes region drawn on birch bark. **Hours:** Tues. 11-5, Sat. 10-3 (also Thurs. noon-6, June-Aug.). Phone ahead to confirm schedule. **Cost:** Free. **Phone:** (207) 743-2980.

SOUTHPORT (J-4) elev. 50'

• Hotels p. 150 • Restaurants p. 150

HENDRICKS HILL MUSEUM, 2 mi. s. via SR 27 to 419 Hendricks Hill Rd., includes a restored early 19th-century house containing such artifacts as period household items, tools from the local fishing industry and navigational instruments and charts. A boat shop contains early fishing boats, woodworking tools and tools from the ice harvesting industry. **Time:** Allow 30 minutes minimum. **Hours:** Tues., Thurs. and Sat. 11-3, July-Aug. **Cost:** Donations. **Phone:** (207) 633-1102.

OCEAN GATE RESORT   (207)633-3321

Hotel
$104-$384

Address: 70 Ocean Gate Rd 04576 **Location:** Waterfront. SR 27, 2.5 mi s of Boothbay Harbor, 0.5 mi s of bridge to Southport Island. Located in a quiet secluded area. **Facility:** 65 units, some two bedrooms, kitchens and cottages. 1-2 stories (no elevator), exterior corridors. **Terms:** closed 10/9-5/10, 2 night minimum stay - seasonal and/or weekends, 7 day cancellation notice-fee imposed. **Pool(s):** heated outdoor. **Activities:** whirlpool, boating, canoeing, paddleboats, boat dock, fishing, miniature golf, tennis court, basketball, horseshoes, exercise room. **Guest Services:** coin laundry. **Free Special Amenities:** full breakfast and high-speed Internet. *(See ad p. 68.)*

ROBINSON'S WHARF   207/633-3830

 Regional Seafood. Casual Dining. $8-$25 **AAA Inspector Notes:** In a scenic cove offering a great view of boats and docks, diners indulge on this restaurant's specialty: generously sized lobster rolls. The menu also features fried seafood and sandwiches served in a charming downeast, no-frills atmosphere. **Bar:** full bar. **Address:** 20 Hendricks Hill Rd 04576 **Location:** 2 mi s of Boothbay Harbor on SR 27, just across bridge to Southport Island.

SOUTH PORTLAND   pop. 25,002, elev. 20'

- Attractions map p. 127
- Hotels & Restaurants map & index p. 98, 131

BEST WESTERN MERRY MANOR INN

(207)774-6151   **30**

Hotel
$99-$209

AAA Benefit: Members save 10% or more with Best Western.

Address: 700 Main St 04106 **Location:** I-95 exit 45, 1.3 mi e to US 1. **Facility:** 153 units. 4 stories, interior/exterior corridors. **Amenities:** *Some:* high-speed Internet. **Pool(s):** heated indoor/outdoor. **Activities:** whirlpool, exercise room. **Guest Services:** valet and coin laundry. **Free Special Amenities:** local telephone calls and high-speed Internet.

COMFORT INN   (207)775-0409   **22**

Hotel
$74-$189

Address: 90 Maine Mall Rd 04106 **Location:** I-95 exit 45, 1 mi n. **Facility:** 127 units. 3 stories, interior corridors. **Terms:** cancellation fee imposed. **Amenities:** high-speed Internet. **Guest Services:** valet and coin laundry, area transportation-Amtrak station, Maine Medical Center & Mercy Hospital. *(See ad p. 135.)*

COURTYARD BY MARRIOTT PORTLAND AIRPORT

(207)253-5005   **28**

Hotel $159-$359 **Address:** 100 Southborough Dr 04106 **Location:** I-95 exit 45, just s. **Facility:** 92 units. 4 stories, interior corridors. **Amenities:** high-speed Internet. **Pool(s):** heated indoor. **Activities:** whirlpool, exercise room. **Guest Services:** valet and coin laundry, area transportation-within 5 mi.

AAA Benefit: AAA hotel discounts of 5% or more.

DAYS INN PORTLAND-SOUTH PORTLAND

(207)772-3450   **26**

Hotel
$45-$350

Address: 461 Maine Mall Rd 04106 **Location:** I-95 exit 45. **Facility:** 149 units. 2 stories, interior corridors. **Amenities:** safes (fee). **Pool(s):** heated indoor. **Activities:** whirlpool, limited exercise equipment. **Guest Services:** area transportation-Amtrak & bus stations.

DOUBLETREE BY HILTON   (207)775-6161   **25**

Hotel
$109-$349

DOUBLETREE

AAA Benefit: Members save 5% or more!

Address: 363 Maine Mall Rd 04106 **Location:** I-95 exit 45. Opposite Maine Mall. **Facility:** 219 units. 7-9 stories, interior corridors. **Terms:** 1-7 night minimum stay, cancellation fee imposed. **Amenities:** video games (fee). **Dining:** 2 restaurants. **Pool(s):** heated indoor. **Activities:** saunas, exercise room. **Guest Services:** valet laundry. **Free Special Amenities:** high-speed Internet and airport transportation.

HAMPTON INN PORTLAND AIRPORT   (207)773-4400   **27**

Hotel $99-$269 **Address:** 171 Philbrook Ave 04106 **Location:** I-95 exit 45, just ne. Opposite Maine Mall. **Facility:** 117 units. 4 stories, interior corridors. **Terms:** 1-7 night minimum stay, cancellation fee imposed. **Pool(s):** heated indoor. **Activities:** whirlpool, exercise room. **Guest Services:** valet laundry.

AAA Benefit: Members save up to 10%!

HOLIDAY INN EXPRESS & SUITES   207/775-3900   **23**

Hotel
Rates not provided

Address: 303 Sable Oaks Dr 04106 **Location:** I-95 exit 45, just n on Maine Mall Rd, then just w on Running Hill Rd. **Facility:** 130 units. 6 stories, interior corridors. **Pool(s):** heated indoor. **Activities:** exercise room. **Guest Services:** valet and coin laundry, area transportation-within 2 mi. **Free Special Amenities:** expanded continental breakfast and local transportation.

HOWARD JOHNSON HOTEL   (207)775-5343   **29**

 Hotel $70-$180 **Address:** 675 Main St 04106 **Location:** I-95 exit 45, 1.3 mi e to US 1. **Facility:** 121 units. 4 stories, interior corridors. **Pool(s):** heated indoor. **Activities:** exercise room. **Guest Services:** valet laundry, area transportation-International Ferry Terminal, Amtrak & bus stations.

(See maps & indexes p. 98, 131.)

PORTLAND MARRIOTT AT SABLE OAKS

(207)871-8000 **24**

▼▼▼▼
Hotel
$129-$329

Marriott
HOTELS & RESORTS

AAA Benefit: AAA hotel discounts of 5% or more.

Address: 200 Sable Oaks Dr 04106 **Location:** I-95 exit 45, just n on Maine Mall Rd, then just w on Running Hill Rd. **Facility:** 226 units. 6 stories, interior corridors. **Terms:** check-in 4 pm. **Pool(s):** heated indoor. **Activities:** saunas, whirlpool, exercise room. **Fee:** golf-18 holes. **Guest Services:** valet and coin laundry, area transportation-within 2 mi. **Free Special Amenities: local telephone calls and high-speed Internet.**

[SAVE] [ECO] [✈] [¶|] CALL [&M] [⇆] [BIZ] [📶] [✕] [▭]
/ SOME UNITS FEE [🐕] [♿]

WHERE TO EAT

JOE'S BOATHOUSE

207/741-2780 **45**

▼▼▼▼ American. Casual Dining. $10-$27 **AAA Inspector Notes:** Lovely views of Casco Bay and the busy marina attract a large following to Joe's Boathouse. The menu, featuring New American cuisine with a number of pasta and seafood items, keeps them coming back. The décor is bright and contemporary with a casual atmosphere. Patio seating is a more than agreeable option in the summer. **Bar:** full bar. **Address:** 1 Spring Point Dr 04106 **Location:** At Spring Point Marina. [L] [D]

Q STREET DINER

207/767-0299 **48**

▼ American. Family Dining. $4-$9 **AAA Inspector Notes:** This diner is a local favorite and I can understand why. The buttery roll, grilled perfectly, holds a tasty burger with crispy lettuce and tomato. The sides (French fries, onion rings and pasta salad) range from moderately healthy to sinful and all are delicious. Do not be dissuaded by the tired look—the old building is bright yellow and hard to miss. Cash only. **Address:** 9 Q St 04106 **Location:** Just w of Ocean St off E St. [B] [L]

SALTWATER GRILLE

207/799-5400 **46**

▼▼▼▼ Regional Seafood. Casual Dining. $12-$28 **AAA Inspector Notes:** On the harbor, this marina-side restaurant offers wonderful sunset views of the city skyline. The innovative kitchen turns out fine preparations of Maine seafood, steak, pasta and vegetarian fare. Deck seating is available seasonally. **Bar:** full bar. **Reservations:** suggested. **Address:** 231 Front St 04106 **Location:** In Ferry Village; on the waterfront. [L] [D] CALL [&M]

SEA DOG BREWING CO

207/871-7000 **50**

▼▼▼ American. Casual Dining. $8-$23 **AAA Inspector Notes:** A bustling atmosphere and good food draw patrons to the nautically decorated restaurant and microbrewery. The bar area is a favorite spot for the after-work crowd. Included on the menu is a fine variety of seafood, vegetarian and beef entrées. **Bar:** full bar. **Address:** 125 Western Ave 04106 **Location:** I-295 exit 3, just w. [B] [L] [D] CALL [&M]

THAI POM'S RESTAURANT

207/347-3000 **49**

▼▼▼ Thai. Casual Dining. $8-$19 **AAA Inspector Notes:** Patrons can rest assured no MSG is used at this popular Thai restaurant whose menu items are made to order. The eatery is located just a couple of miles from the Maine Mall. **Bar:** full bar. **Address:** 209 Western Ave 04106 **Location:** I-295 exit Western Ave, 0.5 mi w. [L] [D]

THAI TASTE RESTAURANT

207/767-3599 **47**

▼▼▼ Thai. Casual Dining. $8-$19 **AAA Inspector Notes:** Menu items are made to order at the popular Thai restaurant, which is on the road to Portland Headlight. Monosodium glutamate is nowhere to be found here. **Bar:** beer & wine. **Reservations:** suggested. **Address:** 435 Cottage Rd 04106 **Location:** 0.9 mi se of jct Broadway. [L] [D]

WEATHERVANE SEAFOOD RESTAURANT

207/772-3856

▼▼▼ Seafood. Family Dining. $8-$25 **AAA Inspector Notes:** The popular, family-oriented restaurant presents a large menu with lobster, fried clams and crisp Cape Cod apple-cranberry cobbler. Flavorful dishes are served in large portions. A fish market is on the premises. **Bar:** full bar. **Address:** 380 Gorham Rd 04106 **Location:** Near Maine Mall. [L] [D] CALL [&M]

WILD WILLY'S GOURMET BURGERS

207/822-9999 **51**

▼ Burgers. Quick Serve. $7-$12 **AAA Inspector Notes:** Thick, juicy Angus beef burgers are the trademark of this popular restaurant. Guests order their items at the counter and wait for their food to be delivered. The barn-style, post and beam dining room has a rustic feel. **Bar:** beer & wine. **Address:** 449 Westbrook St 04106 **Location:** I-295 exit 3, just n on SR 9. [L] [D] CALL [&M]

SOUTH THOMASTON

WATERMAN'S BEACH LOBSTER

207/596-7819

▼ Seafood. Quick Serve. $13-$28 **AAA Inspector Notes:** This award-winning, traditional Maine lobster shack offers counter service and outdoor dining. Guests enjoy fresh local seafood and magnificent views of the ocean. **Address:** 343 Waterman Beach Rd 04858 **Location:** Just e of SR 73. [L] [D] [Ⓥ]

SOUTHWEST HARBOR (I-6) pop. 720, elev. 468'

- Hotels p. 152 • Restaurants p. 152
- Attractions map p. 39
- Hotels & Restaurants map & index p. 49
- Part of Acadia National Park area — see map p. 38

Located on the southwest side of Somes Sound and bordered by a natural fjord, this fishing and boatbuilding center shares Mount Desert Island with Acadia National Park (see place listing p. 38). With about 70 lobster fishermen operating from its wharves, Southwest Harbor is the archetype of the New England coastal village.

Bass Harbor Head Light, 3 miles south on SR 102A, is a favorite spot for photographers. Local conditions are ideal for boating, swimming and other water sports. Schooner cruises, deep-sea fishing excursions and canoe rentals are available.

Southwest Harbor-Tremont Chamber of Commerce: 329 Main St., P.O. Box 1143, Southwest Harbor, ME 04679. **Phone:** (207) 244-9264.

WENDELL GILLEY MUSEUM, Main St. and Herrick Rd., houses more than 200 bird models by the master woodcarver. In addition to the native and foreign species carved by Gilley, the museum offers annual art exhibitions and natural history and art programs. A resident woodcarver demonstrates his skill. Carving workshops are offered throughout the year.

Time: Allow 30 minutes minimum. **Hours:** Tues.-Sat. 10-5, July-Aug.; Tues.-Sat. 10-4 in June and Sept.-Oct.; Fri.-Sun. 10-4 in May and Nov. 1 to mid-Dec. Last admission 30 minutes before closing. Closed major holidays. **Cost:** $5; $2 (ages 5-12). **Phone:** (207) 244-7555.

RECREATIONAL ACTIVITIES

Kayaking

- **Maine State Sea Kayak** departs from 254 Main St. The company offers half-day and sunset tours

(See map & index p. 49.)

on the western side of Mount Desert Island. **Hours:** Tours depart daily, Memorial Day-late Sept. **Cost:** Reservations are recommended. **Phone:** (207) 244-9500 or (877) 481-9500.

ACADIA COTTAGES 207/244-5388 ⓮
◊◊◊◊ Cottage $115-$150 **Address:** 410 Main St 04679 **Location:** Just s on SR 102. **Facility:** 11 cottages. 1 story, exterior corridors. **Terms:** closed 10/15-5/15, 2-4 night minimum stay, 30 day cancellation notice-fee imposed. **Guest Services:** coin laundry.

CLARK POINT INN 207/244-9828 ⓫
◊◊◊◊ Bed & Breakfast $139-$239 **Address:** 109 Clark Point Rd 04679 **Location:** SR 102, just w. **Facility:** This pleasant B&B is just steps away from the center of town and its activities. The tastefully decorated guest rooms have contemporary styling; many offer a lovely harbor view. 5 units. 3 stories (no elevator), interior/exterior corridors. **Terms:** check-in 4 pm, 2 night minimum stay - seasonal, 14 day cancellation notice-fee imposed.

THE INN AT SOUTHWEST 207/244-3835 ⓬
◊◊◊◊ Historic Bed & Breakfast $125-$200 **Address:** 371 Main St 04679 **Location:** Center. **Facility:** This 1884 Victorian has a variety of pleasant guest units, all named after historic lighthouses. Some rooms have gas log stoves. The large sunporch and comfortable parlors are attractive retreats. 7 units. 3 stories (no elevator), interior corridors. **Terms:** closed 11/1-4/30, 2 night minimum stay - seasonal and/or weekends, 14 day cancellation notice-fee imposed.

THE KINGSLEIGH INN 207/244-5302 ⓭
◊◊◊◊ Historic Bed & Breakfast $140-$315 **Address:** 373 Main St 04679 **Location:** On SR 102; center. **Facility:** Turrets add architectural interest to this turn-of-the-20th-century home. Guest rooms vary in size, and some offer harbor views and private balconies. 8 units. 3 stories (no elevator), interior corridors. **Terms:** closed 10/21-5/16, check-in 4 pm, 2 night minimum stay - seasonal and/or weekends, 21 day cancellation notice-fee imposed.

WHERE TO EAT

CAFE 2/EAT-A-PITA 207/244-4344 ⑨
◊◊ American. Casual Dining. $13-$26 **AAA Inspector Notes:** For breakfast, offerings at Eat-a-Pita include three-egg omelets, homemade blueberry pancakes and the signature blueberry-stuffed French toast. During the day, the menu keeps its focus on delicious salads and sandwiches. In the evening, the restaurant transforms into Cafe 2, a more upscale eatery, where the cuisine is American with a European flair. A full-service patio bar serves the full menu. **Bar:** full bar. **Address:** 326 Main St 04679 **Location:** Just n of Clark Point Rd; center. **Parking:** street only. B L D

CAFE DRY DOCK 207/244-5842 ⑩
◊◊ American. Casual Dining. $8-$24 **AAA Inspector Notes:** Located outside the hustle and bustle of Bar Harbor, this restaurant on Main Street features very good burgers, great clam chowder, nicely prepared fresh seafood and sandwiches. The serving staff is pleasant and professional. Deck dining is available. **Bar:** full bar. **Address:** 357 Main St 04679 **Location:** Center. **Parking:** street only. L D

FIDDLER'S GREEN RESTAURANT 207/244-9416 ⓫
◊◊◊ American. Fine Dining. $18-$28 **AAA Inspector Notes:** Gaze out over the harbor as you sit down to the owner-chef's exquisite meat and seafood dishes. Local ingredients are emphasized and pair well with the 150-plus selections from their excellent wine cellar. **Bar:** full bar. **Reservations:** suggested. **Address:** 411 Main St 04679 **Location:** Center. D

SPRUCE HEAD

THE CRAIGNAIR INN & RESTAURANT 207/594-7644
◊◊◊ Historic Country Inn $100-$200 **Address:** 5 Third St 04859 **Location:** Oceanfront. 2.5 mi w on SR 73, 1.5 mi s on Clark Island Rd; 10 mi s of Rockland. Located in a rural area. **Facility:** Built in 1930, this oceanfront former quarrymen's boardinghouse overlooks Clark Island and offers rooms of varying styles, some with an oceanview. 20 units. 2-3 stories (no elevator), interior/exterior corridors. *Bath:* some shared. **Terms:** 14 day cancellation notice-fee imposed. **Dining:** restaurant, see separate listing.

WHERE TO EAT

THE CRAIGNAIR INN & RESTAURANT 207/594-7644
◊◊◊ American. Fine Dining. $15-$27 **AAA Inspector Notes:** House specialties include a delicious lobster Newburg, crab cakes and homemade desserts. The restaurant boasts a country kitchen feel and features outstanding views of the ocean and Clark Cove. **Bar:** full bar. **Reservations:** suggested. **Address:** 5 Third St 04859 **Location:** 2.5 mi w on SR 73, 1.5 mi s on Clark Island Rd; 10 mi s of Rockland. D

STANDISH pop. 469

SEBAGO LAKE LODGE AND COTTAGES (207)892-2698
◊◊ Bed & Breakfast $62-$275 **Address:** 661 White's Bridge Rd 04084 **Location:** Waterfront. 1 mi w on US 302. **Facility:** 19 units, some cottages. 2 stories (no elevator), interior/exterior corridors. *Bath:* some shared. **Terms:** closed 11/2-4/31, 2 night minimum stay - seasonal and/or weekends, 30 day cancellation notice-fee imposed. **Activities:** canoeing, boat dock, fishing, horseshoes, limited exercise equipment.

SURRY

SURRY INN DINING ROOM 207/667-5091
◊◊◊ Continental. Fine Dining. $17-$26 **AAA Inspector Notes:** The owner-chef of this restaurant is quite creative when preparing meals and uses only the freshest ingredients available. The comfortable country-inn setting overlooks Contention Cove. Fireside dining is offered in the fall and winter months. The servers provide friendly and efficient service with a casual flair. **Bar:** full bar. **Reservations:** suggested. **Address:** Surry Rd 04684 **Location:** Jct US 1, 4 mi s on SR 172. D

THE FORKS (G-3)

The Forks is a tiny logging village in the heart of Maine's North Woods, on the Old Canada Road National Scenic Byway (US 201). Situated at the confluence of the Kennebec and Dead rivers, it is a popular white-water rafting area.

RECREATIONAL ACTIVITIES
White-water Rafting

- **Northern Outdoors** is 3.5 mi. s. at 1771 US 201. Other activities are offered. **Hours:** White-water rafting trips depart daily, May-Oct. **Phone:** (207) 663-4466 or (800) 765-7238.

- **Wilderness Expeditions** is on the Penobscot and Kennebec rivers. **Hours:** White-water rafting trips depart daily, May-Oct. **Phone:** (207) 695-8927 or (800) 825-9453.

THOMASTON (J-5) pop. 1,875, elev. 20'

In 1605 Capt. George Weymouth planted a cross on Allen's Island, off the mouth of the St. Georges River, making the first known claim of possession by an Englishman on New England soil. In 1630 a post for trading with the American Indians was established, and in 1736 settlers founded what is now Thomaston.

Village life soon centered on the busy harbor where some of America's finest sailing ships were built. Lime, quarried locally, was an important export. Boatbuilding, fishing, lobstering and clamming are still significant local industries. Many fine Colonial houses stand throughout the town.

THE GENERAL HENRY KNOX MUSEUM/ MONTPELIER, 30 High St. near jct. US 1 and SR 131, is a replica of the home of Gen. Henry Knox, first U.S. Secretary of War. The house contains many of Knox's original furnishings and possessions. Tours conducted by guides in period costumes are available and last between 45 minutes and 1 hour.

Hours: Tues.-Sat. 10-3:30, Memorial Day-Columbus Day; by appointment rest of year. **Cost:** $7; $6 (ages 62+); $4 (ages 5-13); free (active military with ID); $18 (family). **Phone:** (207) 354-8062.

HAMPTON INN & SUITES ROCKLAND/THOMASTON
(207)594-6644

WWWW **Hotel** $145-$399 **Address:** 190 New County Rd 04861 **Location:** On US 1. **Facility:** 85 units. 4 stories, interior corridors. **Terms:** check-in 4 pm, 1-7 night minimum stay, cancellation fee imposed. **Amenities:** high-speed Internet. **Pool(s):** heated indoor. **Activities:** whirlpool, exercise room. **Guest Services:** valet and coin laundry.

| **AAA Benefit:** Members save up to 10%! |

[icons] CALL [icons]

WHERE TO EAT

THE SLIPWAY   207/354-4155

WW **Seafood. Casual Dining.** $6-$25 **AAA Inspector Notes:** On the public landing, this popular restaurant affords wonderful harbor views from the spacious outdoor deck and restaurant. Guests unwind in a casual setting while enjoying fresh local seafood. **Bar:** full bar. **Address:** 24 Town Landing Rd 04861 **Location:** Center; at harbor via Knox St.

THOMASTON CAFE   207/354-8589

WW **Regional American. Family Dining.** $6-$25 **AAA Inspector Notes:** Open for breakfast and lunch seven days a week and for dinner two days a week, this café is a local favorite. Wholesome foods are made from chemical- and hormone-free poultry, as well as fresh, local ingredients when available. This place is known for its wild mushroom hash and haddock fish cakes. **Bar:** full bar. **Address:** 154 Main St 04861 **Location:** On US 1; center. **Parking:** street only.

Ratings
Members
Trust

Learn more at **AAA.com/Diamonds**

TOPSHAM pop. 5,931

SEA DOG BREWING CO   207/725-0162

WWWW **American. Casual Dining.** $8-$23 **AAA Inspector Notes:** In a converted mill, a bustling atmosphere and good food draw patrons to the nautically decorated restaurant and microbrewery, which affords a lovely view of the Androscoggin River falls. Included on the menu is a fine variety of seafood, vegetarian and beef entrées. **Bar:** full bar. **Address:** 1 Main St 04086 **Location:** On SR 24 and 201 at Bath Bridge. [L] [D]

TRENTON
• Hotels & Restaurants map & index p. 49

TRENTON BRIDGE LOBSTER POUND   207/667-2977 [14]

WW **Seafood. Quick Serve.** $9-$18 **AAA Inspector Notes:** In business since 1956, the traditional Maine lobster pound enables diners to choose a lobster from the tank. The à la carte menu emphasizes fresh seafood. Lobsters are caught fresh and cooked in natural seawater outdoors in wood-fired cookers. Those who dine in can sit inside or out. Takeout is another option. **Address:** 1237 Bar Harbor Rd 04605 **Location:** On SR 3, at Trenton Bridge.

[L] [D] [icon]

UNION (I-4) elev. 97'

MATTHEWS MUSEUM OF MAINE HERITAGE, off SR 17 at the Union Fairgrounds at Union and Common rds., displays over 8,000 artifacts relevant to Maine life, including antique tools, vehicles and kitchen utensils as well as innovative, homemade inventions reflecting the ingenuity and craftsmanship of Maine's early settlers. Of interest is the extensive collection of Moxie memorabilia, including a 32-foot-tall Moxie bottle stand. A one-room schoolhouse that operated 1864-1954 houses original furnishings and supplies.

Time: Allow 30 minutes minimum. **Hours:** Wed.-Sat. noon-4, July-Aug.; by appointment in June and Sept. Closed major holidays. **Cost:** $5; $3 (ages 65+); $1 (ages 8-16). **Phone:** (207) 785-3281 or (207) 542-2379.

VAN BUREN (B-7) elev. 496'

More than an international bridge links Van Buren to St. Léonard, New Brunswick, across the St. John River. Settled by displaced Acadians and French Canadians in 1789, Van Buren was incorporated in 1881 and named for the eighth president. Throughout the upper St. John Valley, to which Van Buren is the gateway, signs and citizens are mostly bilingual.

Van Buren's economy is based on potatoes and lumber. For recreation the surrounding woodlands offer hunting and fishing; there is a beach at Long Lake, about 10 miles west. Other popular outdoor activities are snowmobiling, boating and off-roading.

Greater Van Buren Chamber of Commerce: 51 Main St., Suite 101, Van Buren, ME 04785. **Phone:** (207) 868-5059.

ACADIAN VILLAGE, 5 mi. n. on US 1, includes 17 reconstructed buildings. Among them are dwellings and a general store, country schoolhouse, blacksmith shop and chapel, all of which depict the late 18th-century to the early 20th-century culture of the St. John Valley. A museum of local art has permanent and changing art exhibits. **Time:** Allow 1 hour minimum. **Hours:** Daily noon-5, June 15-Sept. 15. **Cost:** $6; $3 (ages 7-16). **Phone:** (207) 868-5042 June-Sept.

VINALHAVEN ISLAND (J-5) elev. 100'

Vinalhaven Island, 9 miles long and 6 miles wide, is the largest of Penobscot Bay's Fox Islands and the third largest along the Maine coast. This working island village is a popular day-trip destination with visitors and locals alike. The Maine State Ferry Service transports passengers, automobiles and trucks on a 1.25-hour cruise from Rockland to Carver's Harbor; phone (207) 596-5450 or (207) 596-5400.

Incorporated in 1789, Vinalhaven at one time had numerous granite quarries that attracted settlers and provided a booming industry. Many buildings in Washington, D.C., and New York were made of Vinalhaven granite. Two abandoned spring-fed quarries are now town parks and popular swimming holes. Another abandoned site, Armbrust Hill, also is a town park.

The island is home to one of the most productive lobster-fishing fleets in the world. Parks, rocky beaches, hiking trails and natural areas offer a variety of recreational opportunities. Lane's Island, south of Vinalhaven and accessible by bridge, is a nature preserve.

Vinalhaven Chamber of Commerce: P.O. Box 703, Vinalhaven, ME 04863. **Phone:** (207) 863-4826.

VINALHAVEN HISTORICAL SOCIETY MUSEUM, 41 High St., exhibits fishing and seafaring artifacts as well as tools and photographs from granite quarrying days. **Time:** Allow 30 minutes minimum. **Hours:** Daily noon-5, July-Aug.; Tues.-Sat. noon-5 in June and Sept.; by appointment rest of year. **Cost:** Donations. **Phone:** (207) 863-4410.

WALDOBORO (J-4) pop. 1,233, elev. 13'

During the 19th century Waldoboro was known for producing five-masted schooners. Shipbuilding has since given way to small industry, farming and other commercial activities. Situated at the headwaters of the Medomak River near Muscongus Bay, the community was settled largely by German families.

Clamming, lobstering and sauerkraut production are the primary industries. Several art galleries feature works by local artists. Waldoboro also is home to the renovated 1936 Waldo Theatre, phone (207) 832-6060, and the locally renowned Moody's Diner, a part of Maine lore and legend.

Town of Waldoboro: P.O. Box J, Waldoboro, ME 04572. **Phone:** (207) 832-5369.

WALDOBORO HISTORICAL SOCIETY MUSEUM, .5 mi. s. on SR 220, comprises three buildings: the 19th-century Boggs Schoolhouse, the Hauck Building and The Barn. The Hauck Building contains a military exhibit, ship models, antique fire engines and tools. The Barn features heirloom quilts, 19th-century hooked rugs, textiles and a ladies' emporium. Also included are a 19th-century farm kitchen, a furnished Victorian bedroom and a country store as well as children's toys and medical equipment. The town's 1800s-era shelter for stray farm animals also is on the property.

Time: Allow 30 minutes minimum. **Hours:** Wed.-Mon. noon-3, mid-June through Labor Day; Sat.-Sun. noon-3, day after Labor Day-Sept. 30. **Cost:** Donations.

MOODY'S DINER   207/832-7785

◆◆ American. Family Dining. $5-$14 **AAA Inspector Notes:** *Classic.* Possibly one of the oldest diners in America as it celebrates 80 years in business. Fish chowder, french fries, onion rings, cheeseburgers, pies galore and more make up only part of their menu. Their old-time diner décor includes chrome edging, counter service (and table service) and local memorabilia hanging on the walls. **Address:** 1885 Atlantic Hwy 04572 **Location:** On US 1, northbound side.

Ⓑ Ⓛ Ⓓ

WALLAGRASS

FOUR SEASONS INN OF SOLDIER POND VILLAGE
                                    207/834-4722

◆◆◆ Historic Bed & Breakfast $99-$199 **Address:** 13 Church St 04781 **Location:** Off SR 11, 0.5 mi e on Strip Rd. **Facility:** Comfortable parlor areas and an attractive breakfast room give you nice spots in which to relax at this splendid 1910 former merchant's home. 6 units. 3 stories (no elevator), interior corridors. **Terms:** 7 day cancellation notice-fee imposed. **Activities:** hiking trails.

Ⓑⓘⓩ 📶 ✕ ✉ 🖥

WATERVILLE (I-4) pop. 15,722, elev. 112'

Abenaki Indians once met for tribal councils and summer encampments at the Kennebec River's Ticonic Falls, near the site of Waterville. The area is now a center for commerce and education.

The city of Waterville was established in 1802. The arrival of the steamship *Ticonic* in 1832 introduced Waterville's era as a prosperous freight and passenger port. By mid-century, as river traffic declined due to railroad advances, energies turned to new possibilities. A dam was erected at Ticonic Falls in 1868; 5 years later the first of many large factories was established. The city is an important industrial center for paper, biotechnology, health care and professional services.

Waterville also benefits from the presence of two colleges and several cultural organizations. Especially popular are theater, dance, music and comedy performances at the Waterville Opera House; phone (207) 873-7000 for ticket information.

West of the city lies the Belgrade Lakes region, whose largest lake, Great Pond, inspired the play and movie "On Golden Pond." Miles of hiking trails lace the city, and fishing and boating on the Kennebec River are other popular outdoor pastimes.

Mid-Maine Chamber of Commerce: 50 Elm St., Waterville, ME 04901. **Phone:** (207) 873-3315.

COLBY COLLEGE occupies a 714-acre campus at 4000 Mayflower Hill. The school, which was founded in 1813, is recognized as a national leader in research- and project-based undergraduate learning. Among the collections in the Miller Library are letters, manuscripts and memorabilia of Maine poet Edwin Arlington Robinson as well as the Thomas Hardy Collection. The campus also includes a 128-acre arboretum and bird sanctuary. **Time:** Allow 1 hour minimum. **Hours:** Collections in the Miller Library may be viewed Mon.-Fri. 10-noon and 1-4:30. **Cost:** Free. Reservations are recommended. **Phone:** (207) 859-5150.

Museum of Art, in Bixler Art and Music Center, features 18th-century American portraits, 19th-century landscapes and 20th-century contemporary American artwork. Among the American artists represented are watercolorist John Marin and contemporary artist Alex Katz. The museum's permanent collection also includes works by Mary Cassatt, John Singleton Copley, Winslow Homer and Andrew Wyeth. Changing exhibits also are displayed.

   Time: Allow 2 hours minimum. **Hours:** Tues.-Sat. 10-5, Sun. noon-5. Closed Jan. 1, Easter, Thanksgiving and Christmas. **Cost:** Free. **Phone:** (207) 859-5600.

REDINGTON MUSEUM, 62 Silver St., Unit A, contains displays about the early history of Waterville. Collections of furniture, household artifacts, toys and weapons are displayed in an elegant 1814 Federal-style home. A replica of a 19th-century apothecary shop in the museum annex contains an impressive set of matching mahogany, brass and glass cases filled with pharmaceutical artifacts and medicines.

   Time: Allow 1 hour, 30 minutes minimum. **Hours:** Tours Tues.-Sat. at 10, 11, 1 and 2, Memorial Day-Labor Day. Closed major holidays. **Cost:** $5; $2 (ages 0-18). **Phone:** (207) 872-9439.

BEST WESTERN PLUS WATERVILLE   (207)873-0111

Hotel
$99-$249

AAA Benefit: Members save 10% or more with Best Western.

Address: 375 Main St 04901 **Location:** I-95 exit 130 (Main St), on SR 104. **Facility:** 138 units. 3 stories, interior corridors. **Pool(s):** heated indoor. **Activities:** whirlpool, exercise room. **Guest Services:** valet and coin laundry. **Free Special Amenities: continental breakfast and high-speed Internet.**

COMFORT INN & SUITES   207/873-2777

Hotel. Rates not provided. **Address:** 332 Main St 04901 **Location:** I-95 exit 130 (Main St), 0.4 mi e on SR 104. **Facility:** 101 units, some two bedrooms and kitchens. 4 stories, interior corridors. **Pool(s):** heated indoor. **Activities:** limited exercise equipment. *Fee:* game room. **Guest Services:** valet and coin laundry.

FIRESIDE INN & SUITES   (207)873-3335

Hotel $89-$249 **Address:** 356 Main St 04901 **Location:** I-95 exit 130 (Main St). **Facility:** 85 units. 2 stories (no elevator), interior corridors. **Amenities:** *Some:* high-speed Internet. **Dining:** Governor's Restaurant & Bakery, see separate listing. **Pool(s):** outdoor. **Activities:** whirlpool, exercise room. **Guest Services:** valet and coin laundry.

HAMPTON INN WATERVILLE   (207)873-0400

Hotel $99-$299 **Address:** 425 Kennedy Memorial Dr 04901 **Location:** I-95 exit 127, just e. **Facility:** 81 units. 4 stories, interior corridors. **Terms:** 1-7 night minimum stay, cancellation fee imposed.

AAA Benefit: Members save up to 10%!

Amenities: video games (fee), high-speed Internet. **Pool(s):** heated indoor. **Activities:** exercise room. **Guest Services:** valet and coin laundry.

WHERE TO EAT

GOVERNOR'S RESTAURANT & BAKERY   207/872-0677

American. Family Dining. $8-$19 **AAA Inspector Notes:** Diners flip through a dozen pages of wonderful seafood and varied Italian dishes, in addition to choices such as homemade meatloaf, steaks, burgers and sandwiches, on Governor's Restaurant's diverse menu. Breakfast dishes also can be ordered at any time of the day. Weekends stay bustling with families filing in to the casual spot to indulge in the daily made bakery treats and desserts. **Bar:** beer & wine. **Address:** 356 Main St 04901 **Location:** I-95 exit 130 (Main St); in Fireside Inn & Suites. B L D

WEATHERVANE SEAFOOD RESTAURANT   207/873-4522

Seafood. Family Dining. $8-$25 **AAA Inspector Notes:** The popular, family-oriented restaurant presents a large menu with lobster, fried clams and crisp Cape Cod apple-cranberry cobbler. Flavorful dishes are served in large portions. A fish market is on the premises. **Bar:** full bar. **Address:** 470 Kennedy Memorial Dr 04901 **Location:** I-95 exit 127, on SR 11 (Kennedy Memorial Dr). L D CALL

WELLS (L-2) elev. 203'

• Hotels p. 156 • Restaurants p. 156
• Hotels & Restaurants map & index p. 98

   Within a year of its settlement in 1640 Wells boasted a mill on the Webhannet River and showed signs of becoming a flourishing trading port. Although it ultimately fulfilled its potential, American Indian hostility made the village's first century precarious. Wells was one of only four English communities to survive the second French and Indian War, which occurred 1688-97.

   Stubborn courage may have been at the heart of Wells' survival. For 2 days in 1692, 15 soldiers ensconced in the Joseph Storer House repulsed the attacks of 500 Indians and French. The house, south on US 1, still stands as a private home and business.

   Wells remained primarily a fishing and farming center until the "discovery" of Wells Beach, Laudholm Beach and Drakes Island Beach by vacationers in the early 20th century. Since then visitors have thronged to the 7-mile-long strand to sun, swim and just relax. The town also is a popular shopping center with a variety of stores, shops and factory outlets.

(See map & index p. 98.)

Wells Chamber of Commerce: 136 Post Rd., P.O. Box 356, Wells, ME 04090. **Phone:** (207) 646-2451.

RACHEL CARSON NATIONAL WILDLIFE REFUGE,

n. on SR 9 to 321 Port Rd., embraces more than 5,600 acres of salt marshes and upland habitat between Kittery and Cape Elizabeth and is a haven for both migratory and resident wildlife. A mile-long interpretive nature trail overlooks marshes and barrier beaches; the Carson Trail begins at the refuge headquarters, which has exhibits and brochures about wildlife. Other trails are available. **Note:** Leashed pets are permitted on Carson Trail only. **Time:** Allow 30 minutes minimum. **Hours:** Trails daily dawn-dusk. Visitor contact station Mon.-Fri. 8-4:30 (also Sat.-Sun. 10-2, Memorial Day to mid-Aug.); closed federal holidays. **Cost:** Donations. **Phone:** (207) 646-9226. 🐾

WELLS NATIONAL ESTUARINE RESEARCH RESERVE / WELLS RESERVE AT LAUDHOLM is off

I-95 (Maine Tpke.) exit 19, 1 mi. e. to US 1 (following signs), 1.5 mi. n. to Laudholm Farm Rd., then .5 mi. e., following signs. An educational, research and recreational facility occupies a 19th-century saltwater farm with Greek Revival architecture. Coastal-themed exhibits are displayed.

The 2,250-acre preserve offers 7 miles of hiking and cross-country skiing trails, providing access to the woodlands, fields, wetlands, beach and dunes. Trail maps are available at the visitor center and the entry kiosk.

Tours: Guided tours are available. **Time:** Allow 2 hours minimum. **Hours:** Reserve daily 7 a.m.-dusk. Visitor center Mon.-Sat. 10-4, Sun. noon-4, Memorial Day weekend-Columbus Day; Mon.-Fri. 10-4, Jan. 16-day before Memorial Day weekend and day after Columbus Day-Dec. 15; by appointment rest of year. Phone for guided tour schedule. **Cost:** Memorial Day weekend-Columbus Day $4; $1 (ages 6-16); $10 maximum per passenger vehicle. Rest of year by donation. Guided tour fees vary; phone ahead. **Phone:** (207) 646-1555.

CARRIAGE HOUSE MOTEL, COTTAGES & SUITES
207/646-2159 **64**
♦♦ Motel $59-$175 **Address:** 1404 Post Rd (US 1) 04090 **Location:** Jct SR 109 and US 1, just s. **Facility:** 27 units, some two bedrooms, efficiencies, kitchens and cottages. 1-2 stories (no elevator), interior/exterior corridors. **Terms:** closed 10/22-4/4, 2 night minimum stay - seasonal and/or weekends, 15 day cancellation notice-fee imposed. **Pool(s):** heated outdoor. **Activities:** whirlpool, playground, basketball, horseshoes, shuffleboard. **Guest Services:** coin laundry.

ELMWOOD RESORT HOTEL   (207)646-1038 **65**

♦♦♦ **Condominium** $79-$459 **Address:** 1351 Post Rd (US 1) 04090 **Location:** Jct SR 109 and US 1, 0.5 mi s. **Facility:** Guest rooms offer individual décor and pleasant surroundings. 50 condominiums. 2 stories (no elevator), exterior corridors. **Terms:** 2 night minimum stay - seasonal and/or weekends, 15 day cancellation notice-fee imposed, resort fee. **Pool(s):** heated outdoor, heated indoor. **Activities:** sauna, playground. **Guest Services:** coin laundry. **Free Special Amenities: local telephone calls and high-speed Internet.**

GARRISON SUITES MOTEL & COTTAGES
207/646-3497 **66**
♦♦♦♦ Motel $69-$229 **Address:** 1099 Post Rd (US 1) 04090 **Location:** Jct SR 109 and US 1, 1.1 mi s. **Facility:** 48 units, some efficiencies and cottages. 1-2 stories (no elevator), exterior corridors. **Terms:** closed 10/17-4/30, 10 day cancellation notice-fee imposed. **Pool(s):** heated outdoor. **Activities:** whirlpool, horseshoes, volleyball.

HAMPTON INN & SUITES   (207)646-0555 **67**

♦♦♦ Hotel $89-$299

AAA Benefit: Members save up to 10%!

Address: 900 Post Rd (US 1) 04090 **Location:** 0.7 mi n of jct SR 9B. **Facility:** 87 units. 3 stories, interior corridors. **Terms:** 1-7 night minimum stay, cancellation fee imposed. **Amenities:** video games (fee). *Some:* high-speed Internet. **Pool(s):** heated indoor. **Activities:** whirlpool, exercise room. **Guest Services:** valet and coin laundry, area transportation-within 5 mi. **Free Special Amenities: full breakfast and high-speed Internet.**

WELLS-MOODY MOTEL   207/646-5601 **68**
♦ Motel $49-$149 **Address:** 119 Post Rd (US 1) 04054 **Location:** I-95 exit 19, jct SR 109 and US 1, 3.4 mi s. **Facility:** 24 units. 1 story, exterior corridors. **Terms:** closed 10/17-5/31, 10 day cancellation notice-fee imposed. **Pool(s):** outdoor.

WHERE TO EAT

BILLY'S CHOWDER HOUSE   207/646-7558 **47**
♦♦ American. Family Dining. $12-$26 **AAA Inspector Notes:** This is an informal restaurant with rustic decor. It provides excellent views of the tidal river and salt marsh. The menu features fresh seafood as well as chicken and steak. They are famous for chowder but the lobster stew is their signature dish. Be sure to try the strawberry shortcake, which is available most of the year. **Bar:** full bar. **Address:** 216 Mile Rd 04090 **Location:** 1 mi s on US 1, 0.5 mi e on Mile Rd to Wells Beach; center. L D

BULL & CLAW   207/646-8467 **42**
♦♦ Regional American. Family Dining. $6-$26 **AAA Inspector Notes:** In business for more than 30 years, the restaurant offers a menu that includes steak, prime rib, pasta and baked, broiled, fried and sautéed seafood. Sandwiches, wraps and burgers are the focus of the lunch menu, and an extensive breakfast buffet is available. **Bar:** full bar. **Address:** 2270 Post Rd 04090 **Location:** 1.8 mi n on US 1. B L D

CONGDON'S DONUTS & FAMILY RESTAURANT

207/646-4219 **46**
♦♦ American Family Dining $3-$12 **AAA Inspector Notes:** The family-run restaurant and bakery is known for its doughnuts. Home-style cooking is at the menu's heart. **Address:** 1090 Post Rd 04090 **Location:** I-95 exit 19, 1.6 mi e on SR 109, then 0.9 mi s on US 1. B L

JAKE'S SEAFOOD RESTAURANT   207/646-6771 **50**
♦ Seafood. Quick Serve. $5-$20 **AAA Inspector Notes:** A favorite of locals and tourists alike, the restaurant serves traditional Maine seafood. Those who do not order for take-out can eat in the cozy dining room or on the seasonal deck. **Bar:** beer only. **Address:** 139 Post Rd (US 1) 04090 **Location:** 3 mi s of jct US 1 and SR 109; 2.5 mi n of center of Ogunquit. B L D

(See map & index p. 98.)

MAINE DINER

American
Family Dining
$6-$30

207-646-4441 (43)

AAA Inspector Notes: The Maine Diner is very popular with local residents and visitors. The menu features a variety of good seafood dishes including their signature lobster pie, as well as breakfast items served all day. The staff is friendly, prompt and attentive. **Bar:** beer & wine. **Address:** 2265 Post Rd (US 1) 04090 **Location:** 1.8 mi n.

(B) (L) (D)

MAINIAX RESTAURANT

American
Family Dining
$8-$25

207-646-0808 (49)

AAA Inspector Notes: Families visit to enjoy the great woods theme of the dining rooms and the lunch and dinner preparations of seafood, pasta, steak and chicken. **Bar:** full bar. **Address:** 526 Post Rd 04090 **Location:** 1.2 mi s on US 1. *Menu on AAA.com*

(L) (D) CALL (&M)

MIKE'S CLAM SHACK

Seafood
Family Dining
$8-$24

207-646-5999 (45)

AAA Inspector Notes: The eatery started out as a clam shack in 1948 but has grown into a popular sit-down restaurant. Seafood is at the heart of the menu. A take-out window is still available seasonally. **Bar:** full bar. **Address:** 1150 Post Rd 04090 **Location:** I-95 exit 19, 1 mi e on SR 109, then 0.8 mi s on US 1. (L) (D)

THE STEAKHOUSE

207/646-4200 (44)

Steak. Family Dining. $15-$27 **AAA Inspector Notes:** The Steakhouse's strawberry shortcake is a mouthwatering treat! Located in a turn-of-the-century barn, this popular restaurant has a rustic setting in which to serve its very well-prepared beef, seafood and chicken dishes--all served in large portions. **Bar:** full bar. **Address:** 1205 Post Rd (US 1) 04090 **Location:** Jct SR 109 and US 1, 1 mi s; center. (D) CALL (&M)

VARANO'S ITALIAN RESTAURANT

207/641-8550 (48)

Italian. Casual Dining. $14-$30 **AAA Inspector Notes:** Dining rooms provide a sweeping view of the salt marshes and a distant view of the Atlantic Ocean. The menu has an extensive list of classic Italian dishes. **Bar:** full bar. **Address:** 60 Mile Rd 04090 **Location:** US 1, just e. (D)

WELLS BEACH
• Hotels & Restaurants map & index p. 98

ATLANTIC OCEANFRONT MOTEL

207/646-7061 (71)

Motel $69-$309 **Address:** 37 Atlantic Ave 04090 **Location:** Oceanfront. US 1, 1 mi e on Mile Rd, just n. **Facility:** 35 units. 3 stories (no elevator), exterior corridors. **Terms:** closed 10/27-4/2, 3 night minimum stay - seasonal and/or weekends, 10 day cancellation notice-fee imposed. **Amenities:** high-speed Internet. **Pool(s):** heated outdoor.

LAFAYETTE'S OCEAN FRONT RESORT AT WELLS BEACH

207/646-2831 (72)

Hotel $49-$500 **Address:** 393 Mile Rd 04090 **Location:** Oceanfront. Jct US 1, 1 mi e. **Facility:** 148 units, some efficiencies. 2-3 stories, interior/exterior corridors. **Terms:** 3-5 night minimum stay - seasonal and/or weekends, 7 day cancellation notice-fee imposed. **Pool(s):** heated indoor. **Activities:** whirlpool, exercise room. **Guest Services:** coin laundry.

WEST BATH (J-3)

HAMILTON SANCTUARY, 4 mi. s. on Foster Point Rd., following signs to sanctuary entrance, has 1.5 miles of trails that lead through fir, pine and spruce forests and open meadows. On a peninsula in the New Meadows River, the 74-acre sanctuary offers views of the rugged Maine coastline. Visitors are likely to see ospreys, great blue herons, kingfishers and an array of other birds. **Hours:** Daily dawn-dusk. **Cost:** Free. **Phone:** (207) 781-2330.

WEST BOOTHBAY HARBOR (J-4) elev. 33'

Encompassing 5 acres, Burnt Island is home to the restored 1821 Burnt Island Light and its accompanying buildings. Transportation to and from the island is provided by boat.

MAINE STATE AQUARIUM is at 194 McKown Point Rd. A gallery evoking Maine's coast holds viewing tanks filled with regional fish and invertebrates. Colorful lobsters, sharks and sport fish may be seen. Sea creatures including sea stars, crabs and sea cucumbers reside in a 20-foot-long touch tank; sharks and invertebrates reside in a second touch tank. A display teaches visitors about lobster trapping. Presentations are offered.

Time: Allow 1 hour minimum. **Hours:** Daily 10-5, Memorial Day weekend-Labor Day; Wed.-Sun. 10-5, day after Labor Day-late Sept. Phone ahead to confirm schedule. **Cost:** $5; $3 (ages 3-12 and 65+). **Phone:** (207) 633-9559, or (207) 633-9500 in the off-season.

WESTBROOK pop. 17,494
• Hotels & Restaurants map & index p. 131

SUPER 8

Hotel
$58-$130

207/854-1881 (19)

Address: 208 Larrabee Rd 04092 **Location:** I-95 exit 48. **Facility:** 105 units. 2 stories (no elevator), interior corridors. **Pool(s):** heated indoor. **Activities:** whirlpool. **Free Special Amenities:** expanded continental breakfast and high-speed Internet.

 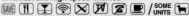

WEST FORKS (G-3) elev. 1,214'

RECREATIONAL ACTIVITIES
White-water Rafting

• **U.S. Rafting** departs from 2981 US 201. **Hours:** Trips depart daily 9-4, May-Oct. **Phone:** (207) 323-3052.

INN BY THE RIVER

Country Inn
$89-$129

(207)663-2181

Address: 2777 US Rt 201 04985 **Location:** Center. **Facility:** 10 units. 2 stories (no elevator), interior corridors. **Terms:** 2 night minimum stay - seasonal and/or weekends, 30 day cancellation notice-fee imposed. **Activities:** fishing, hiking trails. **Fee:** canoes, snowmobiling. **Free Special Amenities:** continental breakfast and high-speed Internet.

WEST PARIS (I-2) elev. 480'

In West Paris, as in many Oxford County communities, it is not the pleasant farm and woodland scenery but what lies beneath it that is of consuming interest. Oxford County is one of Maine's richest sources of minerals, harboring such gemstones as tourmaline, beryl, rose and smoky quartz, amethyst and aquamarine.

Many mines and quarries have been yielding their treasures since the late 1800s. Snow Falls Gorge, 2 miles south on SR 26, includes walkways around the scenic falls as well as picnic facilities.

Oxford Hills Chamber of Commerce: 4 Western Ave., South Paris, ME 04281. **Phone:** (207) 743-2281.

WESTPORT

THE SQUIRE TARBOX INN   (207)882-7693

wwww **Historic Country Inn** $115-$199 **Address:** 1181 Main Rd 04578 **Location:** Jct US 1 and SR 144; in Wiscasset; 8.5 mi s on SR 144, follow signs. Located in a quiet rural area. **Facility:** Located on a quiet country road, the inn is situated on a working farm. Built in 1763, the inn reflects Colonial-style décor. Modern distractions are minimized, which means no TV or phone in the rooms. 11 units. 2 stories (no elevator), interior/exterior corridors. *Bath:* shower only. **Terms:** closed 1/2-4/18, 2 night minimum stay - seasonal and/or weekends, 14 day cancellation notice-fee imposed. **Activities:** boating, boat dock, bicycles.

🍴 BIZ 📶 ✕ 🅦 🄩 / SOME UNITS FEE 🐾

WILTON

FARMINGTON/WILTON COMFORT INN & SUITES
                                         (207)645-5155

wwww **Hotel** $99-$140 **Address:** 1026 US Rt 2 04294 **Location:** On US 2, just w of jct SR 133. **Facility:** 86 units, some efficiencies. 3 stories, interior corridors. **Terms:** cancellation fee imposed. **Amenities:** high-speed Internet. **Pool(s):** heated indoor. **Activities:** whirlpool, exercise room. **Guest Services:** valet and coin laundry.

CALL 🅲M 🕽 BIZ 📶 ✕ 🖵
/ SOME UNITS FEE 🐾 🗋 🖼

WILSON LAKE INN   (207)645-3721

ww **Motel** $70-$139 **Address:** 183 Lake Rd 04294 **Location:** Waterfront. SR 2, 1 mi w of jct SR 4. **Facility:** 30 units, some two bedrooms, efficiencies and kitchens. 2 stories (no elevator), exterior corridors. **Terms:** check-in 4 pm, cancellation fee imposed. **Activities:** boating, canoeing, boat dock, fishing, horseshoes, volleyball. **Guest Services:** coin laundry.

BIZ 📶 ✕ 🗋 / SOME UNITS FEE 🖼

WINDHAM

AMATO'S   207/892-0160

w **Deli. Quick Serve.** $4-$14 **AAA Inspector Notes:** Known for their "Real Italian" sandwich, which was created over 100 years ago by an Italian immigrant who decided to place a little bit of meat, fresh vegetables, cheese, Greek olives, a zesty pickle and a specialty blended olive oil on a freshly made roll. This recipe has built up a loyal following of customers. Other menu choices include hot or cold sandwiches, calzones, specialty pizzas, pasta and freshly prepared salads. Diners may choose to eat in or take out. **Bar:** beer & wine. **Address:** 727 Roosevelt Tr 04062 **Location:** On US 302, just e of jct SR 115/35. L D

WISCASSET   (J-4) pop. 1,097, elev. 11'

Wiscasset at one time was Maine's chief port. The Embargo Act of 1807 seriously crippled its prosperous sea trade, and the town never regained its stature as a seaport. However, the legacy of that era is evidenced by Wiscasset's mansions, built by ship

owners and merchants in the 18th and early 19th centuries.

CASTLE TUCKER HISTORIC HOUSE MUSEUM is at 2 Lee St. Guided tours take visitors through this 1807 Regency-style mansion. Interior furnishings include the Tucker family's original furniture, as well as Federal and Victorian furniture, paintings and household items. A freestanding, elliptical staircase and a 19th-century kitchen also are of note. **Hours:** Tours are given on the hour and half-hour Wed.-Sun. 11-4, June 1-Oct. 15. **Cost:** $5; $4 (ages 65+); $2.50 (ages 6-12). **Phone:** (207) 882-7169.

FORT EDGECOMB STATE HISTORIC SITE—see Edgecomb p. 83.

LINCOLN COUNTY MUSEUM AND OLD JAIL, 133 Federal St., is a fortress-like granite building used as a jail 1811-1913. Original graffiti from the 19th century still exists on cell walls. A brick jailer's home attached to the jail houses antiques and decorative arts as well as changing exhibits. **Time:** Allow 30 minutes minimum. **Hours:** Fri.-Sat. 10-4, Sun. noon-4, July-Aug.; Sat. 10-4, Sun. noon-4, Memorial Day-June 30 and Sept. 1-Columbus Day; by appointment rest of year. **Cost:** $4; free (ages 0-16). **Phone:** (207) 882-6817.

 **MUSICAL WONDER HOUSE** is at 16-18 High St. Built in 1852 for a sea captain, this 32-room mansion contains more than 5,000 antique music boxes, player grand pianos, organettes, phonographs, furniture pieces, porcelains and paintings. The grand entrance hall features a flying staircase surrounded by coin-operated antique music boxes and other machines.

The Grand House Presentation includes a 2-hour mechanical music presentation in eight rooms on two floors. The Full House Presentation includes a 1-hour mechanical music presentation in three rooms on the first floor.

Time: Allow 1 hour minimum. **Hours:** Mon.-Sat. 10-5, Sun. noon-5, Memorial Day weekend-Oct. 31. **Cost:** Grand House Presentation $40; $36 (ages 65+). Full House Presentation $20; $18 (ages 65+). **Phone:** (207) 882-7163.

NICKELS-SORTWELL HOUSE, 121 Main St. (US 1), was built by prominent Maine shipmaster Capt. William Nickels and later owned by Alvin Sortwell, a mayor of Cambridge, Mass. Guided tours take visitors through the 1807 house, which contains the Sortwell family's Colonial Revival-style furnishings. An elliptical staircase is illuminated by a third-floor skylight. **Time:** Allow 30 minutes minimum. **Hours:** Tours are given on the hour and half-hour Fri.-Sun. 11-4, June 1-Oct. 15. **Cost:** $5; $4 (ages 65+); $2.50 (ages 6-12). **Phone:** (207) 882-7169.

LE GARAGE   207/882-5409

▼▼▼
**American
Casual Dining
$8-$28**

AAA Inspector Notes: Le Garage features an excellent view of the Sheepscot River from its glassed-in porch. The exceptional menu offers finnan haddie, charbroiled lamb, seafood Newburg, steak and vegetarian dishes. Large, wrought-iron candelabras provide romantic lighting. **Bar:** full bar. **Address:** 15 Water St 04578 **Location:** Downtown. **Parking:** street only. *Menu on AAA.com*

L D

RED'S EATS   207/882-6128

▼ Regional Seafood. Quick Serve. $5-$20 **AAA Inspector Notes:** Don't be surprised if you have to stand in line to order at this laid-back spot. Don't worry, you'll agree it was worthwhile when you take your first taste of Red's famous lobster roll. **Address:** 41 Water St 04578 **Location:** On US 1; center of village. **Parking:** street only.

L D ✗

SEA BASKET RESTAURANT   207/882-6581

▼ Seafood. Quick Serve. $6-$22 **AAA Inspector Notes:** Colorful seaside murals decorate the walls of the traditional seafood restaurant. Fresh Maine seafood is cooked in a convection fryer for lighter, healthier fried seafood. Patrons can bring their own bottle. **Address:** 303 Bath Rd 04578 **Location:** On US 1, 1.2 mi s of center.

L D

WOOLWICH

MONTSWEAG ROADHOUSE   207/443-6563

▼ American. Casual Dining. $7-$18 **AAA Inspector Notes:** A bevy of New England comfort foods are served at this popular spot. The post-and-beam ceilinged dining room features a rustic ambience, including antique farming and wood tools hanging on the walls. The menu offers such favorites such as fried and baked seafoods, steaks, and meatloaf, as well as sandwiches, burgers, and soups. Seasonal outdoor seating is available. **Bar:** full bar. **Address:** 942 US 1 04579 **Location:** On US 1 S. L D

THE TASTE OF MAINE RESTAURANT   207/443-4554

▼▼
**Seafood
Family Dining
$11-$25**

AAA Inspector Notes: Lobster is the focus, but patrons also can select chicken, steak and a few vegetarian entrees. Fresh seafood arrives daily. The family-friendly restaurant provides an area where children can play while parents eat. **Reservations:** suggested. **Address:** 161 Main St 04579 **Location:** 0.6 mi n of Bath Bridge. L D CALL

YARMOUTH (J-3) pop. 5,869, elev. 87'

Although Yarmouth was first settled in 1636, permanent habitation was not possible until 1713 due to repeated attacks by American Indians. Early residents took advantage of the power provided by four waterfalls on the Royal River, and the economy prospered due to fishing, lumbering, shipbuilding and farming.

Of interest is a 41.5-foot-high rotating globe dubbed EARTHA, on view in the lobby of DeLorme, a mapping company at 2 DeLorme Dr. Exhibits describe data-gathering technology used to create the globe.

Yarmouth is known as a scenic coastal community. Picnicking, strolls on paved pathways and views of picturesque waterfalls are possible at Royal River Park, on Elm Street off SR 115.

Yarmouth Chamber of Commerce: 162 Main St., Yarmouth, ME 04096. **Phone:** (207) 846-3984.

YARMOUTH HISTORY CENTER, 118 E. Elm St., displays photographs, clothing, furnishings and other items reflecting the history of the area. Research materials include journals, documents and historical records. **Time:** Allow 30 minutes minimum. **Hours:** Tues.-Sat. 10-5. **Cost:** Donations. **Phone:** (207) 846-6259.

DOWN-EAST VILLAGE MOTEL   207/846-5161

▼▼
**Motel
$89-$129**

Address: 705 US Rt 1 04096 **Location:** I-295 exit 15 northbound; exit 17 southbound. **Facility:** 30 units. 1 story, exterior corridors. **Pool(s):** outdoor. **Activities:** playground. **Free Special Amenities:** local telephone calls and high-speed Internet. *(See ad p. 89.)*

SAVE 🚗 BIZ 📶 ✕ ▭
/ SOME UNITS FEE 🐾 🔌

WHERE TO EAT

CLAYTON'S   207/846-1117

▼ Deli. Quick Serve. $6-$8 **AAA Inspector Notes:** Homemade bread, generously sized sandwiches, scratch-made soups, fresh coffee and desserts, not to mention an impressive bottled wine selection, are the many reasons why patrons love this place. It's a great spot to pick up a picnic lunch too. **Address:** 447 US 1 04096 **Location:** Just s of SR 115. B L D

GRILL 233   207/846-3633

▼▼ American. Casual Dining. $8-$26 **AAA Inspector Notes:** Although dining rooms are decorated in the style of an Italian eatery in Boston's North End, the cuisine is more of the American bistro style. Among choices are 233 carbonara, pinwheel salmon and wild mushroom soup with puff pastry. Brunch is offered on Sunday. **Bar:** full bar. **Address:** 233 US 1 04096 **Location:** I-295 exit 15, 0.3 mi n. L D

MUDDY RUDDER RESTAURANT   207/846-3082

▼▼ American. Casual Dining. $6-$20 **AAA Inspector Notes:** Soup, stew, salad, lobster pie, and steak and seafood dinners are served at this warm and inviting restaurant, which boasts good views of the wildlife on Cousins River. Downeast clambakes are another popular choice. Adorning the dining room walls are prints with Maine coastal themes, while on the tables are area maps from the 1800s. **Bar:** full bar. **Address:** 1335 US Rt 1 04096 **Location:** US 1, at north end of town limits. L D

ROYAL RIVER GRILLHOUSE   207/846-1226

▼▼▼ American. Casual Dining. $10-$38 **AAA Inspector Notes:** Overlooking the Royal River, this casual restaurant is on the site of a former seafood cannery. Large windows in the dining room give an unrestricted view of the marine activity. The seasonally changing menu features native seafood, including shellfish, as well as beef and poultry entrees. Outdoor dining on the deck is available seasonally. **Bar:** full bar. **Reservations:** suggested. **Address:** 106 Lafayette St 04096 **Location:** I-295 exit 17, just s on US 1, then 1 mi s on SR 88, follow signs. L D

YORK (L-2)
• Restaurants p. 161
• Hotels & Restaurants map & index p. 98

York is one of Maine's oldest, most historic places. First settled in 1624, it was called Agamenticus for the abandoned American Indian village on the site. Six years later an aristocratic group led by

(See map & index p. 98.)

agents of Sir Ferdinando Gorges arrived; their plantation prospered, and they adopted the name of their home city of Bristol in 1638. In 1641 Gorges granted the settlement a city charter under the name of Gorgeana—making it the first chartered English city in America.

After Gorges' dream of a city in the wilderness ended with his death in 1647, the inhabitants formed a body politic with six other outposts and attempted self-rule. Plagued by contradictory land grants, threatened by American Indians and finally realizing the importance of a central government, they became freemen of Massachusetts in 1652. Massachusetts then promptly demoted the city of Gorgeana to a town and renamed it York.

One of the heaviest blows of the French and Indian Wars was struck at York in January 1692. In what became known as the Candlemas Massacre, some 500 Abenaki fell upon the village, killing 80 townspeople, capturing another 50 and burning most of the buildings. Snowshoe Rock, where the American Indians left their snowshoes before the attack, is 5 miles north on Chases Pond Road; a marker commemorates the disaster.

Reminders of York's past include residential areas dating from the 18th century, Colonial churches, farmhouses with large woodpiles of white birch, stone walls along tree-lined streets and an old burying ground where quaint epitaphs are favorites for stone rubbings. Ancient traditions are strong, but there also are new industries and plentiful facilities for recreation. The York River provides a setting for boating, and Agamenticus Mountain has facilities for picnicking, biking and hiking.

The Greater York Region Chamber of Commerce: 1 Stonewall Ln., York, ME 03909. **Phone:** (207) 363-4422.

MUSEUMS OF OLD YORK, 3 Lindsay Rd., maintains nine restored historic house museums representing 4 centuries of life in the coastal village of York and in southern Maine. Tours begin at the Remick Barn visitor center. A research library is on the premises. **Hours:** Each site open Mon.-Sat. 9:30-4, early June-Columbus Day weekend. Research library Thurs.-Fri. 9-noon and 12:30-4, year-round; phone for holiday closures. **Cost:** One building $6; $5 (ages 65+); $3 (ages 4-15); $15 (family, two adults and all accompanying children ages 6-15). Combination ticket for all buildings $12; $10 (ages 65+); $5 (ages 4-15); $25 (family, two adults and all accompanying children ages 4-15). **Phone:** (207) 363-4974.

Elizabeth Perkins House is on the banks of the York River at the s. end of Sewall's Bridge on Southside Rd. Furnishings reflect the eclectic tastes of a family of collectors from the Colonial Revival period. Restored gardens and landscaped grounds also are featured. Guided tours are available by reservation.

Time: Allow 30 minutes minimum. **Hours:** Tours depart Mon.-Sat. by appointment, early June-Columbus Day weekend. **Cost:** $6; $5 (ages 65+); $3 (ages 4-15); $15 (family, two adults and all accompanying children ages 6-15). A combination ticket with other Museums of Old York sites is available. **Phone:** (207) 363-4974.

Emerson-Wilcox House, center of town on York St., has served as a tavern, general store, tailor shop, post office and private residence. The 1742 building contains a series of period rooms furnished with American antiques dating 1750-1850. **Time:** Allow 30 minutes minimum. **Hours:** Tours Mon.-Sat. by appointment, early June-Columbus Day weekend. **Cost:** $6; $5 (ages 65+); $3 (ages 4-15); $15 (family, two adults and all accompanying children ages 6-15). A combination ticket with other Museums of Old York sites is available. **Phone:** (207) 363-4974.

Jefferds' Tavern is just off US 1A, on Lindsay Rd. facing the Old Burying Ground. Built by Capt. Samuel Jefferds in 1750 in Wells, the tavern was moved to York in 1939. **Hours:** Mon.-Sat. 9:30-4, early June-Columbus Day weekend. **Cost:** $6; $5 (ages 65+); $3 (ages 4-15); $15 (family, two adults and all accompanying children ages 6-15). A combination ticket with other Museums of Old York sites is available. **Phone:** (207) 363-4974.

John Hancock Warehouse, on the York River on Lindsay Rd., was owned by John Hancock until 1794. One of the oldest surviving commercial buildings in Maine, it has exhibits that illustrate the maritime history of the Yorks. **Hours:** Mon.-Sat. 9:30-4, Sun. 1-4, early June-Columbus Day weekend. **Cost:** $6; $5 (ages 65+); $3 (ages 4-15); $15 (family, two adults and all accompanying children ages 6-15). A combination ticket with other Museums of Old York sites is available. **Phone:** (207) 363-4974.

Old Gaol, center of town on York St., is one of the oldest English public buildings in the United States and was used as a jail until 1860. The 1719 structure is furnished according to the inventory of William Emerson, gaoler in 1790. Dungeons and cells for felons and debtors and galleries of local historical artifacts are included. A self-guiding tour is available. **Time:** Allow 30 minutes minimum. **Hours:** Mon.-Sat. 9:30-4, early June-Columbus Day weekend. **Cost:** $6; $5 (ages 65+); $3 (ages 4-15); $15 (family, two adults and all accompanying children ages 6-15). A combination ticket with other Museums of Old York sites is available. **Phone:** (207) 363-4974.

Old Schoolhouse, center of town on Lindsay Rd., dates from 1745 and is one of the oldest surviving one-room schoolhouses in the state. **Hours:** Mon.-Sat. 9:30-4, early June-Columbus Day weekend. **Cost:** $6; $5 (ages 65+); $3 (ages 4-15); $15 (family, two adults and all accompanying children ages 6-15). A combination ticket with other Museums of Old York sites is available. **Phone:** (207) 363-4974.

(See map & index p. 98.)

CAPE NEDDICK INN RESTAURANT AND TAVERN
207/351-1145 68

American
Fine Dining
$10-$32

AAA Inspector Notes: The stone hearth fireplace sets an intimate, warm, and inviting tone at the inn. Local, fresh seafood, including haddock, is prepared in a variety of styles. Naturally, the menu features Maine lobster, as well as shrimp. Landlubbers need not worry as there's something to tempt them on the menu as well. **Bar:** full bar. **Reservations:** required. **Address:** 1273 US Rt 1 03902 **Location:** On US 1.

D

Historic, romantic, moderate pricing Maine restaurant

CLAY HILL FARM   207/361-2272 67
American. Fine Dining. $24-$29 **AAA Inspector Notes:** The restaurant's gracious dining rooms offer views of the peaceful country setting. Guests can enjoy the casual elegance while dining on beautifully prepared New England regional cuisine. In season, soothing piano music is played in the dining room. **Bar:** full bar. **Reservations:** suggested. **Address:** 220 Clay Hill Rd 03902 **Location:** 0.5 mi s on US 1, 2 mi w on Agamenticus Rd. **Parking:** valet only.

D

LOBSTER BARN   207/363-4721 69
Seafood. Casual Dining. $7-$35 **AAA Inspector Notes:** The restaurant is well named--it's in a real New England barn displaying many farm artifacts. The setting is warm and cozy, with lanterns and candles on the tables. Maine lobster is the specialty, but the menu also offers steak and blueberry pie. **Bar:** full bar. **Address:** 1000 US Rt 1 03909 **Location:** I-95 exit 7, 2.5 mi n.

D   CALL

LOBSTER COVE   207/351-1100 71
Seafood. Family Dining. $8-$28 **AAA Inspector Notes:** The restaurant boasts lovely water views and is open for breakfast, lunch and dinner. Eclectic menus emphasize fresh seafood. Deck seating is available in season. **Bar:** full bar. **Address:** 756 York St 03910 **Location:** On US 1A.   B   L   D

RUBY'S GENUINE BRICK OVEN   207/363-7980 72
American. Casual Dining. $7-$19 **AAA Inspector Notes:** In addition to brick-oven pizzas, the menu lists pasta, seafood, steak, sizzling fajitas, salads, sandwiches and burgers. **Bar:** full bar. **Address:** 433 US Rt 1 03909 **Location:** I-95 exit 7, just s.

L   D

WILD WILLY'S BURGERS   207/363-9924 70
Burgers. Quick Serve. $7-$9 **AAA Inspector Notes:** Thick, juicy Angus beef burgers are the trademark of Wild Willy's, a popular spot with locals. Step up to the counter to order your food, then take a seat in the colorful dining room, which sports a Rocky Mountain mural on the walls and ceiling. You can also take your burgers to go. **Bar:** beer & wine. **Address:** 765 US Rt 1 03909 **Location:** I-95 exit 7, 1 mi n.   L   D

YORK BEACH (L-2)
• Hotels & Restaurants map & index p. 98

YORK'S WILD KINGDOM ZOO AND AMUSEMENT PARK, I-95 exit 7, then 2 mi. n. to 1 Animal Park Rd., is home to exotic animals from around the world, including bears, lions and a white Bengal tiger. The Butterfly Kingdom exhibit, animal shows and a petting zoo also are offered. An amusement park features 20 rides.

Time: Allow 3 hours minimum. **Hours:** Zoo daily 10-6, July 1-Labor Day; 10-5, Memorial Day-June 30. Amusements daily noon-9, July 1-Labor Day; Sat.-Sun. noon-6, Memorial Day-June 30. Phone for schedule, day after Labor Day to mid-Sept. **Cost:** Zoo $14.75; $9 (ages 4-12); $1 (ages 1-3). Combination zoo and rides $21.25; $16.25 (ages 4-12); $4.75 (ages 1-3). Hours and rates may vary; phone ahead. **Phone:** (207) 363-4911 or (800) 456-4911.

THE ANCHORAGE INN   207/363-5112 101
Hotel $70-$585 **Address:** 265 Long Beach Ave 03910 **Location:** 1.5 mi s on US 1A. **Facility:** 202 units, some two bedrooms, efficiencies and kitchens. 3 stories, interior/exterior corridors. **Terms:** 2 night minimum stay - seasonal and/or weekends, 10 day cancellation notice-fee imposed. **Amenities:** Some: safes. **Pool(s):** 2 heated outdoor, 2 heated indoor. **Activities:** whirlpools, limited beach access, exercise room.

LIGHTHOUSE INN & CARRIAGE HOUSE 207/363-6072 100
Motel $85-$185 **Address:** 18-20 Nubble Rd 03910 **Location:** 0.5 mi s on US 1A, then just e. **Facility:** 31 units, some two bedrooms. 2 stories (no elevator), interior/exterior corridors. **Terms:** closed 10/17-5/12, 1-2 night minimum stay - seasonal, 7 day cancellation notice-fee imposed. **Pool(s):** heated outdoor. **Activities:** whirlpool.

THE UNION BLUFF HOTEL   207/363-1333 99
Hotel $79-$399 **Address:** 8 Beach St 03910 **Location:** Oceanfront. Center. **Facility:** 70 units. 3-5 stories, interior/exterior corridors. **Terms:** 2 night minimum stay - seasonal and/or weekends, 14 day cancellation notice-fee imposed. **Dining:** Union Bluff Pub & Grill, see separate listing. **Activities:** limited beach access.

WHERE TO EAT

CHEF MIMMO'S   207/363-3807 78
Italian. Casual Dining. $21-$28 **AAA Inspector Notes:** Diners will find informal dining across the street from Long Sands Beach. The kitchen prepares ample portions and a good selection of continental Italian dishes and desserts. No alcohol is served, but guests are invited to bring their own. The enclosed porch is pleasant. **Reservations:** suggested. **Address:** 243 Long Beach Ave 03910 **Location:** 1.5 mi s on US 1A.   D

FOX'S LOBSTER HOUSE   207/363-2643 76
Seafood. Family Dining. $14-$39 **AAA Inspector Notes:** Panoramic views of Nubble Lighthouse and the ocean enhance the mood for guests who come to dine on lobster and fried seafood. Landlubbers need not worry, as there is a good selection of pastas, burgers and more. Food can be ordered for dining in or taking out. **Bar:** full bar. **Address:** 8 Sohier Park Rd 03910 **Location:** At Nubble Point.   L   D

SUN & SURF   207/363-2961 77
American. Casual Dining. $8-$30 **AAA Inspector Notes:** This restaurant practically sits on the beach—both the indoor and outdoor dining areas overlook a bank of rose bushes, the beach and the Atlantic beyond. The fanciful décor exudes a cheery quality, while a varied menu satisfies with its fried, broiled, and baked local shellfish and fish. The must-have Maine lobster can be steamed, baked, stuffed, or sautéed, depending on the preference. Landlubbers need not worry: sandwiches, burgers, steaks, and chicken also are featured. **Bar:** full bar. **Address:** 264 Long Beach Ave 03910 **Location:** 1.5 mi s on US 1A.   B   L   D   CALL

UNION BLUFF PUB & GRILL   207/363-1333 75
American. Casual Dining. $7-$28 **AAA Inspector Notes:** Casual dining and a slightly more upscale experience are offered—both are excellent choices. The haddock, regardless of preparation, is moist, fresh and flaky. The many other items on the menu, even those for the landlubber, are equally tasty. **Bar:** full bar. **Address:** 8 Beach St 03910 **Location:** Center; in The Union Bluff Hotel.

L   D

YORK HARBOR (L-2) pop. 3,033, elev. 56'
• Hotels & Restaurants map & index p. 98

The fashionable resort member of the Yorks, York Harbor has enjoyed this role since the Civil War. Well-to-do residents of Boston, Philadelphia and other large cities built rambling three-story "cottages" and grand hotels in which to while away their summers, cooled by the New England sea breezes. York Harbor's summer colony once rivaled those of Bar Harbor (see place listing p. 46) and Newport, R.I.

The harbor itself, with the town wharves and marina, remains as busy now as in the 18th century, when it was the Yorks' marketplace and the scene of lively market fairs. It is a favored stopover among yachtsmen and an equally popular starting point for deep-sea fishing trips.

One block south of SR 1703 and US 1 a footpath leads to Wiggley Bridge, a restored suspension bridge spanning the York River. From York Harbor, Long Sands Beach extends northeastward past York Beach toward Cape Neddick Light, popularly known as the Nubble Light. One of the most photographed lighthouses in Maine, the Nubble extends a rocky thumb into the sea; from a tiny island just off its tip the Cape Neddick Light, built in 1879, once guided seamen.

The Sayward-Wheeler House at 9 Barrell Ln. Ext., open the second and fourth Saturday of each month from June to mid-October, contains antique furniture and items brought back as booty from the expedition against the French at Louisbourg in 1745; phone (207) 384-2454.

DOCKSIDE GUEST QUARTERS   (207)363-2868 **108**
▼▼▼▼ Country Inn $140-$345 Address: 22 Harris Island Rd 03909 Location: Waterfront. Jct US 1A, just s on SR 103 to Harris Island Rd, then just s. Located in a rural area. Facility: A main inn and cottages are situated on a small private island in a harbor setting; phone for seasonal availability. 25 units, some efficiencies. 2 stories (no elevator), interior/exterior corridors. Terms: check-in 4 pm, 2 night minimum stay - seasonal and/or weekends, 14 day cancellation notice-fee imposed. Dining: Dockside Restaurant on York Harbor, see separate listing. Activities: rental boats, fishing, bicycles. Fee: marina.

EDWARDS HARBORSIDE INN   207/363-3037 **106**
▼▼▼▼ Historic Resort Hotel $90-$290 Address: 7 Stage Neck Rd 03911 Location: Waterfront. Off US 1A, 2 mi n of jct US 1. Facility: A picturesque setting overlooking York Harbor enhances this nicely appointed Victorian home. Handsomely decorated, varied-size rooms are rented out individually or collectively as a group. 8 units, some two bedrooms. 3 stories (no elevator), interior corridors. Terms: 2-3 night minimum stay - seasonal and/or weekends, 15 day cancellation notice-fee imposed, resort fee. Activities: beach access, boat dock, fishing.

INN AT HARMON PARK   (207)363-2031 **105**
▼▼▼ Bed & Breakfast $99-$139 Address: 415 York St 03911 Location: I-95 exit 7, 0.3 mi s on US 1, then 1.5 mi n; to York Village. Located in a residential area. Facility: An 1899 Victorian-style home, the inn offers charming décor; the innkeepers provide gracious hospitality. 5 units. 2 stories (no elevator), interior corridors. Terms: closed 1/1-3/31, 2 night minimum stay - seasonal and/or weekends, 7 day cancellation notice-fee imposed.

▼ See AAA listing p. 163 ▼

Location, Amenities, Relaxation, Togetherness ...

Your Seaside Getaway to southern Maine ...

Stage Neck Inn

YORK HARBOR, ME / 800-340-2243 / WWW.STAGENECKINN.US

AAA/CAA travel information:

Available in print, online and on the go!

(See map & index p. 98.)

STAGE NECK INN   207/363-3850   107

Resort Hotel
$182-$444

Address: 8 Stage Neck Rd 03911 **Location:** Oceanfront. Off US 1A via Harbor Beach Rd. **Facility:** A traditional New England-style oceanside inn, the property has good ocean and harbor views and well-tended landscaping. Rooms are richly decorated. 60 units. 3 stories, interior corridors. **Terms:** closed 1/1-1/18, 2-3 night minimum stay - seasonal and/or weekends, 14 day cancellation notice-fee imposed, resort fee. **Amenities:** safes. **Pool(s):** heated outdoor, heated indoor. **Activities:** sauna, whirlpool, 2 tennis courts, exercise room, spa. **Guest Services:** valet and coin laundry. **Free Special Amenities:** full breakfast and high-speed Internet. *(See ad p. 162.)*

[SAVE] [⍦] [⍭] [⊷] [BIZ] [⍢] [⊠] [🔋] [▭]

YORK HARBOR INN   (207)363-5119   104

▽▽▽ **Historic Country Inn** $109-$349 **Address:** 480 York St 03911 **Location:** On US 1A; center. **Facility:** Sections of this inn date from the 1600s, lending a feel of yesteryear combined with modern amenities. Room size varies from compact to more spacious. 54 units. 2-3 stories (no elevator), interior/exterior corridors. **Terms:** 2 night minimum stay - seasonal and/or weekends, 14 day cancellation notice-fee imposed. **Dining:** The York Harbor Inn & Ship's Cellar Pub, see separate listing. **Activities:** whirlpool.

[ECO] [⍦] [⍢] [⊠] / [SOME UNITS] [🛏]

DOCKSIDE RESTAURANT ON YORK HARBOR
207/363-2722   83

▽▽▽ Seafood. Casual Dining. $9-$29 **AAA Inspector Notes:** The restaurant's attractive and informal dining room and screened porch overlook York Harbor and the marina. The menu features a nice variety of seafood dishes as well as chicken and beef. Lighter fare is available at lunch. **Bar:** full bar. **Address:** 22 Harris Island Rd 03909 **Location:** Jct US 1A, just s on SR 103 to Harris Island Rd, then just s; in Dockside Guest Quarters. [L] [D]

FOSTER'S RESTAURANT AND FOSTER'S DOWNEAST
CLAMBAKE   207/363-3255   81

▽ Regional Seafood. Quick Serve. $6-$30 **AAA Inspector Notes:** Old-world charm meets new-world hospitality at this lovely lakeside landmark that serves Continental cuisine with a modern flair. The restaurant, a colonial inn originally constructed in 1787, has been lovingly restored and maintains its place as a favorite of locals and travelers alike. **Bar:** beer & wine. **Address:** 5 Axholme Rd 03911 **Location:** Off US 1A. [L] [D]

THE YORK HARBOR INN & SHIP'S CELLAR PUB
207/363-5119   82

▽▽▽ Regional American. Casual Dining. $7-$29 **AAA Inspector Notes:** In a true historic Colonial country inn, the restaurant showcases an elegant and upscale decor with wide windows offering great views of the ocean. The menu reflects a regional cuisine featuring seafood prepared with international flavors. **Bar:** full bar. **Address:** 480 York St 03911 **Location:** On US 1A; center; in York Harbor Inn. [L] [D]

Portsmouth Harbor historic homes

New Hampshire

Historic Timeline 166
What To Pack 166
Good Facts To Know 167
Annual Events 168
GEM Attraction Index 170
Maps: Atlas Section & Orientation 171
Recreation Areas Chart 175
Alphabetical City Listings 177

Live free or die.

To understand New Hampshire's blunt motto, it's necessary to peek into the state's feisty and pathfinding past.

Twenty years after English sea captain Martin Pring sailed up the lower Piscataqua River to explore the region, Europeans established the first white settlements at Odiorne's Point and Dover in 1623. Others followed in nearly a century of allegiance to the English crown.

When the colonists would have no more, New Hampshire declared independence from England, and in 1776 became the first colony to adopt a provisional constitution and government.

Durham was a hotbed of this Revolutionary activity. Led by native son Maj. Gen. John Sullivan, patriots took gunpowder from the British and stored it in a town meetinghouse; a tablet marks the site. Several historic houses along the Portsmouth Harbour Trail

Canterbury Shaker Village

owe their significance to the strife. A then-renowned haven for dissenters, Exeter now is home to the American Independence Museum.

Out of this epic struggle for freedom, a simple motto was born.

In post-independence New Hampshire, the spirited maxim had even broader implications. It meant immunity from religious persecution to the Shakers, who built villages in Canterbury and Enfield.

The influence of the state's majestic backdrop of mountains, caves, lakes and wide open spaces encouraged creative figures to freely express themselves. Poet John Greenleaf Whittier wrote "Sunset on the Bearcamp" about the river of the same name. An ascent of Mount Monadnock inspired Ralph Waldo Emerson's poem "Monadnoc." Many writings of Robert Frost drew upon his life on a Derry farm.

Author Thomas Bailey Aldrich penned "The Story of a Bad Boy," which includes references to his Portsmouth boyhood home. Composer Edward MacDowell thrived in the woodland retreat of Peterborough, which he later introduced to scores of other artists.

From the White Mountains to Lake Winnipesaukee, the largely pristine Granite State epitomizes much of what is amazing—and liberating—about nature.

Mountain roads like Kancamagus Highway (SR 112) wind through White Mountain National Forest, skirting breathtaking vistas of the peaks. In autumn the vivid hues of changing leaves are unmatched in their glory and beauty.

Railways and tramways climb to the top of Cannon Mountain, Loon Mountain and Mount Washington, the Northeast's tallest peak at 6,288 feet. Well-trodden hiking paths through the entire mountainous region often lead to tumbling waterfalls.

At the Bottom, Looking Up

The low-level vantage points of mountain gaps give a different perspective. Impressive characteristics of Franconia Notch, which splits the Kinsman and Franconia ranges, are The Flume Gorge, a long chasm flanking Mount Liberty; the Lost River, which often disappears as it snakes through boulder caves and potholes in Kinsman Notch; and Dixville Notch, which boasts striking sights like the Cathedral Spires and Table Rock.

Walk amid granite boulders and mineral formations in Plymouth's Polar Caves, seven caves formed by glacial activity more than 20,000 years ago.

Climb aboard a steamship or boat in Portsmouth and cruise through Portsmouth Harbor to the Isles of Shoals. Marvel at Lake Winnipesaukee's natural spectacles—coves and islands set against an outline of mountain peaks; cruises depart from Weirs Beach and Wolfeboro.

Kick back, shake off your encumbrances and live life to its fullest in New Hampshire. It's certainly the better of the motto's two options!

Recreation

If New Hampshire needs a recreation slogan, here's an idea: "Have skis, will travel."

The state sport is unrivaled in popularity.

Like it fast? You'll find more than 150 downhill skiing and snowboarding trails among the White Mountain region's three largest resorts: Attitash Bear Peak in Bartlett, Loon Mountain in Lincoln, and Waterville Valley.

Tubing parks are among the additional facilities at Cranmore Mountain Resort in North Conway, Gunstock Mountain Resort in Gilford, King Pine Ski Area in East Madison, Pats Peak in Henniker and Whaleback in Lebanon.

If you prefer skiing on more level ground, there are 24 cross-country facilities that fit the bill. Lengthy trails and scenic vistas characterize Jackson X-C in Jackson and The Franconia Inn in Franconia.

In the state's northernmost quarter snowmobiling is sure to get your motor running. A 7,000-mile interconnecting trail system weaves through breathtaking scenery.

When the snow melts away, you'll warm to New Hampshire's more temperate pursuits.

Bicyclists are in for a treat when they pedal through the Granite State: endless vistas of dark green mountainsides and clear blue skies. The trail system is extensive, particularly along the Connecticut River, around Lake Winnipesaukee and in the Merrimack Valley region, from Concord to Nashua.

The easy 1-mile hike up Blue Job Mountain, near Strafford, culminates in great views of Boston and Mount Washington. If you have half a day, take on White Dot Trail on Mount Monadnock, one of the most climbed mountains in the world.

Got nerves of steel? Cathedral Ledge, in Echo Lake State Park near Bartlett, and Franconia Notch State Park, near Franconia and Lincoln, are hot spots for rock climbing.

The Swift River beckons to white-water rafting enthusiasts. Kayaking is good on the Androscoggin River, which can be slightly rough upstream from Berlin.

Strong winds over the surface of Lake Winnipesaukee make for excellent sailing. For boating and swimming, check out Newfound, Squam and Sunapee lakes.

Cannon Mountain Aerial Tramway, Franconia Notch

Historic Timeline

1603   English sea captain Martin Pring becomes the first European to visit New Hampshire.

1622   Captain John Mason is given a land grant to the area and names it after the English county of Hampshire.

1776   New Hampshire becomes the first colony to declare independence from England.

1788   New Hampshire is the ninth and deciding state to ratify the U.S. Constitution.

1808   Concord becomes the state capital.

1852   New Hampshire native Franklin Pierce is elected president of the United States.

1920   The state begins holding the first-in-the-nation presidential primary.

1944   At the Bretton Woods Conference, delegates from 44 nations agree on solutions to international monetary problems.

1964   The state adopts the first legal lottery in the 20th-century United States.

1986   Concord teacher Christa McAuliffe, the first educator to fly in space, is killed when the space shuttle *Challenger* explodes.

1999   New Hampshire is the first state to have a female governor, Senate president and House speaker all at the same time.

What To Pack

Temperature Averages Maximum/Minimum	JANUARY	FEBRUARY	MARCH	APRIL	MAY	JUNE	JULY	AUGUST	SEPTEMBER	OCTOBER	NOVEMBER	DECEMBER
Concord	32/11	34/12	42/22	56/32	69/42	78/51	83/56	81/54	72/46	62/36	48/27	35/15
Dixville Notch	21/-3	24/-2	34/9	46/24	60/36	69/47	74/52	72/50	63/42	51/32	38/22	26/7
Franconia	25/5	28/7	36/16	47/28	61/39	70/48	74/53	73/51	65/43	54/33	42/24	31/12
Hanover	29/9	34/12	43/22	57/33	70/44	79/54	83/59	81/57	71/49	59/37	46/28	34/16
Manchester	32/5	36/8	44/18	56/29	68/40	77/50	82/55	80/53	72/44	61/32	50/24	37/12
Portsmouth	34/15	37/18	46/26	56/34	68/44	77/53	83/59	81/57	72/50	61/39	50/32	39/21

From the records of The Weather Channel Interactive, Inc.

Good Facts To Know

ABOUT THE STATE

POPULATION: 1,316,470.

AREA: 9,024 square miles; ranks 44th.

CAPITAL: Concord.

HIGHEST POINT: 6,288 ft., Mount Washington.

LOWEST POINT: Sea level, Atlantic Ocean.

TIME ZONE(S): Eastern. DST.

REGULATIONS

TEEN DRIVING LAWS: For the first 6 months, no more than one unrelated passenger under age 25. Driving is not permitted 1 a.m.-4 a.m. The minimum age for an unrestricted driver's license is 18 years. For more information about New Hampshire driver's license regulations, phone (603) 271-2371.

SEAT BELT/CHILD RESTRAINT LAWS: Children ages 6-18 and at least 55 inches tall are required to be in a seat belt; child restraints are required for children under age 6 and under 55 inches tall.

CELL PHONE RESTRICTIONS: Text messaging is prohibited for all drivers. New Hampshire holds drivers accountable for all distractions causing a crash through its law against negligent driving.

HELMETS FOR MOTORCYCLISTS: Required for all riders under 18.

RADAR DETECTORS: Permitted.

MOVE OVER LAW: Driver is required to slow down and vacate a lane nearest police, fire and rescue vehicles stopped on the side of the road using audible or flashing signals. Law includes tow trucks.

FIREARMS LAWS: Vary by state and/or county. Contact the New Hampshire State Police, Permits and Licensing Unit, 33 Hazen Dr., Concord, NH 03305; phone (603) 223-3873.

HOLIDAYS

HOLIDAYS: Jan. 1 ▪ Martin Luther King Jr. Day, Jan. (3rd Mon.) ▪ Washington's Birthday/Presidents Day, Feb. (3rd Mon.) ▪ Memorial Day, May (last Mon.) ▪ July 4 ▪ Labor Day, Sept. (1st Mon.) ▪ Columbus Day, Oct. (2nd Mon.) ▪ Veterans Day, Nov. 11 ▪ Thanksgiving, Nov. (4th Thurs.) ▪ Christmas, Dec. 25.

MONEY

TAXES: New Hampshire does not have a statewide sales tax. There is a 9 percent Meals & Rentals Tax that includes beverages, and a 9 percent tax on rental vehicles.

VISITOR INFORMATION

INFORMATION CENTERS: State welcome centers provide details about attractions, accommodations, historic sites, parks and events. They are maintained year-round at Canterbury, I-93N between exits 18 and 19 ▪ Hooksett, I-93N and I-93S between exits 10 and 11 ▪ Lebanon, I-89S between exits 17 and 18 ▪ Littleton, I-93S before exit 44 ▪ Nashua, US 3 exit 6 ▪ North Conway, US 16 and US 302 ▪ Salem, I-93N before exit 1 ▪ Sanbornton, I-93S between exits 20 and 22 ▪ Seabrook, I-95N before exit 1 ▪ Springfield, I-89N between exits 12A and 13 ▪ and Sutton, I-89S between exits 9 and 10. Information centers are maintained Memorial Day to mid-October at Antrim ▪ Colebrook ▪ Epsom ▪ Rumney ▪ and Shelburne.

FURTHER INFORMATION FOR VISITORS:
Office of Travel and Tourism
172 Pembroke Rd.
Concord, NH 03302
(603) 271-2665
(800) 386-4664

NATIONAL FOREST INFORMATION:
White Mountain National Forest
71 White Mountain Dr.
Campton, NH 03223
(603) 536-6100
(877) 444-6777 (reservations)

FISHING AND HUNTING REGULATIONS:
Fish and Game Department
11 Hazen Dr.
Concord, NH 03301
(603) 271-3421

New Hampshire Annual Events
Please call ahead to confirm event details.

JANUARY

- Independence Weekend Celebration / Lincoln
  603-745-8111
- New Hampshire Snow Sculpture Competition Jackson
  603-383-9356
- White Mountain Classic 30K Jackson
  603-383-9355

FEBRUARY

- Winter Wine Festival New Castle
  603-422-7322
- Winter Carnival / Newport
  603-863-1510
- Laconia World Championship Sled Dog Derby / Laconia
  603-524-4314

MARCH

- Hannes Schneider Meister Cup Race / North Conway
  603-823-7177
- Loon Mountain Briefcase Race / Lincoln
  603-745-8111, ext. 5516
- Swift Diamond Riders Sno-Deo / Colebrook
  800-698-8939

APRIL

- Intergalactic Cardboard Sled Race / Newbury
  603-763-3500
- Jazzmouth, The Seacoast Poetry and Jazz Festival Portsmouth
  603-436-2400
- Spring Family Farm Day Troy
  603-242-6495

MAY

- Chowder and Microbrew Fest / Waterville Valley
  603-236-8175
- New Hampshire Sheep and Wool Festival / Contoocook
  603-635-8553
- New Hampshire Renaissance Faire and Spring Celebration Kingston
  603-755-9587

JUNE

- WOKQ Chowder Festival Portsmouth
  603-436-2848
- Master Sand Sculpting Competition Hampton Beach
  603-926-8718
- Fields of Lupine Festival Franconia
  603-823-8000

JULY

- Summer Traditions Arts and Crafts Festival / Wolfeboro
  603-528-4014
- Hillsborough Balloon Fest and Fair / Hillsborough
  603-464-0377
- American Independence Festival / Exeter
  603-772-2622

AUGUST

- Pittsfield Rotary Hot Air Balloon Rally / Pittsfield
  603-435-6291
- League of New Hampshire Craftsmen's Fair / Newbury
  603-224-3375
- North Country Moose Festival / Colebrook
  603-237-8939

SEPTEMBER

- Hampton Beach Seafood Festival / Hampton Beach
  800-438-2826
- New Hampshire Highland Games / Lincoln
  603-745-2113
- New England Elvis Festival Manchester
  518-681-7452

OCTOBER

- Attitash Oktoberfest Bartlett
  603-374-2368
- Apple Harvest Day and 5K Road Race / Dover
  603-742-2218
- Return of the Pumpkin People / Jackson
  603-383-9356

NOVEMBER

- New England Craft and Specialty Food Fair / Salem
  603-332-2616
- Canterbury Shaker Village Gift in Hand / Canterbury
  603-783-9511
- Winter Holiday Stroll Nashua
  603-883-5700

DECEMBER

- Candlelight Stroll Portsmouth
  603-422-7504
- Christmas at Canterbury Canterbury
  603-783-9511
- Christmas on the Farm Milton
  603-652-7840

Moffatt-Ladd House, Portsmouth

European Gallery, The Currier Museum of Art, Manchester

The Flume Gorge, Franconia Notch

Winter shopping, North Conway

Wellington State Park, Bristol

Index: Great Experience for Members

AAA editor's picks of exceptional note

Saint-Gaudens
National Historic Site

Crawford Notch

Mount Washington
Cog Railway

Canterbury Shaker
Village

Bretton Woods (C-4)

Mount Washington Cog Railway
(See p. 179.)

Canterbury (E-4)

Canterbury Shaker Village
(See p. 181.)

Cornish (E-2)

Saint-Gaudens National Historic Site
(See p. 187.)

Crawford Notch (C-4)

Crawford Notch *(See p. 187.)*

Franconia Notch (C-4)

Cannon Mountain Aerial Tramway
(See p. 192.)

The Flume Gorge *(See p. 192.)*

Franconia Notch *(See p. 192.)*

Kinsman Notch (D-3)

Lost River Gorge & Boulder Caves
(See p. 206.)

Manchester (F-4)

The Currier Museum of Art *(See p. 213.)*

Pinkham Notch Scenic Area (C-4)

Pinkham Notch Scenic Area *(See p. 235.)*

New Hampshire
Atlas Section

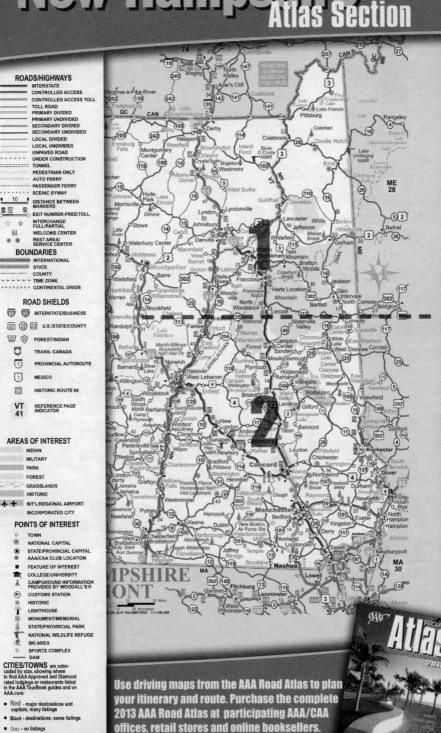

ROADS/HIGHWAYS

- INTERSTATE
- CONTROLLED ACCESS
- CONTROLLED ACCESS TOLL
- TOLL ROAD
- PRIMARY DIVIDED
- PRIMARY UNDIVIDED
- SECONDARY DIVIDED
- SECONDARY UNDIVIDED
- LOCAL DIVIDED
- LOCAL UNDIVIDED
- UNPAVED ROAD
- UNDER CONSTRUCTION
- TUNNEL
- PEDESTRIAN ONLY
- AUTO FERRY
- PASSENGER FERRY
- SCENIC BYWAY
- DISTANCE BETWEEN MARKERS
- EXIT NUMBER-FREE/TOLL
- INTERCHANGE FULL/PARTIAL
- WELCOME CENTER
- REST AREA/SERVICE CENTER

BOUNDARIES

- INTERNATIONAL
- STATE
- COUNTY
- TIME ZONE
- CONTINENTAL DIVIDE

ROAD SHIELDS

- INTERSTATE/BUSINESS
- U.S./STATE/COUNTY
- FOREST/INDIAN
- TRANS- CANADA
- PROVINCIAL AUTOROUTE
- MEXICO
- HISTORIC ROUTE 66
- VT 41 REFERENCE PAGE INDICATOR

AREAS OF INTEREST

- INDIAN
- MILITARY
- PARK
- FOREST
- GRASSLANDS
- HISTORIC
- INT'L/REGIONAL AIRPORT
- INCORPORATED CITY

POINTS OF INTEREST

- TOWN
- NATIONAL CAPITAL
- STATE/PROVINCIAL CAPITAL
- AAA/CAA CLUB LOCATION
- FEATURE OF INTEREST
- COLLEGE/UNIVERSITY
- CAMPGROUND INFORMATION PROVIDED BY WOODALL'S®
- CUSTOMS STATION
- HISTORIC
- LIGHTHOUSE
- MONUMENT/MEMORIAL
- STATE/PROVINCIAL PARK
- NATIONAL WILDLIFE REFUGE
- SKI AREA
- SPORTS COMPLEX
- DAM

CITIES/TOWNS are color-coded by size, showing where to find AAA Approved and Diamond rated lodgings or restaurants listed in the AAA TourBook guides and on AAA.com.

- ● Red - major destinations and capitals; many listings
- ● Black - destinations; some listings
- ● Grey - no listings

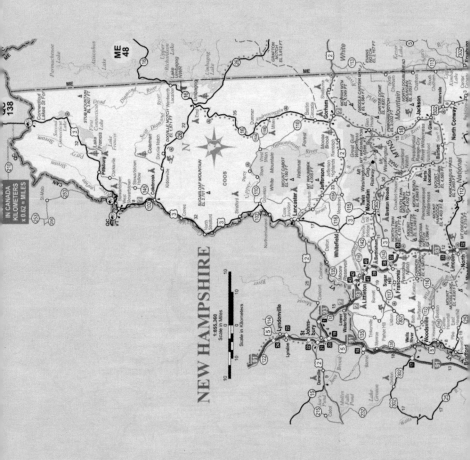

NEW HAMPSHIRE

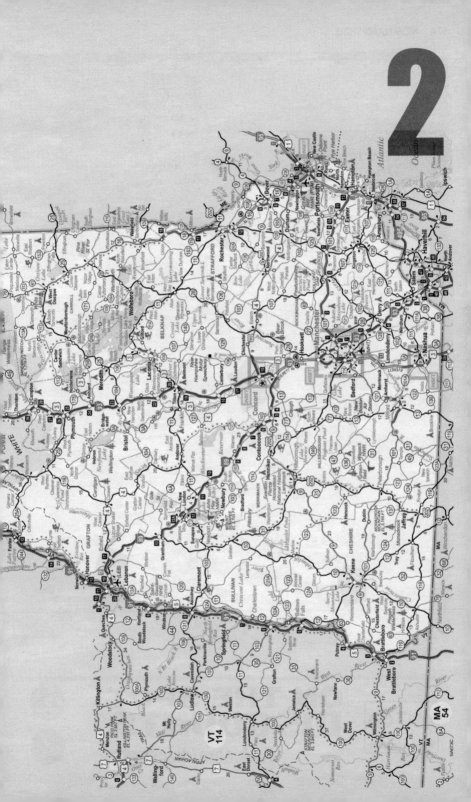

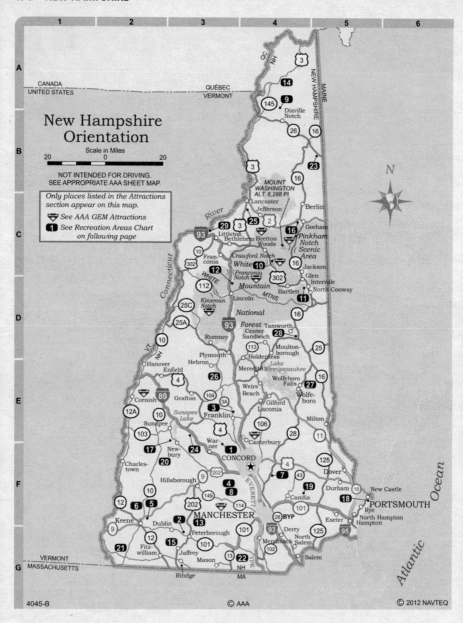

New Hampshire Orientation

Scale in Miles

20   0   20

NOT INTENDED FOR DRIVING.
SEE APPROPRIATE AAA SHEET MAP.

Only places listed in the Attractions
section appear on this map.
See AAA GEM Attractions
1 See Recreation Areas Chart
on following page

CANADA
UNITED STATES

QUÉBEC
VERMONT

QC
NH

3
14
145   9
Dixville
Notch
26
16
23

MOUNT
WASHINGTON
ALT. 6,288 Ft
Lancaster
Jefferson
Berlin

3
16
16

29   3   25   2
Littleton   16   Gorham
Bethlehem   Bretton   Pinkham
Woods   Notch
Scenic
Area

10
Franconia
302
12
Crawford Notch
White   10
Franconia
Notch
302
Jackson
Glen
Intervale
North Conway

112
Mountain
Lincoln

25C
Kinsman
Notch

Rumney
25A
93
Forest   Tamworth
Center
Sandwich
28
113
Moulton-
borough
25

10
Plymouth
Hebron
Holderness
Meredith   Lake
Winnipesaukee

Hanover
Enfield
4
26
Weirs
Beach
Wolfeboro
Falls
27
Wolfe-
boro

Cornish
89
Grafton
104   3A
Gilford
Laconia
16

12A
10
Sunapee
Lake
3
Franklin
4
106
Milton

103
Sunapee
4
28
11

17
Newbury
24
Warner
1
Canterbury

Charlestown
20
CONCORD

Hillsborough
9
202
4
7
43
125
Dover

12
6   5
149
4
8
114
19
Candia
101
18
New Castle
Durham   16
PORTSMOUTH
Rye
North Hampton
Hampton

Keene
9
202
MANCHESTER
28   BYP
Exeter

Dublin
2
13
101
93   North
Salem
125
95

12
15
101
Merrimack
102
Salem

21
Fitzwilliam
Jaffrey
Mason
13
22
NH
MA

Peterborough

Rindge

VERMONT
MASSACHUSETTS

N

White
MTNS
River
Connecticut

Everett
TPK

Atlantic Ocean

VT   NH

4045-B

© AAA

© 2012 NAVTEQ

Recreation Areas Chart

The map location numerals in column 2 show an area's location on the preceding map.

	MAP LOCATION	CAMPING	PICNICKING	HIKING TRAILS	BOATING	BOAT RAMP	BOAT RENTAL	FISHING	SWIMMING	PETS ON LEASH	BICYCLE TRAILS	WINTER SPORTS	VISITOR CENTER	LODGE/CABINS	FOOD SERVICE
NATIONAL FORESTS *(See place listings.)*															
White Mountain (C-4) 770,000 acres. Northern New Hampshire. Scenic. Cross-country and downhill skiing, hunting, rock climbing, snowmobiling, snowshoeing.		•	•	•	•			•	•	•	•	•	•	•	
ARMY CORPS OF ENGINEERS															
Blackwater Dam (F-3) 18 mi. n. of Concord off SR 127. Canoeing, hunting, kayaking; horse trails.	❶		•		•	•		•		•		•			
Edward McDowell Lake (F-3) 1,198 acres 4 mi. w. of Peterborough off SR 101. Hunting, snowshoeing.	❷		•	•	•	•		•		•		•			
Franklin Falls Dam (E-3) 2,800 acres 15 mi. along Pemigewassett River, 2 mi. n. of Franklin off SR 127.	❸		•	•	•	•		•	•	•		•			
Hopkinton-Everett Lake (F-3) 7,992 acres off I-89 exit 6, then 3 mi. w. on SR 127. Hunting; horse trails, model airplane field.	❹		•	•	•	•		•	•	•		•	•		
Otter Brook Lake (F-2) 458 acres 2 mi. e. of Keene off SR 101 on Branch Rd. Cross-country skiing, hunting, ice fishing, snowmobiling, snowshoeing.	❺		•		•	•		•	•	•		•			
Surry Mountain Lake (F-2) 1,865 acres 6 mi. n. of Keene off SR 12A. Cross-country skiing, ice fishing, snowmobiling, snowshoeing; beach, nature trails.	❻		•		•	•		•	•	•		•			
STATE															
Bear Brook (F-4) 9,800 acres 2 mi. e. of Allenstown off SR 28. Horseback riding, mountain biking; archery range, museums.	❼	•	•	•			•	•	•	•	•	•	•		•
Clough (F-3) 140 acres 5 mi. e. of Weare between SRs 114 and 13. Mountain biking; beach.	❽	•	•	•	•			•	•	•					
Coleman (A-4) 1,605 acres 12 mi. e. of Colebrook off SR 26. Cross-country skiing, snowmobiling.	❾	•	•	•				•		•		•			
Crawford Notch (C-4) 5,950 acres 12 mi. w. of Bartlett on US 302. *(See Crawford Notch p. 187.)*	❿	•	•	•				•		•			•		•
Echo Lake (D-4) 396 acres 1.5 mi. w. of US 302 on Westside Rd. in North Conway. Scenic. Rock climbing. *(See North Conway p. 223.)*	⓫		•	•				•	•						
Franconia Notch (C-3) 6,440 acres 5 mi. n. of North Woodstock off US 3. Bike rental. *(See Franconia Notch p. 192.)*	⓬	•	•	•	•			•	•	•	•	•	•		•
Greenfield (F-3) 401 acres 1 mi. w. of Greenfield off SR 136. Canoe rental.	⓭	•	•	•	•	•	•	•	•	•					•
Lake Francis (A-4) 1,684 acres 7 mi. n. of Pittsburg off US 3. Canoeing, cross-country skiing, snowmobiling; playground.	⓮	•	•		•	•		•		•		•			
Monadnock (G-3) 699 acres 4 mi. n.w. of Jaffrey off SR 124. Cross-country skiing, snowshoeing. *(See Dublin p. 189 and Jaffrey p. 203.)*	⓯	•	•	•						•		•	•		•
Moose Brook (C-4) 755 acres 2 mi. w. of Gorham off US 2. Mountain biking trails. Pets restricted to designated areas.	⓰	•	•	•				•	•	•	•	•			
Mount Sunapee (F-2) 2,893 acres w. of Newbury at jct. SRs 103 and 103B. Scenic. Downhill skiing; beach, playground. *(See Newbury p. 221.)*	⓱	•	•	•	•	•		•	•	•			•	•	•
Odiorne Point (F-5) 370 acres on SR 1A in Rye. Science center. *(See Portsmouth p. 236.)*	⓲		•	•				•		•			•		•
Pawtuckaway (F-4) 5,500 acres 4 mi. n.e. of Raymond off SR 156. Cross-country skiing, rock climbing, snowmobiling; beach, playground, tower.	⓳	•	•	•	•	•		•	•	•		•	•		
Pillsbury (F-2) 3,702 acres 3.5 mi. n. of Washington on SR 31. Cross-country skiing, mountain biking, snowmobiling; playground.	⓴	•	•	•	•			•		•		•			
Pisgah (G-2) 13,500 acres off SR 63 in Chesterfield. Horseback riding, hunting, mountain biking, snowmobiling; all-terrain vehicle trails.	21		•	•				•		•	•	•			
Silver Lake (G-4) 80 acres 14 mi. n.e. of Mason on SR 122. Canoeing, kayaking; beach.	22		•	•	•			•	•						

Recreation Areas Chart

The map location numerals in column 2 show an area's location on the preceding map.

	MAP LOCATION	CAMPING	PICNICKING	HIKING TRAILS	BOATING	BOAT RAMP	BOAT RENTAL	FISHING	SWIMMING	PETS ON LEASH	BICYCLE TRAILS	WINTER SPORTS	VISITOR CENTER	LODGE/CABINS	FOOD SERVICE
Umbagog Lake (B-5) 19 mi. s.e. of Dixville Notch on SR 26; some portions accessible only by boat. Canoeing, kayaking; beach.	23	●	●		●	●	●	●	●					●	
Wadleigh (F-3) 8 mi. n.e. of Newbury off Chaulk Pond Rd. Canoeing, kayaking; playground.	24		●	●	●			●	●			●	●		
Weeks (C-4) 420 acres 2 mi. s. of Lancaster off SR 3. Historic. Scenic. Downhill and cross-country skiing, snowmobiling, snowshoeing; tower.	25		●	●						●	●	●	●		
Wellington (E-3) 183 acres 4 mi. n. of Bristol off SR 3A. Beach.	26		●	●	●	●		●	●			●			●
Wentworth (E-5) 50 acres 7 mi e. of Wolfeboro on SR 109.	27		●					●	●						
White Lake (D-4) 603 acres 1 mi. n. of West Ossipee on SR 16. Canoeing, kayaking; playground.	28	●	●	●				●	●			●			
OTHER															
Moore Reservoir (C-3) 3,500 acres 8 mi. w. of Littleton off I-93 via SRs 18 and 135. *(See Littleton p. 212.)*	29		●	●	●	●		●	●	●			●		

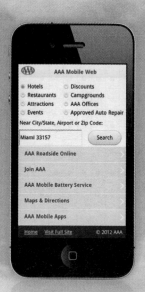

ALBANY
• Hotels & Restaurants map & index p. 225

THE DARBY FIELD INN   (603)447-2181   47

▼▼▼▼
Historic
Country Inn
$150-$300

Address: 185 Chase Hill Rd 03818 **Location:** 1 mi s on SR 16, watch for Bald Hill Rd, then 2 mi w, follow signs. Located in a secluded rural area. **Facility:** In a secluded rural area, this inn sits atop a small mountain and offers commanding views of the surrounding mountains. Beautiful gardens surround the property. 13 units. 3 stories (no elevator), interior corridors. **Terms:** closed 3/31-5/1, 2 night minimum stay - seasonal and/or weekends, age restrictions may apply, 14 day cancellation notice-fee imposed, resort fee. **Pool(s):** heated outdoor. **Activities:** cross country skiing, hiking trails. *Fee:* massage. **Free Special Amenities:** full breakfast and high-speed Internet.

[SAVE] [symbols]
/ SOME UNITS [symbols]

AMHERST   pop. 613

THE BLACK FOREST CAFE & BAKERY   603/672-0500

▼▼▼ American. Casual Dining. $10-$17 **AAA Inspector Notes:** Representative of dishes that might be found on the seasonally inspired menu are pear and goat cheese salad, Vermont cheddar and apple-smoked bacon sandwich and Black Forest meatloaf. Homemade pastries, pies, breads and cakes are delectable. **Bar:** beer & wine. **Address:** 212 SR 101 03031 **Location:** On SR 101.

[L] [D]

JOEY'S DINER   603/577-8955

▼ American. Family Dining. $4-$11 **AAA Inspector Notes:** The newly built eatery was intended to replicate an old-fashioned diner, and it does via its long luncheon counter, chrome-edged Formica tables and sparkling vinyl booths. The menu lists fries with brown gravy, steak tips, a Monte Cristo sandwich and other classics. **Bar:** beer & wine. **Address:** 1 Craftsman Ln 03031 **Location:** Everett Tpke (US 3) exit 8, 6.5 mi w.

[B] [L] [D]

ANDOVER

HIGHLAND LAKE INN BED & BREAKFAST   603/735-6426

▼▼▼ Historic Bed & Breakfast. Rates not provided. **Address:** 32 Maple St 03216 **Location:** Waterfront. I-93 exit 17, 15.5 mi nw on US 4, 3.5 mi e on SR 11, then just w. **Facility:** This handsome Colonial farmhouse dating from 1760 is convenient to Highland Lake and Mount Kearsarge for both summer and winter recreation. The property is beautifully furnished. 10 units. 3 stories (no elevator), interior corridors. **Bath:** shower only. **Activities:** beach access, fishing, cross country skiing, hiking trails.

[symbols] / SOME UNITS [symbols]

ASHLAND   pop. 1,244

GLYNN HOUSE INN   603/968-3775

▼▼▼ Historic Bed & Breakfast. Rates not provided. **Address:** 59 Highland St 03217 **Location:** I-93 exit 24 (SR 25 and US 3), 0.8 mi e to flag pole in center of town (Highland St), then 0.3 mi nw. Located in a quiet area. **Facility:** This attractive inn, which dates from 1895, features handsome furnishings and decor. 12 units. 3 stories (no elevator), interior corridors.

[ECO] [symbols] / SOME UNITS FEE [symbols]

LAKES REGION COMFORT INN   603/968-7668

▼▼▼
Hotel
Rates not provided

Address: 53 West St 03217 **Location:** I-93 exit 24 (SR 25 and US 3), just e. **Facility:** 41 units. 3 stories (no elevator), interior corridors. **Amenities:** safes (fee). **Pool(s):** heated outdoor. **Activities:** game room, exercise room. **Guest Services:** coin laundry.

[SAVE] [symbols] / SOME UNITS FEE [symbols]

WHERE TO EAT

THE COMMON MAN   603/968-7030

▼▼ American. Family Dining. $8-$26 **AAA Inspector Notes:** The restaurant features a charming decor and pleasant upstairs pub. On the menu are steak, seafood, chicken and vegetarian dishes served in generous portions. Lobster corn chowder is popular at lunch; white chocolate mousse is a specialty. **Bar:** full bar. **Address:** 60 Main St 03217 **Location:** I-93 exit 24 (SR 25 and US 3), 0.5 mi e on US 3.

[L] [D]

BARTLETT (D-4) pop. 373, elev. 2,630'
• Hotels & Restaurants map & index p. 225

With Bear Mountain to the south, Mount Parker to the north and symmetrical Mount Carrigan rising at the western end of the valley, Bartlett is a year-round recreation center. The land along the Saco River east of its emergence from Crawford Notch was granted to William Stark and several others for their service in the French and Indian War; the village was incorporated in 1790.

From Bartlett a scenic road runs south through Bear Notch to the Kancamagus Highway *(see attraction listing p. 253).*

RECREATIONAL ACTIVITIES

Alpine Slides
• **Attitash Alpine Slide** is at 775 US 302. Other activities are offered. **Hours:** Daily 10-6, early June-Labor Day; Sat.-Sun. 10-4, late May-early June and day after Labor Day-early Oct. **Phone:** (603) 374-2368. [symbol]

Skiing
• **Attitash Mountain Resort** is at 775 US 302. Other activities are offered. **Hours:** Mon.-Fri. 9-4, Sat.-Sun. 8:30-4, Dec.-Apr. (weather permitting). Last admission 30 minutes before closing. Phone ahead to confirm schedule. **Phone:** (603) 374-2600 or (800) 223-7669.

ATTITASH GRAND SUMMIT HOTEL AND CONFERENCE CENTER   (603)374-1900   15

▼▼▼ Resort Hotel $119-$499 **Address:** 104 Grand Summit Rd (US 302) 03812 **Location:** On US 302, 2.5 mi e. **Facility:** Guests can ski to resort facilities from this hotel set at the base of the Bear Peak ski area. 143 units, some two bedrooms, three bedrooms and kitchens. 4 stories, interior corridors. **Parking:** on-site and valet. **Terms:** check-in 4 pm, 8 day cancellation notice-fee imposed, resort fee. **Amenities:** high-speed Internet. **Dining:** 2 restaurants. **Pool(s):** heated outdoor. **Activities:** sauna, whirlpools, recreation programs in summer, rental bicycles, hiking trails, playground, basketball, horseshoes, volleyball. *Fee:* downhill & cross country skiing, horseback riding, game room, massage. **Guest Services:** valet and coin laundry, area transportation-within resort.

[ECO] [symbols] CALL [GM] [symbols] [BIZ] [symbols]
[symbols] / SOME UNITS [symbols]

THE BARTLETT INN   (603)374-2353   18

▼▼▼
Bed & Breakfast
$109-$248

Address: 1477 US Rt 302 03812 **Location:** On US 302, 7 mi w of jct SR 16. **Facility:** 18 units, some cottages. 2 stories (no elevator), interior/exterior corridors. **Terms:** 14 day cancellation notice-fee imposed. **Pool(s):** heated outdoor. **Activities:** whirlpool, cross country skiing, bicycles, hiking trails, playground. **Free Special Amenities:** full breakfast and high-speed Internet.

[SAVE] [symbols] [BIZ] [symbols]
/ SOME UNITS FEE [symbols]

(See map & index p. 225.)

NORTH COLONY MOTEL (603)374-6679

Motel
$49-$159

Address: 1025 US Rt 302 03812 **Location:** On US 302, 1.5 mi e. **Facility:** 16 units, some cottages. 1 story, exterior corridors. **Terms:** 2 night minimum stay - seasonal and/or weekends, 7 day cancellation notice-fee imposed. **Pool(s):** heated outdoor. **Activities:** cross country skiing, playground, basketball, horseshoes, volleyball. **Free Special Amenities:** local telephone calls and high-speed Internet.

   / SOME UNITS

THE VILLAGER MOTEL 603/374-2742

 **Motel. Rates not provided. Address:** 1126 US 302 03812 **Location:** 1 mi e on US 302; 1.3 mi w of Attitash Mountain. **Facility:** 35 units, some two bedrooms, efficiencies, kitchens, houses and cabins. 1-2 stories (no elevator), exterior corridors. **Pool(s):** heated outdoor. **Activities:** fishing, hiking trails, playground. **Guest Services:** coin laundry.

/ SOME UNITS FEE

BEDFORD

BEDFORD VILLAGE INN (603)472-2001

Historic
Country Inn
$195-$265

Address: 2 Olde Bedford Way 03110 **Location:** On SR 101, 0.3 mi w of jct SR 114. Located in a rural area. **Facility:** Housed in a converted dairy barn dating from 1810, this country inn offers elegant guest rooms with up-to-date amenities and a romantic ambiance. 15 units, some two bedrooms and cottages. 3 stories, interior/exterior corridors. **Terms:** 10 day cancellation notice-fee imposed, resort fee. **Amenities:** safes. **Dining:** Bedford Village Inn Restaurant, see separate listing. **Guest Services:** valet laundry. **Free Special Amenities:** high-speed Internet and airport transportation.

/ SOME UNITS

COUNTRY INN & SUITES BY CARLSON, MANCHESTER AIRPORT 603/666-4600

 Hotel. Rates not provided. Address: 250 S River Rd 03110 **Location:** I-293 exit US 3 (Kilton Rd/S River Rd), 0.7 mi s. **Facility:** 100 units. 4 stories, interior corridors. **Amenities:** high-speed Internet. **Pool(s):** heated indoor. **Activities:** whirlpool, exercise room. *Fee:* game room. **Guest Services:** valet and coin laundry, area transportation-within 5 mi.

HAMPTON INN & SUITES MANCHESTER BEDFORD (603)623-2040

Hotel
$99-$149

AAA Benefit: Members save up to 10%!

Address: 8 Hawthorne Dr 03110 **Location:** Just e of US 3; 1 mi s of jct SR 101. **Facility:** 91 units. 4 stories, interior corridors. **Terms:** 1-7 night minimum stay, cancellation fee imposed. **Amenities:** video games (fee), high-speed Internet. **Pool(s):** heated indoor. **Activities:** sauna, whirlpool, exercise room. **Guest Services:** valet and coin laundry. **Free Special Amenities:** expanded continental breakfast and manager's reception.

Give the gift of security, value and peace of mind: Gift Membership

---

 WHERE TO EAT

BEDFORD VILLAGE INN RESTAURANT 603/472-2001

American
Fine Dining
$10-$38

AAA Inspector Notes: *Historic.* This 1810 farmhouse has been transformed into an elegant setting with authentic antiques and several intimate dining rooms. The menu is creative and offers a variety of dishes and one-of-a-kind desserts and pastries. Semiformal attire. **Bar:** full bar. **Reservations:** suggested. **Address:** 2 Olde Bedford Way 03110 **Location:** On SR 101, 0.3 mi w of jct SR 114; in Bedford Village Inn. *Menu on AAA.com*

CHEN YANG LI CHINESE RESTAURANT 603/641-6922

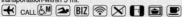 Asian. Casual Dining. $10-$30 **AAA Inspector Notes:** The exceptional restaurant prepares many house specialties and standard favorites. The wonderfully descriptive menu also lists a nice selection of sushi items. An elegant atmosphere and helpful staff make for an enjoyable experience. **Bar:** full bar. **Reservations:** suggested. **Address:** 124 S River Rd 03110 **Location:** US 3, just n of jct I-293; in Woodbury Court Plaza.   CALL

PIZZA BELLA 603/472-8560

Pizza. Quick Serve. $6-$16 **AAA Inspector Notes:** Fantastic pizza is made with fresh ingredients and homemade crusts. Submarine sandwiches and salads are among other choices. **Bar:** beer only. **Address:** 178 SR 101 03110 **Location:** On SR 101, 2.5 mi w of jct SR 114; in Bedford Village Shops.

TAIPEI & TOKYO CHINESE & JAPANESE RESTAURANT 603/622-2588

Japanese. Casual Dining. $8-$37 **AAA Inspector Notes:** In Colby Court Plaza, the restaurant presents a lengthy menu of Japanese and Chinese cuisine. Patrons also can choose selections from the extensive sushi bar. **Bar:** full bar. **Address:** 7 Colby Ct 03110 **Location:** SR 101 exit 3, 1 mi n.

T-BONES GREAT AMERICAN EATERY 603/641-6100

American. Casual Dining. $10-$27 **AAA Inspector Notes:** One of three locations, the local eatery prepares burgers, steaks, sandwiches and more. All menu items are made from scratch on the premises. **Bar:** full bar. **Address:** 25 S River Rd 03110 **Location:** Jct I-293 and US 3, 1 mi n on US 3.

WEATHERVANE SEAFOOD RESTAURANT 603/472-2749

Seafood. Family Dining. $8-$25 **AAA Inspector Notes:** The popular, family-oriented restaurant presents a large menu with lobster, fried clams and crisp Cape Cod apple-cranberry cobbler. Flavorful dishes are served in large portions. A fish market is on the premises. **Bar:** full bar. **Address:** 393 SR 101 W 03110 **Location:** Jct SR 114, 3.7 mi w. CALL

BELMONT pop. 1,301

CHINA GARDEN 603/524-6340

Chinese. Casual Dining. $8-$17 **AAA Inspector Notes:** Representative of traditional fare are sweet and sour dishes, chop suey, chow mein and the pu pu platter. The casual setting is comfortable for families. **Bar:** full bar. **Address:** 200 Daniel Webster Hwy 03220 **Location:** On US 3; center.

BERLIN (C-4) pop. 10,051, elev. 1,010'

Androscoggin Valley Chamber of Commerce: 961 Main St., Berlin, NH 03570. **Phone:** (603) 752-6060.

NORTHERN FOREST HERITAGE PARK & MUSEUM is at 942 Main St. The museum houses interactive displays explaining the history of the local paper mill and the lifestyle of mill workers in the mid-19th century. The park offers 90-minute narrated heritage boat tours along the scenic Androscoggin River. **Time:** Allow 1 hour, 30 minutes minimum. **Hours:** Museum Mon.-Fri. 9-4, year-round. Park daily 10-4, late May-Columbus Day. Boat tours depart daily at 6, late May-Aug. 31; at 5, Sept. 1-Columbus Day (weather permitting). Closed major holidays. **Cost:** Park and museum $6; $3 (ages 5-11). Boat tour $15; $8 (ages 5-11). Reservations are recommended for the boat tour. **Phone:** (603) 752-7202.

BETHLEHEM (C-3) pop. 972

THE ROCKS ESTATE off I-93 exit 40, then .5 mi. e. on US 302 to Glessner Rd., then e. to 4 Christmas Ln. The 1882 estate of Chicago businessman John Jacob Glessner, a founder of International Harvester, sits on the grounds. Scenic trails with wildlife viewing and hiking and skiing opportunities wind throughout the 1,300 acres.

Glessner's grandchildren donated the land to the Society for Protection of New Hampshire Forests in 1978. A sustainable Christmas tree farm with more than 50,000 trees is open to the public, as is an interactive maple sugar house and museum. **Time:** Allow 2 hours minimum. **Hours:** Estate daily dawn-dusk. Maple sugar museum daily 10-4, June 1 to mid-Oct. **Cost:** Donations. **Phone:** (603) 444-6228 or (800) 639-5373. 🎋

ADAIR COUNTRY INN & RESTAURANT   (603)444-2600
▽▽▽▽
Historic
Country Inn
$185-$375
Address: 80 Guider Ln 03574 **Location:** I-93 exit 40, just e on US 302. Located in a quiet area. **Facility:** Furnished with antiques and reproductions, this 1927 Georgian Colonial is on 200 wooded acres with ponds, rolling hills, wide lawns, a gazebo and lovely perennial gardens. 9 units. 3 stories (no elevator), interior/exterior corridors. **Terms:** closed 4/1-4/26 & 11/3-11/29, 2 night minimum stay - seasonal, age restrictions may apply, 15 day cancellation notice-fee imposed. **Activities:** tennis court, cross country skiing, snowmobiling, shuffleboard. **Free Special Amenities: full breakfast and high-speed Internet.** SAVE ECO 🍽 📶 ✖ 🏊 🚭

WHERE TO EAT

ROSA FLAMINGO'S   603/869-3111
▽▽▽ Italian. Family Dining. $10-$24 **AAA Inspector Notes:** This family-style restaurant features good food and friendly, attentive service. The varied menu offers pizza, pasta, pork tenderloin, beef, seafood and chicken dishes, in addition to fresh vegetables and salad. The lounge is on the lower level. **Bar:** full bar. **Reservations:** suggested. **Address:** 2312 Main St (US 302) 03574 **Location:** I-93 exit 40, 3 mi e; in village center. D

BRADFORD pop. 356

CANDLELITE INN BED & BREAKFAST   (603)938-5571
▽▽ Bed & Breakfast $129-$208 **Address:** 5 Greenhouse Ln 03221 **Location:** 0.3 mi n on SR 114, from SR 103. **Facility:** 6 units. 2 stories (no elevator), interior/exterior corridors. **Terms:** 2 night minimum stay - seasonal and/or weekends, age restrictions may apply, 14 day cancellation notice-fee imposed. ECO 🍽 📶 ✖ 🚭 🏊

ROSEWOOD COUNTRY INN   (603)938-5253
▽▽▽▽ Historic Bed & Breakfast $129-$299 **Address:** 67 Pleasant View Rd 03221 **Location:** US 89 exit 9, 7 mi sw on SR 103, then 2.5 mi s on Main St, follow signs. **Facility:** Period oil paintings decorate this 1896 Victorian-style inn, which is on manicured grounds and offers many added amenities. 11 units. 3 stories (no elevator), interior corridors. **Terms:** 2 night minimum stay - weekends, age restrictions may apply, 14 day cancellation notice-fee imposed. **Activities:** cross country skiing, hiking trails. ECO 📶 ✖ 🏊 /SOME UNITS 🚭

WHERE TO EAT

BRADFORD JUNCTION RESTAURANT & BAKERY
603/938-2424
▽ American. Casual Dining. $2-$7 **AAA Inspector Notes:** The restaurant and bakery combines cheap eats and good comfort foods all in one. An attached caboose serves as one of the dining rooms. **Address:** 2370 SR 114 03221 **Location:** On SR 114. B L

BRETTON WOODS (C-4)
• Hotels p. 180 • Restaurants p. 180

With the opening of the Mount Washington Hotel in July 1902, Bretton Woods became a well-known resort. Wealthy families spent pre-Depression summers at this lavish European-style spa. Some 50 trains arrived daily, and private railroad cars sat on a siding by the golf course, waiting to take passengers home.

A second surge of fame came in July 1944 when the International Monetary Conference convened at the hotel, refurbished for the occasion by the federal government. This meeting set the gold standard at $35 an ounce, thereby stabilizing post-World War II currency and establishing the American dollar as the cornerstone of international financial exchange. The conference room is now a small museum.

Twin Mountain-Bretton Woods Chamber of Commerce: P.O. Box 194, Twin Mountain, NH 03595. **Phone:** (800) 245-8946.

MOUNT WASHINGTON COG RAILWAY is 6 mi. n.w. on SR 302, then 6 mi. n.e. to 3168 Base Station Rd. Opened in 1869, the historic railway bills itself as the first mountain-climbing cog railway in the world. Coal-fired steam and biodiesel-powered trains take passengers on a scenic 3-hour round trip to the top of Mount Washington—the highest peak in the Northeast. The base station features a museum that has artifacts, historical displays and video presentations.

Time: Allow 3 hours minimum. **Hours:** Train departs two to 10 times daily on the half-hour beginning at 8:30 or 10:30, late May-early Dec.; Sat.-Sun. at 10:30 and 1:30, May 1-late May. Closed Thanksgiving. Phone ahead to confirm schedule. **Cost:** (Includes Mount Washington Observatory Weather Discovery Center) $64; $59 (ages 65+); $39 (ages 4-12); free (ages 0-3 on adult lap). Advance ticket purchase is recommended; all sales are final and no refunds or exchanges are issued. **Phone:** (603) 278-5404 or (800) 922-8825. 🍽

RECREATIONAL ACTIVITIES
Skiing

- **Bretton Woods** is on US 302. Other activities are offered. **Hours:** Mon.-Fri. 9-4, Sat.-Sun. and holidays 8-4 (also 4-8, late Dec. to mid-Mar.), mid-Nov. to mid-Apr. (weather permitting). **Phone:** (603) 278-3320 or (800) 314-1752.

ABOVE THE NOTCH MOTOR INN   603/846-5156

◈ **Motel** $73-$88 **Address:** 2058 US 302 03595 **Location:** Jct US 3, 4 mi e. **Facility:** 13 units. 1 story, exterior corridors. **Parking:** winter plug-ins. **Terms:** 5 day cancellation notice. **Activities:** snowmobiling, hiking trails, playground.

THE LODGE   (603)278-4000

◈◈◈ **Motel** $79-$269 **Address:** 2653 US 302 03575 **Location:** Center. **Facility:** 50 units. 2 stories (no elevator), exterior corridors. **Terms:** cancellation fee imposed, resort fee. **Pool(s):** heated indoor. **Activities:** sauna, whirlpool, 8 tennis courts, racquetball courts, ice skating, hiking trails, basketball. **Fee:** golf-27 holes, downhill & cross country skiing, horseback riding, game room, massage. **Guest Services:** coin laundry, area transportation-within resort.

OMNI BRETTON ARMS INN   (603)278-3000

◈◈◈ **Historic Country Inn** $129-$479 **Address:** 173 Mount Washington Hotel Rd (US 302) 03575 **Location:** Center. **Facility:** This charming 1896 inn offers an intimate ambiance, elegant décor, lovely gardens, comfortable sitting areas and a beautiful, upscale dining room. 34 units, some two bedrooms. 3 stories, interior corridors. **Parking:** winter plug-ins. **Terms:** 2 night minimum stay - seasonal and/or weekends, 7 day cancellation notice-fee imposed, resort fee. **Dining:** The Dining Room at The Omni Bretton Arms Inn, see separate listing. **Activities:** 4 tennis courts, racquetball courts, ice skating, recreation programs, rental bicycles, hiking trails, jogging, playground. **Fee:** golf-27 holes, downhill & cross country skiing, horseback riding, massage. **Guest Services:** valet laundry, area transportation-within resort.

OMNI MOUNT WASHINGTON HOTEL   (603)278-1000

◈◈◈◈ ◈◈◈◈ **Classic Historic Hotel** $149-$829 **Address:** 310 Mount Washington Hotel Rd (US 302) 03575 **Location:** Center. **Facility:** Built in 1902 and on the National Registry of Historic Places, this landmark hotel sits on expansive, manicured grounds and offers breathtaking mountain views. 200 units. 5 stories, interior corridors. **Parking:** on-site and valet. **Terms:** 2 night minimum stay - seasonal and/or weekends, 7 day cancellation notice-fee imposed, resort fee. **Dining:** 4 restaurants, also, The Dining Room at The Omni Mount Washington Hotel, see separate listing, entertainment. **Pool(s):** heated outdoor, heated indoor. **Activities:** sauna, whirlpool, steamroom, fishing, 4 tennis courts, racquetball courts, snowmobiling, ice skating, recreation programs, rental bicycles, hiking trails, jogging, playground, basketball, volleyball, spa. **Fee:** golf-27 holes, downhill & cross country skiing, horseback riding, game room. **Guest Services:** valet and coin laundry, area transportation-within resort.

THE TOWNHOMES   (603)278-2000

◈◈◈◈ **Vacation Rental House** $229-$1799 **Location:** Center. **Facility:** These accommodations are at the base of a ski hill, and some furnished homes across the street afford views of the skiing action. All units have a fireplace and a kitchen. 65 houses. 1-3 stories (no elevator), exterior corridors. **Terms:** check-in 4 pm, 2 night minimum stay, 7 day cancellation notice-fee imposed, resort fee. **Pool(s):** heated outdoor, 3 heated indoor. **Activities:** sauna, whirlpool, steamrooms, fishing, 8 tennis courts, racquetball courts, ice skating, exercise room. **Fee:** golf-27 holes, downhill & cross country skiing, snowmobiling, horseback riding, massage. **Guest Services:** area transportation-within resort.

THE DINING ROOM AT THE OMNI BRETTON ARMS INN
603/278-3305

◈◈◈ **American Fine Dining** $25-$38 **AAA Inspector Notes:** An intimate dining room creates an enjoyable experience in which waiters are attentive and work to exceed guest expectations. Semiformal attire. **Bar:** full bar. **Reservations:** suggested. **Address:** 300 Mount Washington Hotel Rd 03575 **Location:** Center; in Omni Bretton Arms Inn.

THE DINING ROOM AT THE OMNI MOUNT WASHINGTON HOTEL
603/278-1000

◈◈◈ **Continental Fine Dining** $25-$60 **AAA Inspector Notes:** This elegant dining room has panoramic views of the mountains and the resort's lush grounds, which are breathtaking. Guests will appreciate that each dish is prepared with a creative flair and delectable flavor. Semiformal attire. **Bar:** full bar. **Reservations:** suggested. **Address:** 310 Mount Washington Hotel Rd (US 302) 03575 **Location:** Center; in Omni Mount Washington Hotel. **Parking:** on-site and valet.

FABYAN'S STATION RESTAURANT & LOUNGE   603/278-2222

◈◈ **American. Family Dining.** $7-$20 **AAA Inspector Notes:** This restaurant, located in a restored railroad station in the heart of the White Mountains, is well-known for its nachos, burgers, ribs and seafood dishes. The decor displays train memorabilia, original woodwork and stained-glass windows. Good service. **Bar:** full bar. **Address:** US 302 03575 **Location:** Jct access road to Cog Railway.

BRISTOL   pop. 1,688

KATHLEEN'S COTTAGE   603/744-6336

◈ **Irish. Casual Dining.** $7-$19 **AAA Inspector Notes:** An Irish pub is an unusual find along the busy state highway. The menu features beer-battered fish and chips, shepherd's pie, Guinness beef stew, and bangers and mash among the sampling of homemade items. Enjoy traditional Irish music on Sunday evening with no cover charge from 4 pm-8 pm. **Bar:** full bar. **Address:** 98 Lake St 03222 **Location:** On US 3A.

CAMPTON

DAYS INN CAMPTON/PLYMOUTH   (603)536-3520

◈◈ **Hotel** $75-$189 **Address:** 1513 Daniel Webster Hwy 03223 **Location:** I-93 exit 27, just e, then just n. **Facility:** 99 units. 2 stories (no elevator), interior corridors. **Pool(s):** heated indoor. **Activities:** sauna, whirlpool, steamroom. **Guest Services:** coin laundry.

THE COUNTRY COW RESTAURANT AT BLAIR BRIDGE
603/536-1331

◈◈ **American. Casual Dining.** $8-$24 **AAA Inspector Notes:** This casual eatery affords views of one of the state's historic covered bridges. Steak, chicken and seafood dishes are prepared traditionally. **Bar:** full bar. **Address:** 57 Blair Rd 03223 **Location:** I-93 exit 27, just ne.

MAD RIVER TAVERN   603/726-4290

◈◈ **American. Casual Dining.** $9-$27 **AAA Inspector Notes:** Diners often stop by for a bite of tasty homemade fare on their way to ski or hike the mountains. The pleasant atmosphere makes this a nice place to unwind. **Bar:** full bar. **Address:** SR 49 03223 **Location:** I-93 exit 28, 1 mi e.

SUNSET GRILL   603/726-3108
▼▼ ▼▼ American. Casual Dining. $6-$18 **AAA Inspector Notes:**
The traditional menu lists burgers, steaks, salads, pasta, seafood,
chicken and more. The decor is accented with antique cameras
throughout. **Bar:** full bar. **Address:** 2092 US 3 03223 **Location:** I-93
exit 28, 1 mi w on SR 49. [L] [D]

CANDIA (F-4) elev. 360'

CHARMINGFARE FARM is off I-93 exit 9N, 4.5 mi.
e. on SR 27. The 180-acre farm features agricultural
animals, wildlife, a petting zoo, live animal demonstrations, tractor train rides, horse-drawn wagon or
sleigh rides, pony rides and guided horse trail rides.
Time: Allow 2 hours minimum. **Hours:** Daily 10-4,
May 1-Columbus Day; by appointment rest of year.
Closed Easter. **Cost:** Mon.-Fri. **$11;** free (ages 0-2).
Sat.-Sun. (includes unlimited pony rides, a horse-
drawn wagon ride and a tractor train ride) $17.
Phone: (603) 483-5623.

CANTERBURY (E-4) elev. 375'

▼▼GEM **CANTERBURY SHAKER VILLAGE** is off
I-93 exit 18, following signs. During the village's heyday in the 1850s, more than 300
Shakers—members of a religious sect known for the
ecstatic dancing that took place during church
services—lived, worked and worshipped in the village. Today it's a museum and historic site with 25
restored original buildings and four reconstructions
set among nearly 700 acres of pretty New England
countryside.

The oldest buildings go back all the way to 1792,
when the village was established, about 2 decades
after the Shakers first arrived from England. Canterbury Village was one of the most important of the 19
virtually self-sufficient communities the Shakers established from Maine to Kentucky in the 18th and
19th centuries.

Living a nearly monastic lifestyle that stressed
pacifism, communal ownership, celibacy, gender
equality, industriousness and simple living, the
Shakers built large dormitories, barns and workshops with minimal ornamentation, a feature you'll
notice immediately as you stroll among the un-
adorned utilitarian clapboard buildings. You'll also
notice the separate entrances and sleeping areas
for men and women; another hallmark of the Shaker
lifestyle.

"Hands to work and hearts to God" was one
Shaker motto, and Shaker communities prospered
as they became known for the beautifully crafted objects they made. The village museum houses a
large collection of these items, including Shaker furniture, noted for its elegant simplicity. And at various
locations in the village, you can watch artisans re-
create the traditional Shaker crafts of broom making,
dovetailing, wood turning, oval box making, spinning
and weaving, among others.

There are four guided tours to choose from, each
highlighting different themes including the community's history, its living spaces and the village grounds.

You can learn about the Shakers' close relationship
to the land as you ride among picturesque mill
ponds, orchards, gardens, fields and forests in a hay
wagon. Or, if you want to see the village at your own
pace, you can opt for the self-guiding tour; a printed
guide is available at the Visitor Education Center
that describes the network of nature trails on-site.

Time: Allow 3 hours minimum. **Hours:** Grounds
open daily 10-5, mid-May through Oct. 31. Tours are
offered daily 11-3. **Cost:** $17; $8 (ages 6-17); $42
(family). **Phone:** (603) 783-9511. [🍴]

GREENWOODS AT CANTERBURY SHAKER VILLAGE
                                     603/783-4238
▼▼ ▼▼ Specialty. Casual Dining. $9-$17 **AAA Inspector Notes:**
In a former blacksmith's shop, the restaurant serves traditional
Shaker dishes. Seating is strictly family style. **Reservations:** sug-
gested. **Address:** 288 Shaker Rd 03224 **Location:** I-93 exit 18, 6 mi
e, follow signs on SR 132, then 1 mi n to Shaker Village. [L]

CENTER SANDWICH (D-4) pop. 123

Near the east end of Squam Lake and bordered
on the north by the Sandwich Mountains, Center
Sandwich is the principal village of the Sandwich region. Now a summer resort and craft center, the
area was a favorite of poet John Greenleaf Whittier;
his "Sunset on the Bearcamp" refers to the
Bearcamp River, which lies between Center Sandwich and North Sandwich.

SANDWICH HISTORICAL SOCIETY MUSEUM, 4
Maple St., houses 18th-century to present-day
Americana. The 1850 Elisha Marston House is fur-
nished with antiques; the Wentworth wing contains
changing exhibits, a resource library and archives.
Farm implements, tools and vehicles are displayed
in the Quimby Barn Transportation Museum. **Time:**
Allow 1 hour minimum. **Hours:** Wed.-Sat. 10-4, late
June-early Oct.; by appointment rest of year. **Cost:**
Donations. **Phone:** (603) 284-6269.

CORNER HOUSE INN   603/284-6219
▼▼ ▼▼ Regional American. Casual Dining. $7-$24 **AAA Inspector Notes:** This restaurant, located in a country inn and converted barn, has a Colonial-tavern atmosphere and decor. Superb
cuisine focuses primarily on New England seafood; lobster and
mushroom soup is a delicious specialty. Creations by local artists are
displayed. **Bar:** full bar. **Address:** 22 Main St 03227 **Location:** Jct
SR 109 and 113; center. [L] [D]

CHARLESTOWN (F-2) pop. 1,152, elev. 369'

The 12 families who lived in this northwestern
outpost in 1744 found their position increasingly precarious as King George's War accelerated. In 1746
Abenaki Indian raids confined them to the fortified
village, and that winter they abandoned the settlement. Capt. Phineas Stevens and less than 50 provincial soldiers returned in April. Their withstanding
a 3-day siege by 700 French and Indians was celebrated in Boston.

Charlestown revived as settlers returned to the
fertile Connecticut River Valley. During the Revolutionary War the town's wide main streets supposedly
served as a training ground for the soldiers of Gen.

John Stark, hero of the Battle of Bennington *(see Bennington, Vt., p. 272)*. Main Street has many buildings that date from the late 18th and early 19th century.

FORT AT NO. 4 LIVING HISTORY MUSEUM is on SR 11, .5 mi. e. of I-91 exit 7. This reconstruction of the 1744 fortified village of Charlestown follows detailed drawings made in 1746 and includes the Great Chamber, stockade, watchtower, two barns and 12 other buildings. Furnishings and demonstrations depict 18th-century frontier life. Events include Colonial musters, 18th-century festivals and musical programs.

Time: Allow 1 hour minimum. **Hours:** Mon.-Sat. 10-4:30, Sun. 10-4, May-Oct. **Cost:** $10; $7 (ages 13-17 and 55+); $5 (ages 6-12). **Phone:** (603) 826-5700. 🅰

CHESTERFIELD

CHESTERFIELD INN   603/256-3211
▼▼▼ **Historic Country Inn** $149-$345 **Address:** 20 Cross Rd 03466 **Location:** I-91 exit 3, 2 mi e on SR 9. **Facility:** A farm in the late 18th century, this restored country inn offers well-appointed guest rooms, many with a fireplace and a balcony or patio. A terrific gourmet breakfast is served each morning. 15 units. 2 stories (no elevator), interior/exterior corridors. **Terms:** 5 day cancellation notice. **Dining:** restaurant, see separate listing. **Activities:** *Fee:* massage. **Guest Services:** valet laundry.
🅴🅲🅾 🍴 📶 ⊠ 🔋 / SOME UNITS 🐾 🖵

WHERE TO EAT

CHESTERFIELD INN   603/256-3211
▼▼▼ American. Fine Dining. $18-$30 **AAA Inspector Notes:** In an elegant, romantic inn, the candlelit restaurant offers a feast for the eyes and palate. Guests enjoy the beautiful view of rolling hills and gorgeous sunsets while they dine on crab cakes with honey-sweet potato puree, rosemary- and walnut-encrusted rack of lamb with merlot and red onion glaze, and chocolate cake with crème anglaise. Dishes are prepared using fresh and unusual ingredients with a creative flare. **Bar:** full bar. **Reservations:** suggested. **Address:** 20 Cross Rd 03446 **Location:** I-91 exit 3, 2 mi e on SR 9. D

CHICHESTER

WEATHERVANE SEAFOOD RESTAURANT   603/225-4044
▼▼ ▼ Seafood. Family Dining. $7-$25 **AAA Inspector Notes:** The popular, family-oriented restaurant presents a large menu with lobster, fried clams and crisp Cape Cod apple-cranberry cobbler. Flavorful dishes are served in large portions. A fish market is on the premises. **Bar:** full bar. **Address:** 379 Dover Rd 03301 **Location:** I-93 exit 15E (SR 4), 4.7 mi on I-393, then 0.4 mi e.
L D CALL ♿M

CLAREMONT pop. 13,355

RAMUNTO'S BRICK OVEN PIZZA   603/542-9100
▼▼ ▼ Italian. Casual Dining. $5-$14 **AAA Inspector Notes:** A casual atmosphere makes this riverside restaurant a great gathering spot. The kitchen uses fresh ingredients, and the pizza dough is made each morning. The garlic knots are a standout. **Bar:** beer & wine. **Address:** 71 Broad St 03743 **Location:** At Water St; downtown. L D CALL ♿M

Safety tip: Keep a current AAA/CAA
Road Atlas in every vehicle

COLEBROOK pop. 1,394

NORTHERN COMFORT MOTEL   603/237-4440
▼▼▼
Motel
$79-$89
Address: 1 Trooper Scott Phillips Hwy 03576 **Location:** 1.5 mi s on US 3. **Facility:** 19 units, some two bedrooms and kitchens. 1 story, exterior corridors. **Terms:** 3 day cancellation notice. **Pool(s):** heated outdoor. **Activities:** snowmobiling, playground, sports court. **Free Special Amenities:** local telephone calls and high-speed Internet.
SAVE 🛥 📶 ⊠ 🔋 / SOME UNITS FEE 🐾 🖵

CONCORD (F-4) pop. 42,695, elev. 264'
• Restaurants p. 186

The political and financial center of the state—and capital since 1808—Concord also is a major industrial, transportation and distribution point. At the root of its prosperity is easy accessibility. Historically, settlement and commerce followed the Merrimack River and later, a canal to Boston. Now a convergence of highways forms the city's busy lifelines.

A trading post operating as early as 1660, the locale gained notoriety in 1697 as the place where Hannah Dustin, abducted by Penacook Indians in a raid on Haverhill, Mass., scalped her sleeping captors and escaped.

Settlement came somewhat more slowly. Not until 1725 was the land granted to settlers, who named it the Plantation of Penacook, from the name American Indians gave to a nearby bend in the river. In 1765 the area was renamed Concord.

Because generally peaceful relations with the Penacook people had allowed Concord to grow, by the Revolutionary War it was a sturdy community able to send companies to fight at Lexington and Concord, Mass., Bunker Hill and other battle sites. A tablet at Walker and Bouton streets marks the site where New Hampshire ratified the Constitution on June 21, 1788.

Industry began to develop during the early 1800s. Wheelwright Lewis Downing and coach builder J. Stephens Abbot created a product that was instrumental in opening the frontier—the bouncing, high-wheeled Concord coach used by Wells Fargo and other stage lines throughout the West.

A few reminders of Concord's past stand along some of the town's wide, shaded streets. The Rev. Timothy Walker House, 276 N. Main St., dates from 1734, making it the oldest house in Concord; it is closed to the public. The structure at 132 N. Main St. once was the Eagle Hotel, a popular tavern 1825-56; it is now the site of a restaurant. Tuck Library, established in the early 1900s and operated by the New Hampshire Historical Society, is at 30 Park St.

A community-wide effort resulted in the restoration of the Capitol Theatre, built in the neo-Egyptian style in 1927 to house vaudeville shows. The Capitol Center for the Arts, with the Chubb Theatre as its centerpiece, presents touring Broadway shows, concerts, entertainers and dance troupes. The

1,300-seat theater is at 44 S. Main St.; phone (603) 225-1111.

The city balances its governmental and business orientation with ample opportunities for recreation. Among several city parks offering both summer and winter sports are 20-acre White Park at Centre and Washington streets and 16-acre Merrill Park at Eastman and Carpenter streets.

Greater Concord Chamber of Commerce: 49 S. Main St., Suite 104, Concord, NH 03301. **Phone:** (603) 224-2508.

Self-guiding tours: Concord on Foot, a tour of downtown, includes historical and architecturally interesting buildings. Brochures are available at the chamber of commerce and at the New Hampshire Historical Society Museum *(see attraction listing)* for $2.

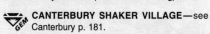 **CANTERBURY SHAKER VILLAGE**—see Canterbury p. 181.

CONSERVATION CENTER is off I-93 exit 16, then s.e. on SR 132, following signs to 54 Portsmouth St. The center showcases passive solar and wood heating methods, including an envelope room, fiberglass water tubes and a wood-chip gasification furnace. The adjacent French Wing, added in 2001, is a timber-framed, three-story addition with a dramatic two-story atrium that uses 60 percent less energy and 90 percent less water than a conventional new building. A 2-mile interpretive hiking trail explores native flora. Self-guiding tours include a map and audiotape. **Hours:** Center Mon.-Fri. 8:30-5. Last admission 30 minutes before closing. Trail daily dawn-dusk. Closed major holidays. **Cost:** Free. **Phone:** (603) 224-9945.

McAULIFFE-SHEPARD DISCOVERY CENTER, off I-393 exit 1, following signs, is said to be New England's largest air and space museum. Dedicated to New Hampshire astronauts Christa McAuliffe and Alan Shepard, the center features state-of-the-art interactive exhibits on aviation, astronomy, and Earth and space sciences. Visitors can enjoy the planetarium, Earth and Planetary Sciences Gallery, special traveling exhibits and educational programs.

Time: Allow 2 hours minimum. **Hours:** Daily 10-5 (also first and second Fri. of the month 6:30-9 p.m.), Memorial Day-Labor Day; Thurs.-Sun. 10-5 (also first and second Fri. of the month 6:30-9 p.m.), rest of year. Show times vary; phone ahead for schedule. Closed major holidays. **Cost:** $9; $8 (ages 62+ and students with ID); $6 (ages 3-12). Ticket sales are by telephone Mon.-Fri. 8-5 or at the sales desk. Planetarium show $4. **Phone:** (603) 271-7827. [T]

McLANE CENTER & SILK FARM SANCTUARY is at 84 Silk Farm Rd. Visitors can view wildlife and observe raptors up close. Miles of well-marked hiking trails and a large picnic area are available. In addition to serving as the headquarters of the New Hampshire Audubon Society, the center offers educational programs year-round. **Hours:** Grounds daily dawn-dusk. Center and sanctuary Mon.-Fri. 9-5. **Cost:** Free. **Phone:** (603) 224-9909. [&]

NEW HAMPSHIRE HISTORICAL SOCIETY MUSEUM, 6 Eagle Sq. off N. Main St., across from the State House, features an overview of the state's history. Exhibits include Revolutionary War and Civil War artifacts, an original Concord stagecoach, 19th-century White Mountain paintings and a re-created fire tower. Changing exhibits relating to art, history and culture also are offered.

Hours: Tues.-Sat. 9:30-5 (also Mon. 9:30-5, July 1-Oct. 15 and in Dec.), Sun. noon-5. **Cost:** $5.50; $4.50 (ages 55+); $3 (ages 6-18); $17 (family). **Phone:** (603) 228-6688.

PIERCE MANSE, 14 Horseshoe Pond Ln., was the 1842-48 home of President Franklin Pierce. Moved from its original location on Montgomery Street, the restored house is furnished in mid-19th-century style with Pierce family furnishings and memorabilia as well as other period items. **Time:** Allow 1 hour minimum. **Hours:** Tues.-Sat. 11-3, mid-June through Labor Day; Fri.-Sat. noon-3, day after Labor Day-early Oct.; otherwise by appointment. Closed major holidays. Phone ahead to confirm schedule. **Cost:** $7; $6 (ages 65+); $3 (ages 4-17); $15 (family). **Phone:** (603) 225-4555.

STATE HOUSE, at 107 N. Main St., is said to be the country's oldest statehouse in which the legislature continues to meet in the original chambers. Constructed of Concord granite and Vermont marble, the 1819 neoclassic structure is the focal point of State House Plaza. Featured are portraits of the state's well-known residents, the Hall of Flags, four mural panels by Barry Faulkner and a visitor center with dioramas and displays. Statues and historical markers adorn the plaza. The Memorial Arch, built in 1891, honors New Hampshire's soldiers and sailors. **Hours:** Mon.-Fri. 8-4. Closed major holidays. **Cost:** Free. **Phone:** (603) 271-2154.

RECREATIONAL ACTIVITIES
Canoeing

• **Contoocook River Canoe Co.,** 9 Horse Hill Rd., Concord, NH 03303. **Hours:** Wed.-Sun. 9-5 (also Thurs. 5-7), mid-May to late Sept. (weather permitting). **Phone:** (603) 753-9804.

BEST WESTERN CONCORD INN & SUITES

(603)228-4300

Hotel
$89-$249

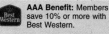
AAA Benefit: Members save 10% or more with Best Western.

Address: 97 Hall St 03301 **Location:** I-93 exit 13, just n on Main St, then 0.5 mi w. **Facility:** 66 units. 3 stories, interior corridors. **Terms:** cancellation fee imposed. **Pool(s):** heated indoor. **Activities:** whirlpool, exercise room. **Guest Services:** valet and coin laundry. **Free Special Amenities:** expanded continental breakfast and high-speed Internet.

[SAVE] [≈] [BIZ] [⌘] [⊟] [⊜] [⊡] / SOME UNITS FEE [🐾]

THE CENTENNIAL HOTEL   (603)227-9000

▽▽▽▽ **Classic Hotel** $119-$400 **Address:** 96 Pleasant St 03301 **Location:** I-93 exit 14, just w to Main St, just s to Pleasant St (SR 9), then 0.5 mi w. **Facility:** Turrets, porches and handsomely furnished common areas enhance this brick Victorian mansion dating from 1892. The inside features contemporary guest rooms. 32 units. 3 stories, interior corridors. *Bath:* shower only. **Terms:** 2 night minimum stay - seasonal, cancellation fee imposed. **Amenities:** high-speed Internet. **Dining:** Granite Restaurant & Bar, see separate listing. **Activities:** exercise room. **Guest Services:** valet laundry.

⊘ ⊘ CALL ⊘ BIZ ⊘ ⊘ ⊘

CONCORD COMFORT INN   (603)226-4100

▽▽▽▽ **Hotel** $59-$179 **Address:** 71 Hall St 03301 **Location:** I-93 exit 13, just n on Main St, then 0.3 mi w. Located in a residential area. **Facility:** 100 units. 3 stories, interior corridors. **Terms:** cancellation fee imposed. **Pool(s):** heated indoor. **Activities:** sauna, whirlpool, limited exercise equipment. **Guest Services:** valet and coin laundry, area transportation-within 20 mi.

FEE ⊘ CALL ⊘ ⊘ BIZ ⊘ ⊘ ⊘ ⊘ ⊘
/ SOME UNITS FEE ⊘

COURTYARD BY MARRIOTT-CONCORD   (603)225-0303

▽▽▽▽ **Hotel** $139-$189 **Address:** 70 Constitution Ave 03301 **Location:** I-93 exit 13, just n on Main St, then 0.3 mi w. Located at Grappone Conference Center. **Facility:** 90 units. 3 stories, interior corridors. **Amenities:** high-speed Internet. **Pool(s):** heated indoor. **Activities:** whirlpool, exercise room. **Guest Services:** valet and coin laundry.

> **AAA Benefit:**
> AAA hotel discounts of 5% or more.

ECO ⊘ FEE ⊘ ⊘ ⊘ CALL ⊘ ⊘ BIZ ⊘
⊘ ⊘ / SOME UNITS ⊘ ⊘

Save on Theme Park Tickets

AAA ⊘ CAA
Show Your Card & Save

AAA.com/discounts

FAIRFIELD INN BY MARRIOTT CONCORD
      (603)224-4011

▽▽▽▽ **Hotel** $99-$160

> **AAA Benefit:** AAA hotel discounts of 5% or more.

Address: 4 Gulf St 03301 **Location:** I-93 exit 13, just n on Main St, then immediate right turn. **Facility:** 104 units. 3 stories, interior corridors. **Pool(s):** heated indoor. **Activities:** whirlpool, limited exercise equipment. **Guest Services:** valet and coin laundry. **Free Special Amenities: expanded continental breakfast and room upgrade (subject to availability with advance reservations).**

SAVE CALL ⊘ ⊘ BIZ ⊘ ⊘ ⊘ / SOME UNITS ⊘ ⊘

HAMPTON INN-CONCORD/BOW   (603)224-5322

▽▽▽▽ **Hotel** $109-$289

> **AAA Benefit:** Members save up to 10%!

Address: 515 South St 03304 **Location:** I-89 exit 1. **Facility:** 145 units. 4 stories, interior corridors. **Terms:** 1-7 night minimum stay, cancellation fee imposed. **Pool(s):** heated indoor. **Activities:** limited exercise equipment. **Guest Services:** valet and coin laundry. **Free Special Amenities: full breakfast and high-speed Internet.** *(See ad this page.)*

SAVE ⊘ CALL ⊘ ⊘ BIZ ⊘ ⊘
/ SOME UNITS ⊘ ⊘

HOLIDAY INN   (603)224-9534

▽▽▽ **Hotel** $89-$169 **Address:** 172 N Main St 03301 **Location:** I-93 exit 14, jct US 3 and 4; downtown. **Facility:** 122 units. 4 stories, interior corridors. **Amenities:** *Some:* safes. **Pool(s):** heated indoor. **Activities:** sauna, whirlpool, exercise room. *Fee:* massage. **Guest Services:** valet laundry.

⊘ ⊘ CALL ⊘ ⊘ BIZ ⊘ ⊘ ⊘ ⊘
/ SOME UNITS ⊘ ⊘

Find Pet-Friendly Places to Stay and Play

Buy *The AAA PetBook®* at participating AAA/
CAA offices — or download in digital format
from your online bookseller.

- Pet-stay details for AAA Approved and
  Diamond Rated hotels
- Pet-friendly campgrounds, attractions
  and national public lands
- Handy tips and resources

Visit **AAA.com/PetBook** for information, travel tips
and AAA PetBook Photo Contest details.

RESIDENCE INN BY MARRIOTT CONCORD (603)226-0012

▼▼▼ **Extended Stay Hotel**
$99-$179 **Address:** 91 Hall St 03301
Location: I-93 exit 13, just n on Main St,
then 0.5 mi w. **Facility:** 92 units, some

AAA Benefit:
AAA hotel discounts
of 5% or more.

two bedrooms, efficiencies and kitchens.
4 stories, interior corridors. **Pool(s):** heated indoor. **Activities:** sports
court, exercise room. **Guest Services:** valet and coin laundry, area
transportation-local area.

[icons] CALL [icons] BIZ [icons] / SOME UNITS FEE [icon]

WHERE TO EAT

ANGELINA'S RISTORANTE ITALIANO 603/228-3313

▼▼ Regional Italian. Fine Dining. $10-$24 **AAA Inspector
Notes:** The veal piccata is delectable at this attractive, intimate restaurant. Well-prepared cuisine is enhanced by an extensive wine list.
Simple decor lends to a casual setting; the entrance is at the building's rear corner. **Bar:** full bar. **Reservations:** suggested. **Address:**
11 Depot St 03301 **Location:** Just off Main St; downtown. **Parking:**
street only. L D

THE BARLEY HOUSE RESTAURANT & TAVERN 603/228-6363

▼▼ American. Casual Dining. $6-$22 **AAA Inspector Notes:**
The casual downtown eatery presents entertainment on most evenings. Representative of menu choices are traditional burgers,
applewood-smoked pork chops and vegetable lasagna. **Bar:** full bar.
Address: 132 N Main St 03301 **Location:** Center. **Parking:** street
only. L D LATE

CHEERS GRILLE AND BAR 603/228-0180

▼▼ American. Casual Dining. $6-$19 **AAA Inspector Notes:**
The large restaurant has big booths and a collection of many things on
the walls. American food is served in hearty portions. The separate bar
is a popular spot to unwind. **Bar:** full bar. **Address:** 17 Depot St 03301
Location: I-93 exit 14, just w, just s, then just e. L D

CHEN YANG LI RESTAURANT & PUB 603/228-8508

▼▼ Chinese. Fine Dining. $9-$25 **AAA Inspector Notes:** The
restaurant's third location continues the tradition of offering excellent
Chinese cuisine, serving many house specialties and standard favorites. The wonderfully descriptive menu also has a nice selection of
sushi items. An elegant dining atmosphere and helpful staff make for
a very enjoyable experience. **Bar:** full bar. **Address:** 520 South St
03304 **Location:** I-89 exit 1. L D

THE COMMON MAN 603/228-3463

▼▼ American. Casual Dining. $9-$24 **AAA Inspector Notes:**
Charming décor, both in the dining room and the pleasant upstairs
pub, sets the stage for a menu filled with steak, seafood, chicken and
vegetarian dishes served in generous portions. Lobster corn chowder
is popular at lunch. For dessert, the specialty white chocolate mousse
is a favorite. **Bar:** full bar. **Address:** 25 Water St 03301 **Location:**
I-93 exit 13, just n. L D

CONSTANTLY PIZZA 603/224-9366

▼ Pizza. Casual Dining. $6-$20 **AAA Inspector Notes:** Patrons
can choose one of the restaurant's creative concoctions or create their
own specialty pizza. If you're not in the mood for pizza, check out one
of their specialty subs or wraps. **Bar:** beer & wine. **Address:** 39 S
Main St 03301 **Location:** I-93 exit 13, 0.7 mi n. L D

GRANITE RESTAURANT & BAR 603/227-9000

▼▼▼ International. Fine Dining. $7-$35 **AAA Inspector
Notes:** *Historic.* Located within the historical Centennial Inn, this attractive and romantic dining room occupies a historic Victorian mansion. Healthful preparations and eye-appealing presentations
characterize specialties of New England cuisine. **Bar:** full bar. **Reservations:** suggested. **Address:** 96 Pleasant St 03301 **Location:** I-93
exit 14, just w to Main St, just s to Pleasant St (SR 9), then 0.5 mi w;
in The Centennial Hotel. B L D

HERMANOS COCINA MEXICANA 603/224-5669

▼▼ **AAA Inspector Notes:** This restaurant
has simple decor with an Aztec flavor.
The extensive menu includes traditional
Mexican favorites, some with a slightly
different twist. Live jazz is played five
nights a week in the lounge. Do not miss
the strawberry burrito for dessert. **Bar:**

**Mexican
Casual Dining
$5-$15**

full bar. **Address:** 11 Hills Ave 03301 **Location:** Center.
L D CALL [icon]

MAKRIS LOBSTER & STEAK HOUSE 603/225-7665

▼▼ **AAA Inspector Notes:** The friendly,
family-run restaurant serves fresh seafood and lobster in a casual, no-
nonsense atmosphere. **Bar:** full bar.
Address: 354 Sheep Davis Rd 03301
Location: I-393 exit 3, 0.5 mi n on SR
106.

**Seafood
Casual Dining
$8-$25**

L D

MARGARITAS MEXICAN RESTAURANT 603/224-2821

▼▼ Regional Mexican. Casual Dining. $8-$20 **AAA Inspector
Notes:** Diners will feel as though they have just stepped south of the
border at this fun Mexican cantina. Traditional music fills the air while
warm terracotta colored walls accented by painted pottery and unique
jeweled star lanterns surround you. Sip on a large margarita while enjoying the freshly prepared fajitas, burritos, enchiladas, or quesadillas.
Bar: full bar. **Address:** 1 Bicentennial Square 03301 **Location:**
Center. **Parking:** street only. D

NEWICK'S LOBSTER HOUSE 603/225-2424

▼▼ Seafood. Casual Dining. $5-$30 **AAA Inspector Notes:**
The family-owned and family-friendly restaurant offers fresh seafood
in portions suitable for small or large appetites. **Bar:** full bar. **Address:** 317 Loudon Rd 03301 **Location:** I-93 exit 14, 2.8 mi e.
L D CALL [icon]

THE RED BLAZER 603/224-4101

▼▼ American. Casual Dining. $8-$27 **AAA Inspector Notes:**
Greek, Brazilian and American dishes are the restaurant's specialty.
A sample of menu items includes pastry-baked chicken, salmon
crusted in roasted ginger and sesame seeds, scallops with bacon,
burgers, sandwiches and salads. Live entertainment is featured
Thursday through Saturday. **Bar:** full bar. **Address:** 72 Manchester
St 03301 **Location:** I-93 exit 13, 0.5 mi e. L D

SIAM ORCHID 603/228-3633

▼▼ Thai. Casual Dining. $6-$16 **AAA Inspector Notes:** The
small storefront restaurant is downtown near the capitol building. The
menu lists an extensive collection of delicious Thai cuisine, including
seafood, chicken, beef, pork and vegetarian entrees. Noodles, fried
rice, soup appetizers and curry selections are available as well. Don't
miss the chicken satay and golden triangle appetizers. **Bar:** full bar.
Address: 158 N Main St 03301 **Location:** Center. **Parking:** street
only. L D

CONTOOCOOK pop. 1,444

COVERED BRIDGE RESTAURANT 603/746-5191

▼▼ American. Casual Dining. $7-$18 **AAA Inspector Notes:**
This family restaurant has large windows that overlook the Contoocook River. A variety of items are offered from steak and potatoes to
pasta and rice. **Bar:** full bar. **Address:** 16 Cedar St 03229 **Location:**
I-89 exit 6, 1 mi s. L D

CONWAY pop. 1,823
• Hotels & Restaurants map & index p. 225

CAFE NOCHE MEXICAN 603/447-5050 (30)

▼▼ Mexican. Casual Dining. $5-$15 **AAA Inspector Notes:**
Colorful Southwestern decor and a casual ambience welcome diners
to the small restaurant. The reasonably priced menu features
Mexican favorites scratch-made from fresh ingredients. More than 80
displayed hot sauces can be ordered to season meals. Everything
can be prepared to accommodate vegetarian tastes. Outdoor seating
is available in the summer. **Bar:** full bar. **Address:** 147 Main St 03818
Location: Center. L D

(See map & index p. 225.)

FIRE 21 PIZZA   603/447-2211 (29)

W Pizza. Family Dining. $2-$12 **AAA Inspector Notes:** Centrally located and open late, menu selections include pizza, subs, sandwiches, salads and spaghetti. **Address:** 9 W Main St 03860 **Location:** Corner of Main and W Main sts; across from Kenneth High School. **Parking:** street only. [L] [D]

JONATHON'S SEAFOOD RESTAURANT & FISH MARKET
                                 603/447-3838 (28)

WW Seafood. Casual Dining. $8-$17 **AAA Inspector Notes:** This restaurant is basic, but serves a wide variety of fresh seafood. A large lobster tank at the entrance lets the visitors know they are fresh. The brownie sundae is great choice for dessert. **Bar:** full bar. **Address:** 280 Eastside Rd 03818 **Location:** 2.1 mi s of jct US 302; 0.5 mi n of village center. [L] [D]

CORNISH (E-2)

In the first decade of the 20th century this township on the Connecticut River gained fame as a major New England art colony. The central force behind the reputation was sculptor Augustus Saint-Gaudens, but Maxfield Parrish and other notables in arts and letters also found a haven in the village.

About 2 miles south of Saint-Gaudens National Historic Site *(see attraction listing)* off SR 12A is one of the longest covered bridges in the United States. Built in 1866 and 450 feet long, the bridge spans the Connecticut River and links New Hampshire to Windsor, Vt.

SAINT-GAUDENS NATIONAL HISTORIC SITE is off SR 12A at 139 Saint-Gaudens

Rd. The 1885-1907 home and studio of sculptor Augustus Saint-Gaudens originally was a country tavern built in the early 1800s. Complemented by formal gardens, the house retains Saint-Gaudens' furnishings.

Other buildings include the Little Studio, which contains bas-reliefs, portraits and monuments; the New Gallery, with casts of some of the sculptor's largest works, cameos and coin models; the Picture Gallery, where contemporary art exhibitions are displayed; and the stable, which features a collection of horse-drawn vehicles. Hiking trails wind through the 150-acre site. Concerts are held on Sundays from early July to mid-August.

Time: Allow 2 hours minimum. **Hours:** Grounds open daily dawn-dusk. Buildings open daily 9-4:30, Memorial Day weekend-Oct. 31. **Cost:** (Valid for 7 days) $5; free (ages 0-15). **Phone:** (603) 675-2175.

CRAWFORD NOTCH (C-4)

Created when the Pleistocene ice sheet pushed through a narrow preglacial pass, majestic Crawford Notch stretches from Bartlett on the south to Saco Lake on the north. The Saco River and US 302 wind along its floor between steep, wooded Webster and Willey mountains. Behind Mount Webster rises Mount Jackson, the southernmost peak of the Presidential Range.

The scars of many landslides mark the mountainsides. In 1826 a landslide thundered down Willey Mountain, killing the fleeing family whose name the peak bears, but sparing the family's home. The event is recounted in "The Ambitious Guest," one of Nathaniel Hawthorne's "Twice-Told Tales." Near the site of the Willey House is the headquarters for Crawford Notch State Park *(see Recreation Areas Chart),* which embraces much of the notch; phone (603) 374-2272.

The Willey Slide also disrupted the Tenth New Hampshire Turnpike, one of a series of roads that laced the notch following Timothy Nash's discovery of the gap during a 1771 hunting expedition. Spurred by the governor's promise of a land grant if Nash could bring a horse through the notch, the hunter and a companion hauled the animal up and down the rocks by ropes.

As improvements made the route passable for freight traffic, the turnpike became instrumental in the opening of New Hampshire's North Country. Promptly repaired after the 1826 landslide, the road served as a channel for commerce until the railroad crossed the notch in 1875.

ARETHUSA FALLS, 1.2 mi. w. of US 302, is at the s. end of Crawford Notch State Park and can be reached by a steep, marked trail. With a drop of 200 feet, it is one of the highest waterfalls in New Hampshire. **Phone:** (603) 374-2272.

SILVER AND FLUME CASCADES are e. of US 302 at the n. end of Crawford Notch State Park. The Silver Cascade shoots across smoothly sloping ledges and bounds over precipices in its 1,000-foot course down Mount Webster. **Phone:** (603) 374-2272.

DERRY (G-4) pop. 22,015, elev. 278'

Water power from nearby Beaver Brook and linen-making skills brought by 18th-century Scot-Irish immigrants combined to make Derry a prosperous linen manufacturing center. Its quality cloth was widely imitated.

The art of weaving sustained Derry well into the 20th century. When the textile industry moved to the Southern states, manufacturing shifted to shoes and palm leaf hats. The city's present economy is based mainly on services and such manufactured products as printed circuit boards and giftware. Derry was the boyhood home of Cmdr. Alan B. Shepard Jr., the first American in space.

Four miles east on Island Pond Road from the junction of SR 28 and the SR 28 bypass in Ballard State Forest is the Taylor Up-and-Down Sawmill, a mechanized version of the old two-man vertical pit saw. Last operated in 1865, the water-powered mill is demonstrated periodically during the summer; it can be viewed from the outside at other times. Contact the Urban Forestry Center, 45 Elwyn Rd. in Portsmouth, for the demonstration schedule; phone (603) 431-6774.

Greater Derry Londonderry Chamber of Commerce: 29 W. Broadway, Derry, NH 03038. **Phone:** (603) 432-8205.

ROBERT FROST FARM, 1.5 mi. s of jct. SR 102 at 122 Rockingham Rd., is where renowned poet Robert Frost lived 1900-11. The farm was the source of inspiration for many of his published works. Restored to its turn-of-the-20th-century condition, the house contains period furniture. Displays in the barn pertain to Frost and his writings. Videotapes feature readings of his works and describe the restoration of the farm. A .5-mile poetry nature trail winds through the farm.

Time: Allow 1 hour, 30 minutes minimum. **Hours:** Grounds open daily year-round. Farm open daily 10-4, late June-early Sept.; Wed.-Sun. 10-4, early May-late June and early Sept. to mid-Oct. **Cost:** Grounds free. Farm $5; $3 (ages 6-17). **Phone:** (603) 432-3091, or (603) 271-3556 during the off-season.

DIXVILLE NOTCH (B-4) elev. 1,600'

The northernmost and most dramatic of the White Mountain notches, rocky Dixville Notch is traversed by SR 26 between Colebrook and Errol. Among its scenic highlights are Lake Gloriette, the Cathedral Spires, Cascade Falls and Table Rock. Much of the area is within Dixville Notch State Park. The town also is renowned for being one of the first places to declare its results for the New Hampshire presidential primary and U.S. presidential elections.

DOVER (F-5) pop. 29,987, elev. 77'

Considered the oldest permanent settlement in the state, Dover was founded in 1623 by fishermen and traders who plied the tidewaters of the Great Bay area and landed at Pomeroy Cove, now called Dover Point. By the late 1600s population growth necessitated moving the settlement from Dover Point, on SR 4 at the Piscataqua River, to its present location.

The harnessing of the Cocheco Falls' water power caused the shift from a fishing and farming economy to one based on industry. Sawmills and gristmills gave way to cotton mills when the embargoes imposed during the War of 1812 curtailed mercantile interests.

Renovations in the downtown area and along the riverfront feature a variety of architectural styles, especially Colonial and Victorian.

Greater Dover Chamber of Commerce: 550 Central Ave., Dover, NH 03820. **Phone:** (603) 742-2218.

CHILDREN'S MUSEUM OF NEW HAMPSHIRE, 6 Washington St., has an assortment of hands-on exhibits. Youngsters can command a yellow submarine, explore kaleidoscopes, learn about life in the mills and experience a music matrix where they can visualize sound waves. **Time:** Allow 1 hour minimum. **Hours:** Tues.-Sat. 10-5 (also Mon. 10-5 during summer, holidays and school vacations), Sun. noon-5. **Cost:** $9; $8 (ages 65+); free (under 1). **Phone:** (603) 742-2002.

WOODMAN INSTITUTE MUSEUM, 182-190 Central Ave., consists of four display buildings. The oldest is the hand-hewn 1675 William Damm Garrison House, with Early American utensils, tools, clothing and furniture. The 1818 Woodman House has exhibits about natural history and science, Civil War rooms, and a collection of Indian artifacts.

Abolitionist Sen. John P. Hale lived in the 1813 Hale House, which features Hale family memorabilia and exhibits showcasing local history. The 1825 Keefe House and carriage barn houses rotating exhibits. Among the most notable items displayed in these homes are a saddle used by Abraham Lincoln and a rare Napoleon cannon from the American Civil War. **Hours:** Wed.-Sun. 12:30-4:30, Apr.-Nov. Closed major holidays. **Cost:** $8; $6 (ages 65+ and students with ID); $3 (ages 6-15); $35 (family). Cash or check only. **Phone:** (603) 742-1038.

COMFORT INN & SUITES   (603)750-7507

▼▼▼▼ Hotel $89-$200 **Address:** 10 Hotel Dr **Location:** SR 16 exit 9, 0.4 mi ne. Located at Weeks Crossing. **Facility:** 96 units. 4 stories, interior corridors. **Terms:** cancellation fee imposed. **Pool(s):** heated indoor. **Activities:** whirlpool, exercise room. **Guest Services:** valet and coin laundry, area transportation-within 10 mi.

DAYS INN   (603)742-0400

▼▼ Motel $89-$179 **Address:** 481 Central Ave 03820 **Location:** Spaulding Tpke exit 7, 2 mi n on SR 108; downtown. **Facility:** 69 units, some two bedrooms and kitchens. 2 stories (no elevator), interior/exterior corridors. **Amenities:** safes. **Pool(s):** heated indoor. **Activities:** whirlpool.

HAMPTON INN   (603)516-5600

▼▼▼ Hotel $99-$199 **Address:** 9 Hotel Dr 03820 **Location:** SR 16 exit 9, 0.4 mi ne. **Facility:** 93 units. 3 stories, interior corridors. **Terms:** 1-7 night minimum stay, cancellation fee imposed. **Amenities:** video games (fee), high-speed Internet. **Pool(s):** heated indoor. **Activities:** whirlpool, exercise room. **Guest Services:** valet and coin laundry, area transportation-within 10 mi.

AAA Benefit: Members save up to 10%!

HOMEWOOD SUITES DOVER   (603)516-0929

▼▼▼ Extended Stay Hotel $129-$229 **Address:** 21 Members Way 03820 **Location:** SR 16 exit 9, 0.4 mi w. **Facility:** 88 efficiencies, some two bedrooms. 4 stories, interior corridors. **Terms:** 1-7 night minimum stay, cancellation fee imposed. **Amenities:** high-speed Internet. **Pool(s):** heated indoor. **Activities:** whirlpool, exercise room. **Guest Services:** valet and coin laundry, area transportation-within 10 mi.

AAA Benefit: Contemporary luxury at a special Member rate.

MICROTEL INN & SUITES BY WYNDHAM DOVER
                                        (603)953-0800

▼▼ Hotel $80-$150 **Address:** 31 Webb Pl 03820 **Location:** SR 16 exit 9, 0.4 mi e. **Facility:** 57 units. 3 stories, interior corridors. **Activities:** exercise room. **Guest Services:** coin laundry.

THE FISH SHANTY   603/749-1001

◆ Seafood. Family Dining. $7-$22 **AAA Inspector Notes:** In the heart of downtown, the popular, family-owned and managed restaurant has a bi-level dining room with clean, simple decor and a casual atmosphere. The menu features fresh seafood as well as steak and chicken entrees. Lots of sandwiches and well-prepared salads can be ordered all day. Don't pass up one of the delicious desserts. **Bar:** full bar. **Address:** 471 Central Ave 03820 **Location:** Spaulding Tpke exit 7, 1 mi e on SR 108 to Central Ave; downtown. **Parking:** street only. L D

NEWICK'S LOBSTER HOUSE   603/742-3205

◆ Seafood. Family Dining. $9-$25 **AAA Inspector Notes:** The menu incorporates a good selection of baked and broiled seafood, steamers and chowders. Guests appreciate the views of Great Bay and geese, eagles and seals. Save space for the heaping strawberry shortcake for dessert. **Bar:** full bar. **Address:** 431 Dover Point Rd 03820 **Location:** SR 4 exit 6W, follow signs to Dover Point business district. L D CALL ⛓M 🅺

ORCHARD STREET CHOP SHOP   603/749-0006

◆◆◆ American. Fine Dining. $17-$38 **AAA Inspector Notes:** In the center of Dover, the modern steakhouse prepares USDA Prime dry-aged beef. Side dishes are ordered a la carte. Those who prefer a more casual setting should head to Top of the Chop on the second floor. **Bar:** full bar. **Reservations:** suggested. **Address:** 1 Orchard St 03820 **Location:** Jct Washington St and Central Ave. D

WEATHERVANE SEAFOOD RESTAURANT   603/749-2341

◆◆ American Seafood. Family Dining. $8-$24 **AAA Inspector Notes:** The popular, family-oriented restaurant presents a large menu with lobster, fried clams and crisp Cape Cod apple-cranberry cobbler. Flavorful dishes are served in large portions. A fish market is on the premises. **Bar:** full bar. **Address:** 2 Dover Point Rd 03820 **Location:** Spaulding Tpke exit 6N, 4 mi n on SR 16. L D CALL ⛓M

DUBLIN (G-3) elev. 1,845'

The name Dublin is a reminder of the group of Scot-Irish immigrants who attempted to settle this densely forested region in 1753. Permanent settlement did not occur for another decade, however, and Dublin was not chartered until 1771. Its slow start and distance from major rivers discouraged industry and kept the community essentially rural.

In the 1800s this isolation began to be viewed as an advantage, and the town at the base of Mount Monadnock became a popular summer resort area.

Mount Monadnock is well known among both geology students and vacationers. Its name has become the term for the type of occurrence it exemplifies: a mountain or hill of resistant rock rising above a plain created by glacial or other erosive action. Monadnock State Park *(see Recreation Areas Chart)* embraces much of the mountain; phone (603) 532-8862.

THE FRIENDLY FARM, 2 mi. w. on SR 101, presents farm livestock and their young in a natural setting. Visitors can feed and touch most of the animals. **Time:** Allow 1 hour minimum. **Hours:** Daily 10-5, Memorial Day weekend-Labor Day; Sat.-Sun. 10-5, day after Labor Day to mid-Sept. (weather permitting). **Cost:** $7.50; $6.50 (ages 1-12). **Phone:** (603) 563-8444. 🏕

AUDREY'S CAFE   603/876-3316

◆ American. Casual Dining. $6-$24 **AAA Inspector Notes:** Off a busy state route, this roadside location welcomes diners in for tasty traditional comfort foods. **Bar:** beer & wine. **Address:** 13 Main St (SR 101) 03444 **Location:** Center. B L D

DURHAM (F-5) pop. 10,345, elev. 81'

Settled in 1635 and separated from Dover in 1732, historic Durham was the home of Maj. Gen. John Sullivan, a Revolutionary War hero and three-time governor of New Hampshire.

A tablet marks the site of the old meetinghouse where, in 1774, Sullivan and his band of Durham patriots supposedly stored the gunpowder they had taken from the British at Fort William and Mary in New Castle *(see place listing p. 221).* Although the British attempted to retrieve the gunpowder, the shallow river halted their frigate at Portsmouth.

The ensuing century of rural and maritime activity ended in 1893. A bequest to the state removed the College of Agriculture and Mechanical Arts (which later became the University of New Hampshire) from Hanover, where it had been founded in association with Dartmouth College in 1866, to Durham. University and community quickly blended, and Durham assumed its role as a college town. The university's Paul Creative Arts Center is a focus for cultural activities; phone (603) 862-2290.

HOLIDAY INN EXPRESS DURHAM-UNH   (603)868-1234

◆◆ Hotel $99-$189 **Address:** 2 Main St 03824 **Location:** On SR 108; center. **Facility:** 68 units. 3 stories, interior corridors. **Terms:** cancellation fee imposed. **Activities:** limited exercise equipment. **Guest Services:** valet and coin laundry.

🛗 🛜 ✕ 💻 / SOME UNITS FEE 🐾 FEE 🚗 FEE 🖼

THREE CHIMNEYS INN   (603)868-7800

◆◆◆
Historic
Country Inn
$139-$239

Address: 17 Newmarket Rd 03824 **Location:** On SR 108; center. **Facility:** Antique artwork, Georgian-era mahogany furniture and four-poster beds with period drapery bring an elegant ambiance to this hilltop inn. 23 units. 4 stories (no elevator), interior/exterior corridors. **Terms:** 7 day cancellation notice-fee imposed. **Amenities:** high-speed Internet. **Dining:** Maples Dining Room and ffrost Sawyer Tavern, see separate listing. **Guest Services:** valet laundry.

SAVE 🍴 FEE 🚲 🛜 ✕ 💻 / SOME UNITS FEE 🐾

MAPLES DINING ROOM AND FFROST SAWYER TAVERN   603/868-7800

◆◆◆
American
Casual Dining
$10-$28

AAA Inspector Notes: *Classic.* In a beautifully renovated 18th-century farmhouse, the restaurant sustains a casual pub atmosphere amid comfortable surroundings. American cuisine emphasizes fresh local ingredients prepared with international influences. **Bar:** full bar. **Reservations:** suggested. **Address:** 17 Newmarket Rd 03824 **Location:** On SR 108; center; in Three Chimneys Inn.

Menu on AAA.com L D

ENFIELD (E-2) pop. 1,540, elev. 760'

In 1782 two Shaker brothers from Mount Lebanon, N.Y., came to a village in the rolling woodlands near the eastern shore of Lake Mascoma. With others they formed the society that led to the establishment of Enfield, one of 19 Shaker communities to flourish in the United States. In 1793 they moved to the west side of the lake, where a permanent settlement was built.

The Enfield Shakers numbered 330 in the 1850s, but entries into the celibate order declined steadily after the Civil War. The last 10 members moved to the Canterbury society *(see Canterbury Shaker Village attraction listing p. 181)* in 1923.

ENFIELD SHAKER MUSEUM, off I-89 exit 17, e. on US 4, then s. on SR 4A following signs, is a restored 19th-century village dedicated to preserving the legacy of the Enfield Shakers. A self-guiding walking tour includes the herb, production and community gardens; the cemetery; the horse barn; the stone mill; the 1854 cow barn; the Great Stone Dwelling; the Mary Keane Chapel; and the laundry and dairy complex.

Museum displays include Shaker artifacts and furniture. Workshops and artisan demonstrations are offered. **Time:** Allow 1 hour minimum. **Hours:** Mon.-Sat. 10-5, Sun. noon-5. Last admission 1 hour before closing. Guided tours are available Fri.-Mon. by appointment. Closed major holidays. **Cost:** $8.50; $7.50 (ages 62+); $6 (students with ID); $4 (ages 7-17). Prices may vary; phone ahead. **Phone:** (603) 632-4346.

LA SALETTE SHRINE AND CENTER is 1.5 mi. w. on SR 4A. The shrine, a replica of the Marian Shrine of the Blessed Virgin Mary at La Salette, France, offers a chapel, the Rosary Pond, the Peace Walk and outdoor Stations of the Cross. **Hours:** Grounds open daily dawn-dusk. **Cost:** Free. **Phone:** (603) 632-7087.

EXETER (F-5) pop. 9,242, elev. 58'

Behind the peaceful charm of Exeter at the falls of the Squamscott River lies a history of outspoken dissent. The settlement was begun in 1638 by the Rev. John Wheelwright, whose radical views and religious nonconformity led to his expulsion from Boston. Wheelwright's individualism seemed to set the tone for the community, for revolutionary attitudes and politics were characteristic from the outset.

Exeter citizenry defied Royal commands, flouted talk of liberty and burned in effigy British lords Bute and North. When the war began, it was natural that the capital was moved from Tory-controlled Portsmouth to this Patriot stronghold.

Exeter is a mixture of industry and academia; Phillips Exeter Academy, a distinguished secondary school, was founded in 1781 and has conducted classes since 1783. Another link to the town's past is its architectural heritage, which is preserved with pride.

Exeter Area Chamber of Commerce: 24 Front St., Suite 101, Exeter, NH 03833. **Phone:** (603) 772-2411.

AMERICAN INDEPENDENCE MUSEUM, 1 Governors Ln., is within the restored Ladd-Gilman House, built in 1721. Formerly known as Cincinnati Hall, the house served as the state treasury during the American Revolution. John Taylor Gilman, an early governor of New Hampshire, lived there during his 14 gubernatorial terms. The museum complex also features the 1775 Folsom Tavern, where George Washington paid a visit in 1789. On display is Nicholas Gilman's draft of the U.S. Constitution.

Time: Allow 1 hour minimum. **Hours:** Wed.-Sat. 10-4, May-Oct. Guided tours depart at 10, noon and 2. **Cost:** $6; $5 (ages 65+); $3 (ages 6-18). **Phone:** (603) 772-2622.

THE EXETER INN   603/772-5901
▼W▼ **Country Inn.** Rates not provided. **Address:** 90 Front St 03833 **Location:** Just w on SR 111. Located at Phillips Exeter Academy. **Facility:** The inn has a Georgian brick exterior and is elegantly decorated with modern, contemporary touches. 46 units. 3 stories, interior corridors. **Dining:** Epoch Restaurant & Bar, see separate listing. **Activities:** limited exercise equipment. **Guest Services:** valet laundry.

FAIRFIELD INN & SUITES BY MARRIOTT (603)772-7411

▼W▼   Hotel $99-$209

AAA Benefit: AAA hotel discounts of 5% or more.

Address: 138 Portsmouth Ave 03833 **Location:** I-101 exit 11, just s. **Facility:** 71 units. 3 stories, interior corridors. **Amenities:** high-speed Internet. **Pool(s):** heated indoor. **Activities:** exercise room. **Guest Services:** valet and coin laundry. **Free Special Amenities: expanded continental breakfast and high-speed Internet.**

SAVE ECO ⏽◄ CALL ⎗M 🌊 BIZ 📶 ✕ 🔋 💻 / SOME UNITS 🛏

HAMPTON INN & SUITES   (603)658-5555

▼W▼   Hotel $109-$179

AAA Benefit: Members save up to 10%!

Address: 59 Portsmouth Ave 03833 **Location:** I-101 exit 11. **Facility:** 111 units. 4 stories, interior corridors. **Terms:** 1-7 night minimum stay, cancellation fee imposed. **Amenities:** high-speed Internet. **Pool(s):** heated indoor. **Activities:** whirlpool, exercise room. **Guest Services:** valet and coin laundry, area transportation-within 5 mi. **Free Special Amenities: full breakfast and high-speed Internet.** *(See ad p. 242.)*

SAVE CALL ⎗M 🌊 BIZ 📶 ✕ 🔋 💻 / SOME UNITS 🛏

Get pet travel tips and enter the photo contest at AAA.com/PetBook

EPOCH RESTAURANT & BAR   603/778-3762

▼▼▼ Regional American. Casual Dining. $10-$32 **AAA Inspector Notes:** In an upscale country inn near Phillips Exeter Academy, the restaurant features creative cuisine made with fresh local ingredients. The wine list is extensive. **Bar:** full bar. **Reservations:** suggested. **Address:** 90 Front St 03833 **Location:** Just w on SR 111; in The Exeter Inn. B L D

LOAF & LADLE   603/778-8955

▼ American. Quick Serve. $6-$8 **AAA Inspector Notes:** Self-described as a natural foods eatery, this place serves a selection of nearly 50 soups and 60 bread varieties, all of which are homemade and prepared daily. **Bar:** beer & wine. **Address:** 9 Water St 03833 **Location:** Center. **Parking:** street only. B L D

TAVERN AT RIVER'S EDGE   603/772-7393

▼▼ American. Casual Dining. $9-$28 **AAA Inspector Notes:** The setting is comfortable in the Victorian-era room. The food includes upscale entrees, as well as lighter tavern fare. Among specialties are New Zealand rack of lamb, filet mignon, fresh salmon and sesame-encrusted tuna. The entrance is on the stoop's right side and downstairs. **Bar:** full bar. **Address:** 163 Water St 03833 **Location:** Center. **Parking:** street only. L D

FITZWILLIAM (G-2) elev. 1,057'

Fitzwilliam is a classic New England community with a village green framed by a meetinghouse, historic houses, several antiques shops and a 1796 inn. Settled in the early 1760s, the town was incorporated in 1773. During its early years Fitzwilliam's manufacturers made the wheels on which much of the yarn for the textile industry was spun.

RHODODENDRON STATE PARK, 2.5 mi. w. off SR 119 following signs, encompasses 2,723 acres and is noted for its 16 acres of native rhododendron maximum, considered to be one of the largest stands of the hardy shrub north of the Alleghenies. The bushes, some of which exceed 20 feet in height, usually bloom in mid-July. A .6-mile path encircles the grove; pets are not permitted on the path. The park offers views of Mount Monadnock and other mountains in the region. **Hours:** Daily dawn-dusk. **Cost:** Free. **Phone:** (603) 532-8862.

FRANCONIA (C-3) elev. 990'
• Restaurants p. 192

In June Franconia hosts the Fields of Lupine Festival, featuring afternoon teas, sporting events, arts and crafts, horse-drawn wagon rides and tours of historic homes and gardens.

THE FROST PLACE, off I-93 exit 38 to SR 116, following signs to Bickford Hill and Ridge rds., is the house that poet Robert Frost purchased after his 1915 return from England. Two rooms contain memorabilia, including signed first editions of each of his books. A narrated videotape, a self-guiding tour of the 1859 farmhouse and a half-mile nature trail marked with

many of the poet's works create a detailed impression of Frost. Each summer a resident poet writes verse and gives readings in the old barn.

Time: Allow 1 hour minimum. **Hours:** Wed.-Mon. 1-5, July 1-Columbus Day; Sat.-Sun. 1-5, Memorial Day-June 30. **Cost:** Donations. **Phone:** (603) 823-5510.

IRON FURNACE INTERPRETIVE CENTER is off I-93 exit 38 near jct. SRs 18 and 117. This park on the Gale River features historical exhibits centered on Franconia's early iron industry. Included are a scale model of the furnace and cast house, production tools and outdoor interpretive panels. Remains of the original stone stack across the river can be viewed from the park. **Time:** Allow 30 minutes minimum. **Hours:** Grounds daily dawn-dusk. Interpretive center Fri.-Sat. 1-4, Memorial Day weekend-Oct. 31; by appointment rest of year. **Cost:** Donations. **Phone:** (603) 823-5000.

NEW ENGLAND SKI MUSEUM, 135 Tramway Dr. next to the Cannon Mountain Aerial Tramway (see attraction listing p. 192), details the history of Nordic and alpine skiing through artworks, a DVD presentation, photographs and exhibits of clothing and equipment. **Hours:** Daily 10-5, June-Mar. **Cost:** Free. **Phone:** (800) 639-4181.

BEST WESTERN WHITE MOUNTAIN INN   (603)823-7422

 Hotel $90-$210

AAA Benefit: Members save 10% or more with Best Western.

Address: 87 Wallace Hill Rd 03580 **Location:** I-93 exit 38, just e. **Facility:** 60 units. 2 stories (no elevator), interior corridors. **Parking:** winter plug-ins. **Terms:** 2 night minimum stay - seasonal, 3 day cancellation notice. **Pool(s):** heated indoor. **Activities:** saunas, whirlpool, exercise room. **Guest Services:** coin laundry. **Free Special Amenities:** expanded continental breakfast and high-speed Internet. (See ad p. 209.)

FRANCONIA INN   (603)823-5542

▼▼▼ Country Inn $129-$249

Address: 1172 Easton Rd (Rt 116) 03580 **Location:** I-93 exit 38, 2.3 mi sw. **Facility:** A scenic mountain is the backdrop for this inn, which offers cozy common areas and varied-size rooms with some antique furnishings. 34 units, some two bedrooms, efficiencies and kitchens. 3 stories (no elevator), interior corridors. **Parking:** winter plug-ins. **Terms:** 7 day cancellation notice. **Dining:** restaurant, see separate listing. **Pool(s):** heated outdoor. **Activities:** whirlpool, fishing, 4 tennis courts, cross country skiing, ice skating, bicycles. **Fee:** horseback riding, game room.

GALE RIVER MOTEL   603/823-5655

▼ Motel $60-$220 **Address:** 1 Main St 03580 **Location:** I-93 exit 38, 0.8 mi n on SR 18. **Facility:** 12 units, some efficiencies and cottages. 1 story, exterior corridors. **Terms:** 7 day cancellation notice-fee imposed. **Pool(s):** heated outdoor. **Activities:** whirlpools, playground, horseshoes, shuffleboard. **Guest Services:** valet laundry.

LOVETTS INN BY LAFAYETTE BROOK   603/823-7761

▼▼▼ **Historic Country Inn** $155-$255 **Address:** 1474 Profile Rd 03580 **Location:** I-93 exit 38, just w on Wallace Hill Rd, then 2.1 mi s on SR 18. **Facility:** This 1784 inn overlooks the mountains and offers attractively furnished guest rooms as well as cottages with fireplaces. 18 units, some cottages. 1-2 stories (no elevator), interior/exterior corridors. **Terms:** closed 4/1-4/30 & 11/1-11/15, 7 day cancellation notice-fee imposed. **Dining:** Lovetts Inn by Lafayette Brook Restaurant, see separate listing. **Pool(s):** outdoor. **Activities:** cross country skiing, bicycle trails, shuffleboard.

🍴 🍸 🐟 ✕ 🏊 / SOME UNITS FEE 🐕 🐾 🛗 🖥

STONYBROOK MOTEL & LODGE   (603)823-5800

▼▼ **Motel** $69-$179 **Address:** 1098 Profile Rd 03580 **Location:** I-93 exit 38, just w on Wallace Hill Rd, then 1.5 mi s on SR 18. **Facility:** 23 units. 1-2 stories (no elevator), interior/exterior corridors. **Terms:** 2 night minimum stay - weekends, 3 day cancellation notice-fee imposed. **Pool(s):** heated outdoor, heated indoor. **Activities:** cross country skiing, hiking trails. *Fee:* game room.

🐟 📶 ✕ 🛗 🖥 / SOME UNITS 🖥

WHERE TO EAT

FRANCONIA INN   603/823-5542

▼▼▼ Regional American. Casual Dining. $19-$29 **AAA Inspector Notes:** *Classic.* The frequently updated menu here offers many meals with a Continental touch. Specialties include lamb and seasonal seafood, with a good selection of health-conscious items. The unpretentious elegance of the decor offers fine views of the White Mountains. **Bar:** full bar. **Reservations:** suggested. **Address:** 1172 Easton Rd (Rt 116) 03580 **Location:** I-93 exit 38, 2.3 mi sw.

B   D

LOVETTS INN BY LAFAYETTE BROOK RESTAURANT
    603/823-7761

▼▼▼ Continental. Fine Dining. $18-$25 **AAA Inspector Notes:** This informal dining room, located in an 18th-century inn, has elegant table tops, antique hard-wood chairs and quality wood trimmed walls. Guests may enjoy such entrees as pasta primavera, chicken forestiere, roast pork tenderloin, roast duck, rack of lamb, beef tenderloin and pan-fried boneless trout. **Bar:** full bar. **Reservations:** suggested. **Address:** 1474 Profile Rd 03580 **Location:** I-93 exit 38, just w on Wallace Hill Rd, then 2.1 mi s on SR 18; in Lovetts Inn by Lafayette Brook. B   D

FRANCONIA NOTCH (C-4)

Franconia Notch is perhaps the most celebrated mountain gap in the East. A gap between the towering Kinsman and Franconia ranges, it has more scenic spots than any other White Mountain notch. It is crossed by I-93 from Echo Lake, southwest of Twin Mountain, to Lincoln.

The grandeur of the notch most likely was first seen by white settlers in the late 18th century. Its fame spread quickly, and by the mid-1800s it was a favorite tourist destination, with huge hotels to accommodate a plethora of visitors. Although the hotels no longer exist, throngs of visitors continue to enjoy the area's scenic and recreational aspects, many of which are within Franconia Notch State Park *(see Recreation Areas Chart).*

Franconia Notch Chamber of Commerce: 421 Main St., P.O. Box 780, Franconia, NH 03580. **Phone:** (603) 823-5661.

THE BASIN, reached by trail from US 3 n. of The Flume Gorge *(see attraction listing),* is a deep glacial pothole at the base of a waterfall. Measuring 20 feet in diameter and 15 feet deep, its sides have been polished smooth by sand, stones and water.

Below the basin the Pemigewasset River tumbles through the Baby Flume, a smaller version of the well-known gorge. The area includes walking paths, hiking trails and picnic tables. **Phone:** (603) 745-8391. 🏕

CANNON MOUNTAIN AERIAL TRAMWAY, off I-93 exit 34B, extends from Valley Station to the top of Cannon Mountain. During the summer, when this popular ski mountain isn't buried in snow and swarming with skiers and snowboarders, you can hop aboard an 80-passenger aerial tram car that will whisk you to the summit where you can enjoy spectacular views of the surrounding mountains and valleys of Franconia Notch State Park and the White Mountain National Forest *(see place listing p. 253).* Foot trails lead from the observation platform to overlooks from which, on a clear day, you can see four states and the province of Québec.

The current tramway, inaugurated in 1980, is the second to operate on this breathtaking spot. Its predecessor is said to have been the first aerial tram in North America, having made its first trip up to the 4,180-foot-high summit back in 1938.

RV campsites are available. **Time:** Allow 1 hour minimum. **Hours:** Daily 9-5, mid-May to mid-Oct. (weather permitting). **Cost:** Round trip $15; $12 (ages 6-12). One-way trip $13; $10 (ages 6-12). **Phone:** (603) 823-8800. 🅰 🍴

ECHO LAKE, at the n. end of Franconia Notch, is bounded by mountains on three sides. Named for the acoustical phenomenon resulting from its setting, the lake is the largest body of water in the notch and offers boating, fishing and swimming. **Hours:** Beach open daily 10-5, late June-Labor Day. **Cost:** Beach $4; $2 (ages 6-11). Boat rental $20 per hour. **Phone:** (603) 823-5563. ✕

THE FLUME GORGE, 852 Daniel Webster Hwy. (SR 3), at the s. end of Franconia Notch State Park, is a chasm extending nearly 800 feet along the flank of Mount Liberty. A mountain stream tumbles in a series of waterfalls and pools between its 60- to 90-foot-high granite walls. An optional shuttle bus takes visitors the first half-mile; it is then a 1.5-mile walk through the flume back to the visitor center. A well-constructed boardwalk leads through the gorge; there are, however, some steep grades. Within the flume are two covered bridges, waterfalls and cascades.

Time: Allow 1 hour minimum. **Hours:** Daily 9-5:30, July-Aug.; 9-5, early May-June 30 and Sept. 1 to mid-Oct. Phone ahead to confirm schedule. **Cost:** $15; $12 (ages 6-12). Prices may vary; phone ahead. **Phone:** (603) 745-8391.

RECREATIONAL ACTIVITIES
Skiing
- **Cannon Mountain** is off I-93 exit 34B. Other activities are offered. **Hours:** Mon.-Fri. 9-4, Sat.-Sun. 8:30-4, Dec.-Mar. Phone ahead to confirm schedule. **Phone:** (603) 823-8800, or (603) 823-7771 for snow information.

FRANKLIN (E-3) pop. 8,477, elev. 354'

Upon separating from the town of Salisbury in 1820, citizens first thought to name their community after New Hampshire native Daniel Webster. But the state already had a town called Webster, so Benjamin Franklin was honored instead.

Franklin flourished as a milling and industrial community, capitalizing on the water power made available by its location at the confluence of the Pemigewasset and Winnipesaukee rivers. Old mill buildings, dams and the upside-down, covered Sulphite Bridge provide a historical perspective on industry and transportation.

Other reminders of the past include the 1892 Franklin Opera House, a Romanesque Revival structure, and the 1820 Congregational Christian Church, Franklin's first church. In front of the church, 47 S. Main St., is a bust of Daniel Webster created by Daniel Chester French, sculptor of the seated Abraham Lincoln in the Lincoln Memorial in Washington, D.C.

The Winnipesaukee River Trail is a multiuse scenic trail with numerous viewing areas near downtown Franklin. White-water kayaking is a popular recreational activity.

DANIEL WEBSTER BIRTHPLACE is off SR 127, 3.5 mi. s. via US 3. Webster was born in the two-room house in 1782. The house contains period antiques and relics. Living-history programs are offered. **Time:** Allow 30 minutes minimum. **Hours:** Sat.-Sun. and holidays 9-5, late June-Labor Day. Last admission 1 hour before closing. **Cost:** $7; $3 (ages 6-11); free (New Hampshire residents). **Phone:** (603) 934-5057, or (603) 271-3556 during the off-season.

TARBIN GARDENS is at 321 Salisbury Rd. English-style gardens include flowering trees, shrubs and perennials; maps are provided to assist visitors. Other highlights include tropical and succulent greenhouses, a children's play area, and koi and water lily ponds. Animals on site include Highland cattle, a hinny, goats, peacocks and chickens. English cream tea can be enjoyed on the grounds June through September. **Time:** Allow 1 hour minimum. **Hours:** Tues.-Sun. and Mon. holidays 10-6, Sat. before Mother's Day-Columbus Day. Guided tours are given Tues.-Sun. at 11. **Cost:** $8.50; $7 (ages 4-17, ages 62+ and students with ID); $25 (family). **Phone:** (603) 934-3518. 🏧

GILFORD (E-4) elev. 738'

RECREATIONAL ACTIVITIES
Recreational Complex
- **Gunstock Mountain Resort** is 7 mi. e. on SR 11A. **Hours:** Various activities are offered year-round, including skiing, tubing, scenic lift rides, a zipline course and Segway tours. Phone ahead to confirm schedule. **Phone:** (603) 293-4341 or (800) 486-7862.

BELKNAP POINT MOTEL   603/293-7511

Motel $77-$150 **Address:** 107 Rt 11 03249 **Location:** Waterfront. 1 mi e of jct SR 11B. **Facility:** 16 units, some efficiencies. 1-2 stories (no elevator), interior/exterior corridors. **Terms:** 2-3 night minimum stay - seasonal and/or weekends, 14 day cancellation notice-fee imposed. **Activities:** limited beach access, fishing. *Fee:* boat dock. 📶 🚫 / SOME UNITS 🍴 🖥 🍺

FIRESIDE RESORT INN & SUITES   (603)293-7526

Hotel $90-$270 **Address:** 17 Harris Shore Rd 03249 **Location:** Jct SR 11 and 11B, 2.5 mi e of jct US 3 N. **Facility:** 83 units, some kitchens. 2 stories (no elevator), interior corridors. **Terms:** cancellation fee imposed. **Pool(s):** heated outdoor, heated indoor. **Activities:** whirlpool, beach access, ice skating, basketball, exercise room. *Fee:* massage. ⏸ CALL 📶 🚫 🍺 / SOME UNITS FEE 🐾 🍴 🖥

THE INN AT SMITH COVE   (603)293-1111

Bed & Breakfast $90-$180 **Address:** 19 Roberts Rd 03249 **Location:** Waterfront. SR 11, 3 mi e of jct US 3 N. **Facility:** Rooms are individually decorated and retain a cottage feel at this restored 1894 Victorian home; a dock and gazebo border the lake. 12 units. 3 stories (no elevator), interior/exterior corridors. **Terms:** 2 night minimum stay - seasonal and/or weekends, 7 day cancellation notice. **Activities:** beach access, fishing. *Fee:* boat dock. 📶 🚫 ☎

TOWNEPLACE SUITES BY MARRIOTT GILFORD   (603)524-5533

Extended Stay Hotel $119-$329 **Address:** 14 Sawmill Rd 03249 **Location:** Just e of jct SR 3 and 11A. **Facility:** 75 units, some two bedrooms, efficiencies and kitchens. 3 stories, interior corridors. **Pool(s):** heated indoor. **Activities:** exercise room. **Guest Services:** valet and coin laundry. CALL 📶 🚫 🖥 / SOME UNITS FEE 🐾

AAA Benefit:
AAA hotel discounts of 5% or more.

WHERE TO EAT

LYONS' DEN RESTAURANT & TAVERN   603/293-8833

American. Casual Dining. $7-$30 **AAA Inspector Notes:** Gaze at the spectacular mountain view at the lakefront eatery, accessible by car or boat. **Bar:** full bar. **Reservations:** suggested. **Address:** 25 Dock Rd 03249 **Location:** 0.5 mi e of SR 11 and 11B, just n on Glendale Pl and Dock Rd; at Glendale Docks. L D

PATRICK'S PUB & EATERY   603/293-0841

Irish. Casual Dining. $8-$18 **AAA Inspector Notes:** This Irish-style pub has two sections: one with a lively bar atmosphere and a quieter area which is appropriate for families. The large-portioned dishes are tasty. A gluten-free menu is available. **Bar:** full bar. **Address:** 18 Weirs Rd 03249 **Location:** Jct SR 11 and 11B; in Gilford Square. L D

PEKING TOKYO   603/524-8150

Japanese. Casual Dining. $5-$16 **AAA Inspector Notes:** The restaurant specializes in Chinese and Japanese cuisine, including fresh sushi that's made-to-order at a sushi bar. It is the perfect place to take a break from shopping. **Bar:** full bar. **Address:** 1458 Lakeshore Dr 03249 **Location:** On SR 11, jct US 3 and SR 11, just s; in Walmart Plaza. L D

Find thousands of places to show your card and save at AAA.com/discounts

GLEN (D-4) elev. 544'
• Hotels & Restaurants map & index p. 225

An access point to both Franconia Notch *(see place listing p. 192)* and Pinkham Notch *(see place listing p. 235)*, Glen is an important link in the chain of communities in the Mount Washington Valley. Nearby ski areas include a large cross-country skiing center.

STORY LAND, .5 mi. n. of US 302 on SR 16, is a family park with familiar fairy tale themes. Visitors can shoot water cannons at Splash Battle: Pharaoh's Reign, experience Dr. Geyser's Remarkable Raft Ride, take an African safari or a journey on the Polar Coaster, visit the Oceans of Fun Sprayground or ride aboard a swan boat or pumpkin coach. Children can meet Cinderella and see how vegetables grow at the Farm Follies Theater.

Time: Allow a full day. **Hours:** Daily 9-6, mid-June through Aug. 31; Fri.-Sun. 9-5, Memorial Day weekend to mid-June and Sept. 1-Columbus Day. Last admission 45 minutes before closing. Phone ahead to confirm schedule. **Cost:** $29.99; $27.99 (ages 60+); $26.99 (active military with ID); free (ages 0-2). Stroller rental $6 (single); $8 (double). Free kennel service is available on a first-come, first-served basis. **Phone:** (603) 383-4186. [icons]

COVERED BRIDGE HOUSE   (603)383-9109 22
WWWW **Historic Bed & Breakfast** $89-$139 **Address:** 404 US 302 03838 **Location:** Waterfront. On US 302, 1.9 mi w of jct SR 16. **Facility:** A covered bridge built in 1850 houses a gift shop at this riverfront B&B, which offers well-appointed accommodations. 5 units, some two bedrooms. 2 stories (no elevator), interior corridors. **Terms:** 2 night minimum stay - seasonal and/or weekends, 14 day cancellation notice-fee imposed. **Activities:** whirlpool, playground.
[icons] / SOME UNITS

GOLDEN APPLE INN   (603)383-9680 21
WW **Motel** $60-$229 **Address:** 322 Route 302 03838 **Location:** On US 302, 1 mi w of jct SR 16. **Facility:** 17 units, some two bedrooms. 2 stories, interior/exterior corridors. **Terms:** 2 night minimum stay - seasonal and/or weekends. **Pool(s):** outdoor. **Activities:** playground. [icons BIZ]

WILL'S INN   603/383-6757 23
W   **Address:** 440 US 302 03838 **Location:**
Motel   On US 302, 2 mi w of jct SR 16. **Facility:** 32 units, some two bedrooms,
$49-$235 kitchens, houses and cabins. 1-2 stories (no elevator), exterior corridors. **Terms:** 10 day cancellation notice-fee imposed. **Pool(s):** heated outdoor. **Activities:** playground, basketball, volleyball. **Guest Services:** coin laundry. **Free Special Amenities:** high-speed Internet and use of on-premises laundry facilities.
[SAVE icons] / SOME UNITS FEE [icons]

GORHAM (C-4) pop. 1,600, elev. 801'

A gateway to the Great North Woods, Gorham is home to several miles of scenic and challenging trails, including a section of the Appalachian Trail.

MOUNT WASHINGTON AUTO ROAD—see Mount Washington p. 219.

RECREATIONAL ACTIVITIES
Winter Activities
• **Great Glen Trails** is on SR 16 at Pinkham Notch, 8 mi. s. of jct. SR 16 and US 2. Other activities are offered. **Hours:** Daily 8:30-4:30, late Nov.-early Apr.; 9-5, rest of year. Phone ahead to confirm schedule. **Phone:** (603) 466-2333.

MOOSE BROOK MOTEL   603/466-5400
W **Motel** $59-$89 **Address:** 65 Lancaster Rd 03581 **Location:** Jct SR 16, 0.5 mi w on US 2. **Facility:** 13 units, some two bedrooms and kitchens. 1 story, exterior corridors. **Terms:** closed 10/21-5/16, 7 day cancellation notice. **Pool(s):** outdoor.
 / SOME UNITS FEE [icons]

ROYALTY INN (603)466-3312

▼▼◆◆ Hotel $69-$169 Address: 130 Main St 03581 Location: On US 2 and SR 16; center. Facility: 88 units, some efficiencies. 1-2 stories (no elevator), interior/exterior corridors. Parking: winter plug-ins. Amenities: high-speed Internet. Pool(s): heated outdoor, heated indoor. Activities: sauna, whirlpool, racquetball courts, basketball. Fee: game room. Guest Services: coin laundry.

[ECO] [🍴] [🍸] CALL [🔊M] [🚭] [🏋️] [📶] [📶] [🛎️] [📺] / SOME UNITS FEE [🐕] [💻]

TOP NOTCH INN (603)466-5496

▼▼▼▼ Motel $69-$149

Address: 265 Main St 03581 Location: On US 2 and SR 16; center. Facility: 37 units, some three bedrooms and kitchens. 1-2 stories (no elevator), interior/exterior corridors. Terms: closed 10/27-5/8. Pool(s): outdoor. Activities: whirlpool. Guest Services: coin laundry. Free Special Amenities: local telephone calls and newspaper.

[SAVE] [🍴] [🚭] [📶] [✕] [📺] / SOME UNITS [🐕] [🛎️] [📺]

TOWN & COUNTRY INN & RESORT (603)466-3315

▼▼◆◆ Hotel $68-$148 Address: 20 SR 2 03581 Location: 0.5 mi e of jct SR 16. Facility: 160 units. 2 stories, interior/exterior corridors. Parking: winter plug-ins. Dining: Town & Country Inn & Resort Dining Room, see separate listing. Pool(s): heated indoor. Activities: sauna, whirlpool, steamroom, snowmobiling, bicycle trails, hiking trails, jogging, exercise room. Fee: golf-18 holes, game room. Guest Services: valet laundry, area transportation-bus station.

[🛫] [🍴] [🍸] [🚭] [BIZ] [📶] [📺] / SOME UNITS FEE [🐕] [🛎️] [📺]

WHERE TO EAT

J'S CORNER RESTAURANT & LOUNGE 603/466-5132

▼▼ American. Casual Dining. $7-$28 AAA Inspector Notes: The family restaurant serves up an array of comfort foods, from barbecue chicken to fried or baked seafood to pasta and steaks. The restaurant has a casual ambience and the lounge area may get more lively as the night continues. Bar: full bar. Address: 277 Main St 03581 Location: On US 2 and SR 16. [L] [D]

MARY'S PIZZA & PASTA 603/752-6150

▼▼▼ Italian Family Dining $5-$17

AAA Inspector Notes: Established in 1947, this third-generation family diner specializes in award-winning pizzas and homemade pasta dishes. Fettuccine Alfredo, spaghetti with white clam sauce, linguine and manicotti are available in both small and large portions. Bar: beer & wine. Address: 9 Cascade Flats 03581 Location: 4 mi n on SR 16 from jct US 2; 2 mi s on SR 16 from jct SR 110. Menu on AAA.com [L] [D]

MR. PIZZA FAMILY RESTAURANT & CRACKER JACK LOUNGE 603/466-5573

▼▼ American. Casual Dining. $6-$19 AAA Inspector Notes: Enjoy more than just pizza at this family restaurant. Steak, seafood, hamburgers and sandwiches are on the menu, too. Not hungry? You can just kick back in the lounge and enjoy a drink. Bar: full bar. Address: 160 Main St 03581 Location: On US 2 and SR 16; center. [L] [D]

TOWN & COUNTRY INN & RESORT DINING ROOM 603/466-3315

▼▼ American. Casual Dining. $10-$30 AAA Inspector Notes: The varied menu features New England prime beef, chops and fresh seafood. The dining room is informal and pleasantly decorated. Menu items include filet mignon, New York sirloin, lamb chops, pork chops, veal cutlets, Maine lobster, filet of haddock, cape scallops and vegetable linguini. Bar: full bar. Address: 20 SR 2 03581 Location: 0.5 mi e of jct SR 16; in Town & Country Inn & Resort. [B] [D]

YOKOHAMA RESTAURANT 603/466-2501

▼▼▼▼ Japanese. Casual Dining. $4-$18 AAA Inspector Notes: The menu features a good selection of American dishes in addition to the well-prepared and nicely presented Japanese offerings. You'll find that the serving staff is home-style friendly and attentive. The traditional decor is comfortable. Bar: full bar. Address: 288 Main St 03581 Location: 0.8 mi n on US 2 and SR 16. [L] [D]

GRAFTON (E-3) elev. 841'

RUGGLES MINE is off SR 4 at the Village Green. Mica was first mined in the area by Sam Ruggles in 1803; by 1868 New Hampshire was the country's sole producer. Visitors can explore the open pit mine as well as tunnels and cave-like rooms with arched ceilings to collect minerals. Findings might include beryl, feldspar, mica and quartz. Splendid views of the surroundings are available from the mine entrance atop Isinglass Mountain.

Time: Allow 1 hour minimum. **Hours:** Daily 9-5, mid-June to mid-Oct.; Sat.-Sun. 9-5, mid-May to mid-June. Last admission 1 hour before closing. **Cost:** $25; $13 (ages 4-11). **Phone:** (603) 523-4275.

GRANTHAM

BISTRO NOUVEAU 603/863-8000

▼▼ American. Casual Dining. $7-$21 AAA Inspector Notes: Located at the golf course, this restaurant offers fresh, creative cuisine. Each entrée is paired with a suggested wine. Bar: full bar. Address: 6 Clubhouse Ln 03753 Location: I-89 exit 13; in Center at Eastman. [D]

HAMPTON (F-5) pop. 9,656, elev. 52'
• Hotels p. 196 • Restaurants p. 196

One of New Hampshire's earliest towns, Hampton was settled in 1638. The town first was called the Plantation of Winnacunnet. *Winnacunnet* is an Abenaki Indian word meaning "pleasant pines." The first tax-supported public school was established in Winnacunnet in 1649 for the education of both boys and girls. The Tuck Museum on Meeting House Green, 40 Park Ave., depicts facets of Hampton's history; phone (603) 929-0781. Across from the Green, Founders Park contains 42 stones representing the town's earliest families.

Hampton Area Chamber of Commerce: 1 Lafayette Rd., Hampton, NH 03842. **Phone:** (603) 926-8718 or (603) 926-8717.

BEST WESTERN PLUS THE INN AT HAMPTON
(603)926-6771

Hotel
$99-$189

Best Western
PLUS

AAA Benefit: Members save 10% or more with Best Western.

Address: 815 Lafayette Rd, US 1 03842 **Location:** 0.5 mi n on US 1. **Facility:** 71 units, some two bedrooms and efficiencies. 2 stories (no elevator), interior corridors. **Amenities:** high-speed Internet, safes. **Pool(s):** heated indoor. **Activities:** exercise room. **Fee:** game room. **Guest Services:** valet and coin laundry. **Free Special Amenities:** local telephone calls and high-speed Internet.

  CALL

LAMIE'S INN AND THE OLD SALT
(603)926-0330

Country Inn
$99-$180

Address: 490 Lafayette Rd 03842 **Location:** Jct SR 27 on US 1. **Facility:** This service-oriented country inn has a cozy atmosphere offering modern amenities and B&B hospitality. 32 units. 2 stories (no elevator), interior corridors. **Terms:** 2 night minimum stay - seasonal and/or weekends, 3 day cancellation notice. **Amenities:** *Some:* high-speed Internet. **Dining:** Old Salt Eating & Drinking Place, see separate listing. **Guest Services:** valet laundry. *(See ad p. 243.)*

 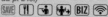

 / SOME UNITS FEE

THE VICTORIA INN
603/929-1437

Bed & Breakfast. Rates not provided. **Address:** 430 High St 03842 **Location:** Jct US 1, 1.7 mi e on SR 27. **Facility:** In summer, English-style gardens grace the grounds of this attractive inn, which dates from 1875. 6 units, some two bedrooms. 3 stories (no elevator), interior corridors. **Bath:** some shared.

---

401 TAVERN
603/926-8800

American. Casual Dining. $8-$24 **AAA Inspector Notes:** The menu at this casual and classic tavern features some traditional pub fare, such as bangers and mash and shepherd's pie, as well as seafood and steaks. **Bar:** full bar. **Reservations:** suggested. **Address:** 401 Lafayette Rd (US 1) 03842 **Location:** On US 1, just s of jct SR 27; center of village. L D LATE

THE GALLEY HATCH RESTAURANT & KAY'S KAFE
603/926-6152

American. Casual Dining. $9-$26 **AAA Inspector Notes:** The freshly-baked desserts, pastries and breads are themselves worth the trip. However, the main dishes are terrific as well, including fresh fish, roasted chicken, New York sirloin and a variety of creative sandwiches. **Bar:** full bar. **Address:** 325 Lafayette Rd (Rt 1) 03842 **Location:** On US 1, just s of jct SR 27. L D

OLD SALT EATING & DRINKING PLACE
603/926-8322

Seafood. Casual Dining. $7-$22 **AAA Inspector Notes:** In a pleasant country inn, this renovated dining room resembles an old barn with high, beamed ceilings and decor fitting a traditional New England theme. The menu features well-prepared steaks and seafood. Everything is made from scratch, including the salad dressing. Portions are huge. **Bar:** full bar. **Address:** 490 Lafayette Rd 03842 **Location:** Jct SR 27 on US 1; in Lamie's Inn and The Old Salt. *(See ad p. 243.)* L D

RON'S LANDING AT ROCKY BEND
603/929-2122

Seafood. Casual Dining. $23-$37 **AAA Inspector Notes:** The restaurant specializes in fresh seafood, but the menu also lists beef, veal, chicken and pasta dishes. Check out the dessert menu, too. The casually elegant dining room affords great views of the ocean. **Bar:** full bar. **Reservations:** suggested. **Address:** 379 Ocean Blvd 03842 **Location:** I-95 exit 2, just e on SR 101 to SR 1A, then 0.3 mi n. D

HAMPTON BEACH   pop. 2,275

ASHWORTH BY THE SEA HOTEL   603/926-6762

▼▼▼▼ **Hotel.** Rates not provided. **Address:** 295 Ocean Blvd 03842 **Location:** Oceanfront. I-95 exit 2, 3 mi e on SR 101. **Facility:** 105 units. 3-4 stories, interior corridors. **Dining:** 3 restaurants, entertainment. **Pool(s):** heated indoor. **Activities:** limited beach access, exercise room. **Guest Services:** valet laundry. *(See ad this page.)*

▼ *See AAA listing this page* ▼

HANCOCK pop. 204

THE HANCOCK INN   603/525-3318
▼▼▼▼ **Historic Country Inn.** Rates not provided. **Address:** 33 Main St 03449 **Location:** Jct SR 123 and 137; center. **Facility:** Circa 1789, this small-town property is one of the oldest continuously operating inns in New England. Front porch rockers offer a pleasant way to relax. First-rate dining is prepared on site. 13 units. 3 stories (no elevator), interior corridors. **Dining:** restaurant, see separate listing.
[🍴] [📶] [✕] / SOME UNITS [🐾]

WHERE TO EAT

FIDDLEHEAD'S CAFE   603/525-4432
▼ **Deli.** Casual Dining. $5-$12 **AAA Inspector Notes:** A local, loyal following patronizes the casual cafe. This eatery uses local ingredients, especially New Hampshire maple syrup and honey. Tasty sandwiches, homemade pies and fresh-brewed coffee are among the favorites. **Address:** 28 Main St 03449 **Location:** Jct SR 123 and 137; center. **Parking:** street only. [B] [L] [D]

THE HANCOCK INN   603/525-3318
▼▼▼ **American.** Casual Dining. $9-$28 **AAA Inspector Notes:** Inside New Hampshire's oldest inn, built in 1789, this gem turns out exquisitely prepared, attractively presented dishes. Service is excellent. **Bar:** full bar. **Reservations:** suggested. **Address:** 33 Main St 03449 **Location:** Jct SR 123 and 137; center. [D]

HANOVER (E-2) pop. 8,636, elev. 603'
• Restaurants p. 200

When Rev. Eleazar Wheelock arrived in Hanover to establish the school that was to be an experiment in spreading Christian education to the Abenaki Indians and other youth, he found a staid agricultural village of about 20 families. The purpose of the school failed so Wheelock enlarged it to include a college for the education of whites in the classics, philosophy and literature. In 1769 and despite objections from Lord Dartmouth, the head of the British Board of Trustees, Wheelock named the school Dartmouth College. The community and the college quickly established a symbiotic relationship that continues to the present, each growing and prospering with the other.

Hanover Area Chamber of Commerce: 53 S. Main St., Suite 208, P.O. Box 5105, Hanover, NH 03755. **Phone:** (603) 643-3115.

DARTMOUTH COLLEGE is centered on the Dartmouth Green at W. Wheelock St. Founded in 1769, Dartmouth is the ninth-oldest college in the nation and the northernmost of the eight Ivy League institutions.

From one log hut built by Rev. Eleazar Wheelock in 1770, the campus has grown to include many structures in several architectural styles. Notable Dartmouth Row includes the college's first four classroom buildings, the oldest of which dates from 1784. The Thompson Arena and the Leverone Field House, both designed by Pier Luigi Nervi, are examples of the modern use of architecture. **Phone:** (603) 646-1110, (603) 646-2466 for athletic tickets, or (603) 646-2422 for performing arts tickets.

Baker-Berry Library, 6025 Baker-Berry Library, faces the Green on the Dartmouth College campus.

This 1928 Georgian structure contains more than 2.5 million volumes. Murals painted by Mexican artist José Clemente Orozco cover 3,200 square feet and depict the story of civilization on the American continents. **Tours:** Guided tours are available. **Hours:** Library Mon.-Fri. 8 a.m.-2 a.m., Sat.-Sun. 10 a.m.-2 a.m. Murals Mon.-Thurs. 8 a.m.-midnight, Fri. 8-6, Sat. 10-6, Sun. 10 a.m.-midnight. Schedule varies during campus holidays; phone ahead to confirm schedule. **Cost:** Free. **Phone:** (603) 646-2560 or (603) 646-2704.

Hood Museum of Art is on the Dartmouth College campus at 6 E. Wheelock St. Permanent collections include ancient and Asian art; European paintings, drawings and sculpture; American silver and paintings; Oceanic, African and American Indian art objects; and contemporary works by artists ranging from Pablo Picasso to Edward Ruscha. Second-floor galleries present changing exhibits. Public programs are held year-round. **Hours:** Tues.-Sat. 10-5 (also Wed. 5-9), Sun. noon-5. Closed major holidays. **Cost:** Free. **Phone:** (603) 646-2808.

Hopkins Center, on the Dartmouth College campus at 2 E. Wheelock St., was architect Wallace Harrison's prototype for his Metropolitan Opera House at Lincoln Center in New York City. Opened in 1962, Hopkins Center presents artists in music, dance and theatre, plus student performances, a film series and galleries with various works. **Hours:** Building open daily 7:30 a.m.-midnight; reduced hours during campus holidays. Box office open Mon.-Fri. 10-6, Sat. 1-6. **Cost:** Building free. Performances priced individually. **Phone:** (603) 646-2422.

SIX SOUTH STREET HOTEL HANOVER   (603)643-0600

▼▼▼ Hotel $259-$389

Address: 6 South St 03755 **Location:** I-89 exit 18, n on SR 120 to Lebanon St, left on Sanborn Rd (which becomes South St). **Facility:** 69 units. 4 stories, interior corridors. **Parking:** on-site (fee) and valet. **Activities:** exercise room. **Free Special Amenities:** high-speed Internet. *(See also p. 199.)*
[SAVE] [🍴] [🍸] [BIZ] [📶] [✕] [🔌] [💻] / SOME UNITS FEE [🐾]

THE HANOVER INN DARTMOUTH   603/643-4300
[fyi] Not evaluated. **Address:** 2 E Wheelock St 03755 **Location:** Center. Facilities, services, and décor characterize an upscale property.

Share a New View on Travel at AAATravelViews.com

▼ *See AAA listing p. 198* ▼

JESSE'S   603/643-4111

▼▼▼
American
Casual Dining
$11-$25

AAA Inspector Notes: Famous for prime rib and fresh Maine lobster dishes, the restaurant offers house specialties such as teriyaki sirloin, peppercorn steak and delectable desserts. The rustic log cabin has three distinct dining rooms: Victorian, Adirondack and Greenhouse. **Bar:** full bar. **Address:** 224 Lebanon St (SR 120) 03755 **Location:** I-89 exit 18, 3 mi n. *Menu on AAA.com* D

LOU'S RESTAURANT & BAKERY   603/643-3321

▼▼ American. Quick Serve. $7-$10 **AAA Inspector Notes:** Since 1947, the establishment has been serving breakfast all day, every day as the specialty. It has been a favorite breakfast spot of many Upper Valley residents for years. Lunch favorites include sandwiches, burgers, salads, quiche and Mexican dishes. Don't miss the delicious pies, cakes and other goodies prepared daily in the on-site bakery. **Address:** 30 S Main St 03755 **Location:** Center. **Parking:** street only. ECO B L

MAI THAI   603/643-9980

▼▼▼ Thai. Casual Dining. $6-$16 **AAA Inspector Notes:** Authentic Thai cuisine is served at this restaurant, located in the heart of this quaint New England town near Dartmouth College. **Bar:** full bar. **Address:** 44 S Main St 03755 **Location:** Corner of Lebanon St; downtown. **Parking:** street only. L D

MOLLY'S RESTAURANT & BAR   603/643-2570

▼▼▼
American
Casual Dining
$8-$17

AAA Inspector Notes: Located on the Dartmouth College campus, this restaurant offers a casual, comfortable atmosphere; a friendly, attentive staff; imaginative offerings of pizza, pasta, stew, soup, burgers, sandwiches, fish and full dinners; and patio dining. **Bar:** full bar. **Address:** 43 S Main St 03755 **Location:** Center. **Parking:** street only. *Menu on AAA.com* L D

HARTS LOCATION

NOTCHLAND INN   603/374-6131

▼▼▼ Historic Country Inn. Rates not provided. **Address:** 2 Morey Rd 03812 **Location:** On US 302, 6.4 mi w of town. **Facility:** A granite mansion built in 1862 in the midst of the White Mountains, the inn offers elegant public areas. 15 units, some cottages. 2 stories (no elevator), interior/exterior corridors. **Activities:** cross country skiing, ice skating, hiking trails.

/SOME UNITS FEE

HEBRON (E-3)

NEWFOUND AUDUBON CENTER is e. on N. Shore Rd., following signs. Owned by New Hampshire Audubon, the center includes Ash Cottage and the Nature Store, Paradise Point Nature Center and Wildlife Sanctuary, the Hebron Marsh Wildlife Sanctuary and the Bear Mountain Sanctuary. Three nature trails on 43 acres offer opportunities to view wildlife and wildflowers. Educational programs are offered. Bordering Newfound Lake, the nature center features interactive exhibits and live animal displays. **Time:** Allow 1 hour, 30 minutes minimum. **Hours:** Paradise Point Nature Center daily 10-4, July-Aug.; Sat.-Sun. 10-4 in June and Sept. Nature trails daily dawn-dusk. **Cost:** Donations. **Phone:** (603) 744-3516, or (603) 224-9909 in the off-season.

COPPERTOPPE INN & RETREAT CENTER   (603)744-3636

▼▼▼ Bed & Breakfast $139-$279 **Address:** 8 Range Rd 03241 **Location:** I-93 exit 23, 6 mi w on SR 104, 8.7 mi n on SR 3A, then 0.6 mi w on N Shore Rd. Located in a rural area. **Facility:** The property sits in a secluded location on a hill with views of Newfound Lake. The individually decorated guest rooms vary in size. 4 units, some two bedrooms. 2 stories (no elevator), interior corridors. **Terms:** check-in 4 pm, 2 night minimum stay - seasonal and/or weekends, 14 day cancellation notice-fee imposed. **Amenities:** high-speed Internet. **Activities:** whirlpool, exercise room. *Fee:* massage.

ECO BIZ 🛜 ✕ 🐾 🛎 / SOME UNITS FEE 🐕 💻

HENNIKER pop. 1,747

COLBY HILL INN   (603)428-3281

▼▼▼▼ Historic Country Inn $150-$289 **Address:** 33 The Oaks St 03242 **Location:** 0.5 mi s of US 202 and SR 9, via SR 114, 0.5 mi w on Western Ave. Located in a quiet area. **Facility:** Set in a quiet New England village, this 1800s farmhouse is furnished with many antiques. Varied-size rooms, some with a fireplace, are housed in a main house and a carriage house. 14 units. 2 stories (no elevator), interior corridors. **Terms:** 2 night minimum stay - seasonal and/or weekends, age restrictions may apply, 14 day cancellation notice-fee imposed. **Dining:** restaurant, see separate listing. **Pool(s):** outdoor. 🍽 🏊 🛜 ✕ / SOME UNITS 🅆 🛎 💻

HENNIKER MOTEL   (603)428-3536

▼▼ Motel $90-$139 **Address:** 61 Craney Pond Rd 03242 **Location:** I-89 exit 5, 6.5 mi w on US 202 and SR 9 to jct SR 114, 3 mi s to Flanders Rd, then 0.5 mi w, follow signs; adjacent to Pat's Peak. **Facility:** 21 units. 2 stories (no elevator), interior/exterior corridors. **Terms:** check-in 4 pm, 14 day cancellation notice-fee imposed. **Pool(s):** heated indoor.

🛗 🏊 🛜 ✕ 🛎 💻 / SOME UNITS 🐕 📶

COLBY HILL INN   603/428-3281

▼▼▼ American. Fine Dining. $20-$36 **AAA Inspector Notes:** *Historic.* New England favorites are prepared with a Continental flair and served in candlelit dining rooms. The highly trained chefs prepare all dishes from scratch. Delightful perennial gardens and a gazebo surround the 1790 farmhouse. **Bar:** full bar. **Reservations:** suggested, weekends. **Address:** 33 The Oaks St 03242 **Location:** 0.5 mi s of US 202 and SR 9, via SR 114, 0.5 mi w on Western Ave. D

COUNTRY SPIRIT RESTAURANT & TAVERN   603/428-7007

▼▼ American. Casual Dining. $7-$28 **AAA Inspector Notes:** This country-style restaurant is a popular spot which serves up a variety of traditional American dishes. **Bar:** full bar. **Address:** 262 Maple St 03242 **Location:** Jct US 202, SR 9 and 114. L D

ST. GEORGE'S CAFE   603/428-4455

▼ Deli. Quick Serve. $4-$6 **AAA Inspector Notes:** This downtown delicatessen-style café--which serves varied sandwiches, wraps, bagels, desserts and coffees--is ideal for starting the day or enjoying a quick lunch. **Address:** 9 Bridge St 03242 **Location:** Center. **Parking:** street only. B L

HILLSBOROUGH (F-3) pop. 1,976, elev. 580'

Hillsborough comprises several villages that feature Early American architecture, some of which is pre-Revolutionary. Stone arch bridges, built 1830-60 by Scottish stonemasons, are made from locally excavated granite. The town also was the home of the 14th president of the United States, Franklin Pierce.

Fox State Forest, on Center Road 2 miles north, covers 1,445 wooded acres. Its 20 miles of hiking paths become cross-country ski trails in winter; snowshoeing and snowmobiling also are available. Information about local plants and wildlife is available at headquarters; phone (603) 464-3453.

Hillsborough Chamber of Commerce: 25 School St., P.O. Box 541, Hillsborough, NH 03244. **Phone:** (603) 464-5858.

FRANKLIN PIERCE HOMESTEAD NATIONAL HISTORIC LANDMARK, 301 2nd New Hampshire Tpke. (SR 31) near jct. SR 9, was the boyhood home of the 14th president of the United States. The restored 1804 mansion, with its hand-stenciling and period furnishings, reflects the lifestyle of the affluent in the 19th century. **Hours:** Fri.-Tues. 10-4, July-Aug.; Sat.-Sun. 10-4, Memorial Day-June 30 and Sept. 1-Columbus Day. Last tour departs 30 minutes before closing. Off-season tours available by reservation. **Cost:** $5; $3 (ages 6-17); free (New Hampshire residents ages 65+ and military with ID). **Phone:** (603) 478-3165. 🅰

THE COMMON MAN   603/429-3463
▼▼ American. Casual Dining. $9-$24 **AAA Inspector Notes:** This eatery's décor is rustic New England and the comfort food is tasty. A menu of original dishes include the signature lobster and corn chowder, chicken Kiev, steaks and seafood. Do not forget to sample the white chocolate mousse served at the end of each meal. **Bar:** full bar. **Address:** 304 Daniel Webster Hwy 03054 **Location:** On US 3 at Continental Blvd. [L] [D]

HOLDERNESS (D-4)

SQUAM LAKES NATURAL SCIENCE CENTER, jct. SRs 3 and 113 at 23 Science Center Rd., has nature trails featuring interactive live animal exhibits. Owls, bears, deer, bobcats, otters, birds of prey, mountain lions and other New Hampshire wildlife are housed in settings that resemble their natural habitats. The center also includes a public garden and children's activity center. Guided cruises on Squam Lake are available for an additional fee. A variety of programs are offered year-round. **Hours:** Daily 9:30-4:30, May-Nov. 1. Last admission 1 hour before closing. **Cost:** $15; $12 (ages 65+); $10 (ages 3-15). **Phone:** (603) 968-7194.

THE MANOR ON GOLDEN POND   (603)968-3348
▼▼▼ ▼▼▼
Historic
Country Inn
$245-$600
Address: 31 Manor Dr 03245 **Location:** I-93 exit 24, 5 mi e on US 3. **Facility:** This English-style mansion sits atop a knoll overlooking Squam Lake and is graced with lovely grounds and some charming cottages. 24 units, some cottages. 1-2 stories (no elevator), interior/exterior corridors. **Terms:** age restrictions may apply, 30 day cancellation notice-fee imposed. **Dining:** 2 restaurants, also, The Manor Dining Room, see separate listing. **Pool(s):** heated outdoor. **Activities:** lighted tennis court, horseshoes, spa. **Guest Services:** valet laundry. **Free Special Amenities:** full breakfast and high-speed Internet.

 SAVE 🍴 🍸 🏊 BIZ 🛜 ✕ 🖥 / SOME UNITS 🛗

WHERE TO EAT

THE MANOR DINING ROOM   603/968-3348
▼▼▼ ▼▼▼
New American Fine Dining
$25-$42
AAA Inspector Notes: *Historic.* The Manor's creative New American cuisine offers three- or five-course fixed-price dinners that are artistically presented and wonderfully flavorful, with a hint of French influence. The decor is elegant and relaxed; service is superb. **Bar:** full bar. **Reservations:** required. **Address:** 31 Manor Dr 03245 **Location:** I-93 exit 24, 5 mi e on US 3; in The Manor on Golden Pond. *Menu on AAA.com* [D]

WALTER'S BASIN   603/968-4412
▼▼ ▼ American. Casual Dining. $8-$25 **AAA Inspector Notes:** Authentic food like the lobster roll and the Fisherman's Platter make this a favorite spot for the locals. The location on Little Squam Lake and the marina accommodates those arriving via boat. **Bar:** full bar. **Address:** 859 US Rt 3 03245 **Location:** I-93 exit 24, 4 mi e. **Parking:** street only. [L] [D]

HOOKSETT pop. 4,147

FAIRFIELD INN & SUITES BY MARRIOTT HOOKSETT
       (603)606-5485
▼▼▼ ▼ Hotel $99-$219 **Address:** 8 Bell Ave 03106 **Location:** I-93 exit 9N, just n on US 3. **Facility:** 59 units. 3 stories, interior corridors. **Amenities:** high-speed Internet. **Pool(s):** heated indoor. **Activities:** exercise room. **Guest Services:** valet and coin laundry.

AAA Benefit: AAA hotel discounts of 5% or more.

CALL 🛗ᴹ 🏊 BIZ 🛜 ✕ 🖥 / SOME UNITS 🛗 🖨

INTERVALE (D-4) elev. 547'
• Hotels & Restaurants map & index p. 225

HARTMANN MODEL RAILROAD, .2 mi. s. of jct. US 302 and SR 16 at 15 Town Hall Rd., offers displays of domestic and foreign model trains, including a number of operating exhibits. Visitors may ride a small train through the surrounding woods. **Time:** Allow 1 hour minimum. **Hours:** Daily 10-5, July-Aug.; Wed.-Mon. 10-5, in June and Sept.-Oct.; Fri.-Mon. 10-5, rest of year. Closed Easter, Mother's Day, Thanksgiving and Christmas. **Cost:** $6; $5 (ages 60+); $4 (ages 0-12). Cash only. **Phone:** (603) 356-9922.

OLD FIELD HOUSE   (603)356-5478 **12**
▼▼ ▼ Hotel $75-$350 **Address:** 347 NH 16A 03845 **Location:** Jct US 302/SR 16, follow SR 16A Intervale Resort Loop. **Facility:** 20 units, some kitchens. 2 stories (no elevator), interior corridors. **Terms:** 7 day cancellation notice. **Pool(s):** heated outdoor. **Activities:** whirlpool, cross country skiing, basketball, game room. **Guest Services:** coin laundry. 🛗⬆ 🏊 🛜 ✕ 🛗

WHERE TO EAT

THE SCARECROW PUB & GRILL   603/356-2287 **10**
▼▼ ▼ American. Casual Dining. $5-$17 **AAA Inspector Notes:** Newcomers shouldn't let the scarecrows keep them away from this popular watering hole, which has been serving patrons for more than 20 years. A cozy atmosphere and home-style cooking await. **Bar:** full bar. **Address:** 283 RT 302 & 16 03845 **Location:** Jct SR 16A, US 302 W and SR 16 N, 1 mi n on US 302 W and SR 16 N. [L] [D]

JACKSON (C-4)
• Hotels & Restaurants map & index p. 225

The village of Jackson, nestled between several mountain peaks in the White Mountain National Forest (see place listing p. 253), offers visitors numerous year-round recreational opportunities in a picturesque setting.

Jackson Area Chamber of Commerce: 18 Main St., P.O. Box 304, Jackson, NH 03846. **Phone:** (603) 383-9356.

RECREATIONAL ACTIVITIES
Skiing

• **Black Mountain** is n. on SR 16A to SR 16B. Other activities are offered. **Hours:** Daily 9-4, Dec.-Mar. **Phone:** (603) 383-4490, or (800) 475-4669 for snow updates.

• **Jackson Ski Touring Foundation** is n. on SR 16A. **Hours:** Daily 8-4:30, Dec.-Mar. Closed Christmas. **Phone:** (603) 383-9355 or (800) 927-6697.

• **Wildcat Mountain** is n. on SR 16. Other activities are available. **Hours:** Daily 9-4, Nov.-May; 10-5, rest of year. Phone ahead to confirm schedule. **Phone:** (603) 466-3326 or (888) 754-9453.

CHRISTMAS FARM INN & SPA 603/383-4313 **4**

▼▼▼▼ **Historic Country Inn.** Rates not provided. **Address:** 3 Blitzen Way (Rt 16B) 03846 **Location:** Jct SR 16, 0.6 mi e on SR 16A (through Jackson Covered Bridge), then 0.4 mi. **Facility:** Guest rooms at this historic country inn, which can be the base for a romantic getaway or family vacation, are individually decorated and vary in size. 41 units, some two bedrooms and cottages. 1-2 stories (no elevator), interior/exterior corridors. **Pool(s):** heated outdoor, heated indoor. **Activities:** whirlpool, steamroom, cross country skiing, shuffleboard, exercise room, spa.

THE EAGLE MOUNTAIN HOUSE & GOLF CLUB (603)383-9111 **3**

▼▼▼ **Classic Historic Hotel** $79-$229 **Address:** 179 Carter Notch Rd 03846 **Location:** Jct SR 16B, from village center follow SR 16B across the Jackson Covered Bridge to immediate right turn, 0.7 mi n. **Facility:** A charming Old World ambiance enhances this restored turn-of-the-century grand hotel, which is in a picturesque mountain setting. 96 units. 5 stories, interior corridors. **Terms:** 2 night minimum stay - seasonal and/or weekends, 3 day cancellation notice-fee imposed. **Dining:** Highfields Tavern, see separate listing. **Pool(s):** heated outdoor. **Activities:** saunas, whirlpool, tennis court, cross country skiing, tobogganing, hiking trails, playground, exercise room. Fee: golf-9 holes, game room. **Guest Services:** coin laundry.

INN AT ELLIS RIVER 603/383-9339 **2**

▼▼▼ **Bed & Breakfast** $129-$329 **Address:** 17 Harriman Rd 03846 **Location:** Waterfront. SR 16 and 16A at Jackson Covered Bridge, 0.5 mi n. Located in a quiet area. **Facility:** A quiet riverfront setting offers tastefully decorated guest rooms furnished with period antiques and equipped with modern amenities. Many rooms have a fireplace. 21 units, some cottages. 3 stories (no elevator), interior corridors. **Terms:** 2-3 night minimum stay - seasonal and/or weekends, age restrictions may apply, 14 day cancellation notice-fee imposed. **Pool(s):** heated outdoor. **Activities:** sauna, fishing, cross country skiing, game room. Fee: massage.

THE INN AT JACKSON 603-383-4321 **8**

▼▼▼▼ **Bed & Breakfast** $119-$259 **Address:** 12 Thorn Hill Rd 03846 **Location:** Jct SR 16, 0.4 mi e on SR 16A (through Jackson Covered Bridge). **Facility:** On a grassy knoll overlooking the village, this large, traditional-style inn features some guest rooms with a four-poster bed. 14 units. 3 stories (no elevator), interior/exterior corridors. **Terms:** 2 night minimum stay - seasonal, 14 day cancellation notice-fee imposed. **Activities:** cross country skiing, hiking trails.

THE INN AT THORN HILL AND SPA (603)383-4242 **7**

▼▼▼▼ Country Inn $169-$440 **Address:** 40 Thorn Hill Rd 03846 **Location:** Off SR 16A. **Facility:** Stanford White designed this turn-of-the-century home. The main inn's 16 luxurious guest rooms each have a gas fireplace; also offered are three pleasant cottages, plus rooms in a carriage house. 25 units. 3 stories, interior/exterior corridors. **Terms:** 2 night minimum stay - weekends, age restrictions may apply, 14 day cancellation notice-fee imposed. **Dining:** The Inn at Thorn Hill, see separate listing. **Pool(s):** outdoor. **Activities:** sauna, whirlpool, cross country skiing, tobogganing, hiking trails, shuffleboard, exercise room, spa. **Guest Services:** valet laundry. **Free Special Amenities:** full breakfast and local telephone calls.

THE LODGE AT JACKSON VILLAGE 603/383-0999 **1**

▼▼▼ **Hotel** $119-$249 **Address:** 153 Rt 16 03846 **Location:** Jct SR 16 and 16A at Jackson Covered Bridge, 0.5 mi n. **Facility:** 32 units. 2 stories (no elevator), interior corridors. **Terms:** 2 night minimum stay - seasonal and/or weekends, 14 day cancellation notice-fee imposed. **Pool(s):** outdoor. **Activities:** fishing, tennis court, cross country skiing, playground.

NORDIC VILLAGE RESORT (603)383-9101 **9**

▼▼▼ Resort Condominium $89-$869 **Address:** Rt 16 03846 **Location:** 1 mi n of jct US 302. **Facility:** Extensive grounds and enhanced luxury-level amenities add appeal to this mountainside, family-oriented property. Many, not all, of the rooms have WiFi and laundry facilities. The office is closed 11 pm-7 am. 225 condominiums, some two and three bedrooms. 2-3 stories (no elevator), interior/exterior corridors. **Terms:** check-in 3:30 pm, 2 night minimum stay - weekends, 7 day cancellation notice-fee imposed. **Amenities:** Some: high-speed Internet. **Pool(s):** 4 heated outdoor, heated indoor. **Activities:** sauna, whirlpools, steamroom, boating, tennis court, cross country skiing, ice skating, recreation programs in summer, hiking trails, playground, basketball, horseshoes, volleyball, exercise room. Fee: game room, massage. **Free Special Amenities:** children's activities and use of on-premises laundry facilities.

SNOWFLAKE INN 603-383-8259 **6**

▼▼▼▼ **Bed & Breakfast** $169-$375 **Address:** 95 Main St (SR 16A) 03846 **Location:** On SR 16A; center. **Facility:** Located on 6 acres of sprawling grounds, this inn offers spacious, luxuriously appointed guest rooms, each with a cozy fireplace and whirlpool tub. 20 units. 2 stories (no elevator), interior corridors. **Terms:** 2 night minimum stay - seasonal and/or weekends, age restrictions may apply, 14 day cancellation notice-fee imposed. **Pool(s):** heated indoor. **Activities:** Fee: massage. **Guest Services:** valet laundry.

Save on theme park tickets
at AAA.com/discounts

(See map & index p. 225.)

THE WENTWORTH   (603)383-9700 **5**

Historic Hotel
$99-$325

Address: 1 Carter Notch Rd 03846 **Location:** Just w of jct SR 16A and 16B. **Facility:** The resort centers on a building dating from 1900; its annexes offer standard and luxury lodgings with upgrades such as whirlpools and fireplaces. 51 units. 3 stories (no elevator), interior/exterior corridors. **Parking:** winter plug-ins. **Terms:** 2-3 night minimum stay - weekends, 7 day cancellation notice-fee imposed. **Dining:** The Wentworth Dining Room, see separate listing. **Pool(s):** heated outdoor. **Activities:** tennis court, cross country skiing. *Fee:* golf-18 holes.

WHERE TO EAT

HIGHFIELDS TAVERN   603/383-9111 **2**

American. Fine Dining. $10-$25 **AAA Inspector Notes:** The vintage hotel's dining room is elegantly decorated, and the service is attentive and friendly. On the varied menu is classic New England cuisine: fresh seafood, beef, poultry and some wild game selections. **Bar:** full bar. **Address:** 179 Carter Notch Rd 03846 **Location:** Jct SR 16B, from village center follow SR 16B across the Jackson Covered Bridge to immediate right turn, 0.7 mi n; in The Eagle Mountain House & Golf Club. L D

THE INN AT THORN HILL   603/383-4242 **7**

Regional American. Fine Dining. $18-$30 **AAA Inspector Notes:** The inn offers the opportunity for informal dining in a setting of homey elegance. The outstanding menu reflects "Big Apple" ingenuity, local market availability and international influences. An extensive wine list perfectly complements the cuisine. **Bar:** full bar. **Reservations:** suggested. **Address:** 40 Thorn Hill Rd 03846 **Location:** Off SR 16A; in The Inn at Thorn Hill and Spa. B D

RED FOX BAR & GRILLE   603/383-4949 **1**

American. Casual Dining. $9-$24 **AAA Inspector Notes:** Many pictures of local landscapes line the walls of this rustic, country-feeling eatery, where American dishes span from steaks to seafood. The good-size lounge offers a place to kick back before or after the meal. **Bar:** full bar. **Address:** 49 New Hampshire (SR 16) 03846 **Location:** Jct US 302 and SR 16, 2.3 mi n. B L D

THOMPSON HOUSE EATERY   603/383-9341 **4**

American. Casual Dining. $14-$32 **AAA Inspector Notes:** In an early 1800s farmhouse, this restaurant includes an ice cream fountain and farm stand. The casual atmosphere extends to a patio that is available for seasonal dining. The owner/chef creates distinctive contemporary dishes from fresh local ingredients, many of which come from the restaurant's organic garden. The smoke-free bar presents a pub-style menu and exhibits a collection of local artwork. The restaurant does not have high chairs or booster seats. **Bar:** full bar. **Reservations:** suggested. **Address:** 193 Main St (SR 16A) 03846 **Location:** In village. D

THE WENTWORTH DINING ROOM   603/383-9700 **3**

Regional
American
Fine Dining
$25-$28

AAA Inspector Notes: This property offers fine lodging and memorable dining in a serene and breathtaking setting. Diners may sample a variety of the freshest fish, fine cuts of meat and wonderful homemade desserts. **Bar:** full bar. **Reservations:** suggested. **Address:** 1 Carter Notch Rd 03846 **Location:** Just w of jct SR 16A and 16B; in The Wentworth. B D

THE WILDCAT INN & TAVERN   603/383-4245 **6**

New American. Casual Dining. $6-$25 **AAA Inspector Notes:** This 19th-century country inn is located in the center of the village and has a pleasant informal atmosphere. Garden dining is available in the summer. The cuisine is described as country gourmet, and entrées are made to order. Ingredients are as fresh as possible. A lighter menu is available in the tavern. **Bar:** full bar. **Reservations:** suggested. **Address:** 94 Main St 03846 **Location:** Jct SR 16 and 16A, at Jackson Covered Bridge, then 0.5 mi ne on SR 16A. L D

YESTERDAYS OF JACKSON VILLAGE   603/383-4457 **5**

American. Casual Dining. $5-$12 **AAA Inspector Notes:** Located in the center of town at the crossroads, this rustic, diner-style restaurant specializes in breakfast items such as pecan-pumpkin French toast served with real maple syrup. Also worth trying are the tasty, house-made soups, salads, sandwiches, wraps and burgers. **Address:** SR 16A 03846 **Location:** Jct SR 16 and 16A, at Jackson Covered Bridge, then 0.5 mi ne. B L

JAFFREY (G-3) pop. 2,757, elev. 1,000'

The Jaffrey area originally was part of a huge land grant owned by Capt. John Mason. Title to Mason's grant was later transferred to a group of men known as proprietors. At least one of these, George Jaffrey, left his mark on the wilderness when the area took his name in 1773.

In the 1840s the region became popular with summer visitors, including Ralph Waldo Emerson, who wrote the poem "Monadnoc" after climbing nearby Monadnock Mountain, reputedly one of the most climbed mountains in the United States. Several easy and intermediate hiking trails start from SR 124 or from Monadnock State Park *(see Recreation Areas Chart).*

Jaffrey is a quiet village surrounding the 1775 white clapboard Meeting House. The building is the site of the Amos Fortune Forum, an annual lecture series established in 1958. The forum honors Amos Fortune, a slave who was granted freedom and later became a prominent Jaffrey citizen.

Jaffrey Chamber of Commerce: 7 Main St., P.O. Box 2, Jaffrey, NH 03452. **Phone:** (603) 532-4549.

SILVER RANCH & SILVER RANCH AIRPARK, 1 mi. e. on SR 124, offers a variety of activities, including scenic airplane rides and horse-drawn carriage and sleigh rides. **Time:** Allow 1 hour minimum. **Hours:** Open daily at 9. **Cost:** Plane rides $99-$239 for up to three passengers. Sleigh and carriage rides $120 for up to 10 passengers. Reservations are recommended. **Phone:** (603) 532-8870 for plane rides, or (603) 532-7363 for stable activities.

THE BENJAMIN PRESCOTT INN OF JAFFREY   603/532-6637

Historic Bed & Breakfast $99-$255 **Address:** 433 Turnpike Rd 03452 **Location:** Jct SR 202, 2 mi e. **Facility:** Each guest room at this classic Colonial-style inn is named for a family member who had the home built in 1853. 10 units. 3 stories (no elevator), interior/exterior corridors. **Terms:** 2 night minimum stay - seasonal and/or weekends, age restrictions may apply, 10 day cancellation notice-fee imposed. **Activities:** cross country skiing, hiking trails.

JAFFREY CENTER

THORNDIKE'S RESTAURANT   603/532-7800

American. Fine Dining. $18-$35 **AAA Inspector Notes:** Creative, home-cooked dishes are well-prepared. Diners can enjoy their meals in the country cottage-style dining room. **Bar:** full bar. **Reservations:** suggested. **Address:** 379 Main St 03452 **Location:** Jct SR 202, 1.7 mi w on SR 124. D

JEFFERSON (C-4) elev. 1,400'

Known locally as Jefferson Hill, Jefferson is primarily a summer resort community. From high on the flank of Mount Starr King, it commands a wide view of the Israel River Valley and the White Mountains southwest to the Franconias.

A marker just west on US 2 commemorates inventor and pioneer aeronaut Thaddeus S.C. Lowe, born nearby in 1823. During the Civil War Lowe organized and directed a Union balloon force; later he invented several important devices for use in atmospheric observation and metallurgical processing.

SANTA'S VILLAGE is 1 mi. n.w. on US 2 at 528 Presidential Hwy. This Christmas theme park, in a landscaped setting, features live entertainment and rides. Children can visit with Santa, feed his reindeer, play the Elfabet Game, become a helper at Santa's Workshop and enjoy live performances at the Polar Theater. Rides include Rudy's Rapid Transit Coaster, the Skyway Sleigh monorail and the Yule Log Flume.

Time: Allow 3 hours minimum. **Hours:** Opens daily at 9:30, day after Father's Day-Labor Day; Sat.-Sun. at 9:30, Memorial Day weekend-Father's Day and day after Labor Day-Columbus Day. Closing times vary. Phone ahead to confirm schedule. **Cost:** $28; $26 (ages 62+); free (ages 0-3). Those entering less than 3 hours before closing receive a pass to return any day throughout the season. **Phone:** (603) 586-4445. 🍴

SIX GUN CITY & FORT SPLASH WATER PARK, just w. of jct. SR 115 at 1492 Presidential Hwy. (US 2), offers 35 buildings in a frontier setting, including a church, schoolhouse and blacksmith shop. The Carriage and Sleigh Museum displays more than 100 horse-drawn vehicles and other antiques. Twelve rides are available, including a raft ride and two waterslides; there also is a wading area for children.

Also included are a miniature horse show, a miniature golf course, a family roller coaster, laser tag facilities, and cowboy and frontier shows. During Ghost Town at Six Gun City: A Halloween Spooktacular in the fall, the park features a children's corn maze, a haunted hayride, haunted houses and other Halloween-themed activities.

Time: Allow 3 hours minimum. **Hours:** Daily 9:30-6, July 1-late Aug.; 10-5, last weekend in May, last week in June and late Aug.-Labor Day weekend. Ghost Town at Six Gun City: A Halloween Spooktacular Sat. 3-9:30, late Sept.-Oct. 31. Phone ahead to confirm schedule. **Cost:** $22.95; $17.95 (ages 65+); free (ages 0-3 with adult). Ghost Town at Six Gun City: A Halloween Spooktacular $20.95; free (ages 0-4 with adult). **Phone:** (603) 586-4592. 🍴

EVERGREEN MOTEL   603/586-4449

🏍 **Motel** $45-$89 **Address:** 537 Presidential Hwy 03583 **Location:** On US 2, 0.6 mi w of jct SR 116. Across from Santa's Village. **Facility:** 18 units. 1 story, exterior corridors. **Terms:** 1-2 night minimum stay - seasonal and/or weekends, 7 day cancellation notice-fee imposed. **Pool(s):** outdoor. **Activities:** miniature golf, snowmobiling.

JEFFERSON INN   603/586-7998

🏵🏵🏵 ◆
Historic Bed
& Breakfast
Rates not provided

Address: 6 Renaissance Ln 03583 **Location:** US 2, 0.5 mi e of SR 116. **Facility:** Perched on a hilltop, the inn offers guest rooms and a veranda with good mountain views. The historic inn is furnished with many antiques. 11 units, some two bedrooms. 3 stories (no elevator), interior corridors. **Activities:** cross country skiing, snowmobiling, ice skating, tobogganing, bicycle trails, hiking trails. **Free Special Amenities:** full breakfast and local telephone calls.

THE LANTERN RESORT   603/586-7151

🏍 🏍 **Motel** $45-$99 **Address:** 571 Presidential Hwy 03583 **Location:** On US 2, 0.4 mi w of jct SR 116. Across from Santa's Village. **Facility:** 30 units. 2 stories (no elevator), exterior corridors. **Terms:** closed 10/13-5/1, 7 day cancellation notice-fee imposed. **Pool(s):** 2 heated outdoor. **Activities:** whirlpools, recreation programs in summer, playground, basketball, horseshoes, volleyball. *Fee:* game room. **Guest Services:** coin laundry.

KEENE (F-2) pop. 23,409, elev. 496'

The 1762 Wyman Tavern, 339 Main St., is one of Keene's important early buildings. In 1770 the well-known inn was the scene of the first meeting of the trustees of Dartmouth College; 5 years later Capt. Isaac Wyman led 29 Minutemen from the tavern to Lexington at the onset of the Revolutionary War. The Historical Society of Cheshire County offers seasonal tours of the tavern; phone (603) 352-1895.

Keene's industrial future was cast during the 19th century when the city became known for the production of glass and pottery. Henry Schoolcraft's flint glass bottles have become collectors' items, as has the white pottery made 1871-1926 by the Hampshire Pottery.

The Keene State College Redfern Arts Center on Brickyard Pond is the locale of plays, concerts and recitals during the academic year; phone (603) 358-2168. The restored Colonial Theatre at 95 Main St. features plays, concerts and opera as well as movies; phone (603) 357-1233.

Six covered bridges can be found on side roads off SR 10 between Keene and Winchester. Three of these bridges span the Ashuelot River: south of SR 119 at Ashuelot; east of SR 10 at West Swanzey; and a mile north of SR 32 at Swanzey Village. Still another covered bridge crosses the South Branch of the Ashuelot River east of SR 32, a half-mile south of Swanzey Village.

Greater Keene Chamber of Commerce: 48 Central Sq., Keene, NH 03431. **Phone:** (603) 352-1303.

Shopping areas: The Colony Mill Marketplace, 222 West St., is a restored woolen mill that contains a group of shops. The Center at Keene, 149 Emerald St., includes a collection of shops in a restored railroad repair depot.

HORATIO COLONY HOUSE MUSEUM is at 199 Main St.; parking is at the rear of St. Bernard's Church adjacent to the museum. Built in 1806, the Federal-style house was sold in 1847 into the Joslin/Colony family, prominent mill owners, and remained in the family for 130 years. The home features all-original eclectic furnishings representing several periods and styles. Horatio Colony, the last of the family to inhabit the house, had a flair for the unusual, mixing heirlooms with souvenirs of his world travels. **Hours:** Wed.-Sun. 11-4, May 1-Oct. 15; by appointment rest of year. Closed July 4. **Cost:** Free. **Phone:** (603) 352-0460.

HORATIO COLONY NATURE PRESERVE, off SR 9, 1 mi. w. of jct. SRs 10, 12 and 101 on Daniels Hill Rd., is a 645-acre refuge for many species of birds and other animals as well as native plants. Five miles of nature trails wind through upland hardwood forest; hiking, cross-country skiing and snowshoeing are popular activities. A self-guiding trail booklet is available at the trailhead kiosk. **Hours:** Daily dawn-dusk. **Cost:** Free. **Phone:** (603) 352-0460.

BEST WESTERN PLUS SOVEREIGN HOTEL
(603)357-3038

 Hotel $89-$299

 AAA Benefit: Members save 10% or more with Best Western.

Address: 401 Winchester St 03431 **Location:** SR 10, just s of jct SR 12 and 101. **Facility:** 131 units. 3 stories, interior corridors. **Amenities:** video games (fee). *Some:* high-speed Internet. **Pool(s):** heated indoor. **Activities:** exercise room. **Guest Services:** valet laundry. **Free Special Amenities:** local telephone calls and high-speed Internet.

   / SOME UNITS FEE

COURTYARD BY MARRIOTT KEENE DOWNTOWN
(603)354-7900

 Hotel $109-$259 **Address:** 75 Railroad St 03431 **Location:** Just off Main St; downtown. **Facility:** 100 units. 5 stories, interior corridors. **Amenities:** high-speed Internet. **Pool(s):** heated indoor. **Activities:** exercise room. **Guest Services:** valet and coin laundry.

AAA Benefit: AAA hotel discounts of 5% or more.

/ SOME UNITS FEE

DAYS INN OF KEENE
(603)352-9780

Hotel $75-$260

Address: 3 Ash Brook Rd 03431 **Location:** Jct SR 9 and 12, just w. **Facility:** 59 units. 2 stories (no elevator), interior corridors. **Terms:** cancellation fee imposed. **Amenities:** safes (fee). **Activities:** limited exercise equipment. **Free Special Amenities:** expanded continental breakfast and high-speed Internet.

/ SOME UNITS FEE

Trust your vehicle to AAA/CAA Approved Auto Repair facilities

---

HOLIDAY INN EXPRESS
(603)352-7616

Hotel $89-$199 **Address:** 175 Key Rd 03431 **Location:** SR 101, just n, via Winchester St, then 0.3 mi w. Located in a business park. **Facility:** 80 units. 2 stories, interior corridors. **Pool(s):** heated indoor. **Activities:** whirlpool, exercise room. **Guest Services:** valet and coin laundry.

/ SOME UNITS FEE

THE LANE HOTEL, AN ASCEND COLLECTION HOTEL
(603)357-7070

Hotel $129-$229 **Address:** 30 Main St 03431 **Location:** Between Church and Roxbury sts; downtown. **Facility:** 40 units. 4 stories, interior corridors. *Bath:* shower only. **Terms:** 2-4 night minimum stay - weekends, cancellation fee imposed. **Amenities:** high-speed Internet. **Activities:** exercise room. **Guest Services:** valet laundry.

CALL / SOME UNITS FEE

WHERE TO EAT

ELM CITY BREWING COMPANY
603/355-3335

American. Gastropub. $6-$24 **AAA Inspector Notes:** Located in historic Colony Mill Marketplace, this brewery provides a great casual spot to relax after work or for a casual gathering. Housemade desserts are a great finish to a meal. Beer only. **Address:** 222 West St 03431 **Location:** Between Island St and Gilbo Ave; in Colony Mill Marketplace. [L] [D]

THE PUB RESTAURANT & CATERERS
603/352-3135

Greek. Family Dining. $4-$15 **AAA Inspector Notes:** This pub's atmosphere is laid-back, and the serving staff is friendly, prompt and courteous. The Greek and Italian flavors of the menu's offerings should please everyone in the family. Meals are hot, well-seasoned, plentiful and tasty. **Bar:** full bar. **Reservations:** suggested. **Address:** 131 Winchester St 03431 **Location:** Jct SR 9/10/101, 0.5 mi n. [B] [L] [D]

WAXY O'CONNOR'S IRISH PUB & RESTAURANT
603/357-9299

Irish. Gastropub. $9-$22 **AAA Inspector Notes:** The decor fits the image the name evokes with the central wrap around dark wood bar, copper fixtures, billiard table, darts and semi-enclosed dining areas. The menu offers standard Irish fare along with classic American dishes. Of course, one must indulge in a pint of Guinness while enjoying the entertainment provided every weekend. **Bar:** full bar. **Address:** 401 Winchester St 03431 **Location:** SR 10, just s of jct SR 12 and 101; adjacent to BEST WESTERN PLUS Sovereign Hotel. [L] [D] CALL

KINGSTON

KINGSTON 1686 HOUSE
603/642-3637

American. Casual Dining. $20-$33 **AAA Inspector Notes:** Historic. An historic 300-year-old house with original fireplaces, hand-cut beams and pine floors is the setting for a wonderful dining experience. Creative, flavorful New England fare reflects Greek influences. Service is good, and the wine list is sensational. **Bar:** full bar. **Reservations:** suggested, weekends. **Address:** 127 Main St 03848 **Location:** Jct Scotland Rd; center of village. [D]

KINSMAN NOTCH (D-3)

Rather than turn back when he found that he had taken the wrong road en route to a land grant at Landaff, pioneer Asa Kinsman, his wife and two Woodstock townsmen hacked their way through the rugged intervening miles to their destination. Thus was traversed—and named—Kinsman Notch, a pass between Mount Moosilauke and the Kinsman Range.

Kinsman, like the other White Mountain notches, was deepened and widened by the Pleistocene ice sheet. As the glaciers melted and frost weakened the fractures in the north face of the notch, huge blocks of granite plunged into Lost River Gorge to form the narrow passages among which the river gets lost.

▼GEM **LOST RIVER GORGE & BOULDER CAVES** is 6 mi. w. of North Woodstock on SR 112. Thousands of years ago, the water from melting glaciers scoured out this 300-feet-deep gorge in Kinsman Notch. As centuries passed, water seeped into cracks within the walls, expanded as it froze and split away massive blocks of granite that tumbled into the gorge, stacking up and hiding the river in places—hence the name "Lost."

But you won't get lost as you explore this heavily wooded setting thanks to a wide loop trail of gravel paths, wooden boardwalks and more stairs than you'd want to count. You'll have postcard-worthy views of the river as it cascades over, around and under the huge, moss-covered boulders. If you're up to it, and don't mind confined spaces and a little dirt, you can clamber down ladders into lantern-lit caves among the rocks with colorful names like Judgment Hall of Pluto, Devil's Kitchen, Cave of Odin, the Dungeon and, if you dare, the Lemon Squeezer.

Informative signs along the way describe various features of the gorge, and platforms and benches offer spots beneath the maple and birch trees where you can pause to catch your breath. A nature garden near the trail's end shows off native plants grouped according to habitat, and the visitor center, where the trail begins and ends, features exhibits about the area.

Self-guiding trails through the gorge cover three-quarters of a mile and take roughly 60 to 90 minutes to complete; sturdy walking shoes are advised. The caves can be individually bypassed. **Note:** Baby strollers are not allowed in the gorge. **Time:** Allow 1 hour minimum. **Hours:** Daily 9-6, July-Aug.; 9-5, May-June and Sept.-Oct. Last admission 1 hour before closing. Evening Lantern Tour departs Sat. at 8 p.m., mid-June through Labor Day weekend. **Cost:** $17; $13 (ages 4-12). Evening Lantern Tour $27; children under 5 are not permitted. Reservations are required for Evening Lantern Tour. **Phone:** (603) 745-8031. 🍴 🎋

Lost River Nature Garden, 1712 Lost River Rd., includes 300 labeled varieties of native flowering plants, shrubs, ferns and mosses. Flowers bloom June through September. **Hours:** Daily 9-6, July-Aug.; 9-5, May-June and Sept.-Oct. Last admission 1 hour before closing. **Cost:** Free. **Phone:** (603) 745-8031.

LACONIA (E-4) pop. 15,951, elev. 507'

A log cabin, the first structure on the site of Laconia, was probably erected in 1766. Before then the presence of Sachem Indians had prevented settlement, although the area had been granted as early as 1727. Growth was slow until the railroad reached the community—then called Meredith

Bridge—in 1848. Thereafter mills and factories proliferated, and Laconia became a trading and manufacturing center.

Paugus Bay and lakes Winnisquam and Opechee extend into Laconia's city limits, bringing opportunities for water sports. About 5 miles north is Lake Winnipesaukee, the largest lake in the state and a major resort center (see Weirs Beach p. 251).

Cultural activities are presented at the Belknap Mill (see attraction listing), a noted center for arts and humanities. Outdoor concerts are presented in spring and summer at the grandstand next to Belknap Mill.

Lakes Region Chamber of Commerce 383 S. Main St., Laconia, NH 03246. **Phone:** (603) 524-5531.

Shopping areas: [SAVE] Tanger Outlet Center, 120 Laconia Rd. in nearby Tilton, offers more than 50 outlet stores, including Eddie Bauer, Gap and Nine West.

BELKNAP MILL is at 25 Beacon St. E. Constructed in 1823, this building houses original circular knitting machines, a renovated wheel house and a 1918 hydroelectric power plant. Live demonstrations explain the mechanics of knitting machines used to make socks. An art gallery has changing exhibits. **Time:** Allow 1 hour minimum. **Hours:** Mon.-Fri. 9-5, Sat. 9-3. Live demonstrations are given on Thurs.; phone ahead to confirm schedule. **Cost:** Donations. **Phone:** (603) 524-8813.

PRESCOTT FARM ENVIRONMENTAL EDUCATION CENTER is at 928 White Oaks Rd. The 160-acre farm offers visitors more than 2 miles of well-marked hiking trails, a three-story historic barn, heritage and heirloom flower and vegetable gardens, a working maple sugar shack and wildlife-viewing opportunities. **Hours:** Trails daily dawn-dusk. Center daily 9-4. **Cost:** Free. **Phone:** (603) 366-5695.

BAY TOP MOTEL   (603)366-2225
🏆 **Motel** $69-$149 **Address:** 1025 Weirs Blvd 03246 **Location:** 0.5 mi s of Weirs Beach on US 3. **Facility:** 12 units. 1 story, exterior corridors. *Bath:* shower only. **Terms:** closed 10/18-3/31, 7 day cancellation notice-fee imposed. **Pool(s):** outdoor. **Activities:** whirlpool.
🛜➕ CALL 🖥️Ⓜ 🏊 🛜 ✕ 📱 🖥️

BIRCH KNOLL MOTEL   (603)366-4958
🏆 **Motel** $69-$169 **Address:** 867 Weirs Blvd 03247 **Location:** 1 mi s of Weirs Beach on US 3. **Facility:** 24 units. 1-2 stories (no elevator), exterior corridors. *Bath:* shower only. **Terms:** closed 10/29-5/9, 2 night minimum stay - seasonal and/or weekends, 7 day cancellation notice-fee imposed. **Pool(s):** heated outdoor. **Activities:** beach access, fishing. *Fee:* game room.
🏊 🛜 ✕ 📱

THE LAKE HOUSE AT FERRY POINT   603/524-0087
🏆🏆🏆 **Historic Bed & Breakfast** $165-$260 **Address:** 100 Lower Bay Rd 03269 **Location:** Waterfront. I-93 exit 20, 4.5 mi n on US 3, at light before bridge, 0.5 mi n on Bay Rd, then 0.5 mi n. **Facility:** Located in a quiet, lakefront residential community on Lake Winnisquam, this Victorian inn overlooking the lake features a wide front porch with hanging flowerpots and wicker furniture. 10 units. 2 stories (no elevator), interior corridors. **Terms:** 2 night minimum stay - weekends, 10 day cancellation notice-fee imposed. **Amenities:** *Some:* high-speed Internet. **Activities:** boat dock, fishing.
🛜 ✕ 🅿️ 🆑 / SOME UNITS 🅺

WHERE TO EAT

FRATELLO'S RISTORANTE ITALIANO   603/528-2022

Italian. Casual Dining. $8-$24 **AAA Inspector Notes:** This popular restaurant presents a menu of such varied Italian favorites as piccata, parmigiana, spaghetti, Caesar salad and terrific desserts, all served in a fun atmosphere. **Bar:** full bar. **Address:** 799 Union Ave 03246 **Location:** 1.5 mi n on Old US 3; center. [L] [D]

WATER STREET CAFE   603/524-4144

American. Casual Dining. $5-$12 **AAA Inspector Notes:** A casual atmosphere makes this cafe a great stop for a quick bite at the counter or a relaxed meal at a table. A wide variety of menu options is available as well as ample on-site parking. **Bar:** beer & wine. **Address:** 141 Water St 03246 **Location:** I-93 exit 20, 7.1 mi n on SR 3, then just w on Fair St. [B] [L]

LANCASTER (C-4) pop. 1,725, elev. 887'

Charming old houses create an atmosphere of the past in this busy trading center, settled in 1764 as the first town in northern New Hampshire. Its setting at the confluence of the Israel and Connecticut rivers is enhanced by the serrated Pilot Range to the northeast and the Presidential Range to the southeast. Abundant recreational activities are available, including hiking, biking, camping, fishing, hunting, skiing and snowmobiling.

Lancaster is a waypoint along the Connecticut River Byway, a scenic, 500-mile route that traverses through more than 50 communities on both sides of the Connecticut River in New Hampshire and Vermont. Brochures and information are available at the Great North Woods Welcome Center (closed in winter), 25 Park St; phone (603) 788-3212.

Northern Gateway Chamber of Commerce: 25 Park St., P.O. Box 537, Lancaster, NH 03584. **Phone:** (603) 788-2530 or (877) 788-2530.

JOHN WINGATE WEEKS HISTORIC SITE consists of 420 acres 2 mi. s. on US 3. The park was the mountaintop summer estate of John Wingate Weeks, the one-time secretary of war and senator who wrote the legislation that established the Eastern national forests.

The fieldstone and stucco mansion contains exhibits and mementos of Senator Weeks' service during the Harding and Coolidge presidential administrations as well as displays that trace the history of the state's conservation efforts. A fieldstone observation tower affords views of Mount Washington and the Presidential Range to the east and Vermont's Green Mountains to the west.

Nature and hiking trails are available. **Time:** Allow 1 hour minimum. **Hours:** Wed.-Sun. 10-5, late June-early Sept.; Sat.-Sun. 10-5, late May-late June and early Sept.-early Oct. Phone ahead to confirm schedule. **Cost:** $7; $3 (ages 6-17). **Phone:** (603) 788-4004, or (603) 271-3556 during the off-season.

THE CABOT INN & SUITES   (603)788-3346

Hotel
$79-$159

Address: 200 Portland St 03584 **Location:** On US 2, 1.5 mi e of jct US 3. **Facility:** 54 units, some two bedrooms, efficiencies and kitchens. 2-3 stories, interior corridors. **Parking:** winter plug-ins. **Terms:** 2 night minimum stay - seasonal and/or weekends, cancellation fee imposed. **Pool(s):** heated indoor. **Activities:** saunas, whirlpool, snowmobiling, bicycles, hiking trails, playground, exercise room. *Fee:* game room. **Guest Services:** coin laundry. **Free Special Amenities: continental breakfast and local telephone calls.** *(See ad p. 209.)*

COOS MOTOR INN   (603)788-3079

Hotel
$49-$110

Address: 209 Main St 03584 **Location:** On US 2 and 3; center. **Facility:** 41 units. 2 stories, interior corridors. **Parking:** winter plug-ins. **Terms:** cancellation fee imposed. **Guest Services:** coin laundry. **Free Special Amenities: continental breakfast and local telephone calls.**

LEBANON pop. 13,151

COURTYARD BY MARRIOTT HANOVER LEBANON
(603)643-5600

Hotel $139-$549 **Address:** 10 Morgan Dr 03766 **Location:** I-89 exit 18, 2 mi n on SR 120 exit Centerra Pkwy, then s. **Facility:** 124 units. 4 stories, interior corridors. **Amenities:** high-speed Internet. **Pool(s):** heated indoor. **Activities:** whirlpool, exercise room. **Guest Services:** valet and coin laundry, area transportation-within 10 mi.

AAA Benefit: AAA hotel discounts of 5% or more.

RESIDENCE INN BY MARRIOTT HANOVER LEBANON
(603)643-4511

Extended Stay Hotel
$139-$259

AAA Benefit: AAA hotel discounts of 5% or more.

Address: 32 Centerra Pkwy 03766 **Location:** I-89 exit 18, 2.5 mi n on SR 120. **Facility:** 114 units, some two bedrooms, efficiencies and kitchens. 3 stories, interior corridors. **Amenities:** high-speed Internet. **Pool(s):** heated indoor. **Activities:** whirlpool, exercise room. **Guest Services:** valet and coin laundry, area transportation-within 5 mi. **Free Special Amenities: full breakfast and local transportation.**

WHERE TO EAT

MARGARITAS MEXICAN RESTAURANT   603/643-8800

Mexican. Casual Dining. $9-$16 **AAA Inspector Notes:** Diners will feel as though they have just stepped south of the border at this fun Mexican cantina. Traditional music fills the air while warm terracotta colored walls accented by painted pottery and unique jeweled star lanterns surround you. Sip on a large margarita while enjoying the freshly prepared fajitas, burritos, enchiladas, or quesadillas. **Bar:** full bar. **Address:** 18 Centerra Pkwy 03766 **Location:** I-89 exit 18, 2.5 mi n on SR 120, then just ne. [L] [D] CALL [&M]

LINCOLN (D-3) pop. 993, elev. 808'
• Restaurants p. 211

Lincoln is the western terminus of one of the state's most popular scenic drives, the Kancamagus Highway *(see attraction listing p. 253)*. With North Woodstock, its sister community across the Pemigewasset River, Lincoln serves those who visit the nearby recreational developments. The North Country Center for the Arts offers year-round productions at the Papermill Theatre; phone (603) 745-6032 for information or (603) 745-2141 for tickets.

In September the 🍁 New Hampshire Highland Games & Festival, featuring Scottish music, dancing and athletic competitions, is held at Loon Mountain Resort *(see attraction listing)*.

Lincoln-Woodstock Chamber of Commerce: at Lincoln Village Shops on SR 112 (Kancamagus Hwy.), P.O. Box 1017, Lincoln, NH 03251. **Phone:** (603) 745-6621 or (800) 227-4191.

CLARK'S TRADING POST, off I-93 exit 33, then 1 mi. s. on US 3, features North American black bear performances and rides on the White Mountain Central Railroad. The 1884 Pemigewasset Hook and Ladder Fire Station displays antique equipment; museum buildings feature early cameras, typewriters, guns and toys. Guests can enjoy a 5-minute ride at Wolfie's White Mountain Wheelin' Segway Park or partake in a 45-minute Segway excursion. Other attractions include Merlin's Mystical Mansion, Tuttle's Rustic House, water blaster boats and performances by the Yandong Chinese Acrobatic Troupe.

Time: Allow 2 hours, 30 minutes minimum. **Hours:** Daily 9:30-5:30, late June-Labor Day; Mon.-Fri. 11:30-2:30, Sat.-Sun. 10-5, mid-Sept. to early Oct.; Sat.-Sun. 10-5, Memorial Day weekend-late June and day after Labor Day to mid-Sept. Last admission 1 hour before closing. Segway excursions depart every hour 10:45-4:45, late June-Labor Day. Phone ahead to confirm schedule. **Cost:** $19; $17 (ages 65+); free (ages 0-3). Segway excursion additional $25; age, height and weight restrictions apply. Prices may vary; phone ahead. **Phone:** (603) 745-8913.

HOBO RAILROAD, off I-93 exit 32 on SR 112, offers 15-mile excursions in vintage, restored coaches along the Pemigewasset River. Specialty tours, including fall foliage trips, are offered. **Time:** Allow 1 hour, 30 minutes minimum. **Hours:** Trips depart daily, late June-Labor Day; schedule varies late May-late June and day after Labor Day-late Oct. Arrive 30 minutes before departure. Phone ahead to confirm schedule. **Cost:** $14; $11 (ages 3-11). Fares may vary; phone ahead. **Phone:** (603) 745-2135.
🍴

LOON MOUNTAIN RESORT is off I-93 exit 32, then 2 mi. e. on the Kancamagus Hwy. (SR 112). A four-passenger gondola travels 7,000 feet from base to summit, where a four-story observation tower offers a panorama of the area, including Mount Washington and the Presidential Range. Self-guiding nature walks explore the summit and glacial caves. A zipline, mountain bike rentals and trails, a bungee trampoline, a climbing wall and the Aerial Forest Adventure Park obstacle course provide summer fun. Winter activities include downhill and cross-country skiing, ice skating, snowboarding and snowshoeing. Guided tours include the Franconia Notch Bike Tour and a 3-hour Segway tour.

Hours: Mountain and gondola daily 9:30-6, June 1-Labor Day; 9:30-5, day after Labor Day to mid-Oct. Winter activities mid-Nov. to mid-Apr. (weather permitting). **Cost:** Gondola $15; $13 (ages 65+); $10 (ages 6-12). Zipline $26. Bungee trampoline $11. Climbing wall $8. Franconia Notch Bike Tour $37; $33 (ages 6-12). Segway tour $69. Combination day pass $39-$59; $29-$49 (ages 6-12). **Phone:** (603) 745-8111 or (800) 229-5666. 🍴

THE WHALE'S TALE WATER PARK, off I-93 exit 33 to US 3, features 18 waterslides including a wave pool with ocean-size breakers, a lazy river, a multi-passenger waterslide, two flume slides, two speed slides, a 310-foot tube slide and a children's area with a splash pool and slides. Also featured are Castaway Cove, a warm-water pool with hot tubs, and two thrill rides: Eye of the Storm and Banzai Pipeline. Free concerts are offered on Saturdays in July and August.

Time: Allow 2 hours minimum. **Hours:** Daily 10-6, late June-late Aug.; 10-4, early June-late June; 11-5, late Aug.-Labor Day weekend. Phone ahead to confirm schedule. **Cost:** Late June-late Aug. $34; free (ages 0-3 and 71+). Mid-June to late June and late Aug.-Labor Day weekend $26; free (ages 0-3 and 71+). Reduced admission is offered after 3 p.m. **Phone:** (603) 745-8810 or (888) 391-4222. 🍴

COMFORT INN & SUITES   (603)745-6700

Hotel
$99-$249

Address: 21 Railroad St 03251 **Location:** I-93 exit 32 (SR 112), just e; at Hobo Railroad. **Facility:** 82 units. 4 stories, interior corridors. **Terms:** check-in 4 pm, 3 day cancellation notice-fee imposed. **Pool(s):** heated indoor. **Activities:** whirlpool, exercise room. **Guest Services:** coin laundry.

SAVE CALL 🚭M ❄ 🛜 BIZ 📶 ✕ 🛗 🖥 🖨
/SOME UNITS FEE 🐕

ECONO LODGE INN & SUITES   (603)745-3661

Motel
$60-$250

Address: 381 US Rt 3 03251 **Location:** I-93 exit 33 (US 3), 0.3 mi ne. **Facility:** 51 units, some two bedrooms. 1-2 stories (no elevator), interior/exterior corridors. **Parking:** winter plug-ins. **Terms:** check-in 4 pm, cancellation fee imposed. **Pool(s):** outdoor, heated indoor. **Activities:** sauna, whirlpool, exercise room. *Fee:* game room. **Guest Services:** coin laundry. *(See ad p. 209.)*

SAVE 🛗 ❄ 🛜 ✕ 🛗
🖨 /SOME UNITS FEE 🐕

▼ See AAA listing p. 208 ▼

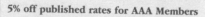

▼ *See AAA listing p. 208* ▼

THE MOUNTAIN CLUB ON LOON (603)745-2244

Resort Hotel
$108-$425

Address: 90 Loon Mountain Rd 03251 **Location:** I-93 exit 32 (SR 112), 3 mi e. Located in Loon Mountain Ski and Recreation Area. **Facility:** Located on Loon Mountain within the national forest, the resort offers ski-in/ski-out access and four-season activities for the entire family. Choose from traditional hotel rooms or studios with Murphy beds. 234 units, some kitchens. 3-4 stories, interior corridors. **Terms:** 14 day cancellation notice-fee imposed. **Dining:** 2 restaurants. **Pool(s):** heated outdoor, heated indoor. **Activities:** saunas, whirlpools, steamrooms, racquetball court, recreation programs, rental bicycles, hiking trails, playground, basketball, volleyball, exercise room, spa. **Fee:** downhill & cross country skiing, ice skating, game room. **Guest Services:** coin laundry, area transportation-Loon area. **Free Special Amenities:** high-speed Internet. (See ad p. 210.)

MOUNT COOLIDGE MOTEL 603/745-8052

 Motel. Rates not provided. **Address:** 386 US 3 03251 **Location:** I-93 exit 33 (US 3), 0.3 mi n. Located along a mountain stream. **Facility:** 20 units, some cottages. 1 story, exterior corridors. **Pool(s):** heated outdoor. **Activities:** fishing, hiking trails.

NORDIC INN CONDOMINIUM RESORT (603)745-2230

Condominium $119-$329 **Address:** 227 Main St 03251 **Location:** I-93 exit 32 (SR 112), 1 mi ne. **Facility:** 60 condominiums. 4 stories, interior corridors. **Terms:** check-in 4 pm, 2 night minimum stay, 14 day cancellation notice-fee imposed, resort fee. **Pool(s):** heated outdoor, heated indoor. **Activities:** game room, exercise room. **Guest Services:** coin laundry, area transportation-Loon Mountain.

PARKER'S MOTEL (603)745-8341

Motel
$59-$99

Address: 750 US Rt 3 03251 **Location:** I-93 exit 33 (US 3), 2 mi ne. **Facility:** 30 units, some two bedrooms, three bedrooms, efficiencies and cottages. 1-2 stories (no elevator), exterior corridors.

Parking: winter plug-ins. **Terms:** 3 day cancellation notice. **Pool(s):** heated outdoor. **Activities:** sauna, whirlpool, playground, basketball, horseshoes. **Fee:** game room. **Guest Services:** coin laundry. **Free Special Amenities:** early check-in/late check-out and high-speed Internet.

PROFILE MOTEL & COTTAGES 603/745-2759

Motel. Rates not provided. **Address:** 391 US Rt 3 03251 **Location:** I-93 exit 33 (US 3), 0.5 mi ne. **Facility:** 19 units, some efficiencies and cottages. 1 story, exterior corridors. **Pool(s):** heated outdoor. **Activities:** snowmobiling, hiking trails, basketball, horseshoes, volleyball.

RIVERGREEN RESORT HOTEL (603)745-2450

Hotel $104-$314 **Address:** 48 Cooper Memorial Dr 03251 **Location:** Waterfront. I-93 exit 32 (SR 112), 1 mi e. **Facility:** 120 units, some two bedrooms and kitchens. 4 stories, interior corridors. **Terms:** check-in 4 pm, 2 night minimum stay - seasonal and/or weekends, 7 day cancellation notice, resort fee. **Pool(s):** heated indoor. **Activities:** whirlpool, exercise room. **Fee:** game room. **Guest Services:** coin laundry, area transportation-Loon Mountain.

RODEWAY INN 603/745-2267

Motel
Rates not provided

Address: 417 US Rt 3 03251 **Location:** I-93 exit 33 (US 3), 0.5 mi ne. **Facility:** 30 units. 2 stories (no elevator), exterior corridors. **Pool(s):** heated outdoor. **Activities:** basketball, shuffleboard. **Guest Services:** coin laundry. **Free Special Amenities:** continental breakfast and room upgrade (subject to availability with advance reservations).

SOUTH MOUNTAIN RESORT (603)745-6261

Hotel $159-$369 **Address:** 23 InnSeason Dr 03251 **Location:** I-93 exit 32 (SR 112), 1 mi e. Adjacent to a market. **Facility:** 69 units, some two bedrooms and kitchens. 4 stories, interior corridors. **Terms:** check-in 4 pm, 2 night minimum stay - seasonal and/or weekends, 3 day cancellation notice-fee imposed. **Pool(s):** heated outdoor, heated indoor. **Activities:** saunas, whirlpools, exercise room. **Fee:** game room. **Guest Services:** area transportation-Loon Mountain.

WOODWARD'S RESORT 603/745-8141

Motel
Rates not provided

Address: 527 US 3 03251 **Location:** I-93 exit 33 (US 3), 1.4 mi ne. **Facility:** 85 units, some two bedrooms and cottages. 1-2 stories (no elevator), interior/exterior corridors. **Parking:** winter plug-ins. **Pool(s):** heated outdoor, heated indoor. **Activities:** sauna, whirlpool, tennis court, ice skating, playground, basketball, horseshoes, shuffleboard, volleyball. **Fee:** racquetball court, game room. **Guest Services:** coin laundry.

WHERE TO EAT

CHIENG GARDENS 603/745-8612

Chinese. Casual Dining. $5-$16 **AAA Inspector Notes:** Near Loon Mountain, the Asian-oriented restaurant serves traditional Chinese cuisine. This place is on the second floor of a small strip mall. **Bar:** full bar. **Address:** 165 Main St (SR 112) 03251 **Location:** I-93 exit 32 (SR 112), 1.5 mi e; in Lincoln Square Mall.

THE COMMON MAN 603/745-3463

American. Casual Dining. $14-$24 **AAA Inspector Notes:** The decor is charming and the cuisine tasty. A menu of original comfort foods includes the signature lobster and corn chowder, chicken Kiev, steaks and seafood. Diners should be sure to sample the white chocolate mousse served at the end of the meal. **Bar:** full bar. **Address:** 10 Pollard Rd (SR 112) 03251 **Location:** I-93 exit 32 (SR 112), 1.6 mi e.

GORDI'S FISH & STEAK HOUSE 603/745-6635

Steak. Family Dining. $9-$32 **AAA Inspector Notes:** The owners, Gordi and Karen Eaton, were on the Olympic ski team spanning the 1960s and '70s, and ski memorabilia graces the walls. The menu lists a wide selection, from prime rib and fresh Maine lobster to sandwiches and Santa Fe chicken. **Bar:** full bar. **Address:** 260 Main St 03251 **Location:** I-93 exit 32 (SR 112), 1.5 mi e.

GYPSY CAFÉ 603/745-4395

Regional American. Casual Dining. $7-$23 **AAA Inspector Notes:** Those who appreciate variety should stop in this small retro-style café for diverse dishes from around the world. For just a drink, check out the bright, neon-colored bar. **Bar:** full bar. **Address:** 117 Main St 03251 **Location:** I-93 exit 32 (SR 112), 1 mi e. **Parking:** street only.

PROFILE ROOM 603/745-8000

American
Casual Dining
$5-$20

AAA Inspector Notes: New England favorites, such as Yankee pot roast and baked stuffed haddock, as well as innovative dishes including sauteed shrimp and feta and veggie medley are among menu choices. The decor has a Native American motif, and the dining room affords scenic views. **Bar:** full bar. **Address:** 664 US Rt 3 03251 **Location:** I-93 exit 33 (US 3), 1.5 mi ne; in Indian Head Resort.

LITTLETON (C-3) pop. 4,412, elev. 875'

Prior to the Civil War Littleton was a station on the branch of the Underground Railroad that led northward to Vermont and Canada. It is now better known as a resort center and stopover for travelers bound for the White Mountains.

The Ammonoosuc River's 235-foot descent through Littleton was the catalyst for the city's transformation into a manufacturing and commercial center. The job of energy production now falls to Moore Station, a hydroelectric plant on the Connecticut River, 8 miles west on SR 18. One of New England's largest such projects, it impounds Moore Reservoir *(see Recreation Areas Chart)*.

Littleton Area Chamber of Commerce: 2 Union St., P.O. Box 105, Littleton, NH 03561. **Phone:** (603) 444-6561.

Self-guiding tours: A free brochure describing a walking tour of 22 historic sites along Main Street is available from the chamber of commerce.

LITTLETON GRIST MILL, just s. of US 302 at 18 Mill St., was built along the banks of the Ammonoosuc River in 1798. Restored to its original appearance, the mill produces stone-ground flours just as it did in the late 18th century. **Hours:** Tues.-Sat. 10:30-3:30. Phone ahead to confirm schedule. **Cost:** Free. **Phone:** (603) 259-3205.

THE BEAL HOUSE INN   603/444-2661
▼▼▼▼ **Historic Country Inn.** Rates not provided. **Address:** 2 W Main St 03561 **Location:** I-93 exit 42, 0.8 mi e on US 302 and SR 10. **Facility:** Built in 1833, this inn has attractive and comfortable guest rooms, many having a cozy gas fireplace. The on-site restaurant makes for delicious, convenient dining. 7 units, some two bedrooms. 3 stories (no elevator), interior corridors. **Dining:** The Beal House Restaurant Inn, see separate listing.

COUNTRY SQUIRE MOTEL   (603)444-5610
▼ **Motel** $59-$79 **Address:** 172 W Main St 03561 **Location:** I-93 exit 43, 1.4 mi s on SR 18. Located in a quiet area. **Facility:** 8 units. 1 story, exterior corridors. *Bath:* shower only. **Terms:** closed 10/29-5/16, 5 day cancellation notice-fee imposed. **Pool(s):** outdoor.

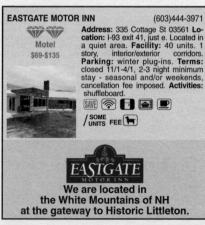

EASTGATE MOTOR INN   (603)444-3971
Motel
$69-$135
Address: 335 Cottage St 03561 **Location:** I-93 exit 41, just e. Located in a quiet area. **Facility:** 40 units. 1 story, interior/exterior corridors. **Parking:** winter plug-ins. **Terms:** closed 11/1-4/1, 2-3 night minimum stay - seasonal and/or weekends, cancellation fee imposed. **Activities:** shuffleboard.

/ SOME UNITS FEE

EASTGATE
MOTOR INN
We are located in the White Mountains of NH at the gateway to Historic Littleton.

EXIT 41 TRAVEL INN   603/259-3085

Motel
$60-$99
Address: 337 Cottage St 03561 **Location:** I-93 exit 41. **Facility:** 12 units. 1 story, exterior corridors. **Parking:** winter plug-ins. **Terms:** cancellation fee imposed. **Pool(s):** outdoor. **Free Special Amenities:** continental breakfast and high-speed Internet.

EXIT 41
Travel Inn
In the heart of the White Mountains near all recreation areas and attractions.

HAMPTON INN   603/444-0025
▼▼▼▼ **Hotel.** Rates not provided.
AAA Benefit: Members save up to 10%!
Address: 580 Meadow St 03561 **Location:** I-93 exit 42, just nw. Located in a commercial area. **Facility:** 88 units. 4 stories, interior corridors. **Parking:** winter plug-ins. **Amenities:** video games (fee), high-speed Internet. **Pool(s):** heated indoor. **Activities:** whirlpool, exercise room. *Fee:* game room. **Guest Services:** valet and coin laundry.

LITTLETON MOTEL   (603)444-5780
▼ **Motel** $68-$98 **Address:** 166 Main St 03561 **Location:** I-93 exit 42, 1.2 mi e on US 302 and SR 10; center. **Facility:** 19 units, some kitchens. 1 story, exterior corridors. **Terms:** closed 11/1-5/1. **Pool(s):** outdoor. **Activities:** shuffleboard.

MAPLE LEAF MOTEL   603/444-5105
▼ **Motel** $64-$101 **Address:** 150 W Main St 03561 **Location:** I-93 exit 43, 1.4 mi s on SR 18. Located in a quiet area. **Facility:** 13 units, some two bedrooms, efficiencies and kitchens. 1 story, exterior corridors. **Parking:** winter plug-ins. **Terms:** closed 4/7-5/17, 3 day cancellation notice-fee imposed. **Pool(s):** outdoor. **Activities:** playground, horseshoes.
/ SOME UNITS

THAYERS INN   603/444-6469
▼ ▼ **Historic Hotel.** Rates not provided. **Address:** 111 Main St 03561 **Location:** I-93 exit 42, 1.3 mi e on US 302 and SR 10; center. **Facility:** This 19th-century hotel in the town center features a model of an 1840s-era guest room. 35 units, some two bedrooms and efficiencies. 4 stories (no elevator), interior corridors. **Parking:** winter plug-ins. **Activities:** spa.
/ SOME UNITS

WHERE TO EAT

ASIAN GARDEN RESTAURANT   603/444-9888
▼▼ ▼ Asian. Casual Dining. $4-$16 **AAA Inspector Notes:** Right off Interstate 93, this easy-to-find restaurant serves traditional Asian dishes in an open dining room. A small full liquor bar serves as a great spot for unwinding. **Bar:** full bar. **Address:** 551 Meadow St 03561 **Location:** I-93 exit 42, just nw. L D CALL

THE BEAL HOUSE RESTAURANT INN   603/444-2661
▼▼▼▼

International Fine Dining
$9-$30
AAA Inspector Notes: An elegant and intimate dining room is enhanced with soft lighting, light jazz playing in the background and pleasant servers. **Bar:** full bar. **Reservations:** suggested. **Address:** 2 W Main St 03561 **Location:** I-93 exit 42, 0.8 mi e on US 302 and SR 10; in The Beal House Inn. D

ITALIAN OASIS RESTAURANT & BREWERY   603/444-6995

▼▼ ▼▼ Italian. Casual Dining. $7-$22 **AAA Inspector Notes:** Good, hearty food and friendly service are the attractions here. A fun menu features pizza, pasta and microbrews. The casual atmosphere includes an atrium and terrace, and there's live entertainment on Fridays during the summer. The lounge is open until 12:30 am. **Bar:** full bar. **Reservations:** suggested. **Address:** 106 Main St 03561 **Location:** US 302 and SR 10; center; in Parker's Marketplace.

[L] [D] [LATE]

LITTLETON DINER   603/444-3994

▼▼ ▼▼ American. Family Dining. $6-$12 **AAA Inspector Notes:** *Classic Historic.* A classic, historic diner with window booths and counter stool seating. Serving generous portions since 1930, menu selections include comfort foods such as breakfast dishes, meatloaf, steak, roast turkey, roast beef and fish and chips. **Address:** 145 Main St 03561 **Location:** Center. **Parking:** street only.

[B] [L] [D]

LONDONDERRY pop. 11,037

SLEEP INN   (603)425-2110

▼▼ Hotel $69-$139 **Address:** 72 Perkins Rd 03053 **Location:** I-93 exit 5. **Facility:** 99 units. 3 stories, interior corridors. **Terms:** cancellation fee imposed. **Pool(s):** heated indoor. **Activities:** whirlpool, exercise room. **Guest Services:** valet and coin laundry.

[✈] CALL [&M] [🖨] [BIZ] [🛜] [✕] [▣] [/SOME UNITS] [📶] [🖼]

WHERE TO EAT

THE COACH STOP RESTAURANT & TAVERN   603/437-2022

▼▼ ▼▼ American. Casual Dining. $9-$30 **AAA Inspector Notes:** There is something for everyone at this family run restaurant. Menu offerings include broiled Boston scrod, chicken parmesan, steak au poivre, and much more to choose from. Several dining rooms are throughout this restored farmhouse and the lounge is located on the second level. **Bar:** full bar. **Address:** 176 Mammoth Rd 03053 **Location:** I-93 exit 4, 1.7 mi w on SR 102. [L] [D]

LOUDON pop. 559

RED ROOF INN LOUDON #586   (603)225-8399

▼▼ ▼▼ Hotel $80-$216

Address: 2 Staniels Rd 03307 **Location:** I-393 exit 3, 1.5 mi n. **Facility:** 73 units. 2 stories (no elevator), interior corridors. **Pool(s):** heated indoor. **Guest Services:** coin laundry. **Free Special Amenities: continental breakfast and high-speed Internet.** *(See ad p. 185.)*

[SAVE] CALL [&M] [🖨] [🛜] [✕] [/SOME UNITS] [🐾] [📶] [🖼]

MANCHESTER (F-4) pop. 109,565, elev. 210'
• Hotels p. 214 • Restaurants p. 215

Logging helped to sustain early settlers in Manchester, and by 1810 the first cotton and woolen mills were in operation. The village was on its way to becoming the American counterpart of its British namesake, then the largest textile producing city in the world. In 1831 a group of Boston financiers bailed out a struggling cotton mill called the Amoskeag Cotton and Woolen Factory and reincorporated it as the Amoskeag Manufacturing Co.

Nearly 5 million yards of cloth were shipped each week from the brick mills, which employed thousands of workers and covered more than 8 million square feet. The mills thrived until the 1920s when a combination of stresses on the industry such as obsolete machinery, labor unrest and strong competition from the South, sapped its strength. In 1935 Amoskeag filed for bankruptcy and the mills fell silent.

But Manchester was not doomed to obscurity. A group of local businessmen pooled $5 million, purchased the mile-long ranks of mills and reactivated them with a diversified array of industries. Manchester is the state's industrial giant as well as its largest city and the home of nearly 10 percent of its population.

Just as the mills and the company houses have new tenants, so does the 1915 Palace Theatre at 80 Hanover St. The theater was known for its excellent acoustics and large stage. The New Hampshire Symphony and the Opera League of New Hampshire as well as national touring companies and various community groups perform at the fully restored theater; phone (603) 668-5588.

Manchester also is noted for its association with Gen. John Stark, who was born in Londonderry in 1728 and moved with his family to Derryfield—now Manchester—when he was 8. Stark fought the Abenaki Indians with Maj. William Rogers and his Rogers' Rangers, a backwoods fighting team that is considered the forerunner of today's Army Rangers. Stark died in 1822, having outlived every Patriot general except Marquis de Lafayette. His childhood home stands at 2000 Elm St.; his grave is in Stark Park, off N. River Road overlooking the river.

Greater Manchester Chamber of Commerce— Manchester: 54 Hanover St., Manchester, NH 03101. **Phone:** (603) 666-6600.

Shopping areas: The Mall of New Hampshire, 1500 S. Willow St., features JCPenney, Macy's and Sears. Elm Street and Hanover Street in downtown boast dozens of locally owned shops.

◆▼ **THE CURRIER MUSEUM OF ART,** 150 Ash St., is in a 1929 Beaux Arts building reminiscent of an Italian Renaissance palace. The museum showcases an internationally respected collection of European and American paintings, sculpture and decorative arts from the 13th century to the present. More than 11,000 objects are displayed, including works by Winslow Homer, Henri Matisse, Claude Monet, Georgia O'Keeffe, Pablo Picasso and Andrew Wyeth. Also included are American furniture and works by New Hampshire artists and craftsmen. Changing exhibitions, lectures and concerts are offered.

Time: Allow 1 hour, 30 minutes minimum. **Hours:** Sun.-Mon. and Wed.-Fri. 11-5 (also first Thurs. of the month 5-8), Sat. 10-5. Closed Jan. 1, Easter, July 4, Thanksgiving and Christmas. **Cost:** $10; $9 (ages 65+); $8 (students with ID); free (ages 0-17 and to all Sat. 10-noon). Combination ticket with Zimmerman House $20; $19 (ages 65+); $16 (students with ID); $8 (ages 7-17). **Phone:** (603) 669-6144. [🍽]

Zimmerman House is reached by van from The Currier Museum of Art, 150 Ash St. A 90-minute tour of the house and grounds provides an introduction to one of Frank Lloyd Wright's Usonian houses. The house, designed for Isadore J. and Lucille Zimmerman in 1950, contains original built-in and freestanding furniture, textiles and landscaping designed by Wright.

Time: Allow 1 hour, 30 minutes minimum. **Hours:** Tours depart Thurs.-Mon. at 11:30 and 2, Apr.-Oct.; Mon. and Thurs.-Fri. at 2, Sat.-Sun. at 11:30 and 2, Nov. 1 to mid-Jan. Closed Jan. 1, Easter, July 4, Thanksgiving and Christmas. Phone ahead to confirm schedule. **Cost:** (Includes The Currier Museum of Art) $20; $19 (ages 65+); $16 (students with ID); $8 (ages 7-17). Reservations are required. **Phone:** (603) 669-6144.

LAWRENCE L. LEE SCOUTING MUSEUM AND MAX I. SILBER LIBRARY, off I-93 exit 5 to Camp Carpenter on Bodwell Rd., features a collection of Boy Scout memorabilia dating from the late 19th century. The Max I. Silber Library houses a collection of scouting periodicals and handbooks. Hiking is available. **Time:** Allow 30 minutes minimum. **Hours:** Tues.-Thurs. and Sat. 10-4, July-Aug.; Sat. 10-4 or by appointment rest of year. Phone ahead to confirm schedule. **Cost:** Donations. **Phone:** (603) 669-8919.

MANCHESTER HISTORIC ASSOCIATION MILLYARD MUSEUM is in Mill #3 at 200 Bedford St., Suite 103. Exhibits survey area history and the development of the city's textile industry from the 1830s to the 1930s. Topics include Native Americans, Revolutionary War hero John Stark and immigrants who came to work in the mills. The museum is housed in one of the historic mills. A research library contains the records of the Amoskeag Manufacturing Co. as well as regional maps, diaries, photographs and other documents.

Time: Allow 1 hour minimum. **Hours:** Tues.-Sat. 10-4. Closed major holidays. **Cost:** $8; $6 (ages 62+ and students with ID); $4 (ages 12-18). **Phone:** (603) 622-7531.

NEW HAMPSHIRE INSTITUTE OF ART, 148 Concord St. at Pine St., is a fine arts college. Changing exhibitions by local and nationally known artists are featured in three galleries, and demonstrations and lectures are offered. **Time:** Allow 30 minutes minimum. **Hours:** Mon.-Fri. 9-5, Sat. 9-noon. Closed major holidays. **Cost:** Free. **Phone:** (603) 623-0313 or (866) 241-4918.

SEE SCIENCE CENTER, 200 Bedford St., has interactive exhibits that focus on a variety of topics including electricity, momentum, light and gravity. A LEGO mill yard exhibit features more than 3 million LEGOs. **Time:** Allow 1 hour minimum. **Hours:** Mon.-Fri. 10-4, Sat.-Sun. 10-5. Closed major holidays. **Cost:** $8; free (ages 0-2). **Phone:** (603) 669-0400.

BEST WESTERN PLUS EXECUTIVE COURT INN & CONFERENCE CENTER (603)627-2525

 Hotel $107-$117

AAA Benefit: Members save 10% or more with Best Western.

Address: 13500 S Willow St 03103 **Location:** I-293 exit 1, 0.5 mi s on SR 28, then 1 mi e. **Facility:** 136 units. 3 stories, interior corridors. **Terms:** cancellation fee imposed. **Amenities:** *Some:* safes. **Dining:** The Yard Seafood & Steak House, see separate listing. **Pool(s):** heated indoor. **Activities:** whirlpool, exercise room. *Fee:* game room. **Guest Services:** valet and coin laundry, area transportation-within 5 mi. **Free Special Amenities: local telephone calls and high-speed Internet.**

COMFORT INN (603)668-2600

 Hotel $79-$119

Address: 298 Queen City Ave 03102 **Location:** I-293 exit 4, just w. **Facility:** 104 units. 5 stories, interior corridors. **Terms:** cancellation fee imposed. **Pool(s):** heated indoor. **Activities:** exercise room. **Guest Services:** valet and coin laundry. **Free Special Amenities: expanded continental breakfast and airport transportation.**

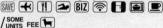

COURTYARD BY MARRIOTT MANCHESTER BOSTON REGIONAL AIRPORT (603)641-4900

 Hotel $89-$199 **Address:** 700 Huse Rd 03103 **Location:** I-293 exit 1, 0.5 mi se on SR 28. **Facility:** 139 units. 3 stories, interior corridors. **Amenities:** *Some:* high-speed Internet.

AAA Benefit: AAA hotel discounts of 5% or more.

Pool(s): heated indoor. **Activities:** whirlpool, exercise room. **Guest Services:** valet and coin laundry, area transportation-local area.

FAIRFIELD INN BY MARRIOTT-MANCHESTER AIRPORT (603)625-2020

 Hotel $79-$169 **Address:** 860 S Porter St 03103 **Location:** I-293 exit 1, just ne on SR 28. **Facility:** 102 units. 4 stories, interior corridors. **Pool(s):** outdoor. **Guest Services:** valet laundry.

AAA Benefit: AAA hotel discounts of 5% or more.

FOUR POINTS BY SHERATON (603)668-6110

 Hotel $89-$195

AAA Benefit: Members get up to 20% off, plus Starwood Preferred Guest® bonuses.

Address: 55 John E Devine Dr 03103 **Location:** I-293 exit 1, just nw on SR 28. **Facility:** 120 units. 4 stories, interior corridors. **Terms:** 3 day cancellation notice-fee imposed. **Amenities:** video games (fee). **Dining:** Nutfield Ale & Steak House, see separate listing. **Pool(s):** heated indoor. **Activities:** exercise room. **Guest Services:** valet laundry, area transportation-within 5 mi. **Free Special Amenities: local telephone calls and newspaper.**

Learn the local driving laws
at DrivingLaws.AAA.com

HILTON GARDEN INN MANCHESTER DOWNTOWN
(603)669-2222

▼▼◇ Hotel $129-$199 **Address:** 101 S Commercial St 03101 **Location:** I-293 exit 5, just e; jct W Granite and S Commercial sts, just s. Located at Northeast Delta Dental Stadium (Fisher Cats) baseball field. **Facility:** 125 units. 6 stories, interior corridors. **Terms:** 1-7 night minimum stay, cancellation fee imposed. **Amenities:** high-speed Internet. **Dining:** entertainment. **Pool(s):** heated indoor. **Activities:** whirlpool, exercise room. **Guest Services:** valet and coin laundry, area transportation-within 5 mi.

AAA Benefit: Unparalleled hospitality at a special Member rate.

HOLIDAY INN EXPRESS HOTEL & SUITES - MANCHESTER AIRPORT
603/669-6800

▼▼▼ Hotel. Rates not provided. **Address:** 1298 S Porter St 03103 **Location:** I-293 exit 1. **Facility:** 107 units. 3 stories, interior corridors. **Pool(s):** heated indoor. **Activities:** whirlpool, exercise room. **Guest Services:** complimentary and valet laundry, area transportation-within 2 mi.

HOLIDAY INN MANCHESTER AIRPORT
(603)641-6466

▼▼▼ Hotel $109-$134 **Address:** 2280 Brown Ave 03103 **Location:** I-293 exit 2, just s. **Facility:** 96 units. 4 stories, interior corridors. **Terms:** cancellation fee imposed. **Amenities:** video games (fee), high-speed Internet. **Dining:** Airport Diner, see separate listing. **Pool(s):** heated indoor. **Activities:** whirlpool, exercise room. **Guest Services:** complimentary and valet laundry.

HOMEWOOD SUITES BY HILTON
(603)668-2200

▼▼▼ **Extended Stay Hotel** $103-$189 **Address:** 1000 Perimeter Rd 03103 **Location:** I-293 exit 2, follow signs to Manchester-Boston Regional Airport. **Facility:** 124 units, some two bedrooms, efficiencies and kitchens. 4 stories, interior corridors. **Terms:** 1-7 night minimum stay, cancellation fee imposed. **Amenities:** video games (fee), high-speed Internet. **Pool(s):** heated indoor. **Activities:** whirlpool, sports court, exercise room. **Guest Services:** valet and coin laundry.

AAA Benefit: Contemporary luxury at a special Member rate.

LA QUINTA INN & SUITES MANCHESTER
(603)669-5400

▼▼▼ Hotel $68-$287 **Address:** 21 Front St 03102 **Location:** I-293 exit 6, just se. **Facility:** 109 units. 4 stories, interior corridors. **Pool(s):** outdoor. **Activities:** exercise room. **Guest Services:** valet and coin laundry.

RADISSON HOTEL MANCHESTER DOWNTOWN
(603)625-1000

▼▼▼ Hotel $119-$209 **Address:** 700 Elm St 03101 **Location:** Jct Granite St; downtown. **Facility:** 250 units. 12 stories, interior corridors. **Parking:** on-site (fee). **Amenities:** Some: safes. **Pool(s):** heated indoor. **Activities:** saunas, whirlpool. **Guest Services:** valet laundry, area transportation-within 10 mi. **Free Special Amenities:** high-speed Internet and airport transportation.

SPRINGHILL SUITES BY MARRIOTT MANCHESTER-BOSTON REGIONAL AIRPORT
(603)668-9400

▼▼▼ Hotel $89-$169 **Address:** 975 Perimeter Rd 03103 **Location:** I-293 exit 2, follow signs to Manchester-Boston Regional Airport. **Facility:** 100 units. 3 stories, interior corridors. **Amenities:** high-speed Internet. **Pool(s):** heated indoor. **Activities:** whirlpool, exercise room. **Guest Services:** valet and coin laundry, area transportation-local area.

AAA Benefit: AAA hotel discounts of 5% or more.

TOWNEPLACE SUITES BY MARRIOTT MANCHESTER-BOSTON REGIONAL AIRPORT
(603)641-2288

▼▼▼ **Extended Stay Hotel** $89-$179 **Address:** 686 Huse Rd 03103 **Location:** I-293 exit 1, 0.5 mi se on SR 28. **Facility:** 77 kitchen units, some two bedrooms. 3 stories, interior corridors. **Amenities:** high-speed Internet. **Pool(s):** heated indoor. **Activities:** exercise room. **Guest Services:** valet and coin laundry, area transportation-within 2 mi.

AAA Benefit: AAA hotel discounts of 5% or more.

WHERE TO EAT

AIRPORT DINER
603/623-5040

▼▼ American. Casual Dining. $5-$13 **AAA Inspector Notes:** In a handy location near the airport, it's easy for travelers to grab a bite at this place. The stainless-steel boxcar and 1950s décor make for a fun dining experience. Enjoy diner favorites such as melts, burgers and shepherd's pie. Breakfast is served all day. **Bar:** full bar. **Address:** 2280 Brown Ave 03103 **Location:** I-293 exit 2, just s; in Holiday Inn Manchester Airport. B L D 24

BILLY'S SPORTS BAR & GRILL
603/625-6294

▼▼ American. Casual Dining. $5-$16 **AAA Inspector Notes:** Off the beaten track about three miles from the center of town, this lively and casual sports bar is decorated in the traditional style, with lots of sports memorabilia and TVs surrounding the perimeter. Typical American fare--soups, burgers, salads and sandwiches--makes up the menu. **Bar:** full bar. **Address:** 34 Tarrytown Rd 03103 **Location:** 1.5 mi e of Elm St (SR 3). L D LATE

CHEN'S GARDEN
603/836-5608

▼▼ Chinese. Casual Dining. $8-$18 **AAA Inspector Notes:** New to the area, the restaurant serves fresh, tasty traditional Chinese-American items, such as standard and varied preparations of noodles, rice, chicken, beef, pork, pea pods and much more. **Bar:** full bar. **Address:** 956 Second St 03102 **Location:** On US 3. L D CALL

CJ'S GREAT WEST GRILL
603/627-8600

▼▼ American. Casual Dining. $7-$21 **AAA Inspector Notes:** The popular, lively restaurant prepares American cuisine from scratch with a Southwestern flair. Dishes range from soups, pastas, steaks, quesadillas, and terrific desserts. Call-ahead seating is encouraged. **Bar:** full bar. **Address:** 782 S Willow St 03103 **Location:** I-293 exit 1, 1 mi nw on SR 28. L D

COTTON
603/622-5488

▼▼▼ New American. Casual Dining. $7-$30 **AAA Inspector Notes:** In a restored textile mill overlooking the Merrimack River, the trendy bistro offers an incredible and memorable dining experience. The inviting, upscale decor is crisp and sleek. Highly trained servers are eager to share their knowledge of the menu and offer a wine suggestion. **Bar:** full bar. **Reservations:** suggested. **Address:** 75 Arms St 03101 **Location:** At Arms Park on the River, just off Commercial St; downtown. L D

FRATELLO'S RISTORANTE ITALIANO   603/624-2022

▼▼▼ Italian. Casual Dining. $9-$24 **AAA Inspector Notes:** In a renovated turn-of-the-20th-century textile mill, the popular restaurant presents a menu of such varied Italian favorites as piccata, parmigiana and Caesar salad. The atmosphere is fun. **Bar:** full bar. **Address:** 155 Dow St 03101 **Location:** I-293 exit 6 (W Bridge St), 0.3 mi e, 0.3 mi n on Canal St, then just e. L D

GAUCHOS BRAZILIAN STEAK HOUSE   603/669-9460

▼▼ Brazilian. Casual Dining. $15-$30 **AAA Inspector Notes:** In downtown Manchester, the steakhouse offers a dining experience like no other. There is a set price for the large variety of salads and meats that are brought to diners throughout the evening. Live music infuses the place on Friday and Saturday. **Bar:** full bar. **Address:** 62 Lowell St 03101 **Location:** Jct Elm St, just e; downtown. **Parking:** street only. L D

HANOVER STREET CHOPHOUSE   603/644-2467

▼▼▼▼ Steak. Fine Dining. $10-$55 **AAA Inspector Notes:** This upscale surf-and-turf restaurant is great for a nice lunch or dinner downtown. Relax amid classic steak house décor as you savor dry-aged steaks, veal and Maine lobster. Special function rooms also are available. **Bar:** full bar. **Reservations:** suggested. **Address:** 149 Hanover St 03101 **Location:** Just e of Elm St; jct Pine and Hanover sts; downtown. L D

JW HILL'S SPORTS BAR & GRILL   603/645-7422

▼▼ American. Gastropub. $8-$18 **AAA Inspector Notes:** This upscale sports bar and grill offers a large dining room surrounding a rectangular bar. Many flat screen TVs let you see whatever you would like. The menu offers items from steak tips to salmon. **Bar:** full bar. **Address:** 795 Elm St 03101 **Location:** Jct Elm and Merrimack sts; downtown. **Parking:** street only. L D

LA CARRETA   603/628-6899

▼▼ Mexican. Casual Dining. $10-$17 **AAA Inspector Notes:** Locals and travelers alike pack into this popular eatery for the large portions. The menu is made up of traditional Mexican fare but it is very fresh and affordable. The bar in the back of the dining room also is a popular hangout. **Bar:** full bar. **Address:** 545 Daniel Webster Hwy 03104 **Location:** I-93 exit 9, 0.5 mi s; in Maple Tree Mall. L D

MARGARITAS MEXICAN RESTAURANT   603/647-7717

▼▼ Regional Mexican. Casual Dining. $8-$20 **AAA Inspector Notes:** Diners will feel as though they have just stepped south of the border at this fun Mexican cantina. Traditional music fills the air while warm terracotta colored walls accented by painted pottery and unique jeweled star lanterns surround you. Sip on a large margarita while enjoying the freshly prepared fajitas, burritos, enchiladas, or quesadillas. **Bar:** full bar. **Address:** 1037 Elm St 03101 **Location:** Jct Elm and Concord sts; downtown. **Parking:** street only. L D

NINETY NINE RESTAURANT   603/641-5999

▼▼ American. Casual Dining. $7-$18 **AAA Inspector Notes:** This popular pub is committed to serving large portions of great food at reasonable prices. Guest favorites include hot wings, burgers, seafood, barbecue ribs and chicken. While reservations are not taken, call-ahead seating is offered. A children's menu is also available. **Bar:** full bar. **Address:** 1685 S Willow St 03103 **Location:** I-293 exit 1, just s. L D

NUTFIELD ALE & STEAK HOUSE   603/668-6110

▼▼ American. Casual Dining. $10-$26 **AAA Inspector Notes:** The locally known Nutfield Ale Company also has a restaurant. Guests can expect a casual atmosphere, friendly servers, good food and great beer. **Bar:** full bar. **Address:** 55 John E Devine Dr 03103 **Location:** I-293 exit 1, just nw on SR 28; in Four Points by Sheraton. B L D

OLLIE'S FOOD & SPIRITS   603/626-3711

▼▼ American. Casual Dining. $5-$19 **AAA Inspector Notes:** Local charm is found at the restaurant, where the menu consists mostly of traditional comfort foods. Among choices are fried chicken, barbecue lamb, fried haddock, burgers and delicatessen sandwiches. **Bar:** full bar. **Reservations:** suggested. **Address:** 761 Mast Rd 03102 **Location:** On SR 114A. L D

PEKING GARDEN CHINESE RESTAURANT   603/623-8880

▼▼▼ Chinese. Casual Dining. $6-$13 **AAA Inspector Notes:** Easy to find in the center of town, the Chinese restaurant serves up fresh food in a small dining room with wood walls and Asian art. Takeout and delivery service are options here. **Bar:** full bar. **Address:** 967 Elm St 03101 **Location:** Between Concord and Amherst sts; center. **Parking:** on-site (fee) and street. L D

PICCOLA RISTORANTE   603/606-5100

▼▼ Italian. Casual Dining. $10-$25 **AAA Inspector Notes:** This is an attractive but small bistro with tightly spaced seating. Ultimately, the dishes are terrific with homemade pastas, sauces and desserts. **Bar:** full bar. **Reservations:** suggested. **Address:** 815 Elm St 03101 **Location:** Between Merrimack and Manchester sts; downtown. **Parking:** street only. L D

PURITAN BACKROOM   603/669-6890

▼▼ American. Casual Dining. $6-$28 **AAA Inspector Notes:** Established in 1917, the popular eatery is a local landmark. Favorite libations and edibles include mudslides, fried chicken tenders, the Texasburger and Greek specialty pizza. **Bar:** full bar. **Address:** 245 Hooksett Rd 03104 **Location:** I-93 exit 9 southbound, 1 mi s. L D CALL ♿M

THE SHASKEEN IRISH PUB & RESTAURANT   603/625-0246

▼▼ Irish. Casual Dining. $7-$14 **AAA Inspector Notes:** Irish décor and a wide-ranging menu of bar entrées—from sandwiches to wraps to steaks—are what you'll find at this fun downtown spot. Nightlife picks up after 10 pm; Irish bands perform certain days of the week. **Bar:** full bar. **Address:** 909 Elm St 03101 **Location:** Between Amherst and Hanover sts; center. **Parking:** on-site (fee) and street. L D LATE

SHOGUN JAPANESE STEAK HOUSE   603/669-8122

▼▼ Japanese. Casual Dining. $8-$24 **AAA Inspector Notes:** The Japanese restaurant offers two styles of dining rooms: one with hibachi grills where chefs prepare food in front of guests and one with more typical restaurant-style service of items ranging from sushi to filet mignon. **Bar:** full bar. **Address:** 545 Hooksett Rd 03104 **Location:** I-93 exit 9, 0.5 mi s; in Maple Tree Mall. L D

SHORTY'S MEXICAN ROADHOUSE   603/625-1730

▼▼ Mexican. Casual Dining. $6-$18 **AAA Inspector Notes:** Casual, vibrant décor enlivens the festive setting, where helpful servers hustle to your table with well-prepared Mexican specialties, including nachos, quesadillas, fajitas, chimichangas, burritos and enchiladas, as well as chili, soups and pasta. **Bar:** full bar. **Address:** 1050 Bicentennial Dr 03105 **Location:** I-93 exit 9; in Northside Plaza Shopping Center. L D

THOUSAND CRANE   603/634-0000

▼▼ Chinese. Casual Dining. $7-$25 **AAA Inspector Notes:** A full sushi bar may seem incongruous in a spot that prepares mostly Chinese (rather than Japanese) dishes, but both offerings coexist nicely at this centrally located restaurant. **Bar:** full bar. **Address:** 1000 Elm St, Unit 6 03101 **Location:** Downtown; in Hampshire Plaza. **Parking:** street only. L D

TINKER'S SEAFOOD   603/622-4272

▼ Seafood. Casual Dining. $5-$23 **AAA Inspector Notes:** Fresh seafood is fried to order immediately after diners order at the counter and wait for a number. Take-out is popular, as is the adjacent seafood market. **Bar:** beer & wine. **Address:** 545 Daniel Webster Hwy (Hooksett Rd) 03104 **Location:** I-93 exit 9, 0.5 mi s on SR 28/US 3; in Maple Tree Mall. L D

UNWINE'D   603/625-9463

▼▼ Small Plates. Fine Dining. $12-$26 **AAA Inspector Notes:** Perfect for a first date, this contemporary/retro dining room puts its primary focus on wine, but the food is great as well. **Bar:** wine only. **Address:** 865 Second St 03102 **Location:** I-293 exit 4, just s; in Mallard Pond Plaza. D LATE

THE WAY WE COOK DINING
603/625-5454

WWW Italian. Fine Dining. $14-$30 **AAA Inspector Notes:** Rekindle romance and dine on often-changing Italian selections at this cozy spot on the north side of downtown. The sophisticated bar whips up some interesting concoctions. **Bar:** full bar. **Address:** 1361 Elm St, Suite 108 03101 **Location:** Jct Myrtle and Elm sts; downtown. **Parking:** street only. [D]

XO ON ELM
603/560-7998

WWWW Northern American. Casual Dining. $8-$29 **AAA Inspector Notes:** This happening and hip bistro has become a favorite among locals. Diners may opt to nosh on tasty small plates and entrées at the bar or at a table. A few enticing examples are truffle goat cheese and wild mushroom strudel, dates stuffed with cream cheese and a chorizo filling, coriander dusted crab cakes and a raspberry-glazed half duck. The servers are enthusiastic about the dishes and happy to assist with recommendations. **Bar:** full bar. **Reservations:** suggested. **Address:** 827 Elm St 03101 **Location:** At Manchester St; downtown. **Parking:** street only. [L] [D]

THE YARD SEAFOOD & STEAK HOUSE
603/623-3545

WW Steak. Casual Dining. $7-$26 **AAA Inspector Notes:** The casual, cozy restaurant has floral wallpaper and comfortable booths. Among offerings of American fare are sandwiches, chicken and steaks. **Bar:** full bar. **Address:** 1211 S Mammoth Rd 03109 **Location:** I-293 exit 1, 0.5 mi s on SR 28, then 1 mi e; next to BEST WESTERN PLUS Executive Court Inn & Conference Center.
[L] [D]

MASON (G-3) elev. 760'

PICKITY PLACE is at 248 Nutting Hill Rd. The site consists of themed gardens and the woods and cottage that inspired award-winning illustrator Elizabeth Orton Jones' drawings of the classic children's story "Little Red Riding Hood." Illustrations from the 1948 edition of the story are displayed. Workshops about herbs and gardening are offered. **Time:** Allow 1 hour, 30 minutes minimum. **Hours:** Daily 10-5, Apr.-Dec.; 10-4, rest of year. Closed Jan. 1, Easter, July 4, Thanksgiving and Christmas. **Cost:** Free. **Phone:** (603) 878-1151, ext. 0. [T1]

PARKER'S MAPLE BARN
603/878-2308

WW Breakfast Sandwiches. Casual Dining. $5-$13 **AAA Inspector Notes:** On a snaky country road sits the 200-year old converted barn restaurant which is noted for its hearty breakfasts (served all day) and overstuffed sandwiches. Maple syrup is produced on site each spring and is bottled and sold, along with other sweets created from this amber liquid. It is even incorporated into the menu, simmered into the baked beans, the brewing coffee and there is even a maple Swiss burger. **Address:** 1316 Brookline Rd 03048 **Location:** Jct SR 101 and 13, 6 mi s, 3 mi w on Mason Rd.
[B] [L] [AC]

MEREDITH (E-4) pop. 1,718

WINNIPESAUKEE SCENIC RAILROAD departs Meredith and Weirs Beach stations. A 2-hour train ride takes visitors along the scenic shore of Lake Winnipesaukee. **Time:** Allow 2 hours minimum. **Hours:** Train departs daily at 10:30, 12:30 and 2:30, mid-June through Labor Day; Sat.-Sun. at 10:30, 12:30 and 2:30, Memorial Day to mid-June and day after Labor Day-late Oct. Phone ahead to confirm schedule. **Cost:** $15; $11 (ages 3-11). Fares may vary; phone ahead. **Phone:** (603) 279-5253. [T1]

BAY POINT AT MILL FALLS
(603)279-7006

WWW Hotel $209-$379 **Address:** 1 SR 25 03253 **Location:** Waterfront. Jct US 3 and SR 25; center. **Facility:** 24 units. 4 stories, interior corridors. **Terms:** 2-3 night minimum stay - seasonal and/or weekends, 3 day cancellation notice-fee imposed, resort fee. **Activities:** boat dock, ice skating. **Guest Services:** valet laundry.
[icons]

CHASE HOUSE AT MILL FALLS
(603)279-7006

WWW Hotel $199-$369 **Address:** 300 Daniel Webster Hwy 03253 **Location:** Jct US 3 and SR 25; center. **Facility:** 21 units. 4 stories, interior corridors. **Terms:** 2-3 night minimum stay - seasonal and/or weekends, 3 day cancellation notice-fee imposed, resort fee. **Dining:** Camp, see separate listing. **Guest Services:** valet laundry.
[icons]

CHURCH LANDING AT MILL FALLS
(603)279-7006

WWWW Hotel $239-$509 **Address:** 281 Daniel Webster Hwy 03253 **Location:** Waterfront. Jct US 3 and SR 104, 0.6 mi n. **Facility:** 73 units, some cottages. 4 stories, interior/exterior corridors. **Terms:** 2-3 night minimum stay - seasonal and/or weekends, 3 day cancellation notice-fee imposed, resort fee. **Amenities:** *Some:* safes. **Pool(s):** heated indoor/outdoor. **Activities:** whirlpools, limited beach access, rental canoes, rental paddleboats, boat dock, fishing, ice skating, game room, exercise room, spa. *Fee:* charter fishing. **Guest Services:** valet laundry.
[icons] / SOME UNITS FEE

THE INN AT MILL FALLS
(603)279-7006

WWWW Hotel $109-$289 **Address:** 312 Daniel Webster Hwy 03253 **Location:** Jct US 3 and SR 25; center. **Facility:** 54 units. 5 stories, interior corridors. **Terms:** 2-3 night minimum stay - seasonal and/or weekends, 3 day cancellation notice-fee imposed, resort fee. **Pool(s):** heated indoor. **Activities:** whirlpool, spa. **Guest Services:** valet laundry.
ECO [icons] / SOME UNITS FEE

MEREDITH INN B & B
(603)279-0000

WWW Bed & Breakfast $119-$219 **Address:** 2 Waukewan St 03253 **Location:** Jct US 3 and SR 25, 0.4 mi sw on Main St. **Facility:** A renovated Victorian painted lady, the inn was built in 1897 and features many antique furnishings. Guest rooms are spacious, two have a fireplace and six have a whirlpool tub. 8 units. 2 stories (no elevator), interior corridors. **Terms:** closed 4/1-4/30, 2 night minimum stay - seasonal and/or weekends, 14 day cancellation notice-fee imposed. [icons]

WHERE TO EAT

CAMP
603/279-3003

WW American. Casual Dining. $9-$24 **AAA Inspector Notes:** Fashioned after an Adirondack camp complete with a fieldstone fireplace and tin ceiling, this casual restaurant prepares comfort food (steaks, pot roast, chicken, pork and seafood) with a trendy twist. And of course, there are s'mores for dessert. **Bar:** full bar. **Address:** 300 Daniel Webster Hwy 03253 **Location:** Jct US 3 and SR 25; center; in Chase House at Mill Falls. [D]

GIUSEPPE'S SHOW TIME PIZZERIA
603/279-3313

WW Italian. Casual Dining. $8-$22 **AAA Inspector Notes:** In a bustling marketplace, the restaurant serves large portions of antipasti, gourmet pizza, scampi, parmigiana and more. **Bar:** full bar. **Address:** 312 Daniel Webster Hwy 03253 **Location:** Jct US 3 and SR 25; in Mill Falls Marketplace. [L] [D]

HART'S TURKEY FARM RESTAURANT
603/279-6212

WWW
American Family Dining
$5-$22

AAA Inspector Notes: Operated by the Hart family since 1954, the popular family restaurant specializes in home-style cooking, particularly turkey preparations. Also on the menu are beef, pasta and seafood dishes. Almost everything is made on the premises. Contributing to the decor is an extensive collection of turkey plates. **Bar:** full bar. **Address:** 233 Daniel Webster Hwy 03253 **Location:** Jct US 3 and SR 104. [L] [D]

MAME'S RESTAURANT   603/279-4631

▼▼ ▼▼ American. Casual Dining. $7-$25 **AAA Inspector Notes:** *Historic.* Close to shops and lodgings, the cozy, informal restaurant was converted from a private residence dating to 1825. The cuisine includes seafood, steak and pasta entrees; flavorful prime rib is a specialty. Lighter fare is served in the pub. **Bar:** full bar. **Address:** 8 Plymouth St 03253 **Location:** Just w of jct US 3 and SR 25; center.

L   D

SUNSHINE & PA'S RESTAURANT   603/279-5280

▼▼ ▼▼ American. Casual Dining. $5-$10 **AAA Inspector Notes:** The restaurant is great for breakfast and lunch, serving traditional breakfast fare along with soup, sandwiches and homemade desserts daily. **Address:** 11 Main St 03253 **Location:** Just w of US 3 and SR 104. **Parking:** street only.   B   L

TOWN DOCKS   603/279-3445

▼▼ Seafood. Casual Dining. $6-$20 **AAA Inspector Notes:** On Bay of Meredith, this seafood restaurant lets guests dine outdoors on a sandy beach overlooking the water. If the weather is bad, everything is moved indoors. **Bar:** full bar. **Address:** 289 Daniel Webster Hwy (US 3) 03253 **Location:** At the public dock on the bay.

B   L   D   ℵ

MERRIMACK (G-4) elev. 122'

ANHEUSER-BUSCH INC. is e. off Everett Tpke. exit 10 at 221 Daniel Webster Hwy. Tours include a visit to the brew hall, cold cellars, sampling room, packaging facilities and Clydesdale stables. A time-line exhibit chronicles the history of Anheuser-Busch Inc. Behind-the-scenes Beermaster Tours include a visit to the brewhouse, hop room, primary fermentation cellar, lager cellar, packaging facility, quality as-

surance room and finishing cellar.

Note: Pants and closed-toe shoes are required for the Beermaster Tour. **Time:** Allow 1 hour, 30 minutes minimum. **Hours:** Daily 10-5, June-Aug.; daily 10-4, Sept.-Dec.; Thurs.-Mon. 10-4, rest of year. Beermaster Tour schedule varies; phone ahead. Closed Jan. 1, Easter, Thanksgiving, Christmas Eve, Christmas and Dec. 31. **Cost:** Regular tours free. Beermaster Tours $25 (ages 21+); $10 (ages 13-20). Children must be with an adult. Reservations are required for Beermaster Tours. **Phone:** (603) 595-1202.

**RESIDENCE INN BY MARRIOTT
NASHUA-MERRIMACK**   (603)424-8100

▼▼ ▼▼   **AAA Benefit:** AAA hotel discounts of 5% or more.

Extended Stay Hotel
$94-$179

Address: 246 Daniel Webster Hwy 03054 **Location:** Everett Tpke exit 11, just e, then 0.6 mi s on US 3. **Facility:** 129 kitchen units, some two bedrooms. 2-3 stories (no elevator); interior/exterior corridors. **Amenities:** *Some:* high-speed Internet. **Pool(s):** outdoor. **Activities:** whirlpool, sports court, exercise room. **Guest Services:** valet and coin laundry. **Free breakfast and high-speed Internet.**

Special Amenities: full breakfast and high-speed Internet. *(See ad this page.)*

SAVE ECO CALL &M 🐾 BIZ 📶 ✕ 📶 🖥 📼 / SOME UNITS FEE 🐕

▼ See AAA listing this page ▼

WHERE TO EAT

BUCKLEY'S GREAT STEAKS AT RIDDLE'S TAVERN
603/424-0995

▼▼▼▼ Steak. Fine Dining. $13-$39 **AAA Inspector Notes:** Excellent wood-grilled steaks are served here in a variety of A-one cuts. Traditional side options with a modern twist include the must-have creamed spinach, garlic mashed potatoes and bacon and potato rustic griddle hash. **Bar:** full bar. **Reservations:** suggested. **Address:** 438 Daniel Webster Hwy 03054 **Location:** On US 3. D

THE LOBSTER BOAT RESTAURANT
603/424-5221

▼▼ Seafood. Casual Dining. $7-$20 **AAA Inspector Notes:** The friendly staff at this highly casual local favorite serves fried seafood, burgers and more. **Bar:** beer & wine. **Address:** 453 Daniel Webster Hwy 03054 **Location:** 1.5 mi n on US 3. L D

MILFORD pop. 8,835

MILE AWAY RESTAURANT
603/673-3904

▼▼▼▼ European. Casual Dining. $15-$33 **AAA Inspector Notes:** Located on a tranquil country road with high trees and rock walls, this hidden treasure offers a blend of European and American favorites. Schnitzels, filet mignon, parmigiana, rack of lamb and surf and turf are just a few of the menu offerings. Four course all inclusive meals are an exceptional value. Housed in a converted barn built in 1812, the interior features two dining rooms, both with huge open hearth fire places and antique wood panel walls. **Bar:** full bar. **Reservations:** suggested. **Address:** 52 Federal Hill Rd 03055 **Location:** Jct SR 101 and 13, just s on SR 13, just e on Emerson Rd, then just s. D

MILTON (E-5) pop. 575, elev. 440'

NEW HAMPSHIRE FARM MUSEUM is off SR 16 exit 18, then .7 mi. s. on SR 125. The museum, housed on two historic farmsteads, reflects New Hampshire's agricultural past through tours of the Jones farmhouse, displays of antique farm implements, heritage breeds of farm animals and demonstrations of rural arts. The farmsteads are considered the best preserved examples of connected farm structures in the state. A cider mill and blacksmith shop also are on the premises.

Tours: Guided tours are available. **Time:** Allow 1 hour minimum. **Hours:** Wed.-Sun. 10-5, mid-June to mid-Oct.; Sat.-Sun. 10-4, mid-May to mid-June and mid-Oct. to mid-Nov. Last tour departs 30 minutes before closing. **Cost:** $7; $6 (ages 65+); $4 (ages 4-17); $20 (family). **Phone:** (603) 652-7840. 🅰🅣

MOULTONBOROUGH (D-4) elev. 808'

CASTLE IN THE CLOUDS, 3 mi. s. of jct. SRs 25 and 109, then 2 mi. e. on SR 171 to 455 Old Mountain Rd., is a turn-of-the-20th-century mansion set amid the Ossipee Mountains. A self-guiding tour provides visitors with an overview of the castle's history and technology. Spectacular views of Lake Winnipesaukee and the surrounding area can be seen from virtually every room. Twenty-eight miles of hiking trails traverse the property. Horseback and carriage rides are available.

Time: Allow 1 hour, 30 minutes minimum. **Hours:** Daily 10-4, mid-June to late Oct.; Sat.-Sun. 10-4, mid-May to mid-June. **Cost:** $16; $12 (ages 65+ and students ages 16-20 with ID); $8 (ages 5-15).

Grounds only $5 (ages 7+). **Phone:** (603) 476-5900. 🍴

THE LOON CENTER, jct. Blake Rd. and SR 25, 1 mi. s.w. on Blake Rd., then s. on Lee's Mills Rd., offers loon exhibits, videotapes and nature trails showcasing woodlands, wetlands, lakeshore and more. **Time:** Allow 1 hour, 30 minutes minimum. **Hours:** Daily 9-5, July 1-Columbus Day; Mon.-Sat. 9-5, May-June and day after Columbus Day-Dec. 31; Thurs.-Sat. 9-5, rest of year. Nature trails daily dawn-dusk. Closed Jan. 1, Thanksgiving and Christmas. **Cost:** Free. **Phone:** (603) 476-5666.

THE WOODSHED RESTAURANT
603/476-2311

▼▼▼ American. Casual Dining. $19-$34 **AAA Inspector Notes:** The popular restaurant is housed in a 200-year-old farmhouse and barn. Handsome, rustic surroundings add to a pleasant dining experience. Among the nicely prepared offerings are tasty, slow-roasted prime rib and fresh seafood. **Bar:** full bar. **Reservations:** suggested. **Address:** 128 Lee Rd 03254 **Location:** Jct SR 25 and Old SR 109 by airport, 1.1 mi s on SR 109, then 0.7 mi w. D

MOUNT WASHINGTON (C-4) elev. 6,288'

At 6,288 feet, Mount Washington, in the Presidential Range of the White Mountains, is the Northeast's highest peak. The weather at its summit rivals that of Antarctica: the average annual temperature is below freezing. Fifteen feet of snow is the winter norm, and summer temperatures rarely exceed 72 F. The highest wind velocity ever recorded—231 mph—occurred in April 1934.

Conditions can change in minutes from balmy to subfreezing. Nevertheless, in clear weather, the summit rewards visitors with a panorama that includes the Atlantic Ocean, Maine, New Hampshire, Québec and Vermont.

MOUNT WASHINGTON AUTO ROAD is reached via SR 16, about 8 mi. s. of Gorham. The scenic trip requires 30 to 45 minutes each way; frequent turnouts provide views. Low gear should be used both ways. Because of steep grades and sharp curves, driving instructions are available at the toll house and should be heeded. For those who prefer not to drive, guided tours are available with a 1-hour stop at the summit.

Note: For safety, towed trailers, motor homes, pickup campers, certain vehicles with full passenger loads, vehicles with a wheelbase longer than 161 inches or wider than 85 inches (including mirrors) are not permitted. Allow 2 hours minimum for the driving tour or the guided tour.

Hours: Daily 7:30-6, early June-Labor Day; schedule varies early May-early June and day after Labor Day-late Oct. (weather permitting). Guided tours daily 8:30-5, mid-May through Sept. 30; 8:30-4:30, Oct. 1-third week in Oct. (weather permitting). SnowCoach guided tours daily 8:30-3, Dec.-Mar. (weather permitting). **Cost:** Driving tour (includes CD) $26 (driver); $8 (passengers); $6 (ages 5-12);

$16 (motorcycle and driver). Guided tour $35; $30 (ages 62+ and military with ID); $15 (ages 5-12). SnowCoach tour $45; $30 (ages 5-12). **Phone:** (603) 466-3988.

 MOUNT WASHINGTON COG RAILWAY — see Bretton Woods p. 179.

SHERMAN ADAMS SUMMIT BUILDING, atop Mount Washington, offers a 360-degree view of the northern Presidential Range. Visitors can see the restored 1853 Tip Top House, one of the oldest mountaintop buildings in the country and the first hotel on Mount Washington. The summit building honors Sherman Adams, a former governor of New Hampshire and one of the state's best-known political, civic and business leaders. An information desk, a glass-enclosed viewing area and a weather museum are in the building.

The building is accessible via hiking trails, the Mount Washington Auto Road or the Cog Railway. **Time:** Allow 1 hour minimum. **Hours:** Daily 9-6, Memorial Day-late Oct. (weather permitting). **Cost:** Free. **Phone:** (603) 466-3347. 🍴

NASHUA pop. 86,494

BEST WESTERN GRANITE INN (603)883-7700

 Motel $80-$231 | Best Western | **AAA Benefit:** Members save 10% or more with Best Western.

Address: 10 St. Laurent St 03060 **Location:** US 3 (Everett Tpke) exit 7E, just e. **Facility:** 100 units. 2 stories (no elevator), interior corridors. **Terms:** cancellation fee imposed. **Amenities:** high-speed Internet, safes. **Pool(s):** outdoor. **Guest Services:** valet and coin laundry. **Free Special Amenities: expanded continental breakfast and use of on-premises laundry facilities.**

 / SOME UNITS FEE 🐕

COURTYARD BY MARRIOTT NASHUA (603)880-9100

Hotel $99-$249 **Address:** 2200 Southwood Dr 03063 **Location:** US 3 (Everett Tpke) exit 8, just w. Located in Southwood Corporate Park. **Facility:** 245 units. 4 stories, interior corridors. **Amenities:** high-speed Internet. **Pool(s):** heated indoor. **Activities:** whirlpool, exercise room. **Guest Services:** valet and coin laundry.

AAA Benefit: AAA hotel discounts of 5% or more.

 / SOME UNITS

CROWNE PLAZA HOTEL NASHUA (603)886-1200

Hotel $129-$179 **Address:** 2 Somerset Pkwy 03063 **Location:** US 3 (Everett Tpke) exit 8, just w. **Facility:** 230 units, some two bedrooms. 8 stories, interior corridors. **Terms:** cancellation fee imposed. **Amenities:** video games (fee), high-speed Internet. **Dining:** Speaker's Corner Restaurant, see separate listing. **Pool(s):** heated indoor. **Activities:** saunas, whirlpool, spa. **Guest Services:** valet laundry, area transportation-within 5 mi.

/ SOME UNITS

HAMPTON INN NASHUA (603)883-5333

Hotel $89-$169 **Address:** 407 Amherst St 03063 **Location:** US 3 (Everett Tpke) exit 8. **Facility:** 102 units. 4 stories, interior corridors. **Terms:** 1-7 night minimum stay, cancellation fee imposed. **Amenities:** high-speed Internet. **Pool(s):** heated indoor. **Activities:** whirlpool, exercise room. **Guest Services:** valet and coin laundry.

AAA Benefit: Members save up to 10%!

/ SOME UNITS FEE 🐕

HOLIDAY INN & SUITES NASHUA 603/888-1551

Hotel. Rates not provided. **Address:** 9 Northeastern Blvd 03062 **Location:** US 3 (Everett Tpke) exit 4, just w, then 0.3 mi n. **Facility:** 198 units, some efficiencies. 4 stories, interior corridors. **Terms:** check-in 4 pm. **Pool(s):** outdoor. **Activities:** exercise room. **Guest Services:** valet and coin laundry.

/ SOME UNITS FEE

MOTEL 6 #2019 (603)888-1893

Motel $53-$59 **Address:** 77 Spitbrook Rd 03060 **Location:** US 3 (Everett Tpke) exit 1, just e. **Facility:** 115 units. 3 stories, exterior corridors. **Guest Services:** coin laundry.

CALL / SOME UNITS 🐕

RADISSON HOTEL NASHUA (603)888-9970

Hotel $89-$219 | **Address:** 11 Tara Blvd 03062 **Location:** US 3 (Everett Tpke) exit 1, just w. **Facility:** 326 units. 7 stories, interior corridors. **Terms:** cancellation fee imposed. **Amenities:** video games (fee). **Pool(s):** outdoor, heated indoor. **Activities:** sauna, whirlpool, steamrooms, spa. **Guest Services:** valet laundry. **Free Special Amenities:** newspaper and high-speed Internet.

/ SOME UNITS FEE FEE

WHERE TO EAT

COUNTRY TAVERN RESTAURANT AND LOUNGE 603/889-5871

American. Casual Dining. $8-$20 **AAA Inspector Notes:** Some diners may feel the presence of Elizabeth the "friendly ghost." The menu lists a vast selection of comfort foods. **Bar:** full bar. **Address:** 452 Amherst St 03063 **Location:** US 3 (Everett Tpke) exit 8, 1 mi w on SR 101A. L D

JOE'S AMERICAN BAR & GRILL 603/891-2060

American. Casual Dining. $12-$25 **AAA Inspector Notes:** If it's Americana you want, you'll get all that and more at Joe's, where the bill of fare includes all-American favorites like hearty burgers, fresh-from-the-oven chicken pot pies, Maryland lump crab cakes, and Joe's classic meatloaf. Pizzas, pastas, steaks and salads round out the extensive menu, giving diners the freedom to choose from a vast selection of offerings. There's nothing more American than that, except, of course, for apple pie, so save some room. **Bar:** full bar. **Address:** 310 Daniel Webster Hwy 03060 **Location:** In Pheasant Lane Mall. L D

LA CARRETA RESTAURANTE MEXICANO 603/891-0055

Mexican. Casual Dining. $10-$17 **AAA Inspector Notes:** In a small strip mall, this Mexican eatery offers colorful décor, a friendly staff and a wide selection of favorites. **Bar:** full bar. **Address:** 139 Daniel Webster Hwy 03060 **Location:** US 3 (Everett Tpke) exit 2, just n. L D

LILAC BLOSSOM 603/886-8420

Chinese. Casual Dining. $7-$19 **AAA Inspector Notes:** The restaurant serves Asian cuisine in a casual atmosphere and is very popular among the locals. **Bar:** full bar. **Address:** 650 Amherst St 03063 **Location:** 3 mi w of US 3 (Everett Tpke) on SR 101A; in Greystone Plaza. L D

MARTHA'S EXCHANGE RESTAURANT & BREWING CO
603/883-8781
▼▼ ▼▼ American. Casual Dining. $7-$22 **AAA Inspector Notes:** The friendly neighborhood pub serves up a good variety of comfort foods and an excellent selection of homemade specialty brews. **Bar:** full bar. **Address:** 185 Main St 03060 **Location:** Between High and Garden sts; downtown. **Parking:** street only. [L] [D]

MT'S LOCAL KITCHEN & WINE BAR
603/595-9334
▼▼▼▼ Regional American. Casual Dining. $10-$34 **AAA Inspector Notes:** The food quality along with the service at this bistro-style kitchen is solid. The menu includes creative pizza, burgers and meatloaf—all best described as gourmet comfort foods. **Bar:** full bar. **Reservations:** suggested. **Address:** 212 Main St 03060 **Location:** US 3 (Everett Tpke) exit 7, 1.5 mi se on SR 101A, 0.5 mi s. **Parking:** street only. [D]

NATHANIEL'S FAMILY EATERY
603/883-4052
▼▼ ▼▼ American. Family Dining. $7-$19 **AAA Inspector Notes:** This family-run restaurant is strictly casual and serves up dishes of homemade pasta, steak, salads and more. **Bar:** full bar. **Address:** 537 Amherst St 03063 **Location:** US 3 (Everett Tpke) exit 8, 2 mi w on SR 101A. [B] [L] [D]

SHORTY'S MEXICAN ROADHOUSE
603/882-4070
▼▼ ▼▼ Mexican. Casual Dining. $5-$19 **AAA Inspector Notes:** Located in the Nashua Mall parking lot, this popular Mexican-American spot is ever-popular with hungry shoppers and the lunch crowd. **Bar:** full bar. **Address:** 48 Gusabel Ave 03060 **Location:** US 3 (Everett Tpke) exit 6, just w; in Nashua Mall parking lot.
[L] [D] CALL [M]

SPEAKER'S CORNER RESTAURANT
603/886-1200
▼▼ ▼▼ American. Casual Dining. $8-$25 **AAA Inspector Notes:** The restaurant is convenient from the adjacent strip mall and nearby businesses. Menu selections consist of New York sirloin and chicken and pasta dishes. **Bar:** full bar. **Address:** 2 Somerset Pkwy 03063 **Location:** US 3 (Everett Tpke) exit 8, just w; in Crowne Plaza Hotel Nashua. [B] [L] [D]

SURF
603/595-9293
▼▼▼▼ American. Fine Dining. $15-$28 **AAA Inspector Notes:** On par with its sister restaurant, Michael Timothy's, the menu is creative and filled with fresh fish and extensive raw-bar offerings. Preparations are delicious and flavorful, and the knowledgeable staff is proficient in making suggestions. **Bar:** full bar. **Address:** 207 Main St 03060 **Location:** US 3 (Everett Tpke) exit 7, 1.5 mi se on SR 101A, then 0.5 mi s. [D]

VILLA BANCA
603/598-0500
▼▼▼▼ Italian. Casual Dining. $7-$24 **AAA Inspector Notes:** The chef-owned downtown restaurant provides fantastic Italian fare, with homemade pasta and other creatively prepared traditional dishes. Intimate dining is enhanced with muted background music, trendy and tasteful décor and thoughtful service. **Bar:** full bar. **Reservations:** suggested. **Address:** 194 Main St 03060 **Location:** US 3 (Everett Tpke) exit 7, 1.5 mi se on SR 101A, then 0.4 mi s. **Parking:** street only. [L] [D]

NEWBURY (E-3)

Beginning the first Saturday in August, Newbury's 9-day ▼ League of New Hampshire Craftsmen's Fair is said to be the oldest craft fair in the country; phone (603) 224-3375.

THE FELLS HISTORIC ESTATE AND GARDENS is 2.2 mi. n. on SR 103A. The Fells, which overlooks Lake Sunapee, was the early 20th-century summer estate of three generations of the Hay family. John M. Hay, a diplomat and writer, served as President Abraham Lincoln's private secretary and secretary of state under presidents William McKinley and Theodore Roosevelt. The estate includes a 22-room

house; a rock garden with more than 600 varieties of alpine plants; nature trails for hiking and snow-shoeing; and period gardens with roses, rhododendrons and azaleas.

Pets are not permitted. **Time:** Allow 1 hour minimum. **Hours:** Grounds open daily 9-5. House open Wed.-Sun. and Mon. holidays 10-4, mid-June through Labor Day; Sat.-Sun. and Mon. holidays 10-4, Memorial Day to mid-June and day after Labor Day-Columbus Day. **Cost:** $10; $8 (ages 65+ and students with ID); $4 (ages 6-17); $25 (family). **Phone:** (603) 763-4789.

MOUNT SUNAPEE STATE PARK is 3 mi. s. at jct. SRs 103 and 103B. This 2,893-acre recreation area includes a 200-acre network of trails for skiing and hiking. Chairlifts transport winter skiers *(see Recreational Activities)* and summer sightseers 1.2 miles to the 2,743-foot top of Mount Sunapee. The summit building has an observation platform. There is an exhibition trout pool near the base building. A beach with a bathhouse borders the lake. Boating, fishing, hiking and swimming are permitted. *See Recreation Areas Chart.*

Hours: Park open Mon.-Fri. 9-dusk, Sat.-Sun. 8:30-dusk, Memorial Day-Labor Day. Summer chairlift operates daily 10-4:30, mid-June through Labor Day; Sat.-Sun. 9-5, late May to mid-June. Phone ahead to confirm schedule. **Cost:** Free. Beach $5; $2 (ages 6-11). Round-trip lift fare $7; $6 (ages 13-18 and 65-69); $5 (ages 6-12 and 70+). One-way lift fare $5. Fees may vary; phone ahead. **Phone:** (603) 763-5561. [icons]

RECREATIONAL ACTIVITIES

Skiing
• **Mount Sunapee** is at 1398 SR 103. Other activities are offered. **Hours:** Mon.-Fri. 9-4, Sat.-Sun. and holidays 8-4, mid-Dec. to early Apr. (weather permitting). **Phone:** (603) 763-3500, or (603) 763-4020 for snow updates.

BEST WESTERN SUNAPEE LAKE LODGE
603/763-2010

Hotel
Rates not provided

AAA Benefit: Members save 10% or more with Best Western.
Address: 1403 SR 103 03255 **Location:** Jct SR 103B, just e. **Facility:** 55 units. 3 stories, interior corridors. **Amenities:** high-speed Internet. **Pool(s):** heated indoor. **Activities:** ice skating, volleyball, exercise room. **Guest Services:** coin laundry. **Free Special Amenities:** local telephone calls and high-speed Internet.
[SAVE] [icons] CALL [M] [icons] [BIZ] [icons] [X] [icons] [icons] [icons]
/ SOME UNITS FEE [icon]

NEW CASTLE (F-5)
• Hotels p. 222 • Restaurants p. 222
• Hotels & Restaurants map & index p. 239

Narrow streets with old houses flush to the curbs lend a Colonial air to New Castle, founded as a fishing village on Great Island in the late 1600s. To the east of the square is a historic site containing the

(See map & index p. 239.)

remnants of Fort Constitution, the site of the first overt acts of rebellion against the British Crown.

Originally Fort Constitution was the British stronghold Fort William and Mary. On Dec. 14, 1774, following a little-known warning ride by Paul Revere, Portsmouth's Sons of Liberty, accompanied by Durham and New Castle patriots, captured the fort and seized the British powder and arms. Stored in Durham (see place listing p. 189), the munitions were used against the British 4 months later at the battle of Bunker Hill.

President Theodore Roosevelt won a Nobel Peace Prize for work done in New Castle. In 1905 he negotiated the Treaty of Portsmouth, which ended the Russo-Japanese War.

WENTWORTH BY THE SEA MARRIOTT HOTEL & SPA
(603)422-7322 **19**

Historic Hotel
$199-$469

AAA Benefit: AAA hotel discounts of 5% or more.

Address: 588 Wentworth Rd 03854 **Location:** Waterfront. On SR 1B, 2 mi e of SR 1A. **Facility:** Once host to many dignitaries, this grand and luxurious 19th-century hotel is nestled oceanside. Although restored, the property retains an ambiance of bygone times. 161 units, some two bedrooms and kitchens. 4 stories, interior/exterior corridors. **Parking:** on-site and valet. **Terms:** check-in 4 pm, 3 day cancellation notice. **Amenities:** high-speed Internet, safes. **Dining:** The Dining Room at Wentworth By The Sea, see separate listing. **Pool(s):** 2 heated outdoor, heated indoor. **Activities:** whirlpools, steamrooms, lighted tennis court, exercise room, spa. Fee: golf-18 holes. **Guest Services:** valet laundry, area transportation-within 5 mi. **Free Special Amenities: local telephone calls and high-speed Internet.**

SAVE ❘❙ 🍴 �̶ 🏊 BIZ 🛜 ✕ 📹 ▄ 🖥
/ SOME UNITS FEE 🐕 📷

WHERE TO EAT

THE DINING ROOM AT WENTWORTH BY THE SEA
603/373-6566 **28**

▼▼▼ New American. Fine Dining. $10-$40 **AAA Inspector Notes:** Not only does this destination offer fine lodging but memorable dining as well. The waterfront location is serene and breathtaking. Diners may sample a variety of the freshest of fish, fine cuts of meat and wonderful homemade desserts. **Bar:** full bar. **Reservations:** suggested. **Address:** 588 Wentworth Rd 03854 **Location:** On SR 1B, 2 mi e of SR 1A; in Wentworth By The Sea Marriott Hotel & Spa. **Parking:** on-site and valet. B L D

NEWFIELDS pop. 301

SHIP TO SHORE FOOD & SPIRITS   603/778-7898
▼▼▼ Regional American. Casual Dining. $17-$29 **AAA Inspector Notes:** Ship to Shore's lively setting is in a 1793 New England barn. It was built by a master shipbuilder who formed the beams of the attic as though for a mast of a ship. The unusual atmosphere features a quaint decor and menu offerings of char-grilled steak, homemade pasta and fresh seafood. The serving staff is prompt, friendly and knowledgeable. **Bar:** full bar. **Reservations:** suggested. **Address:** SR 108 03856 **Location:** On SR 108, 0.5 mi n of SR 85. D

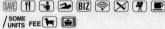

Visit your AAA/CAA Travel office to book a AAA Vacations® Disney package

---

NEW LONDON pop. 1,415

FAIRWAY MOTEL AT LAKE SUNAPEE COUNTRY CLUB
603/526-0202

▼ Motel $69-$109 **Address:** 344 Andover Rd 03257 **Location:** I-89 exit 11, 3 mi e on SR 11. **Facility:** 12 units. 2 stories (no elevator), exterior corridors. **Terms:** 2 night minimum stay - seasonal and/or weekends, 14 day cancellation notice-fee imposed. **Pool(s):** outdoor. ❘❙ 🚶 🛜 ✕ / SOME UNITS FEE 🐕 🖥

THE INN AT PLEASANT LAKE   (603)526-6271
▼▼▼ Country Inn $185-$225 **Address:** 853 Pleasant St 03257 **Location:** Waterfront. I-89 exit 12 (SR 11), 3 mi se, then 1.5 mi ne from center. **Facility:** This attractive 1790 farmhouse overlooks Pleasant Lake. A five-course dinner is served Wednesday through Sunday in season. 10 units. 3 stories (no elevator), interior corridors. **Terms:** 2 night minimum stay - weekends, 14 day cancellation notice-fee imposed. **Dining:** restaurant, see separate listing. **Activities:** beach access, canoeing, boat ramp, fishing, 3 tennis courts, ice skating, basketball, volleyball, exercise room.
❘❙ 🛜 ✕ 🏊 / SOME UNITS 📺

NEW LONDON INN   603/526-2791
▼▼▼
Country Inn
$144-$259
Address: 353 Main St 03257 **Location:** Center. Adjacent to Colby-Sawyer College. **Facility:** Antiques and reproductions are among the furnishings at this inn dating from 1792. 23 units. 3 stories (no elevator), interior corridors. **Terms:** 2 night minimum stay - seasonal and/or weekends, 3 day cancellation notice. **Activities:** ice skating. **Free Special Amenities: expanded continental breakfast and local telephone calls.**
SAVE ❘❙ 🍷 🛜 ✕ / SOME UNITS 🐕 🖥

WHERE TO EAT

FLYING GOOSE BREW PUB & GRILLE   603/526-6899
▼▼ American. Casual Dining. $7-$19 **AAA Inspector Notes:** Well-prepared American cuisine is served in an informal setting. The microbrewery serves Flying Goose and 16 house brews in a rustic pub-style atmosphere. Try the chocolate hazelnut porter cake while admiring views of Mount Kearsarge. **Bar:** full bar. **Reservations:** suggested. **Address:** 40 Andover Rd 03257 **Location:** I-89 exit 11, 1 mi e to jct SR 11 and 114. L D

THE INN AT PLEASANT LAKE   603/526-6271
▼▼▼ Continental. Fine Dining. $55 **AAA Inspector Notes:** Guests can expect to enjoy a glass of wine before the chef comes out to explain the menu for the evening at this inn. The highly skilled chef/owner serves amazing flavorful food in an elegant dining room overlooking Lake Pleasant. A perfect place for a romantic date. Semiformal attire. **Bar:** full bar. **Reservations:** required. **Address:** 853 Pleasant St 03257 **Location:** I-89 exit 12 (SR 11), 3 mi se, 1.5 mi ne from center. D

MACKENNA'S RESTAURANT   603/526-9511
▼▼ American. Casual Dining. $4-$14 **AAA Inspector Notes:** In the parking lot of a small strip mall, this family restaurant prepares most of its dishes in house. A country feel makes this a comfortable spot to stop for a bite after shopping. **Address:** 293 Newport Rd 03257 **Location:** I-89 exit 12 (SR 11), 2 mi e.
B L D

MILLSTONE RESTAURANT   603/526-4201
▼▼▼ American. Fine Dining. $11-$24 **AAA Inspector Notes:** The light, airy setting has a casual elegance that fits perfectly with the cuisine of well-prepared seafood, wild game, pasta, vegetarian dishes and desserts. A full wine list is presented. Servers are knowledgeable. **Bar:** full bar. **Address:** 74 Newport Rd 03257 **Location:** I-89 exit 12 (SR 11), 2.2 mi e. L D

NORTH CONWAY (D-5) pop. 2,349, elev. 546'
• Hotels p. 228 • Restaurants p. 233
• Hotels & Restaurants map & index p. 225

So taken was he with the view of Mount Washington from North Conway's main street that artist Benjamin Champney set up his easel in the middle of the road in August 1850 and painted the scene. Subsequently he and other artists depicted Thompson's Falls and many other nearby spots. Champney supposedly sold several of his New Hampshire landscapes to a chromolithograph company that circulated reproductions.

As the commercial center of the Mount Washington Valley recreation area, the community thrives on a year-round throng of visitors who come not only for outdoor sports and sightseeing, but also for dining, shopping and nightlife. The arts scene is another attraction. The Mount Washington Valley Theatre Company offers a varied repertoire during July and August; phone (603) 356-5776.

Mount Washington Valley Chamber of Commerce: 2617 White Mountain Hwy. at Village Sq., P.O. Box 2300, North Conway, NH 03860. **Phone:** (603) 356-3171, or (800) 367-3364 out of N.H.

Shopping areas: Bargain hunters enjoy Main Street, where the L.L. Bean Shopping Center, Red Barn Factory Stores, Settler's Green and White Mountain Outlets feature such stores as Brooks Brothers, Geoffrey Beene, Nautica and Ralph Lauren.

CONWAY SCENIC RAILROAD, off SR 16 and US 302, offers nostalgic, narrated, round-trip train rides of varying duration. Excursions are powered by early diesel locomotives over tracks laid in the 1870s. A 1921 steam engine pulls the Conway train from mid-September to mid-October and some weekends in early winter. Trains depart from the 1874 North Conway Station. The Valley Train runs to Conway and Bartlett, while the Crawford Notch train travels into the mountains. First-class dining cars are available.

Time: Allow 1 hour, 30 minutes minimum. **Hours:** Trains to Conway and Bartlett depart mid-Apr. through Dec. 31. Crawford Notch train runs late June to mid-Oct. Phone ahead to confirm schedule. **Cost:** $15.50-$80; $11-$64 (ages 4-12); free-$40 (ages 0-3). Reservations are recommended. **Phone:** (603) 356-5251, or (800) 232-5251 out of N.H. 🍴 🎁

ECHO LAKE STATE PARK, 1.5 mi. w. of US 302 off Old West Side Rd., covers 396 acres. A scenic road near the top of Cathedral Ledge, 700 feet above the river valley, offers a view of the White Mountains and the Saco River Valley. Just south is Echo Lake, which offers swimming, hiking and climbing opportunities, with White Horse Ledge providing a spectacular backdrop. *See Recreation Areas Chart.*

Time: Allow 1 hour minimum. **Hours:** Daily 9-6, mid-June through Labor Day. Phone ahead to confirm schedule. **Cost:** $4; $2 (ages 6-11). **Phone:** (603) 356-2672, or (603) 323-2087 in the off-season. 🍽 🏕

FARM BY THE RIVER BED AND BREAKFAST WITH STABLES, 2555 West Side Rd., offers 1-hour horseback sightseeing rides through 70 acres of meadows, woods and maple trees and along the Saco River, with panoramic views of surrounding mountains. Also offered is a 45-minute tour aboard a horse-drawn Victorian sleigh, a 12-passenger sleigh, a carriage or a 12-passenger wagon. Pony rides also are available. Allow 1 hour minimum for riding tours.

Hours: Trips depart four to five times daily starting at 10. Passengers should arrive 30 minutes before departure. **Cost:** Two- to four-person Victorian sleigh or carriage rides $85-$120. Large sleigh or wagon $15.50 per adult; $10.50 (ages 3-11). Horseback tours $50. Reservations are recommended. **Phone:** (603) 356-6640 or (603) 356-2694.

MOUNT WASHINGTON OBSERVATORY WEATHER DISCOVERY CENTER is at 2779 White Mountain Hwy. Interactive exhibits explore the science of climate and weather. Visitors can speak with meteorologists at the Mount Washington summit, forecast the weather in a mock television studio, and learn how tornadoes form. Mount Washington is said to have some of the world's most extreme weather, and the observatory plays an important role in recording and researching atmospheric conditions.

Time: Allow 1 hour minimum. **Hours:** Daily 10-5. Closed Jan. 1, Easter, Thanksgiving and Christmas. Phone ahead to confirm schedule. **Cost:** Donations. **Phone:** (603) 356-2137, or (800) 706-0432 for schedule confirmation.

▼ See AAA listing p. 253 ▼

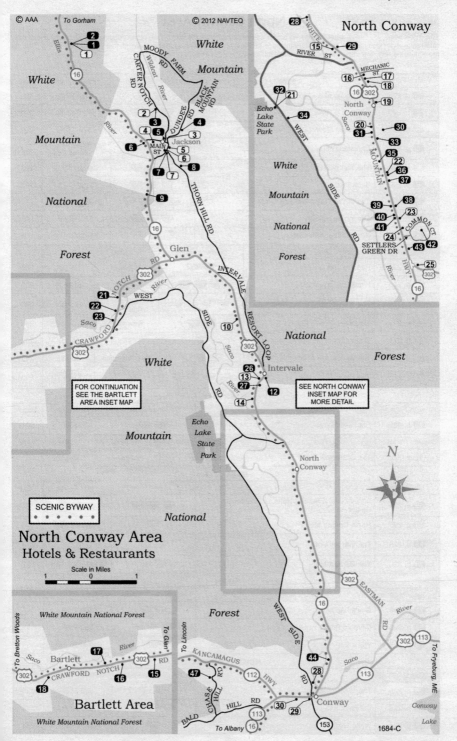

North Conway

White
Mountain

White

Mountain

National

Forest

FOR CONTINUATION
SEE THE BARTLETT
AREA INSET MAP

SEE NORTH CONWAY
INSET MAP FOR
MORE DETAIL

White

Mountain

National

Forest

Echo
Lake
State
Park

Jackson

Glen

Intervale

North
Conway

N

SCENIC BYWAY

North Conway Area
Hotels & Restaurants

Scale in Miles
1   0   1

White Mountain National Forest

Bartlett

To Breton Woods

Bartlett Area
White Mountain National Forest

Forest

To Lincoln

To Albany

Conway

Conway
Lake

To Fryeburg, ME

1684-C

North Conway Area

This index helps you "spot" where approved hotels and restaurants are located on the corresponding detailed maps. Hotel daily rate range is for comparison only. Restaurant price range is a combination of lunch and/or dinner. Turn to the listing page for more detailed rate and price information and consult display ads for special promotions.

JACKSON

Map Page	Hotels	Diamond Rated	Rate Range	Page
1 p. 225	The Lodge at Jackson Village	◆◆	$119-$249	202
2 p. 225	Inn at Ellis River	◆◆◆	$129-$329	202
3 p. 225	The Eagle Mountain House & Golf Club	◆◆◆	$79-$229	202
4 p. 225	Christmas Farm Inn & Spa	◆◆◆	Rates not provided	202
5 p. 225	**The Wentworth**	◆◆◆	$99-$325 [SAVE]	203
6 p. 225	Snowflake Inn	◆◆◆	$169-$375	202
7 p. 225	**The Inn at Thorn Hill and Spa**	◆◆◆◆	$169-$440 [SAVE]	202
8 p. 225	The Inn at Jackson	◆◆◆	$119-$259	202
9 p. 225	**Nordic Village Resort**	◆◆◆	$89-$869 [SAVE]	202

Map Page	Restaurants	Diamond Rated	Cuisine	Price Range	Page
① p. 225	Red Fox Bar & Grille	◆◆	American	$9-$24	203
② p. 225	Highfields Tavern	◆◆◆	American	$10-$25	203
③ p. 225	**The Wentworth Dining Room**	◆◆◆◆	Regional American	$25-$28	203
④ p. 225	Thompson House Eatery	◆◆	American	$14-$32	203
⑤ p. 225	Yesterdays of Jackson Village	◆	American	$5-$12	203
⑥ p. 225	The Wildcat Inn & Tavern	◆◆◆	New American	$6-$25	203
⑦ p. 225	The Inn at Thorn Hill	◆◆◆◆	Regional American	$18-$30	203

INTERVALE

Map Page	Hotel	Diamond Rated	Rate Range	Page
12 p. 225	Old Field House	◆◆	$75-$350	201

Map Page	Restaurant	Diamond Rated	Cuisine	Price Range	Page
⑩ p. 225	The Scarecrow Pub & Grill	◆◆	American	$5-$17	201

BARTLETT

Map Page	Hotels	Diamond Rated	Rate Range	Page
15 p. 225	Attitash Grand Summit Hotel and Conference Center	◆◆◆	$119-$499	177
16 p. 225	**North Colony Motel**	◆	$49-$159 [SAVE]	178
17 p. 225	The Villager Motel	◆◆	Rates not provided	178
18 p. 225	**The Bartlett Inn**	◆◆	$109-$248 [SAVE]	177

GLEN

Map Page	Hotels	Diamond Rated	Rate Range	Page
21 p. 225	Golden Apple Inn	◆◆	$60-$229	194
22 p. 225	Covered Bridge House	◆◆◆	$89-$139	194
23 p. 225	**Will's Inn**	◆	$49-$235 [SAVE]	194

NORTH CONWAY

Map Page	Hotels	Diamond Rated	Rate Range	Page
26 p. 225	The 1785 Inn & Restaurant	◆◆	$69-$199	228
27 p. 225	Cabernet Inn	◆◆◆	$99-$239	228
28 p. 225	White Trellis Motel	◆	$59-$269	232

NORTH CONWAY (cont'd)

Map Page	Hotels (cont'd)	Diamond Rated	Rate Range	Page
29 p. 225	**Eastern Inns** (See ad p. 228.)	♦♦	$55-$155 SAVE	228
30 p. 225	Red Elephant Inn	♦♦♦	Rates not provided	231
31 p. 225	**Briarcliff Motel**	♦♦	$59-$249 SAVE	228
32 p. 225	**White Mountain Hotel & Resort** (See ad p. 232.)	♦♦♦	$109-$269 SAVE	232
33 p. 225	**Red Jacket Mountain View Resort and Indoor Water Park**	♦♦♦	$109-$339 SAVE	232
34 p. 225	**The Farm by the River Bed & Breakfast with Stables**	♦♦	$100-$200 SAVE	229
35 p. 225	**North Conway Mountain Inn**	♦♦	$79-$199 SAVE	231
36 p. 225	**Comfort Inn & Suites**	♦♦♦	$99-$209 SAVE	228
37 p. 225	**Fox Ridge Resort**	♦♦	$99-$209 SAVE	229
38 p. 225	**Residence Inn by Marriott, North Conway**	♦♦♦	$94-$236 SAVE	232
39 p. 225	**Golden Gables Inn**	♦♦	$60-$229 SAVE	229
40 p. 225	North Conway Hampton Inn & Suites	♦♦♦	$85-$225	231
41 p. 225	**Holiday Inn Express Hotel & Suites** (See ad p. 230.)	♦♦♦	$105-$260 SAVE	230
42 p. 225	**North Conway Grand Hotel** (See ad p. 231.)	♦♦♦	$79-$229 SAVE	231
43 p. 225	**Green Granite Inn and Conference Center** (See ad p. 229.)	♦♦	$70-$280 SAVE	229
44 p. 225	**Merrill Farm Inn**	♦♦	Rates not provided SAVE	231

Map Page	Restaurants	Diamond Rated	Cuisine	Price Range	Page
13 p. 225	The 1785 Inn Restaurant	♦♦♦	Continental	$16-$36	233
14 p. 225	Moat Mt Smokehouse & Brewing Co.	♦♦	Barbecue	$9-$25	233
15 p. 225	Delaney's Hole in the Wall	♦♦	American	$7-$25	233
16 p. 225	**Hooligan's**	♦♦	American	$9-$21	233
17 p. 225	Horsefeather's	♦♦	American	$9-$23	233
18 p. 225	A Taste of Thai Restaurant	♦♦	Thai	$8-$26	233
19 p. 225	Peach's Restaurant	♦♦	American	$5-$9	233
20 p. 225	Muddy Moose Restaurant & Pub	♦♦	American	$6-$20	233
21 p. 225	Ledges Dining Room (See ad p. 232.)	♦♦♦	American	$21-$29	233
22 p. 225	China Chef	♦♦	Chinese	$5-$15	233
23 p. 225	The Blueberry Muffin	♦	American	$3-$8	233
24 p. 225	Merlino's Family Steakhouse	♦♦	American	$9-$35	233
25 p. 225	The Peking Sunrise Restaurant Lounge	♦♦	Chinese	$5-$20	233

ALBANY

Map Page	Hotel	Diamond Rated	Rate Range	Page
47 p. 225	**The Darby Field Inn**	♦♦♦	$150-$300 SAVE	177

CONWAY

Map Page	Restaurants	Diamond Rated	Cuisine	Price Range	Page
28 p. 225	Jonathon's Seafood Restaurant & Fish Market	♦♦	Seafood	$8-$17	187
29 p. 225	Fire 21 Pizza	♦	Pizza	$2-$12	187
30 p. 225	Cafe Noche Mexican	♦♦	Mexican	$5-$15	186

(See map & index p. 225.)

THE 1785 INN & RESTAURANT   (603)356-9025 **26**

▼▼ ▼▼ **Historic Country Inn** $69-$199 **Address:** 3582 White Mountain Hwy 03860 **Location:** 2 mi n on US 302/SR 16. **Facility:** Mountain views enhance guests' stay. Rooms are furnished with antiques and reproductions. 17 units, some kitchens. 3 stories (no elevator), interior corridors. *Bath:* some shared. **Parking:** winter plugins. **Terms:** 7 day cancellation notice-fee imposed. **Dining:** The 1785 Inn Restaurant, see separate listing. **Pool(s):** outdoor. **Activities:** cross country skiing, hiking trails, jogging, shuffleboard, volleyball.

ECO ❙❙↑ 🏊 📶 ✕ ☎
/ SOME UNITS AC 🅿 🖥 📠 🖥

BRIARCLIFF MOTEL   603/356-5584 **31**

▼▼▼ **Motel** $59-$249
Address: 2304 White Mountain Hwy 03860 **Location:** 0.5 mi s on SR 16; village center. **Facility:** 31 units. 1 story, exterior corridors. **Terms:** 2 night minimum stay - seasonal and/or weekends, 7 day cancellation notice-fee imposed. **Pool(s):** heated outdoor. **Activities:** shuffleboard. **Guest Services:** coin laundry. **Free Special Amenities: local telephone calls and newspaper.**

SAVE 🏊 FEE📶↑ 📶 ✕ 🖥 🖥

CABERNET INN   603/356-4704 **27**

▼▼▼ **Historic Bed & Breakfast** $99-$239 **Address:** 3552 White Mountain Hwy 03860 **Location:** On US 302/SR 16, 1.5 mi nw of village center. **Facility:** On grounds highlighted by picturesque gardens, this 1842 property features some guest rooms with fireplaces. 11 units. 3 stories (no elevator), interior/exterior corridors. **Terms:** 2 night minimum stay - seasonal and/or weekends, age restrictions may apply, 15 day cancellation notice-fee imposed. **Activities:** cross country skiing, hiking trails.

ECO ❙❙↑ FEE📶↑ 📶 ✕ / SOME UNITS 🅿 🖥

COMFORT INN & SUITES   (603)356-8811 **36**

▼▼ ▼▼ **Hotel** $99-$209
Address: 2001 White Mountain Hwy 03860 **Location:** 1.4 mi s on US 302/SR 16. **Facility:** 59 units. 3 stories, interior corridors. **Terms:** check-in 4 pm, cancellation fee imposed. **Amenities:** safes. **Pool(s):** heated indoor. **Activities:** exercise room. *Fee:* miniature golf. **Guest Services:** coin laundry. **Free Special Amenities: full breakfast and high-speed Internet.**

SAVE ❙❙↑ 🏊 📶 ✕ 🖥
🖥 🖥

Located in the heart of the White Mountains with Free Hot Breakfast Buffet & Free WiFi.

EASTERN INNS   (603)356-5447 **29**

▼▼ **Hotel** $55-$155
Address: 2955 White Mountain Hwy 03860 **Location:** 0.5 mi n on US 302/SR 16. **Facility:** 56 units. 2 stories (no elevator), interior corridors. **Terms:** 3 day cancellation notice-fee imposed. **Pool(s):** heated indoor. **Activities:** cross country skiing, playground, basketball, exercise room. *Fee:* game room. **Guest Services:** coin laundry. **Free Special Amenities: expanded continental breakfast.** *(See ad this page.)*

SAVE 🏊 📶 ✕
/ SOME UNITS 🖥 🖥

▼ *See AAA listing this page* ▼

Learn about inspections and Diamond Ratings at AAA.com/Diamonds

(See map & index p. 225.)

THE FARM BY THE RIVER BED & BREAKFAST WITH STABLES
(603)356-2694 **34**

Historic Bed & Breakfast

$100-$200

Address: 2555 West Side Rd 03860 **Location:** Jct SR 16/113 (Main St in Conway), just n on Washington St, then 5.3 mi n. Located in a quiet rural area. **Facility:** Covering 70 acres, this is a former working farm with pastures and sugar maple orchards. Guided trail rides originate from a stable on the property. Some rooms include a fireplace. 7 units, some two bedrooms. 2 stories (no elevator), interior corridors. **Terms:** check-in 4 pm, 2 night minimum stay - weekends, 14 day cancellation notice-fee imposed. **Activities:** fishing. *Fee:* horseback riding. **Free Special Amenities: full breakfast and high-speed Internet.** SAVE ECO 📶 ✕ ☎ / SOME UNITS 📺

FOX RIDGE RESORT
(603)356-3151 **37**

Hotel

$99-$209

Address: 1979 White Mountain Hwy 03860 **Location:** 1 mi s on US 302/SR 16. Located in a quiet area. **Facility:** 136 units, some two bedrooms. 2 stories (no elevator), interior corridors. **Terms:** closed 10/27-5/15, 2 night minimum stay - seasonal and/or weekends, cancellation fee imposed. **Pool(s):** heated outdoor, heated indoor. **Activities:** whirlpool, miniature golf, tennis court, recreation programs in summer, hiking trails, playground, basketball, shuffleboard. *Fee:* game room. **Guest Services:** coin laundry. **Free Special Amenities: full breakfast and high-speed Internet.**
SAVE 🍴 CALL &M 🏊 BIZ 📶 ✕ 🔌 💻

GOLDEN GABLES INN
(603)356-2878 **39**

Motel

$60-$229

Address: 1814 White Mountain Hwy 03860 **Location:** Jct US 302/SR 16, 1 mi n. **Facility:** 58 units. 1-2 stories (no elevator), exterior corridors. **Terms:** 2 night minimum stay - seasonal and/or weekends. **Pool(s):** heated outdoor. **Activities:** whirlpool, snowmobiling, playground, horseshoes. **Guest Services:** coin laundry. SAVE 🍴 🏊 📶 ✕ 🔌 / SOME UNITS 📺

GREEN GRANITE INN AND CONFERENCE CENTER
(603)356-6901 **43**

Hotel

$70-$280

Address: 1515 White Mountain Hwy (Rt 16) 03860 **Location:** 2.3 mi s on US 302/SR 16; village center. **Facility:** 91 units, some two bedrooms and kitchens. 2 stories (no elevator), interior/exterior corridors. **Terms:** check-in 4 pm, 3 day cancellation notice-fee imposed. **Pool(s):** heated outdoor, heated indoor. **Activities:** whirlpool, playground, exercise room. *Fee:* game room. **Guest Services:** valet and coin laundry. **Free Special Amenities: continental breakfast and high-speed Internet.** *(See ad this page.)*

SAVE 🍴 🏊 BIZ 📶 ✕ 💻 / SOME UNITS 🔌 📺

▼ See AAA listing this page ▼

(See map & index p. 225.)

Visit AAA.com/Travel
or CAA.ca/Travel for
complete trip planning
and reservations

HOLIDAY INN EXPRESS HOTEL & SUITES

(603)356-2551   41

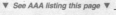

Hotel
$105-$260

Address: 1732 White Mountain Hwy 03860 **Location:** 2 mi s on US 302/SR 16; village center. **Facility:** 78 units. 3 stories, interior corridors. **Terms:** check-in 4 pm, 2 night minimum stay - seasonal and/or weekends. **Pool(s):** heated indoor. **Activities:** whirlpool. *Fee:* game room. **Guest Services:** coin laundry. **Free Special Amenities: expanded continental breakfast and high-speed Internet.** *(See ad this page.)*

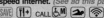

▼ *See AAA listing p. 252* ▼

(See map & index p. 225.)

MERRILL FARM INN
603/447-3866

Motel
Rates not provided

Address: 428 White Mountain Hwy 03860 **Location:** Jct SR 16 and US 302, 1.5 mi s on SR 16; 0.5 mi n of village center. **Facility:** 60 units, some two bedrooms and cabins. 2 stories (no elevator), interior/exterior corridors. **Pool(s):** heated outdoor. **Activities:** sauna, whirlpool, canoeing, putting green, horseshoes, shuffleboard, volleyball, exercise room. **Guest Services:** coin laundry. **Free Special Amenities: continental breakfast and high-speed Internet.**

NORTH CONWAY GRAND HOTEL
(603)356-9300

Hotel
$79-$229

Address: 72 Common Ct SR 16 at Settlers' Green 03860 **Location:** 0.5 mi n of southern jct US 302/SR 16, 0.3 mi e at sign. **Facility:** 200 units. 4 stories, interior corridors. **Terms:** 2 night minimum stay - weekends, 3 day cancellation notice-fee imposed. **Amenities:** safes. **Pool(s):** outdoor, heated outdoor, heated indoor. **Activities:** saunas, whirlpools, ice skating, recreation programs in summer, exercise room. *Fee:* game room. **Guest Services:** valet and coin laundry. **Free Special Amenities: high-speed Internet and children's activities.**

(See ad this page.)

NORTH CONWAY HAMPTON INN & SUITES
(603)356-7736

Hotel $85-$225 Address: 1788 White Mountain Hwy 03860 **Location:** Jct US 302/SR 16, 1 mi n. **Facility:** 97 units. 4 stories, interior corridors. **Terms:** check-in 4 pm, 1-7 night minimum stay, cancellation fee imposed. **Amenities:** video games (fee). **Activities:** whirlpool, waterslide, exercise room. *Fee:* game room. **Guest Services:** valet and coin laundry.

AAA Benefit:
Members save up to 10%!

NORTH CONWAY MOUNTAIN INN
(603)356-2803

Motel
$79-$199

Address: 2114 White Mountain Hwy 03860 **Location:** 1 mi s on US 302/SR 16. **Facility:** 34 units. 2 stories (no elevator), exterior corridors. **Terms:** cancellation fee imposed. **Free Special Amenities: preferred room (subject to availability with advance reservations) and high-speed Internet.**

RED ELEPHANT INN
603/356-3548

Historic Bed & Breakfast. Rates not provided. **Address:** 28 Locust Ln 03860 **Location:** 0.5 mi s on US 302/SR 16, then just e. Located in a quiet area. **Facility:** This cozy inn is off the main highway and offers quiet, comfortable rooms. Modern upgrades and amenities make for a pleasant stay. 8 units. 2 stories (no elevator), interior corridors. **Pool(s):** outdoor.

▼ See AAA listing this page ▼

(See map & index p. 225.)

RED JACKET MOUNTAIN VIEW RESORT AND INDOOR WATER PARK

(603)356-5411 33

Resort Hotel
$109-$339

Address: 2251 White Mountain Hwy 03860 **Location:** 1 mi s on US 302/SR 16. **Facility:** Guest rooms at this property have either mountain or garden views, and many of the rooms have a balcony. Attractively landscaped grounds with scenic views surround the property. 160 units, some two bedrooms. 3 stories, interior/exterior corridors. **Terms:** cancellation fee imposed. **Pool(s):** heated outdoor. **Activities:** whirlpool, cross country skiing, snowmobiling, tobogganing, playground, exercise room, spa. *Fee:* waterslide, game room. **Guest Services:** valet and coin laundry. **Free Special Amenities:** local telephone calls and high-speed Internet.

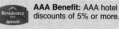

RESIDENCE INN BY MARRIOTT, NORTH CONWAY

(603)356-3024 38

Extended Stay Hotel
$94-$236

AAA Benefit: AAA hotel discounts of 5% or more.

Address: 1801 White Mountain Hwy 03860 **Location:** Jct US 302/SR 16, 1 mi n. **Facility:** 108 units, some two bedrooms, efficiencies and kitchens. 4 stories, interior corridors. **Terms:** check-in 4 pm. **Amenities:** high-speed Internet. **Pool(s):** heated indoor. **Activities:** putting green, sports court, exercise room. **Guest Services:** coin laundry. **Free Special Amenities:** full breakfast and high-speed Internet.

WHITE MOUNTAIN HOTEL & RESORT

(603)356-7100 32

Hotel
$109-$269

Address: 2660 West Side Rd 03860 **Location:** Jct SR 16/113/153 at Conway traffic light, turn onto Washington St to West Side Rd (do not cross covered bridge), then 5 mi on left. **Facility:** 80 units. 3 stories, interior corridors. **Terms:** 2 night minimum stay - seasonal and/or weekends, 5 day cancellation notice-fee imposed. **Dining:** Ledges Dining Room, see separate listing. **Pool(s):** heated outdoor. **Activities:** saunas, whirlpool, tennis court, cross country skiing, hiking trails, exercise room. *Fee:* golf-9 holes, game room, massage. **Guest Services:** coin laundry. **Free Special Amenities:** continental breakfast and high-speed Internet. *(See ad this page.)*

WHITE TRELLIS MOTEL

(603)356-2492 28

Motel $59-$269 **Address:** 3245 White Mountain Hwy 03860 **Location:** 0.8 mi n on US 302/SR 16; village center. **Facility:** 22 units. 1 story, exterior corridors. **Terms:** 3 day cancellation notice-fee imposed.

THE EASTERN SLOPE INN RESORT

603/356-6321

fyi Not evaluated. **Address:** 2760 Main St 03860. Facilities, services, and décor characterize a mid-scale property.

▼ *See AAA listing this page* ▼

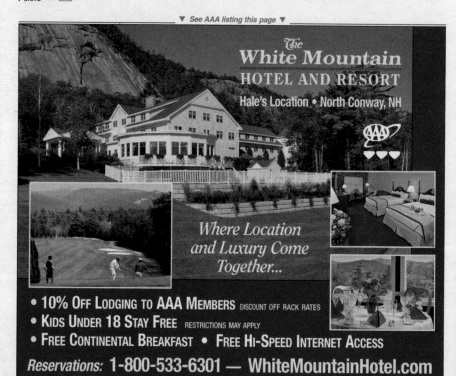

(See map & index p. 225.)

WHERE TO EAT

THE 1785 INN RESTAURANT   603/356-9025   13
WWW Continental. Fine Dining. $16-$36 **AAA Inspector Notes:** In the original section of a Colonial inn, the restaurant overlooks a scenic vista. Entrees are made to order with fresh ingredients and include duckling, rabbit, veal, elk, lamb, chicken, beef and seafood preparations. Desserts are also made on the premises, and the wine list is award-winning. Diners seeking a romantic atmosphere should request a table near the fireplace. **Bar:** full bar. **Reservations:** suggested. **Address:** 3582 White Mountain Hwy 03860 **Location:** 2 mi n on US 302/SR 16; in The 1785 Inn & Restaurant. D

A TASTE OF THAI RESTAURANT   603/356-7624   18
WW Thai. Casual Dining. $8-$26 **AAA Inspector Notes:** The restaurant presents a menu of great-tasting upscale Thai dishes. A friendly staff further adds to the dining experience. **Address:** 27 Seavey St 03860 **Location:** 2.4 mi n on US 302/SR 16, just e. L D

THE BLUEBERRY MUFFIN   603/356-2811   23
W American. Family Dining. $3-$8 **AAA Inspector Notes:** Casual, diner-style atmosphere and fare are popular with locals. Service is swift, and portions are large. **Address:** 1769 White Mountain Hwy 03860 **Location:** 1.3 mi s on US 302/SR 16; center; in Yankee Clipper Inn. B L

CHINA CHEF   603/356-3788   22
WW Chinese. Casual Dining. $5-$15 **AAA Inspector Notes:** This restaurant offers a large selection and makes a perfect choice for the Chinese food lover. **Bar:** full bar. **Address:** 2025 White Mountain Hwy 03860 **Location:** 1.4 mi s on US 302/SR 16. L D

DELANEY'S HOLE IN THE WALL   603/356-7776   15
WW American. Casual Dining. $7-$25 **AAA Inspector Notes:** In the heart of town, the restaurant was named after a member of the infamous Hole in the Wall Gang of Butch Cassidy and the Sundance Kid. Decor is reminiscent of the period, and the atmosphere is casual and family-focused. On the menu are seafood, steaks, pasta, burgers, soup and salads. Made-from-scratch dishes employ fresh ingredients, whenever possible, and are served in large portions. **Bar:** full bar. **Address:** 2966 White Mountain Hwy 03860 **Location:** 1 mi n on US 302/SR 16. L D

FLATBREAD COMPANY   603/356-4470
WW American. Casual Dining. $9-$18 **AAA Inspector Notes:** This small regional chain offers a variety of gourmet brick-oven pizza's with many organic ingredients. The brownie for dessert is a must. **Bar:** full bar. **Address:** 2760 White Mountain Hwy 03860 **Location:** Center; North Conway Village. D

HOOLIGAN'S   603/356-6110   16

American
Casual Dining
$9-$21
AAA Inspector Notes: Popular with the locals, the rustic, pub-style restaurant has planked walls and beamed ceilings. On the menu is a good selection of meat and seafood entrees, as well as basic comfort foods. **Bar:** full bar. **Address:** 21 Kearsarge Rd 03860 **Location:** Just e of US 302/SR 16; village center. **Parking:** street only. L D

HORSEFEATHER'S   603/356-6862   17
WW American. Casual Dining. $9-$23 **AAA Inspector Notes:** In the heart of North Conway Village, this popular restaurant offers everything from sandwiches to steaks. Reservation aren't accepted, so get there early. **Bar:** full bar. **Address:** 2679 White Mountain Hwy 03860 **Location:** 1 mi s on US 302/SR 16. **Parking:** street only. L D

LEDGES DINING ROOM   603/356-7100   21
WWW American. Fine Dining. $21-$29 **AAA Inspector Notes:** In a beautiful mountain setting, the elegant dining room affords great views of the colorful gardens. Representative of creative cuisine is a casserole with couscous, shrimp, scallops, mussels and haddock. A pianist performs nightly in season, weekends in the off season. **Bar:** full bar. **Reservations:** suggested. **Address:** 2560 West Side Rd 03860 **Location:** Jct SR 16/113/153 at Conway traffic light, turn onto Washington St to West Side Rd (do not cross covered bridge), then 5 mi on left; in White Mountain Hotel & Resort. *(See ad p. 232.)* B D

MERLINO'S FAMILY STEAKHOUSE   603/356-6006   24
WW American. Casual Dining. $9-$35 **AAA Inspector Notes:** The family friendly restaurant maintains a casual country atmosphere. Entrees range from steaks to Italian dishes. This is a great place to have a good meal at a good price. **Bar:** full bar. **Address:** 1717 White Mountain Hwy 03860 **Location:** 2 mi s on US 302/SR 16. L D

MOAT MT SMOKEHOUSE & BREWING CO.   603/356-6381   14
WW Barbecue. Casual Dining. $9-$25 **AAA Inspector Notes:** Specializing in barbecue items, the restaurant serves richly flavored ribs and chicken, homemade soups and other traditional favorites. The casual dining room, with paneled walls and diner-styled tables, offers a great atmosphere for families and the after-skiing crowd. **Bar:** full bar. **Address:** 3378 White Mountain Hwy 03860 **Location:** 1.5 mi n on US 302/SR 16. L D

MUDDY MOOSE RESTAURANT & PUB   603/356-7696   20
WW American. Casual Dining. $6-$20 **AAA Inspector Notes:** In a convenient site on a busy highway, the fun and upbeat restaurant serves traditional American fare. **Bar:** full bar. **Address:** 2344 White Mountain Hwy 03860 **Location:** On US 302/SR 16, 1 mi s. L D

NINETY NINE RESTAURANT   603/356-9909
WW American. Casual Dining. $9-$16 **AAA Inspector Notes:** This popular pub is committed to serving large portions of great food at reasonable prices. Guest favorites include hot wings, burgers, seafood, barbecue ribs and chicken. While reservations are not taken, call-ahead seating is offered. A children's menu is also available. **Bar:** full bar. **Address:** 1920 White Mountain Hwy 03860 **Location:** 1.6 mi s on US 302/SR 16. L D

PEACH'S RESTAURANT   603/356-5860   19
WW American. Casual Dining. $5-$9 **AAA Inspector Notes:** This small, homey restaurant is open for breakfast and lunch. The chef/owner prepares great homemade dishes. **Address:** 2506 White Mountain Hwy 03860 **Location:** 1.1 mi s on US 302/SR 16; village center. **Parking:** street only. B L

THE PEKING SUNRISE RESTAURANT LOUNGE   603/356-6976   25
WW Chinese. Casual Dining. $5-$20 **AAA Inspector Notes:** The dining room surrounds a colorful water fountain and the walls are covered with bamboo. Traditional Chinese dishes make up a large menu. Pool tables and table tennis lend to the lounge's popularity. **Bar:** full bar. **Address:** 1179 Eastman Rd (SR 302) 03860 **Location:** Jct US 302 and SR 16, just e. L D

NORTH HAMPTON (F-5) elev. 77'
• Restaurants p. 234

Its position on the seacoast about midway between Portland, Maine, and Boston prompted many of the wealthy from both cities to build summer homes in North Hampton in the late 19th and early 20th centuries. One such estate was Runnymede-by-the-Sea, belonging to former Massachusetts governor Alvan T. Fuller. Although the house no longer exists, the gardens remain as an attractive legacy of the era.

FULLER GARDENS occupies 3 acres off SR 1A at 10 Willow Ave. Designed and built in the early 1920s in the Colonial Revival style, the gardens feature 2,000 rose bushes that bloom from June through October, azaleas, rhododendrons, a Japanese garden, English perennial borders, annual displays and a conservatory. Period statuary and fountains are interspersed throughout the grounds.

Time: Allow 30 minutes minimum. **Hours:** Daily 10-5:30, mid-May to mid-Oct. **Cost:** $9; $8 (ages 65+); $6 (students with ID); $4 (ages 1-11). **Phone:** (603) 964-5414.

BETTY'S KITCHEN   603/964-9870

▼ American. Family Dining. $5-$9 **AAA Inspector Notes:** Well known for its all-day breakfasts, the popular eatery has been an area fixture for years. This is a good spot for a quick bite. **Bar:** beer & wine. **Address:** 164 Lafayette Rd 03862 **Location:** On US 1, 2 mi n of SR 101D. [B] [L]

THE COPPER LANTERN   603/964-5008

▼▼ American. Casual Dining. $7-$20 **AAA Inspector Notes:** In a convenient location, the cozy little restaurant serves good home-made comfort foods. Menu items include deep-fried and baked seafood, burgers and sirloin steak. **Bar:** full bar. **Address:** 54 Lafayette Rd 03862 **Location:** On US 1, 0.5 mi s of SR 101D. [B] [L] [D]

RONALDO'S ITALIAN RESTAURANT   603/964-5064

[fyi] Not evaluated. The popular bistro is situated in a small strip mall off the northbound stretch of US 1. **Address:** 69 Lafayette Rd 03862 **Location:** On US 1.

NORTH SALEM (G-4) elev. 147'

Low wooded hills and numerous ponds characterize the region around North Salem, a farming and residential community.

AMERICA'S STONEHENGE, 5 mi. e. of I-93 exit 3 on SR 111, then 1 mi. s. to 105 Haverhill Rd., encompasses prehistoric stone structures proven by carbon dating to form the oldest known megalithic site on this continent. Continuing research indicates the site may be 4,000 years old; inscriptions deciphered offer possible evidence that Celt-Iberians used this site from about 800 to 300 B.C. Inscriptions are displayed and reading material is available. Eight alpacas are on the premises.

Time: Allow 1 hour minimum. **Hours:** Daily 9-5. Last admission 1 hour before closing. Closed Thanksgiving and Christmas. **Cost:** $11; $9.50 (ages 65+); $7.50 (ages 6-12). **Phone:** (603) 893-8300.

NORTHWOOD

JOHNSON'S SEAFOOD & STEAK   603/942-7300

▼ Seafood. Casual Dining. $5-$23 **AAA Inspector Notes:** Diners can choose to sit down and order inside or, during the summer months, order at the outdoor counter before plunking down on a picnic bench. The seafood is fresh and tasty. Dishes are primarily fried. **Bar:** full bar. **Address:** 1334 First NH Tpke 03261 **Location:** On US 4/202. [L] [D]

NORTH WOODSTOCK pop. 528

AUTUMN BREEZE MOTOR LODGE   603/745-8549

▼ Motel. Rates not provided. **Address:** 183 Main St 03262 **Location:** I-93 exit 32, 0.5 mi w on SR 112, then just n on US 3. **Facility:** 6 units, some kitchens. 1 story, exterior corridors.

WILDERNESS INN BED & BREAKFAST   603/745-3890

▼▼▼ Bed & Breakfast $70-$185 **Address:** 57 Main St (SR 3) 03262 **Location:** I-93 exit 32, 0.5 mi w on SR 112, then just s on US 3. **Facility:** Just south of downtown, the inn is convenient to year-round area activities. Common rooms have a comfortable country feel. A full menu is offered for breakfast, which is served on the all-weather porch. 8 units, some two bedrooms and cottages. 2 stories (no elevator), interior corridors. **Terms:** 2 night minimum stay - seasonal and/or weekends, 14 day cancellation notice-fee imposed.

WOODSTOCK INN, STATION & BREWERY
                                                 603/745-3951

▼▼▼ Historic Country Inn   Rates not provided   **Address:** 135 Main St 03262 **Location:** I-93 exit 32, 0.5 mi w on US 3. **Facility:** Located in the center of town, the inn is close to White Mountains' year-round activities. A mix of Victorian-style guest rooms and lodge-style rooms are available. 33 units. 2-3 stories (no elevator), interior corridors. *Bath:* some shared. **Dining:** Clement Room Grille, Woodstock Station, see separate listings. **Free Special Amenities: full breakfast and high-speed Internet.**

CLEMENT ROOM GRILLE   603/745-3951

▼▼▼ American Casual Dining $17-$30   **AAA Inspector Notes:** The attractive dining room features Victorian decor, intriguing cuisine and a pleasant, well-informed staff. Flavorful broiled salmon has an appealing presentation. Servers are professional and friendly. **Bar:** full bar. **Reservations:** suggested. **Address:** 135 Main St 03262 **Location:** I-93 exit 32, 0.5 mi w on SR 112, then just n on US 3; in Woodstock Inn, Station & Brewery. [B] [D]

WOODSTOCK STATION   603/745-3951

▼▼ American Gastropub $7-$21   **AAA Inspector Notes:** An old railroad station is the setting for relaxed dining. Among lunch and dinner offerings are chimichangas, homemade root beer and salads. Servers are prompt, friendly and attentive. The patio is open seasonally. **Bar:** full bar. **Address:** 135 Main St 03262 **Location:** I-93 exit 32, 0.5 mi w on SR 112, then just n on US 3; in Woodstock Inn, Station & Brewery. [L] [D]

CAFE LAFAYETTE DINNER TRAIN   603/745-3500

[fyi] Not evaluated. Preparations of area-friendly contemporary cuisine center around fresh regional ingredients. Enjoy an elegant dinner while taking in the White Mountains. **Address:** 3 Crossing at River Place (Rt 112) 03262 **Location:** I-93 exit 32, just w.

PETERBOROUGH (G-3) pop. 3,103, elev. 723'

Peterborough and the arts have been virtually synonymous since the late 19th century. In 1907 composer Edward MacDowell decided to share with other artists the peace and inspiration he had found at his nearby woodland retreat. Although he died the next year, the MacDowell Colony flourished. Pulitzer Prizes, Guggenheim Fellowships and many other international awards have been bestowed upon painters, sculptors, printmakers, filmmakers, writers and composers who have worked in Peterborough.

Because the colony closely guards the privacy of its resident artists, only Colony Hall and MacDowell's gravesite are accessible to the public; phone (603) 924-3886.

Nearly as venerable is the Peterborough Players, a professional summer theater company that performs in a theater within a converted 18th-century barn at Stearns Farm, just 3 miles from downtown at 55 Hadley Rd.; phone (603) 924-7585.

Greater Peterborough Chamber of Commerce: 10 Wilton Rd. (SR 101), P.O. Box 401, Peterborough, NH 03458. **Phone:** (603) 924-7234.

MILLER STATE PARK covers 533 acres 3 mi. e. off SR 101. The state's oldest state park was founded in 1891 and offers a scenic drive and a foot trail to the 2,290-foot summit of Pack Monadnock Mountain. The Wapack Trail between North Pack Monadnock Mountain, 2 miles north, and Mount Watatic, in Massachusetts, also crosses the park. On clear days the view from the summit reaches from Mount Washington to Boston.

Hiking is a popular activity. **Time:** Allow 1 hour, 30 minutes minimum. **Hours:** Gates open daily 9-5, mid-Aug. through Oct. 31; Fri.-Sun. 9-4:30, Memorial Day weekend to mid-Aug. (weather permitting). Trails open daily dawn-dusk year-round. **Cost:** $4; $2 (ages 6-11). **Phone:** (603) 924-3672.

PETERBOROUGH HISTORICAL SOCIETY MUSEUM, 19 Grove St. near Main St., has items pertaining to state and local history. Changing exhibits include quilts, ceramics, pewter, textiles and toys. **Tours:** Guided tours are available. **Time:** Allow 1 hour minimum. **Hours:** Wed.-Sat. 10-4. **Cost:** $3; free (ages 0-11). **Phone:** (603) 924-3235.

SHARON ARTS CENTER, 30 Grove St., has two fine arts and crafts galleries featuring a permanent collection and changing exhibits. An arts library and an arts and crafts school are nearby. **Hours:** Mon.-Sat. 10-6, Sun. 11-5. **Cost:** Free. **Phone:** (603) 924-2787 or (603) 924-7676.

PINKHAM NOTCH SCENIC AREA (C-4)

Walled by the Presidential Range on the west and by Mount Moriah, North Carter Mountain, Carter Dome and other mountains on the east, Pinkham Notch is one of the easternmost of the New Hampshire White Mountain notches.

In 1790 Joseph Pinkham, whose name was bestowed on the notch, allegedly brought his possessions to his new home via pig-drawn sled. The rough trace that Pinkham and his companions followed has since evolved into scenic SR 16, which threads through the pass between Jackson and Gorham. On the south slope the road parallels the Ellis River and offers access to such spots as Glen Ellis Falls and Crystal Cascade along the Tuckerman Ravine Trail.

The ravine's sheer west wall challenges expert downhill skiers. The notch and its attractions are within the White Mountain National Forest *(see White Mountains and White Mountain National Forest p. 253).*

A visitor center on SR 16 between North Conway and Gorham is sponsored by the Appalachian Mountain Club. The center offers hikers and other travelers trail and weather information, food, educational displays about outdoor recreation in the White Mountains, free guided walks and evening lectures; phone (603) 466-2721.

PITTSBURG

THE GLEN   603/538-6500

Cabin. Rates not provided. **Address:** 118 Glen Rd 03592 **Location:** Waterfront. 9 mi n on US 3, from jct SR 145 to Varney Rd, then 0.3 mi s to Glen Rd, follow signs. Located in a rustic area. **Facility:** 16 cabins. 1-2 stories (no elevator), interior/exterior corridors. **Activities:** rental boats, boat dock, fishing, hiking trails, horseshoes.

PLYMOUTH (D-3) pop. 4,456, elev. 514'
• Restaurants p. 236

POLAR CAVES PARK is 5 mi. w. on SR 25 (Tenney Mountain Hwy.). The caves were formed by glacial action more than 20,000 years ago. Paths lead through a series of eight caves and passages featuring granite boulders as well as mineral formations of quartz, mica, garnet and beryl. The park is home to peacocks, pheasants and European fallow deer. Nature trails offer educational plaques about native plants and natural history; there also is a mining sluice.

A picnic area with barbecue grills is available. **Time:** Allow 1 hour, 30 minutes minimum. **Hours:** Daily 9-6, mid-May through Labor Day; 10-5:30, day after Labor Day to mid-Oct. Last admission 1 hour before closing. **Cost:** $16; $11 (ages 4-10). **Phone:** (603) 536-1888.

RED CARPET INN & SUITES   (603)536-2155

Motel
$40-$166

Address: 166 Highland St 03264 **Location:** 1 mi w of center. **Facility:** 21 units. 2 stories (no elevator), exterior corridors. **Terms:** cancellation fee imposed. **Free Special Amenities:** continental breakfast and local telephone calls.

WHERE TO EAT

ITALIAN FARMHOUSE   603/536-4536

▼▼ Italian. Casual Dining. $9-$22 **AAA Inspector Notes:** In an old farmhouse in the center of town, this popular restaurant serves Italian dishes and never-ending fresh bread at the bread bar. Locals enjoy watching activity in the open kitchen. **Bar:** full bar. **Address:** 337 Daniel Webster Hwy (SR 3) 03264 **Location:** From Main St, 1.4 mi s on Daniel Webster Hwy. [D]

PORTSMOUTH (F-5) pop. 20,779, elev. 14'

- Hotels p. 241 • Restaurants p. 244
- Hotels & Restaurants map & index p. 239

To their delight, when the sea-weary travelers on the *Pied Cow* disembarked on the west bank of the Piscataqua River in 1630, they found the ground covered with wild strawberries. Thus was founded and named Strawbery Banke, the little settlement that took root around a tidal inlet and grew into the seaport of Portsmouth.

The passengers on the *Pied Cow* were not the first to settle in the area. In 1623 members of the Laconia Co. had come to the Piscataqua to establish a plantation and fishery. Part of the group continued upriver to Dover. The remainder settled at Odiorne Point, 2 miles east of Portsmouth, where they built the first house in New Hampshire. Odiorne Point is a state park that preserves an area little changed in the last 3 centuries *(see Recreation Areas Chart)*.

Strawbery Banke, however, changed greatly. Fishing and farming sustained residents at first, but the ready supply of good timber and an excellent harbor soon engaged them in shipbuilding. Portsmouth—the name was changed in 1653— began attracting the merchant class in large numbers.

The community also served as the seat of the provincial government. As a center of political activity and a vital trade circuit that linked it with Great Britain and the West Indies, Portsmouth naturally was the focus of many Patriot vs. Tory confrontations prior to the Revolutionary War. British ammunition and stores taken from Fort William and Mary by Portsmouth patriots on Dec. 14, 1774, were used in the first battles of the revolution.

Private shipbuilding reached its apex in the early 19th century, producing many of the swift clipper ships that graced the sea. Two of America's first warships, the *Ranger* and the *America*, were built in Portsmouth Harbor under the direction of John Paul Jones. Thereafter, shipping and shipbuilding declined as steamships and the competing Massachusetts ports gained popularity.

In 1800 the historic U.S. Navy Yard on Seavey's Island *(see Kittery, Maine, p. 107)* became the impetus behind Portsmouth's economy, since augmented by diversified industry and a healthy summer resort trade.

Portsmouth's history is documented in many restored buildings and neighborhoods. Colonial structures as well as the finely detailed houses built by wealthy 19th-century sea captains line the narrow, winding streets of these sections.

The Old Harbor area at Bow and Ceres streets once was the focus of a thriving mercantile seaport; craft shops, restaurants and boutiques now occupy its chandleries and warehouses. Seacoast Repertory Theatre, an all-year equity theater, is in a renovated brewery at 125 Bow St.; phone (603) 433-4793 for general information or (603) 433-4472 for tickets.

Similarly the 14 Federal and Georgian buildings of The Hill, at Deer and High streets, have been refurbished and now are used as offices. Seven of the structures were erected during or before the Revolutionary War. Across Mechanic Street from Prescott Park is the city's oldest cemetery, Point of Graves, which contains gravestones dating from 1682.

Greater Portsmouth Chamber of Commerce: 500 Market St., P.O. Box 239, Portsmouth, NH 03802. **Phone:** (603) 610-5510 or (603) 436-3988.

ISLES OF SHOALS STEAMSHIP CO., Barker's Wharf at 315 Market St., offers trips to the historic Isles of Shoals and around Portsmouth Harbor aboard the late 19th-century steamship replica MV *Thomas Laighton.* Sights along the cruise include forts, lighthouses, a naval prison and a shipyard. Dinner cruises and fall foliage excursions also are available.

Hours: Two-and-a-half-hour trips depart twice daily, mid-June through Labor Day. **Cost:** Fares $28; $25 (ages 13-17, ages 60+ and military with ID); $18 (ages 6-12). Reservations are recommended. **Parking:** $5. **Phone:** (603) 431-5500 or (800) 441-4620.

PORTSMOUTH HARBOR CRUISES, 64 Ceres St., travels around the 14 islands of Portsmouth Harbor to the Isles of Shoals and up the Piscataqua River as far as Dover and Great Bay via a 49-passenger vessel. Cruises lasting 1.5 and 2.5 hours are available. **Hours:** Trips depart daily, early June-late Oct.; Sat.-Sun., early May-early June (weather permitting). Phone for departure times. **Cost:** $14-$24; $12-$21 (ages 60+ and military with ID); $10-$17 (ages 3-12). A fuel surcharge may apply. Reservations are recommended. **Phone:** (603) 436-8084 or (800) 776-0915. [¶]

PORTSMOUTH HARBOUR TRAIL, beginning at Market Square, tours the waterfront and downtown. Guides provide information about early settlers and their homes. **Hours:** Tours Tues.-Thurs. and Sat. at 10:30, late June-Columbus Day. **Cost:** $12; $10 (ages 60+ and students with ID); $8 (ages 8-14). Cash or check only. **Phone:** (603) 610-5518.

Governor John Langdon House, 143 Pleasant St., was built in 1784 by John Langdon, a three-time governor of the state, signer of the Constitution and first president of the Senate. In 1789 George Washington described the Georgian mansion as "the finest house in Portsmouth." The main portion of the structure retains its original balustrade and stately

(See map & index p. 239.)

portico. Ornate woodwork and period furniture highlight the interior; behind the house is an enclosed garden with a rose arbor and pavilion.

Time: Allow 1 hour minimum. **Hours:** Guided tours are offered on the hour Fri.-Sun. 11-5, June 1 to mid-Oct. Last tour begins 1 hour before closing. **Cost:** $6; $5 (ages 65+); $3 (ages 6-12). **Phone:** (603) 436-3205.

Moffatt-Ladd House is at 154 Market St. Best known as the home of William Whipple, a signer of the Declaration of Independence, the house was built in 1763 by Whipple's father-in-law, John Moffatt, a wealthy sea merchant. Paneled halls and chambers, an ornate staircase and original furniture distinguish the house, which is set amid formal gardens with turf steps and raised beds. **Time:** Allow 30 minutes minimum. **Hours:** Mon.-Sat. 11-5, Sun. 1-5, mid-June to mid-Oct. Last tour begins 30 minutes before closing. **Cost:** House and garden $6; $2.50 (ages 7-12). Garden only $2. **Phone:** (603) 436-8221.

Portsmouth Historical Society Museum at the John Paul Jones House, Middle and State sts., was built in 1758 by Capt. Gregory Purcell. After his death Purcell's widow operated the house as a genteel guesthouse. Most notable of her guests was Capt. John Paul Jones, who lived in the house while supervising the outfitting of the *Ranger* in 1777 and again in 1781 while the *America* was being built. China, silver, glass, portraits, costumes and a model of the *Ranger* are displayed.

Time: Allow 30 minutes minimum. **Hours:** Daily 11-5, May-Oct. **Cost:** $6; $5 (ages 65+); free (ages 0-14 with adult). **Phone:** (603) 436-8420.

Rundlet-May House, 364 Middle St., is a three-story 1807 Federal mansion. Built by textile merchant James Rundlet, the house retains its original character while reflecting the varying lifestyles of successive generations of the family. Several pieces of furniture were made by noted Portsmouth craftsmen. **Time:** Allow 1 hour minimum. **Hours:** Tours are given on the hour first and third Sat. of the month 11-5, June 1 through mid-Oct. Last tour begins 1 hour before closing. Closed July 4. **Cost:** $6; $5 (ages 65+); $3 (ages 6-12). **Phone:** (603) 436-3205.

Warner House, Daniel and Chapel sts., is a noted example of Georgian architecture. The 1716 house has brick walls 18 inches thick, fine paneling and wall murals. The lightning rod on the west wall is said to have been installed in 1762 under the supervision of Benjamin Franklin, a frequent visitor. **Time:** Allow 1 hour minimum. **Hours:** Wed.-Mon. noon-4, early June to mid-Oct. **Cost:** $5; $4 (ages 65+ and students with ID); $2.50 (ages 7-12). **Phone:** (603) 436-5909.

Wentworth-Gardner House, at Mechanic and Gardner sts., is said to rank among the finest Georgian-style buildings in the country. The restored blocked-front 1760 house is known for its doorway and woodcarvings. **Time:** Allow 30 minutes minimum. **Hours:** Wed.-Sun. noon-4, mid-June to mid-Oct. **Cost:** $5; $2 (ages 0-14). **Phone:** (603) 436-4406.

PRESCOTT PARK is on Marcy St., between the riverfront and Strawbery Banke Museum *(see attraction listing)*. In addition to gardens, fountains and a fishing pier, the park contains two old warehouses. The 1705 Sheafe Warehouse, where John Paul Jones outfitted the *Ranger*, now houses changing

(See map & index p. 239.)

art exhibits during the summer. **Time:** Allow 1 hour minimum. **Hours:** Daily 5 a.m.-midnight. **Cost:** Free. **Phone:** (603) 431-8748.

ST. JOHN'S EPISCOPAL CHURCH is on Chapel St. Built in 1807, it is the successor to the 1732 Queen's Chapel. The church contains 17th- and 18th-century antiques, including a steeple bell that came from France to Nova Scotia in the mid-1700s. Colonial soldiers took the bell as a souvenir and presented it to Queen's Chapel in 1745. Damaged when the chapel burned in 1806, the bell was recast by Paul Revere. The church has one of four American copies of the 1717 "Vinegar Bible," so named because vineyard is misspelled "vinegar." **Time:** Allow 30 minutes minimum. **Hours:** Mon.-Thurs. 9-3, except during services. **Cost:** Free. **Phone:** (603) 436-8283.

STRAWBERY BANKE MUSEUM is bounded by Marcy, Court, Washington and Hancock sts. The 10-acre historic waterfront neighborhood offers more than 30 buildings from the period 1695-1955, in various stages of restoration and adaptation.

The 1770 William Pitt Tavern, 1780 Wheelwright House, 1795 Drisco House, 1796 Walsh House, 1815 Chase House, 1830 Rider-Wood House, 1860 Goodwin Mansion and 1919 Shapiro House have been restored and furnished in different periods to show the changes in lifestyle and architectural fashion over 350 years. The boyhood home of editor and author Thomas Bailey Aldrich, known as the Nutter House to readers of his book "The Story of a Bad Boy," is another highlight.

Information about self-guiding tours, guided walking tours and holiday events is available at the Tyco Visitor Center at 14 Hancock St.

Time: Allow 1 hour, 30 minutes minimum. **Hours:** Daily 10-5, May-Oct. Guided garden tours depart daily at 1. Guided 90-minute museum tours are given Sat.-Sun. on the hour 10-2, in Nov. Candlelight Stroll holiday event Sat. 5-9, Sun. 4-8, first three weekends in Dec. Closed Christmas Eve, Christmas and Dec. 31. Phone ahead to confirm schedule. **Cost:** (Valid for 2 consecutive days) $15; $10 (ages 5-17); $40 (family). Garden tour free. Museum or holiday house tour $12; $10 (ages 5-17); $30 (family). **Phone:** (603) 433-1100, or (603) 433-1107 for the visitor center. [TI] [A]

URBAN FORESTRY CENTER is 2.5 mi. s. on US 1 (Lafayette Rd.), then .1 mi. e. to 45 Elwyn Rd. Set on 182 acres of marshland, woods and meadows bordering Sagamore Creek, the center offers trails and gardens in a peaceful setting. Programs about forestry and natural resources are offered. **Hours:** Trails open daily 7:30 a.m.-8 p.m. **Cost:** Free. **Phone:** (603) 431-6774.

USS *ALBACORE*, off I-95 exit 7, then .2 mi. e. off Market St. in Albacore Park and Memory Garden, was built in 1952 and served as an experimental prototype for modern submarines. Its radical hull design enabled it to set an underwater speed record that marked the beginning of the era of high-speed undersea fleets. From 1953 to 1972 the *Albacore* was used to test innovations in sonar, dive brakes and emergency escape systems. The Memorial Garden pays tribute to those killed in the line of duty in the submarine service. Audio tours also are available.

Time: Allow 1 hour minimum. **Hours:** Daily 9:30-5:30, Memorial Day-Columbus Day; Thurs.-Mon. 9:30-4:30, rest of year. Last admission 30 minutes before closing. **Cost:** $5; $4 (military with ID); $3 (ages 7-17); $10 (family, two adults and two children). **Phone:** (603) 436-3680.

WATER COUNTRY, 3 mi. s. on US 1, features a variety of water-related amusements, including a tube ride on a gentle river, a large wave pool, family raft ride, children's attractions and 16 large waterslides. **Hours:** Daily 10-6:30, late June to mid-Aug.; 10-5:30, mid-June to late June and mid-Aug. through Labor Day. Phone ahead to confirm schedule. **Cost:** $37.99; $25.99 (ages 65+ and under 48 inches tall); free (ages 0-2). Reduced admission is offered after 3 p.m. **Phone:** (603) 427-1111. [TI]

WENTWORTH-COOLIDGE MANSION STATE HISTORIC SITE, off Sagamore Rd. on Little Harbor Rd., was the official residence of Benning Wentworth, first royal governor 1741-67. The mansion's interior reflects aristocratic life in the area around the 1700s. Contemporary art pieces can be viewed at the Coolidge Center for the Arts. The 1.5-mile Little Harbor Loop Trail is on the premises. **Time:** Allow 1 hour minimum. **Hours:** Wed.-Sun. 10-4, late June-Labor Day; Sat.-Sun. and holidays, late May-late June and day after Labor Day-late Oct. House tours are given at 10, 11:40, 12:45, 2 and 3. **Cost:** $5; $3 (ages 6-17). **Phone:** (603) 436-6607. [A]

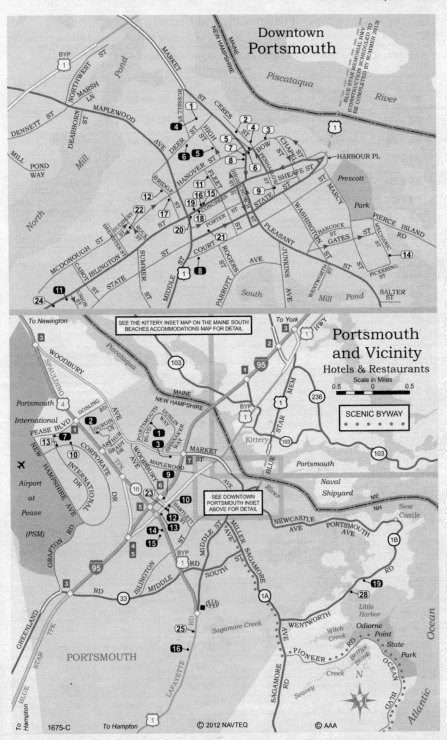

Portsmouth and Vicinity

This index helps you "spot" where approved hotels and restaurants are located on the corresponding detailed maps. Hotel daily rate range is for comparison only. Restaurant price range is a combination of lunch and/or dinner. Turn to the listing page for more detailed rate and price information and consult display ads for special promotions.

PORTSMOUTH

Map Page	Hotels	Diamond Rated	Rate Range	Page
❶ p. 239	Homewood Suites by Hilton	◈◈◈	$129-$399	242
❷ p. 239	Hampton Inn-Portsmouth	◈◈◈	Rates not provided	242
❸ p. 239	Courtyard by Marriott	◈◈◈	$129-$239	241
❹ p. 239	**Sheraton Portsmouth Harborside Hotel & Conference Center**	◈◈◈	$139-$649 [SAVE]	243
❺ p. 239	Hilton Garden Inn Portsmouth Downtown	◈◈◈	$159-$439	242
❻ p. 239	Residence Inn by Marriott Downtown/Waterfront	◈◈◈	$129-$489	243
❼ p. 239	Residence Inn by Marriott	◈◈◈	$139-$339	242
❽ p. 239	**Sise Inn**	◈◈◈	$119-$289 [SAVE]	243
❾ p. 239	**Anchorage Inn & Suites**	◈◈◈	$89-$349 [SAVE]	241
❿ p. 239	America's Best Inn	◈◈	Rates not provided	241
⓫ p. 239	Martin Hill Inn	◈◈◈	$125-$225	242
⓬ p. 239	Holiday Inn Portsmouth	◈◈◈	$129-$229	242
⓭ p. 239	**BEST WESTERN PLUS Wynwood Hotel & Suites**	◈◈◈	$89-$329 [SAVE]	241
⓮ p. 239	**The Port Inn**	◈◈◈	$79-$199 [SAVE]	242
⓯ p. 239	Fairfield Inn by Marriott - Portsmouth Seacoast	◈◈◈	$99-$229	241
⓰ p. 239	Comfort Inn Portsmouth	◈◈◈	$110-$210	241

Map Page	Restaurants	Diamond Rated	Cuisine	Price Range	Page
① p. 239	Harbor's Edge Restaurant	◈◈◈	American	$11-$35	244
② p. 239	The Oar House Restaurant	◈◈◈	American	$10-$45	244
③ p. 239	The Wellington Room	◈◈◈	Italian	$25-$35	245
④ p. 239	Old Ferry Landing	◈	Seafood	$8-$28	244
⑤ p. 239	The Dolphin Striker	◈◈◈	Seafood	$10-$28	244
⑥ p. 239	Fat Belly's	◈◈	American	$9-$19	244
⑦ p. 239	Portsmouth Gas Light Co	◈◈	American	$10-$29	245
⑧ p. 239	**The Portsmouth Brewery**	◈◈	American	$11-$25	245
⑨ p. 239	Ristorante Massimo	◈◈◈	Italian	$22-$34	245
⑩ p. 239	Cataqua Public House at Redhook Brewery	◈◈	American	$10-$17	244
⑪ p. 239	Coat of Arms	◈◈	British	$9-$17	244
⑫ p. 239	Thai Paradise	◈◈	Thai	$9-$20	245
⑬ p. 239	Paddy's An American Grille	◈◈	American	$9-$26	244
⑭ p. 239	Geno's Chowder and Sandwich Shop	◈	American	$4-$15	244
⑮ p. 239	Café Mediterraneo	◈◈	Italian	$9-$26	244
⑯ p. 239	Friendly Toast	◈	American	$8-$14	244
⑰ p. 239	Cafe Mirabelle	◈◈	French	$16-$27	244

Map Page	Restaurants (cont'd)	Diamond Rated	Cuisine	Price Range	Page
⑱ p. 239	Jumpin' Jays Fish Café	▽▽▽	Seafood	$20-$30	244
⑲ p. 239	Sake Japanese Restaurant	▽▽▽	Japanese	$8-$23	245
⑳ p. 239	Radici Ristorante	▽▽▽	Italian	$14-$24	245
㉑ p. 239	The Library Restaurant & Steakhouse	▽▽▽	American	$8-$35	244
㉒ p. 239	Blue Mermaid Island Grill	▽▽	Seafood	$5-$22	244
㉓ p. 239	Roundabout Diner Lounge	▽▽	American	$6-$18	245
㉔ p. 239	The Portsmouth Bread Box	▽	Pizza	$4-$12	245
㉕ p. 239	Dinnerhorn Restaurant & Bratskellar Pub	▽▽	Seafood	$7-$23	244

NEW CASTLE

Map Page	Hotel	Diamond Rated	Rate Range	Page
⑲ p. 239	Wentworth By The Sea Marriott Hotel & Spa	▽▽▽▽	$199-$469 SAVE	222

Map Page	Restaurant	Diamond Rated	Cuisine	Price Range	Page
㉘ p. 239	The Dining Room at Wentworth By The Sea	▽▽▽	New American	$10-$40	222

AMERICA'S BEST INN   603/431-4400   **10**
▽▽ **Hotel.** Rates not provided. **Address:** 383 Woodbury Ave 03801 **Location:** I-95 exit 5 at Portsmouth Traffic Circle. **Facility:** 61 units. 4 stories, interior corridors. **Activities:** limited exercise equipment. **Guest Services:** coin laundry.
CALL ♿M BIZ 🛜 / SOME UNITS 🛏 📷

ANCHORAGE INN & SUITES   (603)431-8111   **9**

▽▽▽
Hotel
$89-$349
Address: 417 Woodbury Ave 03801 **Location:** Jct US 1 and I-95; at Portsmouth Traffic Circle. **Facility:** 92 units. 3 stories, interior corridors. **Pool(s):** heated indoor. **Activities:** sauna, whirlpool, exercise room. **Guest Services:** valet and coin laundry.
SAVE 🏊 BIZ 🛜 🛏 📷 ☕ / SOME UNITS FEE 🐾

BEST WESTERN PLUS WYNWOOD HOTEL & SUITES   (603)436-7600   **13**

▽▽▽
Hotel
$89-$329
[Best Western PLUS logo] **AAA Benefit:** Members save 10% or more with Best Western.
Address: 580 US Hwy 1 Bypass 03801 **Location:** I-95 exit 5, jct US 1 Bypass and Portsmouth Traffic Circle. **Facility:** 169 units, some two bedrooms and efficiencies. 2-6 stories, interior/exterior corridors. **Terms:** check-in 4 pm. **Amenities:** high-speed Internet. **Dining:** Roundabout Diner Lounge, see separate listing. **Pool(s):** outdoor, heated indoor. **Activities:** whirlpool, exercise room. **Guest Services:** valet and coin laundry. **Free Special Amenities:** local telephone calls and high-speed Internet.
SAVE 🍴 CALL ♿M 🏊 BIZ 🛜 🛏 📷 ☕

COMFORT INN PORTSMOUTH   (603)433-3338   **16**
▽▽▽ **Hotel** $110-$210 **Address:** 1190 Lafayette Rd (US 1) 03801 **Location:** I-95 exit 5 at Portsmouth Traffic Circle, 1.5 mi s. **Facility:** 121 units. 6 stories, interior corridors. **Terms:** cancellation fee imposed. **Amenities:** Some: high-speed Internet. **Pool(s):** heated indoor. **Activities:** whirlpool, exercise room. **Guest Services:** valet laundry. 🍴 🏊 BIZ 🛜 🛏 📷 ☕

COURTYARD BY MARRIOTT   (603)436-2121   **3**
▽▽▽ **Hotel** $129-$239 **Address:** 1000 Market St 03801 **Location:** I-95 exit 7, just w. **Facility:** 133 units. 4 stories. Some: high-speed Internet. **Pool(s):** heated indoor. **Activities:** whirlpool, exercise room. **Guest Services:** valet and coin laundry.
AAA Benefit: AAA hotel discounts of 5% or more.
ECO 🍴 🍽 CALL ♿M 🏊 BIZ 🛜 ✕ 🛏 📷 ☕

FAIRFIELD INN BY MARRIOTT - PORTSMOUTH SEACOAST   (603)436-6363   **15**
▽▽▽ **Hotel** $99-$229 **Address:** 650 Borthwick Ave 03801 **Location:** I-95 exit 5, jct US 1 Bypass and Portsmouth Traffic Circle. **Facility:** 105 units. 4 stories, interior corridors. **Guest Services:** valet and coin laundry.
AAA Benefit: AAA hotel discounts of 5% or more.
CALL ♿M 🏊 🏃 BIZ 🛜 ✕ ☕ / SOME UNITS 🛏 📷

(See map & index p. 239.)

HAMPTON INN-PORTSMOUTH   603/431-6111 ②

WWW **Hotel**. Rates not provided. **Address:** 99 Durgin Ln 03801 **Location:** I-95 exit 7, 1 mi w via Market St and Woodbury Ave to Durgin Ln, then 0.3 mi s. **Facility:** 125 units. 5 stories, interior corridors. **Pool(s):** heated indoor. **Activities:** whirlpool, sports court, exercise room. **Guest Services:** valet and coin laundry, area transportation-within 5 mi.

AAA Benefit: Members save up to 10%!

CALL &M ⊇ BIZ 🛜 ✕ 🖭 🖼 🖳 / SOME UNITS FEE 🐾

HILTON GARDEN INN PORTSMOUTH DOWNTOWN
(603)431-1499 ⑤

WWW **Hotel** $159-$439 **Address:** 100 High St 03801 **Location:** Downtown. Adjacent to city parking garage. **Facility:** 131 units. 5 stories, interior corridors. **Parking:** valet only. **Terms:** 1-7 night minimum stay, cancellation fee imposed. **Amenities:** video games (fee), high-speed Internet. **Dining:** name entertainment. **Pool(s):** heated indoor. **Activities:** whirlpool, exercise room. **Guest Services:** valet and coin laundry.

AAA Benefit: Unparalleled hospitality at a special Member rate.

🍽 🍴 🍸 CALL &M 🏊 BIZ 🛜 ✕ 🎥 🖭 🖳

HOLIDAY INN PORTSMOUTH   (603)431-8000 ⑫

WWW **Hotel** $129-$229 **Address:** 300 Woodbury Ave 03801 **Location:** I-95 exit 5 at Portsmouth Traffic Circle. **Facility:** 130 units. 6 stories, interior corridors. **Amenities:** video games (fee). *Some:* high-speed Internet. **Pool(s):** heated indoor. **Activities:** exercise room. **Guest Services:** valet and coin laundry.

🍽 🍴 🍸 CALL &M 🏊 BIZ 🛜 ✕ 🎥 🖳 / SOME UNITS 🖭 🖼

Be a better driver.
Keep your mind on the road.

HOMEWOOD SUITES BY HILTON   (603)427-5400 ①

WWWW **Extended Stay Hotel** $129-$399 **Address:** 100 Portsmouth Blvd 03801 **Location:** I-95 exit 7, 0.5 mi w, then 0.3 mi n. **Facility:** 116 units, some efficiencies and kitchens. 4 stories, interior corridors. **Terms:** check-in 4 pm, 1-7 night minimum stay, cancellation fee imposed. **Amenities:** video games (fee), high-speed Internet. **Pool(s):** heated indoor. **Activities:** sports court, exercise room. **Guest Services:** valet and coin laundry, area transportation-within 5 mi.

AAA Benefit: Contemporary luxury at a special Member rate.

CALL &M ⊇ BIZ 🛜 🎥 🖭 🖼 🖳 / SOME UNITS FEE 🐾

MARTIN HILL INN   603/436-2287 ⑪

WWW **Historic Bed & Breakfast** $125-$225 **Address:** 404 Islington St 03801 **Location:** I-95 exit 6, Portsmouth Traffic Circle, exit Woodbury Ave, just e on Bartlett St, under bridge, then just n. **Facility:** Convenient to downtown, this early-19th-century inn is furnished with antiques and offers colorful perennial gardens in season. 7 units. 2 stories (no elevator), interior corridors. **Terms:** check-in 4 pm, 2-3 night minimum stay - seasonal and/or weekends, age restrictions may apply, 14 day cancellation notice-fee imposed, resort fee.

🛜 ✕ 🗺

THE PORT INN   (603)436-4378 ⑭

WWW
Motel
$79-$199

Address: 505 US 1 Bypass 03801 **Location:** I-95 exit 5, jct US 1 Bypass and Portsmouth Traffic Circle. **Facility:** 57 units, some two bedrooms and kitchens. 1-2 stories (no elevator), exterior corridors. **Amenities:** high-speed Internet. **Pool(s):** heated outdoor. **Guest Services:** valet and coin laundry. **Free Special Amenities: continental breakfast and high-speed Internet.**

SAVE ⊇ BIZ 🛜 🖭 🖼 🖳

RESIDENCE INN BY MARRIOTT   (603)436-8880 ⑦

WWW **Extended Stay Hotel** $139-$339 **Address:** 1 International Dr 03801 **Location:** SR 4/16 exit 1, just s. **Facility:** 90 units, some two bedrooms, efficiencies and kitchens. 3 stories, interior corridors. **Pool(s):** heated indoor. **Activities:** whirlpool, sports court, exercise room. **Guest Services:** valet and coin laundry.

AAA Benefit: AAA hotel discounts of 5% or more.

ECO CALL &M 🏊 ⊇ BIZ 🛜 ✕ 🖭 🖼 🖳 / SOME UNITS FEE 🐾

▼ See AAA listing p. 190 ▼

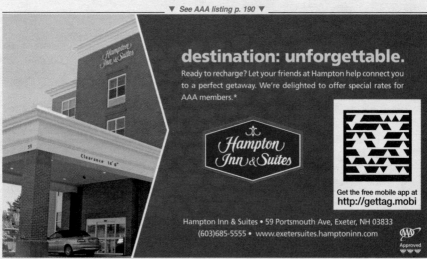

(See map & index p. 239.)

RESIDENCE INN BY MARRIOTT DOWNTOWN/WATERFRONT
(603)422-9200 **6**

 Extended Stay Contemporary Hotel $129-$489 **Address:** 100 Deer St 03801 **Location:** Downtown. **Facility:** 128 efficiencies. 5 stories, interior corridors. **Parking:** no self-parking. **Amenities:** high-speed Internet. **Pool(s):** heated indoor. **Activities:** exercise room. **Guest Services:** valet and coin laundry.

AAA Benefit: AAA hotel discounts of 5% or more.

CALL BIZ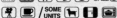

/SOME UNITS FEE

SHERATON PORTSMOUTH HARBORSIDE HOTEL & CONFERENCE CENTER   (603)431-2300 **4**

 **Hotel** $139-$649

Sheraton HOTELS & RESORTS

AAA Benefit: Members get up to 20% off, plus Starwood Preferred Guest® bonuses.

Address: 250 Market St 03801 **Location:** Downtown. **Facility:** 200 units, some two bedrooms and kitchens. 5 stories, interior corridors. **Parking:** on-site (fee). **Terms:** cancellation fee imposed. **Amenities:** video games (fee). **Dining:** Harbor's Edge Restaurant, see separate listing, entertainment. **Pool(s):** heated indoor. **Activities:** sauna, exercise room, spa. **Guest Services:** valet laundry.

SAVE ECO  CALL /SOME UNITS

SISE INN   (603)433-1200 **8**

 Historic Hotel $119-$289

Address: 40 Court St 03801 **Location:** At Middle St; downtown. Located in historic district. **Facility:** Notable for its fine interior woodwork, this handsome downtown Victorian inn with striking interior woodwork dates from 1881 and houses attractively decorated guest rooms with modern amenities. 34 units, some efficiencies. 4 stories, interior/exterior corridors. **Terms:** check-in 4 pm. **Guest Services:** valet laundry. **Free Special Amenities:** expanded continental breakfast and high-speed Internet.

SAVE /SOME UNITS

▼ See AAA listing p. 196 ▼

(See map & index p. 239.)

WHERE TO EAT

BLUE MERMAID ISLAND GRILL   603/427-2583 22
▼▼ Seafood. Casual Dining. $5-$22 **AAA Inspector Notes:** The restaurant's eclectic menu offers Asian, Moroccan, Jamaican and Caribbean cuisine. The dishes are creatively prepared, including calypso seasoned hanger steak, plantain-encrusted grouper, island rubbed grilled pork chops and much more. **Bar:** full bar. **Address:** 409 The Hill 03801 **Location:** Corner of Hanover and High sts; behind Hilton Garden Inn Portsmouth Downtown.
L D X

CAFÉ MEDITERRANEO   603/427-5563 15
▼▼ Italian. Casual Dining. $9-$26 **AAA Inspector Notes:** Well-prepared, traditional Mediterranean dishes are on the bistro-style eatery's menu. Among favorites are baked salmon, lobster ravioli and tiramisu. Service is friendly, and the European-style decor is casual. A municipal parking lot is adjacent. **Bar:** full bar. **Reservations:** suggested, for weekends. **Address:** 119 Congress St 03801 **Location:** Between Middle and Fleet sts; downtown. L D

CAFE MIRABELLE   603/430-9301 17
▼▼ French. Casual Dining. $16-$27 **AAA Inspector Notes:** At this warm, cozy and casually elegant café, the French cuisine may feature nicely prepared bouillabaisse, steak au poivre and profiterole. Two levels of dining space provide seating for 60 people. **Bar:** full bar. **Reservations:** suggested. **Address:** 64 Bridge St 03801 **Location:** Corner of Hanover and Bridge sts; downtown. **Parking:** street only. D

CATAQUA PUBLIC HOUSE AT REDHOOK BREWERY   603/430-8600 10
▼▼ American. Casual Dining. $10-$17 **AAA Inspector Notes:** Traditional pub fare is on the menu at the popular restaurant attached to Redhook Brewery. In season, patrons can enjoy lunch or dinner in the beer garden or take a tour of the brewery. **Bar:** beer & wine. **Address:** 35 Corporate Dr 03801 **Location:** At Pease International Tradeport. L D

COAT OF ARMS   603/431-0407 11
▼ British. Casual Dining. $9-$17 **AAA Inspector Notes:** The lively British-style pub features fish and chips, beef Wellington, steak and kidney pie, chicken curry, bangers and mash, shepherd's pie and a good selection of beers and ales. The bar area has dartboards, snooker tables and live music on Thursday. **Bar:** full bar. **Address:** 174 Fleet St 03801 **Location:** Corner of Fleet and Hanover sts; downtown. **Parking:** street only. L D

DINNERHORN RESTAURANT & BRATSKELLAR PUB
    603/436-0717 25

Seafood
Casual Dining
$7-$23

AAA Inspector Notes: Convenient to businesses south of downtown, the casual restaurant displays pleasant contemporary decor. The menu focuses primarily on seafood, including raw bar items, but also includes steak, chicken, pizza and pasta entrees. Smaller portions are available at lunch. **Bar:** full bar. **Address:** 980 Lafayette Rd 03801 **Location:** I-95 exit 5, 1.3 mi s on US 1.
L D

THE DOLPHIN STRIKER   603/431-5222 5
▼▼ Seafood. Fine Dining. $10-$28 **AAA Inspector Notes:** Historic. In a restored 18th-century waterfront warehouse, the restaurant's lower level contains a spring-fed well that once was used to replenish sailing ships. Representative of New American cuisine are flavorful seafood, chicken, pork, beef and pasta dishes. **Bar:** full bar. **Reservations:** suggested. **Address:** 15 Bow St 03801 **Location:** Corner of Bow and Ceres sts; downtown. **Parking:** street only. L D

FAT BELLY'S   603/610-4227 6
▼▼ American. Casual Dining. $9-$19 **AAA Inspector Notes:** In the heart of Portsmouth, the contemporary restaurant specializes in hamburgers. The second-floor bar is popular at night. **Address:** 2 Bow St 03801 **Location:** Downtown. **Parking:** street only. L D

FRIENDLY TOAST   603/430-2154 16
▼ American. Family Dining. $8-$14 **AAA Inspector Notes:** Open 24 hours on weekends and regular hours on weekdays, the restaurant tempts customers with such breakfast favorites as Almond Joy pancakes and green eggs and ham. **Bar:** beer & wine. **Address:** 113 Congress St 03801 **Location:** Between Fleet St and Maplewood Ave; downtown. **Parking:** street only. B L D

GENO'S CHOWDER AND SANDWICH SHOP   603/427-2070 14
▼ American. Casual Dining. $4-$15 **AAA Inspector Notes:** On the river, this small restaurant offers outdoor seating in the summer. Fresh food and homemade desserts make up this family-owned spot's menu. **Address:** 177 Mechanic St 03801 **Location:** Off Marcy St; downtown.

HARBOR'S EDGE RESTAURANT   603/559-2626 1
▼▼ American. Casual Dining. $11-$35 **AAA Inspector Notes:** Superb lobster chowder and rack of lamb are two flavorful choices at the pleasant restaurant, which overlooks historic Portsmouth Harbor. The menu also lists a variety of seafood, beef, chicken and pasta entrees, as well as mouthwatering local desserts. **Bar:** full bar. **Reservations:** suggested. **Address:** 250 Market St 03801 **Location:** Downtown; in Sheraton Portsmouth Harborside Hotel & Conference Center. B L D

JUMPIN' JAYS FISH CAFÉ   603/766-3474 18
▼▼▼ Seafood. Casual Dining. $20-$30 **AAA Inspector Notes:** The busy restaurant serves seafood, including fish from around the world. The bar offers a variety of wines and cocktails. **Bar:** full bar. **Address:** 150 Congress St 03801 **Location:** Corner of Maplewood Ave and Congress St; downtown. **Parking:** street only. D CALL ⚑M

THE LIBRARY RESTAURANT & STEAKHOUSE   603/431-5202 21
▼▼▼ American. Fine Dining. $8-$35 **AAA Inspector Notes:** The popular restaurant lives up to its name. The warm, cozy decor features bookcases, stone fireplaces and lighting fixtures from 1785. The creative menu lists delicious rack of lamb, salmon with barbecue sauce and eggplant parmigiana. **Bar:** full bar. **Reservations:** suggested. **Address:** 401 State St 03801 **Location:** State and Chestnut sts; downtown; at Rockingham House. **Parking:** street only. L D

MARGARITAS MEXICAN RESTAURANT   603/431-5828
▼▼ Mexican. Casual Dining. $8-$20 **AAA Inspector Notes:** Diners will feel as though they have just stepped south of the border at this fun Mexican cantina. Traditional music fills the air while warm terracotta colored walls accented by painted pottery and unique jeweled star lanterns surround you. Sip on a large margarita while enjoying the freshly prepared fajitas, burritos, enchiladas, or quesadillas. **Bar:** full bar. **Address:** 775 Lafayette Rd 03801 **Location:** I-95 exit 5 at Portsmouth Traffic Circle, 2 mi s on US 1. D

THE OAR HOUSE RESTAURANT   603/436-4025 2
▼▼▼ American. Fine Dining. $10-$45 **AAA Inspector Notes:** Historic. Beautifully located on the water in a circa-1800 warehouse, the restaurant displays memorabilia of ships built in Portsmouth. The menu lists seafood casseroles, baked haddock, pan-seared salmon and chocolate raspberry Bavarian cake. Deck seating can be requested in summer. **Bar:** full bar. **Reservations:** suggested. **Address:** 55 Ceres St 03801 **Location:** Downtown; on waterfront. L D

OLD FERRY LANDING   603/431-5510 4
▼ Seafood. Casual Dining. $8-$28 **AAA Inspector Notes:** Most of the off-the-boat-fresh seafood is fried, but broiled selections also are an option. **Bar:** full bar. **Address:** 10 Ceres St 03801 **Location:** Along the waterfront, just n of Bow St; downtown. **Parking:** street only. L D

PADDY'S AN AMERICAN GRILLE   603/430-9450 13
▼▼ American. Casual Dining. $9-$26 **AAA Inspector Notes:** On what was the former Pease Air Force Base campus, the popular restaurant resides amid many thriving businesses. **Bar:** full bar. **Address:** 27 International Dr 03801 **Location:** SR 4/16 exit 1, just s. L D

(See map & index p. 239.)

THE PORTSMOUTH BREAD BOX   603/436-1631   (24)

◆ Pizza. Quick Serve. $4-$12 **AAA Inspector Notes:** Located just south of downtown, the small quick-serve restaurant serves everything from hot dogs to pizza - even take-and-bake varieties. The restaurant is popular with locals for a fast bite to eat. **Address:** 460 Islington St 03801 **Location:** I-95 exit 6, 0.5 mi e on Woodbury Ave, just e on Bartlett St under bridge, then just n. [L] [D]

THE PORTSMOUTH BREWERY   603/431-1115   (8)

American
Casual Dining
$11-$25

AAA Inspector Notes: The downtown restaurant gives diners an occasional glimpse of the brew masters at work. Menu favorites include burgers, sandwiches and fresh fish. **Bar:** full bar. **Address:** 56 Market St 03801 **Location:** Downtown. **Parking:** street only.

 [L] [D]

PORTSMOUTH GAS LIGHT CO   603/430-9122   (7)

◆◆ American. Casual Dining. $10-$29 **AAA Inspector Notes:** In historic downtown, the restaurant is the site of the city's former gaslight utility company. The main dining room is at street level, while the pizza parlor, where pies are made in a wood-fired brick oven, is downstairs. Outdoor seating can be requested in the summer months, with live entertainment Thursday through Saturday. The menu lists sandwiches and burgers, as well as pasta, chicken, seafood and steak. While no reservations are accepted, a call-ahead program is offered. **Bar:** full bar. **Address:** 64 Market St 03801 **Location:** Center. **Parking:** street only. [L] [D]

RADICI RISTORANTE   603/373-6464   (20)

◆◆◆ Italian. Fine Dining. $14-$24 **AAA Inspector Notes:** Pasta and vegetarian dishes are central to the restaurant's menu. High- and low-top tables are placed around the contemporary dining space. The wine list is large. **Bar:** full bar. **Reservations:** suggested, weekends. **Address:** 142 Congress St 03801 **Location:** Downtown. **Parking:** street only. [D]

RISTORANTE MASSIMO   603/436-4000   (9)

◆◆◆ Italian. Fine Dining. $22-$34 **AAA Inspector Notes:** Dishes are prepared to order and paired nicely with popular Italian wines. This intimate bistro serves authentic Italian dishes, such as a traditional antipasto, pappardelle alla Bolognese or wine-braised beef short ribs. The impressive wine list focuses on Italian and California vineyards. **Bar:** full bar. **Reservations:** suggested. **Address:** 59 Penhallow St 03801 **Location:** Downtown. **Parking:** street only. [D]

ROUNDABOUT DINER LOUNGE   603/431-1440   (23)

◆◆◆ American. Family Dining. $6-$18 **AAA Inspector Notes:** This retro diner evokes the 1950s with its metallic painted walls and bebop music playing in the background. Choose from a menu of American fare, including burgers, soups and an array of fried items. Closed Christmas Day. **Bar:** full bar. **Address:** 580 US Hwy 1 Bypass 03801 **Location:** I-95 exit 5, jct US 1 Bypass and Portsmouth Traffic Circle; in BEST WESTERN PLUS Wynwood Hotel & Suites.

[B] [L] [D] CALL[&M]

SAKE JAPANESE RESTAURANT   603/431-1822   (19)

◆◆ Japanese. Casual Dining. $8-$23 **AAA Inspector Notes:** Traditional decor fills the restaurant, which offers Japanese cuisine and a full sushi bar. **Bar:** full bar. **Address:** 141 Congress St 03801 **Location:** Between Maplewood Ave and Fleet St; downtown. [L] [D]

THAI PARADISE   603/431-9193   (12)

◆◆ Thai. Casual Dining. $9-$20 **AAA Inspector Notes:** Tasty Thai cuisine is prepared to order. The atmosphere is cozy and the decor eclectic. **Bar:** beer & wine. **Address:** 96 Bridge St 03801 **Location:** Corner of Hanover St; downtown. **Parking:** street only. [L] [D]

THE WELLINGTON ROOM   603/431-2989   (3)

◆◆◆ Italian. Casual Dining. $25-$35 **AAA Inspector Notes:** The small, intimate dining room affords a great river view. Traditional Southern Italian cuisine uses authentic recipes, superb preparation methods and attractive presentations. The serving staff is pleasant and knowledgeable. **Bar:** full bar. **Reservations:** suggested. **Address:** 67 Bow St, 2nd Floor 03801 **Location:** Downtown; overlooking the river. [D]

GILLEY'S   603/431-6343

[fyi] Not evaluated. Since 1912, this hamburger and hot dog joint has offered animated counter service and good food. Breakfast sandwiches are offered in the morning. Seating is limited to 10 people. **Address:** 175 Fleet St 03801

RINDGE (G-3)

Overlooking the rolling Monadnock Region from its hilltop location, the village of Rindge is the site of 1,200-acre Franklin Pierce University. Recreational activities are available year-round. Many nearby ponds and lakes offer boating and bass fishing.

CATHEDRAL OF THE PINES, 2 mi. n.e. off SR 119, is dedicated to all those killed in war. Sanderson Sloane, a B-17 bomber pilot, was lost over Germany Feb. 22, 1944; he had planned to build a home on this site. This outdoor shrine contains memorial stones donated by American presidents, a museum with war memorabilia, gardens and chapels, and the Memorial Bell Tower, which honors women. Hilltop House has war relics and art objects. **Time:** Allow 1 hour minimum. **Hours:** Daily 9-5, May-Oct. **Cost:** Donations. **Phone:** (603) 899-3300.

ROCHESTER pop. 29,752
• Restaurants p. 246

ANCHORAGE INN   (603)332-3350

◆
Motel
$89-$159

Address: 13 Wadleigh Rd 03867 **Location:** Jct Spaulding Tpke and SR 125 exit 12. **Facility:** 31 units. 1 story, exterior corridors. **Terms:** 2-3 night minimum stay - seasonal and/or weekends. **Pool(s):** outdoor. **Activities:** basketball, horseshoes.

[SAVE] [BIZ] [] [] / UNITS FEE []

THE GOVERNOR'S INN   603/332-0107

◆◆◆◆ Historic Country Inn. Rates not provided. **Address:** 78 Wakefield St 03867 **Location:** On SR 125 and 108, just n of monument; center. **Facility:** A Georgian Colonial built in 1920, the inn features fine woodwork, marble fireplaces and attractive grounds. 20 units, some efficiencies. 3 stories (no elevator), interior corridors. **Activities:** horseshoes.

[] [] [X] / SOME UNITS [] [] [] []

HOLIDAY INN EXPRESS HOTEL & SUITES ROCHESTER   (603)994-1175

◆◆◆ Hotel $79-$159 **Address:** 77 Farmington Rd 03867 **Location:** I-16 exit 15, 1 mi w on SR 11. **Facility:** 77 units. 3 stories, interior corridors. **Terms:** cancellation fee imposed. **Amenities:** high-speed Internet. **Pool(s):** heated indoor. **Activities:** whirlpool, limited exercise equipment. **Guest Services:** valet and coin laundry.

[] CALL[&M] [BIZ] [] []
/ SOME UNITS FEE [] [] []

WHERE TO EAT

SPAULDING STEAK & ALE   603/332-0107

[fyi] Not evaluated. Diners appreciate a pleasant dining experience in this traditional New England country inn. **Address:** 78 Wakefield St 03867 **Location:** On SR 125 and 108, just n of monument; center; in The Governor's Inn.

RUMNEY (D-3) elev. 527'

A mountain, brook and lake near Rumney bear the name of David Stinson, a colleague of Gen. John Stark. The community, established in the 1760s near the confluence of Stinson Brook and the Baker River, serves summer travelers and the surrounding farming area.

The Mary Baker Eddy Historic House is at 58 Stinson Lake Rd. The founder of Christian Science, Eddy lived in the house 1860-62. Tours of the home are available May through October; phone (603) 786-9943 or (800) 277-8943.

RYE (F-5)

GRANITE STATE WHALE WATCH, 1870 Ocean Blvd. (SR 1A), offers whale-watching expeditions and sightseeing cruises from Rye Harbor to the Isles of Shoals. Highlights of the Isles of Shoals cruise include a boat tour of nine islands and a local fireworks display. Whale-watch tours are conducted by research biologists, with humpback, finback and minke whales being the most common species in these waters.

Allow 3 hours minimum for island trips, 4 hours minimum for whale-watching trips. **Hours:** Whale-watching trips depart daily at 8:30 and 2, mid-June to late Aug.; daily at 11, late Aug.-Labor Day; Wed. and Fri. at 10, Sat.-Sun. at 8:30 and 2, day after Labor Day to mid-Sept.; Wed. and Fri. at 10, Sat.-Sun. at 11, mid-Sept. through Columbus Day; Sat.-Sun. at 11, mid-May to mid-June (weather permitting). Island trips depart Wed. at 7 p.m., early July-late Aug. Phone ahead to confirm schedule. **Cost:** Whale-watching trip $36; $28 (ages 60+); $23 (ages 4-17). Island trip $24; $19 (ages 60+); $16 (ages 4-17). Reservations are recommended. **Phone:** (603) 964-5545 or (800) 964-5545.

SEACOAST SCIENCE CENTER, 570 Ocean Blvd. (SR 1A) in Odiorne Point State Park *(see Recreation Areas Chart),* has cultural, marine and natural history exhibits as well as a tide pool touch tank. Interpretive programs are offered. **Time:** Allow 1 hour minimum. **Hours:** Park open daily 8-dusk. Science center daily 10-5, Mar.-Oct.; Sat.-Mon. 10-5, rest of year. Closed Jan. 1, Thanksgiving and Christmas. **Cost:** Park Memorial Day-Labor Day $4; $2 (ages 6-11). Park free rest of year. Science center $5; $2 (ages 3-12). **Phone:** (603) 436-8043 for the science center, or (603) 436-1552 for the park.

ATLANTIC FOUR WINDS COTTAGES   603/436-5140

[fyi] Not evaluated. **Address:** 1215 Ocean Blvd 03870 **Location:** On US 1A. Facilities, services, and décor characterize an economy property.

CROWN COLONY COTTAGES   603/436-8923

[fyi] Not evaluated. **Address:** 1381 Ocean Blvd 03870 **Location:** On US 1A. Facilities, services, and décor characterize an economy property.

WHERE TO EAT

THE CARRIAGE HOUSE   603/964-8251

▼▼▼ American. Casual Dining. $11-$32 **AAA Inspector Notes:** The restaurant features excellent seafood and veal specialties with some Italian inspired dishes such as haddock piccata or sea scallop Florentine. A gluten-free menu is also offered. **Bar:** full bar. **Reservations:** suggested. **Address:** 2263 Ocean Blvd 03870 **Location:** Jct US 1A and SR 11, 2.4 mi n on US 1A. [D]

PETEY'S SUMMERTIME SEAFOOD & BAR   603/433-1937

▼▼ Seafood. Casual Dining. $7-$32 **AAA Inspector Notes:** The super-casual spot prepares super-good seafood. Homemade chowders are made daily. Steamed lobster and fried clams are among dishes worth the wait. **Bar:** full bar. **Address:** 1323 Ocean Blvd 03870 **Location:** On US 1A. [L] [D]

SALEM (G-4) elev. 147'

[SAVE] **CANOBIE LAKE PARK** is .2 mi. e., then 1 mi. n. of I-93 exit 2 to 85 N. Policy St. The amusement park offers more than 85 rides, games and activities and features live entertainment. Highlights include three roller coasters, a giant sky wheel, an 1890s carousel with hand-carved horses, a lake cruise, two log flume water rides, a water coaster and an interactive water-play complex. During the park's annual SCREEEMFEST in October, visitors can brave haunted houses, play Halloween-themed games and sample seasonal foods in addition to enjoying the park's regular ride offerings.

Time: Allow 4 hours minimum. **Hours:** Daily 11-10, Memorial Day-Labor Day; hours vary Sat.-Sun., late Apr.-day before Memorial Day and day after Labor Day-late Sept. SCREEEMFEST Fri.-Sun. in Oct. Phone ahead to confirm schedule. **Cost:** (includes rides and shows) $33; $24 (ages 60+ and children under 48 inches tall); free (ages 0-3). After 5 p.m. $23. SCREEEMFEST $33; $17.99 (ages 60+ and children under 48 inches tall). **Phone:** (603) 893-3506. [❯❮] [✂]

HOLIDAY INN-SALEM NEW HAMPSHIRE   603/893-5511

▼▼▼ Hotel. Rates not provided. **Address:** 1 Keewaydin Dr 03079 **Location:** I-93 exit 2, just sw. **Facility:** 109 units. 6 stories, interior corridors. **Dining:** 2 restaurants. **Pool(s):** outdoor, heated indoor. **Activities:** whirlpool, exercise room. *Fee:* game room. **Guest Services:** valet and coin laundry.

[❯❮] [Y] CALL [&M] [➜] [BIZ] [📶] [✕] [👤] [▯]
/SOME UNITS [🐾] [❢] [🖼]

LA QUINTA INN & SUITES SALEM   (603)893-4722

▼▼ Hotel. $75-$188 **Address:** 8 Keewaydin Dr 03079 **Location:** I-93 exit 2, just sw. Located in a quiet area. **Facility:** 105 units. 4 stories, interior corridors. **Pool(s):** outdoor. **Activities:** exercise room. **Guest Services:** valet and coin laundry.

[❯❮] CALL [&M] [➜] [BIZ] [📶] [▯]
/SOME UNITS [🐾] [❢] [🖼]

PARK VIEW INN

(603)898-5632

▽▽▽
Motel
$53-$90

Address: 109 S Broadway (Rt 28) 03079 **Location:** I-93 exit 1, 1 mi e, then just n on SR 28. **Facility:** 58 units, some efficiencies. 1 story, exterior corridors. **Terms:** cancellation fee imposed. **Guest Services:** coin laundry.

SAVE BIZ 🛜 📞 💻 / SOME UNITS 🖥

RED ROOF INN #151

(603)898-6422

▽▽▽
Motel
$50-$110

Address: 15 Red Roof Ln 03079 **Location:** I-93 exit 2, just se. **Facility:** 108 units. 2 stories (no elevator), exterior corridors. **Amenities:** safes. **Free Special Amenities:** local telephone calls and high-speed Internet.

SAVE CALL 🔊Ⓜ 🛜 / SOME UNITS 🐾 📞 🖥 💻

WHERE TO EAT

THE COLOSSEUM RESTAURANT

603-898-1190

▽▽▽ Italian. Casual Dining. $9-$37 **AAA Inspector Notes:** This family-owned-and-operated eatery serves homemade traditional delights. The casual atmosphere is welcoming to families and friends. **Bar:** full bar. **Address:** 264 N Broadway 03079 **Location:** I-93 exit 1, 1 mi w to SR 28, then 2.3 mi n; in Breckenridge Mall. L D

T-BONES GREAT AMERICAN EATERY

603/893-3444

▽▽ American. Casual Dining. $10-$27 **AAA Inspector Notes:** One of three locations, the local eatery prepares burgers, steaks, sandwiches and more. All menu items are made from scratch on the premises. **Bar:** full bar. **Address:** 311 S Broadway 03079 **Location:** 1 mi s of Rockingham Park on US 28. L D

WEATHERVANE SEAFOOD RESTAURANT

603/893-6269

▽▽ Seafood. Family Dining. $8-$25 **AAA Inspector Notes:** The popular, family-oriented restaurant presents a large menu with lobster, fried clams and crisp Cape Cod apple-cranberry cobbler. Flavorful dishes are served in large portions. A fish market is on the premises. **Bar:** full bar. **Address:** 41 S Broadway 03079 **Location:** I-93 exit 1, 1 mi n on SR 28. L D CALL 🔊Ⓜ

SEABROOK

HAMPSHIRE INN   603/474-5700

Motel
Rates not provided

Address: 20 Spur Rd 03874 **Location:** I-95 exit 1 on SR 107. **Facility:** 35 units. 3 stories, interior corridors. **Pool(s):** heated indoor. **Activities:** whirlpool, exercise room. *Fee:* game room. **Guest Services:** valet and coin laundry. **Free Special Amenities:** continental breakfast and high-speed Internet.

HOLIDAY INN EXPRESS HOTEL & SUITES   (603)474-1150

Hotel $99-$179 **Address:** 11 Rocks Rd 03874 **Location:** I-95 exit 1, e on SR 107, then just n on SR 1. **Facility:** 78 units. 3 stories, interior corridors. **Terms:** 2 night minimum stay - seasonal and/or weekends, cancellation fee imposed. **Amenities:** high-speed Internet. **Pool(s):** heated indoor. **Activities:** exercise room. **Guest Services:** coin laundry.

SEABROOK INN   603/474-3078

Motel
$69-$120

Address: 9 Stard Rd 03874 **Location:** I-95 exit 1, just w on SR 107. **Facility:** 195 units. 2 stories (no elevator), exterior corridors. **Terms:** check-in 4 pm, cancellation fee imposed. **Pool(s):** heated outdoor. **Activities:** waterslide, paddleboats, playground. **Guest Services:** coin laundry. **Free Special Amenities:** continental breakfast and children's activities. *(See ad this page.)*

Keep seasonal vehicles travel-ready with a AAA/CAA Battery Tender®

▼ *See AAA listing this page* ▼

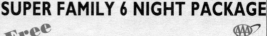

Ratings Members Trust

AAA's professional, in-person hotel and restaurant inspections are based on qualities members say matter most.

Learn more at **AAA.com/Diamonds**

SUGAR HILL

THE HILLTOP INN
603/823-5695

▼▼▼ **Historic Bed & Breakfast** $120-$195 **Address:** 9 Norton Ln 03586 **Location:** I-93 exit 38, 0.5 mi n on SR 18, then 2.8 mi w on SR 117. **Facility:** This attractive turn-of-the-20th-century home is in the village center and features cable television in the common area. 6 units, some two bedrooms. 2 stories (no elevator), interior corridors. **Terms:** 2 night minimum stay - seasonal and/or weekends, 8 day cancellation notice-fee imposed. **Activities:** cross country skiing, hiking trails.

SUGAR HILL INN
(603)823-5621

▼▼▼▼ **Historic Country Inn** $175-$490 **Address:** 116 SR 117 03586 **Location:** I-93 exit 38, 0.5 mi n on SR 18, then 0.4 mi w. Located in a quiet area. **Facility:** Converted to an inn in 1929, this property originated as a farmhouse in 1789. Set in attractively landscaped grounds, the property offers historic guest rooms and beautifully designed cottages. 14 units, some cottages. 1-2 stories (no elevator), interior/exterior corridors. **Terms:** 1-3 night minimum stay - seasonal and/or weekends, 14 day cancellation notice-fee imposed. **Pool(s):** heated outdoor. **Activities:** Fee: massage.

SUNSET HILL HOUSE-A GRAND INN
(603)823-5522

▼▼▼ **Historic Country Inn** $149-$499 **Address:** 231 Sunset Hill Rd 03586 **Location:** I-93 exit 38, 0.5 mi n on SR 18, 2.2 mi w on SR 117, then 0.5 mi s. Across from golf course. **Facility:** Perched on a 1,700-foot-high ridge, this turn-of-the-20th-century inn is elegantly and comfortably restored and offers commanding mountain views. 29 units. 3 stories (no elevator), interior corridors. **Terms:** 2 night minimum stay - seasonal and/or weekends, 14 day cancellation notice-fee imposed. **Dining:** Sunset Hill House/The Restaurant at Sunset Hill, see separate listing. **Pool(s):** heated outdoor. **Activities:** cross country skiing, hiking trails, horseshoes. Fee: golf-9 holes, massage.

WHERE TO EAT

POLLY'S PANCAKE PARLOR
603/823-5575

◆ ▼ American. Casual Dining. $5-$20 **AAA Inspector Notes:** Patrons come from far and near to feast upon the family's own pancake recipe that they have been grilling up for generations. Visitors to the rustic eatery, set on a working maple sugar farm, can occasionally catch a glimpse of wandering moose. **Address:** 672 Rt 117 03585 **Location:** I-93 exit 38, 0.5 mi n on SR 18, then 1.4 mi w.

[B] [L] [⟨]

SUNSET HILL HOUSE/THE RESTAURANT AT SUNSET HILL
603/823-5522

▼▼▼ Continental. Fine Dining. $21-$36 **AAA Inspector Notes:** You'll appreciate the views of gorgeous mountains and dramatic sunsets from this elegant restaurant's huge picture windows. The seasonal menu highlights innovative preparation including house-smoked fish, herbed lamb, and grilled seafood soup. **Bar:** full bar. **Reservations:** required. **Address:** 231 Sunset Hill Rd 03586 **Location:** I-93 exit 38, 0.5 mi n on SR 18, 2.2 mi w on SR 117, then 0.5 mi s; in Sunset Hill House-A Grand Inn. [B] [D]

SUNAPEE (E-3) elev. 914'

Sunapee is one of several resort communities that line many-lobed, 10-square-mile Lake Sunapee. A vacation spot since the mid-19th century, the area affords a variety of year-round outdoor recreation. Located in west-central New Hampshire, the locale should not be confused with the "Lakes Region," located in the eastern part of the state. The lake's name is derived from a Penacook Indian word believed to mean "goose lake." Boat cruises may be taken on the lake.

During the 1860s Sunapee seemed to attract residents with a flair for invention. In 1868 John Smith devised a machine that permitted the local clothespin factory—a major industry at the time—to produce 125 finished clothespins per minute.

The following year, after a decade of study, Enos Clough drove a horseless carriage throughout the area, but its tendency to terrify horses resulted in its being banned. Clough sold the contraption to a Laconia man who ran it into a fence; the engine was finally installed in a boat.

Lake Sunapee Region Chamber of Commerce: 328 Main St., P.O. Box 532, New London, NH 03257. **Phone:** (603) 526-6575 or (877) 526-6575.

LAKE SUNAPEE CRUISES, off SR 11 at Sunapee Harbor at 1 Main St., offers 1.5-hour narrated cruises around Lake Sunapee aboard the MV *Mt. Sunapee II.* Loon Island, Georges Mills Bay, Fishers Bay and Mount Kearsarge are among the sights. Dinner cruises aboard the MV *Kearsarge* also are available.

Hours: Trips depart daily at 2, day after Father's Day-Labor Day; Sat.-Sun. at 2, Memorial Day-Father's Day and day after Labor Day-Columbus Day. Dinner cruises depart Tues.-Sun. at 6:30, day after Father's Day-Labor Day; Sat.-Sun. at 6:30, Memorial Day-Father's Day; Sat.-Sun. at 5:30, day after Labor Day-Columbus Day. **Cost:** $20; $18 (ages 65+ and military with ID); $10 (ages 4-12). Dinner cruise $36.99; $25.99 (ages 4-12). **Phone:** (603) 938-6465.

BURKEHAVEN MOTEL AND LODGE
603/763-2788

▼▼▼ Motel $89-$149 **Address:** 179 Burkehaven Hill Rd 03782 **Location:** I-89 exit 12, 5 mi w on SR 11, 0.4 mi e on Main St (Lake Ave), then 0.8 mi se, follow signs to harbor. **Facility:** 10 units. 1 story, exterior corridors. Bath: shower only. **Terms:** 14 day cancellation notice-fee imposed. **Pool(s):** heated outdoor. **Free Special Amenities:** expanded continental breakfast and high-speed Internet.

DEXTER'S INN
(603)763-5571

▼▼ **Historic Country Inn** $110-$185 **Address:** 258 Stagecoach Rd 03782 **Location:** Jct SR 103B and 11, 0.4 mi e on SR 11, then 1.8 mi s on Winn Hill Rd. Located in a quiet area. **Facility:** A main inn and a converted barn annex both offer accommodations at this inn set on sprawling grounds in a scenic area. 19 units, some two bedrooms and cottages. 2 stories (no elevator), interior/exterior corridors. **Terms:** 1-2 night minimum stay - seasonal and/or weekends, 7 day cancellation notice. **Pool(s):** heated outdoor. **Activities:** 3 tennis courts, basketball, game room, horseshoes, shuffleboard, volleyball. Fee: cross country skiing.

TAMWORTH (D-4)

REMICK COUNTRY DOCTOR MUSEUM AND FARM is at 58 Cleveland Hill Rd. The museum preserves the heritage of Dr. Edwin C. Remick and his son, Dr. Edwin Crafts Remick, who practiced medicine in the village of Tamworth 1894-1993. Farm exhibits interpret 200 years of rural New England domestic and agricultural life while contrasting historic and modern methods.

Hands-on activities in summer include grinding corn and milking cows. An interpretive hiking trail and live farm animals also are on the premises. **Time:** Allow 1 hour minimum. **Hours:** Mon.-Fri. 10-4 (also Sat. 10-3, Memorial Day-Labor Day). **Cost:** $3; free (ages 0-4); $10 (family). **Phone:** (603) 323-7591 or (800) 686-6117.

THORNTON

SHAMROCK MOTEL   603/726-3534

▼▼ **Motel** $63-$85 **Address:** 2913 US 3 03285 **Location:** I-93 exit 29, 2.3 mi n. **Facility:** 8 units, some efficiencies and cottages. 1 story, exterior corridors. **Terms:** closed 11/1-4/30, 7 day cancellation notice-fee imposed. **Pool(s):** outdoor. **Activities:** game room, horseshoes.

ECO 🛥 📶 ✕ 🎮 🚭
/SOME UNITS FEE 🐕 🍳 🛗 📺 💻

TILTON

BLACK SWAN INN   (603)628-4524

▼▼▼ **Historic Bed & Breakfast** $99-$159 **Address:** 354 W Main St 03276 **Location:** I-93 exit 20 southbound, 1.5 mi w on SR 3 and 11. Adjacent to park. **Facility:** An attractive 1880 Victorian estate, this inn offers lovely guest rooms and elegant décor throughout. 9 units. 3 stories (no elevator), interior corridors. **Terms:** age restrictions may apply, 10 day cancellation notice-fee imposed.

📶 ✕ 🚭 /SOME UNITS 🐕 📶 🛗 📺 💻

HAMPTON INN & SUITES   603/286-3400

▼▼▼▼
Hotel
Rates not provided

AAA Benefit: Members save up to 10%!

Address: 195 Laconia Rd 03276 **Location:** I-93 exit 20, 1 mi e on US 3. **Facility:** 92 units. 4 stories, interior corridors. **Pool(s):** heated indoor. **Activities:** whirlpool, exercise room. **Guest Services:** coin laundry. **Free Special Amenities:** full breakfast and high-speed Internet.

SAVE CALL 📶 🛥 BIZ 📶 ✕ 💻 /SOME UNITS 🛗 📺

HOLIDAY INN EXPRESS & SUITES   (603)286-4550

▼▼▼ **Hotel** $89-$149 **Address:** 75 Tilton Rd 03276 **Location:** I-93 exit 20, 0.4 mi e on SR 140. **Terms:** cancellation fee imposed. **Amenities:** high-speed Internet. **Pool(s):** heated indoor. **Activities:** sauna, exercise room. **Guest Services:** coin laundry.

🛥 BIZ 📶 ✕ 🛗 📺 💻

SUPER 8 OF TILTON   (603)286-8882

▼▼ **Motel** $69-$249 **Address:** 7 Tilton Rd 03276 **Location:** I-93 exit 20; behind McDonald's. **Facility:** 63 units. 2 stories (no elevator), interior corridors.

🍴 CALL 📶 📶 🛗 📺 /SOME UNITS 📺

WHERE TO EAT

NINETY NINE RESTAURANT   603/286-4994

▼▼▼ American. Casual Dining. $9-$16 **AAA Inspector Notes:** This popular pub is committed to serving large portions of great food at reasonable prices. Guest favorites include hot wings, burgers, seafood, barbecue ribs and chicken. While reservations are not taken, call-ahead seating is offered. A children's menu is also available. **Bar:** full bar. **Address:** 154 Laconia Rd 03276 **Location:** I-93 exit 20, 0.5 mi e on US 3. ⌐L⌐ ⌐D⌐

TILT'N DINER   603/286-2204

▼ American. Family Dining. $4-$15 **AAA Inspector Notes:** The "old-time" traditional diner specializes in the expected burgers, cheese fries, hot dogs, salads and sandwiches. **Bar:** full bar. **Address:** 61 Laconia Rd 03276 **Location:** I-93 exit 20, just n on US 3. ⌐B⌐ ⌐L⌐ ⌐D⌐

TROY

THE INN AT EAST HILL FARM   603/242-6495

▼▼ **Country Inn** $248-$292 **Address:** 460 Monadnock St 03465 **Location:** Waterfront. Jct SR 12 and Monadnock St, 2 mi e. **Facility:** 49 units, some two and three bedrooms. 1-3 stories (no elevator), interior/exterior corridors. **Terms:** 2 night minimum stay - seasonal and/or weekends, 21 day cancellation notice-fee imposed. **Pool(s):** outdoor, heated outdoor, heated indoor. **Activities:** whirlpools, canoeing, paddleboats, boat dock, waterskiing, fishing, tennis court, cross country skiing, ice skating, recreation programs, hiking trails, jogging, playground, basketball, game room, horseshoes, shuffleboard, volleyball. **Fee:** horseback riding, massage. **Guest Services:** coin laundry.

ECO 🍴 🛥 ✕ 🚭 🛗 /SOME UNITS FEE 🐕 🎮 📺

TWIN MOUNTAIN

CARLSON'S LODGE   603/846-5501

▼▼ **Hotel** $69-$119 **Address:** 330 Rt 302 W 03595 **Location:** On US 302, 0.7 mi w of jct US 3. **Facility:** 27 units, some two bedrooms and efficiencies. 2 stories (no elevator), interior corridors. **Terms:** 2-3 night minimum stay - seasonal and/or weekends, 14 day cancellation notice-fee imposed. **Pool(s):** outdoor. **Activities:** cross country skiing, snowmobiling, bicycle trails, hiking trails, jogging, playground. **Fee:** game room.

🛥 BIZ 📶 ✕ 💻 /SOME UNITS 🚭 🛗 📺

PROFILE DELUXE MOTEL   603/846-5522

▼ **Motel** $80-$165 **Address:** 580 Rt 3 S 03595 **Location:** On US 3, 1.3 mi s of US 302. **Facility:** 15 units, some two bedrooms and cabins. 1 story, exterior corridors. **Terms:** 7 day cancellation notice-fee imposed. **Pool(s):** heated outdoor. **Activities:** cross country skiing, snowmobiling, bicycles, hiking trails, playground, basketball, horseshoes, volleyball.

ECO 🛥 📶 ✕ 🚭 🛗 💻 /SOME UNITS 🎮 📺

WAKEFIELD

LAKE IVANHOE INN   603/522-8824

▼▼ **Bed & Breakfast** $85-$150 **Address:** 631 Acton Ridge Rd 03830 **Location:** Waterfront. N on SR 16 to jct Wakefield Rd, 0.5 mi e to jct SR 153, 2.5 mi n to Acton Ridge Rd, then 1.3 mi e. Located within a camping resort. **Facility:** 6 units, some efficiencies. 2 stories (no elevator), interior corridors. **Bath:** some shared. **Terms:** closed 10/16-4/30, 2-3 night minimum stay - seasonal and/or weekends, 14 day cancellation notice-fee imposed. **Activities:** limited beach access, rental canoes, rental paddleboats, fishing, recreation programs, playground, basketball, horseshoes, shuffleboard, volleyball. **Fee:** game room. **Guest Services:** coin laundry.

📶 ✕ 🚭 /SOME UNITS 📺 🛗 📺 💻

WAKEFIELD INN BED & BREAKFAST   (603)522-8272

▼▼▼ **Historic Bed & Breakfast** $109-$209 **Address:** 2723 Wakefield Rd 03872 **Location:** SR 16, 0.5 mi e. Located in historic district. **Facility:** Located in the Lakes Region in the historic district, this 19th-century Colonial-style inn features a spiral staircase in the entryway and an original stone fireplace in the breakfast area. 7 units, some two bedrooms. 3 stories (no elevator), interior corridors. **Terms:** 2 night minimum stay - seasonal and/or weekends, 14 day cancellation notice-fee imposed.

[ECO] [¶] [🛜] [✕] [☎] / SOME UNITS [W]

WHERE TO EAT

POOR PEOPLE'S PUB   603/522-8681

▼ American. Casual Dining. $5-$16 **AAA Inspector Notes:** This casual restaurant is a favorite among the locals. **Bar:** beer & wine. **Address:** 1 Witchtrot Rd 03830 **Location:** Jct SR 109 and 153.

[L] [D]

WARNER (F-3) pop. 444, elev. 498'

A quiet agricultural village with a few structures dating from the late 1700s, Warner was the birthplace of three of New Hampshire's governors.

MT. KEARSARGE INDIAN MUSEUM, off I-89 exit 8N, 1 mi. e. on SR 103, then 1 mi. n. on Kearsarge Mountain Rd., depicts the culture and heritage of American Indians. An 8-minute videotape introduces visitors to the museum, thereafter they may embark on a self-guiding tour of exhibits featuring baskets, canoes, quillwork, beadwork and other artifacts. The adjacent Medicine Woods area offers a walking tour of 2 acres of plants, shrubs and trees used by various tribes for food, medicine and dyes.

Hours: Mon.-Sat. 10-5, Sun. noon-5, May-Oct.; Sat. 10-5, Sun. noon-5, Nov. 1 to mid-Dec. Guided tours are given daily at 2. **Cost:** $8.50; $7.50 (ages 62+ and students with ID); $6.50 (ages 6-12); $26 (family). **Phone:** (603) 456-2600.

NEW HAMPSHIRE TELEPHONE MUSEUM 22 E. Main St. Exhibits of antique telephones, telephone equipment and tools spanning more than 130 years of telephone history are on display at the museum. Visitors can see a replica of Alexander Graham Bell's first phone as well as use a hand-cranked phone and a plug-in switchboard. An introductory video depicts the life of a telephone operator and the telephone's evolution over the years.

Tours: Guided tours are available. **Hours:** Tues. and Sat. 10-4 (also Thurs. 10-4, May-Oct.). **Cost:** $5; $4 (ages 60+); $3 (ages 6-17). **Phone:** (603) 456-2234.

ROLLINS STATE PARK is 5 mi. n. off SR 103. A scenic road winds 3.5 miles up the slope of Mount Kearsarge. A .5-mile trail continues to the 2,937-foot granite summit, with a view encompassing Lake Sunapee, the White Mountains and mountains in Massachusetts and Vermont. **Hours:** Daily 9-5, mid-June to late Oct. Last admission 1 hour before closing. **Cost:** $4; $2 (ages 6-11). **Phone:** (603) 456-3808. [🐾] [⛱]

WATERVILLE VALLEY

BEST WESTERN SILVER FOX INN   603/236-3699

 ◈◈ ◈ Hotel   Rates not provided   **AAA Benefit:** Members save 10% or more with Best Western.

Address: 70 Packards Rd 03215 **Location:** I-93 exit 28, 11 mi e on SR 49, then just n. **Facility:** 32 units. 3 stories, interior corridors. **Terms:** check-in 4 pm. **Activities:** recreation programs in summer, bicycles. **Guest Services:** coin laundry, area transportation-ski area. **Free Special Amenities:** local telephone calls and high-speed Internet.

[SAVE] [BIZ] [🛜] [✕] [▦] / SOME UNITS FEE [🐾]

INNS OF WATERVILLE VALLEY-THE BIRCHES   603/236-8366

[fyi] Not evaluated. **Address:** 46 Packards Rd 03215 **Location:** I-93 exit 28, 11 mi e on SR 49, just n. Facilities, services, and décor characterize a mid-scale property.

WHERE TO EAT

DIAMOND'S EDGE NORTH RESTAURANT   603/236-2006

▼▼ American. Casual Dining. $11-$28 **AAA Inspector Notes:** Diners make their way to the easy-to-find Town Square, which houses this restaurant known for its appetizing American cuisine, such as stuffed chicken breast, roasted salmon and New York sirloin. Specials change each night. The lounge is a popular gathering spot. **Bar:** full bar. **Address:** 6 Village Rd (Town Square) 03215 **Location:** I-93 exit 28, 11 mi e on SR 49, then just n; in Town Square.

[D]

COYOTE GRILL   603/236-4919

[fyi] Not evaluated. Creativity infuses the restaurant's American preparations of seafood, steak and pasta. **Address:** Rt 49 03215

WEIRS BEACH (E-4)

A boardwalk, waterslide, weekly fireworks displays, yachting, fishing, swimming and other water sports are among the diversions at Weirs Beach, New Hampshire's inland version of a seaside resort.

Weirs Beach lies on the shore of Lake Winnipesaukee. Its name is thought to mean "Smile of the Great Spirit." The title is apt, for island-studded Winnipesaukee is considered one of the most picturesque lakes in the state. It also is the largest; the many bays and deep coves create a 283-mile shoreline.

Endicott Rock, a large boulder, was marked by emissaries of Gov. John Endicott of Massachusetts Colony. Proceeding 3 miles north, they established the northern boundary of Massachusetts, a line that held until the separation of New Hampshire and Massachusetts in 1740.

MOUNT WASHINGTON CRUISES depart from Weirs Beach docks. The MS *Mount Washington* offers scenic excursions and dinner dance cruises on Lake Winnipesaukee, New Hampshire's largest lake. The 72-square-mile lake is dotted with islands and surrounded by mountains. The popular U.S. mail boat *Sophie C.* takes on passengers as it delivers mail to the islands. The MV *Doris E.* offers 1- and 2-hour scenic and sunset cruises on the lake. A seasonal dinner dance cruise also is available.

Hours: MS *Mount Washington* scenic cruises depart daily at 10 and 12:30, late May-late Oct. MV *Sophie C.* cruises depart Mon.-Sat. at 11 and 2, mid-June to early Sept. MV *Doris E.* cruises depart daily, late June-Labor Day. Phone ahead to confirm schedule.

Cost: MS *Mount Washington* cruise $27-$49; $14 (ages 5-12); $68-$122 (family, two adults and two children). MV *Sophie C.* cruise $24; $12 (ages 5-12). MV *Doris E.* cruise $16-$24; $8-$12 (ages 5-12). Fares vary according to cruise type. **Phone:** (603) 366-5531 or (888) 843-6686.

WEST LEBANON

A FIRESIDE INN AND SUITES   (603)298-5900

Hotel $120-$200 **Address:** 25 Airport Rd 03784 **Location:** I-89 exit 20 (SR 12A), just s. **Facility:** 126 units. 2 stories (no elevator), interior corridors. **Pool(s):** heated indoor. **Activities:** whirlpool, exercise room. **Guest Services:** coin laundry.

BAYMONT INN   (603)298-8888

Motel
$90-$250

Address: 45 Airport Rd 03784 **Location:** I-89 exit 20 (SR 12A), just s, then just e. **Facility:** 55 units. 4 stories, interior corridors. **Amenities:** safes (fee). **Pool(s):** outdoor. **Guest Services:** coin laundry. **Free Special Amenities: expanded continental breakfast and high-speed Internet.**

SUNSET MOTOR INN   603/298-8721

Motel. Rates not provided. **Address:** 305 N Main St 03784 **Location:** SR 10, 2 mi s of Dartmouth College. **Facility:** 18 units. 1 story, exterior corridors.

WHERE TO EAT

LUI LUI   603/298-7070

Italian. Casual Dining. $6-$22 **AAA Inspector Notes:** Lui Lui (pronounced Louie Louie) means "he he" in Italian. The topic of conversation for first timers will surely be the brick oven encased in a giant red tomato. Savor one of the many tempting Italian dishes the menu offers inside one of the multiple level dining areas or on the outdoor riverside patio. The atmosphere is lighthearted. **Bar:** full bar. **Address:** 8 Glen Rd 03784 **Location:** I-89 exit 20 (SR 12A), just n, then just e; in Power House Mall Plaza.

THE SEVEN BARREL BREWERY   603/298-5566

American. Casual Dining. $4-$20 **AAA Inspector Notes:** Just off the Interstate, the brewery turns out house-brewed beers that go down easy with varied steaks, chicken dishes, sandwiches, salads and soups. The rustic setting incorporates exposed wood beams and beer barrels. **Bar:** full bar. **Address:** 5 Airport Rd, Suite 16 03784 **Location:** I-89 exit 20 (SR 12A), just s.

WEATHERVANE SEAFOOD RESTAURANT   603/298-7805

Seafood. Family Dining. $8-$25 **AAA Inspector Notes:** The popular, family-oriented restaurant presents a large menu with lobster, fried clams and crisp Cape Cod apple-cranberry cobbler. Flavorful dishes are served in large portions. A fish market is on the premises. **Bar:** full bar. **Address:** Rt 12A 03874 **Location:** I-89 exit 20 (SR 12A), 0.3 mi s.

WEST OSSIPEE

WHITTIER HOUSE RESTAURANT & TAVERN   603/539-4513

American. Casual Dining. $8-$19 **AAA Inspector Notes:** Traditional American fare is at the heart of the busy eatery's menu. Good food, reasonable prices and the casual atmosphere are what attract the local clientele. **Bar:** full bar. **Address:** 2415 SR 16 03890 **Location:** Jct 16 and 25 W, just n.

THE YANKEE SMOKEHOUSE WILD HOG PIZZERIA   603/539-7427

Barbecue
Casual Dining
$9-$20

AAA Inspector Notes: Patrons should ask for extra napkins to prepare for the terrific barbecue ribs, chicken and more. **Bar:** beer & wine. **Address:** Rt 16/25 03890 **Location:** Jct SR 16 and 25.

WHITEFIELD pop. 1,142

MOUNTAIN VIEW GRAND RESORT & SPA
(603)837-2100

Classic Historic
Hotel
$149-$790

Address: 101 Mountain View Rd 03598 **Location:** 2.5 mi n on US 3, just e. **Facility:** Outfitted with many luxury touches, this stately hotel offers sweeping views and an ambience of yesteryear. 144 units, some two bedrooms. 4 stories, interior corridors. **Parking:** on-site and valet. **Terms:** 2 night minimum stay - seasonal and/or weekends, 7 day cancellation notice-fee imposed. **Amenities:** *Some:* safes. **Dining:** 3 restaurants, also, Mountain View Grand Resort and Spa Main Dining Room, see separate listing. **Pool(s):** heated outdoor, heated indoor. **Activities:** sauna, whirlpool, 4 tennis courts, cross country skiing, ice skating, recreation programs, bicycles, hiking trails, playground, game room, horseshoes, shuffleboard, volleyball, spa. *Fee:* golf-9 holes, snowmobiling, horseback riding. **Guest Services:** complimentary laundry. (See ad p. 230.)

WHERE TO EAT

MOUNTAIN VIEW GRAND RESORT AND SPA MAIN DINING ROOM   603/837-2100

Continental
Fine Dining
$23-$50

AAA Inspector Notes: From its location in the historic hotel, this restaurant offers panoramic views of the Presidential Range. Guests are treated to a memorable dining experience by the exceptional chef. For those seeking a more unique atmosphere, inquire about the downstairs chef's table and wine cellar dining room, stocked with some 9,000 bottles. Semiformal attire. **Bar:** full bar. **Reservations:** required. **Address:** 101 Mountain View Rd 03598 **Location:** 2.5 mi n on US 3, just e; in Mountain View Grand Resort & Spa. **Parking:** valet and street only.

SPRING HOUSE CHINESE RESTAURANT   603/837-8898

Asian. Casual Dining. $4-$11 **AAA Inspector Notes:** Sitting all alone on Lancaster Road, this restaurant affords views of the grand mountains through its large windows. Guests sit down to Mandarin, Szechuan and Cantonese dishes in the open dining room. A small lounge sustains a laid-back atmosphere. **Bar:** full bar. **Address:** 140 Lancaster Rd 03598 **Location:** I-93 exit 35, 19.3 mi n on US 3.

WHITE MOUNTAINS AND WHITE MOUNTAIN NATIONAL FOREST (C-4)

Elevations in the forest range from 440 ft. south of Deer Hill near Colton Brook to 6,288 ft. on Mount Washington. Refer to AAA maps for additional elevation information.

North of New Hampshire's central plateau, the White Mountains rise in dramatic relief, cloaked with forests and laced with streams. Among the ranges and ridges are the highest mountains in the Northeast, the Presidential Range, which culminate in the bare granite summit of 6,288-foot Mount Washington (see place listing p. 219). Mounts Adams, Jefferson, Monroe and Madison also exceed 5,000 feet in elevation.

Passes known as notches pierce the uplift; Crawford, Dixville, Franconia, Kinsman and Pinkham notches (see place listings p. 187, 188, 192, and 205) provide some of the best scenic features in the state. Some 796,400 acres of the region lie within the White Mountain National Forest, which extends into Maine.

The names of several mountains in the southern section of the forest commemorate some of the state's best-known American Indians. Mount Passaconaway honors the chieftain who united 17 tribes into the Penacook Confederacy in the mid-17th century. Mount Kancamagus remembers Passaconaway's grandson Kancamagus, the last sagamore of the confederacy, who strove for peace with white settlers until he was provoked to attack Dover in 1689.

Because the White Mountains are as noted for outdoor recreation—particularly skiing and hiking—as for their beauty, they are one of the nation's most heavily used forest areas. Some of the ski resorts are world renowned. In summer anglers ply the rivers for several species of trout, and campers take advantage of the numerous campgrounds.

From spring through late fall the extensive network of trails, including the Appalachian Trail along the mountains' spine, lures hikers and backpackers. Many places, such as the Great Gulf Wilderness, are accessible only on foot. Only experienced backcountry travelers thoroughly familiar with the terrain and weather should attempt the higher elevations—in any season.

There are visitor information centers at the Pemigewasset Ranger Station, 71 White Mountain Dr. in Campton, phone (603) 536-6100; at the Saco Ranger Station, 33 Kancamagus Highway (SR 112) near Conway, phone (603) 447-5448; and at the Androscoggin Ranger Station, 300 Glen Rd. in Gorham, phone (603) 466-2713. White Mountains Visitor Center (See ad p. 224.), 200 Kancamagus Hwy. (SR 112) in North Woodstock, is open daily 8:30-5; phone (603) 745-8720.

For further information write to the Supervisor, White Mountain National Forest, 71 White Mountain Dr., Campton, NH 03223; phone (603) 536-6100, or TTY (603) 536-3665. See Recreation Areas Chart.

KANCAMAGUS HIGHWAY (SR 112), traverses the forest between Conway and Lincoln. It follows the Swift River Valley, passing Rocky Gorge Scenic Area, old Passaconaway and Sabbaday Falls. After crossing 2,860-foot Kancamagus Pass, the highway drops into the Pemigewasset Valley. Overlooks, picnic sites and campgrounds are scattered along the 34.5-mile route.

Self-guiding trails are near Covered Bridge Campground and at the Passaconaway Historic Site, 12 miles from Conway near the junction with Bear Notch Road, which leads to Bartlett (see place listing p. 177). About 1.5 miles west of Lincoln (see place listing p. 208) is the White Mountains Visitor Center, which dispenses recreation information year-round. Seasonal interpretive programs and brochures detailing the history of the area are available. **Phone:** (603) 447-5448 for the Saco Visitor Center, or (603) 745-8720 for the White Mountains Visitor Center. 🅰 ❎ 🔺

WINDHAM

THE COMMON MAN   603/898-0088
▼▼ American. Casual Dining. $14-$24 **AAA Inspector Notes:** Amid charming décor you'll browse a menu of tasty comfort foods, including the signature lobster and corn chowder, chicken Kiev, steaks, seafood and more. Leave room for the white chocolate mousse served at the end of each meal. **Bar:** full bar. **Address:** 88 Range Rd (Rt 111A) 03087 **Location:** I-93 exit 3, 1 mi e. [D]

WOLFEBORO (E-4) pop. 2,838, elev. 508'
• Hotels p. 254 • Restaurants p. 254

Known as one of the oldest summer resorts in America, Wolfeboro attained this status in 1768 when Gov. John Wentworth of Massachusetts built the country's first summer home. A marker at the site, 5 miles east on SR 109, commemorates the estate. By the time the governor's manor house burned in 1820, it was no longer unique. Summer homes and resorts now line Lake Wentworth and the southeastern shore of Lake Winnipesaukee. Although it has an air of sedate venerability, modern Wolfeboro is a major lake port.

Wolfeboro Area Chamber of Commerce: 32 Central Ave., P.O. Box 547, Wolfeboro, NH 03894. **Phone:** (603) 569-2200 or (800) 516-5324.

CLARK HOUSE MUSEUM COMPLEX, across from Huggins Hospital at 233 S. Main St., is a cluster of historic buildings on the village green. Pleasant Valley School, an 1820 one-room schoolhouse, features 19th-century desks and the Wolfeboro Historical Society Library. The Monitor Engine Co. Firehouse Museum is a replica of an 1862 firehouse with restored firefighting equipment, including a horse-drawn hose wagon and an 1872 steam pumper. The 1778 Clark House is a typical Colonial farmhouse furnished in period. An 1870s vintage barn also is located here.

Time: Allow 30 minutes minimum. **Hours:** Wed.-Fri. 10-4, Sat. 10-2, July-Aug; by appointment in June and Sept. **Cost:** $4; $3 (ages 55+); $2 (students with ID); free (ages 0-11). **Phone:** (603) 569-4997.

LIBBY MUSEUM is 3.7 mi. n.w. on SR 109. Natural history and early life in Wolfeboro and the Lakes Region are depicted through collections of mounted animals and Abenaki Indian artifacts. Changing art exhibits, lectures and special programs are offered throughout the season, and children's nature classes are presented in July and August. **Hours:** Tues.-Sat. 10-4, Sun. noon-4, June 1-Labor Day; Fri.-Sat. 10-4, Sun. noon-4, day after Labor Day-Columbus Day. **Cost:** $2; $1 (ages 6-12). **Phone:** (603) 569-1035.

THE WRIGHT MUSEUM OF WORLD WAR II HISTORY, n.w. of jct. SRs 109 and 28 at 77 Center St., displays memorabilia of the U.S. home front 1939-45. Exhibits illustrate details of American life as well as major events of World War II as they unfolded in Europe and the Pacific. An extensive collection of vehicles, equipment, clothing and other relics is on permanent display and enhanced by music and news broadcasts of the period, film clips and vintage periodicals.

Time: Allow 1 hour minimum. **Hours:** Mon.-Sat. 10-4, Sun. noon-4, May-Oct. **Cost:** $10; $8 (ages 60+ and military veterans with ID); $6 (ages 5-17). **Phone:** (603) 569-1212.

PIPING ROCK RESORT (603)569-1915

Motel
$63-$279

Address: 680 N Main St 03894 **Location:** Waterfront. 3.1 mi n on SR 109 N. **Facility:** 18 units, some two bedrooms, efficiencies, kitchens and cottages. 2 stories (no elevator), exterior corridors. **Terms:** 2-7 night minimum stay - seasonal and/or weekends, 30 day cancellation notice-fee imposed. **Activities:** canoeing, fishing, snowmobiling, playground, basketball, horseshoes, volleyball. *Fee:* boat dock. **Free Special Amenities:** high-speed Internet and children's activities.

WOLFEBORO INN (603)569-3016

Hotel $119-$399 **Address:** 90 N Main St 03894 **Location:** Waterfront. On SR 109, 0.5 mi n of jct SR 28; center. **Facility:** 44 units. 3 stories, interior corridors. **Terms:** 2 night minimum stay - seasonal and/or weekends, 14 day cancellation notice, resort fee. **Dining:** Wolfe's Tavern, see separate listing. **Activities:** limited beach access, boat dock, fishing, cross country skiing, ice skating, volleyball. *Fee:* massage. **Guest Services:** valet laundry.

THE CIDER PRESS 603/569-2028

American
Casual Dining
$17-$24

AAA Inspector Notes: The casual, family friendly restaurant specializes in delicious grilled ribs and chops and flavorful seafood dishes. Several dining rooms feature country decor, with a fireplace and raised hearth. Prompt, friendly service is the norm. **Bar:** full bar. **Reservations:** suggested. **Address:** 30 Middleton Rd 03894 **Location:** 2.8 mi s on SR 28, just s. Ⓓ

STRAWBERRY PATCH 603/569-5523

American. Casual Dining. $3-$8 **AAA Inspector Notes:** Hearty breakfasts and lunches are served at the country-style, smoke-free restaurant, where everything is homemade and fresh. Diners seated at tables set with berry-pattern plates and antique milk-glass vases filled with fresh flowers can gaze outside through bay windows. **Address:** 50 N Main St 03894 **Location:** Center.

Ⓑ Ⓛ

WOLFE'S TAVERN 603/569-3016

American. Casual Dining. $9-$28 **AAA Inspector Notes:** The restaurant builds its menu on the regional cuisine of seafood and aged Angus beef. **Bar:** full bar. **Address:** 90 N Main St 03894 **Location:** On SR 109, 0.5 mi n of jct SR 28; center; in Wolfeboro Inn. Ⓑ Ⓛ Ⓓ

WOLFEBORO FALLS (E-4)

NEW HAMPSHIRE BOAT MUSEUM, 399 Center St., has a rotating collection of antique race boats, rowboats and sailboats. Photographs, trophies, models and other boating-related memorabilia are on display; classes and special events are held throughout the year. **Time:** Allow 1 hour minimum. **Hours:** Mon.-Sat. 10-4, Sun. noon-4, Memorial Day weekend-Columbus Day. **Cost:** $7; $5 (ages 65+); $3 (ages 7-17); $17 (family, two adults and two children). **Phone:** (603) 569-4554.

WOODSVILLE pop. 1,126

ALL SEASONS MOTEL (603)747-2157

Motel
$60-$125

Address: 36 Smith St 03785 **Location:** I-91 exit 17, 4.1 mi e on US 302, then just s. **Facility:** 14 units, some efficiencies. 1 story, exterior corridors. **Terms:** 3 day cancellation notice-fee imposed. **Pool(s):** outdoor. **Activities:** playground, basketball. **Free Special Amenities:** local telephone calls and high-speed Internet.

NOOTKA LODGE (603)747-2418

Motel
$75-$235

Address: 4982 Dartmouth College Hwy 03785 **Location:** I-91 exit 17, 4.5 mi e on US 302. **Facility:** 34 units, some two bedrooms, efficiencies and kitchens. 2 stories (no elevator), exterior corridors. **Terms:** 3 day cancellation notice-fee imposed. **Amenities:** *Some:* high-speed Internet. **Pool(s):** outdoor. **Activities:** whirlpool, hiking trails, jogging, game room, exercise room. **Free Special Amenities:** local telephone calls and high-speed Internet.

SHILOH'S RESTAURANT 603/747-2525

American. Casual Dining. $6-$21 **AAA Inspector Notes:** This small, family-run restaurant serves casual and very fresh items. Sandwiches and limited entrée selections are offered for lunch while larger steak and seafood items are available at dinner. Most of the salad dressings are made in house and the ranch dressing is amazing. **Address:** 202 Central St 03785 **Location:** Center.

Ⓑ Ⓛ Ⓓ

Keep Your Children Safe in the Car

AAA and the timeless characters of best-selling children's author Richard Scarry have partnered to promote child passenger safety. Visit **AAA.com/SafeSeats4Kids** for car seat guidelines, and go to **SeatCheck.org** or call **866-SEAT-CHECK (732-8243)** for installation information. In Canada, visit the Child Safety section of Transport Canada's website at **tc.gc.ca.**

Remember, car seats save lives!

Lake Dunmore

Vermont

Historic Timeline 258
What To Pack 258
Good Facts To Know 259
Annual Events 260
GEM Attraction Index 262
Maps: Atlas Section & Orientation 263
Recreation Areas Chart 268
Alphabetical City Listings 270

Samuel de Champlain, the French explorer who in 1609 visited what is now Vermont, called it *les verts mont*—"green mountains"—after the lush ridges that form the spine of the state. Visit Vermont and you'll discover its namesake hue just about everywhere.

Take the Green Mountains and Green Mountain National Forest in central Vermont: From a distance, peaks appear swathed in deep blue-green, the palette of balsam, hemlock and white pine trees.

Maple trees adorned with emerald, five-fingered leaves contribute to the state's maple syrup production. Light green apples hang on orchard trees throughout the state in late summer, awaiting harvest. Fields of kelly green crops display the state's green thumb.

Rainbow-colored hot air balloons float over dark green valleys and aqua lakes. And various shades of green can be found stitched

Varying grades of Vermont maple syrup

or woven into quilts, baskets and other Vermont handicrafts.

The Green Mountain State

In an attic, an elderly woman discovers a book containing portraits of the "Green Mountain State." Images fill her head as she recalls her childhood in Vermont. Deciding to revisit a pleasant past, she dusts off the cover and cracks the binding.

Page one: A stark white steeple pierces the deep blue sky. Lofty, green-leafed trees surround the church.

It's summer in Stowe, and Mount Mansfield, the state's tallest peak, keeps watch over the town. The outline of the mountain resembles a face, so much so that it's easy to make out the formations locals call the Forehead, Nose and Chin.

The woman sips her tea and flips to page 11: A light blue truck is parked under a red covered bridge. Bands of soft light filter through the wooden lattice on one side wall, and the outlines of two lip-locked lovers can be seen in the glow of the setting sun.

Page 14: Light from a full moon cloaked in clouds casts a violet glow over a field quilted in white.

She clutches the afghan around her shoulders and turns to page 16. Buckets are crookedly attached to the trunks of sugar maple trees, tapped to catch oozing sap in spring. Page 17 shows beige, gallon-sized jugs filled with the sugary stuff lining a shelf.

Flames of fall color dominate pages 20 and 21. She can easily distinguish the softwoods from the hardwoods in a photograph of

Green Mountain National Forest. Softwoods remain a deep green, while the leaves on oak, maple, beech, ash and cherry trees showcase the same hues as school buses, blackberries, pumpkins and rosy lips.

Next, a father searches for the perfect pick off an apple tree while his son slyly taste-tests those already in the bucket. The flush of the boy's cheeks matches the red of the apples, and the scene calls to mind a Norman Rockwell painting—the artist lived in Arlington 1939-53 and used many townsfolk as models.

She flips to page 26: The granite spire of the Bennington Battle Monument reaches 306 feet into the cloudless sky. The monument honors the 1777 defeat of the British forces at this site by the Green Mountain boys, a Vermont militia group.

Turning to the last page, she is greeted by the gap-toothed grins of two young girls. Their fingers are covered with dripping ice cream, their faces a sticky delight. The sugar cone wrappers display "Ben & Jerry's" in trademark bubble letters, and one of the girls' shirts reads "I loVERMONT."

As she slowly closes the book, she can't think of a reason not to love Vermont.

Recreation

Mogul maniacs hit the slopes at Killington/Pico (the "Beast of the East"); Mount Snow; Stratton, known as the birthplace of snowboarding; Bromley in Manchester Center; Okemo in Ludlow; Sugarbush in Warren; Mad River Glen in Waitsfield; Stowe; Smugglers' Notch in Jeffersonville; Burke Mountain in East Burke; and Bolton Valley.

Snowmobiling on more than 1,800 miles of well-marked "corridor" throughout the state heats up winter chills. Cross-country skiing trails are at Hildene, The Lincoln Family Home in Manchester Village; Prospect Mountain; and Viking and Wild Wings, both near Arlington.

But Vermont is versatile. Hiking and biking trails also accommodate cross-country skiers and snowmobilers; fishing and boating become ice fishing and ice boating in winter; and ski slopes run alpine slides in summer.

Biking is best in central Vermont's Green Mountains. In fall, blueberries grow on wild bushes that crowd the Hogback Mountain Trail on the south side of Hogback Mountain.

For another good Green Mountains ride, head to Ripton and catch the Natural Turnpike, a 23-mile paved path that circles to South Lincoln and offers a great view of Mount Abraham. Linking to the Natural Turnpike is Steammill Road, where you may glimpse moose relaxing near a former steam mill.

Hikers love Camel's Hump Trail. Crossing brooks and passing stands of birch trees, it runs between Burlington and Montpelier. Aptly named, the 270-mile Long Trail ascends to the Camel's Hump summit.

In Mount Mansfield State Forest, numerous paths lead trekkers to the Chin of Mount Mansfield for a spectacular 360-degree panorama. The famed Appalachian Trail meanders along the Green Mountains' crown; continue south at Shelburne Pass to intersect with the lower portion of the Long Trail.

Put the wind in your sails on expansive Lake Champlain. More than 400 other freshwater lakes—especially Lake Seymour, Lake Willoughby, and Caspian and Crystal lakes in the north—are also good places to row a boat.

Rafters and canoeists put in and paddle the waters of the Connecticut, Batten Kill and White rivers. Otter Creek, the longest river in the state, provides a good view of the Green Mountains. The Winooski River starts at Montpelier and runs 58 miles through deep Winooski Gorge, around dams and eventually to Lake Champlain.

Ben & Jerry's Ice Cream Factory Tours, Waterbury

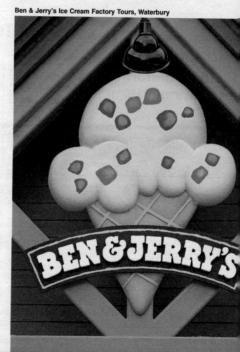

Historic Timeline

1609 — French explorer Samuel de Champlain discovers the Green Mountains and the lake that now bears his name.

1775 — Ethan Allen, the Green Mountain Boys and Benedict Arnold capture Fort Ticonderoga from the British.

1785 — The nation's first marble quarry is begun in East Dorset by Isaac Underhill.

1864 — Confederate soldiers raid St. Albans in the northernmost land battle of the Civil War.

1881 — Native son Chester A. Arthur becomes the 21st president of the United States following James A. Garfield's assassination.

1923 — Calvin Coolidge of Plymouth Notch becomes the 30th president.

1940 — Ida M. Fuller of Ludlow becomes the first recipient of a monthly Social Security check, for $22.54.

1968 — Vermont becomes the first state to ban roadside billboards.

1984 — Madeleine M. Kunin becomes the first woman governor of Vermont.

1987 — The Growth Management Law sets statewide goals to protect natural resources and to promote land preservation.

2008 — South Burlington-based ice cream icon Ben & Jerry's celebrates its 30th anniversary.

What To Pack

Temperature Averages Maximum/Minimum	JANUARY	FEBRUARY	MARCH	APRIL	MAY	JUNE	JULY	AUGUST	SEPTEMBER	OCTOBER	NOVEMBER	DECEMBER
Bennington	29/9	32/10	41/20	53/31	66/42	74/50	79/55	77/53	69/45	58/35	45/28	34/16
Burlington	27/9	29/10	38/20	53/33	67/44	77/54	82/59	80/57	71/49	57/39	44/29	31/15
Derby Line	26/6	31/8	41/19	54/31	69/43	77/52	81/57	79/55	70/47	57/37	43/27	31/13
Montpelier	25/7	28/10	38/20	51/32	65/43	73/52	78/57	76/55	67/46	55/36	42/28	31/14
Norwich	29/9	34/12	43/22	57/33	70/44	79/54	83/59	81/57	71/49	59/37	46/28	34/16
Shoreham	27/9	30/10	41/22	55/34	68/46	76/55	81/59	78/57	69/48	57/37	45/28	33/16

From the records of The Weather Channel Interactive, Inc.

Good Facts To Know

POPULATION: 625,741.

AREA: 9,609 square miles; ranks 43rd.

CAPITAL: Montpelier.

HIGHEST POINT: 4,393 ft., Mount Mansfield.

LOWEST POINT: 95 ft., Lake Champlain.

TIME ZONE(S): Eastern. DST.

GAMBLING

MINIMUM AGE FOR GAMBLING: Because most games of chance are illegal in Vermont, no minimum gambling age has been established.

REGULATIONS

TEEN DRIVING LAWS: No passengers are allowed for the first 3 months without a licensed parent, guardian or other licensed adult at least 25 years old. No passengers, except for immediate family (of any age), are allowed for the following 3 months. The minimum age for an unrestricted driver's license is 16 years, 6 months. Phone (802) 828-2011 for more information about Vermont driver's license regulations.

SEAT BELT/CHILD RESTRAINT LAWS: Seat belts are required for driver and all passengers ages 18 and over. Children ages 8-18 are required to be in a child restraint or seat belt; child restraints are required for children under age 8.

CELL PHONE RESTRICTIONS: Drivers under 18 are banned from using cell phones. Text messaging is prohibited for all drivers.

HELMETS FOR MOTORCYCLISTS: Required for all riders.

RADAR DETECTORS: Permitted.

MOVE OVER LAW: Driver is required to slow down and vacate the lane nearest stopped police, fire, rescue and tow truck vehicles using audible or flashing signals.

FIREARMS LAWS: Vary by state and/or county. Contact the Vermont State Police Headquarters, Waterbury State Office Complex, 103 S. Main St., Waterbury, VT 05671; phone (802) 244-8727.

HOLIDAYS

HOLIDAYS: Jan. 1 ▪ Martin Luther King Jr. Day, Jan. (3rd Mon.) ▪ Washington's Birthday/Presidents Day, Feb. (3rd Mon.) ▪ Town Meeting Day, Mar. (1st Tues.) ▪ Memorial Day, May (4th Mon.) ▪ July 4 ▪ Bennington Battle Day, Aug. 16 ▪ Labor Day, Sept. (1st Mon.) ▪ Veterans Day, Nov. 11 ▪ Thanksgiving, Nov. (4th Thurs.) ▪ Christmas, Dec. 25.

MONEY

TAXES: Vermont's statewide sales tax is 6 percent; the towns of Burlington, Dover, Killington, Manchester, Middlebury, Rutland Town, South Burlington, Stratton, Williston, Winhall and Wilmington impose an additional 1 percent sales tax. The state's Meals and Rooms Tax assesses a tax of 9 percent on lodgings and food and 10 percent on alcoholic beverages; 12 Vermont communities impose an extra 1 percent tax on lodgings, food and alcoholic beverages.

VISITOR INFORMATION

INFORMATION CENTERS: Year-round welcome centers are open in Montpelier (daily 8-8) ▪ on I-91 near the Canadian border at Derby Line ▪ on SR 4A at Fair Haven ▪ on I-91 at Guilford ▪ on I-93 at Lower Waterford ▪ and on I-91 at Lyndonville.

State and visitor information booths, open during the summer, are in Alburg ▪ Barre ▪ Bellows Falls ▪ Bennington ▪ Brandon ▪ Brattleboro ▪ Bristol ▪ Burlington ▪ Castleton ▪ Chester ▪ Hardwick ▪ Island Pond ▪ Jeffersonville ▪ Killington ▪ Ludlow ▪ Manchester ▪ Middlebury ▪ Montpelier ▪ Quechee ▪ Randolph ▪ Rutland ▪ St. Albans ▪ St. Johnsbury ▪ Swanton ▪ Vergennes ▪ Waitsfield ▪ Wells River ▪ White River Junction ▪ Wilmington ▪ and Woodstock.

FURTHER INFORMATION FOR VISITORS:
Vermont Department of Tourism and Marketing
National Life Building
1 National Life Dr., 6th floor
Montpelier, VT 05620-0501
(802) 828-3237
(800) 837-6668 *(See ad on inside front cover.)*

NATIONAL FOREST INFORMATION:
Green Mountain and Finger Lakes National Forest
231 N. Main St.
Rutland, VT 05701
(802) 747-6700
(877) 444-6777 (reservations)

FISHING AND HUNTING REGULATIONS:
Vermont Department of Fish and Wildlife
103 S. Main St., Bldg. 10 S.
Waterbury, VT 05671
(802) 241-3700

RECREATION INFORMATION:
State of Vermont Parks and Reservations
103 S. Main St., Bldg. 10 S.
Waterbury, VT 05671
(802) 241-3655

Vermont Annual Events

Please call ahead to confirm event details.

JANUARY

- Lake Morey Winterfest
  Fairlee
  802-649-9075
- Stowe Winter Carnival
  Stowe
  802-253-7321
- Vermont Farm Show
  Essex Junction
  802-828-1319

FEBRUARY

- Middlebury College Winter
  Carnival / Middlebury
  802-443-3103
- Burlington Winter Festival
  Burlington
  802-864-0123
- Winter Carnival / Brattleboro
  802-254-5808

MARCH

- Maple Open House
  Weekend / Ludlow
  802-899-9926
- Audubon Sugar on Snow
  Party / Huntington
  802-434-3068
- North American Telemark
  Festival / Waitsfield
  802-496-3551

APRIL

- Vermont Maple Festival
  St. Albans
  802-524-5800
- Pond Skimming / Killington
  802-422-6200
- Sugar Slalom / Stowe
  802-253-7704

MAY

- Kids' Day / Burlington
  802-864-0123
- Cheese and Dairy
  Celebration / Woodstock
  802-457-2355
- Gardening and Lilac Sunday
  Shelburne
  802-985-3346

JUNE

- Discover Jazz Festival
  Burlington
  802-863-7992
- Vermont Quilt Festival
  Essex Junction
  802-872-0034
- Quechee Balloon Festival
  and Crafts Fair / Quechee
  802-295-7900

JULY

- Stoweflake Hot Air Balloon
  Festival / Stowe
  802-253-7355
- Old Vermont 4th
  Woodstock
  802-457-2355
- Warren 4th of July / Warren
  802-485-7092

AUGUST

- Plymouth Old Home Day
  Plymouth
  802-672-3773
- Quechee Scottish Festival
  and Celtic Fair / White River
  Junction
  802-295-7900
- Central Vermont Chamber
  Music Festival / Randolph
  802-728-6464

SEPTEMBER

- Vermont State Fair
  Rutland
  802-775-5200
- Colors of the Kingdom
  St. Johnsbury
  802-748-3678
- Oktoberfest / Stowe
  802-253-3928

OCTOBER

- 19th-Century Apple and
  Harvest Festival / Strafford
  802-765-4288
- Harborween Celebration
  Vergennes
  802-475-2311
- Harvest Weekend
  Woodstock
  802-457-2355

NOVEMBER

- Veterans Day Observance
  Northfield
  802-485-2080
- Manchester Tree Lighting
  Manchester
  802-362-2100
- Santa Claus Parade and
  Holiday Lighting Ceremony
  Burlington
  802-863-1648

DECEMBER

- Vermont International
  Festival / Essex Junction
  802-863-6713
- Christmas at the Farm
  Woodstock
  802-457-2355
- Coolidge Christmas Open
  House / Plymouth
  802-672-3773

Traditional red barn, Stowe

Quechee Balloon Festival and Crafts Fair, Quechee

Shelburne Farms, Shelburne

Vermont State Fair, Rutland

Covered bridge, Woodstock

Index: Great Experience for Members

AAA editor's picks of exceptional note

Marsh-Billings-Rockefeller
Mansion

Billings Farm &
Museum

Shelburne Museum

Hildene, The Lincoln
Family Home

Bennington (G-1)
Bennington Battle Monument *(See p. 272.)*
Bennington Museum *(See p. 273.)*

Manchester (F-2)
Hildene, The Lincoln Family Home
(See p. 290.)

Marsh-Billings-Rockefeller National Historical Park (D-3)
Marsh-Billings-Rockefeller Mansion
(See p. 294.)

North Bennington (G-1)
Park-McCullough Historic Estate *(See p. 299.)*

Norwich (D-3)
Montshire Museum of Science *(See p. 300.)*

Plymouth (E-3)
President Calvin Coolidge State Historic Site
(See p. 301.)

Proctor (E-2)
Wilson Castle *(See p. 302.)*

Shelburne (C-1)
Shelburne Museum *(See p. 307.)*

Woodstock (E-3)
Billings Farm & Museum *(See p. 322.)*

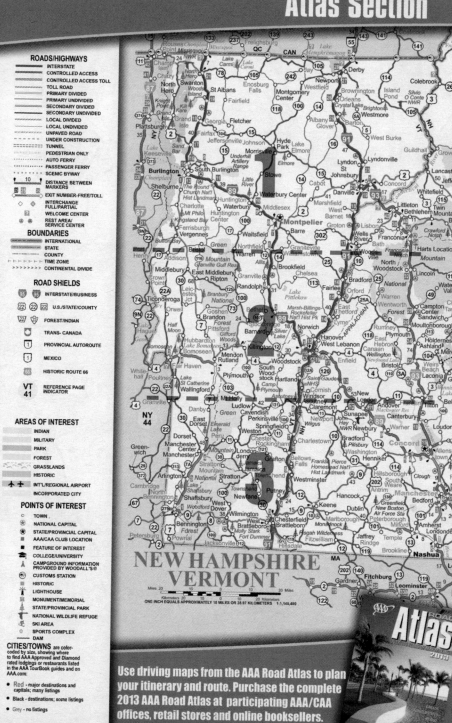

2

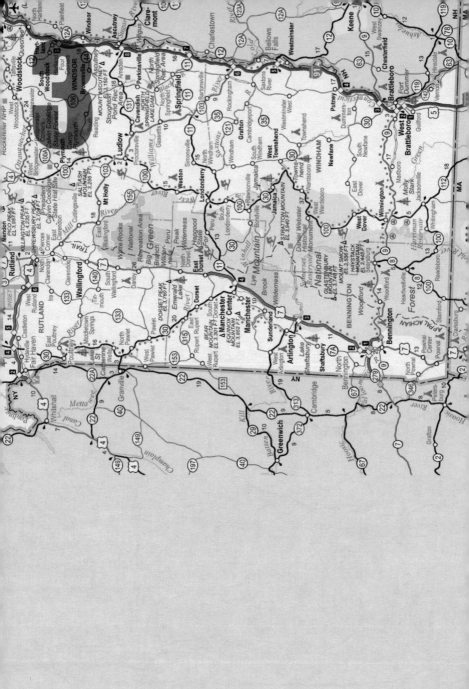

	1	2	3	4	5	6

A

QUÉBEC
NEW YORK

CAN
USA

QC

QC
VT

LAKE CHAMPLAIN
ISLANDS

Swanton
78

78
24
105

Jay
101

Newport

Derby
Line

VT

114

34

St
Albans
36

108

Fairfield

105

91

105

Brownington

41
8

7

23

Jefferson-
ville

100

Barton
Glover
12

7
105

17
21

104

36

Green
River
Reservoir

5

114

102
27

B

I-89

15
32
31
29

Morrisville
Wolcott
14

16

East
Burke

Lake
Champlain

BURLINGTON
Bolton Valley

MOUNT MANSFIELD
EL 4,393 FT
Stowe

15

91

2

Shelburne

Richmond
30

Waterbury
Center

Cabot

St
Johnsbury

93

River

C

Huntington
Charlotte

Water-
bury

42
14

MONTPELIER
★

East
Montpelier
Barre

18

33
22

Huntington
Center
Waitsfield

116

12

302

9

Ferrisburgh
Vergennes

Warren

North-
field

Granite-
ville

Addison

17

Granville

100

14

25

D

13

125

Middle-
bury

125

Strafford
4

Connecticut NH

91

132

22A
30

6

Bethel

89

Sharon

Shoreham

7

73

Green

107

37

Barnard

Marsh-
Billings-
Rockefeller
NHP

35

Norwich

Orwell

73

22A

Pittsford
100

White River Junction

19

16

1

Quechee

E

5

Proctor

Killington

Rutland

4

Wood-
stock

Castle-
ton

4

11

28

25

Plymouth

103

10

Ludlow

131

Windsor

30

2
39

100

Weston

Springfield

F

15

London-
derry

11

103

Manchester

Peru

Rockingham

30

Stratton
Mountain

100

20

Bellows
Falls

Arlington

26

Townshend

91

7A

Nat'l

100

3
38

Newfane

North
Bennington

40

MOUNT SNOW
EL 3,583 FT

30

Putney

G

9

Benning-
ton

Marlboro

Brattleboro

7

100

GREEN

Forest

112

VERMONT
MASSACHUSETTS

NEW HAMPSHIRE
MASSACHUSETTS

Vermont Orientation

Scale in Miles

15   0   15

NOT INTENDED FOR DRIVING.
SEE APPROPRIATE AAA SHEET MAP.

Only places listed in the Attractions section appear on this map.

⛤ *See AAA GEM Attractions*

1 *See Recreation Areas Chart on following page*

4048-B

© AAA

© 2012 NAVTEQ

AAA.com/
TourBook
Comments

Tell Us How We're Doing

If your visit to a TourBook-listed property doesn't meet your expectations, tell us about it.

AAA.com/TourBookComments

Recreation Areas Chart

The map location numerals in column 2 show an area's location on the preceding map.

	MAP LOCATION	CAMPING	PICNICKING	HIKING TRAILS	BOATING	BOAT RAMP	BOAT RENTAL	FISHING	SWIMMING	PETS ON LEASH	BICYCLE TRAILS	WINTER SPORTS	VISITOR CENTER	LODGE/CABINS	FOOD SERVICE
NATIONAL FORESTS *(See place listings.)*															
Green Mountain (E-2) 420,000 acres. South-central Vermont. Cross-country and downhill skiing, horseback riding, hunting, snowboarding, snowmobiling, snowshoeing.		•	•	•	•			•	•	•	•	•			
ARMY CORPS OF ENGINEERS															
North Hartland Lake (E-3) 1 mi. n. of North Hartland off US 5. Cross-country skiing, snowmobiling, snowshoeing; playground. Non-motorized boats only.	1	•	•	•	•	•	•	•	•	•	•		•	•	
North Springfield Lake (E-3) 1,361 acres .5 mi. n.e. of North Springfield off SR 106. Cross-country skiing, hunting, snowmobiling, snowshoeing. Canoes and flat-bottomed boats only.	2		•		•	•		•	•			•			
Townshend Lake (F-2) 6 mi. n. of Townshend on SR 30. Cross-country skiing, hunting, snowmobiling, snowshoeing.	3	•	•	•	•			•	•						
Union Village Dam (D-4) 5 mi. s. of Thetford Center on SR 132. Cross-country skiing, hunting, snowmobiling.	4		•	•				•	•			•			
STATE															
Bomoseen (E-1) 3,576 acres (two areas) .5 mi. n. of West Castleton. Historic. Beach, nature center, nature trails.	5	•	•	•	•	•	•	•	•			•			•
Branbury (D-2) 64 acres 3 mi. e. of Salisbury off US 7 on SR 53. Beach, nature center, nature trails, waterfalls.	6	•	•	•	•	•	•	•	•	•				•	•
Brighton (B-4) 610 acres 2 mi. e. of Island Pond off SR 105. Amphitheater, beach, nature center, nature trails, theater.	7	•	•	•	•	•	•	•	•	•		•			•
Burton Island (A-2) 253 acres in Lake Champlain; access by boat only from Kill Kare State Park. Marina, nature center, nature trails.	8	•	•	•	•	•	•	•	•	•					•
Button Bay (C-1) 253 acres .5 mi. w. of Vergennes on SR 22A, then 6.5 mi. n. w. via Panton and Basin Harbor rds. Nature center, nature trails, swimming pool.	9	•	•	•	•	•	•	•	•			•			•
Camp Plymouth (E-3) 295 acres off SR 100 n. of Ludlow. Beach.	10	•	•	•	•	•	•	•	•	•					
Coolidge (E-3) 21,416 acres 2 mi. n. of Plymouth via SR 100A. Snowmobiling.	11	•	•	•				•		•		•			
Crystal Lake (B-4) 16 acres in Barton on SR 16. Beach. *(See Barton p. 271.)*	12		•	•	•	•		•	•					•	•
D.A.R. (D-1) 95 acres 1 mi. n. of Chimney Point on SR 17. Bird-watching, sailing.	13	•	•		•	•		•		•					
Elmore (B-3) 700 acres at Elmore on SR 12. Beach.	14	•	•	•	•	•	•	•	•	•					•
Emerald Lake (F-2) 430 acres at North Dorset on US 7. Historic. Beach, cemetery, nature center, nature trails. Non-motorized boats only.	15	•	•	•	•		•	•	•	•		•			•
Gifford Woods (E-2) 285 acres 2 mi. n. of Killington on SR 100.	16	•	•	•				•		•			•		
Grand Isle (B-1) 226 acres 5 mi. n. of South Hero off US 2. Nature center.	17	•	•		•	•	•	•	•	•		•			
Groton State Forest (C-4) 26,175 acres (seven areas) midway between Montpelier and St. Johnsbury. Snowmobiling.	18	•	•	•	•	•	•	•	•	•		•			
Half Moon Pond (E-1) 50 acres 10 mi. n.w. of Castleton off SR 30. Nature programs. Beach, nature trails. Non-motorized boats only.	19	•		•	•			•	•	•		•			
Jamaica (F-3) 772 acres 1 mi. e. of Jamaica on SR 30. Nature center.	20	•	•	•				•	•	•		•			
Kill Kare (B-2) 17.75 acres 4 mi. w. of St. Albans on SR 36, then 3.5 mi. s.w. on Point Rd.	21		•		•	•		•	•			•			
Kingsland Bay (C-1) 264 acres 3 mi. n.w. of Ferrisburgh off Hawkins Rd. Historic. Sailing.	22		•	•	•		•	•	•	•		•			
Knight Point (B-1) 54 acres 3 mi. s. of North Hero off US 2. Art center, beach.	23		•	•	•	•		•	•			•			
Lake Carmi (A-2) 482 acres 3 mi. s. of East Franklin on SR 236. Beach, nature trails.	24	•	•	•	•	•	•	•	•			•		•	•

Recreation Areas Chart

The map location numerals in column 2 show an area's location on the preceding map.

	MAP LOCATION	CAMPING	PICNICKING	HIKING TRAILS	BOATING	BOAT RAMP	BOAT RENTAL	FISHING	SWIMMING	PETS ON LEASH	BICYCLE TRAILS	WINTER SPORTS	VISITOR CENTER	LODGE/CABINS	FOOD SERVICE
Lake St. Catherine (F-1) 117 acres 3 mi. s. of Poultney on SR 30. Nature center, nature trails.	25	•	•	•	•	•	•	•	•	•			•		•
Lake Shaftsbury (E-2) 84 acres 10 mi. n. of Bennington via US 7A. Beach, nature trail. *(See Bennington p. 272.)*	26		•	•				•	•	•				•	•
Maidstone (B-5) 469 acres 5 mi. s. of Bloomfield on SR 102, then 5 mi. s.w. on State Forest Hwy. Beach, nature trails.	27	•	•	•	•	•		•	•	•					
Mt. Ascutney (E-3) 2,506 acres 3 mi. s.w. of Windsor on SR 44 off US 5. Scenic. Hang gliding, snowmobiling.	28	•	•	•						•			•		
Mount Mansfield State Forest (B-3) 39,765 acres. Cross-country and downhill skiing, snowmobiling. *(See Mount Mansfield p. 298.)*	29	•	•	•						•		•	•	•	
Little River (C-2) 60 acres 1.5 mi. w. of Waterbury on US 2, then 3.5 mi. n. on Little River Rd. Water skiing; beach.	30	•	•	•	•	•		•	•	•		•	•		
Smugglers Notch (B-2) 32 acres 8 mi. w. of Stowe on SR 108. Historic. *(See Stowe p. 309.)*	31	•	•	•						•		•			
Underhill (B-2) 1 mi. n.e. of Underhill Center on Pleasant Valley Rd., then 2.6 mi. e. on Mountain Rd.	32	•	•	•						•		•			
Mount Philo (C-1) 168 acres 14 mi. s. of Burlington off US 7. Scenic.	33	•	•	•						•			•		
North Hero (A-1) 400 acres 8 mi. n. of North Hero off US 2. Nature trails.	34	•	•		•	•	•	•	•	•			•		
Quechee (E-3) 688 acres 7 mi. w. of White River Junction off US 4.	35	•	•					•		•			•		
Sand Bar (B-1) 15 acres n.w. of Burlington using I-89, exit 17 (Champlain Islands) then 4 mi n on US 2. Beach.	36		•		•		•	•	•						•
Silver Lake (D-3) 34 acres .5mi. e. of Barnard off SR 12. Beach.	37	•	•		•		•	•	•	•					•
Townshend (F-3) 1,095 acres 17 mi. n.w. of Brattleboro via SR 30. Boats with 10 hp maximum motors only.	38	•	•	•	•	•		•	•	•					
Wilgus (E-3) 89 acres 1 mi. s. of Ascutney on US 5. Canoeing, kayaking; nature trails.	39	•	•	•	•			•		•				•	
Woodford (G-2) 398 acres 10 mi. e. of Bennington on SR 9. Nature trails. *(See Bennington p. 272.)*	40	•	•	•	•			•	•	•					
Woods Island (A-2) 125 acres 4 mi. n. of Burton Island State Park in Lake Champlain; accessible by private boat only. Permit camping only.	41	•	•					•		•					
OTHER															
Wrightsville Beach (C-3) 4 mi. n. of Montpelier off SR 12. Disc golf (18 holes).	42		•	•	•	•		•	•	•					

ADDISON (C-1)

A small crossroads town, Addison is bounded on the west by sweeping plains that lead to Lake Champlain. At Chimney Point, 8 miles west, a steel bridge spans the lake to connect Vermont with New York. It is said that Samuel de Champlain stood at Chimney Point on July 30, 1609, and gave his name to the huge body of water that lay before him.

CHIMNEY POINT STATE HISTORIC SITE is 8 mi. w. at jct. SRs 17 and 125, at the Lake Champlain Bridge. This late 18th-century tavern has displays and artifacts relating to the region's history, including the Native American, Colonial French and early American heritage in Vermont. **Hours:** Wed.-Sun. 9:30-5, late May to mid-Oct. **Cost:** $3; free (ages 0-15). **Phone:** (802) 759-2412.

STRONG MANSION MUSEUM is 1 mi. n. of Crown Point Bridge at 6656 SR 17W. Built in 1785, the mansion is a restored, two-story Federal-style brick house—once home to a Revolutionary War patriot and his family—that contains period room displays. The grounds are accented by Colonial herb and perennial gardens.

Time: Allow 1 hour minimum. **Hours:** Guided tours Sat.-Sun. 10-5, Memorial Day weekend-Labor Day; by appointment rest of year. Last tour begins 1 hour before closing. **Cost:** $5; $3 (ages 62+ and students with ID); $10 (family). **Phone:** (802) 759-2309.

ALBURG pop. 497

RANSOM BAY INN & RESTAURANT   802/796-3399

▼▼ **Historic Bed & Breakfast** $120-$135 **Address:** 4 Center Bay Rd 05440 **Location:** Jct SR 78, 0.5 mi s on US 2, then just e. **Facility:** Spacious, tastefully decorated guest rooms with modest baths are offered at this long-established inn, built in 1795 as an inn and tavern. 4 units. 2 stories (no elevator), interior corridors. **Terms:** 7 day cancellation notice. **Activities:** bicycles. **Guest Services:** area transportation-Bay Beach & train station.

🍴 🍸 📶 ✕ 🚫 ⓩ / SOME UNITS FEE 🐾

ARLINGTON (F-2) pop. 1,213, elev. 689'

Chartered in 1761 by Benning Wentworth, governor of New Hampshire, Arlington's early history found it in the middle of a tug-of-war; its land was claimed by both New York and New Hampshire. New York was given control of the area by the British crown and refused to respect the New Hampshire grants and town charters. The vast majority of settlers rejected the authority of New York. With several hundred members, the Green Mountain Boys (led by Ethan Allen) were fairly successful in promoting the cause of the New Hampshire grantees.

Arlington became the center of another struggle caused by America's Declaration of Independence from England in 1776. Many of its citizens remained loyal to the king, and to this day Arlington is sometimes referred to as "Tory Hollow."

For a journey back in time, visit St. James Church Cemetery on SR 7, where the earliest stone is from 1777. Many of the Green Mountain Boys, both officers and enlisted men, lay beneath the little flags that dot the green lawn. Historic SR 7A offers 11 miles of scenic driving for those going north to Manchester Center.

THE NORMAN ROCKWELL EXHIBIT AND SUGAR SHACK is at 1 Sugar Shack Ln. This small country store has a room dedicated to many of Norman Rockwell's *The Saturday Evening Post* covers, illustrations, advertisements and prints. A 15-minute video presentation outlines Rockwell's career. The artist lived in Arlington 1939-53, and many local residents modeled for his illustrations.

Time: Allow 30 minutes minimum. **Hours:** Daily 10-5, mid-Apr. through Dec. 31. Closed Jan. 1, Thanksgiving and Christmas. **Cost:** Country store free. Rockwell exhibit $2.50; free (ages 0-12). **Phone:** (802) 375-6747.

CANDLELIGHT MOTEL   802/375-6647

▼ Motel $59-$115

Address: 4893 SR 7A 05250 **Location:** Historic SR 7A, 1 mi n. **Facility:** 17 units. 1 story, exterior corridors. **Terms:** 2 night minimum stay - seasonal and/or weekends, 14 day cancellation notice-fee imposed. **Pool(s):** outdoor. **Free Special Amenities:** continental breakfast and high-speed Internet.

SAVE 🏊 📶 🛗 / SOME UNITS FEE 🐾 🖥

WHERE TO EAT

ARLINGTON'S SOUTHSIDE CAFE & RESTAURANT   802/375-9900

▼▼ American. Casual Dining. $6-$13 **AAA Inspector Notes:** The simple, casual restaurant offers friendly service and their New England clam chowder is a must-try if you enjoy it thick and creamy. **Bar:** full bar. **Address:** Historic SR 7A 05250 **Location:** In Arlington Plaza. L D

ASCUTNEY pop. 540

MR. G'S RESTAURANT   802/674-2486

▼▼ American. Casual Dining. $5-$15 **AAA Inspector Notes:** The restaurant is a local favorite, offering good food in a simple, casual atmosphere. **Bar:** beer & wine. **Address:** SR 131 05030 **Location:** I-91 exit 8, just e. B L

BARNARD (D-3)

A town of summer cottages and winter hideaways, Barnard has been home to some of the state's most elite citizens. Journalist Dorothy Thompson and her husband, novelist Sinclair Lewis, lived at their picturesque white frame house, Twin Farms, during the 1930s. Thompson was one of the few female correspondents during World War II. She is buried in Village Cemetery on North Road.

THE MAPLE LEAF INN   (802)234-5342

▼▼▼▼ ▼▼▼▼
Bed & Breakfast
$160-$290

Address: 5890 VT 12 05031 **Location:** Just s on SR 12 from center. **Facility:** This newly constructed Victorian-style farmhouse sits in a serene, rural setting near picturesque Silver Lake. The guest rooms, some with a fireplace, are well furnished. 7 units. 3 stories (no elevator), interior corridors. **Terms:** 2 night minimum stay - seasonal and/or weekends, age restrictions may apply, 15 day cancellation notice-fee imposed. **Activities:** cross country skiing, snowmobiling, bicycles. **Free Special Amenities: full breakfast and high-speed Internet.** [SAVE] 🛜 ✕

TWIN FARMS   802/234-9999

[fyi] Not evaluated. **Address:** Stage Rd 05031 **Location:** 1.5 mi e of SR 12. Facilities, services, and décor characterize an upscale property.

WHERE TO EAT

BARNARD INN RESTAURANT & TAVERN   802/234-9961

▼▼▼▼ New American. Fine Dining. $15-$30 **AAA Inspector Notes:** Off the beaten path, this place occupies a lovely inn near beautiful Silver Lake in a quaint, picturesque town and offers intimate dining in one of four elegant dining rooms. The chef/owners specialize in a diverse three-course prix fixe menu from which patrons can select eclectic cuisine prepared using the freshest seasonal ingredients. The extensive wine list offers a choice of more than 300 selections. **Bar:** full bar. **Reservations:** required. **Address:** 5518 Vermont Rt 12 05031 **Location:** I-89 exit 3, just s. [D]

BARRE (C-3) pop. 9,052, elev. 515'

Although Barre (BARE-ie) started out not much different than other fledgling late 18th-century New England towns, a quirk of geology established its fate.

Originally chartered as Wildersburgh in 1780, the area's first settlers arrived in 1788, followed soon thereafter by emigrants from New Hampshire and Massachusetts. A name change resulted in Barre replacing Wildersburgh, though exactly how the change occurred has been lost to history. Two stories prevail—one version involves a bout of fisticuffs, the other has to do with offering naming rights to the person who contributed the most money towards the construction of a meeting house (the winning bid, by the way, was £62).

The huge quantity of granite found nearby is the geological phenomenon that altered the course of Barre's history. Shortly after the conclusion of the War of 1812, many highly skilled stonecutters from Italy, Scotland and other nations came to ply their trade. The arrival of the railroad simplified transportation, and the city adopted the moniker Granite Center of the World. Barre has been the largest granite-producing district in the country since 1900.

Barre granite, known for its almost flawless texture, comes in two shades: white and blue-gray. Fine works created from the local stone can be found throughout the region, including the state house in nearby Montpelier (see place listing p. 296).

You don't have to go far, though, to find some prime examples of granite craftsmanship. Pay a visit to Barre Opera House at 6 N. Main St.; phone (802) 476-8188. Hope Cemetery, established in 1895, has many artistic, often whimsical memorials, all crafted out of Barre gray granite. And the Robert Burns Monument, at 60 Washington St., was cut by local artisans in 1899 and is considered one of the finest pieces of granite sculpture in the world. In addition to a statue of Burns, the sculpture includes four panels that depict scenes from his poems and from his cottage in Ayr, Scotland.

Many large plants still produce granite sculpture for use in monuments and tombstones, and factory and quarry tours are available in nearby Graniteville at Rock of Ages Visitors Center (see attraction listing p. 284).

Central Vermont Chamber of Commerce: 33 Stewart Rd., P.O. Box 336, Barre, VT 05641. **Phone:** (802) 229-5711 or (802) 229-4619.

Self-guiding tours: A downtown walking tour covers the town's common, memorials, a number of 19th-century churches, the Opera House, Masonic Temple, library, post office and fire station. You can pick up a walking tour brochure at the chamber of commerce, the library and local merchants.

ROCK OF AGES VISITORS CENTER—see Graniteville p. 284.

MR. Z'S   802/479-3259

▼▼ Italian. Casual Dining. $6-$12 **AAA Inspector Notes:** The cute Italian bistro-themed restaurant offers a variety of burgers, grinders, pizza and pasta dishes. **Bar:** beer & wine. **Address:** 379 N Main St 05641 **Location:** Jct SR 14/US 302. [L] [D]

THE STEAK HOUSE RESTAURANT   802/479-9181

▼▼ Steak. Casual Dining. $10-$21 **AAA Inspector Notes:** This dining room has a comfortable, rustic-style consisting of timbers from old barns that were knocked down and reassembled. The menu features teriyaki steak, baked haddock, chicken and pasta dishes, and a salad and dessert bar. Enjoy the prompt, friendly service. **Bar:** full bar. **Reservations:** suggested, weekends. **Address:** 1239 US 302 05641 **Location:** Jct SR 14 N, 3 mi w. [D]

BARTON (B-4) pop. 737, elev. 945'

The Town of Barton was first granted by the legislature in response to a petition from some 60 Revolutionary War veterans in 1781, under the name "Providence" after their hometown in Rhode Island. However, it was not chartered until Oct. 20, 1789, at which time Colonel (later General) William Barton, a war hero, changed the name to Barton. Crystal Lake State Park (see Recreation Areas Chart) is popular with water enthusiasts.

Barton Area Chamber of Commerce: P.O. Box 776, Barton, VT 05822. **Phone:** (802) 239-4147.

THE SUGARMILL FARM, off I-91 exit 25, then .2 mi. s. on SR 16S to 1296 Glover Rd., offers self-guiding tours of its maple syrup-making facilities. Between mid-February and mid-April visitors can view syrup production, grading, storage and packaging techniques by appointment. The grounds include a maple museum with a 15-minute videotape presentation about the history of maple syrup, a travel information plaza and a fish farm.

Time: Allow 1 hour minimum. **Hours:** Daily 10-5, May-Oct.; by appointment rest of year. **Cost:** Free. **Phone:** (802) 525-3701 or (800) 688-7978. 🏧

BELLOWS FALLS (F-3) pop. 3,148, elev. 298'

Bellows Falls' namesake and most prominent feature is the falls. Once called the Great Falls, they now are reduced frequently to a trickle because of the power demands of industry. A canal was constructed nearby 1792-1802 for navigation on the Connecticut River from Long Island Sound to Barnet. Its nine locks raised small steamers and barges over the falls until the 1840s, when railroads took over the role of transportation.

Notoriety came to Bellows Falls in the person of Hetty Green, the Witch of Wall Street. Her house, now a bank, was at School and Westminster streets. Proclaimed the richest woman in the world at the time of her death in 1916, her worth was estimated at more than $100 million (over $17 billion in today's dollars). Green was known nationwide for her fabled money management as well as for her parsimony. She is said to have once spent half a night looking for a two-cent stamp, and she wore the same black dress day after day until it was in tatters.

The Connecticut River Byway (US 5), the scenic route that follows the Connecticut River, passes through the historic towns of Bellows Falls, Bradford, Brattleboro, St. Johnsbury, White River Junction and Windsor. From Memorial Day weekend through Labor Day, an interesting stop in Bellows Falls is the town's fish ladder on Bridge Street. Completed in 1982, the fish ladder reintroduced salmon to the upper Connecticut River for the first time since the 1790s, when the river was dammed for the canal. Now fish move up the ladder much the same way earlier canal boats moved up the locks. A visitor center offers exhibits; phone (802) 843-2111.

Great Falls Regional Chamber of Commerce: 5 Westminster St., Bellows Falls, VT 05101. **Phone:** (802) 463-4280.

BLUE HAVEN CHRISTIAN BED & BREAKFAST   (802)463-9008
▼▼ **Historic Bed & Breakfast** $99-$159 **Address:** 6963 US Rt 5 05158 **Location:** I-91 exit 5, 1.7 mi n. **Facility:** Quaint common areas at this restored 1830 house in Connecticut River Valley are adorned with original paintings by the owner, who happens to be a charming host. 4 units, some two bedrooms. 2 stories (no elevator), interior corridors. *Bath:* shower only. **Parking:** street only. **Terms:** check-in 4 pm, 10 day cancellation notice.
🛜 ✕ 🕅 ✕ / SOME UNITS 🍴 🖥 📼

BENNINGTON (G-1) pop. 9,074, elev. 728'
• Hotels p. 274 • Restaurants p. 276

Bennington is set in a valley between Mount Anthony, part of the Taconic Range, and the foothills of the Green Mountains *(see place listing p. 284).* In the Battle of Bennington on Aug. 16, 1777, the Americans under Gen. John Stark defeated a British expedition sent by Gen. John Burgoyne. The conflict

is commemorated each year in mid-August during the Bennington Battle Day Celebration.

Bennington's three covered bridges are reminders of times gone by. The Silk Road Bridge, Paper Mill Village Bridge and Henry Bridge all are easily accessible from off SR 67A on Murphy Road. US 7A north to Manchester and SR 9 east to Brattleboro provide scenic drives.

Hemmings Sunoco Filling Station and Exhibits displays vintage automobiles and automobile memorabilia in an old-fashioned, full-service gas station at 216 Main St.; phone (802) 447-9652.

Three miles north at 121 Historic SR 7A in Shaftsbury is the Robert Frost Stone House Museum, in which the Pulitzer Prize-winning poet lived and composed poetry from 1920-29. Educational and literary displays cover Frost's life and art; phone (802) 447-6200.

Outdoor activities available in the area include cross-country skiing, snowshoeing, snowmobiling, canoeing, kayaking, hiking and fishing. Popular recreational areas are Lake Paran, Woodford State Park *(see Recreation Areas Chart)* and Lake Shaftsbury State Park *(see Recreation Areas Chart).*

Bennington Area Chamber of Commerce: 100 Veterans Memorial Dr., Bennington, VT 05201. **Phone:** (802) 447-3311 or (800) 229-0252.

Self-guiding tours: Maps of two walking tours of historic buildings, houses and streets are available from the chamber of commerce. The chamber also has bike tour maps and driving tour maps that feature covered bridges.

Shopping areas: Bennington Potters Yard, 324 County St., offers free self-guiding tours of the pottery works which produce fine and decorative art pottery for the home; phone (802) 447-7531 or (800) 205-8033. Works in other media are offered in galleries throughout town.

BENNINGTON BATTLE MONUMENT, 1 mi. w. on SR 9 (Main St.), then .3 mi. n. on Monument Ave. to 15 Monument Cir., commemorates the Revolutionary War battle of Aug. 16, 1777, between British General John Burgoyne's forces and a group of Vermont, New Hampshire and Massachusetts volunteers led by General John Stark.

The British, running low on supplies, were attempting to reach the depot in Bennington where U.S. military provisions and food were stocked. The Americans met the redcoats before they could reach the storage site, however, and the Battle of Bennington, which ensued, was actually fought about 5 miles west at Walloomsac, N.Y. The loss to the Americans (both in manpower and the failure to restock their supplies) proved to be a factor in Burgoyne's surrender following the Battle of Saratoga in October, said to be a major turning point in the war.

The stone obelisk, when completed in 1889, was the tallest battle monument in the world; at 306 feet, it is still the tallest structure in Vermont. The monument was not dedicated, though, until 1891, with President Benjamin Harrison in attendance.

From the upper lookout chamber, reached by elevator, three states (Vermont, New York and Massachusetts) can be seen. A diorama and exhibits illustrate the battle, and an iron kettle belonging to General Burgoyne is displayed. A granite monument to Seth Warner who, with the Green Mountain Boys, helped win the battle, a statue of Stark and other monuments surround the attraction. Events are scheduled throughout the season.

Time: Allow 30 minutes minimum. **Hours:** Daily 9-5, second weekend in Apr.-Oct. 31. **Cost:** $3; $1 (ages 6-14). **Phone:** (802) 447-0550.

BENNINGTON CENTER FOR THE ARTS, 44 Gypsy Ln., is home to seven visual arts galleries and a covered bridge museum. The center's 700-piece collection is displayed on a rotating basis; a Native American exhibit, Floyd Scholz bird carvings and Eric Sloane paintings are displayed year-round. Concerts, lectures and workshops are offered throughout the year.

Time: Allow 30 minutes minimum. **Hours:** Daily 10-5, in Oct.; Mon.-Sat. 10-5, Jan. 8-May 31; Wed.-Mon. 10-5, June-Sept. and Nov. 1-Dec. 20. Closed Jan. 1, Thanksgiving and Christmas. **Cost:** (Includes entire complex) $9; $8 (ages 62+ and students ages 13-22 with ID); free (ages 0-12); $20 (family). **Phone:** (802) 442-7158.

Vermont Covered Bridge Museum, inside the Bennington Center for the Arts at 44 Gypsy Ln., describes the history of the state's and nation's covered bridges, many of which were destroyed in a late 1920s flood. Visitors view miniature replicas of covered bridges and learn about the bridges' builders, architectural styles and locations. Also of interest is the working train display. **Time:** Allow 30 minutes minimum. **Hours:** Daily 10-5, in Oct.; Mon.-Sat. 10-5, Jan. 17-May 31; Wed.-Mon. 10-5, June-Sept. and Nov. 1-Dec. 20. **Cost:** (Includes entire Bennington Center for the Arts complex) $9; $8 (ages 62+ and students ages 13-22 with ID); free (ages 0-12); $20 (family). **Phone:** (802) 442-7158.

BENNINGTON MUSEUM, 75 Main St., 1 mi. w. of jct. SRs 7 and 9, houses a collection of art and artifacts reflective of Vermont and associated areas of New York and Massachusetts. The Grandma Moses Gallery displays her paintings and belongings as well as photographs and family memorabilia. The gallery is adjacent to the Grandma Moses Schoolhouse, a family and children's activity center where visitors can barter in a country store and learn what it was like to attend school in the 19th century.

Permanent exhibits include the Bennington Flag, one of the oldest Stars and Stripes flags in existence; firearms; American paintings and sculpture; and American furniture from the 18th and 19th centuries.

The Bennington Pottery Gallery showcases a renowned collection of 19th-century ceramics produced by local companies. Another gallery features the Martin-Wasp, a 1924 luxury touring car. Changing exhibits are available year-round. A genealogy research area and the Hadwen Woods and George Aiken Wildflower Trail also are on the grounds.

Cell phone audio tours are available. **Time:** Allow 1 hour minimum. **Hours:** Daily 10-5, July-Oct.; Thurs.-Tues. 10-5, Feb.-June and Nov.-Dec. Closed Jan. 1, July 4, Thanksgiving and Christmas. **Cost:** $10; $9 (ages 62+); free (ages 0-17). **Phone:** (802) 447-1571.

OLD FIRST CHURCH (Congregational) is on Monument Ave. in Old Bennington Village. The church organization, dating from 1762, is among the oldest in Vermont. Built 1805-06, the church is regarded as one of the more beautiful in New England. The restored building features vaulted ceilings of plaster and wood as well as historic box pews. **Hours:** Mon.-Sat. 10-noon and 1-4, Sun. 1-4, July 1-Columbus Day; Sat. 10-noon and 1-4, Sun. 1-4, Memorial Day weekend-June 30. **Cost:** Donations. **Phone:** (802) 447-1223.

Old Burying Ground, on the Old First Church grounds, contains the graves of the founders of Bennington, soldiers killed in the Battle of Bennington, six Vermont governors and the poet Robert Frost, whose epitaph is "I had a lover's quarrel with the world." **Hours:** Daily 24 hours. **Cost:** Free.

ALEXANDRA BED & BREAKFAST INN   802/442-5619

▼▼▼▼ **Bed & Breakfast.** Rates not provided. **Address:** 916 Orchard Rd 05201 **Location:** 1 mi n on Historic SR 7A. **Facility:** This 1859 farmhouse-style B&B sits on a knoll offering good views of the surrounding countryside and distant mountains. 12 units. 2 stories (no elevator), interior/exterior corridors. **Parking:** winter plug-ins. **Terms:** age restrictions may apply. 🌿 📶 ✕

BENNINGTON MOTOR INN   (802)442-5479

Motel
$65-$169

Address: 143 W Main St 05201 **Location:** Jct US 7, 0.4 mi w on SR 9. **Facility:** 16 units, some two bedrooms. 2 stories (no elevator), exterior corridors. **Parking:** winter plug-ins. **Terms:** 3 day cancellation notice-fee imposed. **Free Special Amenities: continental breakfast and high-speed Internet.** *(See ad this page.)*

SAVE FEE 📶 🛗 🖥 💻 /SOME UNITS FEE 🐾

BEST WESTERN PLUS NEW ENGLANDER MOTOR INN   (802)442-6311

Motel
$69-$169

AAA Benefit: Members save 10% or more with Best Western.

Address: 220 Northside Dr 05201 **Location:** Jct US 7, then 0.7 mi n on Historic SR 7A. **Facility:** 58 units. 1-2 stories (no elevator), interior/exterior corridors. **Parking:** winter plug-ins. **Terms:** 2 night minimum stay - seasonal and/or weekends, cancellation fee imposed. **Amenities:** high-speed Internet, safes. **Pool(s):** heated outdoor. **Activities:** exercise room. **Guest Services:** valet and coin laundry. **Free Special Amenities: local telephone calls and high-speed Internet.** *(See ad p. 275.)*

SAVE CALL 📞M 🚗 BIZ 📶 🛗 🖥 💻

FOUR CHIMNEY'S INN & RESTAURANT   (802)447-3500

▼▼▼▼ **Country Inn** $129-$299 **Address:** 21 West Rd (Vt Rt 9 W) 05201 **Location:** On SR 9, 1.3 mi w of jct US 7. **Facility:** Built in 1910, this property sits on 11 landscaped acres so it's situated back from the road in a quiet, serene country setting. 10 units. 3 stories (no elevator), interior/exterior corridors. **Terms:** 2 night minimum stay - weekends, 10 day cancellation notice-fee imposed. **Amenities:** high-speed Internet. **Dining:** Four Chimney's Restaurant, see separate listing. **Activities:** hiking trails. *Fee:* massage.

🍽 FEE ♿ 📶 ✕

HAMPTON INN-BENNINGTON   (802)440-9862

▼▼▼▼
Hotel
$139-$199

AAA Benefit: Members save up to 10%!

Address: 51 Hannaford Square 05201 **Location:** SR 279 exit 1, just s. **Facility:** 80 units. 3 stories, interior corridors. **Terms:** 1-7 night minimum stay, cancellation fee imposed. **Amenities:** video games (fee), high-speed Internet. **Pool(s):** heated indoor. **Activities:** sauna, whirlpool, exercise room. **Guest Services:** valet and coin laundry.

SAVE 🍽 CALL 📞M 🚗 BIZ 📶 ✕ 📹 🖥 💻 /SOME UNITS 🛗 🖥

HARWOOD HILL MOTEL   802/442-6278

▼▼▼
Motel
$67-$99

Address: 864 Harwood Hill Rd (SR 7A) 05201 **Location:** Jct SR 9, 1.2 mi n on US 7, then 1.7 mi n on Historic SR 7A. **Facility:** 17 units, some cottages. 1 story, exterior corridors. **Terms:** 3 day cancellation notice-fee imposed. **Free Special Amenities: local telephone calls and high-speed Internet.**

SAVE 🍽 ✕ 🛗 💻 /SOME UNITS FEE 🐾 🚭 🖥

KNOTTY PINE MOTEL   802/442-5487

▼ **Motel** $79-$99 **Address:** 130 Northside Dr (SR 7A) 05201 **Location:** Jct SR 9, 1.2 mi n on US 7, then just n on Historic SR 7A. **Facility:** 19 units, some efficiencies and kitchens. 1 story, exterior corridors. **Parking:** winter plug-ins. **Terms:** 2 night minimum stay - seasonal and/or weekends, cancellation fee imposed. **Pool(s):** outdoor.

🍽 🚗 📶 ✕ 🛗 🖥 💻 /SOME UNITS 🐾

▼ See AAA listing this page ▼

▼ See AAA listing p. 274 ▼

ALLEGRO RISTORANTE   802/442-0990

▼▼▼▼ Italian. Fine Dining. $12-$21 **AAA Inspector Notes:** In the heart of the village, this intimate bistro offers some interesting variations on Italian cuisine. **Bar:** full bar. **Reservations:** suggested. **Address:** 520 Main St 05201 **Location:** Between School and Valentine sts; center. **Parking:** street only. [D] CALL [M]

BENNINGTON STATION   802/442-7900

▼▼▼▼ Seafood. Fine Dining. $7-$28 **AAA Inspector Notes:** Built in 1897 from locally quarried blue marble, this former rail station has been restored and transformed into a fine-dining establishment. The menu offers a wide variety of seafood dishes along with steaks, poultry and some New England staples such as Yankee pot roast, Vermont tom turkey and New England clam chowder. **Bar:** full bar. **Address:** 150 Depot St 05201 **Location:** Jct US 7, just s; corner of River St. [L] [D] CALL [M]

CARMODY'S   802/447-5748

▼▼ American. Casual Dining. $7-$19 **AAA Inspector Notes:** At this inviting tavern, patrons can enjoy a variety of American dishes. **Bar:** full bar. **Address:** 421 Main St 05201 **Location:** Center. **Parking:** street only. [L] [D] [LATE] CALL [M]

FOUR CHIMNEY'S RESTAURANT   802/447-3500

▼▼▼ American. Casual Dining. $20-$38 **AAA Inspector Notes:** In a former private mansion, this charming country inn combines American and Continental-style dishes on its menu. Local ingredients are used in such menu highlights as seafood pasta, filet mignon, crab cakes, New York strip steak, New Zealand lamb, New York strip steak, salmon and chicken Florentine. The casually attired waitstaff is friendly and helpful. **Bar:** full bar. **Reservations:** suggested. **Address:** 21 West Rd (Vt Rt 9 W) 05201 **Location:** On SR 9, 1.3 mi w of jct US 7; in Four Chimney's Inn & Restaurant. [D]

THE GRILLE AT MT ANTHONY COUNTRY CLUB
                                                            802/442-2617

▼▼ American. Casual Dining. $8-$27 **AAA Inspector Notes:** A laid back, no-frills atmosphere awaits at this country club eatery, in a quiet residential area overlooking the golf course. An attractive stone fireplace, wood floors and decorative sconce lighting make up the decor. The menu lists a varied selection of well-prepared American cuisine, including seafood, steak and chicken served in large portions. **Bar:** full bar. **Address:** 180 Country Club Dr 05201 **Location:** Jct US 7, 0.5 mi w on SR 9, then 0.5 mi n on Convent Ave. [L] [D]

LIL' BRITAIN FISH & CHIP SHOP   802/442-2447

▼ British. Casual Dining. $5-$11 **AAA Inspector Notes:** The Union Jack flag proudly displayed outside this modest café makes it easy to find. It's owned and operated by a native British couple who have brought their homeland favorites to the states. Along with fish and chips you can order a variety of meat pies, burgers and fried shrimp, scallops and clams. **Address:** 116 North St 05201 **Location:** Center; near corner of Main St on SR 7. **Parking:** street only. [L] [D]

MADISON BREWING CO. PUB & RESTAURANT 802/442-7397

▼▼ American. Casual Dining. $8-$22 **AAA Inspector Notes:** This relaxed brewpub serves traditional pub fare, such as tasty sandwiches and burgers, as well as chicken, seafood, pasta and beef dishes. Among yummy desserts include chocolate mousse pie with a ladyfinger crust. **Bar:** full bar. **Address:** 428 Main St 05201 **Location:** On SR 9; center. [L] [D]

THE PUBLYK HOUSE   802/442-7500

▼▼▼ American. Casual Dining. $9-$36 **AAA Inspector Notes:** This restored three-story horse barn was relocated to be situated in an apple orchard overlooking the village, battle monument and the lush rolling hills. The tasteful, rustic décor adds to its charm. Serving a variety of hearty New England dishes as well as lighter tavern fare. Multiple beers from area microbreweries are on tap. The fresh home-baked bread is served with Vermont maple butter. **Bar:** full bar. **Address:** 782 Harwood Hill 05201 **Location:** 0.8 mi n on Historic SR 7A. [D] CALL [M]

BERLIN

COMFORT INN & SUITES AT MAPLEWOOD LTD
                                                         (802)229-2222

▼▼▼
Hotel
$150-$210

Address: 213 Paine Tpke N 05602 **Location:** I-89 exit 7 (SR 62), 0.3 mi e. **Facility:** 89 units. 3 stories (no elevator), interior corridors. **Parking:** winter plug-ins. **Terms:** cancellation fee imposed. **Amenities:** high-speed Internet. **Activities:** exercise room. **Guest Services:** coin laundry. **Free Special Amenities:** expanded continental breakfast and local telephone calls.

[SAVE] [TI+] CALL [M] 🛜 ✕ 🚪 💼 💻

WAYSIDE RESTAURANT & BAKERY   802/223-6611

▼ American. Quick Serve. $4-$12 **AAA Inspector Notes:** Historic. This popular family restaurant and bakery has been a local favorite for breakfast, lunch and dinner since 1918. The menu features familiar New England dishes, including fried clams, fried tripe, scallops and haddock, as well as pasta, burgers, steak, chicken, meatloaf, roast beef, ham, sandwiches, daily specials and freshly made pies. **Bar:** full bar. **Address:** 1873 US Rt 302 05602 **Location:** I-89 exit 7 (SR 62), 0.3 mi w. [B] [L] [D]

BETHEL (D-3) pop. 569, elev. 569'

Bethel was the first town created by the independent Republic of Vermont. One of the grantees, while surveying the town with his associates, woke one morning and told of having dreamed about the Biblical story in which Jacob slept in a field with only a stone for a pillow; Jacob subsequently named the place Bethel (meaning "sacred place"). The grantee and his associates were so moved by his dream, they agreed to name their town the same. When the Baptist church was built in 1824 in the village of East Bethel, stones from the old church at Bethel Gilead, SR 12 between Bethel and Randolph, were incorporated into the foundation.

WHITE RIVER NATIONAL FISH HATCHERY, 2 mi. w. on SR 107, following signs, has a visitor center with displays depicting the hatchery's work of restoring Atlantic salmon to the Connecticut River. The fish once thrived in New England rivers and streams, but by the mid-1800s dam construction and overfishing had drastically reduced their population.

At the outdoor aquaculture pond, visitors can view fish at various developmental stages. The hatchery also raises lake trout for planting in lakes Erie and Ontario. **Note:** The hatchery is closed due to damage sustained in 2011 from Tropical Storm Irene; reconstruction is scheduled to be completed in 2014. **Time:** Allow 30 minutes minimum. **Hours:** Daily 8-3. **Cost:** Free. **Phone:** (802) 234-5241 or (802) 234-5400. 🎍

BOLTON VALLEY (C-2) elev. 1,591'

RECREATIONAL ACTIVITIES
Skiing

- **Bolton Valley Resort** is at 4302 Bolton Access Rd. Other activities are available. **Hours:** Daily early Dec.-early Apr. (weather permitting). **Phone:** (802) 434-3444 or (877) 926-5866.

BRADFORD pop. 788

COLATINA EXIT
802/222-9008

▼▼▼ Italian. Casual Dining. $7-$21 **AAA Inspector Notes:** Patrons will find fresh food and friendly, casual service at this restaurant with an Italian bistro atmosphere, rough hewn walls and a painted tin ceiling. **Bar:** full bar. **Address:** 164 Main St 05033 **Location:** Center. **Parking:** street only. [L] [D]

THE PERFECT PEAR CAFE
802/222-5912

▼▼▼ American. Casual Dining. $9-$20 **AAA Inspector Notes:** This charming eatery offers patrons a definite twist when it comes to comfort foods. Creative and delicious is the best way to describe them. **Bar:** full bar. **Address:** 48 Main St 05033 **Location:** Just s of center. [L] [D]

BRANDON pop. 1,648

BRANDON MOTOR LODGE
802/247-9594

▼▼▼
Motel
$69-$145

Address: 2095 Franklin St 05733 **Location:** 2 mi s on US 7. **Facility:** 26 units. 1 story, exterior corridors. **Pool(s):** heated outdoor. **Activities:** whirlpool, playground, horseshoes, volleyball. **Free Special Amenities:** local telephone calls and high-speed Internet.

[SAVE] [ECO] 🏊 📶 ✕ ▯ / SOME UNITS FEE 🐾 📷

THE LILAC INN
(802)247-5463

▼▼▼ Historic Country Inn $145-$375 **Address:** 53 Park St 05733 **Location:** Just e on SR 73. Located in historic district. **Facility:** The restored 1909 mansion offers spacious guest rooms, some with a fireplace. Public areas are furnished with antiques and artwork. A gazebo, waterfall and two acres of perennial landscaping bring serenity. 9 units. 2 stories (no elevator), interior corridors. **Terms:** 2 night minimum stay - seasonal, age restrictions may apply, 30 day cancellation notice-fee imposed.

[ECO] 🍴 🍸 📶 ✕ ☎ / SOME UNITS FEE 🐾

PATRICIA'S RESTAURANT AKA SULLY'S
802/247-3223

▼▼ American. Casual Dining. $5-$25 **AAA Inspector Notes:** Casual dining in an atmosphere featuring Vermont wildlife, antique creels, rods and wildlife prints adorns the walls. Diners also can enjoy the outdoor deck and umbrella tables in the summer, as well as a fine brunch on Sunday. **Bar:** full bar. **Address:** 18-20 Center St 05733 **Location:** Center. **Parking:** street only. [L] [D]

BRATTLEBORO (G-3) pop. 7,414, elev. 226'

It was here that the state's first permanent English settlement, Fort Dummer, was established in 1724.

Rudyard Kipling, in collaboration with New York architect Henry Rutgers Marshall, built a house for his American bride north of Brattleboro in Dummerston and named it Naulakha, which means "precious jewel." Kipling wrote "Captains Courageous" and the two "Jungle Book" stories during his residence there. The Landmark Trust USA, a non-profit foundation dedicated to preserving historic British homes, restored the house, which is available for rent by reservation and accommodates up to eight guests at a time; phone (802) 254-6868.

Also of interest is Brooks Memorial Library, which has changing art and photography exhibits, an extensive genealogy room and a children's room; phone (802) 254-5290. Running west to Bennington

is SR 9, which offers scenic views in the vicinity of Hogback Mountain.

Brattleboro Area Chamber of Commerce: 180 Main St., Brattleboro, VT 05301. **Phone:** (802) 254-4565 or (877) 254-4565.

BRATTLEBORO MUSEUM & ART CENTER, off I-91 via SR 5 to Main and Vernon sts., is in the former Union Station. Six galleries present changing exhibits of contemporary visual arts. **Time:** Allow 30 minutes minimum. **Hours:** Thurs.-Mon. 11-5 (also first Fri. of the month 5-8:30). Closed Jan. 1, July 4, Thanksgiving, Christmas and between exhibits. Phone ahead to confirm schedule. **Cost:** $8; $6 (ages 60+); $4 (ages 6-17 and students with ID). **Phone:** (802) 257-0124.

ECONO LODGE
802/254-2360

▼▼▼
Motel
Rates not provided

Address: 515 Canal St 05301 **Location:** I-91 exit 1, 0.3 mi n on US 5. **Facility:** 40 units. 1-2 stories (no elevator), interior/exterior corridors. **Parking:** winter plug-ins. **Pool(s):** outdoor. Free **Special Amenities:** full breakfast and local telephone calls.

[SAVE] 🏊 📶 ✕ ▯ 📷 🖥 / SOME UNITS FEE 🐾

HAMPTON INN BRATTLEBORO
(802)254-5700

▼▼▼
Hotel
$139-$289

AAA Benefit: Members save up to 10%!

Address: 1378 Putney Rd 05301 **Location:** I-91 exit 3, 0.6 mi n on US 5. **Facility:** 73 units. 4 stories, interior corridors. **Terms:** 1-7 night minimum stay, cancellation fee imposed. **Amenities:** video games (fee), high-speed Internet. **Pool(s):** heated indoor. **Activities:** whirlpool, limited exercise equipment. **Guest Services:** valet and coin laundry. Free **Special Amenities:** full breakfast and high-speed Internet.

[SAVE] 🏊 [BIZ] 📶 ✕ ▯ 📷 🖥

HOLIDAY INN EXPRESS HOTEL & SUITES
(802)257-2400

▼▼▼
Hotel
$139-$299

Address: 100 Chickering Dr 05301 **Location:** I-91 exit 3, just e on SR 9, then 0.5 mi s on US 5. **Facility:** 86 units. 3 stories, interior corridors. **Terms:** cancellation fee imposed. **Amenities:** high-speed Internet. **Pool(s):** heated indoor. **Activities:** whirlpool, exercise room. **Guest Services:** valet and coin laundry. Free **Special Amenities:** expanded continental breakfast and high-speed Internet.

[SAVE] [ECO] 🍴 CALL 🔔M 🏊 [BIZ] 📶 ✕ ▯ 📷 🖥

PANDA NORTH CHINESE & JAPANESE RESTAURANT
802/257-4578

▼▼▼ Asian. Casual Dining. $8-$20 **AAA Inspector Notes:** Szechuan, Hunan, Shanghai, Peking and Cantonese cuisine is offered at this restaurant and selections include seafood, chicken, pork, beef and vegetarian entrees. General Tso's chicken is superb! Lunch specials include soup and rice. The prompt, friendly service and casual atmosphere are delightful. **Bar:** full bar. **Address:** 1332 Putney Rd 05301 **Location:** I-91 exit 3, 0.4 mi n on US 5. [L] [D]

SHIN-LA RESTAURANT AND SUSHI BAR 802/257-5226

 Asian. Casual Dining. $5-$13 **AAA Inspector Notes:** Located in the center of town this restaurant is very popular with the locals. The décor is made up of wood booths and mismatched chairs. The dishes served are a variety of Korean and Japanese specialties. Fresh sushi is served for lunch and dinner. **Bar:** beer & wine. **Address:** 57 Main St 05301 **Location:** Center of downtown. **Parking:** on-site (fee) and street. [L] [D]

BRISTOL pop. 2,030

INN AT BALDWIN CREEK-MARY'S RESTAURANT
802/453-2432

Regional
American
Fine Dining
$9-$28

AAA Inspector Notes: *Historic.* Famous for its cream of garlic soup, this historic restaurant uses fresh products from local farms. The menu is changed seasonally and supplemented with daily specials to take advantage of the freshest ingredients. The 1790 farmhouse setting at foot of Green Mountains is warm and cozy. **Bar:** full bar. **Reservations:** suggested. **Address:** 1868 Route 116 N 05443 **Location:** Jct SR 116 N and 17 E; center. [D]

BROOKFIELD

ARIEL'S RESTAURANT 802/276-3939

American. Fine Dining. $14-$30 **AAA Inspector Notes:** The restaurant is in Pond Village, aptly named for beautiful Sunset Lake, which is known for its floating bridge. On weekends, patrons can sample exceptionally prepared cuisine in the dining room. Offerings include butternut squash soup with hazelnuts, locally raised grilled quail and such international favorites as traditional Pad Thai. **Bar:** full bar. **Reservations:** suggested. **Address:** 29 Stone Rd 05036 **Location:** Center. [D] [AC]

BROWNINGTON (A-4)

OLD STONE HOUSE MUSEUM, 2.5 mi. n. at 109 Old Stone House Rd., is in a four-story granite structure known as Athenian Hall. Built by Alexander Twilight, the country's first African-American college graduate, and completed in 1836, it served as a dormitory for schoolchildren.

Displays include the collections of the Orleans County Historical Society, early American furniture, paintings, textiles, tools, toys and folk art. **Time:** Allow 1 hour minimum. **Hours:** Wed.-Sun. 11-5, May 15-Oct. 15. **Cost:** $8; $5 (students); free (ages 0-4). **Phone:** (802) 754-2022.

Theme Park Savings

Show Your Card & Save

AAA.com/discounts

BROWNSVILLE

HOLIDAY INN CLUB VACATIONS AT ASCUTNEY MOUNTAIN RESORT (802)484-7711

Hotel
$119-$299

Address: 485 Hotel Rd 05037 **Location:** I-91 exit 9, 5 mi s on US 5/SR 12, then 5.4 mi w on SR 44 to Ski Tow Rd; exit 8 northbound, just e on SR 131, 1.2 mi n on US 5/SR 12, 3 mi w on SR 44A, then 2 mi w on SR 44 to Ski Tow Rd. **Facility:** 134 units, some two bedrooms, three bedrooms and kitchens. 4-5 stories, interior corridors. **Terms:** check-in 4 pm, 3 day cancellation notice-fee imposed. **Amenities:** safes. **Pool(s):** outdoor, heated indoor. **Activities:** saunas, 4 tennis courts (1 lighted), racquetball courts, ice skating, recreation programs, rental bicycles, hiking trails, playground, basketball, horseshoes, exercise room. **Fee:** cross country skiing, game room. **Guest Services:** complimentary and valet laundry. **Free Special Amenities:** early check-in/late check-out and high-speed Internet.

Peaceful mountainside resort offering spacious villas, outdoor activities and comforting amenities.

BURLINGTON (B-1) pop. 42,417, elev. 112'
• Hotels p. 280 • Restaurants p. 281

Built on the terraced slopes of Lake Champlain, Burlington is the largest city in Vermont and is an important industrial, retail and educational center. It is the headquarters of navigation on the lake and a principal port of air entry on the United States-Canada border.

The area first was settled in 1775, but most of its inhabitants left with the onset of the American Revolution, and settlement did not resume until after the war. Revolutionist Ethan Allen tended a farm north of the city and is buried in Greenmount Cemetery on Colchester Avenue. The Ethan Allen Monument, a 35-foot-tall Doric column topped with an 8-foot-tall statue of the patriot, marks the site of his grave.

The city's oldest section is along Battery Street near the lakefront. Other historic areas are Pearl, South Willard and Church streets, the University Green and City Hall Park. Church Street Marketplace, a five-block pedestrian mall, is in the historic district.

On the upper level of town is the University of Vermont, founded in 1791. Champlain College, established in 1878 as the Burlington Collegiate Institute but renamed in 1958, spreads out along S. Willard Street in the city's Hill Section, within walking distance of downtown. Some dormitories occupy handsomely renovated Victorian-era mansions. Free campus tours of Champlain College are available; phone (802) 860-2727 for reservation information.

The Burlington Bikepath, a 7.5-mile scenic route from Oakledge Park to the path's terminus at the Winooski River, traverses Burlington's historic waterfront, skirts Lake Champlain's shoreline, passes through woodland areas and ultimately connects to the Colchester Bike Path.

Burlington is at the end of the scenic portion of two highways: I-89, which runs 95 miles southeast to White River Junction, and SR 7, which runs south to Middlebury.

Lake Champlain Regional Chamber of Commerce: 60 Main St., Suite 100, Burlington, VT 05401. **Phone:** (802) 863-3489 or (877) 686-5253.

Shopping areas: Burlington Town Center, I-89 exit 14W, features some 50 stores, including Ann Taylor LOFT, Chico's, Coldwater Creek, J. Crew, Macy's and Williams-Sonoma.

Downtown, Church Street Marketplace provides shops, services and restaurants in a festive atmosphere that includes street musicians and sidewalk cafés. University Mall on Dorset Street offers more than 70 stores including anchors The Bon-Ton, JCPenney, Kohl's and Sears.

BATTERY PARK, downtown at the top of Battery St., was the 1812 scene of an engagement between U.S. land batteries and British vessels on Lake Champlain. The park has year-round scenic views and an ice skating rink in winter. Burlington City Arts presents free summer concerts Thursday and Sunday. **Hours:** Daily dawn-dusk. **Cost:** Free. **Phone:** (802) 864-0123. ⊠ 🎋

ECHO LAKE AQUARIUM AND SCIENCE CENTER is downtown on the waterfront, just w. of jct. College and Battery sts. in the Leahy Center for Lake Champlain at 1 College St. At ECHO, which stands for *E*cology, *C*ulture, *H*istory and *O*pportunity, visitors learn how these terms relate to the Lake Champlain basin.

Numerous tanks hold 70 species of fish, amphibians, invertebrates and reptiles which can be found in the area, and more than 100 hands-on experiences are available to enhance learning. Animal feedings and demonstrations take place daily.

Permanent exhibits include FrogWorld, home to colorful, unusual reptiles from six continents; Indigenous Expressions, a look at the American Indians who lived in the Lake Champlain basin; Be a Watershed Weather Reporter, a chance to learn about the Vermont watershed and then create and film your own weather report; and Voices for the Lake, an opportunity to capture a personal photo, video or story.

Time: Allow 1 hour, 30 minutes minimum. **Hours:** Daily 10-5. Closed Thanksgiving, Christmas Eve and Christmas. **Cost:** $12.50; $10.50 (ages 60+ and college students with ID); $9.50 (ages 3-17). **Parking:** Apr.-Oct. $8. Rest of year free. **Phone:** (802) 864-1848 or (877) 324-6386. 🍴

ETHAN ALLEN PARK is 2.5 mi. n. on North Ave. A tower offers good views of Green Mountain, the Adirondacks and Lake Champlain, and walking paths crisscross the grounds. **Hours:** Park daily 9-9. Tower daily 9-dusk, Mother's Day-Labor Day (based

on volunteer availability); phone ahead to confirm schedule. **Cost:** Free. **Phone:** (802) 865-7247. ⊠ 🎋

LAKE CHAMPLAIN FERRIES—see Lake Champlain p. 287.

***NORTHERN LIGHTS* CRUISES** departs from 1 King St. Narrated 90-minute scenic cruises on Lake Champlain are offered on the M/V *Northern Lights*, a 115-foot-long cruise boat designed to resemble a 19th- and early 20th-century lake steamboat. The boat's name is a reference to the aurora borealis that sometimes can be seen over the lake at night. An optional lunch buffet is offered on the noon cruise; dinner and summer concert cruises also are available. **Time:** Allow 1 hour, 30 minutes minimum. **Hours:** Scenic cruises depart daily at noon, 2 and 4, mid-June through Columbus Day. **Cost:** $15.99; $5.99 (ages 3-11). Optional lunch buffet on noon cruise $9.99; $6.99 (ages 3-11). A fuel surcharge may apply. Reservations are recommended. **Phone:** (802) 864-9669. 🍴

ROBERT HULL FLEMING MUSEUM, 61 Colchester Ave. on the University of Vermont campus, opened in 1931. Displays of European, American, African, ancient Egyptian, and Middle Eastern art and anthropology as well as paintings by 20th-century American artists are featured. Rotating exhibits are shown periodically.

Hours: Tues.-Fri. 9-4 (also Wed. 4-8), Sat.-Sun. 1-5, day after Labor Day to mid-Dec. and mid-Jan. through Apr. 30; Tues.-Fri. noon-4, Sat.-Sun. 1-5, May 1-Labor Day. Closed major holiday weekends and spring recess in Mar. **Cost:** $5; $3 (ages 7-17 and 60+); $10 (family, two adults and all minor children). **Phone:** (802) 656-0750.

 SHELBURNE MUSEUM—see Shelburne p. 307.

SPIRIT OF ETHAN ALLEN III departs from the Burlington Boat House, at the bottom of College St. The 400-passenger, triple-deck cruise ship offers sightseeing cruises on Lake Champlain; an audiotape provides information about Revolutionary War battles and local history. Brunch, lunch and nightly dinner cruises with live entertainment also are offered.

Hours: Ninety-minute sightseeing cruises depart daily every 2 hours 10-4, mid-May to mid-Oct. **Cost:** $15.49; $7.49 (ages 3-11). Fares may vary; phone ahead. Reservations are required for all but sightseeing cruises. **Phone:** (802) 862-8300. 🍴

HILTON BURLINGTON

Hotel
$99-$199

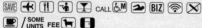

(802)658-6500

AAA Benefit: Members save 5% or more!

Hilton

Address: 60 Battery St 05401 **Location:** At Battery and College sts; just n of ferry terminal; center. **Facility:** 258 units. 8 stories, interior corridors. **Parking:** on-site (fee). **Terms:** 1-7 night minimum stay, cancellation fee imposed. **Amenities:** high-speed Internet (fee), safes. **Pool(s):** heated indoor. **Activities:** whirlpool, exercise room. **Guest Services:** valet laundry, area transportation-within 5 mi. **Free Special Amenities:** newspaper and airport transportation.

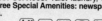

▼ See AAA listing p. 317 ▼

▼ See AAA listing p. 308 ▼

WHERE TO EAT

AMERICAN FLATBREAD
802/861-2999

▼▼▼ Pizza. Casual Dining. $9-$20 **AAA Inspector Notes:** This bustling café features salads and creative pizzas using local, organic and seasonal products. A table in front of the pizza oven provides a mesmerizing show. **Bar:** beer & wine. **Address:** 115 St. Paul St 05401 **Location:** Just s of jct College St; across from City Hall Park. **Parking:** street only. [L] [D]

BLUEBIRD TAVERN
802/540-1786

▼▼▼ New American. Casual Dining. $9-$30 **AAA Inspector Notes:** Enjoy the cuisine that comes from the creative kitchen of this popular eatery, featuring the freshest Vermont farm-to-table products plus Atlantic seafood. **Bar:** full bar. **Reservations:** required. **Address:** 86 St. Paul St 05401 **Location:** Jct College St, just n. **Parking:** street only. [L] [D]

THE FARMHOUSE TAP & GRILL
802/859-0888

▼▼ Regional American. Gastropub. $5-$19 **AAA Inspector Notes:** This tap and grill uses local farm-fresh ingredients to create gourmet burgers, comfort entrées, homemade charcuterie and cheese plates. The seasonal outdoor beer garden has become the talk of this college town for its great variety of highly-prized microbrewed and international beers. The menu is affordable for the type of fare served. A staple on the seasonally changing menu is the Western North Carolina-style barbecue with pulled house-smoked pig, corn bread and homemade coleslaw. **Bar:** full bar. **Address:** 160 Bank St 05401 **Location:** Between Church and St. Paul sts; downtown. **Parking:** street only. [L] [D] CALL [&M]

HALVORSON'S UPSTREET CAFE
802/658-0278

▼▼ American. Casual Dining. $7-$20 **AAA Inspector Notes:** As the eatery is located on a pedestrian street, most patrons wander in and enjoy the atmosphere of this English pub. Outdoor dining in the summer months makes people-watching easy. **Bar:** full bar. **Address:** 16 Church St 05401 **Location:** Between Cherry and Pearl sts. **Parking:** street only. [L] [D] CALL [&M]

THE ICE HOUSE
802/864-1800

▼▼ American. Casual Dining. $6-$30 **AAA Inspector Notes:** A lovely view of Lake Champlain awaits visitors to this converted turn-of-the-20th-century former icehouse. On the menu are seafood, steaks and delicatessen and grilled sandwiches. Brunch is served Sundays, except during winter months. Smoking is allowed on the deck, which is open seasonally. **Bar:** full bar. **Reservations:** suggested. **Address:** 171 Battery St 05401 **Location:** Lakeside; at ferry entrance. [L] [D]

RI-RA IRISH PUB
802/860-9401

▼▼ Irish. Casual Dining. $9-$19 **AAA Inspector Notes:** The restaurant specializes in traditional Irish cuisine with a contemporary twist. Some examples include beef and Guinness pie and classic fish and chips. The noise level can be loud at times due to the pub's popularity and folk bands that regularly play. **Bar:** full bar. **Address:** 123 Church St 05401 **Location:** Between College and Main sts; downtown. **Parking:** street only. [L] [D] CALL [&M]

THE SCUFFER STEAK & ALE HOUSE
802/864-9451

▼▼ American. Casual Dining. $9-$26 **AAA Inspector Notes:** On pedestrian Church Street, the restaurant encourages guests to cut loose. Golfers will appreciate the golf equipment and pictures on the walls. **Bar:** full bar. **Address:** 148 Church St 05401 **Location:** Between College and Main sts; downtown. **Parking:** street only. [L] [D]

SWEETWATERS
802/864-9800

▼▼ American. Casual Dining. $10-$23 **AAA Inspector Notes:** This popular restaurant located in a former bank building has a Southwestern theme. The varied menu offers unusual variations of traditional dishes and includes wood-grilled specialties, pasta, seafood and chicken offerings. Seasonal patio dining. **Bar:** full bar. **Reservations:** suggested, weekends. **Address:** 120 Church St 05401 **Location:** Corner of Church and College sts; downtown. **Parking:** street only. [L] [D]

TRATTORIA DELIA
802/864-5253

▼▼ Italian. Casual Dining. $17-$33 **AAA Inspector Notes:** With such tempting menu selections as wild boar, veal, hand-made sausage and rack of lamb, guests might have a hard time considering the specials, which are just as inventive and delicious. The restaurant boasts an extensive wine list with by-the-glass or bottle choices. **Bar:** beer & wine. **Reservations:** suggested. **Address:** 152 St. Paul St 05401 **Location:** Between Main and King sts. **Parking:** street only. [D] CALL [&M]

CABOT (C-3) pop. 233

Cabot was named in honor of settler Major Lyman Hitchcock's bride, Miss Cabot of Connecticut. The first settlement in the area was on Cabot Plains, also known as Bayley-Hazen Road.

Cabot was the birthplace of Zerah Colburn, a mathematical genius who, before he could read or write, could multiply two six-digit numbers in his head, calculating the correct answer in seconds. Born in 1804, Colburn was hailed as a boy wonder throughout America and Europe. He later became a teacher and clergyman at Norwich University *(see Northfield p. 299)*.

CABOT CREAMERY, 2878 Main St., is a working creamery dating back to 1893 and cooperatively owned since 1919 by the dairy farmers who ship milk to town. Guided tours include a video presentation and a walk down Cheddar Hall. Free cheddar samples also are offered.

Hours: Tours daily 9:30-4:30, June-Oct.; Mon.-Sat. 9:30-3:30, Feb.-May and Nov.-Dec.; Mon.-Sat. 10:30-3:30, rest of year. Phone ahead for cheese-making schedule. **Cost:** Tour $2; free (ages 0-11). **Phone:** (802) 229-9361, ext. 3978 or (800) 837-4261.

GOODRICH'S MAPLE FARM, 2427 US 2, offers tours that outline the production process for maple syrup from tree to table. On display is one of the world's largest maple sap evaporators. Visitors can talk with the people who do the sugaring. Antique implements used in this family business begun in 1840 can be seen. Free syrup samples are available. **Hours:** Mon.-Sat. 9-5. Closed major holidays. **Cost:** Free. **Phone:** (802) 426-3388 or (800) 639-1854.

CASTLETON (E-2) pop. 1,485, elev. 441'

A resort area around Lake Bomoseen, Castleton is a town of historic significance and architectural charm. It was at Zadock Remington's tavern that the Green Mountain Boys, led by Ethan Allen and Seth Warner, planned their successful attack on Fort Ticonderoga during the Revolutionary War.

Marked by Ionic and Corinthian columns, porticoes, archways and Palladian motifs, many houses represent the style of architect Thomas Dake, who became a town resident around 1807. These well-preserved houses delight photographers and sightseers. Another pleasant diversion is the scenic drive along SR 30 south to Manchester Center.

HUBBARDTON BATTLEFIELD STATE HISTORIC SITE is off US 4 exit 5, 3 mi. n. on US 30, 1 mi. n. on Pencil Mill Rd., 1.5 mi. e. on Howland Rd. and St. John Rd. to 5696 Monument Hill Rd. in East Hubbardton. This is the site of the only Revolutionary War battle fought entirely on Vermont soil. On July 7, 1777, Colonial troops in retreat from Mount Independence and Fort Ticonderoga delayed the pursuing British and Hessian forces. A diorama, interpretive display and narrated relief map depict the battle.

Time: Allow 1 hour minimum. **Hours:** Thurs.-Sun. 9:30-5, late May to mid-Oct. **Cost:** $2; free (ages 0-14). **Phone:** (802) 273-2282, or (802) 759-2412 in the off-season.

CAVENDISH pop. 179

THE POINTE AT CASTLE HILL RESORT & SPA (802)226-7688
▼▼▼ Hotel $79-$299 **Address:** 2940 SR 103 05142 **Location:** On SR 103, just n of jct SR 131. **Facility:** 96 units, some kitchens. 2 stories, interior corridors. **Parking:** winter plug-ins. **Terms:** 14 day cancellation notice-fee imposed. **Pool(s):** 2 heated indoor. **Activities:** whirlpools, exercise room, spa. *Fee:* game room.

CHARLOTTE (C-1) elev. 176'

Established in the late 18th century on the stagecoach route between Burlington and Troy, Charlotte (char-LOT) rivaled nearby Burlington in size during the early 1800s. The historic district east of SR 7 has many notable buildings dating from the town's early days. Charlotte also boasts three covered bridges: one spans Holmes Creek on a town road north of the Charlotte ferry; two others cross Lewis Creek in East Charlotte.

LAKE CHAMPLAIN FERRIES—see Lake Champlain p. 287.

VERMONT WILDFLOWER FARM, 3488 Ethan Allen Hwy. (US 7), has 6 acres of public display gardens. Interpretive markers along a self-guiding trail explain the legends behind and practical uses for the hundreds of species in the gardens. **Hours:** Daily 10-5, early Apr. to mid-Oct. **Cost:** Free. **Phone:** (802) 425-3641.

COLCHESTER

DAYS INN COLCHESTER (802)655-0900
▼▼ Hotel $70-$150 **Address:** 124 College Pkwy 05446 **Location:** I-89 exit 15 northbound, just e on SR 15; exit 16 southbound, 1.1 mi s on US 7, then 1 mi e on SR 15. **Facility:** 73 units. 4 stories, interior corridors. **Parking:** winter plug-ins. **Amenities:** safes. **Pool(s):** heated indoor. **Activities:** limited exercise equipment. **Guest Services:** coin laundry.

CALL ⬛M 🔁 BIZ 🛜 💻 / SOME UNITS FEE 🐕 🛗 🖨

HAMPTON INN & EVENT CENTER (802)655-6177
▼▼▼ Hotel $129-$229 **Address:** 42 Lower Mountain View Dr 05446 **Location:** I-89 exit 16, just n on US 7. **Facility:** 187 units, some efficiencies. 5 stories, interior corridors. **Parking:** winter plug-ins. **Terms:** 1-7 night minimum stay, cancellation fee imposed. **Amenities:** video games (fee). **Pool(s):** heated indoor. **Activities:** exercise room. **Guest Services:** valet and coin laundry.

AAA Benefit: Members save up to 10%!

ECO ➡ 📶 CALL ⬛M 🔁 BIZ 🛜 ✖ 🎦 🍴
🖨 💻 / SOME UNITS 🐕

MOTEL 6 #1407 (802)654-6860
▼▼ Hotel $59-$89 **Address:** 74 S Park Dr 05446 **Location:** I-89 exit 16, just s on US 7. **Facility:** 106 units. 3 stories, interior corridors. **Parking:** winter plug-ins. **Pool(s):** outdoor. **Guest Services:** coin laundry. 📶 🔁 🛜 / SOME UNITS 🐕

QUALITY INN COLCHESTER BURLINGTON AREA
(802)655-1400

Hotel
$109-$209

Address: 84 S Park Dr 05446 **Location:** I-89 exit 16, just s on US 7. **Facility:** 113 units. 3 stories, interior/exterior corridors. **Parking:** winter plug-ins. **Terms:** cancellation fee imposed. **Amenities:** safes. **Pool(s):** heated outdoor. **Activities:** limited exercise equipment. **Guest Services:** valet and coin laundry. **Free Special Amenities:** full breakfast and use of on-premises laundry facilities.

SAVE 📶 CALL ⬛M 🔁 BIZ 🛜 💻
/ SOME UNITS FEE 🐕 🛗 🖨

RESIDENCE INN BY MARRIOTT, BURLINGTON-COLCHESTER
(802)655-3100
▼▼▼ Extended Stay Hotel $159-$299 **Address:** 71 Rathe Rd 05446 **Location:** I-89 exit 16, 0.6 mi n on US 2 W/7 N, then just w. **Facility:** 108 units, some two bedrooms, efficiencies and kitchens. 4 stories, interior corridors. **Terms:** check-in 4 pm. **Amenities:** high-speed Internet. **Pool(s):** heated indoor. **Activities:** whirlpool, sports court, exercise room. **Guest Services:** valet and coin laundry, area transportation-within 5 mi.

AAA Benefit: AAA hotel discounts of 5% or more.

➡ CALL ⬛M 🔁 BIZ 🛜 ✖ 🛗 🖨 💻
/ SOME UNITS FEE 🐕

DANVILLE pop. 383

DANVILLE INN (802)684-3484
▼▼ Historic Bed & Breakfast $89 **Address:** 86 US 2 W 05828 **Location:** Center. **Facility:** The ground floor of this 1840s Victorian-style farmhouse has been converted to a full-service restaurant. Guest rooms are accessed through a discreet side staircase that leads to the upper level. 4 units. 2 stories (no elevator), interior corridors. **Bath:** shared. **Terms:** 7 day cancellation notice.

🍴 🍷 ✖ 🎦 🌀

WHERE TO EAT

THE CREAMERY 802/684-3616
▼▼ American. Casual Dining. $14-$20 **AAA Inspector Notes:** This country-style restaurant features very nicely prepared dishes served in a pub-style atmosphere. Fairly elaborate choices including fresh seafood, beef and chicken. **Bar:** full bar. **Address:** 46 Hill St 05828 **Location:** Just n of US 2; center. ⒟

DERBY

DERBY FOUR SEASONS MOTEL 802/334-1775

Motel
$89-$160

Address: 4412 US 5 05829 **Location:** I-91 exit 28, just nw. Adjacent to a truck stop. **Facility:** 52 units. 2 stories (no elevator), interior corridors. **Parking:** winter plug-ins (fee). **Terms:** cancellation fee imposed. **Free Special Amenities:** continental breakfast and high-speed Internet.

SAVE 〔†〕 CALL 〔&M〕 〔BIZ〕 〔 � 〕 〔 📺 〕 / SOME UNITS 🛢 🖼

DERBY LINE (A-4) pop. 673, elev. 1,042'

HASKELL FREE LIBRARY AND OPERA HOUSE (La Bibliothèque Haskell et la Salle d'Opéra) is situated directly on the international boundary between Canada and the United States at 93 Caswell Ave. The stage sits in Canada and most of the 400 seats are in the United States. Guided opera house tours are available. **Hours:** Library open Tues.-Fri. 10-5 (also Thurs. 5-6), Sat. 10-2. Opera House tours Tues.-Fri. 10-4, Sat. 10-1, May-Oct. Closed Jan. 1, day before Easter, Christmas and Québec's major holidays. **Cost:** Library free. Opera house tour $5. Performance ticket prices vary; phone ahead. **Phone:** (802) 873-3022, or (819) 876-2471 in Québec.

DORSET pop. 249

INN AT WEST VIEW FARM (802)867-5715

▼▼ ◆ **Historic Country Inn** $140-$210 **Address:** 2928 SR 30 05251 **Location:** On SR 30, 0.5 mi s. **Facility:** This countryside inn, which was once a farmhouse, offers comfortable common areas and variable-size guest units decorated with antique furniture. 10 units. 2 stories (no elevator), interior corridors. **Terms:** 2 night minimum stay - seasonal and/or weekends, 14 day cancellation notice-fee imposed. 〔†〕 〔Y〕 〔 fish 〕 〔X〕 〔☎〕 / SOME UNITS 〔W〕

WHERE TO EAT

BARROWS HOUSE 802/867-4455

▼▼▼ Regional American. Casual Dining. $25-$38 **AAA Inspector Notes:** Market-fresh ingredients and artistic presentations make the dishes stand out at this pleasant, comfortable restaurant. Seating can be requested in the main dining room, the atrium or a small tavern area. Fresh local Vermont produce is used in season. **Bar:** full bar. **Reservations:** suggested. **Address:** 3156 Rt 30 05251 **Location:** Center. 〔B〕 〔D〕

EAST BURKE (B-4) pop. 132, elev. 866'

RECREATIONAL ACTIVITIES
Skiing

- **Burke Mountain Ski Area** is 1.1 mi. e. on Mountain Rd., then .2 mi. s. on Sherburne Lodge Rd. Other activities are available. **Hours:** Daily early Dec.-early Apr. (weather permitting). **Phone:** (802) 626-7300 or (888) 287-5388.

EAST DORSET

MARBLEDGE MOTOR INN (802)362-1418

▼▼ **Motel** $82-$185 **Address:** 2123 US 7 05253 **Location:** On US 7, 0.6 mi n of jct Historic SR 7A. **Facility:** 20 units, some cottages. 1-2 stories (no elevator), exterior corridors. **Parking:** winter plug-ins. **Terms:** 2 night minimum stay, 14 day cancellation notice-fee imposed. **Activities:** hiking trails.

〔 fish 〕 〔X〕 🛢 〔 📺 〕 / SOME UNITS 🖼

WHERE TO EAT

CHANTECLEER 802/362-1616

▼▼▼ Continental. Fine Dining. $28-$48 **AAA Inspector Notes:** Ensconced in the beautiful countryside, the converted dairy barn features provincial, decorative accents and intriguing French and European dishes that incorporate fresh, high-quality ingredients. Renowned among local residents, the restaurant is well worth a drive. **Bar:** full bar. **Reservations:** suggested. **Address:** 8 Read Farm Ln (Historic SR 7A) 05253 **Location:** Jct SR 11/30 N, 3.5 mi n. 〔D〕

EAST MIDDLEBURY pop. 425

WAYBURY INN DINING ROOM 802/388-4015

▼▼▼ American. Fine Dining. $13-$30 **AAA Inspector Notes:** Traditional Vermont cooking served in a comfortable dining room can be found here. Homemade muffins, bread and relish. A cheerful pub is located below the dining room. The overall atmosphere is graced with a roaring gas fireplace and soft music. **Bar:** full bar. **Reservations:** suggested. **Address:** 457 Main St (SR 125) 05740 **Location:** On SR 125; 1.3 mi e of jct US 7. 〔L〕 〔D〕

EAST MONTPELIER (C-3) pop. 80

BRAGG FARM SUGARHOUSE, 1005 SR 14N, is an eighth-generation, family-operated maple sugar house offering educational tours that describe the history and practices regarding the production of maple sugar. Visitors can hike through 50 acres of maple woods. Free tastings are offered. **Hours:** Daily 8:30-8, May-Aug.; 8:30-6, rest of year. Closed Jan. 1, Thanksgiving and Christmas. **Cost:** Free. **Phone:** (802) 223-5757 or (800) 376-5757.

ESSEX JUNCTION pop. 9,271

THE ESSEX RESORT & SPA (802)878-1100

Contemporary
Hotel
$169-$349

Address: 70 Essex Way 05452 **Location:** SR 289 exit 10, 0.3 mi s. **Facility:** This contemporary country inn features individually decorated rooms, some with a fireplace. Relax in the beautiful spa or enjoy a culinary workshop. 120 units, some two bedrooms and kitchens. 3 stories, interior corridors. **Terms:** 1-2 night minimum stay - weekends, 7 day cancellation notice-fee imposed, resort fee. **Amenities:** Some: high-speed Internet. **Dining:** 2 restaurants. **Pool(s):** heated outdoor, heated indoor. **Activities:** whirlpool, 6 tennis courts, recreation programs, hiking trails, jogging, playground, sports court, exercise room, spa. Fee: saunas, steamrooms, golf-18 holes, bicycles. **Guest Services:** valet and coin laundry, area transportation-local businesses & Amtrak station.

SAVE 〔ECO〕 〔⟷〕 〔†〕 〔↑〕 〔Y〕 CALL 〔&M〕 〔➤〕 〔BIZ〕 〔 fish 〕
〔X〕 〔 🐾 〕 〔 📺 〕 / SOME UNITS FEE 〔 🐾 〕 🛢 🖼

HANDY SUITES-ESSEX   (802)872-5200

▼▼▼ **Extended Stay Hotel** $69-$249 **Address:** 27 Susie Wilson Rd 05452 **Location:** I-89 exit 15 northbound, 2 mi e, then just n. **Facility:** 53 units, some two bedrooms, efficiencies and kitchens. 4 stories, interior corridors. **Parking:** winter plug-ins. **Terms:** cancellation fee imposed. **Amenities:** high-speed Internet, safes. **Pool(s):** heated indoor. **Activities:** waterslide. **Guest Services:** coin laundry.

CALL ⓁⓂ �"> BIZ 📶 🔌 📷 💻 / SOME UNITS FEE 🐾

FAIRFIELD (B-2) elev. 356'

PRESIDENT CHESTER A. ARTHUR STATE HIS-TORIC SITE is 7 mi. n.e. on SR 36, following signs to 4588 Chester Arthur Rd. The replica of the Arthur house contains an interpretive exhibit about the life of the 21st president of the United States, who was born in Fairfield in 1829. The brick church where Arthur's father preached stands nearby and features an exhibit about meetinghouse and church architecture in Vermont.

Time: Allow 1 hour minimum. **Hours:** Sat.-Sun. 11-5, July 4 to mid-Oct. **Cost:** Donations. **Phone:** (802) 828-3051.

FERRISBURGH (C-1) elev. 176'

ROKEBY MUSEUM, 4334 US 7, was the home of the Robinson family for four generations. The most notable residents include Rowland Thomas and Rachel Robinson, devout Quakers and radical abolitionists, and their son Rowland E., the late 19th-century author, illustrator and naturalist. This National Historic Landmark, one of the best-documented Underground Railroad sites in the country, looks much as it did at the end of the 19th century.

Guided tours of the fully furnished Federal-style house view personal items spanning the Quaker family's occupancy from the 1790s to the 1960s. The Free and Safe exhibit allows visitors to follow the lives of two slaves, Simon and Jesse, who were sheltered at Rokeby in the 1800s. On the grounds are hiking trails and eight historic farm buildings.

Time: Allow 1 hour minimum. **Hours:** Guided tours are given Thurs.-Sun. at 11, 12:30 and 2, Memorial Day weekend-Columbus Day weekend. Phone ahead to confirm schedule. **Cost:** $6; $4 (ages 65+ and students with ID); $2 (ages 0-12). **Phone:** (802) 877-3406. 🏕

FLETCHER

THE INN AT BUCK HOLLOW FARM   (802)849-2400

▼▼▼ **Historic Bed & Breakfast** $100-$130 **Address:** 2150 Buck Hollow Rd 05454 **Location:** 6 mi n of jct SR 104 via Buck Hollow Rd. Located in a rural area. **Facility:** This 1790 carriage house is on 400 acres and features themed rooms; an antiques shop is on the grounds. 4 units. 2 stories (no elevator), interior corridors. **Terms:** 14 day cancellation notice-fee imposed. **Pool(s):** heated outdoor. **Activities:** whirlpool, cross country skiing, hiking trails.

🚐 BIZ 📶 ✕ 🐕 / SOME UNITS FEE 🐾

GLOVER (B-4) pop. 303, elev. 946'

BREAD AND PUPPET MUSEUM, 2 mi. s. off SR 16 to 753 Heights Rd. (SR 122), is housed in a transformed 19th-century barn that contains an extensive puppet collection—including some of the largest puppets in the United States—as well as masks and graphics associated with the Bread and Puppet Theater.

The theater presents traveling puppet shows ranging from theater pieces presented by members of the company to extensive outdoor pageants. **Time:** Allow 1 hour minimum. **Hours:** Daily 10-6, June-Oct.; by appointment rest of year. **Cost:** Donations. **Phone:** (802) 525-3031 or (802) 525-1271.

GRAFTON

THE OLD TAVERN AT GRAFTON   802/843-2231

▼▼▼ Regional American. Fine Dining. $19-$29 **AAA Inspector Notes:** Set in a beautifully restored 1801 inn, this restaurant serves an excellent and attractively presented turkey breast and mashed potatoes with gravy dinner. The grilled salmon, roasted rack of lamb and beef tenderloin meals also are good choices. **Bar:** full bar. **Reservations:** suggested. **Address:** 92 Main St 05146 **Location:** On SR 121; center. Ⓑ Ⓓ

GRANITEVILLE (C-3) pop. 784

ROCK OF AGES VISITORS CENTER is at 558 Graniteville Rd., following signs from I-89 exit 6. Guided tours of the 1880 quarry show the drilling, blasting and removal of granite from the 550-foot-deep, 50-acre hole carved out of the hillside over the last century. The company's manufacturing division operates one of the largest granite plants in the world; the plant can be seen on a self-guiding tour. The observation deck overlooks cutting, polishing and rubber-cutting operations. Visitors can engage in a hands-on sandblast activity.

Time: Allow 2 hours minimum. **Hours:** Visitor center daily 9-5, Sept.-Oct.; Mon.-Sat. 9-5, mid-May through Aug. 31. Self-guiding plant tours Mon.-Fri. 8-3:30. A 40-minute shuttle tour of the active quarry departs Mon.-Sat. (also Sun., Sept. 1 to mid-Oct.) about every 45 minutes 9:15-3:35, Memorial Day weekend to mid-Oct. (weather permitting). Closed July 4. **Cost:** Free. Shuttle $5; $4.50 (ages 62+); $2.50 (ages 6-12). **Phone:** (802) 476-3119 or (866) 748-6877.

GREEN MOUNTAINS AND GREEN MOUNTAIN NATIONAL FOREST (E-2)

> Elevations in the forest range from 878 ft. near Rochester to 4,083 ft. Mount Ellen in Warren. Refer to AAA maps for additional elevation information.

Extending the length of Vermont, the Green Mountains comprise several distinct ranges. The highest peaks lie in the north; several—including

Mount Mansfield *(see place listing p. 298)*, the tallest mountain in Vermont—exceed 4,000 feet.

The 420,000-acre Green Mountain National Forest was established in 1932 after uncontrolled logging, fire and flooding had ravaged Vermont. It stretches across nearly two-thirds of the state's length, following the main range of the Green Mountains. The forest is divided into two sections. The southern half extends from the Vermont-Massachusetts border to SR 140 near Wallingford; the northern half extends from US 4 northeast of Rutland to SR 17 near Bristol.

The forest encompasses six wilderness areas as well as the White Rocks National Recreation Area, south of Wallingford, and the Moosalamoo National Recreation Area, east of Lake Dunmore. Ranger stations are located at 2538 Depot St. in Manchester Center, phone (802) 362-2307; 1007 SR 7S in Middlebury, phone (802) 388-4362; and 99 Ranger Rd. in Rochester, phone (802) 767-4261.

Natural resources in this area play an important role in the economy of Vermont and the Northeast. In addition, the region's scenic beauty and a broad range of recreational opportunities attract thousands of visitors annually. Along with 60,000 acres of designated wilderness, there are 900 miles of hiking trails—including the Appalachian/Long Trail and the Robert Frost Interpretive Trail—approximately 400 miles of snowmobile trails, six cross-country ski areas and three downhill ski areas.

Developed campgrounds (no RV hook-ups) and picnic sites are available as well. For more information write the Forest Supervisor, Green Mountain National Forest, 231 N. Main St., Rutland, VT 05701; phone (802) 747-6700. *See Recreation Areas Chart.*

HARTLAND pop. 380

SKUNK HOLLOW TAVERN   802/436-2139
♥♥ ♥♥ American. Casual Dining. $13-$29 **AAA Inspector Notes:** Enjoy a casual or intimate dinner in an authentic 18th-century country tavern. **Bar:** full bar. **Reservations:** suggested. **Address:** Hartland 4 Corners 05049 **Location:** I-91 exit 9 (Hartland/Windsor). D

HUNTINGTON (C-2)

The Green Mountain Audubon Center is a 255-acre expanse of fields, thickets, ponds, streams, woodlands and swamplands that provides sanctuary for many different types of wildlife. Some 5 miles of walking trails wind through the various habitats. A rope-guided sensory trail for the visually impaired has signs in Braille; phone (802) 434-3068.

BIRDS OF VERMONT MUSEUM, 1 mi. w. at 900 Sherman Hollow Rd., contains 175 exhibits, including 501 life-size carvings of birds painted to show typical or breeding plumage. The Vermont nesting bird gallery shows the male, female, nest and eggs in typical habitat vegetation. There also are exhibits depicting birds of prey, winter species, wetland birds and some of North America's endangered and extinct birds. Carving demonstrations and classes are offered. A bird-viewing window provides a great place to see and hear birds at their feeders.

Time: Allow 1 hour minimum. **Hours:** Daily 10-4, May-Oct.; by appointment rest of year. **Cost:** $6; $5 (ages 60+); $3 (ages 3-17). **Phone:** (802) 434-2167. 🅐

HUNTINGTON CENTER (C-2)

CAMEL'S HUMP STATE PARK can be reached via Camel's Hump Road to the park trailhead. Within the park is 4,083-foot Camel's Hump. Called "Le Lion Couchant" (the sleeping lion) by French explorers, it has a distinctive double-humped profile—created by glaciers—that graces the Vermont state seal. Camel's Hump is the state's third-highest peak. Scenic hiking trails lead to the summit, where such fragile alpine vegetation as crowberry, mountain cranberry and Labrador tea grows. The Long Trail, which extends the length of the state along the Green Mountains, traverses the park.

Hours: Daily 24 hours. Trails are closed during mud season, typically early Apr.-Memorial Day weekend. **Cost:** Free. A fee is charged for shelter and lodge use on a first-come, first-served basis. **Phone:** (802) 879-6565. 🅐 🅐

HYDE PARK pop. 462

FITCH HILL INN   (802)888-3834
♥♥♥♥ Historic Bed & Breakfast $99-$225 **Address:** 258 Fitch Hill Rd 05655 **Location:** Jct SR 100, 1.8 mi w on SR 15, then 0.3 mi n. **Facility:** Set on spacious landscaped grounds, this restored 1797 home is tastefully furnished with antiques and has some rooms with a fireplace. 6 units. 2 stories (no elevator), interior/exterior corridors. **Terms:** 2 night minimum stay - seasonal, age restrictions may apply, 30 day cancellation notice-fee imposed. ECO BIZ 🛜 ✕ / SOME UNITS 🚫 🔒 🖼 🖳

JAMAICA

THREE MOUNTAIN INN   802/874-4140
♥♥♥♥ Historic Country Inn $199-$375 **Address:** 3732 Main St/Rt 100/30 05343 **Location:** On SR 30; center. **Facility:** In the village center, this 1790s inn has a rustic ambiance with fireplaces, original wood-plank floors and antique furnishings. 15 units, some cottages. 2-3 stories (no elevator), interior/exterior corridors. **Parking:** winter plug-ins. **Terms:** closed 3/15-5/1, 2-3 night minimum stay - seasonal and/or weekends, 15 day cancellation notice-fee imposed. **Pool(s):** outdoor. **Activities:** hiking trails, jogging. *Fee:* massage. 🏊 🛜 ✕ / SOME UNITS 🅦

JAY (A-3)

Near the Canadian border in the shadow of Jay Peak, Jay is named after statesman John Jay. Known for its winter sports facilities, the town serves as a base for the year-round recreation opportunities at nearby Jay Peak State Forest.

Jay Peak Area Chamber of Commerce: P.O. Box 426, Jay, VT 05859. **Phone:** (802) 744-6523.

RECREATIONAL ACTIVITIES
Recreation Complex

- **Jay Peak Resort** is at 830 Jay Peak Rd., off SR 242 just before Jay State Forest. Year-round facilities include the Jay Peak Pump House indoor water park and the Ice Haus Arena, an ice skating and hockey rink. Seasonal activities include tram rides, downhill skiing and golf (18 holes). **Hours:** Skiing daily, week before Thanksgiving-Apr. 30 (weather permitting). Tram rides daily, mid-May to mid-Oct.; Mon.-Fri., mid-Oct. to mid-Nov. Water park and ice arena hours vary; phone ahead to confirm schedule. **Phone:** (802) 988-2611, (802) 988-2724 for ice arena, (802) 988-4653 for golf course, (802) 988-2710 for water park or (800) 451-4449.

JEFFERSONVILLE (B-2) pop. 729, elev. 460'

BRYAN MEMORIAL GALLERY, 180 Main St., exhibits New England landscapes by local, regional and national artists. Exhibitions change each season. **Hours:** Daily 11-5, June 1-late Oct.; Thurs.-Sun. 11-4, Feb.-May and late Oct.-Dec. 31. **Cost:** Free. **Phone:** (802) 644-5100.

RECREATIONAL ACTIVITIES
Skiing

- **Smugglers' Notch** is 5 mi. s. on SR 108. Other activities are available. **Hours:** Daily 8:30-4, day after Thanksgiving to mid-Apr. (weather permitting). **Phone:** (802) 644-8851 or (800) 451-8752.

Ziplines

- **Arbortrek Canopy Adventures** is at 1239 Edwards Rd. **Hours:** Trips daily dawn-dusk. **Phone:** (802) 644-9300.

KILLINGTON (E-2)

With its long snow season and challenging peaks, today's Killington is home to one of the largest ski resorts in the East. Other popular winter recreational activities include snowmobiling, snowshoeing, cross-country skiing and dog sledding. When green returns to the mountains, the area provides abundant opportunities for hiking, mountain biking, tennis and golf.

Killington Chamber of Commerce: 2046 US 4, P.O. Box 114, Killington, VT 05751. **Phone:** (802) 773-4181 or (800) 337-1928.

RECREATIONAL ACTIVITIES
Skiing

- **Killington Resort** is w. via US 4 in Calvin Coolidge State Forest. Other activities are available. **Hours:** Sun.-Fri. 9-4, Sat. and holidays 8-4, early Nov. to mid-Apr. (weather permitting). **Phone:** (800) 621-6867.

BIRCH RIDGE INN   (802)422-4293

▼▼▼▼ **Country Inn** $100-$325 **Address:** 37 Butler Rd 05751 **Location:** 2.2 mi s on Killington Rd from jct SR 100/US 4, then just w. **Facility:** Fine dining is offered at this modern, well-furnished inn perched on the slopes of the Killington ski area. 10 units. 2 stories (no elevator), interior corridors. **Terms:** 2 night minimum stay - weekends, age restrictions may apply, 14 day cancellation notice-fee imposed. **Dining:** restaurant, see separate listing.

THE CASCADES LODGE   (802)422-3731

▼▼▼▼
Hotel
$115-$299

Address: 58 Old Mill Rd 05751 **Location:** 3.6 mi s on Killington Rd from jct SR 100/US 4, then just e. **Facility:** 45 units. 2-3 stories (no elevator), interior corridors. **Parking:** winter plug-ins. **Terms:** closed 6/1-6/30 & 11/1-11/15, 21 day cancellation notice-fee imposed, resort fee. **Dining:** The Cascades Restaurant, see separate listing. **Pool(s):** heated indoor. **Activities:** sauna, whirlpool, downhill skiing, hiking trails, exercise room. **Fee:** massage. **Guest Services:** valet laundry. **Free Special Amenities:** expanded continental breakfast and high-speed Internet.

GREENBRIER INN   802/775-1575

▼▼ **Motel.** Rates not provided. **Address:** 2057 US 4 05751 **Location:** 0.4 mi w of jct SR 100 N. **Facility:** 21 units. 2 stories (no elevator), interior corridors. **Parking:** winter plug-ins. **Pool(s):** outdoor. **Activities:** hiking trails.

THE INN OF THE SIX MOUNTAINS   (802)422-4302

▼▼▼
Hotel
$89-$299

Address: 2617 Killington Rd 05751 **Location:** 2.7 mi s from jct SR 100/US 4. **Facility:** 103 units, some efficiencies. 4 stories, interior corridors. **Terms:** closed 3/30-5/22 & 10/20-11/20, check-in 4 pm, 2 night minimum stay - seasonal, 8 day cancellation notice, resort fee. **Amenities:** safes. **Pool(s):** heated outdoor, heated indoor. **Activities:** whirlpools, tennis court, exercise room. **Fee:** game room, massage. **Guest Services:** area transportation-ski area. **Free Special Amenities: continental breakfast and local telephone calls.**

KILLINGTON CENTER INN AND SUITES   (802)422-4222

▼▼▼
Hotel
$89-$179

Address: 905 Killington Rd 05751 **Location:** 1 mi s of jct SR 100/US 4. **Facility:** 66 units, some efficiencies. 2 stories (no elevator), exterior corridors. **Terms:** closed 4/27-5/23, check-in 4 pm, 2 night minimum stay - seasonal and/or weekends, 7 day cancellation notice-fee imposed, resort fee. **Pool(s):** heated outdoor. **Guest Services:** coin laundry. **Free Special Amenities: continental breakfast and high-speed Internet.**

KILLINGTON GRAND RESORT HOTEL   (802)422-5001

▼▼▼▼ **Resort Hotel** $155-$515 **Address:** 228 E Mountain Rd 05751 **Location:** 3.6 mi s on Killington Rd from jct SR 100/US 4, then just e. **Facility:** The property's attractive and spacious guest rooms are designed to combine all the conveniences of home with the luxuries of a resort hotel. 200 units, some two bedrooms, three bedrooms and kitchens. 4 stories, interior corridors. **Parking:** on-site and valet. **Terms:** check-in 5:30 pm, 2 night minimum stay - seasonal and/or weekends, 7 day cancellation notice-fee imposed, resort fee. **Amenities:** video games, safes. **Pool(s):** heated outdoor. **Activities:** sauna, whirlpools, steamroom, downhill skiing, recreation programs, hiking trails, jogging, spa. **Fee:** golf-18 holes, bicycles, game room. **Guest Services:** coin laundry.

KILLINGTON MOTEL   (802)773-9535

 Motel $68-$178 **Address:** 1946 Rt 4 05751 **Location:** Jct SR 100 N, 0.3 mi w. **Facility:** 20 units. 1 story, exterior corridors. **Terms:** 2 night minimum stay - seasonal and/or weekends, 14 day cancellation notice-fee imposed. **Pool(s):** outdoor.

MOUNTAIN GREEN SKI & GOLF RESORT
                                     (802)422-3000

Resort
Condominium
$92-$1025

Address: 133 E Mountain Rd 05751 **Location:** 3.7 mi s on Killington Rd from jct SR 100/US 4. **Facility:** The year-round resort is in close proximity to the ski area, and the large suites are very spacious for families. 190 condominiums. 7 stories, interior corridors. **Parking:** winter plug-ins. **Terms:** check-in 6 pm, 2-5 night minimum stay - seasonal, 21 day cancellation notice-fee imposed, resort fee. **Amenities:** Some: safes. **Pool(s):** heated outdoor, heated indoor. **Activities:** sauna, whirlpools, steamroom, spa. Fee: game room. **Guest Services:** coin laundry, area transportation-ski mountain. **Free Special Amenities: high-speed Internet and use of on-premises laundry facilities.**

THE MOUNTAIN INN   802/422-3595

Hotel
Rates not provided

Address: 47 Old Mill Rd 05751 **Location:** 3.6 mi s on Killington Rd from jct SR 100/US 4, then just e. **Facility:** 51 units. 3 stories (no elevator), interior corridors. **Parking:** winter plug-ins. **Pool(s):** heated outdoor. **Activities:** sauna. Fee: game room. **Guest Services:** coin laundry.

MOUNTAIN SPORTS INN   (802)422-3315

 Hotel $64-$250 **Address:** 813 Killington Rd 05751 **Location:** 0.8 mi s from jct SR 100/US 4. **Facility:** 27 units, some two bedrooms, three bedrooms and kitchens. 2-3 stories (no elevator), interior corridors. **Parking:** winter plug-ins. **Terms:** closed 5/1-7/26 & 10/15-11/1, check-in 4 pm, 15 day cancellation notice-fee imposed. **Activities:** sauna, whirlpool.

SNOWED INN   (802)422-3407

Bed & Breakfast
$90-$200

Address: 104 Miller Brook Rd 05751 **Location:** 2 mi s on Killington Rd from jct SR 100/US 4, then just w. **Facility:** Contemporary country accommodations are in just set on the slopes of the Killington ski resort. 20 units, some two bedrooms, efficiencies and kitchens. 2-3 stories (no elevator), interior/exterior corridors. **Terms:** closed 6/1-6/14 & 10/23-11/14, 2-3 night minimum stay - seasonal and/or weekends, 15 day cancellation notice-fee imposed, resort fee. **Activities:** whirlpool, game room. **Free Special Amenities: expanded continental breakfast and high-speed Internet.**

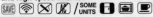

THE SUMMIT LODGE   (802)422-3535

 Hotel $89-$299 **Address:** 200 Summit Rd 05751 **Location:** 1.3 mi s on Killington Rd from jct SR 100/US 4. **Facility:** 45 units. 3 stories (no elevator), interior corridors. **Parking:** winter plug-ins. **Terms:** closed 6/1-10/20 & 11/20-4/20, 21 day cancellation notice. **Dining:** 2 restaurants. **Pool(s):** outdoor, heated outdoor. **Activities:** saunas, whirlpool, 4 tennis courts, ice skating, horseshoes, shuffleboard. Fee: game room, massage. **Guest Services:** coin laundry, area transportation-ski area.

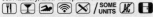

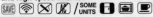
WHERE TO EAT

BIRCH RIDGE INN   802/422-4293

 American. Fine Dining. $19-$35 **AAA Inspector Notes:** This pleasant little dining room is one of the jewels of Killington's dining establishments. Its somewhat limited but inspired menu is sure to please the more refined palate with such creations as pistachio-encrusted rack of New Zealand lamb served with fresh mint pesto or the pan-seared diver scallops served with shellfish risotto and braised fennel cream. The atmosphere is intimate and relaxed, and service very capable. Enjoy a cocktail or an after-dinner drink in the lounge. **Bar:** full bar. **Reservations:** suggested. **Address:** 37 Butler Rd 05751 **Location:** 2.2 mi s on Killington Rd from jct SR 100/US 4, then just w.

THE CASCADES RESTAURANT   802/422-3731

 American. Casual Dining. $12-$24 **AAA Inspector Notes:** Featuring country décor with striking views of the mountains. The menu has a wide variety and offers large portions of the freshest ingredients. Try the flavorful gazpacho or swordfish with fresh sea scallops. **Bar:** full bar. **Address:** 58 Old Mill Rd 05751 **Location:** 3.6 mi s on Killington Rd from jct SR 100/US 4, then just e; in The Cascades Lodge.

PEPPINO'S   802/422-3293

 Italian. Casual Dining. $13-$23 **AAA Inspector Notes:** This restaurant offers diners plentiful, hearty Italian dishes in a casual, yet intimate, setting. **Bar:** full bar. **Address:** Killington Rd 05751 **Location:** 0.7 mi n from jct US 4/Killington Rd.

PIZZA JERKS   802/422-4111

 Pizza. Casual Dining. $7-$19 **AAA Inspector Notes:** The basic, functional restaurant offers walk-up counter service and the food is fresh and tasty, especially the calzones. **Bar:** beer & wine. **Address:** 1307 Killington Rd 05751 **Location:** Jct US 4/Killington Rd, 1.3 mi n.

THE WOBBLY BARN   802/422-6171

 Steak. Casual Dining. $10-$25 **AAA Inspector Notes:** This restaurant is a seasonal eatery which has been locally popular for more than 35 years now. **Bar:** full bar. **Address:** 2229 Killington Rd 05751 **Location:** Jct US 4/Killington Rd, 1.3 mi s.

LAKE CHAMPLAIN (B-1)

Extending from Canada southward for 120 miles, Lake Champlain varies from a quarter of a mile to 12 miles wide. Two-thirds of its area lies in Vermont; the rest, except for a small Canadian portion, is in New York. Lake Champlain—with its Hudson River connector, the Champlain Canal—accommodates large vessels to make navigation possible from New York City to Montréal and the Great Lakes. It briefly became the sixth Great Lake in 1998 after president Bill Clinton signed a Senate bill reauthorizing the Sea Grant Program, but 2 months later the designation was rescinded.

Legends of Lake Champlain's own version of the Loch Ness Monster have persisted since French explorer Samuel de Champlain, the lake's discoverer, allegedly sighted what he described as a serpentine creature 20 feet long, as thick as a barrel and with a head like a horse. Occasional sightings of the elusive creature, affectionately named "Champ," still occur, but whether a distant cousin of the legendary Scottish sea serpent really resides in the lake remains a matter of speculation.

LAKE CHAMPLAIN FERRIES depart from Burlington, Charlotte and Grand Isle. Offered are scenic links between Vermont and New York via three crossings: Burlington to Port Kent, N.Y. (crossing time 1 hour); Charlotte to Essex, N.Y. (crossing time 25 minutes); and Grand Isle to Plattsburgh, N.Y. (crossing time 12 minutes).

Hours: Grand Isle ferry operates daily 24 hours year-round. Charlotte ferry operates year-round (ice conditions permitting); hours vary. Burlington ferry runs late June-Columbus Day; hours vary. Phone ahead to confirm schedule. **Cost:** Grand Isle or Charlotte round-trip fare $7.50; $6.40 (ages 65+); $3 (ages 6-12). Burlington round-trip fare $9.90; $8.50 (ages 65+); $4.40 (ages 6-12). One-way and vehicle fares also are available. A fuel surcharge may apply. Cash only. **Phone:** (802) 864-9804.

LAKE CHAMPLAIN ISLANDS (A-1)

The Lake Champlain Islands are a picturesque summer resort area, affording a broad expanse of inland sea with the Adirondack Mountains on the west and the Green Mountains on the east. US 2 off I-89 connects the islands with the Vermont mainland, New York and Canada.

St. Anne's Shrine on Isle La Motte is on the site of Fort Ste. Anne, the first European settlement in Vermont. The shrine contains a statue of Samuel de Champlain that was sculpted at Expo '67 in Montréal; phone (802) 928-3362.

Lake Champlain Islands Chamber of Commerce: 3501 US 2, P.O. Box 213, North Hero, VT 05474. **Phone:** (802) 372-8400 or (800) 262-5226.

HYDE LOG CABIN is on US 2 in Grand Isle. Built in 1783 and considered the oldest existing log cabin in the nation, it is furnished with domestic items depicting rural life. Also on the premises is a block one-room schoolhouse. **Time:** Allow 30 minutes minimum. **Hours:** Fri.-Sun. 11-5, Memorial Day-Columbus Day. **Cost:** $3; free (ages 0-13). **Phone:** (802) 372-8830.

LONDONDERRY (F-2) elev. 1,115'

RECREATIONAL ACTIVITIES
Skiing

• **Magic Mountain Ski Area** is at 495 Magic Mountain Access Rd. **Hours:** Mon.-Fri. 9-4, Sat.-Sun. and holidays 8:30-4, early Dec.-early Apr. **Phone:** (802) 824-5645.

• **Viking Nordic Center** is at 615 Little Pond Rd. **Hours:** Daily, mid-Dec. to mid-Mar. (weather permitting). **Phone:** (802) 824-3933.

SNOWDON MOTEL   (802)824-6047
▼ **Motel** $65-$125 **Address:** 4071 VT Rt 11 05148 **Location:** Jct SR 100, 2 mi e. **Facility:** 12 units. 1-2 stories (no elevator), exterior corridors. **Parking:** winter plug-ins. **Terms:** 2 night minimum stay - seasonal and/or weekends, 7 day cancellation notice-fee imposed.
📶 ⊠ 🅿 🛏 🖥 / SOME UNITS FEE 🐾 🐾

WHERE TO EAT

THE GARDEN CAFE & GALLERY   802/824-9574
▼▼▼ Continental. Fine Dining. $21-$35 **AAA Inspector Notes:** Enter into the colorful, uniquely shaped structure to find a welcoming sunroom dining area filled with plants, artwork by local artisans and a focal-point circular brick fireplace. A seasonally changing menu assures the freshest ingredients available, which the owner-chef prepares expertly and presents with an artistic flair. **Bar:** full bar. **Reservations:** suggested. **Address:** SR 11/100 05148 **Location:** Center. [D]

JAKE'S RESTAURANT & TAVERN   802/824-6614
▼▼ American. Casual Dining. $8-$25 **AAA Inspector Notes:** This eatery has a fun chili-pepper theme, casual friendly service and good food, especially the soup. Closed for lunch Monday through Thursday. **Bar:** full bar. **Address:** Mountain Marketplace 05148 **Location:** Jct SR 100 and 11. [D]

NEW AMERICAN GRILL   802/824-9844
▼▼ International. Casual Dining. $7-$24 **AAA Inspector Notes:** A diner-style atmosphere prevails here with friendly service. The broad menu has something for everyone from burritos to shrimp scampi, pasta and create-your-own stir fry. A wide range of hot and cold sandwiches are available for both lunch and dinner. **Bar:** full bar. **Address:** 10719 Rt 100 05148 **Location:** Jct SR 100 and 11; in Mountain Marketplace. [L] [D] CALL [&M]

LOWER WATERFORD

RABBIT HILL INN   802/748-5168
▼▼▼ Historic Country Inn $239-$450 **Address:** 48 Lower Waterford Rd 05848 **Location:** I-93 exit 44 northbound, 2.6 mi n on SR 18; exit 1 southbound, 6 mi s on SR 18. **Facility:** This handsome 1825 New England inn sits prominently in a sleepy little town and offers individually decorated guest rooms. The original inn was built in 1825, and the second guest house in 1795. 19 units. 2-3 stories (no elevator), interior/exterior corridors. **Terms:** closed 11/1-11/18, 2 night minimum stay - weekends, age restrictions may apply, 14 day cancellation notice-fee imposed. **Dining:** Rabbit Hill Inn Dining Room, see separate listing. **Activities:** fishing, cross country skiing, hiking trails, shuffleboard. Fee: massage.
🍴 🍸 📶 ⊠ 🅆 🖇 🖥 / SOME UNITS 🐾

WHERE TO EAT

RABBIT HILL INN DINING ROOM   802/748-5168
▼▼▼ **AAA Inspector Notes:** You'll appreciate this candlelit experience in a charming inn. The seasonally changed prix-fixe menu offers many exciting food combinations featuring beef, chicken, vegetarian, fresh seafood, pasta, wild-game and local ingredients. **Bar:** full bar. **Reservations:** required. **Address:** 48 Lower Waterford Rd 05848 **Location:** I-93 exit 44 northbound, 2.6 mi n on SR 18; exit 1 southbound, 6 mi s on SR 18; in Rabbit Hill Inn. [D]

Regional American Fine Dining $53

LUDLOW (E-3) pop. 811, elev. 1,064'

Situated on SRs 100/103 along the Black River, Ludlow offers views of mountain ranges, lakes and fertile farmland. Vermonters in this area pioneered the manufacture of reworked wool to combat cloth shortages after the Civil War.

Ludlow is home to the 600-acre campus of the Fletcher Farm School for the Arts and Crafts, 611 SR 103S, where artisans and craftspeople have been teaching the general public traditional techniques and exploring new media and methods since 1947. Classes last from 2 to 5 days. In the summer a shop features items made by members of the Society of Vermont Artists and Craftsmen; phone (802) 228-8770 for class information and shop schedule.

Okemo Valley Regional Chamber of Commerce: 57 Pond St., P.O. Box 333, Ludlow, VT 05149. **Phone:** (802) 228-5830.

BLACK RIVER ACADEMY MUSEUM is at 14 High St. The academy was founded in 1835 and drew students from all over New England. The original building was destroyed by fire in 1844, and the present Richardsonian-style building was completed around 1890, with future U.S. President Calvin Coolidge graduating that year.

In 1972 the building became a museum with a turn-of-the-20th-century school room; exhibits that include furniture, clothing, quilts and china, set in Victorian Era rooms; replicas of late 19th-century Main Street Ludlow businesses; and Calvin Coolidge memorabilia.

Time: Allow 30 minutes minimum. **Hours:** Tues.-Sat. noon-4, Memorial Day weekend-Columbus Day weekend; by appointment rest of year. **Cost:** $2; $1 (students with ID). **Phone:** (802) 228-5050.

RECREATIONAL ACTIVITIES
Skiing
* **Okemo Mountain Resort** is .3 mi. n. on SR 100, .5 mi. w. on Mountain Rd., then .2 mi. n. on Okemo Ridge Rd. Other activities are available year-round. **Hours:** Mon.-Fri. 9-4, Sat.-Sun. and holidays 8-4, mid-Nov. to late Apr. **Phone:** (802) 228-5222 or (866) 706-5366.

ANDRIE ROSE INN   802/228-4846

◆◆◆ Historic Bed & Breakfast $110-$364 **Address:** 13 Pleasant St 05149 **Location:** Corner of Depot St; center. **Facility:** Attractive furnishings and gas fireplaces add charm to guest rooms at this fully restored 1829 house located in the heart of Ludlow. Some units have a whirlpool bath. 15 units. 2 stories (no elevator), interior corridors. **Parking:** winter plug-ins. **Terms:** 2 night minimum stay - weekends, 20 day cancellation notice-fee imposed. **Activities:** whirlpool. **Guest Services:** valet laundry.

BEST WESTERN PLUS LUDLOW COLONIAL MOTEL
                                                   802/228-8188

◆◆ Motel
Rates not provided

AAA Benefit: Members save 10% or more with Best Western.

Address: 93 Main St 05149 **Location:** On SR 103; center. **Facility:** 43 units, some two bedrooms, efficiencies and kitchens. 2-3 stories (no elevator), interior/exterior corridors. **Parking:** winter plug-ins. **Pool(s):** outdoor. **Activities:** exercise room. **Guest Services:** coin laundry. **Free Special Amenities:** local telephone calls and high-speed Internet.

WHERE TO EAT

DJ'S RESTAURANT AND OAK LOUNGE   802/228-5374

◆◆ American. Casual Dining. $15-$29 **AAA Inspector Notes:** This popular downtown restaurant cooks up a variety of steak and seafood entrees. Oak walls and booths lend to an Irish pub/ski lodge decor. Small party seats are limited in the dining room. The full menu also is presented in the lounge in the front of the restaurant. **Bar:** full bar. **Address:** 146 Main St 05149 **Location:** Center. **Parking:** on-site and street. [D]

SAM'S STEAKHOUSE   802/228-2087

◆◆◆ Steak. Casual Dining. $14-$38 **AAA Inspector Notes:** After a long day of skiing guests can find a nice selection of thick and delicious steaks at this steakhouse. A large salad bar and plenty of fish or chicken choices also are on the menu for you. **Bar:** full bar. **Address:** 91 Rt 103 05149 **Location:** On SR 103, 0.9 mi e.
[D]

LYNDON

BRANCH BROOK BED & BREAKFAST   802/626-8316

◆◆ Historic Bed & Breakfast $100-$138 **Address:** 36 Branch Brook Ln 05849 **Location:** I-91 exit 23, just s on US 5, then just w on S Wheelock Rd. Located in a quiet area. **Facility:** Set in a quiet village that some call the covered bridge capital of Vermont, this restored 1850s Federal-style house has a quaint ambiance. 5 units. 2 stories (no elevator), interior corridors. *Bath:* some shared. **Parking:** winter plug-ins. **Terms:** 2 night minimum stay - seasonal and/or weekends, 14 day cancellation notice-fee imposed.

LYNDONVILLE pop. 1,207

ASIA   802/626-3368

◆◆ Chinese. Casual Dining. $4-$10 **AAA Inspector Notes:** The restaurant prepares a nice selection of Mandarin, Szechuan and Cantonese dishes for both lunch and dinner. **Bar:** full bar. **Reservations:** suggested, weekends. **Address:** 17 Depot St 05851 **Location:** I-91 exit 23, 1.4 mi n on US 5; center. [L] [D]

MISS LYNDONVILLE DINER   802/626-9890

◆◆ American. Family Dining. $5-$8 **AAA Inspector Notes:** A veritable Vermont icon for nearly a quarter of a century, the restaurant keeps folks coming back for its memorable breakfasts served all day, as well as its fresh fruit pies and delicious burgers prepared on homemade bread with Vermont cheese. **Address:** 686 Broad St (US 5 N) 05851 **Location:** I-91 exit 23, 1 mi n. [B] [L] [D]

MANCHESTER (F-2) pop. 749, elev. 695'
• Hotels p. 290 • Restaurants p. 290

Manchester, a year-round resort area guarded by Mount Equinox to the west, encompasses the communities of Manchester, Manchester Depot and Manchester Center. Elm-lined streets and marble sidewalks characterize Manchester, which is primarily residential; Manchester Center is more of a retail area.

Manchester & The Mountains Regional Chamber of Commerce: 39 Bonnet St., Suite 1, Manchester Center, VT 05255. **Phone:** (802) 362-6313 or (800) 362-4144.

Shopping areas: Battenkill & Highridge Outlet Centers, Manchester Designer Outlets and Manchester Marketplace on Depot Street (SR 11/30) all house factory outlets.

AMERICAN MUSEUM OF FLY FISHING, 4104 Main St. (SR 7A), chronicles the history of fly fishing dating back to A.D. 200. The museum has a library, angling-related art and an impressive collection of rods, reels and flies. **Hours:** Tues.-Sat. 10-4 (also Sun. 10-4, May-Oct.). Closed major holidays. **Cost:** $5; $3 (ages 5-14); $10 (family). **Phone:** (802) 362-3300.

HILDENE, THE LINCOLN FAMILY HOME, 1.5 mi. s. on SR 7A to 1005 Hildene Rd., is a 24-room Georgian Revival mansion built in 1905 as a summer home for Robert Todd Lincoln, Abraham Lincoln's only child to live to maturity.

Robert Lincoln, who became president and chairman of the Pullman Co., was so impressed by the beauty of the Manchester area when he visited with his mother and brother Tad in 1863 that he returned years later to build this 412-acre estate. Lincoln descendants lived in the house until 1975.

Visitors can watch a brief video orientation in the welcome center, take a self-guiding tour of the home, hear an original Aeolian 1,000-pipe organ and stroll through the formal gardens. Displays include personal Lincoln artifacts. Cheese-making can be viewed at the Hildene Farm. Interpretative walking trails wind through woods and meadows, and cross-country skiing and snowshoeing are available in winter.

Tours for the visually impaired are available by appointment. **Time:** Allow 1 hour, 30 minutes minimum. **Hours:** Daily 9:30-4:30. Cross-country skiing and snowshoeing are available mid-Dec. to early Mar. (weather permitting). Closed major holidays. **Cost:** $16; $5 (ages 6-14). Phone ahead for skiing and snowshoeing fees; equipment rental is available. **Phone:** (802) 362-1788. 🅿️

MOUNT EQUINOX, on SR 7A, 5 mi. s. of jct. SRs 11 and 30, is owned by a Carthusian monastery. At 3,848 feet, the mountain is the highest peak in the Taconic Range. The view from the summit encompasses parts of New York, New Hampshire, Massachusetts and Québec. The summit is reached by a 5.2-mile paved road with guardrails, steep grades and sharp curves. The Saint Bruno Scenic Viewing Center features exhibits detailing the history of the monastery and the mountain; a two-level deck affords grand views. Hiking trails are available.

Note: Vehicles larger than a 15-passenger van or a small camper are not permitted. Motor homes are prohibited. **Hours:** Daily 9 a.m.-dusk, May-Oct. (weather permitting). Phone ahead to confirm schedule. **Cost:** $15 (private vehicle driver); $12 (motorcycle driver); $5 (per passenger in private vehicle); free (ages 0-10 and motorcycle passenger). **Phone:** (802) 362-1114. 🅿️

Mount Equinox Skyline Drive begins on SR 7A between Manchester and Arlington (toll house). The 5.2-mile winding route takes you to the 3,848-foot summit of Mount Equinox. Parking areas offer panoramic views of the Green, White, Adirondack, Taconic and Berkshire mountains as well as rivers, lakes and valley communities along the way.

Note: Have your brakes checked and be sure your vehicle is in good condition before attempting the drive. **Time:** Allow 1 hour minimum. **Hours:** Daily 9 a.m.-dusk, July-Oct.; Thurs.-Sun. 9 a.m.-dusk, Mon.-Wed. 9-5, May-June (weather permitting). **Cost:** $15 (private vehicle driver); $12 (motorcycle driver); $5 (per passenger in private vehicle); free (ages 0-10 and motorcycle passenger). **Phone:** (802) 362-1115 or (802) 362-1114. 🐾 🅿️

SOUTHERN VERMONT ARTS CENTER is off SR 7A to West Rd., following signs to 902 Southern Vermont Arts Center Dr. Situated on a 407-acre campus on the slope of Mount Equinox, the center includes the Elizabeth de C. Wilson Museum of paintings and sculptures; the 400-seat Louise Arkell Pavilion; the Yester House art galleries; a sculpture garden; and a botany hiking trail.

Food is available early May to mid-Oct. **Time:** Allow 2 hours minimum. **Hours:** Complex open Tues.-Sat. 10-5, Sun. noon-5, May-Dec. Museum open late July to mid-Oct. Hiking trails, art galleries and sculpture garden open year-round. Phone ahead to confirm schedule. **Cost:** Free. Museum $6; $3 (students with ID); free (ages 0-12). **Phone:** (802) 362-1405. 🍽️

BRITTANY MOTEL   802/362-1033
◆◆ **Motel** $79-$140 **Address:** 1056 Main St (Historic SR 7A) 05254 **Location:** Jct SR 11/30, 3.8 mi s. **Facility:** 12 units. 1 story, exterior corridors. **Terms:** 2 night minimum stay - seasonal and/or weekends, 14 day cancellation notice-fee imposed.
ⒺⒸⓄ 📶 ✕ 🔌 ▭

THE INN AT ORMSBY HILL   (802)362-1163
◆◆◆ ◆◆◆ **Address:** 1842 Main St 05255 **Location:** On Historic SR 7A, 3 mi s of jct SR 11/30. **Facility:** A hot breakfast, complete with the inn's house granola and a breakfast dessert, is the specialty at this historic B&B built in 1764. Guest rooms have gas or wood-burning fireplaces and canopy beds. 10 units. 2 stories (no elevator), interior/exterior corridors. **Parking:** winter plug-ins. **Terms:** 2-3 night minimum stay - weekends, age restrictions may apply, 10 day cancellation notice-fee imposed. **Activities:** hiking trails. **Fee:** massage. **Free Special Amenities:** full breakfast and local telephone calls.
Historic Bed
& Breakfast
$175-$535
🆂🅰🆅🅴 📶 ✕ /SOME UNITS 🔌

NORTH SHIRE LODGE   802/362-2336
◆◆ **Motel** $119-$169 **Address:** 97 Main St 05254 **Location:** 4.5 mi s on Historic SR 7A, from jct SR 11/30. **Facility:** 14 units. 1 story, exterior corridors. **Terms:** 2 night minimum stay - weekends, 14 day cancellation notice-fee imposed. **Pool(s):** heated outdoor.
🍽️ 🍸 🏊 📶 ✕ 🔌 ▭

WEATHERVANE MOTEL   802/362-2444
◆◆ **Motel.** Rates not provided. **Address:** 2212 Main St (Historic SR 7A) 05254 **Location:** Jct SR 11/30, 2.3 mi s. **Facility:** 22 units. 1 story, exterior corridors. **Pool(s):** outdoor.
🏊 📶 ✕ ▭ /SOME UNITS FEE 🐾 🔌

WHERE TO EAT

MANCHESTER BAR & GRILL   802/366-8282
◆◆ American. Casual Dining. $8-$20 **AAA Inspector Notes:** After a day of skiing or hiking, adventurers can sit back and relax here with good old-fashioned comfort food. **Bar:** full bar. **Address:** 1844 Depot St 05255 **Location:** 1 mi e of jct SR 11/30. Ⓓ CALL Ⓜ

MULLIGAN'S OF MANCHESTER   802/362-3663
◆◆ American. Casual Dining. $11-$21 **AAA Inspector Notes:** This casual restaurant serves a wide variety of dishes to please nearly everyone--from creative pasta to burgers and deli sandwiches. Specialties include traditional New England clam chowder and New York strip cooked to the diner's specifications. **Bar:** full bar. **Address:** 3912 Main St 05254 **Location:** On Historic SR 7A. Ⓛ Ⓓ

MANCHESTER CENTER pop. 2,120

THE ASPEN AT MANCHESTER
802/362-2450

 Motel $90-$150 **Address:** 5669 Main St (Rt 7A) 05255 **Location:** Jct SR 11/30, 0.9 mi n on Historic SR 7A. Located in a quiet area. **Facility:** 25 units, some two bedrooms, kitchens and cottages. 1 story, exterior corridors. **Parking:** winter plug-ins. **Terms:** 2-3 night minimum stay - seasonal and/or weekends, 14 day cancellation notice-fee imposed. **Pool(s):** outdoor. **Activities:** horseshoes, shuffleboard.

CASABLANCA MOTEL
802/362-2145

 Motel $72-$125 **Address:** 5927 Main St (Rt 7A) 05255 **Location:** Jct SR 11/30, 1 mi n on Historic SR 7A. **Facility:** 25 units, some cottages. 1 story, exterior corridors. **Parking:** winter plug-ins. **Terms:** 14 day cancellation notice-fee imposed. **Activities:** horseshoes, volleyball.

CHALET MOTEL
(802)362-1622

Motel $90-$170 **Address:** 1875 Depot St (SR 11/30) 05255 **Location:** On SR 11/30, 0.3 mi e of jct US 7. **Facility:** 43 units. 1 story, exterior corridors. **Parking:** winter plug-ins. **Terms:** 2-3 night minimum stay - seasonal and/or weekends, 30 day cancellation notice-fee imposed. **Pool(s):** heated outdoor. **Activities:** sauna, whirlpool, game room, horseshoes. **Free Special Amenities:** local telephone calls and high-speed Internet.

MANCHESTER VIEW FINE LODGING   (802)362-2739

Hotel $95-$325 **Address:** 77 High Meadows Way 05255 **Location:** On Historic SR 7A, 2 mi n of jct SR 11/30 N, then just e. **Facility:** 36 units, some two bedrooms. 1-2 stories (no elevator), interior/exterior corridors. **Terms:** 2-3 night minimum stay - seasonal and/or weekends, 14 day cancellation notice-fee imposed. **Pool(s):** heated outdoor.

The Manchester View

Enjoy fine lodging in Southern VT with great views, fireplaces, golf, tennis and ski packages

PALMER HOUSE RESORT MOTEL
802/362-3600

Hotel $95-$300 **Address:** 5383 Main St (Rt 7A N) 05255 **Location:** Jct SR 11/30, 0.5 mi n on Historic SR 7A. **Facility:** 41 units, some two bedrooms. 1 story, exterior corridors. **Parking:** winter plug-ins. **Terms:** 2 night minimum stay - seasonal and/or weekends, age restrictions may apply, 15 day cancellation notice-fee imposed. **Pool(s):** heated outdoor, heated indoor. **Activities:** whirlpools, fishing, golf-9 holes, 2 tennis courts, hiking trails, shuffleboard, exercise room. **Fee:** massage. **Free Special Amenities:** local telephone calls and high-speed Internet.

TOLL ROAD INN
802/362-1711

 Motel $89-$160 **Address:** 2220 Depot St 05255 **Location:** On SR 11/30, 0.8 mi e of jct US 7 exit 4. **Facility:** 16 units. 2 stories (no elevator), interior corridors. **Terms:** 2-3 night minimum stay - seasonal and/or weekends, 14 day cancellation notice-fee imposed. **Pool(s):** outdoor. **Activities:** whirlpool.

 WHERE TO EAT

BISTRO HENRY'S
802/362-4982

Mediterranean Fine Dining $25-$35 **AAA Inspector Notes:** Bistro Henry features a Mediterranean cuisine with a touch of fun! The contemporary menu offers pasta, seafood, chicken, certified Angus beef dishes and a terrific selection of wine. The ambience is open, airy and relaxed. **Bar:** full bar. **Reservations:** suggested. **Address:** 1942 SR 11/30 05255 **Location:** On SR 11/30, 0.3 mi e of jct US 7. [D]

CHINA CITY
802/366-8281

Chinese. Quick Serve. $4-$14 **AAA Inspector Notes:** The basic restaurant offers mostly deep-fried or stir-fried foods via walk-up counter service. **Address:** 263 Depot St (SR 11/30), Suite 3 05255 **Location:** In Manchester Shopping Center. [L] [D]

CHRISTOS' PIZZA & PASTA
802/362-2408

Greek. Quick Serve. $5-$17 **AAA Inspector Notes:** This popular eatery offers pizza, pasta, subs and salads via counter service. Enjoy specialty pies including Buffalo chicken, Greek and Philly cheesesteak in addition to traditional favorites. **Bar:** beer & wine. **Address:** 4931 Historic SR 7A 05255 **Location:** Just n of jct SR 11/30. **Parking:** street only. [L] [D]

GARLIC JOHN'S
802/362-9843

Italian. Casual Dining. $7-$24 **AAA Inspector Notes:** The restaurant serves plentiful, well-prepared portions of both Southern and Northern Italian cuisine in a rustic, casual atmosphere. Hundreds of Chianti bottles hang from the wood-beamed ceiling. Dinner can be enjoyed both inside, as well as outside on the deck, where views of the mountains are stunning. **Bar:** full bar. **Address:** 1610 Depot St 05255 **Location:** US 7 exit 4, just e. [D]

THE GOURMET DELI & CAFE
802/362-1254

American Casual Dining $5-$13 **AAA Inspector Notes:** This restaurant offers patrons fresh delicious foods in a quaint café atmosphere. For those who like beans, do not miss the fifteen-bean soup. Menu offerings include some vegetarian and gluten-free options. **Bar:** beer & wine. **Address:** 4961 Main St, Suite 2 05255 **Location:** In Green Mountain Village Shoppes. [B] [L]

GRAZE AT MANCHESTER
802/366-8018

American. Casual Dining. $9-$28 **AAA Inspector Notes:** Located in a former Cape Cod residential home, this intimate bistro offers two dining areas. One is a casual deli-style café by the entryway; the other has a more formal dining setting in a side room. Lunch is standard fare of soups, sandwiches and salads. The continually changing dinner menu is limited but more enticing. You can opt for the inclusive three-course meal or order à la carte. **Bar:** beer & wine. **Reservations:** suggested, for dinner. **Address:** 32 Bonnet St 05255 **Location:** Jct Historic SR 7A, just n on SR 11/30. **Parking:** on-site and street. [L] [D]

MANCHESTER PIZZA HOUSE
802/362-3338

Pizza. Casual Dining. $4-$27 **AAA Inspector Notes:** This neat, simple restaurant offers limited seating with walk-up counter service. **Bar:** beer & wine. **Address:** 263 Depot St 05255 **Location:** In Manchester Shopping Center. [L] [D]

MISTRAL'S AT TOLL GATE
802/362-1779

French. Fine Dining. $28-$40 **AAA Inspector Notes:** This restaurant presents a sophisticated yet intimate atmosphere offering guests fresh, delightful dishes. Window seats offer a memorizing rushing riverside view. **Bar:** full bar. **Reservations:** suggested. **Address:** 10 Toll Gate Rd 05255 **Location:** US 7 exit 4, 2 mi e on SR 11. [D]

PANDA GARDEN RESTAURANT & LOUNGE   802/362-9133

Chinese. Casual Dining. $8-$32 **AAA Inspector Notes:** This restaurant has an upscale, modern décor and offers well-prepared, tasty food in both Chinese and Japanese traditions. Enjoy traditional Chinese fare, including chicken, pork, beef, seafood and vegetable dishes including Hunan pork and beef in black bean sauce. The Japanese menu features an array of sushi and sashimi selections and maki rolls, as well as udon, a traditional noodle soup. **Bar:** full bar. **Address:** 4519 Main St 05255 **Location:** In Highridge Plaza. L D

THE PERFECT WIFE   802/362-2817

American. Fine Dining. $18-$35 **AAA Inspector Notes:** The restaurant's noticeably distinct interior features a solarium ceiling and stained-glass hanging panels, while the second dining room has unusual stone walls and a knotty pine vaulted ceiling. The food is fresh, innovative and tasty. **Bar:** full bar. **Reservations:** suggested. **Address:** 2594 Depot St (SR 11/30) 05255 **Location:** US 7 exit 4, 3.9 mi e on SR 11/30. D

SHERRIE'S CAFE   802/362-3468

American. Casual Dining. $4-$10 **AAA Inspector Notes:** The restaurant offers a bistro-style atmosphere with casual service and delicious foods. A wide selection of breakfast items also is available. **Bar:** full bar. **Address:** 709A Depot St (Rt 11/30) 05255 **Location:** On SR 11/30; center. B L CALL M

UP FOR BREAKFAST   802/362-4204

American. Casual Dining. $4-$10 **AAA Inspector Notes:** This local favorite for breakfast offers patrons creative choices made from Vermont products. They close at 1 pm on weekdays and 2 pm on weekends. **Address:** 4935 Main St 05255 **Location:** Center. **Parking:** street only. B L

YE OLDE TAVERN   802/362-0611

American. Casual Dining. $17-$36 **AAA Inspector Notes:** Originally built in 1790, this restaurant has a rich history. The current owners have expanded and upgraded the menu to include such selections as Alaskan king crab and bison rib-eye steak, and each evening there is a different game meat available. **Bar:** full bar. **Reservations:** suggested. **Address:** 5183 Main St 05255 **Location:** Jct SR 11/30, 0.3 mi n on Historic SR 7A. D

MANCHESTER VILLAGE
• Restaurants p. 294

THE EQUINOX, A LUXURY COLLECTION GOLF RESORT & SPA (802)362-4700

THE LUXURY COLLECTION
Hotels & Resorts

Resort Hotel
$199-$569

AAA Benefit: Inspiring travels with your AAA Preferred rates.

Address: 3567 Main St 05254 **Location:** 1.3 mi s on Historic SR 7A, from jct SR 11/30. **Facility:** This restored 1769 hotel in the center of a quaint village features upscale décor and a variety of luxurious guest rooms and suites. Guests can relax in the spa or on the large deck next to the fire pit. 136 units. 3-4 stories, interior corridors. **Terms:** 2 night minimum stay - seasonal and/or weekends, 21 day cancellation notice-fee imposed, resort fee. **Amenities:** video games (fee), safes. **Dining:** 3 restaurants, also, The Marsh Tavern at The Equinox, see separate listing, entertainment. **Pool(s):** heated indoor. **Activities:** saunas, whirlpool, steamrooms, cross country skiing, bicycles, hiking trails, playground, spa. *Fee:* golf-18 holes, 3 tennis courts, horseback riding. **Guest Services:** valet laundry, area transportation-within 2 mi. *(See ad this page.)*

SAVE ECO FEE 🐕 🍴 🛁 🍸 CALL 🛗M 🏊
FEE 📺 BIZ 📶 ✕ 🐾 / SOME UNITS FEE 🐕 📶

Plan.
Map.
Go.

TripTik® Travel Planner

Where premier mapping technology meets complete travel information. Only on AAA.com and CAA.ca.

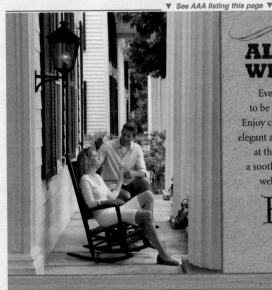

Safety tip: Keep a current AAA/CAA Road Atlas in every vehicle

WHERE TO EAT

THE MARSH TAVERN AT THE EQUINOX   802/362-7833

▼▼▼ American. Fine Dining. $12-$40 **AAA Inspector Notes:** In addition to offering a comfortable, upscale tavern atmosphere, the eatery also offers creative American cuisine with traditional New England flair. The menu makes use of authentic Vermont ingredients whenever possible and always incorporates the freshest in local produce. The main dining room closes between lunch and dinner but light fare is always available in the tavern portion. **Bar:** full bar. **Reservations:** suggested. **Address:** 3567 Main St 05254 **Location:** 1.3 mi s on Historic SR 7A, from jct SR 11/30; in The Equinox, A Luxury Collection Golf Resort & Spa. **Parking:** valet and street only.

(B) (L) (D)

MARLBORO (G-2) elev. 1,736'

Marlboro was settled in 1763 by two families who separately endured the hardships of pioneer life for more than a year before discovering they were neighbors. Today the town is the site of Marlboro College, with an enrollment of more than 300, and a summer music school and festival founded by pianist Rudolf Serkin.

MARSH-BILLINGS-ROCKEFELLER NATIONAL HISTORICAL PARK (D-3)

The nation's only national park focusing on conservation history and the evolution of land stewardship in the United States, Marsh-Billings-Rockefeller National Historical Park is located off SR 12 near Woodstock. The park's woodlands, covering 550 acres, comprise an area known for its scenic beauty and are managed not only to preserve natural resources but also to maintain sustainable forestry.

The park was an outgrowth of the first environmental crisis faced by Vermonters: the large-scale deforestation of the Green Mountains in the mid-19th century as a result of settlement that began after the end of the American Revolution. It was named for George Perkins Marsh, an early conservationist who also served as a diplomat and member of Congress, and Frederick Billings, a railroad president and philanthropist who was a successful attorney in San Francisco before returning to his native state.

Billings purchased the Marsh family farm, not only establishing a progressive dairy operation but also developing one of the country's first blueprints for scientific forest management. His work was carried on by three generations of women—his wife Julia, their three daughters and Billings' granddaughter, Mary French. French subsequently married Laurance S. Rockefeller, bringing together two families with a strong commitment to conservation. The Rockefellers gifted their estate's residential and forestlands to the people of the United States, making possible the creation in 1992 of Vermont's first national park.

A fine way to experience the parkland is by walking some of the 20 miles of carriage roads and trails that crisscross Mount Tom. **Note:** Due to repairs to some facilities, portions of the trails may be closed. Hike to the top of Mount Tom for beautiful views of Woodstock and the surrounding hills. In winter the roads are groomed for cross-country skiing and snowshoeing. Also within the national park is the Marsh-Billings-Rockefeller Mansion (see attraction listing).

The Carriage Barn, the park's visitor center, has an exhibit about land stewardship. The visitor center is open daily 10-5, Memorial Day weekend-Oct. 31. The carriage roads and trails are open year-round. Park admission is free. A fee is charged for cross-country skiing and snowshoeing. For park information phone (802) 457-3368, ext. 22.

▼GEM **MARSH-BILLINGS-ROCKEFELLER MANSION,** just inside the entrance to Marsh-Billings-Rockefeller National Historical Park, is the childhood home of pioneering environmentalist George Perkins Marsh. Conservationist Frederick Billings purchased the property in 1869 and built the Queen Anne-style residence that his granddaughter, Mary French Rockefeller, modernized in the 1950s. The house features Tiffany glass windows and beautifully detailed woodwork.

Ranger-guided tours of the mansion and gardens explore the history of conservation, the stewardship ethic of the Marsh, Billings and Rockefeller families, and community-based conservation in a more modern context. In addition to original furnishings and personal items, the mansion displays works of art that include some of America's finest landscape paintings, highlighting the influence painting and photography had on the conservation movement.

Hours: Guided tours are given daily on the hour 10-4, Memorial Day weekend-Oct. 31. **Cost:** $8; $4 (ages 62+); free (ages 0-15). Reservations are recommended. **Phone:** (802) 457-3368, ext. 22.

MIDDLEBURY (D-2) pop. 6,588, elev. 366'

Midway between Salisbury and New Haven, Middlebury was founded in 1761. A ranger district office at 1007 SR 7S provides maps and guides for hiking in nearby Green Mountain National Forest (see place listing p. 284); phone (802) 388-4362.

Middlebury College was chartered in 1800; the present enrollment exceeds 2,500. The campus includes Painter Hall, Vermont's oldest college building, built in 1816. Emma Hart Willard, a pioneer in American women's education, began her work in 1807 when she became the principal of Middlebury Female Academy. The school plays host to the Bread Loaf Writers' Conference in summer.

Addison County Chamber of Commerce: 93 Court St., Middlebury, VT 05753. **Phone:** (802) 388-7951 or (800) 733-8376.

Self-guiding tours: Walking-tour maps are available from the chamber of commerce.

HENRY SHELDON MUSEUM OF VERMONT HISTORY is at 1 Park St. In operation since 1882 and housed in the 1829 Judd-Harris House, it showcases objects depicting small-town life in 19th-century Vermont, including furniture, textiles, paintings and household artifacts. The Walter Cerf Gallery presents changing exhibits related to art and history. The Stewart-Swift Research Center preserves a collection of 19th-century books, letters, newspapers and genealogical records.

Time: Allow 30 minutes minimum. **Hours:** Museum open Tues.-Sat. 10-5 (also Sun. 1-5, Memorial Day to mid-Oct.). Research center open Thurs.-Fri. 1-5. Museum and research center closed major holidays. Phone ahead to confirm schedule. **Cost:** Museum $5; $4.50 (ages 60+); $4 (students with ID); $3 (ages 6-18); $12 (family, two adults and their children). Research center $5; free (students with ID). **Phone:** (802) 388-2117.

UVM MORGAN HORSE FARM is n.w. of US 7 off SR 23, following signs for 2.5 mi. The Morgan horse, state animal of Vermont, is said to be America's first breed of horse. After a guided tour and videotape presentation about the history and lineage of the Morgan horse, visitors can view a working horse farm.

Comfortable shoes are recommended. **Time:** Allow 1 hour minimum. **Hours:** Grounds open daily 9-4, May-Oct. Tours depart 10 minutes before the hour 9-3, May-Oct.; by appointment rest of year. **Cost:** Grounds (includes tour) $5; $4 (ages 13-19); $2 (ages 5-12). **Phone:** (802) 388-2011. 🎨

COURTYARD BY MARRIOTT MIDDLEBURY
(802)388-7600

Hotel
$145-$259

AAA Benefit: AAA hotel discounts of 5% or more.

Address: 309 Court St 05753 **Location:** 1 mi s on US 7. **Facility:** 89 units. 3 stories, interior corridors. **Parking:** winter plug-ins. **Amenities:** video games (fee), high-speed Internet. *Some:* safes. **Pool(s):** heated indoor. **Activities:** whirlpool, hiking trails, exercise room. **Guest Services:** valet and coin laundry. **Free Special Amenities:** newspaper and high-speed Internet.

 ▨⌘ CALL 🅵M 🏊 🅱🅸🆉 📶 ✕ 🎾 📱 🖨
📼

THE MIDDLEBURY INN (802)388-4961
▼▼▼ **Historic Hotel** $129-$299 **Address:** 14 Court Square 05753 **Location:** On US 7; center. **Facility:** Built in 1827, this imposing red-brick Georgian inn offers rooms in a range of sizes. To the rear of the property is a section of motel rooms. 71 units, some two bedrooms and efficiencies. 1-4 stories, interior/exterior corridors. **Parking:** winter plug-ins. **Terms:** 3 day cancellation notice-fee imposed. **Activities:** spa. **Guest Services:** valet laundry.

🄴🄲🄾 ▨ 🍸 ⚕ 🅱🅸🆉 📶 ✕
/SOME UNITS FEE 🐾 📱 🖨 📼

SWIFT HOUSE INN (802)388-9925
▼▼▼ **Historic Country Inn** $129-$299 **Address:** 25 Stewart Ln 05753 **Location:** 0.3 mi n on US 7 from jct SR 125 W. **Facility:** Set on spacious, well-manicured grounds, this Federal-style 1815 home features individually decorated rooms, some with a fireplace. 20 units. 2 stories (no elevator), interior/exterior corridors. **Parking:** winter plug-ins. **Terms:** off-site registration, 7 day cancellation notice-fee imposed. **Activities:** sauna, steamroom, hiking trails, jogging.

🄴🄲🄾 ▨ 🍸 ⚕ 📶 ✕ /SOME UNITS FEE 🐾 📼

AMERICAN FLATBREAD 802/388-3300
▼▼ ▼▼ Pizza Small Plates. Casual Dining. $6-$19 **AAA Inspector Notes:** The flatbread pizza concept is catching on in Vermont. Pizzas are made from organic grains, topped with local and regional fresh ingredients (organic whenever possible), prepared in the open kitchen and baked in a primitive wood-fired oven. Located in the historic district, the Marbleworks Building is made of scrap marble blocks from the area's marble-making era. **Bar:** beer & wine. **Address:** 137 Maple St 05753 **Location:** In historic Marble Works district. 🄳

FIRE & ICE RESTAURANT 802/388-7166
▼▼ ▼▼
American
Casual Dining
$9-$31
AAA Inspector Notes: A city landmark for more than a quarter of a century, this restaurant features hand-cut steaks, prime rib, fresh seafood and its own homemade mashed potatoes, as well as an impressive 55-item salad bar. Informal dining rooms display an eclectic collection of World War I wooden airplane propellers, a 1921 Hacker Craft motorboat, 50 model boats and 200 antique skis. **Bar:** full bar. **Reservations:** suggested. **Address:** 26 Seymour St 05753 **Location:** Jct SR 125 and US 7, just w. *Menu on AAA.com* 🄳

GREEN PEPPERS RESTAURANT 802/388-3164
▼ Pizza. Casual Dining. $5-$15 **AAA Inspector Notes:** Pick your own toppings for your salad from an extensive list. The list of pizza toppings will keep you busy also. A friendly staff member could also choose for you. **Bar:** beer & wine. **Address:** 10 Washington St 05753 **Location:** Just e of US 7. 🅛 🄳 CALL 🅵M

NOONIES DELI 802/388-0014
▼ Deli. Quick Serve. $6-$9 **AAA Inspector Notes:** This busy deli offers fresh soups, generous-sized salads, sandwiches and wraps made from fresh homemade breads and ingredients. Located in the historic Marbleworks District and on the banks of Otter Creek Falls for a great view. **Address:** 137 Maple St 05753 **Location:** In historic Marble Works district. 🅱 🅛 🄳

ROSIE'S 802/388-7052
▼ American. Fine Dining. $5-$18 **AAA Inspector Notes:** Rosie's is a popular, cheerful, family-style roadside restaurant offering table and counter service. The diverse menu features a great selection of appetizers, sandwiches, pasta dishes, beef plates and side dishes. **Bar:** full bar. **Address:** 886 US 7 05753 **Location:** 1.3 mi s on US 7, on west side. 🅱 🅛 🄳

THE STORM CAFE 802/388-1063
▼▼ American. Casual Dining. $6-$18 **AAA Inspector Notes:** On the river, this restaurant originally functioned as an old mill. The menu lists delicious sandwiches and homemade soups. **Bar:** beer & wine. **Address:** 3 Mill St 05753 **Location:** Jct SR 125 and US 7, just w, then just n. 🅛 🄳

MONTGOMERY CENTER

PHINEAS SWANN BED & BREAKFAST INN 802/326-4306
▼▼ ▼▼ **Historic Boutique Bed & Breakfast** $129-$425 **Address:** 195 Main St 05471 **Location:** Center. **Facility:** This B&B will surely please with its well-coordinated rooms and homey touches, including a collection of over 4,000 antique figurines, most of which are inspired by man's best friend. 9 units, some two bedrooms. 2 stories (no elevator), interior/exterior corridors. **Parking:** winter plug-ins. **Terms:** 2 night minimum stay - seasonal and/or weekends, 30 day cancellation notice-fee imposed, resort fee. **Amenities:** high-speed Internet. **Activities:** cross country skiing, bicycles, hiking trails. *Fee:* canoes, massage.

▨⌘ 🅱🅸🆉 📶 ✕ /SOME UNITS 🐾 📱 📼

MONTPELIER (C-3) pop. 7,855, elev. 484'
• Restaurants p. 298

Capital of the state, Montpelier is a center for the insurance and granite-quarrying industries. The city was the birthplace of Adm. George Dewey, hero of Manila Bay during the Spanish-American War. Hubbard Park, covering 185 acres on a hill behind the Capitol, offers a good view of the Worcester Mountains and the Winooski River Valley.

Also of architectural interest is the Supreme Court Building at 111 State St., which was constructed from Barre granite. The State Office Building, directly across from the Capitol, is a fine example of modern architecture. It is built of reinforced concrete, with Vermont marble facing on the exterior and polished, matched marble in the lobby.

MORSE FARM MAPLE SUGARWORKS, 2.7 mi. n. on Main St. to 1168 County Rd., following signs, shows a videotape about the sugaring process. A sample of maple syrup is included. Tours show processing techniques as well as the history of syrup making. Also on the premises is the Outdoor Museum of Folk Art.

Tours: Guided tours are available. **Time:** Allow 30 minutes minimum. **Hours:** Daily 8-8, June 1-Labor Day; 8-6, day after Labor Day-Oct. 31; 9-5, rest of year. Closed Jan. 1, Easter, Thanksgiving and Christmas. **Cost:** Free. **Phone:** (802) 223-2740.

T.W. WOOD GALLERY AND ART CENTER, 46 Barre St., was founded in 1896 and presents changing exhibitions featuring works by Vermont artists. Rotating exhibitions from the gallery's permanent collection include the work of Wood and other American artists of the 19th and early 20th centuries.

Note: At press time, the center was closed for renovations and was scheduled to reopen in early 2013. **Time:** Allow 30 minutes minimum. **Hours:** Tues.-Sun. noon-4. Closed major holidays and between exhibitions. Phone ahead to confirm schedule. **Cost:** Donations. **Phone:** (802) 249-5352.

VERMONT HISTORY MUSEUM, in the Pavilion Building at 109 State St., houses the permanent exhibit Freedom and Unity, which explores the history of Vermont from 1600 to the present. **Time:** Allow 1 hour minimum. **Hours:** Tues.-Sat. 10-4. Closed

state and federal holidays. **Cost:** $5; $3 (ages 6-17, ages 62+ and students with ID); $12 (family). **Phone:** (802) 828-2291.

VERMONT STATE HOUSE, 115 State St., is built of Barre granite in an impressive Renaissance Revival style. The gilded dome is surmounted by a statue of Agriculture. Inside the portico stands a marble statue of Ethan Allen and a brass cannon captured from Hessians in the 1777 Battle of Bennington. **Hours:** Mon.-Fri. 8-4 (also Sat. 11-2:30, July-Oct.). Thirty-minute tours are given Mon.-Fri. 10-3:30, Sat. 11-2:30, July-Oct.; by appointment rest of year. **Cost:** Donations. **Phone:** (802) 828-2228.

BETSY'S B&B   (802)229-0466

▼▼▼▼ Bed & Breakfast $95-$160 **Address:** 74 E State St 05602 **Location:** 0.3 mi e of Main St; center. Located in a residential area. **Facility:** Two picturesque Victorian homes make up this quaint B&B, which is on a quiet street within walking distance of the city. 12 units, some two bedrooms and kitchens. 2 stories (no elevator), interior corridors. **Terms:** check-in 4 pm, 3 day cancellation notice.

[ECO] [📶] [✕] / SOME UNITS [🐾] [❓] [📷] [💬]

CAPITOL PLAZA HOTEL & CONFERENCE CENTER
(802)223-5252

▼▼▼▼
Hotel
$147-$320

Address: 100 State St 05602 **Location:** Center; 1 blk from state capitol building. **Facility:** 64 units. 4 stories, interior corridors. **Terms:** 3 day cancellation notice-fee imposed. **Amenities:** safes. **Activities:** exercise room. **Guest Services:** valet laundry. (See ad p. 297.)

[SAVE] [ECO] [🍴] [🛎] [🍷]

[CALL] [🖥M] [BIZ] [📶] [✕] [💬]

/ SOME UNITS FEE [🛗]

THE INN AT MONTPELIER
(802)223-2727

▼▼▼▼
Bed & Breakfast
$160-$280

Address: 147 Main St 05602 **Location:** Just e of State St; center. **Facility:** This inn, consisting of two adjacent 19th-century homes, features typical New England architecture and antique and reproduction furnishings. 19 units. 2 stories (no elevator), interior corridors. **Terms:** 14 day cancellation notice-fee imposed. **Guest Services:** valet laundry. **Free Special Amenities:** continental breakfast and high-speed Internet.

[SAVE] [🍷] [📶] [✕]

▼ See AAA listing p. 296 ▼

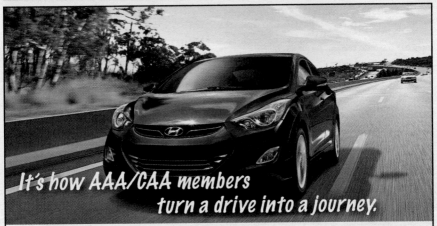

WHERE TO EAT

ANGELENO'S   802/229-5721

▼▼ ▼▼ Italian. Casual Dining. $6-$22 **AAA Inspector Notes:** The casual Italian-themed restaurant offers a variety of Italian and American dishes. **Bar:** beer & wine. **Address:** 15 Barre St 05602 **Location:** Just e of jct Main and Barre sts. [L] [D]

CAPITOL GROUNDS   802/223-7800

▼ American. Quick Serve. $3-$7 **AAA Inspector Notes:** The restaurant is a pleasant coffeehouse with great fresh-brewed coffee and delicious desserts served via walk-up counter service. **Address:** 27 State St 05602 **Location:** Center. **Parking:** street only.

[B] [L] [D]

LA BRIOCHE BAKERY & CAFE   802/229-0443

▼ American. Quick Serve. $4-$7 **AAA Inspector Notes:** The eatery is simple and basic overall but offers tasty food and walk-up counter service. **Address:** 89 Main St 05602 **Location:** I-89 exit 8; center. **Parking:** street only. [B] [L]

MCGILLICUDDY'S IRISH PUB   802/223-2721

▼▼ ▼▼ American. Casual Dining. $7-$16 **AAA Inspector Notes:** The restaurant offers mostly fried or grilled menu items in a simple, casual atmosphere; be sure to try the beer cheddar or French onion soup. **Bar:** full bar. **Address:** 14 Langdon St 05602 **Location:** Center. **Parking:** street only. [L] [D] [LATE]

NECI ON MAIN   802/223-3188

▼▼ ▼▼ American. Casual Dining. $7-$23 **AAA Inspector Notes:** Operated by students of the New England Culinary Institute. This pleasant, informal café atmosphere offers creative and internationally influenced American cuisine. Specialties include grilled meats, seafood, salmon and vegetarian dishes. Pub menu available from 2 pm. **Bar:** full bar. **Reservations:** suggested. **Address:** 118 Main St 05602 **Location:** Between School and State sts; center. **Parking:** street only. [L] [D]

SARDUCCI'S RESTAURANT AND BAR   802/223-0229

▼▼ ▼▼ Italian. Casual Dining. $7-$17 **AAA Inspector Notes:** The casual family restaurant specializes in Northern Italian dishes, many of which are prepared in the wood-burning oven. **Bar:** full bar. **Address:** 3 Main St 05602 **Location:** Just n of US 2; center.

[L] [D]

THE SKINNY PANCAKE   802/262-2253

▼▼ ▼▼ Natural/Organic. Casual Dining. $7-$15 **AAA Inspector Notes:** This rustic little café features a wide variety of savory and sweet crêpes plus soups and salads using Vermont's freshest local and organic ingredients. Gluten-free crêpes are a welcome option. **Bar:** beer & wine. **Address:** 89 Main St 05602 **Location:** Center. **Parking:** street only. [B] [L] [D]

MORRISVILLE (B-3) pop. 1,958, elev. 646'

Morrisville, like Vermont's other mountain-bound towns, grew rapidly when railroad service reached the area. Visible reminders of that event remain on Portland Street, where structures more closely resemble those of a Western boomtown than a New England village.

Lamoille Region Chamber of Commerce: 34 Pleasant St., Morrisville, VT 05661. **Phone:** (802) 888-7607 or (800) 849-9985.

NOYES HOUSE MUSEUM, 122 Lower Main St., is a two-story Federal-style brick building that contains local and regional history exhibits, photographs, furnishings, toys, household and farm tools, quilts, costumes and military artifacts. **Hours:** Fri.-Sat. 10-4,

early June-Aug. 31; Sat. 10-4, Sept. 1 to mid-Oct. **Cost:** Donations. **Phone:** (802) 888-7617.

SUNSET MOTOR INN   802/888-4956

▼▼ ▼▼ ◆
Motel
$85-$142

Address: 160 SR 15 W 05661 **Location:** Jct SR 100, just w on SR 15. **Facility:** 55 units. 2 stories (no elevator), interior/exterior corridors. **Parking:** winter plug-ins. **Terms:** 7 day cancellation notice-fee imposed. **Pool(s):** outdoor. **Activities:** playground. **Free Special Amenities:** local telephone calls and high-speed Internet.

[SAVE] [🛏] [🍽] CALL [&M] [🏊] [📶] [💻]
/ [SOME UNITS] FEE [🐕] [🚭] [🍳]

VILLAGE VICTORIAN BED & BREAKFAST   (802)888-8850

▼▼ ▼▼ ▼▼ Bed & Breakfast $80-$170 **Address:** 107 Union St 05661 **Location:** Just e on Congress St, then just n. **Facility:** The B&B is a charming, quaint, 1890s Victorian inn that offers guests great service and many personal touches. 4 units. 2 stories (no elevator), interior corridors. **Terms:** check-in 4 pm, 15 day cancellation notice-fee imposed. **Activities:** playground, basketball. **Guest Services:** complimentary laundry. [ECO] [📶] [📵] [🔇]

MOUNT HOLLY

HARRY'S CAFE   802/259-2996

▼▼ ▼▼ International. Casual Dining. $10-$24 **AAA Inspector Notes:** Diners here come for the inspirational food loaded with flavorful elements and prepared with care. The international cuisine borrows from many culinary traditions such as Asian, Italian and Caribbean. The mussels in green curry sauce are a great hearty appetizer as is the corn and shrimp bisque. Entrées include baked stuffed pork chops with peach chutney and ginger hoisin-glazed steelhead trout. Save room for the in-house prepared desserts such as Key lime pie, chocolate mousse and carrot cake. **Bar:** full bar. **Reservations:** suggested. **Address:** 3621 SR 103 05758 **Location:** 5 mi n of Ludlow. [D]

MOUNT MANSFIELD (B-2) elev. 4,393'

The loftiest peak in both the Green Mountains and in Vermont, Mount Mansfield is 4,393 feet high and 5 miles long. Covering 34,000 acres of the mountain is Mount Mansfield State Forest *(see Recreation Areas Chart)*. The forest can be reached by roads from Stowe through Smugglers' Notch or from Underhill Center.

The profile of Mount Mansfield is said to resemble a human face. The Long Trail and other trails lead to scenic spots and picnic areas. Campgrounds are available. The east side is a game refuge; hunting is permitted on the west side.

STOWE AUTO TOLL ROAD—see Stowe p. 310.

MOUNT SNOW (F-2) elev. 3,583'

In southern Vermont's Green Mountains, Mount Snow is a year-round resort. Recreational activities include alpine skiing from early November to early May and golf, tennis, swimming, boating, fishing and mountain biking the rest of the year.

RECREATIONAL ACTIVITIES
Skiing

• **Mount Snow Resort** is on SR 100N. Other activities are available. **Hours:** Mon.-Fri. 9-4, Sat.-Sun.

and holidays 8-4, late Nov.-late Apr. (weather permitting). **Phone:** (802) 464-3333 or (800) 245-7669.

NEWFANE (F-3) pop. 118, elev. 536'

WINDHAM COUNTY HISTORICAL SOCIETY MUSEUM, just s. of the village green on SR 30, offers items illustrating the history of the county. Displays include early portraits, Vermont furniture from the 18th and 19th centuries, clothing and textiles, and Civil War artifacts. Exhibits change annually. **Time:** Allow 30 minutes minimum. **Hours:** Wed. and Sat.-Sun. noon-5, late May to mid-Oct. **Cost:** Free. **Phone:** (802) 365-4148.

RICK'S TAVERN   802/365-4310
▼ American. Casual Dining. $7-$20 **AAA Inspector Notes:** Originally a tool shed adjacent to a 1956 sawmill, this tavern offers a casual, relaxed and rustic atmosphere with a large pizza and burger menu. Wednesday is discounted pizza night, Thursday is live jazz night and Friday is all-you-can-eat fish fry. There is a take-out window for those on the run. Free Wi-Fi is offered. **Bar:** full bar. **Address:** 386 VT Rt 30 05345 **Location:** From town green, 0.8 mi s.
L D

NEWPORT (A-4) pop. 4,589

"The Border City," Newport is a gateway between New England and Canada. The city lies on the southern side of Lake Memphremagog, whose name is derived from an Abenaki Indian word meaning "beautiful waters." In Canada on the western side of the 32-mile-long lake rises Owl's Head, named after an American Indian chief. Its 3,360-foot summit offers impressive views.

On Prospect Hill, the granite towers of St. Mary's Star of the Sea Church rise above the city; phone (802) 334-5066.

Vermont's North Country Chamber of Commerce: 246 The Causeway, Newport, VT 05855-1701. **Phone:** (802) 334-7782 or (800) 635-4643.

NEWPORT CITY MOTEL   802/334-6558
◆◆◆ **Address:** 444 E Main St 05855 **Location:** I-91 exit 27, 1.7 mi n on SR 191, Motel just e on Sias Ave, then just n. **Facility:** $88-$260 83 units, some kitchens. 2 stories (no elevator), interior/exterior corridors. **Terms:** cancellation fee imposed. **Parking:** winter plug-ins (fee). **Pool(s):** heated indoor. **Activities:** whirlpool, exercise room. **Guest Services:** coin laundry. **Free Special Amenities:** continental breakfast and high-speed Internet.
SAVE ECO ▦+ ⊠ BIZ 🛜 ▣ /SOME UNITS 🛏 🖼

WHERE TO EAT

THE EASTSIDE RESTAURANT & PUB   802/334-2340
▼▼ American. Casual Dining. $9-$27 **AAA Inspector Notes:** This locally popular restaurant is bustling with activity and offers great mountain and lake views. Hearty portions of such dishes as chicken and biscuits and fried scallops are featured, and the pub has a cozy fireplace. A large deck along the water's edge offers additional seating in season. **Bar:** full bar. **Address:** 47 Landing St 05855 **Location:** Jct SR 191, just n via US 5, SR 105 and Union St; entrance under railway bridge. L D CALL Ⓛ M

NORTH BENNINGTON (G-1) pop. 1,643, elev. 287'

◆ **PARK-McCULLOUGH HISTORIC ESTATE** GEM is 1 blk. w. off SR 67A at jct. Park and West sts. Built in 1865, this 35-room Victorian "summer home" contains original furnishings, decorative art pieces and period clothing belonging to the Park and McCullough families. The home and 800-acre grounds remain essentially as they were more than 140 years ago.

Also on the premises are gardens, a carriage house with a collection of carriages, the 1904 Grapery Greenhouse, the 1865 Playhouse and a farmhouse dating from 1779. Hiking trails are available.

Time: Allow 1 hour minimum. **Hours:** Guided tours are given by appointment; reservations are required at least 24 hours in advance. **Cost:** $15. Cash or check only. **Phone:** (802) 442-5441. 🅿

PANGAEA RESTAURANT   802/442-7171
▼▼▼ American. Fine Dining. $30-$39 **AAA Inspector Notes:** A former storefront in the center of a quaint New England village now hosts a fine-dining establishment that offers a seasonally rotating menu to ensure the freshest and most flavorful ingredients are incorporated to create its innovative offerings. **Bar:** full bar. **Reservations:** suggested. **Address:** 1 Prospect St 05257 **Location:** Center; across from village green. **Parking:** on-site and street. D

NORTH CHITTENDEN (D-2) elev. 1,001'

DWIGHT D. EISENHOWER NATIONAL FISH HATCHERY, just w. on Holden Rd., raises brook and lake trout for restocking lakes around Vermont and Atlantic salmon for Lake Champlain and the Connecticut River restoration program. Visitors can feed adult salmon in a display pool. **Hours:** Daily 8-4. **Cost:** Free. **Phone:** (802) 483-6618. 🅿

NORTHFIELD (C-3) pop. 2,101, elev. 732'

Norwich University was founded in 1819 by Capt. Alden Partridge, a former superintendent at West Point, and is considered the country's oldest private military college. It was one of the first universities to institute military programs, which later formed the basis for the Reserve Officer Training Corps (ROTC). Current enrollment is 2,300 cadets and civilian students.

The Sullivan Museum and History Center has exhibits about the history of the university and the achievements of its alumni, including Adm. George Dewey, Maj. Gen. Grenville Dodge and Gen. I.D. White. Other collections include Norwich uniforms, flags, weapons and military equipment as well as themed changing exhibits; phone (802) 485-2183.

Guided tours of the Norwich University campus can be arranged at the admissions office in Roberts Hall, near the north entrance; phone (802) 485-2001 or (800) 468-6679.

Also of interest in Northfield are five covered bridges—three on Cox Brook Road, one on Stony

Brook Road and one on Slaughterhouse Road. This is one of only two places in Vermont where two covered bridges are in sight of one another.

NORTH HERO

THE NORTH HERO HOUSE
802/372-4732

Historic Country Inn $125-$350

Address: 3643 US 2 05474 **Location:** Waterfront. Center. **Facility:** Part of a village on a Lake Champlain Island, this property dates from 1891 and is a rambling complex of four buildings offering a variety of rooms. 26 units. 2-3 stories (no elevator), interior/exterior corridors. **Terms:** 2 night minimum stay - seasonal and/or weekends, 30 day cancellation notice-fee imposed. **Dining:** 2 restaurants, also, The North Hero House Restaurant, see separate listing. **Activities:** whirlpool, rental boats, rental canoes, shuffleboard. *Fee:* boat dock, massage. **Free Special Amenities:** local telephone calls and high-speed Internet.

SHORE ACRES INN
802/372-8722

Country Inn $95-$250 **Address:** 237 Shore Acres Dr 05474 **Location:** Waterfront. 0.5 mi s on US 2. **Facility:** Situated on 50 acres, this lakefront inn is set back from the highway on the shores of Lake Champlain with panoramic views of the Green Mountains. 23 units. 1-2 stories (no elevator), interior/exterior corridors. **Terms:** closed 1/1-3/31, 2 night minimum stay - weekends, 21 day cancellation notice-fee imposed. **Dining:** Shore Acres Restaurant, see separate listing. **Activities:** boat dock, fishing, 2 tennis courts, playground, horseshoes, shuffleboard.

WHERE TO EAT

THE NORTH HERO HOUSE RESTAURANT
802/372-4732

American Fine Dining $12-$32

AAA Inspector Notes: This comfortable, relaxed restaurant offers a good selection of beer, wine and cocktails with an á la carte menu. A Friday night lobster buffet lures patrons in July and August. Seating is available on a three-season porch with lake views, on the patio or in the peaceful dining room with some garden views. **Bar:** full bar. **Reservations:** suggested. **Address:** 3643 US 2 05474 **Location:** Center; in The North Hero House. *Menu on AAA.com* B D

SHORE ACRES RESTAURANT
802/372-8722

Regional American. Casual Dining. $17-$37 AAA Inspector Notes: The restaurant specializes in fresh grilled fish, steak and chops as well as homemade breads, pastries, desserts, nightly specials and health-conscious appetizers. The decor is cozy New England, and the site overlooks Lake Champlain. **Bar:** full bar. **Reservations:** suggested. **Address:** 237 Shore Acres Dr 05474 **Location:** 0.5 mi s on US 2; in Shore Acres Inn. D

NORWICH (D-3) pop. 878, elev. 398'

The King Arthur Flour Baking Education Center, Bakery and The Baker's Store at 135 SR 5S draws visitors from all over the United States and Canada. The store is staffed with experienced bakers who delight in answering technical baking questions and are quick to provide demonstrations and samples. The education center offers registrants the chance to work alongside some of the nation's finest master bakers. Classes from half a day to a full week cover subjects from chocolate to artisan breads to pasta; phone (802) 649-3881, or (800) 827-6836 to order a catalog.

MONTSHIRE MUSEUM OF SCIENCE, I-91 exit 13 to 1 Montshire Rd. off SR 10A, features more than 100 hands-on exhibits about science, natural history and technology. Permanent displays include freshwater aquariums, live animals and mounted specimens from New England and around the world.

The museum is on 110 acres of woodland along the Connecticut River. Nature trails and an outdoor park with water activities are available. **Time:** Allow 4 hours minimum. **Hours:** Daily 10-5. Closed Thanksgiving and Christmas. **Cost:** $12; $10 (ages 2-17). **Phone:** (802) 649-2200.

THE NORWICH INN
802/649-1143

International. Fine Dining. $9-$25 AAA Inspector Notes: This inn is a fine example of true historic Vermont style. Charming decor with some Victorian touches set a relaxed mood for creative dining. Entrées show the chef's flair for the unusual such as New Zealand lamb lollipops, seared Canadian duck breast with chestnut puree and seared antelope filet with huckleberry gastrique. **Bar:** full bar. **Reservations:** suggested. **Address:** 325 Main St 05055 **Location:** I-91 exit 13, 0.4 mi w; center. L D

ORWELL (D-1) elev. 385'

Settled shortly before the American Revolution by a Scotsman from Montréal, John Charter, Orwell began as a sheep-raising center. The town lies in the Champlain Valley near the southern end of Lake Champlain.

MOUNT INDEPENDENCE STATE HISTORIC SITE is 6 mi. w. of jct. SR 22A and SR 73. The site also is accessible by taking the MV *Carillon (see attraction listing p. 307)* from Shoreham. Location of the Revolutionary War's largest military fortifications, the remains include the foundation of a stockade, blockhouses, gun batteries and a hospital.

A visitor center/museum presents a 12-minute orientation video and tells the story of military life on Mount Independence, featuring many of the artifacts recovered during recent archeological investigations. Trails—including an accessible trail with interpretive signs—with views of Lake Champlain traverse 300 acres of woodland and pasture.

Time: Allow 2 hours minimum. **Hours:** Site and visitor center open daily 9:30-5, late May to mid-Oct. The trails are accessible year-round. **Cost:** $5; free (ages 0-14). **Phone:** (802) 948-2000, or (802) 759-2412 in the off-season.

PERKINSVILLE pop. 130

THE INN AT WEATHERSFIELD
802/263-9217

Historic Country Inn. Rates not provided. Address: 1342 Rt 106 05151 **Location:** On SR 106, 2 mi n of jct SR 10. **Facility:** This farmhouse, set well back from the road, dates from 1792. Guest rooms feature country-style décor and many have a gas or wood-burning fireplace. The old farmhouse and additions create an impressive image. 12 units. 3 stories (no elevator), interior corridors. **Terms:** age restrictions may apply. **Dining:** Restaurant Verterra, see separate listing. **Activities:** hiking trails.

RESTAURANT VERTERRA   802/263-9217

▽▽▽▽ Regional American. Fine Dining. $23-$29 **AAA In-spector Notes:** This romantic room in a rustic inn features regional cuisine that is sensational. The prix fixe dinner offers five courses and selections are changed daily. Fresh local, seasonal ingredients are used. The desserts are delightful. **Bar:** full bar. **Reservations:** suggested. **Address:** 1342 Rt 106 05151 **Location:** On SR 106, 2 mi n of jct SR 10; in The Inn at Weathersfield. D

PERU (F-2) elev. 1,686'

RECREATIONAL ACTIVITIES
Skiing
• **Bromley Mountain Ski Resort** is 6 mi. e. of Manchester Center on SR 11 on Bromley Mountain. Other activities are available. **Hours:** Mon.-Fri. 9-4, Sat.-Sun. 8:30-4, Thanksgiving weekend to mid-Apr. (weather permitting). **Phone:** (802) 824-5522 or (866) 856-2201.

• **Wild Wings Ski Touring Center** is at 246 Styles Ln. **Hours:** Daily 9-4, mid-Dec. to mid-Mar. (weather permitting). **Phone:** (802) 824-6793.

PITTSFORD (D-2) pop. 740, elev. 370'

Pittsford is named in honor of British statesman William Pitt. As prime minister of England "the Great Commoner" was the colonists' best friend, fully supporting them in the passionate demand for "no taxation without representation."

The town is home to four covered bridges: the Hammond, the Depot, the Cooley and the Gorham. The first U.S. patent was granted in Pittsford; it was given to Samuel Hopkins for devising a way to create potash and pearl ash out of wood ash for making soap.

DWIGHT D. EISENHOWER NATIONAL FISH HATCHERY—see North Chittenden p. 299.

NEW ENGLAND MAPLE MUSEUM, n. on US 7, offers self-guiding tours describing the maple sugaring process since American Indian times. Dioramas, antiques and a slide show tell the history of "sweet water." Demonstrations are conducted, and visitors can sample specialty foods and different grades of maple syrup.

Time: Allow 30 minutes minimum. **Hours:** Daily 8:30-5:30, Fri. before Memorial Day-Oct. 31; 10-4, mid-Mar. through Thurs. before Memorial Day and Nov. 1-Dec. 23. Closed Easter and Thanksgiving. Phone ahead to confirm schedule. **Cost:** $2.50; $2 (ages 62+); 75c (ages 6-12). **Phone:** (802) 483-9414 or (800) 639-4280.

PLYMOUTH (E-3)

The small Green Mountain town of Plymouth was the birthplace of Calvin Coolidge. Vice President Coolidge was at home Aug. 3, 1923, when he heard the news of President Warren G. Harding's death. His father, a notary public, administered the oath of office to him in the parlor by the light of a kerosene lamp.

◆ **PRESIDENT CALVIN COOLIDGE STATE HISTORIC SITE,** 3780 SR 100A, includes the birthplace, boyhood home and grave of Calvin Coolidge, the 30th president of the United States. The birthplace and homestead have original furnishings.

Other buildings include the President Calvin Coolidge Museum & Education Center, with an exhibit about Coolidge's career and changing displays of gifts presented to the president while in office; Wilder House, the childhood home of Coolidge's mother, which is now a restaurant; Wilder Barn, displaying a collection of 19th-century farm implements; the Plymouth Cheese Factory, built in 1890 by Coolidge's father and still making cheese using the original 1890 recipe; the 1850s General Store; the office of the 1924 summer White House; and Union Christian Church, an 1840 meetinghouse. The Aldrich House contains exhibits pertaining to the village and to Coolidge.

Time: Allow 2 hours minimum. **Hours:** Complex open daily 9:30-5, late May to mid-Oct. **Cost:** $8; $2 (ages 6-14); $20 (family). **Phone:** (802) 672-3773.

INN AT WATER'S EDGE   802/228-8143

▽▽▽▽ ▽▽▽▽ **Address:** 45 Kingdom Rd 05149 **Location:** On SR 100, 3.6 mi n of jct SR 103.
Historic Country Inn **Facility:** Beautifully restored, this 1878 Victorian farmhouse sits on the edge of
$125-$250 Black River and Echo Lake and features its own small beach. 11 units, some two bedrooms. 2 stories (no elevator), interior corridors. **Parking:** winter plug-ins. **Terms:** age restrictions may apply, 14 day cancellation notice. **Activities:** whirlpool, beach access, boating, canoeing, boat dock, fishing, cross country skiing, bicycles, hiking trails, horseshoes. **Fee:** massage. **Guest Services:** area transportation-bus station. **Free Special Amenities: full breakfast and room upgrade (subject to availability with advance reservations).**

ECHO LAKE INN DINING ROOM   802/228-8602

▽▽▽▽ Regional American. Casual Dining. $17-$28 **AAA Inspector Notes:** Located in a Victorian-era hotel, this restaurant in the lakes region features sumptuous New England cuisine that includes rainbow trout in Chablis sauce, wild rice, local vegetables and Creole seafood soup. **Bar:** full bar. **Reservations:** suggested. **Address:** 2 Dublin Rd 05056 **Location:** On SR 100; in Tyson Village. D

RIVER TAVERN   802/672-3811

▽▽▽▽ American. Casual Dining. $9-$32 **AAA Inspector Notes:** This upscale restaurant offers well-prepared cuisine with an emphasis on New England favorites. The decor is formal, but the atmosphere is casual and comfortable. **Bar:** full bar. **Reservations:** suggested. **Address:** 75 Billings Rd 05056 **Location:** 2 mi s on SR 100; in Hawk Inn & Mountain Resort. B D CALL

PROCTOR (E-2) elev. 477'

In the narrow Otter Creek Valley, Proctor was named for Redfield Proctor, governor of the state 1878-80 and founder of the Vermont Marble Co., an international corporation. Appropriately, sidewalks and public buildings are constructed from the local marble. Central Vermont Public Service on Main Street is a major source of the town's power supply.

VERMONT MARBLE MUSEUM is at 52 Main St. Said to contain one of the largest displays of its kind in the world, the museum illustrates the origin, quarrying and finishing of marble. More than 100 exhibits feature custom marble work, historic photographs, varied artifacts and the Earth Alive geology display room. The Hall of Presidents contains white marble relief statues of past U.S. presidents. The Tomb of the Unknown Soldier exhibit chronicles the history of the shrine, from the quarrying of the marble to the burial vault's arrival at Arlington National Cemetery.

Visitors also can observe the museum's sculptor in residence create marble carvings. **Hours:** Daily 9-4:30, mid-May to late Oct. **Cost:** $7; $5 (ages 62+); $4 (ages 13-18). **Phone:** (802) 459-2300 or (800) 427-1396.

WILSON CASTLE, 3.5 mi. s. on W. Proctor Rd., was built in 1867 on a 115-acre estate. Nineteen open proscenium arches overlooked by a towering turret, parapet and balcony dominate the elaborate facade of English brick and marble. The castle's 32 rooms feature 84 stained-glass windows and 13 fireplaces finished with domestic tiles and bronze; not all rooms are included in the tour.

Furnishings include European and Far Eastern antiques and museum pieces, along with statuary, Chinese scrolls and Oriental rugs. Paintings, sculpture and photographs are displayed in an art gallery. Cattle barns, stables and a carriage house are on the grounds.

Hours: Guided tours of two of the three floors depart continuously daily 9-5, Memorial Day weekend to mid-Oct. **Cost:** $10.75; $9.50 (ages 62+); $5.50 (ages 6-12). **Phone:** (802) 773-3284.

PUTNEY pop. 523, elev. 251'

THE PUTNEY INN   802/387-5517
▼▼ ▼▼ **Hotel.** Rates not provided. **Address:** 57 Putney Landing Rd 05346 **Location:** I-91 exit 4, just e. **Facility:** 25 units. 2 stories (no elevator), exterior corridors. **Dining:** restaurant, see separate listing.

WHERE TO EAT

J.D. MCCLIMENT'S PUB   802/387-4499
▼▼ ▼▼ International. Gastropub. $9-$19 **AAA Inspector Notes:** Be transported to Ireland with just a short drive to Putney and enjoy some tasty cuisine that is a notch above the typical pub fare. Diners come here for the variety of salads, fish and chips, flatbread pizza, Guinness beef stew and flat iron pork steak. Friday and Saturday special theme nights include Mexican or Thai. On Wednesday live Celtic music is featured and there is occasional live music on the weekends. **Bar:** full bar. **Address:** 26 Bellows Falls Rd 05346 **Location:** I-91 exit 4, 1.5 mi n.

THE PUTNEY INN   802/387-5517
▼▼▼ ▼▼ New England. Fine Dining. $12-$31 **AAA Inspector Notes:** Hand-hewn beams highlight this restaurant featuring New England country décor in a comfortable and relaxing atmosphere. The creative New England menu offers all fresh, local and regional ingredients. The wine cellar offers an expanded and diverse wine selection. **Bar:** full bar. **Reservations:** suggested. **Address:** 57 Putney Landing Rd 05346 **Location:** I-91 exit 4, just e.

QUECHEE (E-3) pop. 656

A scenic portion of Quechee Gorge, Vermont's Little Grand Canyon, lies west of Quechee (pronounced KWEE-chee). The bridge on US 4 that spans the gorge 165 feet above the Ottauquechee River provides a good view of this natural spectacle. A covered bridge leads into this small village, known in the 19th century for its busy woolen mills.

White River Welcome Center: 100 Railroad Row, White River Junction, VT 05001. **Phone:** (802) 281-5050.

Shopping areas: The Mill, 1760 Quechee Main St., is a complex of shops including Simon Pearce Glass, where visitors can observe the glass-blowing process. The Fat Hat Clothing Company, 1 Quechee Main St., sells clothing. Quechee Gorge Village, at Quechee Gorge, offers antiques, arts and crafts, seasonal miniature steam train rides and an antique carousel.

VERMONT INSTITUTE OF NATURAL SCIENCE is on SR 4, 3.5 mi. w. of I-89 exit 1 at 6565 Woodstock Rd. Located adjacent to scenic Quechee Gorge, this environmental learning center encompasses 47 acres inhabited by migratory songbirds, amphibians and other Vermont wildlife. Such raptors as owls, bald eagles, red-tailed hawks and peregrine falcons can be viewed in a series of outdoor enclosures. Educational programs allow visitors to get an up-close look at live raptors, and nature trails encourage exploration.

Tours: Cell phone and MP3 audio tours are available. **Hours:** Daily 10-5:30, late June-Oct. 31. Schedule varies rest of year; phone ahead. Closed Thanksgiving and Christmas. **Cost:** $12; $11 (ages 65+); $10 (ages 4-17). **Phone:** (802) 359-5000.

THE QUECHEE INN AT MARSHLAND FARM
                                             (802)295-3133

▼▼▼ ▼▼
Historic
Country Inn
$90-$255
Address: 1119 Quechee Main St 05059 **Location:** 1 mi n of US 4. Located in a quiet area. **Facility:** Dating from the 18th century, this Colonial-style farmhouse provides a lovely retreat in a tranquil countryside setting. 25 units. 2 stories (no elevator), interior corridors. **Terms:** 2 night minimum stay - seasonal and/or weekends, 14 day cancellation notice-fee imposed. **Dining:** The Dining Room at The Quechee Inn, see separate listing. **Activities:** rental canoes, fishing, cross country skiing, rental bicycles, hiking trails.

WHERE TO EAT

THE DINING ROOM AT THE QUECHEE INN

802/295-3133

American
Fine Dining
$18-$33

AAA Inspector Notes: The restaurant occupies the beautiful, historic 1793 former home and farm of Col. John Marsh, Vermont's first lieutenant governor, and is recorded on the National Register of Historic Places. Innovative chefs prepare a variety of complex recipes with fresh ingredients, resulting in excellent flavors. Dishes are presented with careful attention to colors and textures. The experience is wonderful. **Bar:** full bar. **Reservations:** suggested. **Address:** 1119 Quechee Main St 05059 **Location:** 1 mi n of US 4; in The Quechee Inn at Marshland Farm. D

FIRE STONES

802/295-1600

American. Family Dining. $8-$24 **AAA Inspector Notes:** The restaurant offers patrons a fun, rustic atmosphere. Many dishes are prepared in the large wood-burning oven. **Bar:** full bar. **Address:** Waterman, US Rt 4 Pl 05059 **Location:** I-89 exit 1 (Woodstock). L D

PARKER HOUSE INN

802/295-6077

Regional French. Fine Dining. $24-$37 **AAA Inspector Notes:** *Historic.* Along the Ottauquechee River, this restored 1857 Victorian-style inn is on the National Register of Historic Places. The chef-owner prepares innovative beef, lamb, pork and seafood dishes using only the freshest, locally grown produce. Summer guests can enjoy a relaxing yet elegant dinner on the outside patio with a beautiful view of the sun setting over the river. **Bar:** full bar. **Reservations:** suggested. **Address:** 1792 Quechee Main St 05059 **Location:** 0.3 mi n on Waterman Hill Place from flashing light on US 4. D

SIMON PEARCE RESTAURANT

802/295-1470

Regional American. Casual Dining. $9-$35 **AAA Inspector Notes:** In a restored mill where hand-blown glass and pottery demonstrations are given, this restaurant features good views, Irish and Continental dishes and place settings with its own glassware and pottery. It is well worth the usual wait at the popular establishment. Semiformal attire. **Bar:** full bar. **Address:** 1760 Quechee Main St 05059 **Location:** 0.3 mi n on Waterman Hill Place from flashing light on US 4. L D

RANDOLPH   pop. 1,974

THREE STALLION INN

(802)728-5575

Country Inn
$125-$195

Address: 665 Stock Farm Rd 05060 **Location:** I-89 exit 4 (SR 66), 2 mi w; jct SR 12, just e on SR 66, then just s. **Facility:** This all-season resort is close to town and convenient to the interstate, yet it's in an idyllic country setting. 14 units, some two bedrooms. 3 stories (no elevator), interior/exterior corridors. *Bath:* some shared. **Terms:** 15 day cancellation notice-fee imposed. **Pool(s):** outdoor. **Activities:** whirlpool, tennis court, cross country skiing, hiking trails, volleyball, exercise room. *Fee:* golf-18 holes, massage. **Free Special Amenities: expanded continental breakfast and local telephone calls.**

SAVE Y ⛵ 🛜 ✕ / SOME UNITS FEE 🐾 🖥

WHERE TO EAT

PATRICK'S PLACE

802/728-6062

American. Casual Dining. $8-$15 **AAA Inspector Notes:** The busy, popular restaurant serves home-style dishes made from the owner's own recipes. Food is prepared fresh daily in a casual, country atmosphere. Among favorites are Belgian waffles, muffins, cinnamon French toast and other freshly baked goodies. **Bar:** beer & wine. **Address:** 2 Merchants Row 05060 **Location:** I-89 exit 4 (SR 66), 3 mi w. L D

RANDOLPH VILLAGE PIZZA

802/728-9677

Pizza. Quick Serve. $4-$15 **AAA Inspector Notes:** The very simple, basic operation offers good food and self-service at the walk-up counter. **Address:** 1 S Main St 05060 **Location:** Center; just over railroad tracks. **Parking:** street only. L D

RICHMOND   (C-2) pop. 723, elev. 321'

THE ROUND CHURCH NATIONAL HISTORIC LANDMARK, I-89 exit 11, 2 mi. e. on US 2, then .5 mi. s. on Bridge St., is a 16-sided polygon built 1812-13 as a place of worship for five different denominations. The building was renovated in 1981 and is now used for events, concerts, weddings and public gatherings.

Hours: Daily 10-4, mid-June through Labor Day and during fall foliage season; Sat.-Sun. 10-4, Memorial Day to mid-June and day after Labor Day-Columbus Day. May be closed weekends for weddings. Phone ahead to confirm schedule. **Cost:** Donations. **Phone:** (802) 434-3654, or (802) 434-2556 for guided tour information.

RECREATIONAL ACTIVITIES

Skiing

- **Cochran's Ski Area** is on Cochran Rd. 1 mi. s.e. of The Round Church National Historic Landmark. **Hours:** Tues. and Thurs.-Fri. 2:30-5, Sat.-Sun. and holidays 9-4, mid-Dec. to late Mar. (weather permitting). **Phone:** (802) 434-2479 to verify schedule.

RIPTON

THE CHIPMAN INN

(802)388-2390

Historic Bed & Breakfast $125-$240 **Address:** 1233 Rt 125 05766 **Location:** Jct US 7, 4.4 mi e on SR 125. **Facility:** In a quiet area, the inn is relaxing and features nice common areas and individually decorated rooms. 8 units. 2 stories (no elevator), interior corridors. **Terms:** age restrictions may apply, 7 day cancellation notice. Y 🛜 ✕ 🅦 🆉 / SOME UNITS 🅚

ROCKINGHAM   (F-3) elev. 357'

THE OLD ROCKINGHAM MEETING HOUSE is on SR 103 at 11 Meeting House Rd., 3 mi. n.w. of jct. I-91 and SR 103. The oldest public building in original condition in Vermont, this 1787-1801 structure has been preserved as an example of Georgian architecture complete with original box pews and ornate woodwork. The adjoining graveyard contains early slate headstones and two crypts. Views from this hilltop site are excellent. **Time:** Allow 30 minutes minimum. **Hours:** Daily 10-4, Memorial Day-Columbus Day. **Cost:** Free. **Phone:** (802) 463-3964.

ROYALTON

EATON'S SUGARHOUSE RESTAURANT & COUNTRY STORE

802/763-8809

American. Family Dining. $4-$10 **AAA Inspector Notes:** Satisfying customers since 1963, the restaurant is more than just a great place to eat breakfast. Guests can experience the Vermont tradition of maple-syrup making--watching as maple sap is boiled to create delicious maple-sugar candy and maple cream--or browse the antiques and collectibles on the front porch. **Address:** Jct SR 14 & 107 05068 **Location:** I-89 exit 3 (SR 107). B L

RUTLAND (E-2) pop. 16,495, elev. 562'

The immense quarrying and finishing industries in Rutland are responsible for the community's reputation as the "Marble City." An industrial center in the Otter Creek Valley, Rutland is protected by the Taconic Mountains to the west and three striking Green Mountain peaks—Killington, Pico and Shrewsbury—to the east. It is the closest city to Killington (see place listing p. 286) and functions as a base for visits to the Green Mountain National Forest (see place listing p. 284).

The state's oldest continuously published newspaper, the Rutland Herald, was founded in 1794. Rutland also was the birthplace of John Deere, a journeyman blacksmith who developed the first commercially successful, self-scouring steel plow and began a plow-building business that became today's well-known manufacturer of agricultural machinery and equipment.

The Chaffee Art Center, 16 S. Main St., occupies an elegant Victorian-era mansion and offers eight galleries displaying works by Vermont artists; phone (802) 775-0356.

Rutland Region Chamber of Commerce: 50 Merchants Row, Rutland, VT 05701. **Phone:** (802) 773-2747 or (800) 756-8880.

NORMAN ROCKWELL MUSEUM OF VERMONT,
2 mi. e. of jct. US 7 at 654 US 4E, contains more than 2,500 published works, including illustrations for children's books, advertisements and covers for The Saturday Evening Post, Literary Digest, Life, Country Gentleman and other magazines.

Time: Allow 1 hour minimum. **Hours:** Daily 9-5, June-Dec.; 9-4, rest of year. Closed Jan. 1, Easter, Thanksgiving and Christmas. **Cost:** $6.50; $6 (ages 62+); $2.50 (ages 8-17). **Phone:** (802) 773-6095 or (877) 773-6095.

BEST WESTERN PLUS INN & SUITES RUTLAND/ KILLINGTON
(802)773-3200

Hotel $89-$209

AAA Benefit: Members save 10% or more with Best Western.

Address: 5 Best Western Pl 05701 **Location:** Jct US 7, 2.6 mi e on US 4. **Facility:** 112 units, some kitchens. 2 stories (no elevator), exterior corridors. **Parking:** winter plug-ins. **Terms:** check-in 4 pm. **Amenities:** video games (fee). **Pool(s):** heated outdoor. **Activities:** 2 tennis courts, playground, basketball, game room, volleyball, bank. **Guest Services:** valet and coin laundry. **Free Special Amenities:** expanded continental breakfast and high-speed Internet.

COMFORT INN AT TROLLEY SQUARE
802/775-2200

Hotel. Rates not provided. **Address:** 19 Allen St 05701 **Location:** On US 7, 1 mi s from jct US 4 W; 1.5 mi n from US 4 E. **Facility:** 104 units. 3 stories, interior corridors. **Parking:** winter plug-ins. **Pool(s):** heated indoor. **Activities:** whirlpool. **Guest Services:** valet laundry.

HAMPTON INN RUTLAND/KILLINGTON
802/773-9066

Hotel. Rates not provided. **Address:** 47 Farrell Rd 05701 **Location:** 2.4 mi s on US 7 from US 4 W; 0.4 mi n on US 7 from US 4 E. **Facility:** 88 units. 3 stories, interior corridors. **Terms:** check-in 4 pm. **Amenities:** video games (fee), high-speed Internet. **Pool(s):** heated indoor. **Activities:** exercise room. **Guest Services:** valet and coin laundry.

AAA Benefit: Members save up to 10%!

HOLIDAY INN RUTLAND/KILLINGTON
(802)775-1911

Hotel $99-$249 **Address:** 476 Holiday Dr 05701 **Location:** 2.4 mi s on US 7 from US 4 W; 0.4 mi n on US 7 from US 4 E. Located in a commercial area. **Facility:** 151 units. 2 stories (no elevator), interior corridors. **Parking:** winter plug-ins. **Pool(s):** heated indoor. **Activities:** sauna, whirlpools, exercise room. Fee: game room. **Guest Services:** valet and coin laundry, area transportation-mall, bus & train stations.

RED ROOF INN RUTLAND-KILLINGTON
(802)775-4303

Hotel $60-$250

Address: 401 US Hwy 7 S 05701 **Location:** 0.8 mi s on US 7 and 4. **Facility:** 101 units. 2 stories (no elevator), interior corridors. **Parking:** winter plug-ins. **Amenities:** video games (fee). **Pool(s):** heated indoor. **Activities:** sauna. Fee: game room. **Guest Services:** coin laundry.

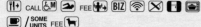

THE COUNTRYMAN'S PLEASURE RESTAURANT
802/773-7141

Continental. Fine Dining. $17-$33 **AAA Inspector Notes:** Historic. The charming, 19th-century, farmhouse-style restaurant specializes in a nice selection of Austrian-German-American dishes. Preparations of seafood, venison, duck, veal, vegetarian fare and sauerbraten go well with a good selection of German wines and beers. Desserts are excellent. **Bar:** full bar. **Reservations:** suggested. **Address:** 63 Town Line Rd 05701 **Location:** Jct US 7, 2.5 mi e on US 4, just s. D

KELVANS
802/775-1550

American. Casual Dining. $8-$19 **AAA Inspector Notes:** The lively downtown Kelvans features an-ever changing menu of diverse items. Grab a seat outdoors when the weather is nice. **Bar:** full bar. **Address:** 128 Merchants Row 05701 **Location:** Downtown; across from shopping center. L D

LITTLE HARRY'S
802/747-4848

International. Casual Dining. $16-$24 **AAA Inspector Notes:** This eatery is a funky and fun, yet intimate, atmosphere offering guests good food and casual service. The spicy cornbread is delicious. **Bar:** full bar. **Address:** 121 West St 05701 **Location:** Center of downtown. **Parking:** street only. D

NINETY NINE RESTAURANT
802/775-9288

American. Casual Dining. $9-$16 **AAA Inspector Notes:** This popular pub is committed to serving large portions of great food at reasonable prices. Guest favorites include hot wings, burgers, seafood, barbecue ribs and chicken. While reservations are not taken, call-ahead seating is offered. A children's menu is also available. **Bar:** full bar. **Address:** 315 S Main St 05701 **Location:** Jct US 7 and 4 W, 1.7 mi w; jct US 7 and 4 E, 1.1 mi n. L D CALL

SAL'S ITALIAN RESTAURANT
802/775-3360

Italian. Casual Dining. $8-$22 **AAA Inspector Notes:** This coordinated, Italian-themed restaurant offers simple fare and casual service. **Bar:** beer & wine. **Address:** 148 West St 05701 **Location:** Downtown. **Parking:** street only. D

SOUTH STATION 802/775-1736

◆◆ American. Casual Dining. $8-$19 **AAA Inspector Notes:** South Station features a salad bar with 35 offerings and a potato salad that is worth writing home about. Steaks, seafood and Italian foods. The extensive casual bar offers a dine-in option. **Bar:** full bar. **Reservations:** suggested. **Address:** 170 S Main St 05701 **Location:** 0.8 mi s on US 7; in Trolley Barn Center. [L] [D]

THREE TOMATOES TRATTORIA 802/747-7747

◆◆ Italian. Casual Dining. $11-$20 **AAA Inspector Notes:** Traditional Italian-American entrées and pasta are served in this modern spot, which has an open chrome kitchen in the rear. This place is a local favorite for Italian wines, which are served in Tuscan ceramic chicken carafes. **Bar:** full bar. **Address:** 88 Merchants Row 05701 **Location:** Center. **Parking:** street only. [D] CALL [&M]

TOKYO HOUSE 802/786-8080

◆◆ Japanese. Casual Dining. $7-$29 **AAA Inspector Notes:** All your favorites, including sushi, are available at this casual Japanese restaurant. **Bar:** beer & wine. **Address:** 106 West St 05701 **Location:** In Grand Theatre Building. **Parking:** street only. [L] [D]

THE YELLOW DELI 802/775-9800

◆ Deli. Casual Dining. $5-$15 **AAA Inspector Notes:** The health-conscious spot is decorated to resemble a forest, with a tangle of branches overhead, plank tables and log benches. Fresh soups, salads and wrap sandwiches are favorites, but many patrons stop in just for such desserts as maple cream cookies and such teas as maté, an alternative to coffee. **Address:** 23 Center St 05701 **Location:** Just n of Merchants Row; downtown. **Parking:** street only. [L] [D]

ST. ALBANS (B-2) pop. 6,918, elev. 383'

Nestled between Lake Champlain and the Green Mountains, the town once described by Henry Ward Beecher as "a place in the midst of a greater variety of scenic beauty than any other I can remember in America" had anything but a placid history to match its serene setting. St. Albans was a notorious center for smuggling operations on Lake Champlain in the early 1800s and was an important link on the Underground Railroad.

Its rowdy days left behind, St. Albans is headquarters for the New England Central Railway, a production and distribution center for dairy products and a manufacturing center of such products as maple sugar, sugar-making equipment, medical technology equipment, batteries and ice cream.

Franklin County Regional Chamber of Commerce: 2 N. Main St., Suite 101, St. Albans, VT 05478. **Phone:** (802) 524-2444.

ST. ALBANS HISTORICAL MUSEUM, 9 Church St., is in a renovated 1861 three-story brick schoolhouse. The museum exhibits quilts, clothing, china, glass, dolls, maps, photographs, Revolutionary and Civil War relics, and information about the St. Albans Raid of 1864. Other collections feature railroad memorabilia, children's toys and medical antiques. An interactive, narrated diorama depicts the history of St. Albans and the Lake Champlain region.

Time: Allow 1 hour minimum. **Hours:** Tues.-Fri. 1-4, Sat. 10-2, June 1-early Oct.; by appointment rest of year. **Cost:** $5; $3 (ages 12-16); $12 (family). **Phone:** (802) 527-7933.

ECONO LODGE 802/524-5956

◆◆ Motel. Rates not provided. **Address:** 287 S Main St (US 7) 05478 **Location:** I-89 exit 19, 1 mi w on Interstate Access Rd, then 0.5 mi s. **Facility:** 29 units. 1-2 stories (no elevator), interior/exterior corridors.

[SAVE] 🛜 🍴 🍽 / SOME UNITS FEE 🐾 🖥

LA QUINTA INN & SUITES ST. ALBANS (802)524-3300

◆◆ Hotel. $99-$232 **Address:** 813 Fairfax Rd 05478 **Location:** I-89 exit 19, just w on Interstate Access Rd, then just s. **Facility:** 81 units. 3 stories, interior corridors. **Parking:** winter plug-ins. **Pool(s):** heated indoor. **Activities:** limited exercise equipment. *Fee:* game room. **Guest Services:** coin laundry.

CALL [&M] 🏊 [BIZ] 🛜 🍴 🖥 / SOME UNITS 🐾 🖥

━━━ WHERE TO EAT ━━━

JEFF'S MAINE SEAFOOD 802/524-6135

◆◆ Seafood. Casual Dining. $6-$26 **AAA Inspector Notes:** This easily accessible, downtown full-service restaurant also offers options other than seafood which include chicken and prime rib. An excellent selection of boutique Vermont cheese is available in the café or for sale by the pound in the wine shop. **Bar:** full bar. **Reservations:** suggested. **Address:** 65 N Main St (US 7) 05478 **Location:** On US 7; corner of Bank St; center. **Parking:** street only. [L] [D]

ST. JOHNSBURY (C-4) pop. 6,193, elev. 556'
• Hotels p. 306 • Restaurants p. 306

The converging valleys of the Moose, Passumpsic and Sleeper's rivers create a striking range of elevations upon which St. Johnsbury grew. The town was named after the French consul in New York, Saint Jean de Crèvecoeur, a friend of Ethan Allen and author of "Letters of an American Farmer." Crèvecoeur suggested the addition of "bury" to the town's name to distinguish it from the many towns named St. John.

Much of St. Johnsbury's history and growth centered on Thaddeus Fairbanks' invention of the platform scale in 1830 and George Cary's idea of flavoring plug tobacco with maple sugar. The town prospered with the success of the Fairbanks Scale and maple-sugar industries, still major contributors to the local economy. It is the industrial, retail and cultural center of the part of Vermont known as the Northeast Kingdom.

Northeast Kingdom Chamber of Commerce: 2000 Memorial Dr., Suite 11, St. Johnsbury, VT 05819. **Phone:** (802) 748-3678 or (800) 639-6379.

FAIRBANKS MUSEUM AND PLANETARIUM, 1302 Main St., houses a large collection that includes more than 170,000 mounted birds and mammals, art and antiques, and village and crafts tools. The museum also is home to the Northern New England Weather Center and Vermont's only public planetarium. The 1891 building was designed by noted architect Lambert Packard to house the collections of Franklin Fairbanks, nephew of Thaddeus Fairbanks, the inventor of the platform scale.

Time: Allow 1 hour, 30 minutes minimum. **Hours:** Tues.-Sat. 9-5 (also Mon. 9-5, Apr.-Oct.), Sun. 1-5. Planetarium shows Sat.-Sun. at 1:30 (also Mon.-Fri. at 11, July-Aug.). Closed Jan. 1, Easter, July 4,

Thanksgiving and Christmas. **Cost:** Museum $8; $6 (ages 5-17 and 62+); $20 (family, two adults and all minor children). Planetarium $5. **Phone:** (802) 748-2372.

MAPLE GROVE FARMS SUGAR HOUSE MUSEUM is 1 mi. e. on US 2. The museum has exhibits about maple syrup and the process of boiling down maple sap. A videotape presentation illustrates the sugaring process. **Time:** Allow 1 hour minimum. **Hours:** Daily 9-5, July 4-Dec. 31; Mon.-Fri. 9-5, Mar. 1-July 3. Closed major holidays. **Cost:** Free. **Phone:** (802) 748-5141, ext. 4 or (800) 525-2540, ext. 4.

ST. JOHNSBURY ATHENAEUM, 1171 Main St., is a public library and art gallery containing 19th-century landscape paintings from the Hudson River School. The collection includes Albert Bierstadt's monumental "The Domes of the Yosemite." The National Historic Landmark, donated to the town by Horace Fairbanks in 1871, has Victorian reading rooms showcasing elaborate woodwork and spiral staircases.

   Time: Allow 30 minutes minimum. **Hours:** Mon.-Fri. 10-5:30, Sat. 10-4. Closed major holidays. **Cost:** Art gallery admission $8; free (ages 0-17). **Phone:** (802) 748-8291.

COMFORT INN & SUITES NEAR BURKE MOUNTAIN
(802)748-1500
▼▼▼ **Hotel** $139-$249 **Address:** 703 US RT 5 S 05819 **Location:** I-91 exit 20, just sw. **Facility:** 107 units. 4 stories, interior corridors. **Parking:** winter plug-ins. **Terms:** cancellation fee imposed. **Amenities:** video games (fee), high-speed Internet. **Pool(s):** heated indoor. **Activities:** sauna, whirlpool, snowmobiling, exercise room. *Fee:* game room. **Guest Services:** valet and coin laundry.
ECO CALL ✦M ⊇ BIZ ⊚ ✕ ✈ 🛏 🖥 🖵

FAIRBANKS INN
802/748-5666
▼▼ **Motel.** Rates not provided. **Address:** 401 Western Ave 05819 **Location:** I-91 exit 21, 0.8 mi e on US 2. **Facility:** 46 units, some efficiencies. 3 stories (no elevator), exterior corridors. **Pool(s):** heated outdoor.
⊇ ✦ BIZ ⊚ ✕ 🛏 🖥 / SOME UNITS FEE 🛏

HOLIDAY MOTEL
(802)748-8192
▼▼ **Motel** $59-$159 **Address:** 222 Hastings St 05819 **Location:** Jct US 5 and Alternate Rt US 5. **Facility:** 32 units. 1 story, exterior corridors. **Terms:** cancellation fee imposed. **Pool(s):** heated outdoor. ✦ ⊇ BIZ ⊚ 🛏 / SOME UNITS 🖥

WHERE TO EAT

ANTHONY'S DINER
802/748-3613
▼▼ American. Casual Dining. $4-$20 **AAA Inspector Notes:** Located downtown, the diner offers homemade wholesome meals. Daily specials and homemade desserts are featured at this eatery. **Bar:** beer & wine. **Address:** 321 Railroad St 05819 **Location:** I-91 exit 20, just n on US 5. B L D

KHAM'S THAI CUISINE
802/751-8424
▼▼ Thai. Casual Dining. $8-$16 **AAA Inspector Notes:** Delicious traditional Thai dishes are served in a cozy atmosphere. A take-out menu is available. **Bar:** beer & wine. **Address:** 1112 Memorial Dr 05819 **Location:** I-91 exit 20, 3.5 mi n on US 5.
L D CALL ✦M

SHAFTSBURY

HILLBROOK MOTEL
802/447-7201
▼▼ ▼ **Motel.** Rates not provided. **Address:** 2629 Rt 7A 05262 **Location:** SR 7 exit 2, 2 mi n. **Facility:** 16 units, some kitchens. 1 story, exterior corridors. **Terms:** check-in 4 pm. **Pool(s):** outdoor. **Activities:** horseshoes.
⊇ ⊚ ✕ 🛏 🖥 / SOME UNITS FEE 🐾 🖵

SERENITY MOTEL
802/442-6490
▼ **Cottage** $70-$90 **Address:** 4379 Rt 7A 05262 **Location:** Jct SR 67, 3.3 mi n on Historic SR 7A. **Facility:** 8 cottages. 1 story, exterior corridors. *Bath:* shower only. **Terms:** closed 10/29-5/9.
⊚ ✕ 🛏 🖥 🖵 / SOME UNITS 🐾

SHARON (D-3) elev. 500'

   In the White River Valley and bordered by mountains on three sides, Sharon is the birthplace of Joseph Smith, founder of the Mormon faith. Born in 1805, Smith lived in the area until he was 11, when his family moved to New York.

JOSEPH SMITH BIRTHPLACE MEMORIAL is 4 mi. n. on SR 14, 1.8 mi. n.e. on Dairy Hill Rd., then .3 mi. e. on LDS Ln. A solid, 38.5-foot granite monument, surrounded by landscaped grounds, hiking trails and a picnic area, marks the site of the Mormon prophet's birth. In the visitor center are pictures, paintings and a theater. Christmas decorations feature more than 150,000 lights and can be seen the night after Thanksgiving through Jan. 1.

   Hours: Tours are given Mon.-Sat. 9-7, Sun. 1:30-7, May-Oct.; Mon.-Sat. 9-5, Sun. 1:30-5, rest of year. **Cost:** Free. **Phone:** (802) 763-7742.

SHELBURNE (C-1) pop. 592, elev. 159'

   Shelburne, with the Adirondack Mountains to the west and the Green Mountains to the east, was settled in 1763 by two German lumbermen and later named for an English earl. Many downtown shops occupy renovated farm buildings dating from the 1800s.

SHELBURNE FARMS, 1.5 mi. w. of US 7 at jct. Bay and Harbor rds., is a 1,400-acre working dairy farm. At the welcome center a 15-minute slide show chronicles the evolution of the property from an agricultural estate into an environmental, non-profit organization dedicated to environmental education. Their award-winning Farmhouse Cheddar cheese is available for sampling and purchase.

   The property has 8 miles of walking trails. Visitors also can explore the Farm Barn and Children's Farmyard, where they can see farm animals, participate in scheduled daily farm chores or watch Farmhouse Cheddar being made from the milk of Brown Swiss cows.

   Pets on leash are permitted November through March only. **Time:** Allow 2 hours minimum. **Hours:** Daily 9-5:30, mid-May to mid-Oct.; 10-5, rest of year. Guided 90-minute tours are available every 2 hours. Closed Thanksgiving and Christmas. **Cost:** $8; $6 (ages 62+); $5 (ages 3-17). Guided property tours (includes admission fee) $11; $9 (ages 62+); $7 (ages 3-17). **Phone:** (802) 985-8686. 🍴

SHELBURNE MUSEUM, on US 7, consists of several galleries and 25 historic structures. Spread over 45 acres, the buildings house diverse collections of fine and folk art and artifacts depicting early New England life. Among the structures are a horseshoe barn, jail, country store, schoolhouse, smithy, meetinghouse, stagecoach inn, lighthouse, hunting lodge, apothecary and furnished houses representing 4 centuries.

Attractions include a railroad depot, a private rail car and locomotive, a two-lane covered bridge, a round barn, a hand-crafted model circus parade more than 500 feet long and the side-wheeler *Ticonderoga*.

Displays of Americana feature a sizable group of wooden cigar-store figures; fine, folk and decorative art; tools; and coaches, carriages and wagons. The Electra Havemeyer Webb Memorial houses European furnishings, sculpture and paintings by Jean Baptiste Corot, Gustave Courbet, Edgar Degas, Edouard Manet and Claude Monet, as well as works by American artist Mary Cassatt.

The Webb Gallery of American Art contains works by Albert Bierstadt, John Copley, Winslow Homer, Fitz Hugh Lane, Grandma Moses, William Prior, Andrew Wyeth and other 18th-, 19th- and 20th-century artists. Formal gardens, ornamental trees and shrubs, and seasonal roses and lilacs adorn the grounds.

Time: Allow 4 hours minimum. **Hours:** Daily 10-5 (also Wed. 5-7, July-Aug.), mid-May to late Oct.; Tues.-Sun. and Mon. holidays 10-5, rest of year. Closed most major holidays. **Cost:** $20; $10 (ages 5-18 and students with ID); $50 (family, two adults and minor children). **Phone:** (802) 985-3346. 🍴 🛏

VERMONT TEDDY BEAR CO., 1 mi. s. of Shelburne Village at 6655 Shelburne Rd. (US 7), offers a glimpse of the step-by-step creative process required to hand craft these jointed teddy bears. Visitors may create personalized bears in the BearShop.

Hours: Guided 30-minute tours depart daily 10-4. Closed Jan. 1, Easter, Thanksgiving and Christmas. Phone ahead to confirm schedule. **Cost:** Tours $3; free (ages 0-12). A fee is charged for making a teddy bear. **Phone:** (802) 985-3001 or (800) 829-2327.

VERMONT WILDFLOWER FARM—see Charlotte p. 282.

QUALITY INN   (802)985-8037

▼▼▼▼ ▼▼▼▼
Motel
$90-$200

Address: 2572 Shelburne Rd 05482 **Location:** I-89 exit 13 (I-189/US 7), 2.1 mi s. **Facility:** 73 units. 2-3 stories (no elevator), interior/exterior corridors. **Parking:** winter plug-ins. **Terms:** check-in 4 pm, cancellation fee imposed. **Pool(s):** heated indoor. **Activities:** sauna, whirlpool, exercise room. **Guest Services:** valet and coin laundry.

SAVE 🆓 🛅 BIZ 🛜 🅱 🖥 📺 / SOME UNITS FEE

T-BIRD MOTOR INN   (802)985-3663

▼▼▼ ▼▼▼
Motel
$78-$248

Address: 4405 Shelburne Rd 05482 **Location:** I-89 exit 13 (I-189/US 7), 4 mi s. **Facility:** 24 units. 1 story, exterior corridors. **Terms:** closed 10/20-5/11, 7 day cancellation notice-fee imposed. **Amenities:** high-speed Internet. **Pool(s):** outdoor. **Free Special Amenities:** continental breakfast and preferred room (subject to availability with advance reservations).

SAVE 🆓 🛅 🛜 ✖ / SOME UNITS 🅱

WHERE TO EAT

CAFE SHELBURNE   802/985-3939

▼▼▼ French. Fine Dining. $19-$29 **AAA Inspector Notes:** This intimate dining room gives patrons a hint of the delights that await. Owner/chef Patrick Grangien prepares classic French cuisine to perfection. Dishes are as much a delight to the eye as to the palate. **Bar:** full bar. **Reservations:** suggested. **Address:** 5573 US 7 05482 **Location:** On US 7; opposite Shelburne Museum.
Ⓓ

CHEF LEU'S HOUSE   802/985-5258

▼▼ Chinese. Casual Dining. $6-$16 **AAA Inspector Notes:** A large selection of Szechuan, Hunan, Mandarin and Vietnamese specialties are prepared in moo shu, kung pao, yu hsiang and chang liu styles. Buddha's delight, as well as the house special egg roll with Vietnamese sauce, are sure to please the vegetarian. Beautifully embroidered silk murals accent simple decor with oil cloth lampshades suspended from the ceiling. Three rooms offer various degrees of intimate dining. **Bar:** full bar. **Address:** 3761 Shelburne Rd 05482 **Location:** I-89 exit 13 (I-189/US 7), 3 mi s. Ⓛ Ⓓ

THE INN AT SHELBURNE FARMS   802/985-8498

▼▼▼ American. Fine Dining. $21-$35 **AAA Inspector Notes:** *Historic.* At this inn, guests can dine in a stately 1886 Vanderbilt mansion with dramatic views of Lake Champlain and New York's Adirondack Mountains beyond. Marble-tiled floors, fabric-covered walls and candlelight illumination set an elegant mood. The food is locally grown, much of it raised on this very farm using environmentally-friendly agriculture methods. As only the freshest local produce is used, the menu changes daily. **Bar:** full bar. **Reservations:** required. **Address:** 1611 Harbor Rd 05482 **Location:** 3.6 mi w of US 7; at Shelburne Farms. Ⓑ Ⓓ 🅰🅲

SHOREHAM (D-1) elev. 333'

Fourteen years after Shoreham's 1761 founding, Ethan Allen and his troops, including volunteer Benedict Arnold, captured Fort Ticonderoga from the British. The town is the birthplace of Levi Morton, vice president to Benjamin Harrison.

The Ticonderoga Ferry provides 7-minute Lake Champlain crossings to Ticonderoga, N.Y., from mid-June to late October; phone (802) 897-7999.

MV *CARILLON*, departing from Larrabees Point on SR 74W, provides a cruise along unspoiled southern Lake Champlain with a historical narrative about Revolutionary War sites. By appointment only and depending on water levels, the boat will dock at Mount Independence State Historic Site *(see attraction listing p. 300),* allowing an opportunity to explore the fortification remains, hike one of the walking trails and stop at the site's visitor center.

Time: Allow 1 hour, 30 minutes minimum. **Hours:** Cruises depart Shoreham Thurs.-Sun. at 1, July-Aug. (also Thurs.-Sun. at 1, mid-Sept. to mid-Oct. during fall foliage season). Schedule varies rest of year. Phone ahead to confirm schedule. **Cost:** $14; $10 (ages 0-11). **Phone:** (802) 897-5331.

SOUTH BURLINGTON pop. 17,904

BEST WESTERN PLUS WINDJAMMER INN & CONFERENCE CENTER (802)863-1125

Hotel
$115-$195

AAA Benefit: Members save 10% or more with Best Western.

Address: 1076 Williston Rd 05403 **Location:** I-89 exit 14E, 0.3 mi e on US 2. **Facility:** 158 units. 2 stories, interior corridors. **Parking:** winter plug-ins. **Terms:** 2 night minimum stay - seasonal and/or weekends, cancellation fee imposed. **Amenities:** video games (fee). *Some:* high-speed Internet. **Dining:** Windjammer, see separate listing. **Pool(s):** outdoor, heated indoor. **Activities:** whirlpool, exercise room. **Guest Services:** valet and coin laundry, area transportation-hospital. **Free Special Amenities: expanded continental breakfast and local telephone calls.**

SAVE ECO [symbols] CALL [symbols] BIZ [symbols]
[symbols] / SOME UNITS FEE [symbols]

COMFORT SUITES (802)860-1112

[symbols] **Hotel** $80-$259 **Address:** 1712 Shelburne Rd 05403 **Location:** I-89 exit 13 (I-189/US 7), w to US 7, then 1.5 mi s. **Facility:** 84 units, some efficiencies. 3 stories, interior corridors. **Parking:** winter plug-ins. **Terms:** cancellation fee imposed. **Amenities:** high-speed Internet. **Activities:** exercise room. **Guest Services:** valet and coin laundry.

[symbols] CALL [symbols] BIZ [symbols] / SOME UNITS [symbols]

DOUBLETREE BY HILTON HOTEL BURLINGTON (802)658-0250

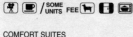

Hotel
$129-$299

DOUBLETREE

AAA Benefit: Members save 5% or more!

Address: 1117 Williston Rd 05403 **Location:** I-89 exit 14E, just e on US 2. **Facility:** 161 units. 2 stories, interior corridors. **Parking:** winter plug-ins, cancellation fee imposed. **Amenities:** video games (fee). *Some:* high-speed Internet. **Pool(s):** heated indoor. **Activities:** whirlpool, exercise room. **Guest Services:** valet laundry. **Free Special Amenities: high-speed Internet and airport transportation.** *(See ad p. 280.)*

SAVE ECO [symbols] CALL [symbols] BIZ [symbols]
[symbols] / SOME UNITS FEE [symbols]

GREEN MOUNTAIN SUITES HOTEL (802)860-1212

[symbols] **Extended Stay Hotel** $149-$489 **Address:** 401 Dorset St 05403 **Location:** I-89 exit 14E, just e on US 2, then 0.8 mi s. **Facility:** 104 units, some two bedrooms, efficiencies and kitchens. 3 stories, interior corridors. **Terms:** 3 day cancellation notice-fee imposed. **Pool(s):** heated indoor. **Activities:** whirlpool, exercise room. **Guest Services:** valet and coin laundry, area transportation-hospital.

ECO [symbols] CALL [symbols] BIZ [symbols]
[symbols] / SOME UNITS FEE [symbols]

HOLIDAY INN BURLINGTON (802)863-6363

[symbols]

Hotel
$109-$329

Address: 1068 Williston Rd 05403 **Location:** I-89 exit 14E, just e on US 2. **Facility:** 173 units. 4 stories, interior corridors. **Parking:** winter plug-ins. **Amenities:** high-speed Internet. **Pool(s):** heated outdoor, heated indoor. **Activities:** sauna, exercise room. **Guest Services:** valet and coin laundry. **Free Special Amenities: high-speed Internet and airport transportation.**

SAVE [symbols] CALL [symbols] BIZ [symbols]
[symbols] / SOME UNITS [symbols]

HOLIDAY INN EXPRESS (802)860-6000

[symbols] **Hotel. Rates not provided. Address:** 1720 Shelburne Rd 05403 **Location:** I-89 exit 13 (I-189/US 7) to US 7, 1.5 mi s. **Facility:** 121 units. 4-5 stories, interior corridors. **Parking:** winter plug-ins. **Pool(s):** heated indoor. **Activities:** saunas, whirlpool, exercise room. **Guest Services:** valet and coin laundry.

[symbols] BIZ [symbols] / SOME UNITS [symbols]

LA QUINTA INN & SUITES SOUTH BURLINGTON (802)865-3400

[symbols] **Hotel** $90-$239 **Address:** 1285 Williston Rd 05403 **Location:** I-89 exit 14E, 0.5 mi e on US 2. **Facility:** 104 units, some efficiencies. 3 stories, interior corridors. **Parking:** winter plug-ins. **Pool(s):** heated outdoor. **Activities:** limited exercise equipment. **Guest Services:** valet and coin laundry.

[symbols] CALL [symbols] BIZ [symbols]
/ SOME UNITS [symbols]

SHERATON BURLINGTON HOTEL & CONFERENCE CENTER (802)865-6600

[symbols]

Hotel
$129-$329

Sheraton
HOTELS & RESORTS

AAA Benefit: Members get up to 20% off, plus Starwood Preferred Guest® bonuses.

Address: 870 Williston Rd 05403 **Location:** I-89 exit 14W, just w on US 2. **Facility:** 309 units, some efficiencies. 2-4 stories, interior corridors. **Parking:** winter plug-ins. **Terms:** cancellation fee imposed. **Amenities:** video games (fee). *Some:* high-speed Internet (fee). **Pool(s):** heated indoor. **Activities:** exercise room. **Guest Services:** valet laundry, area transportation-within 2 mi & hospital. **Free Special Amenities: airport transportation.**

SAVE ECO [symbols] BIZ [symbols]
[symbols] / SOME UNITS [symbols] FEE [symbols] FEE [symbols]

SMART SUITES (802)860-9900

[symbols] **Extended Stay Hotel** $99-$199 **Address:** 1700 Shelburne Rd 05403 **Location:** I-89 exit 13 (I-189/US 7) to US 7, 1.5 mi s. **Facility:** 81 units, some two bedrooms, efficiencies and kitchens. 3-4 stories, interior corridors. **Parking:** winter plug-ins. **Amenities:** high-speed Internet. **Activities:** exercise room. **Guest Services:** valet and coin laundry.

[symbols] BIZ [symbols] / SOME UNITS FEE [symbols]

SMART SUITES ON THE HILL (802)860-1986

[symbols] **Hotel. Rates not provided. Address:** 1702 Shelburne Rd 05403 **Location:** I-89 exit 13 (I-189/US 7) to US 7, 1.5 mi s. **Facility:** 74 units, some two bedrooms, efficiencies and kitchens. 4 stories, interior corridors. **Parking:** winter plug-ins. **Amenities:** high-speed Internet. **Activities:** limited exercise equipment. **Guest Services:** valet and coin laundry. [symbols]

WHERE TO EAT

AL'S FRENCH FRYS (802)863-6511

[symbols] American. Family Dining. $2-$6 **AAA Inspector Notes:** Selected by Yankee Magazine's Travel Guide to New England as "one of the outstanding reasons to visit New England," the restaurant is known for its great French fries. Long, yet quickly moving, lines are worth the wait for Al's chili dogs, burgers, fries and other old-time favorites. The atmosphere evokes the feel of a '50s-style malt shop. This place has been a Vermont landmark since 1948. **Address:** 1251 Williston Rd 05403 **Location:** I-89 exit 14E, 0.5 mi e.

L D [symbols]

LAKE VIEW HOUSE RESTAURANT (802)865-3900

[symbols] American. Casual Dining. $6-$25 **AAA Inspector Notes:** The casual eatery occupies a restored Victorian mansion built in the mid-1800s on land that was originally part of the Lake View Farm. Away from the hustle and bustle of the city, this place is a welcoming respite for travelers. On the menu are traditional chicken, fish, pasta and beef dishes. **Bar:** full bar. **Address:** 1710 Shelburne Rd 05403 **Location:** I-89 exit 13 (I-189/US 7), 1.5 mi s on US 7.

L D

PAULINE'S CAFE
802/862-1081

New American. Casual Dining. $8-$30 **AAA Inspector Notes:** The restaurant has come a long way from the early days when it operated as a truck stop serving up comfort food. The establishment features innovative, nouvelle, regional cuisine. Diners can choose seating in either the casual ground-floor dining room, the more intimate upstairs dining room or the enclosed seasonal patio. **Bar:** full bar. **Reservations:** suggested. **Address:** 1834 Shelburne Rd 05403 **Location:** I-89 exit 13 (I-189/US 7), 2 mi s.

L D

WINDJAMMER
802/862-6585

American. Casual Dining. $8-$39 **AAA Inspector Notes:** This spot offers specialties of fresh seafood from New England ports and flavorful prime rib. Nightly specials, a salad bar with 40 choices and local seasonal produce, a popular pub menu and pleasant service also are offered. **Bar:** full bar. **Reservations:** suggested, for dinner & weekends. **Address:** 1076 Williston Rd 05403 **Location:** I-89 exit 14E, 0.3 mi e on US 2; in BEST WESTERN PLUS Windjammer Inn & Conference Center. L D

SOUTH WOODSTOCK

KEDRON VALLEY INN
(802)457-1473

Historic Country Inn $149-$329 **Address:** 4778 South Rd 05071 **Location:** Jct US 4, 5 mi s. **Facility:** Minutes from historic Woodstock, this country inn features spacious, attractive grounds and a private beach. Many rooms offer a fireplace. The inn features many antiques and well-appointed rooms. 25 units, some two bedrooms and kitchens. 1-3 stories (no elevator), interior/exterior corridors. **Terms:** closed 3/16-4/18 & 11/3-11/19, check-in 3:30 pm, 2 night minimum stay - seasonal and/or weekends, 15 day cancellation notice-fee imposed. **Dining:** restaurant, see separate listing. **Activities:** limited beach access.

WHERE TO EAT

KEDRON VALLEY INN
802/457-1473

American. Fine Dining. $14-$28 **AAA Inspector Notes:** Off the beaten track in the scenic countryside, the picturesque inn is the site of the famous Anheuser-Busch commercial. The experience here is relaxing yet elegant. **Bar:** full bar. **Reservations:** suggested. **Address:** 4778 South Rd 05071 **Location:** Jct US 4, 5 mi s.

D

SPRINGFIELD (F-3) pop. 3,979

The Black River powered a variety of Springfield mills in the 18th and early 19th centuries. Though some mills still exist along the river, none uses waterpower.

Two state historic sites are nearby. The restored Eureka Schoolhouse is east of Springfield on SR 11. Begun in 1785 and completed 5 years later, this one-room schoolhouse is said to be the state's oldest and is one of Vermont's few remaining 18th-century public buildings. Today it houses an information center. Next to it stands the 37-foot-long Baltimore Covered Bridge, built in 1870. The bridge originally spanned Great Brook in North Springfield; it was moved to its present location in 1970.

D'oh! On a more current note, Springfield has declared itself "Home of the Simpsons" after being chosen as the fictional hometown of Homer, Marge, Bart, Lisa and Maggie from the animated television series "The Simpsons."

Springfield Regional Chamber of Commerce: 56 Main St., Springfield, VT 05156. **Phone:** (802) 885-2779.

HOLIDAY INN EXPRESS
802/885-4516

Hotel. Rates not provided. **Address:** 818 Charlestown Rd 05156 **Location:** I-91 exit 7. **Facility:** 88 units. 2 stories, interior corridors. **Amenities:** high-speed Internet. **Pool(s):** heated indoor. **Activities:** exercise room. **Fee:** game room. **Guest Services:** coin laundry.

CALL   BIZ 📶 ✕ 🛏 🖼 💻
/ SOME UNITS FEE 🐾

WHERE TO EAT

SHANGHAI GARDEN
802/885-5555

Chinese. Casual Dining. $5-$14 **AAA Inspector Notes:** This old-time yellow dining car is hard to miss. The restaurant provides a simple atmosphere with casual friendly service. **Address:** 129 Clinton St 05156 **Location:** I-91 exit 7, 3 mi w on SR 11.

L D

STOWE (B-3) pop. 495

- **Hotels p. 313** • **Restaurants p. 314**
- **Hotels & Restaurants map & index p. 311**

In the heart of the Green Mountains, Stowe is a year-round vacation destination offering fall foliage viewing and other outdoor pursuits. This historic, picture-perfect New England village, complete with a white-steepled church, is nestled beside 4,393-foot Mount Mansfield, Vermont's highest peak. The Von Trapps of "The Sound of Music" fame settled in Stowe in the 1940s; today family descendants operate an alpine lodge offering classical concerts and sing-alongs.

The area includes some of New England's best downhill ski runs. Cross-country skiing, snowshoeing, sleighing and ice-skating also are popular cold-weather endeavors. Once it warms up, visitors can indulge in hiking, rock climbing, golf, horseback riding and polo. Hikers, cyclists and skaters head to the Stowe Recreation Path *(see attraction listing),* starting in the town center behind the village church (parking areas provide access along the route). Area outfitters rent bikes and in-line skates. For more challenging terrain, hikers venture to nearby Smugglers Notch State Park *(see Recreation Areas Chart).*

Recreational activities aside, Stowe also presents a thriving cultural and arts scene. Visitors can enjoy musical, theatrical and dance performances as well as outdoor concerts by the Vermont Symphony Orchestra. Artists and craftspeople display their wares in the village's assorted shops and galleries—works include glass, pottery, jewelry, woodcarvings, painting, hand-dyed yarns, sculpture and photography.

During the summer months, Stowe Mountain Resort's gondola takes passengers on a 7,000-foot ride to a point just below Mount Mansfield's summit, where they can view sweeping panoramas of lush mountain valleys; phone (802) 253-3000 or (800) 253-4754.

(See map & index p. 311.)

On Sundays from mid-May to mid-October, the Stowe Farmers' Market is the place to shop for fresh produce, garden supplies, locally made products and other Vermont specialties; the market is next to the Red Barn shops on SR 108.

In addition to the area's brilliant foliage, a highlight of Stowe's fall season is the traditional harvest festival 📹 Oktoberfest. Don your lederhosen and dirndls and celebrate the 3-day event that is held, surprisingly enough, in late September. Oompah bands, German food and beers, a parade, pumpkin and face painting, music, dancing and crafts are part of the fun.

Stowe Area Association: 51 Main St., P.O. Box 1320, Stowe, VT 05672. **Phone:** (802) 253-7321 or (877) 467-8693.

THE HELEN DAY ART CENTER, 1 mi. s.e. on Mountain Rd. (SR 108), .1 mi. e. on Main St., then e. 1 blk. on School St. to 90 Pond St., is in an 1860 Greek Revival building. It presents changing exhibitions of the works of well-known local, national and international visual artists.

Time: Allow 30 minutes minimum. **Hours:** Wed.-Sun. noon-5. Closed major holidays. Phone ahead to confirm schedule. **Cost:** Donations. **Phone:** (802) 253-8358.

MOUNT MANSFIELD, n.w. of town, rises to 4,393 feet and is Vermont's highest peak. From the summit visibility averages 50 to 70 miles on clear days, affording views of parts of Vermont, New Hampshire, New York and Québec.

Stowe Auto Toll Road, entered from SR 108, 6 mi. n.w., is a 4.3-mile unpaved road traversing heavily forested slopes to about the 3,600-foot level; several hiking trails ranging from moderate to difficult continue to the summit areas. Parking and restrooms are available at the end of the road; facilities also are available at the base of the mountain.

Motorcycles and bicycles are not permitted. **Note:** The winding road has some sharp, steep curves and is not recommended for novice drivers or for vehicles longer than a pickup truck. The vehicle should be in good condition; brakes, radiator and transmission should be checked.

Hours: Daily 9-4, early June to mid-Oct. **Cost:** $27 per private vehicle (additional $10 per person

for more than six passengers). **Phone:** (802) 253-3000 or (800) 253-4754.

STOWE ALPINE SLIDE is 7.5 mi. n.w. on SR 108 to 5781 Mountain Rd. The Alpine Chairlift at Spruce Peak climbs to the top of the slide in about 10 minutes. Riders descend 2,300 feet down the mountain on sleds and control their speed of descent, which takes approximately 2 to 3 minutes.

Note: Children ages 0-5 or under 48 inches tall may not ride alone. **Hours:** Daily 10:30-4:30, mid-June through Labor Day; Sat.-Sun. and holidays 10:30-4:30, day after Labor Day to mid-Oct. (weather permitting). **Cost:** Single ride $21; $19 (ages 6-12 and 65+). Four-ride package $44; $38 (ages 6-12 and 65+). **Phone:** (802) 253-3000 or (800) 253-4754. 🍽️ 🅰️

STOWE RECREATION PATH starts in the center of the village at 51 Main St.; parking areas provide access along the route. This is a 5.5-mile scenic pathway that follows a mountain stream north toward Mount Mansfield, past cornfields, woodlands, pastures and swimming holes. This was the first such path where land was donated by individual owners rather than purchased by a government.

Note: Use is restricted to pedestrians and non-motorized vehicles. **Hours:** Daily 24 hours. **Cost:** Free. **Phone:** (802) 253-7321, or (877) 669-8693 out of Vt. and in Canada.

VERMONT SKI & SNOWBOARD MUSEUM is at jct. SR 100 and SR 108, in the Old Town Hall at 1 S. Main St. The museum utilizes permanent and changing exhibits to relate Vermont's skiing and snowboarding history—from handcrafted 8-foot-long skis to lost ski areas to the story of the 10th Mountain Division to Vermont Olympians. **Time:** Allow 1 hour minimum. **Hours:** Generally open Wed.-Mon. noon-5. Closed Thanksgiving and Christmas. Phone ahead to confirm schedule. **Cost:** $3. **Phone:** (802) 253-9911.

RECREATIONAL ACTIVITIES
Skiing

- **Stowe Mountain Resort** is 7.5 mi. n.w. on SR 108 to 5781 Mountain Rd. Other activities are offered. **Hours:** Mon.-Fri. 8-4, Sat.-Sun. 7:30-4, mid-Nov. to late Apr. (weather permitting). **Phone:** (802) 253-3000 or (800) 253-4754.

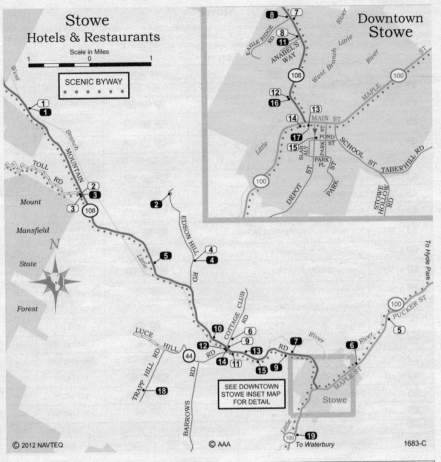

Stowe
Hotels & Restaurants

Scale in Miles

SCENIC BYWAY

Downtown
Stowe

© 2012 NAVTEQ

© AAA

1683-C

SEE DOWNTOWN
STOWE INSET MAP
FOR DETAIL

Stowe

This index helps you "spot" where approved hotels and restaurants are located on the corresponding detailed maps. Hotel daily rate range is for comparison only. Restaurant price range is a combination of lunch and/or dinner. Turn to the listing page for more detailed rate and price information and consult display ads for special promotions.

STOWE

Map Page	Hotels	Diamond Rated	Rate Range	Page
1 p. 311	**Stowe Mountain Lodge**	◆◆◆◆	$199-$829 SAVE	314
2 p. 311	Edson Hill Manor	◆◆◆	$139-$239	313
3 p. 311	Inn at the Mountain	◆◆◆	Rates not provided	313
4 p. 311	Stowehof Inn	◆◆◆	$65-$299	314
5 p. 311	**Topnotch Resort and Spa**	◆◆◆◆	$175-$595 SAVE	314
6 p. 311	**Brass Lantern Inn**	◆◆◆	$115-$275 SAVE	313
7 p. 311	Town & Country Resort Motor Inn	◆◆	$79-$169	314
8 p. 311	**Golden Eagle Resort**	◆◆◆	$99-$299 SAVE	313
9 p. 311	The Mountain Road Resort at Stowe	◆◆◆	Rates not provided	313
10 p. 311	Hob Knob Inn & Restaurant	◆◆	$90-$300	313
11 p. 311	1066 Ye Olde England Inne	◆◆◆	Rates not provided	313
12 p. 311	The Snowdrift Motel	◆◆	$90-$160	313
13 p. 311	**Stoweflake Mountain Resort & Spa**	◆◆◆	$199-$559 SAVE	313
14 p. 311	Stowe Motel	◆◆	$90-$175	314
15 p. 311	**Sun & Ski Inn and Suites**	◆◆	$79-$199 SAVE	314
16 p. 311	**The Stowe Inn & Tavern**	◆◆◆	$99-$379 SAVE	314
17 p. 311	Green Mountain Inn	◆◆◆	$139-$799	313
18 p. 311	Trapp Family Lodge	◆◆◆	$215-$515	314
19 p. 311	**Commodores Inn**	◆◆	$98-$198 SAVE	313

Map Page	Restaurants	Diamond Rated	Cuisine	Price Range	Page
1 p. 311	Solstice	◆◆◆◆	Continental	$27-$36	315
2 p. 311	The Cottage at Spruce Peak	◆◆◆	American	$10-$37	314
3 p. 311	The Cliff House	◆◆◆	New American	$16-$27	314
4 p. 311	Emily's	◆◆◆	American	$22-$35	315
5 p. 311	Foxfire Inn & Italian Restaurant	◆◆◆	Italian	$12-$28	315
6 p. 311	Sunset Grille & Tap Room	◆◆	American	$5-$22	315
7 p. 311	Pie in the Sky	◆◆	Pizza	$7-$15	315
8 p. 311	Mr. Pickwick's Gastropub and Steakhouse	◆◆◆	American	$9-$36	315
9 p. 311	The Cactus Cafe	◆◆	Mexican	$9-$21	314
11 p. 311	Piecasso Pizzeria & Lounge	◆◆	Pizza	$9-$16	315
12 p. 311	River House	◆◆◆	International	$12-$60	315
13 p. 311	The Whip Bar & Grill	◆◆◆	Regional American	$9-$31	315
14 p. 311	Harrison's Restaurant	◆◆◆	New American	$12-$28	315
15 p. 311	Depot Street Malt Shop	◆	American	$4-$8	315

(See map & index p. 311.)

1066 YE OLDE ENGLAND INNE 802/253-7558 **11**

▼▼▼▼ **Country Inn.** Rates not provided. **Address:** 433 Mountain Rd 05672 **Location:** Jct SR 100, 0.4 mi n on SR 108. **Facility:** The main inn, a reproduction of an Old English inn, offers smaller units while the rear unit situated on a bluff offers spacious guest rooms. 28 units, some cottages. 3-4 stories (no elevator), interior/exterior corridors. **Dining:** Mr. Pickwick's Gastropub and Steakhouse, see separate listing. **Pool(s):** heated outdoor. **Activities:** whirlpool. **Fee:** massage.

[ECO] [FEE ⚓] [🛜] [✕] [▣]
/ SOME UNITS FEE [🐾] [🔲]

BRASS LANTERN INN (802)253-2229 **6**

▼▼▼▼
Historic Bed & Breakfast
$115–$275

Address: 717 Maple St 05672 **Location:** Jct SR 108, 0.8 mi n on SR 100. **Facility:** Comprised of a converted 1800 farmhouse and carriage barn, the inn overlooks Mount Mansfield. Rooms are attractively appointed and furnished with antiques. Some units have a wood-burning fireplace. 9 units. 2 stories (no elevator), interior corridors. **Parking:** winter plug-ins. **Terms:** 2 night minimum stay - weekends, 14 day cancellation notice-fee imposed. **Activities:** whirlpool. **Free Special Amenities:** full breakfast and high-speed Internet.

[SAVE] [ECO] [🛜] [✕] [🗗] / SOME UNITS [W] [🔲] [▣]

COMMODORES INN (802)253-7131 **19**

▼▼▼▼
Hotel
$98–$198

Address: 823 S Main St 05672 **Location:** Jct SR 108, 0.8 mi s on SR 100. **Facility:** 72 units. 3 stories, interior corridors. **Parking:** winter plug-ins. **Terms:** check-in 4 pm, 3 day cancellation notice-fee imposed. **Pool(s):** outdoor, heated indoor. **Activities:** saunas, whirlpools, canoeing, fishing, cross country skiing, bicycle trails, hiking trails. **Fee:** game room. **Free Special Amenities:** local telephone calls and high-speed Internet.

[SAVE] [🍴] [▶] [🛏] [BIZ] [🛜] [✕] [🗗] / SOME UNITS FEE [🐾]

EDSON HILL MANOR (802)253-7371 **2**

▼▼▼▼ **Country Inn** $139–$239 **Address:** 1500 Edson Hill Rd 05672 **Location:** Jct SR 100, 3.4 mi w on SR 108, 1.3 mi n. Located in a quiet area. **Facility:** Nestled on 60 acres of rolling countryside, the inn offers accommodations in a restored manor and in separate carriage houses. 25 units. 1-2 stories (no elevator), interior/exterior corridors. **Parking:** winter plug-ins. **Terms:** 15 day cancellation notice. **Pool(s):** outdoor. **Activities:** cross country skiing, hiking trails. **Fee:** horseback riding, massage.

[🍴] [👶] [▶] [🛏] [🛜] [✕] / SOME UNITS [🐾] [K] [W]

GOLDEN EAGLE RESORT (802)253-4811 **8**

▼▼▼▼
Resort Motel
$99–$299

Address: 511 Mountain Rd 05672 **Location:** Jct SR 100, 0.5 mi w on SR 108. **Facility:** A highlight on the resort's 80 acres of landscaped and wooded grounds is a gazebo overlooking a fishpond. The property offers a variety of rooms in several buildings, some with a fireplace and porch or balcony. 88 units, some two bedrooms, efficiencies and kitchens. 1-2 stories (no elevator), exterior corridors. **Parking:** winter plug-ins. **Terms:** 7 day cancellation notice-fee imposed, resort fee. **Pool(s):** heated outdoor, heated indoor. **Activities:** sauna, whirlpool, fishing, tennis court, cross country skiing, ice skating, recreation programs, hiking trails, playground, horseshoes, shuffleboard, exercise room. **Fee:** game room, massage. **Guest Services:** coin laundry, area transportation-within 5 mi & Amtrak station. **Free Special Amenities:** local telephone calls and high-speed Internet.

[SAVE] [ECO] [🍴] [▶] [🛏] [BIZ] [🛜] [✕] [🗗] [▣]
/ SOME UNITS FEE [🐾] [🔲]

Located on 40 acres at the edge of historic Stowe Village. Walking distance to shops & restaurants.

GREEN MOUNTAIN INN (802)253-7301 **17**

▼▼▼▼ **Historic Country Inn** $139–$799 **Address:** 18 Main St 05672 **Location:** Jct SR 108 and 100; center. **Facility:** This restored 1833 inn in the village center reflects the ambience of the era and offers tastefully decorated rooms and suites. 105 units, some two bedrooms and kitchens. 3 stories, interior/exterior corridors. **Parking:** winter plug-ins. **Terms:** 2-4 night minimum stay - seasonal and/or weekends, 14 day cancellation notice-fee imposed, resort fee. **Amenities:** *Some:* video games, high-speed Internet, safes. **Dining:** The Whip Bar & Grill, see separate listing. **Pool(s):** heated outdoor. **Activities:** sauna, whirlpool, exercise room. **Fee:** game room, massage. **Guest Services:** valet laundry.

[ECO] [🍴] [▶] [🛏] [BIZ] [🛜] [✕] [▣]
/ SOME UNITS [🗗] [🔲]

HOB KNOB INN & RESTAURANT (802)253-8549 **10**

▼▼▼ **Motel** $90–$300 **Address:** 2364 Mountain Rd 05672 **Location:** Jct SR 100, 2.5 mi w on SR 108. **Facility:** 20 units, some efficiencies and kitchens. 2 stories (no elevator), interior/exterior corridors. **Terms:** 14 day cancellation notice-fee imposed, resort fee. **Pool(s):** outdoor.

[ECO] [🍴] [▶] [🛏] [🛜] [✕] [▣]
/ SOME UNITS FEE [🐾] [🗗] [🔲]

INN AT THE MOUNTAIN 802/253-3656 **3**

▼▼▼▼ **Resort Hotel.** Rates not provided. **Address:** 5837 Mountain Rd 05672 **Location:** Jct SR 100, 6 mi w on SR 108. Located at Stowe Mountain Resort. **Facility:** All rooms have a private balcony and mountain view at this country-style inn at the base of Mount Mansfield. 33 units. 2-3 stories (no elevator), interior corridors. **Terms:** check-in 4 pm. **Pool(s):** 3 heated outdoor. **Activities:** 6 tennis courts, hiking trails, exercise room. **Fee:** downhill & cross country skiing, game room. **Guest Services:** valet laundry, area transportation-within Stowe Mountain Resort.

[ECO] [🍴] [▶] [🛏] [BIZ] [🛜] [✕] [🗗] / SOME UNITS [🔲]

THE MOUNTAIN ROAD RESORT AT STOWE
802/253-4566 **9**

▼▼▼▼ **Motel.** Rates not provided. **Address:** 1007 Mountain Rd 05672 **Location:** Jct SR 100, 1 mi w on SR 108. **Facility:** 30 units, some efficiencies, kitchens and condominiums. 1-2 stories (no elevator), exterior corridors. **Parking:** winter plug-ins. **Amenities:** *Some:* high-speed Internet. **Pool(s):** heated outdoor, heated indoor. **Activities:** sauna, whirlpools, bicycles, jogging, game room, exercise room. **Guest Services:** valet and coin laundry.

[🍴] [▶] [🛏] [BIZ] [🛜] [✕] [🗗] [▣] / SOME UNITS FEE [🐾] [🔲]

THE SNOWDRIFT MOTEL (802)253-7629 **12**

▼▼▼ **Motel** $90–$160 **Address:** 2135 Mountain Rd 05672 **Location:** Jct SR 100, 2.1 mi w on SR 108. **Facility:** 40 units, some efficiencies. 1-2 stories, interior/exterior corridors. **Terms:** 2 night minimum stay - seasonal and/or weekends, 7 day cancellation notice. **Pool(s):** heated outdoor. **Activities:** whirlpool, tennis court, bicycles. **Fee:** game room.

[🍴] [▶] [🛏] [BIZ] [🛜] [✕] [🗗] / SOME UNITS FEE [🐾] [🔲] [▣]

STOWEFLAKE MOUNTAIN RESORT & SPA
(802)253-7355 **13**

▼▼▼▼
Resort Hotel
$199–$559

Address: 1746 Mountain Rd 05672 **Location:** Jct SR 100, 1.4 mi w on SR 108. **Facility:** Located near Mount Mansfield and the village center, this resort on 60 acres of manicured lawns and gardens offers many rooms with mountain views. 117 units. 2 stories, interior corridors. **Parking:** on-site and valet. **Terms:** 2 night minimum stay - seasonal and/or weekends, 15 day cancellation notice. **Amenities:** high-speed Internet. **Dining:** 3 restaurants. **Pool(s):** heated outdoor, heated indoor. **Activities:** sauna, whirlpool, steamroom, golf-9 holes, 2 tennis courts, cross country skiing, ice skating, recreation programs, hiking trails, jogging, playground, game room, exercise room, spa. **Fee:** bicycles. **Guest Services:** valet laundry. **Free Special Amenities:** preferred room (subject to availability with advance reservations).

[SAVE] [🍴] [👶] [▶] [🏌] [🛏] [BIZ] [🛜] [✕] [▣]
/ SOME UNITS FEE [🐾] [🗗] [🔲]

(See map & index p. 311.)

STOWEHOF INN
(802)253-9722 **4**

▽▽▽▽ **Country Inn** $65-$299 **Address:** 434 Edson Hill Rd 05672 **Location:** Jct SR 100, 3.4 mi w on SR 108, then 0.5 mi n. Located in a rustic area. **Facility:** Thirty acres of forested and landscaped grounds surround this property; rooms come in a variety of shapes and sizes, all individually decorated. 46 units, some efficiencies. 2-3 stories, interior corridors. **Terms:** 2 night minimum stay - weekends, 15 day cancellation notice-fee imposed, resort fee. **Dining:** Emily's, see separate listing. **Pool(s):** outdoor, heated indoor. **Activities:** sauna, whirlpool, fishing, 4 tennis courts, cross country skiing, tobogganing, hiking trails, horseshoes, shuffleboard, volleyball, exercise room. **Fee:** massage. **Guest Services:** complimentary laundry.

🍽️ 👤 🍸 🏊 📶 ✕
/ SOME UNITS 🐾 🅰️🅲 🖥️ 📷 💻

THE STOWE INN & TAVERN
(802)253-4030 **16**

▽▽▽ **Country Inn** $99-$379

Address: 123 Mountain Rd 05672 **Location:** Jct SR 100, just n. **Facility:** This historic inn is within walking distance to shops, galleries and restaurants. 38 units, some kitchens. 1-3 stories (no elevator), interior corridors. **Terms:** 3 day cancellation notice-fee imposed, resort fee. **Free Special Amenities: continental breakfast and high-speed Internet.**

SAVE 🍽️ 🍸 🏊 BIZ 📶 ✕
/ SOME UNITS FEE 🐾 🖥️ 📷

STOWE MOTEL
(802)253-7629 **14**

▽▽ **Motel** $90-$175 **Address:** 2043 Mountain Rd 05672 **Location:** Jct SR 100, 2.1 mi w on SR 108. **Facility:** 21 units, some two bedrooms, efficiencies, kitchens and houses. 1-2 stories (no elevator), exterior corridors. **Parking:** winter plug-ins. **Terms:** 2 night minimum stay - seasonal and/or weekends, 7 day cancellation notice. **Pool(s):** heated outdoor. **Activities:** whirlpool, tennis court, bicycles. **Fee:** game room.

🍽️+ 🏊 BIZ 📶 ✕ 🖥️ 📷 💻

STOWE MOUNTAIN LODGE
(802)253-3560 **1**

▽▽▽▽▽ **Resort Hotel** $199-$829

Address: 7412 Mountain Rd 05672 **Location:** Jct SR 100, 7.3 mi w on SR 108. **Facility:** Located adjacent to the ski area, guests just have to step outside to reach ski lifts or the gondola to Mount Mansfield. Relax year-around in the outdoor pool, or rejuvenate and enjoy the views from the spa. 318 units, some two bedrooms, three bedrooms, efficiencies, kitchens and condominiums. 5 stories, interior corridors. **Parking:** on-site (fee) and valet. **Terms:** check-in 4 pm, 1-4 night minimum stay - seasonal and/or weekends, 14 day cancellation notice imposed. **Amenities:** high-speed Internet, safes. *Some:* video games (fee). **Dining:** 2 restaurants, also, Solstice, see separate listing, entertainment. **Pool(s):** heated outdoor. **Activities:** whirlpools, 6 lighted tennis courts, recreation programs, hiking trails, jogging, playground, shuffleboard, exercise room, spa. **Fee:** saunas, steamrooms, golf-18 holes, downhill & cross country skiing, snowmobiling, tobogganing, bicycles, horseback riding, game room. **Guest Services:** valet and coin laundry, area transportation-Stowe Village.

SAVE ECO 🍽️ 👤 🍸 🏊 BIZ 📶 ✕ 🎮 🖥️
💻 / SOME UNITS FEE 🐾 📷

SUN & SKI INN AND SUITES
(802)253-7159 **15**

▽▽▽ **Motel** $79-$199

Address: 1613 Mountain Rd 05672 **Location:** Jct SR 100, 1.7 mi w on SR 108. **Facility:** 25 units, some efficiencies. 1 story, exterior corridors. **Parking:** winter plug-ins. **Terms:** 2-3 night minimum stay - seasonal and/or weekends, 15 day cancellation notice imposed, resort fee. **Pool(s):** heated indoor/outdoor. **Activities:** whirlpool, fishing, jogging. **Fee:** miniature golf. **Free Special Amenities: expanded continental breakfast and preferred room (subject to availability with advance reservations).**

SAVE 🏊 BIZ 📶 ✕ 🖥️ 💻 / SOME UNITS FEE 🐾

TOPNOTCH RESORT AND SPA
(802)253-8585 **5**

▽▽▽▽ **Resort Hotel** $175-$595

Address: 4000 Mountain Rd 05672 **Location:** Jct SR 100, 4.2 mi w on SR 108. **Facility:** Close to the ski slopes, this upscale hotel also specializes in tennis, fitness facilities and a full-service spa. Offered is varied well-appointed rooms, some with mountain views, and townhomes. 91 units, some efficiencies, kitchens and houses. 3 stories, interior/exterior corridors. **Parking:** on-site and valet. **Terms:** 14 day cancellation notice-fee imposed, resort fee. **Amenities:** safes. **Pool(s):** outdoor, heated outdoor, heated indoor. **Activities:** saunas, whirlpools, steamrooms, cross country skiing, recreation programs, hiking trails, jogging, exercise room, spa. **Fee:** 10 tennis courts (4 indoor, 6 lighted), bicycles, horseback riding, game room. **Guest Services:** valet laundry, area transportation-ski area & Stowe village. **Free Special Amenities: newspaper and high-speed Internet.** Affiliated with A Preferred Hotel.

SAVE 🍽️ 🍸 🏋️ 🏊 BIZ 📶 ✕ 🖥️
/ SOME UNITS 🐾 📷

TOWN & COUNTRY RESORT MOTOR INN
(802)253-7595 **7**

▽▽ ▽▽ **Motel** $79-$169 **Address:** 876 Mountain Rd 05672 **Location:** Jct SR 100, 0.9 mi w on SR 108. **Facility:** 46 units, some houses. 1-2 stories (no elevator), exterior corridors. **Parking:** winter plug-ins. **Terms:** 2 night minimum stay - seasonal and/or weekends, 7 day cancellation notice-fee imposed. **Pool(s):** outdoor, heated indoor. **Activities:** sauna, whirlpool, fishing, tennis court, jogging, volleyball.

🍽️ 🍸 🏊 BIZ 📶 ✕ 💻 / SOME UNITS 🖥️

TRAPP FAMILY LODGE
(802)253-8511 **18**

▽▽▽ **Hotel** $215-$515 **Address:** 700 Trapp Hill Rd 05672 **Location:** Jct SR 100, 2.1 mi w on SR 108, 1.4 mi s on Luce Hill Rd, follow signs. **Facility:** 96 units, some two bedrooms. 2-4 stories, interior corridors. **Parking:** on-site and valet, winter plug-ins. **Terms:** 14 day cancellation notice-fee imposed. **Dining:** 2 restaurants, entertainment. **Pool(s):** 2 heated outdoor, heated indoor. **Activities:** sauna, whirlpool, fishing, 4 tennis courts, cross country skiing, ice skating, recreation programs, hiking trails, playground, game room, volleyball, exercise room. **Fee:** bicycles, massage. **Guest Services:** valet and coin laundry.

ECO 🍽️ 🍸 🏋️ 🏊 BIZ 📶 ✕
/ SOME UNITS FEE 🐾 🅰️🅲 🖥️ 📷 💻

WHERE TO EAT

THE CACTUS CAFE
802/253-7770 **9**

▽▽ Mexican. Casual Dining. $9-$21 **AAA Inspector Notes:** Featuring traditional Mexican entrees and appetizers with a Vermont flair, such as buffalo-style wings served with a Vermont-produced, spicy, honey sauce. **Bar:** full bar. **Reservations:** suggested. **Address:** 2160 Mountain Rd 05672 **Location:** I-89 exit 10, jct SR 100, 2.1 mi w on SR 108. L D

THE CLIFF HOUSE
802/253-3558 **3**

▽▽▽ New American. Casual Dining. $16-$27 **AAA Inspector Notes:** Incredible views and creative comfort foods await you at the top of Stowe Mountain. The gondola ride adds to the great dining experience. In addition to the well-prepared lunch, seasonal chef dinners are periodically scheduled. **Bar:** full bar. **Reservations:** suggested. **Address:** 5781 Mountain Rd 05672 **Location:** Jct SR 100, 7.3 mi w on SR 108; gondola ride to top of Stowe Mountain. L 🅰️🅲

THE COTTAGE AT SPRUCE PEAK
802/253-3000 **2**

▽▽▽ American. Casual Dining. $10-$37 **AAA Inspector Notes:** Located next to the golf course, this stunning post-and-beam cottage features lovely stone, slate and exposed wood accents. A two-story window overlooks the distant ski slopes. Casual fare with farm fresh ingredients is offered. Options include tasty nachos, ale-battered tilapia and chips with homemade tartar sauce, slow-cooked local barbecue pulled pork sandwiches and Angus burgers. An outdoor covered patio is available during warmer months. **Bar:** full bar. **Reservations:** suggested, weekends. **Address:** 5781 Mountain Rd 05672 **Location:** Jct SR 100, 6 mi n on SR 108. **Parking:** on-site and valet. L D CALL 🅶🅼

(See map & index p. 311.)

DEPOT STREET MALT SHOP   802/253-4269   15
▼ American. Family Dining. $4-$8 **AAA Inspector Notes:** This coordinated 1950s malt shop offers casual service and traditional menu items. **Address:** 57 Depot St 05672 **Location:** Center. **Parking:** street only.   L   D

EMILY'S   802/253-9722   4
▼▼▼ American. Fine Dining. $22-$35 **AAA Inspector Notes:** The dining room offers beautiful views and exceptionally prepared dishes, such as a Western rack of lamb, Muscovy duck breast and the house specialty steak Diane, prepared with brandy and a morel mushroom demi-glace. **Bar:** full bar. **Reservations:** suggested. **Address:** 434 Edson Hill Rd 05672 **Location:** Jct SR 100, 3.4 mi w on SR 108, then 0.5 mi n; in Stowehof Inn.   B   D

FOXFIRE INN & ITALIAN RESTAURANT   802/253-4887   5
▼▼ Italian. Fine Dining. $12-$28 **AAA Inspector Notes:** In a circa 1850s country farmhouse, this restaurant specializes in Northern and Southern Italian cuisine. On the menu are excellent steak, veal, chicken, seafood and pasta dishes. **Bar:** full bar. **Reservations:** suggested. **Address:** 1606 Pucker St (SR 100 N) 05672 **Location:** Jct SR 108, 1.6 mi n.   D

HARRISON'S RESTAURANT   802/253-7773   14
▼▼▼ New American. Casual Dining. $12-$28 **AAA Inspector Notes:** This popular and cozy dining room features the freshest Vermont farm-to-table products. Creative New American cuisine is prepared by a skilled kitchen staff. The Prince Edward Island mussels are a delectable house specialty. **Bar:** full bar. **Reservations:** required. **Address:** 25 Main St (SR 100) 05672 **Location:** Just s of jct Mountain Rd (SR 108).   D

MR. PICKWICK'S GASTROPUB AND STEAKHOUSE   802/253-7558   8
▼▼▼ American. Casual Dining. $9-$36 **AAA Inspector Notes:** Patrons shouldn't let the casual, pub atmosphere fool them. The British brew pub specializes in the preparation of Old English specialty dishes, as well as interesting, creative wild game selections. The impressive "connoisseur's collection" includes an extensive selection of fine, rare ales, wines, cordials, vintage ports and single malts. **Bar:** full bar. **Reservations:** suggested. **Address:** 433 Mountain Rd 05672 **Location:** Jct SR 100, 0.4 mi w on SR 108; in 1066 Ye Olde England Inne.   B   L   D

PIECASSO PIZZERIA & LOUNGE   802/253-4411   11
▼▼ Pizza. Casual Dining. $9-$16 **AAA Inspector Notes:** This popular spot features creative hand-tossed pizzas and a variety of salads, sandwiches and entrées showcasing Vermont local, fresh and organic products. Gluten-free pizzas are available. Live music on the weekends makes this a fun night spot. **Bar:** full bar. **Address:** 1899 Mountain Rd 05672 **Location:** Jct Main St (SR 100), 1.9 mi n.   L   D   CALL M

PIE IN THE SKY   802/253-5100   7
▼▼ Pizza. Casual Dining. $7-$15 **AAA Inspector Notes:** Diners patronize this whimsically-named eatery for wood-fired pizza with varied toppings and several kinds of crust, including garlic pesto and wheat. The menu also features hearty pasta entrées, salads and sandwiches. **Bar:** beer & wine. **Address:** 492 Mountain Rd 05672 **Location:** Jct SR 100, 0.5 mi w on SR 108.   L   D

RIVER HOUSE   802/253-4030   12
▼▼▼ International. Casual Dining. $12-$60 **AAA Inspector Notes:** Featuring an expansive garden view and creative local cuisine, including steaks and seafood. **Bar:** full bar. **Address:** 123 Mountain Rd 05672 **Location:** Just n of jct SR 100 and 108.   D

SOLSTICE   802/760-4735   1
▼▼▼▼ Continental. Fine Dining. $27-$36 **AAA Inspector Notes:** This upscale restaurant with ski-slope views portrays a truly unique Vermont experience. The host stand is a piece of pickled wood salvaged from trees at the site. Other features include pottery from Vermont artists, handcrafted tables and an open kitchen. Servers can trace the origins of the food to the local farms and find out exactly which boat the Maine lobster arrived on. **Bar:** full bar. **Reservations:** suggested. **Address:** 7412 Mountain Rd 05672 **Location:** Jct SR 100, 7.3 mi w on SR 108; in Stowe Mountain Lodge. **Parking:** on-site and valet.   B   D   CALL M

SUNSET GRILLE & TAP ROOM   802/253-9281   6
▼▼ American. Casual Dining. $5-$22 **AAA Inspector Notes:** The restaurant offers simple foods and laid-back service in a sports bar atmosphere. **Bar:** full bar. **Address:** 140 Cottage Club Rd 05672 **Location:** Jct SR 100 and 108, 2.2 mi n, just e.   L   D

THE WHIP BAR & GRILL   802/253-7301   13
▼▼▼ Regional American. Casual Dining. $9-$31 **AAA Inspector Notes:** The warm, inviting dining room displays plenty of wood and brass, as well as an interesting collection of old buggy whips. On the varied menu are fresh seafood, hand-cut steaks, vegetarian dishes, daily specials, homemade desserts and bread and a good selection of wines. The patio is a nice dining spot in warm weather. **Bar:** full bar. **Reservations:** suggested. **Address:** 18 Main St 05672 **Location:** Jct SR 108 and 100; center; in Green Mountain Inn.   L   D

STRAFFORD (D-3) elev. 500'

JUSTIN SMITH MORRILL STATE HISTORIC SITE, on Justin Smith Morrill Hwy. in the center of Strafford Village, is a furnished Gothic Revival house built 1848-51 by Sen. Morrill, author of the Morrill Land Grant College Acts of 1862 and 1890. Exhibits featuring the Land Grant College Act and the Gothic Revival movement in 19th-century America are displayed in the carriage barn. Seven outbuildings as well as period gardens and plantings also are on the grounds.

Time: Allow 1 hour, 30 minutes minimum. **Hours:** Sat.-Sun. 11-5, late May to mid-Oct. **Cost:** $5; free (ages 0-14). **Phone:** (802) 765-4484, or (802) 828-3051 in the off-season.

STRATTON

MULLIGAN'S OF STRATTON   802/297-9293
▼▼ International. Gastropub. $12-$25 **AAA Inspector Notes:** This eatery offers steaks, chicken, seafood, burgers and a variety of appetizers in a sports pub atmosphere. Sunday is Prime Rib night and Thursday is Tijuana Mexican special night. **Bar:** full bar. **Address:** 11B Village Square 05155 **Location:** In The Village Square at Stratton Mountain.   L   D

VERDE RESTAURANT   802/297-9200
▼▼▼ Regional American. Fine Dining. $24-$38 **AAA Inspector Notes:** This fine dining restaurant, without the usual stuffiness, is high in the mountains. Featuring cuisine utilizing the concept of farm to table, the menu changes frequently based on the seasonality of ingredients. A value prix-fixe menu is featured Wednesday and Thursday with another prix-fixe menu on Friday paired with wines. Some of the popular dishes include pan-seared venison loin, Berkshire pork chops, duck breast and grass-fed rack of lamb with a Madeira glacé. **Bar:** full bar. **Reservations:** suggested. **Address:** 19 Village Lodge Rd 05155 **Location:** In The Village Square at Stratton Mountain.   D

STRATTON MOUNTAIN (F-2) elev. 3,859'

RECREATIONAL ACTIVITIES
Skiing
- **Stratton Mountain Resort** is on Stratton Mountain Rd. Other activities are offered. **Hours:** Mon.-Fri. 9-4, Sat.-Sun. and holidays 8:30-4, mid-Nov. to mid-Apr. (weather permitting). **Phone:** (802) 297-2200 or (800) 787-2886.

SWANTON (A-2) pop. 2,386, elev. 148'

In the past, smuggling was one of Swanton's more lucrative businesses. This town near the Vermont-Québec border was the scene of controversy when enterprising Vermonters drove cattle across the border into Canada, where the livestock was sold to British soldiers during the War of 1812. Twentieth-century smugglers followed in their predecessors' footsteps during Prohibition when they ran liquor into the state by automobile.

Before 1700 the St. Francis Indians, guided by French Jesuits, built the first chapel in the Vermont territory at Swanton. After France lost the land to the English, the Indians moved the chapel stone by stone to St. Hyacinthe, Québec.

Missisquoi National Wildlife Refuge, 3 miles northwest off SR 78, covers 6,792 acres along the Missisquoi River delta and Lake Champlain. Waterfowl and other wildlife can be seen along a 1.5-mile interpretive trail. Several other refuge trails are open for wildlife observation. Hunting is allowed in season with a permit. Phone (802) 868-4781.

SWANTON MOTEL   (802)868-4284

Motel
$75-$183

Address: 112 Grand Ave (US 7) 05488 **Location:** I-89 exit 21, 0.8 mi w on SR 78, then 0.5 mi s. **Facility:** 13 units, some two bedrooms. 1 story, exterior corridors. **Parking:** winter plug-ins. **Terms:** cancellation fee imposed. **Amenities:** *Some:* high-speed Internet. **Pool(s):** outdoor. **Free Special Amenities: high-speed Internet and manager's reception.**

TOWNSHEND (F-3)

Townshend is the site of Scott Covered Bridge, built in 1870 over the West River. This 276-foot bridge consists of two king post trusses and a 166-foot town lattice truss. The latter is the longest wooden span in the state.

VERGENNES (C-1) pop. 2,588, elev. 176'

Settled in 1766 and incorporated in 1788, Vergennes is one of America's oldest incorporated cities and one of the smallest, at less than 2 square miles. During the War of 1812, 177 tons of cannon balls were cast in the city. The restored, 300-seat 1897 Vergennes Opera House, 120 Main St., is open weekdays for self-guiding tours; phone (802) 877-6737.

Bixby Memorial Free Library displays a collection of Abenaki Indian artifacts and items from other tribes; phone (802) 877-2211.

LAKE CHAMPLAIN MARITIME MUSEUM, on the eastern shore of Lake Champlain at 4472 Basin Harbor Rd., has over a dozen exhibit buildings chronicling the maritime history and nautical archeology of the Champlain Valley through interactive learning stations, video and audio displays, historical artifacts, and images. One of the most popular deciphers the stories of some unusual and dramatic shipwrecks in the lake. Also of interest is a full-size replica of a Revolutionary War gunboat from Lake Champlain's fleet.

Summer workshops on boat-building, blacksmithing and maritime skills are available, along with on-water ecology and historical excursions. **Time:** Allow 2 hours minimum. **Hours:** Daily 10-5, late May to mid-Oct. **Cost:** $10; $9 (ages 62+); $6 (ages 5-17). **Phone:** (802) 475-2022.

STRONG HOUSE INN   (802)877-3337

Historic
Country Inn
$140-$340

Address: 94 W Main St 05491 **Location:** 0.6 mi s on SR 22A. **Facility:** The lovely 1834 country inn and newer Rabbit Ridge Country House with seven working fireplaces are set on six acres of beautifully maintained grounds. 15 units. 2 stories (no elevator), interior corridors. **Terms:** 2 night minimum stay - seasonal, age restrictions may apply, 14 day cancellation notice-fee imposed. **Activities:** hiking trails, game room. **Free Special Amenities: full breakfast and high-speed Internet.**

WAITSFIELD (C-2) pop. 164

Founded by Gen. Benjamin Wait in 1782 in a region known as Mad River Valley—which also comprises the towns of Warren, Fayston and Moretown—this former dairying and lumbering center is now in the heart of a premier winter sports region. Hunting, fishing, canoeing and downhill and cross-country skiing are popular activities. The Village Bridge, an old covered bridge located in the middle of town, was built in 1833.

Mad River Valley Chamber of Commerce: 4061 Main St., P.O. Box 173, Waitsfield, VT 05673. **Phone:** (802) 496-3409 or (800) 828-4748.

RECREATIONAL ACTIVITIES
Skiing

• **Mad River Glen** is on SR 17 off SR 100. **Hours:** Mon.-Fri. 9-4, Sat.-Sun. and holidays 8:30-4, mid-Dec. to mid-Apr. (weather permitting). **Phone:** (802) 496-3551.

THE INN AT THE ROUND BARN FARM   (802)496-2276

Historic Bed & Breakfast $175-$330 **Address:** 1661 E Warren Rd 05673 **Location:** Jct SR 100, 1.8 mi e on E Warren Rd, over covered bridge. Located in a quiet rural area. **Facility:** Set on 245 acres, this lovely inn functioned as a dairy farm up until 1969; rooms are elegant with a mix of contemporary and antique furnishings. 12 units. 2-3 stories (no elevator), interior corridors. **Terms:** 2-3 night minimum stay - seasonal and/or weekends, age restrictions may apply, 21 day cancellation notice-fee imposed. **Pool(s):** indoor. **Activities:** hiking trails, horseshoes, exercise room. *Fee:* massage.

TUCKER HILL INN   (802)496-3983

Bed & Breakfast $119-$299 **Address:** 65 Marble Hill Rd 05673 **Location:** On SR 17, 1.1 mi w of SR 100. **Facility:** Set on 14 acres with perennial gardens, this lovely renovated inn offers attractively decorated guest rooms and family suites of varying sizes. 18 units, some two and three bedrooms. 2 stories (no elevator), interior/exterior corridors. **Terms:** 2-3 night minimum stay - seasonal and/or weekends, age restrictions may apply, 21 day cancellation notice-fee imposed. **Amenities:** high-speed Internet. **Pool(s):** outdoor. **Activities:** 2 tennis courts, hiking trails, game room.

AMERICAN FLATBREAD
802/496-8856

▼▼ Pizza. Casual Dining. $8-$24 **AAA Inspector Notes:** Located on a working organic farm, this restaurant is the original location and concept from more than 30 years ago. They offer all-natural pizzas made from organic-grain wheat with restored wheat germ and topped with fresh local ingredients that are organic whenever possible. Pizzas are assembled in their open kitchen and baked in the primitive wood-fired oven central to the dining room. Natural sausage and smoked bacon have no preservatives. Incredibly fresh salads. **Bar:** beer & wine. **Address:** 46 Lareau Rd 05673 **Location:** On SR 100. [D]

JAY'S RESTAURANT
802/496-8282

▼▼ American. Casual Dining. $4-$21 **AAA Inspector Notes:** Jay's is a family restaurant with a lounge area separated from the main room. Meals are very satisfying. The menu offers Italian dishes, steak, chicken, chops, pizza and dessert such as the chocolate cappuccino pie. **Bar:** full bar. **Address:** 114 SR 100 05673 **Location:** 0.8 mi s of center; in Mad River Green Shopping Center.

[B] [L] [D]

WALLINGFORD pop. 830

MOM'S COUNTRY KITCHEN
802/446-2606

▼ American. Casual Dining. $4-$7 **AAA Inspector Notes:** Located in a circa 1824 historic house-the first house in town with electricity-the restaurant offers mostly short-order items and the service is casual yet friendly. **Address:** 27 N Main St 05773 **Location:** Center. [B] [L]

SAL'S SOUTH
802/446-2935

▼▼ Italian. Casual Dining. $10-$20 **AAA Inspector Notes:** This family-friendly restaurant offers seating either on the outdoor porch or in the cozy interior. The focus of the menu is on pasta and pizza. **Bar:** beer & wine. **Address:** 15 S Main St 05773 **Location:** Jct SR 140/US 7; center. **Parking:** street only. [L] [D]

WARREN (C-2)

Named for physician and general Joseph Warren, who died in action at Bunker Hill, Warren is one of the trio of Mad River Valley communities.

GRANVILLE GULF RESERVATION, covering 1,200 acres between Warren and Granville, protects the scenic beauty of the 6 miles of highway that bisect this steep, forested gorge. Deer Hollow Brook cascades 75 feet to create picturesque Moss Glen Falls at a stopping point along SR 100; a 200-foot boardwalk provides access to a view of the entire falls. The reservation is at its most impressive during fall foliage season. **Hours:** Daily 24 hours. **Cost:** Free. **Phone:** (802) 241-3655.

RECREATIONAL ACTIVITIES
Skiing

• **Sugarbush Resort** is at 1840 Sugarbush Access Rd. off SR 100. Other seasonal activities are available. **Hours:** Mon.-Fri. 9-4, Sat.-Sun. and holidays 8-4, early Nov.-early May. Extended hours are possible in spring; phone ahead. **Phone:** (802) 583-6300 or (800) 537-8427.

AGA AT THE SUGARTREE INN
802/583-3211

▼▼▼ **Bed & Breakfast.** Rates not provided. **Address:** 2440 Sugarbush Access Rd 05674 **Location:** 1.7 mi n on SR 100, then 2.5 mi w. **Facility:** Half a mile from its base lodge, this inn offers a variety of individually decorated guest rooms. All rooms include a hair dryer in the bathroom, and one unit features a fireplace. 9 units, some two bedrooms. 3 stories (no elevator), interior corridors. **Terms:** age restrictions may apply. **Activities:** whirlpool.

 / SOME UNITS

THE BRIDGES FAMILY RESORT & TENNIS CLUB
(802)583-2922

▼▼▼▼
Resort Condominium
$170-$690

Address: 202 Bridges Cir 05674 **Location:** 1.7 mi n on SR 100, 2.6 mi w on Sugarbush Access Rd, then just s. **Facility:** Fireplaces are featured in all of these condominium-style apartments, most with laundry facilities. A shared base lodge is half a mile away. 63 condominiums. 1-3 stories (no elevator), exterior corridors. **Parking:** winter plug-ins. **Terms:** check-in 6 pm, 2 night minimum stay, 21 day cancellation notice-fee imposed. **Pool(s):** 2 heated outdoor, heated indoor. **Activities:** saunas, whirlpool, 10 tennis courts (2 indoor), recreation programs in summer, playground, sports court, basketball, game room, horseshoes, volleyball. **Fee:** massage. **Guest Services:** area transportation-base lodge & downtown. **Free Special Amenities:** high-speed Internet and children's activities. (See ad p. 280.)

THE PITCHER INN
(802)496-6350

▼▼▼▼
Country Inn
$325-$800

Address: 275 Main St 05674 **Location:** Center. **Facility:** Located in the quiet town of Warren, this inn offers luxury appointments with individually decorated rooms, some with a balcony. 11 units, some two bedrooms and kitchens. 3 stories, interior/exterior corridors. **Terms:** closed 4/13-5/9 & 10/27-11/26, 30 day cancellation notice-fee imposed, resort fee. **Amenities:** high-speed Internet. **Dining:** 275 Main, see separate listing. **Activities:** bicycles, hiking trails, jogging, game room, shuffleboard. **Fee:** massage. **Free Special Amenities:** full breakfast and room upgrade (subject to availability with advance reservations).

THE SUGAR LODGE
(802)583-3300

▼▼ Hotel $79-$149 **Address:** 2197 Sugarbush Access Rd 05674 **Location:** 1.7 mi n on SR 100, 2.2 mi w. **Facility:** 24 units, some efficiencies. 2 stories (no elevator), interior corridors. **Terms:** check-in 4 pm, 2 night minimum stay - seasonal and/or weekends, 14 day cancellation notice-fee imposed. **Amenities:** high-speed Internet. **Pool(s):** outdoor. **Guest Services:** coin laundry, area transportation.

275 MAIN
802/496-6350

▼▼▼▼ Regional American. Fine Dining. $18-$36 **AAA Inspector Notes:** The restaurant features a refined, sophisticated atmosphere with a warm, inviting wood-burning fireplace. Gracious, attentive servers circulate through the dining area with delightful and deliciously creative dishes that continually change with the market and season. **Bar:** full bar. **Reservations:** suggested. **Address:** 275 Main St 05674 **Location:** Center; in The Pitcher Inn. [D]

CHEZ HENRI
802/583-2600

▼▼▼ French. Fine Dining. $8-$35 **AAA Inspector Notes:** This bistro restaurant features a classic cuisine including dinner and lighter fare. There's a fireplace in the dining room, and the summer terrace overlooks a small brook. The location allows easy ski-in/ski-out access. **Bar:** full bar. **Reservations:** suggested. **Address:** 80 Sugarbush Village 05674 **Location:** 1.4 mi n on SR 100, 3 mi w on Sugarbush Access Rd, then just n on Village Rd to parking area, cross foot bridge; in Sugarbush Village. [L] [D]

THE COMMON MAN 802/583-2800

⚜️⚜️ American. Casual Dining. $19-$29 **AAA Inspector Notes:** This 19th century barn was renovated and the rafters are open and hand hewn and the large fireplace has an open hearth. The chef has a weekly special that is always a treat. **Bar:** full bar. **Reservations:** suggested. **Address:** 3209 German Flats Rd 05674 **Location:** 1.7 mi n on SR 100, 1.8 mi w on Sugarbush Access Rd, then just n.

[D]

WATERBURY (C-2) pop. 1,763, elev. 427'

For a town with only two traffic lights, Waterbury sure has a lot going on. It's near some of the east's major ski resorts—Mad River Glen, Stowe Mountain Resort and Sugarbush Resort are all close by. It's a quintessentially quaint and charming New England village with an impressive historic district. You'll also find interesting 19th-century architecture, a restored train station and even a covered bridge or two nearby.

In addition to the aforementioned skiing—cross country as well as downhill—there's plenty to keep you outside enjoying the fresh air and beautiful scenery. There are trails to hike and mountain biking adventures to experience. You can fish in lakes or catch a trout in the Winooski River, launch a boat or canoe, or go for a swim or a picnic. Nearby Green Mountain National Forest and Mount Mansfield (see Recreation Areas Chart and place listings p. 284 and 298) and Waterbury Reservoir provide opportunities for many of these endeavors.

Take a break from recreational activities and enjoy a sample of Cherry Garcia or Chunky Monkey at hometown favorite Ben & Jerry's Ice Cream Factory Tours (see attraction listing), or try a cup of the house blend at Waterbury's own Green Mountain Coffee Roasters Visitor Center.

Self-guiding tours: A brochure detailing a historical walking tour of Waterbury Village is available at local convenience stores.

BEN & JERRY'S ICE CREAM FACTORY TOURS, off I-89 exit 10, then 1 mi. n. on SR 100 to 1281 Waterbury-Stowe Rd., provides guided 30-minute tours detailing each step in making ice cream. Tours feature the 7-minute "moovie" about the company's founders and its history, a bird's-eye view of the production room and samples of various flavors.

Hours: Guided tours are given daily every 30 minutes 9-9, July 1 to mid-Aug.; 9-7, mid-Aug. to late Oct.; 10-6, rest of year. Last tour begins 1 hour before closing. Tour and production schedule may vary. Closed Jan. 1, Thanksgiving and Christmas. Phone ahead to confirm schedule. **Cost:** $4; $3 (ages 62+); free (ages 0-12). **Phone:** (802) 882-1240 or (866) 258-6877.

THE BEST WESTERN PLUS WATERBURY STOWE (802)244-7822

⚜️⚜️⚜️
Hotel
$120-$200

AAA Benefit: Members save 10% or more with Best Western.

Address: 45 Blush Hill Rd 05676 **Location:** I-89 exit 10, just nw on SR 100. **Facility:** 84 units. 2 stories (no elevator), interior corridors. **Parking:** winter plug-ins. **Amenities:** Some: high-speed Internet, safes. **Pool(s):** heated indoor. **Activities:** whirlpool, tennis court, cross country skiing, snowmobiling, exercise room. Fee: game room, massage. **Guest Services:** valet and coin laundry. **Free Special Amenities:** local telephone calls and high-speed Internet.

THE OLD STAGECOACH INN 802/244-5056

⚜️⚜️⚜️
Historic Bed
& Breakfast
$90-$150

Address: 18 N Main St 05676 **Location:** I-89 exit 10, just s on SR 100, then just e. **Facility:** A former stagecoach stop, this restored property is within walking distance of restaurants and shops. 11 units, some two bedrooms and kitchens. 2-3 stories (no elevator), interior/exterior corridors. Bath: some shared. **Terms:** 2 night minimum stay - seasonal and/or weekends, 14 day cancellation notice-fee imposed.

THATCHER BROOK INN 802/244-5911

⚜️⚜️⚜️ Country Inn. Rates not provided. **Address:** 1017 Waterbury-Stowe Rd (SR 100) 05676 **Location:** I-89 exit 10, 0.6 mi n. **Facility:** A renovated 1899 Victorian home with newer wings, this inn offers large rooms, many accented by hardwood trim. Some units include a fireplace. 17 units. 2 stories (no elevator), interior/exterior corridors.

WHERE TO EAT

ARVAD'S GRILL & PUB 802/244-8973

⚜️
American
Casual Dining
$6-$22

AAA Inspector Notes: This casual, pub-like eatery serves more than 10 Vermont brews with a large selection of sandwiches, salads, burgers, seafood, meat and pasta preparations. Dishes are prepared with Vermont-made products and seasonal produce. **Bar:** full bar. **Address:** 3 S Main St 05676 **Location:** I-89 exit 10, just s on SR 100, then just e. **Parking:** street only. *Menu on AAA.com*

[L] [D]

MARSALA SALSA 802/244-1150

⚜️⚜️ Caribbean. Casual Dining. $7-$20 **AAA Inspector Notes:** The restaurant features an interesting Indian and Caribbean theme throughout; the walls are filled with Indian tapestries and rugs which have been hand painted in a variety of colors and patterns. **Bar:** full bar. **Reservations:** suggested. **Address:** 13-15 Stowe St 05676 **Location:** Center. **Parking:** street only. [L] [D]

WATERBURY CENTER (C-3)

COLD HOLLOW CIDER MILL, off I-89 exit 10, then 3.5 mi. n on SR 100, produces approximately 1 million gallons of cider annually. Self-guiding tours allow visitors to view many aspects of the mill's cider production. An 8-minute video explains the process from apple harvesting to cider bottling.

Time: Allow 30 minutes minimum. **Hours:** Daily 8-7, first Sun. in July-late Oct.; 8-6, rest of year. Closed Thanksgiving and Christmas. **Cost:** Free. **Phone:** (802) 244-8771 or (800) 327-7537. 🅰️

MICHAEL'S ON THE HILL   802/244-7476
▽▽▽ Continental. Fine Dining. $25-$43 **AAA Inspector Notes:** Located in a 1820 farmhouse, the restaurant offers guests an intimate and delightful dining experience. **Bar:** full bar. **Reservations:** suggested. **Address:** 4182 Waterbury-Stowe Rd (SR 100) 05677 **Location:** I-89 exit 10, 4.2 mi n of jct SR 100. D

TANGLEWOODS RESTAURANT   802/244-7855
▽▽ American. Casual Dining. $12-$25 **AAA Inspector Notes:** This restaurant's noticeably distinct yet charmingly rustic interior features a wood-burning fireplace, exposed beams and knotty pine walls. **Bar:** full bar. **Address:** 179 Guptil Rd 05677 **Location:** I-89 exit 10, 1.5 mi n on SR 100, then just e. D

WELLS RIVER pop. 399

P & H TRUCK STOP   802/429-2141
▽ American. Quick Serve. $4-$15 **AAA Inspector Notes:** The basic eatery offers pleasant service and mostly short-order menu items. **Address:** 2886 US Rt 302 05081 **Location:** I-91 exit 17, just w. B L D 24

WEST BRATTLEBORO pop. 2,740

MOLLY STARK MOTEL   (802)254-2440
▽ Motel $45-$95 **Address:** 829 Marlboro Rd 05301 **Location:** I-91 exit 2, 3.3 mi w on SR 9. **Facility:** 14 units, some two bedrooms. 1 story, exterior corridors. *Bath:* shower only.
🛜 🖥️ 📷 💻 / SOME UNITS FEE 🐾

WHERE TO EAT

DALEM'S CHALET   802/254-4323

Continental Casual Dining $13-$24

AAA Inspector Notes: This eatery features an inviting Bavarian atmosphere with a dining room overlooking mountains and a pond with swans. The menu offers Swiss, German, Austrian and American dishes. The wiener schnitzel is flavorful. Open and close days may vary depending on the season. **Bar:** full bar. **Reservations:** suggested. **Address:** 78 South St 05301 **Location:** I-91 exit 2, 1.1 mi w on SR 9, then just s. B D 🆇

SUNNY'S DELI & BAKERY   802/257-4994
▽▽ Deli. Quick Serve. $4-$14 **AAA Inspector Notes:** This popular cafe and bakery is the source for the wonderful breads and baked goods featured at its more formal sibling restaurant, The Putney Inn, a few miles north. Desserts are not only extraordinary but also almost a meal unto themselves. **Address:** 849 Western Ave 05301 **Location:** I-91 exit 2, 0.9 mi w. **Parking:** street only.
B L

WEST DOVER

BIG BEAR'S LODGE   802/464-5591
▽▽ Motel $80-$185 **Address:** 344 Rt 100 N 05356 **Location:** Jct SR 9, 8.7 mi n on SR 100. **Facility:** 24 units. 2 stories (no elevator), interior/exterior corridors. **Terms:** cancellation fee imposed. **Pool(s):** heated outdoor. **Activities:** whirlpool, hiking trails, playground, horseshoes, volleyball.
🏊 BIZ 🛜 🖥️ 🆇 🈂️

GRAND SUMMIT RESORT HOTEL & CONFERENCE CENTER   (802)464-6600
▽▽▽ Resort Hotel $110-$446 **Address:** 89 Grand Summit Way 05356 **Location:** Jct SR 9 and 100, 9 mi n on SR 100, then w, follow signs. **Facility:** Located at the base of Mount Snow, this attractive resort offers tastefully decorated guest rooms, many with full kitchens and some with fireplaces. 196 units, some two bedrooms, three bedrooms and kitchens. 3 stories, interior corridors. **Terms:** check-in 4 pm, 2 night minimum stay - seasonal and/or weekends, 8 day cancellation notice-fee imposed, resort fee. **Dining:** 2 restaurants. **Pool(s):** heated outdoor. **Activities:** sauna, whirlpools, steamroom, recreation programs, hiking trails, playground, volleyball, exercise room, spa. **Fee:** golf-18 holes, downhill & cross country skiing, snowmobiling, bicycles, game room. **Guest Services:** coin laundry.
ECO 🍴 🍸 🛗 CALL 🆓Ⓜ️ 🏊 BIZ 🛜 🖥️ 💻 / SOME UNITS 🖥️ 📷

THE HERMITAGE INN   (802)464-3511
▽▽▽ ▽▽▽ Country Inn $170-$295 **Address:** 25 Handle Rd 05356 **Location:** Jct SR 9 and 100, 9 mi n on SR 100, then just w. **Facility:** Wonderful scenic views and grounds complete the garden and guest recreation areas. This well-appointed inn also offers fine on-site dining and an upscale lounge area. 15 units. 2 stories, interior/exterior corridors. **Terms:** check-in 4 pm, 30 day cancellation notice-fee imposed, resort fee. **Amenities:** safes. **Dining:** restaurant, see separate listing. **Activities:** sauna, whirlpools, fishing, bicycles, hiking trails, game room, exercise room. **Fee:** cross country skiing, ice skating, massage. **Guest Services:** area transportation-within 5 mi. 🍴 🏋️ 🍸 🛜 🖥️ 🖥️ 📷 💻

WHERE TO EAT

THE HERMITAGE INN   802/464-3511
▽▽▽ American. Fine Dining. $8-$46 **AAA Inspector Notes:** Offering an elegant dining experience, the establishment features an innovative bill of fare prepared using local ingredients. **Bar:** full bar. **Reservations:** suggested. **Address:** 25 Handle Rd 05356 **Location:** Jct SR 9 and 100, 9 mi n on SR 100, then just w.
B L D

WESTMORE

WILLOUGHVALE INN ON LAKE WILLOUGHBY   (802)525-4123
▽▽▽ Country Inn $79-$329 **Address:** 793 SR 5A 05860 **Location:** Waterfront. Jct SR 16 and 5A, just s. **Facility:** The rooms at this contemporary country inn overlook beautiful Lake Willoughby; each lakefront cottage offers a fireplace, screened porch and deck. 19 units, some cottages. 2 stories (no elevator), interior/exterior corridors. **Terms:** 2 night minimum stay - seasonal, 30 day cancellation notice-fee imposed, resort fee. **Activities:** canoeing, sailboats, fishing, cross country skiing, bicycles, hiking trails. **Fee:** boats.
🍴 🍸 BIZ 🛜 📷 / SOME UNITS FEE 🐾 🖥️ 📷 💻

WESTON (F-2) elev. 1,300'
• Hotels p. 320

Weston nestles in a valley below the source of the West River. Its many restored buildings help to preserve the atmosphere of a 19th-century Vermont village. The Weston Priory, 3 miles north of the village at 58 Priory Hill Rd., is a Benedictine monastery that welcomes the public; phone (802) 824-5409.

WESTON PLAYHOUSE, on the village green, is Vermont's oldest professional theater company. The building's white-columned, Greek Revival facade was restored after a fire in 1962. Following the final curtain during the summer season the Act IV Cabaret, in the downstairs lounge, presents a music and comedy revue.

Hours: Performances are offered Tues.-Sat. at 7:30 p.m. (also Wed. and Sat. at 2, Sun. at 3), late June-early Sept. **Cost:** $30-$58. **Phone:** (802) 824-5288.

BRANDMEYER'S MOUNTAINSIDE LODGE   802/824-5851

◆ **Motel** $109-$159 **Address:** 913 Rt 100 05161 **Location:** On SR 100, 1.7 mi n. **Facility:** 10 units. 1-3 stories (no elevator), interior/exterior corridors. **Terms:** 2 night minimum stay - seasonal and/or weekends, 14 day cancellation notice-fee imposed. **Amenities:** safes. **Activities:** snowmobiling.

WEST TOWNSHEND

WINDHAM HILL INN   (802)874-4080

◆◆◆ ◆◆◆
Historic Country Inn
$255-$545

Address: 311 Lawrence Dr 05359 **Location:** 1.1 mi n on Windham Hill Dr, just e. **Facility:** This restored circa 1825 farmhouse is situated on a quiet hillside with mountain views and extensive gardens. Many rooms feature a fireplace and deck. Ten units have soaking tubs. 21 units. 3 stories (no elevator), interior corridors. **Terms:** closed 4/1-4/18, 2-3 night minimum stay - seasonal and/or weekends, age restrictions may apply, 30 day cancellation notice-fee imposed. **Dining:** Windham Hill Restaurant, see separate listing. **Pool(s):** heated outdoor. **Activities:** tennis court, cross country skiing, hiking trails, spa. **Guest Services:** valet laundry.

WHERE TO EAT

WINDHAM HILL RESTAURANT   802/874-4080

◆◆◆ ◆◆◆
Regional American Fine Dining
$65-$85

AAA Inspector Notes: This elegant intimate dining room offers views of a small pond. Enjoy a drink in the lounge before dinner. The eclectic menu fuses European-style techniques with the frequent use of local farm products including vegetables and herbs from the on-site garden. This spot specializes in chef tasting and prix fixe menus in order to saturate the palate with flavor. **Bar:** full bar. **Reservations:** required. **Address:** 311 Lawrence Dr 05359 **Location:** 1.1 mi n on Windham Hill Dr, just e; in Windham Hill Inn.

WHITE RIVER JUNCTION (E-3) pop. 2,286

WHITE RIVER FLYER departs from Union Station at 102 Railroad Row. Diesel locomotives provide the power for 2.5-hour trips from White River Junction to Thetford. The trains travel along the Connecticut River and make brief stops at the Montshire Museum of Science. **Time:** Allow 2 hours minimum. **Hours:** Departs Thurs. and Sat.-Sun. at noon, mid-July through Oct. 31. Phone ahead to confirm schedule. **Cost:** $25; $20 (ages 3-12). Fares may vary for special events. Reservations are recommended. **Phone:** (802) 463-3069 or (800) 707-3530.

COMFORT INN   (802)295-3051

◆◆ **Hotel** $99-$199 **Address:** 56 Ralph Lehman Dr 05001 **Location:** I-91 exit 11, just e. **Facility:** 91 units. 4 stories, interior corridors. **Parking:** winter plug-ins. **Terms:** cancellation fee imposed. **Amenities:** *Some:* high-speed Internet. **Pool(s):** heated indoor. **Activities:** exercise room. **Guest Services:** coin laundry.

FAIRFIELD INN & SUITES BY MARRIOTT   (802)291-9911

◆◆◆ **Hotel** $139-$459 **Address:** 102 Ballardvale Dr 05001 **Location:** I-91 exit 11, just s. **Facility:** 67 units. 3 stories, interior corridors. **Amenities:** high-speed Internet. **Activities:** exercise room. **Guest Services:** valet and coin laundry.

AAA Benefit: AAA hotel discounts of 5% or more.

HAMPTON INN WHITE RIVER JUNCTION   (802)296-2800

◆◆◆ **Hotel** $139-$459 **Address:** 104 Ballardvale Dr 05001 **Location:** I-91 exit 11, just s on US 5. **Facility:** 96 units. 3 stories, interior corridors. **Parking:** winter plug-ins. **Terms:** 1-7 night minimum stay, cancellation fee imposed. **Pool(s):** heated indoor. **Activities:** exercise room. **Guest Services:** coin laundry.

AAA Benefit: Members save up to 10%!

HOLIDAY INN EXPRESS HOTEL & SUITES   802/299-2700

◆◆◆ **Hotel.** Rates not provided. **Address:** 121 Ballardvale Dr 05001 **Location:** I-91 exit 11. **Facility:** 77 units, some efficiencies and kitchens. 4 stories, interior corridors. **Parking:** winter plug-ins. **Amenities:** high-speed Internet. **Activities:** exercise room. **Guest Services:** valet and coin laundry.

THE WHITE RIVER INN AND SUITES   802/295-3015

◆◆ **Hotel.** Rates not provided. **Address:** 91 Ballardvale Dr 05001 **Location:** I-91 exit 11, just s on US 5. **Facility:** 75 units, some kitchens. 2 stories, interior corridors. **Parking:** winter plug-ins. **Amenities:** high-speed Internet. **Pool(s):** heated indoor. **Guest Services:** valet and coin laundry.

WILLISTON

COURTYARD BY MARIOTT BURLINGTON WILLISTON   (802)879-0100

◆◆◆ **Hotel** $159-$499 **Address:** 177 Hurricane Ln 05495 **Location:** I-89 exit 12, just s on SR 2A, then just e. **Facility:** 90 units. 3 stories, interior corridors. **Parking:** winter plug-ins. **Amenities:** high-speed Internet. **Pool(s):** heated indoor. **Activities:** whirlpool, exercise room. **Guest Services:** valet and coin laundry.

AAA Benefit: AAA hotel discounts of 5% or more.

FAIRFIELD INN BY MARRIOTT-BURLINGTON/WILLISTON   (802)879-8999

◆◆◆ **Hotel** $79-$229 **Address:** 2844 St George Rd 05495 **Location:** I-89 exit 12, just n on SR 2A. **Facility:** 105 units. 3 stories, interior corridors. **Pool(s):** outdoor. **Guest Services:** valet and coin laundry.

AAA Benefit: AAA hotel discounts of 5% or more.

RESIDENCE INN BY MARRIOTT BURLINGTON WILLISTON   (802)878-2001

◆◆◆ **Extended Stay Hotel** $99-$239 **Address:** 35 Hurricane Ln 05495 **Location:** I-89 exit 12, just s on SR 2A, then just e. **Facility:** 96 kitchen units, some two bedrooms. 2 stories, exterior corridors. **Amenities:** *Some:* high-speed Internet. **Pool(s):** heated indoor. **Activities:** whirlpool, playground, sports court, exercise room. **Guest Services:** valet and coin laundry.

AAA Benefit: AAA hotel discounts of 5% or more.

TOWNEPLACE SUITES BY MARRIOTT BURLINGTON
WILLISTON   (802)872-5900

[fyi] **Extended Stay Hotel** $129-$179
Under major renovation, scheduled to
be completed September 2012. **Last
Rated:** ▼▼▼ **Address:** 66
Zephyr Rd 05495 **Location:** I-89 exit
12, 1.1 mi on SR 2A. **Facility:** 95 kitchen units, some two bedrooms. 3 stories, interior corridors. **Amenities:** *Some:* high-
speed Internet. **Pool(s):** heated indoor. **Activities:** limited
exercise equipment. **Guest Services:** valet and coin laundry.

AAA Benefit: AAA
hotel discounts of
5% or more.

CALL 🔥M 🛄 BIZ 🛜 ✕ 🔲 🔳 🖥
/ SOME UNITS FEE 🐾

CHEF'S CORNER CAFE & BAKERY   802/878-5524
▼▼ American. Quick Serve. $7-$13 **AAA Inspector Notes:**
Since opening its doors in 1997, this trendy bakery-cafe continues to
delight both locals and visitors alike with its selection of sweet treats
and entrees. Open for breakfast and lunch, this cafe offers a healthier
alternative for the more health-conscious. Menu offerings include
sandwiches, soups, quiche and traditional house items like blackened
chicken panini or the Corner veggie burger. A full weekend brunch is
available, as is outdoor seating. **Bar:** beer & wine. **Address:** 2121
Essex Rd 05495 **Location:** I-89 exit 12, 0.8 mi n on SR 2A.
[B] [L]

MEXICALI   802/879-9492
▼▼ Mexican. Casual Dining. $5-$15 **AAA Inspector Notes:**
This unusual restaurant has its own self-service salsa and salad
dressing bar. Mixing salsa to create a hotter variety is part of the fun.
Bar: full bar. **Address:** 28 Walnut St, Suite 180 05495 **Location:** I-89
exit 12, 0.4 mi n on SR 2A, then just e; in Maple Tree Place; behind
Majestic 10 Cinema. [L] [D] CALL 🔥M

WILMINGTON pop. 463

HORIZON INN   802/464-2131
▼▼▼◆◆◆◆   **Address:** 861 SR 9 E, Molly Stark Tr
  Hotel   05363 **Location:** On SR 9, 4 mi e. Lo-
  $75-$155 cated in a rural area. **Facility:** 28 units. 2
      stories (no elevator), interior/exterior cor-
ridors. **Parking:** winter plug-ins. **Terms:**
14 day cancellation notice. **Pool(s):** heated indoor. **Activities:**
sauna, whirlpool, tobogganing, shuffleboard, exercise room.
Fee: game room.
[SAVE] 🍴 🍸 🛄 🛜 ✕ 🖥 / SOME UNITS 🔲 🔳

WHITE HOUSE INN   802/464-2135
▼▼▼ Continental. Fine Dining. $25-$37 **AAA Inspector
Notes:** This spot is an elegant English-style dining room in a country
inn high on a hill. The setting offers lovely views. The cuisine reveals
hints of French influences. **Bar:** full bar. **Reservations:** suggested.
Address: 178 Rt 9 E 05363 **Location:** On SR 9, 0.5 mi e.
[B] [D] 🆔

WINDSOR (E-3) pop. 2,066, elev. 321'

"The Birthplace of Vermont," Windsor is where,
after a 6-day convention, the state constitution was
adopted July 8, 1777. The general assembly often
met in Windsor until 1805, when Montpelier became
the permanent capital. The city was a center of invention during the 19th century, spawning such
products as firearms, the hydraulic pump, the coffee
percolator and the sewing machine.

The 1866 Cornish-Windsor Covered Bridge, one
of the longest wooden bridges in the nation, spans

the Connecticut River between Windsor and Cornish, N.H.

**Greater Mt. Ascutney Regional Chamber of Com-
merce:** 3 Railroad Ave., Windsor, VT 05089.
Phone: (802) 674-5910.

AMERICAN PRECISION MUSEUM, 196 Main St.,
is housed in the 1846 Robbins and Lawrence Armory. Highlights include a collection of historic precision machine tools, guns, working scale models
and special exhibits detailing the story of America's
industrial heritage. **Hours:** Daily 10-5, Memorial
Day-Oct. 31. **Cost:** $7.50; $4 (students with ID); free
(ages 0-6); $19.50 (family, two adults and two chil-
dren). **Phone:** (802) 674-5781.

OLD CONSTITUTION HOUSE is at 16 N. Main St.
The constitution of the Free and Independent State
of Vermont was adopted in this former tavern in
1777. The building is now a museum devoted to
Vermont history. Exhibits pertain to the Republic of
Vermont, slavery prohibition, voting rights for men
and the implementation of a public school system.
Time: Allow 30 minutes minimum. **Hours:** Sat.-Sun.
11-5, late May to mid-Oct. **Cost:** $2.50; free (ages
0-14). **Phone:** (802) 672-3773.

JUNIPER HILL INN   802/674-5273
▼▼▼ Historic Country Inn. Rates not provided. **Address:**
153 Pembroke Rd 05089 **Location:** I-91 exit 9, 2.9 mi s on US 5 to
Juniper Hill Rd, then 0.5 mi w. **Facility:** This stately turn-of-the-20th-
century Colonial Revival mansion offers a picturesque hilltop setting
and well-appointed guest rooms, many with a fireplace. 16 units. 3
stories (no elevator), interior corridors. **Activities:** bicycles, hiking
trails. *Fee:* massage.
🍴 🛄 🛜 ✕ 🛄 / SOME UNITS FEE 🐾 🐾

WOLCOTT (B-3)

Wolcott is the home of Fisher Bridge, one of two
remaining covered railroad bridges in Vermont; both
are retired, and the tracks have been removed. It
also is the only railroad bridge with a full-length cu-
pola, which allowed smoke to escape. Built in 1908,
the bridge spans the Lamoille River. Heavy steel
beams were placed beneath the bridge in 1968 so it
could remain in use.

WOODSTOCK (E-3) pop. 900, elev. 700'
• Hotels p. 322 • Restaurants p. 323

A resort and residential community, Woodstock is
noted for its historic Federal-style homes and
charming village green. Four local church bells were
cast in Boston by either Paul Revere or a worker at
his foundry.

Three covered bridges can be seen along scenic
US 4. The Middle Bridge stands on Union Street; the
Taftsville Bridge stands 3 miles east of the village;
and the Lincoln Bridge is in West Woodstock, 4
miles west.

Although it is best known for skiing, Woodstock
also offers summer recreation, including golf, horseback riding and hiking. Holiday decorations and

lights create a magical atmosphere during Woodstock's well-known Wassail Weekend in early December; the festivities include caroling, carriage rides and a parade with horseback riders in 19th-century garb.

Woodstock Area Chamber of Commerce: 4 Mechanic St., P.O. Box 486, Woodstock, VT 05091. **Phone:** (802) 457-3555, (802) 432-1100 or (888) 496-6378.

BILLINGS FARM & MUSEUM is .5 mi. n. on SR 12 across the Elm Street Bridge to Old River Road. It encompasses both a modern working dairy farm and a museum depicting rural Vermont farm life in the late 19th century. In 1871 Vermont native Frederick Billings purchased the Woodstock farm where early conservationist George Perkins Marsh had grown up nurturing his love of nature. The restored farmhouse is now a living-history center offering a look at Billings Farm's domestic farming and forestry operations circa the 1890s.

The museum, housed in four renovated 19th-century barns, portrays daily chores such as butter and cheese-making in addition to seasonal activities like ice cutting and sugaring. Tools, home furnishings, machinery and a re-created workshop, kitchen and country store are displayed. Visitors also can observe the daily activities of the modern dairy operation, including the afternoon milking, and participate in special activities.

Self-guiding tours of the farmhouse are available. **Time:** Allow 2 hours minimum. **Hours:** Daily 10-5, May-Oct.; Sat.-Sun. 10-3:30, Nov.-Feb. **Cost:** $12; $11 (ages 62+); $6 (ages 5-15); $3 (ages 3-4). **Phone:** (802) 457-2355.

DANA HOUSE MUSEUM AT THE WOODSTOCK HISTORICAL SOCIETY, n. of jct. SR 12 and US 4 at 26 Elm St., occupies a Federal-style dwelling built in 1807. It houses paintings, decorative arts, silver, china, textiles, clothing, tools, toys, furniture and furnishings. The Gallery exhibits locally made furniture and works by regional artists. The John Cotton Dana Research Library and an heirloom garden are on the premises.

Time: Allow 1 hour minimum. **Hours:** Tues.-Sat. 1-5, Sun. 11-3, late June-late Oct. Phone ahead to confirm schedule. **Cost:** $5; free (ages 0-16). **Phone:** (802) 457-1822.

SUGARBUSH FARM is .5 mi. n. on SR 12, 1.5 mi. e. on Old River Rd., then 2.6 mi. n. on High Pastures Rd. to Sugarbush Farm Rd. (some of the road is gravel). The farm produces maple syrup and cheeses. Exhibits and a video presentation about farm life and syrup making detail production processes, and free samples are provided. Visitors can walk through the woods and see some of the equipment used in collecting maple sap and making syrup.

Time: Allow 1 hour minimum. **Hours:** Mon.-Fri. 8-5, Sat.-Sun. and holidays 9-5. Phone for winter hours and road conditions. Closed Thanksgiving and Christmas. **Cost:** Free. **Phone:** (802) 457-1757 or (800) 281-1757.

BRAESIDE MOTEL   802/457-1366

◆◆ **Motel** $98-$168 **Address:** 908 US 4 E (Woodstock Rd) 05091 **Location:** 1 mi e. **Facility:** 12 units. 1 story, exterior corridors. **Terms:** 2 night minimum stay - seasonal and/or weekends, 15 day cancellation notice-fee imposed.

🌿 FEE 🛏️ 🛜 ✖️ 🔒 ▯

THE JACKSON HOUSE INN   802/457-2065

◆◆◆ **Bed & Breakfast** $185-$325 **Address:** 43 Senior Ln 05091 **Location:** 1.8 mi w of Village Green on US 4. **Facility:** This service-oriented inn is found on scenic grounds not far from a main street of galleries and shops. 11 units. 3 stories (no elevator), interior corridors. **Terms:** check-in 4 pm, 2 night minimum stay - seasonal and/or weekends, age restrictions may apply, 14 day cancellation notice-fee imposed.

🌿 🍽️ 🛜 ✖️ 🅿️ / SOME UNITS 🌐

THE SHIRE RIVERVIEW INN   802/457-2211

◆◆ **Motel** $98-$228 **Address:** 46 Pleasant St 05091 **Location:** Waterfront. 0.4 mi e on US 4; downtown. **Facility:** 42 units. 2 stories (no elevator), interior/exterior corridors. **Terms:** 2 night minimum stay - seasonal and/or weekends, 14 day cancellation notice-fee imposed.

🛏️ 🛜 ✖️ 🔒 / SOME UNITS FEE 🐾

THE VILLAGE INN OF WOODSTOCK   802/457-1255

◆◆◆ **Historic Bed & Breakfast** $150-$350 **Address:** 41 Pleasant St (US 4) 05091 **Location:** On US 4, 0.5 mi e of jct SR 106. **Facility:** Common areas in this 1899 house feature original woodwork, ornate tin ceilings and stained-glass windows. Guest rooms, many with four-poster beds, have Victorian décor. 8 units. 3 stories (no elevator), interior corridors. **Terms:** 2 night minimum stay - seasonal and/or weekends, age restrictions may apply, 14 day cancellation notice-fee imposed, resort fee.

🍽️ 🛜 ✖️ 🅿️ / SOME UNITS 🔒

THE WOODSTOCKER INN   802/457-3896

◆◆◆ **Historic Bed & Breakfast** $130-$395 **Address:** 61 River St 05091 **Location:** 0.5 mi w on US 4. Located in a residential area. **Facility:** An 1830 Cape Dutch-style house, the B&B is in a picturesque area within walking distance of the Village Green. Rooms feature lively, contemporary decor. 9 units. 2 stories (no elevator), interior corridors. **Terms:** check-in 4 pm, 2 night minimum stay - seasonal, age restrictions may apply, 14 day cancellation notice. **Activities:** hiking trails. **Free Special Amenities:** full breakfast and early check-in/late check-out.

SAVE 🌿 🛏️ 🛜 ✖️ 🅿️ / SOME UNITS 🅰️

WOODSTOCK INN & RESORT   (802)457-1100

◆◆◆◆ **Resort Hotel** $195-$864 **Address:** 14 The Green 05091 **Location:** On US 4; center. Located on Village Green. **Facility:** Spacious public areas, large guest rooms and manicured grounds characterize this traditional in-town white brick building. The lobby is graced by a massive stone fireplace, stone floors and hardwood accents. 142 units. 4 stories, interior corridors. **Parking:** on-site and valet. **Terms:** 2-3 night minimum stay - seasonal and/or weekends, 14 day cancellation notice-fee imposed, resort fee. **Amenities:** video games (fee), safes. *Some:* high-speed Internet. **Dining:** 3 restaurants, also, The Red Rooster, see separate listing. **Pool(s):** heated outdoor, heated indoor. **Activities:** saunas, whirlpools, steamrooms, spa. *Fee:* golf-18 holes, 12 tennis courts (2 indoor), racquetball court, downhill & cross country skiing, snowmobiling, bicycles. **Guest Services:** valet laundry, area transportation-recreation facility. **Free Special Amenities:** newspaper and high-speed Internet.

SAVE 🌿 🍽️ 🛁 🅿️ 🍽️ CALL 🔊M 🏊 🛏️ BIZ 🛜 ✖️ 🐾 🔒 ▯

WHERE TO EAT

BENTLEY'S 802/457-3232

◆◆ American. Casual Dining. $9-$24 **AAA Inspector Notes:** This is a favorite spot for locals and tourists alike, located near the Village Green. They serve traditional New England fare with the freshest of ingredients and home-style cooking. The casual decor has a hodgepodge of wall hangings. Often crowded, dining at non-peak times is wise. **Bar:** full bar. **Address:** 3 Elm St 05091 **Location:** Center (US 4). **Parking:** street only. [L] [D]

MANGOWOOD RESTAURANT 802/457-3312

◆◆◆ Continental. Fine Dining. $21-$53 **AAA Inspector Notes:** *Historic.* Classically trained European chefs emphasize food quality and unusual flavors with an Asian flair. The menu features outstanding filet mignon, lamb chops, duck and trout entrées as well as homemade desserts. The décor is a mixture of antiques and modern, eclectic art. **Bar:** full bar. **Reservations:** suggested. **Address:** US 4 W, 530 Woodstock Rd 05091 **Location:** 3 mi w on US 4 from Village Green; in The Lincoln Inn at The Covered Bridge. [D]

MOUNTAIN CREAMERY 802/457-1715

American Family Dining $4-$9

AAA Inspector Notes: For those with fond memories of a soda fountain, this eatery offers a nice nostalgic retreat. Patrons can sample hand-made ice cream and homemade pies and pastries. Also on a menu of from-scratch items are traditional breakfast dishes and deli sandwiches. **Address:** 33 Central St 05091 **Location:** Center. **Parking:** street only. *Menu on AAA.com* [B] [L]

PI BRICK OVEN TRATTORIA 802/457-9277

◆◆ Pizza. Casual Dining. $16-$25 **AAA Inspector Notes:** Hearty and flavorful wood-fired pizzas are the specialty at this modern and friendly eatery right on the main drag. Also, try the antipasto or the delicious shrimp cocktail. **Bar:** full bar. **Address:** 49 Central St 05091 **Location:** Center. **Parking:** street only. [D]

THE PRINCE & THE PAUPER 802/457-1818

◆◆◆ Continental. Fine Dining. $27-$36 **AAA Inspector Notes:** This restaurant, located just off Woodstock's main street, features very creative and flavorful entrees prepared with a local flair. The comfortable rustic atmosphere offers outdoor dining as the weather permits. This is an exceptional dining experience. **Bar:** full bar. **Reservations:** suggested. **Address:** 24 Elm St 05091 **Location:** Just e of the Village Green; in town. **Parking:** street only. [D]

THE RED ROOSTER 802/457-6671

Regional American Fine Dining $16-$32

AAA Inspector Notes: The dining room features contemporary décor, including light hardwood surfaces, an atrium skylight and a view of the gardens. The menu features local ingredients, including many Vermont cheeses and heirloom varieties of vegetables and fruits. Start your meal with clam chowder or a bibb lettuce salad or perhaps a slow-poached pear with warm bleu cheese. Hearty entrées include the bavette steak with turnip potato gratin and a house-made sage cavatelli with duck leg confit. **Bar:** full bar. **Reservations:** suggested. **Address:** 14 The Green 05091 **Location:** On US 4; center; in Woodstock Inn & Resort. **Parking:** on-site and valet. [B] [L] [D] CALL [&M]

NEW!
Disney's Art of Animation Resort

©Disney/Pixar

Disneyland® Resort Hotel

ENJOY A MAGICAL DISNEY VACATION

What's the best way to experience all the enchantment of a vacation to the *Walt Disney World*® Resort in Florida or the *Disneyland*® Resort in California? How do you squeeze the most magic out of the Theme Parks and the whimsically themed *Disney Resort* hotels? And how can you enjoy great savings and exclusive benefits not available anywhere else? By booking a *AAA Vacations*® package from AAA Travel, of course!

DISNEYLAND® RESORT, CALIFORNIA

- Stay just steps away from the magic at a *Disneyland*® Resort Hotel.

- **Now open!**
  Get ready to be floored—cruise into the amazing new Cars Land at *Disney California Adventure*® Park.

WALT DISNEY WORLD RESORT, FLORIDA

- Stay in the middle of the magic at a *Walt Disney World* Resort hotel.

- **Now open!**
  New *Fantasyland*®—immersing you in Disney stories like never before at the *Magic Kingdom*®.

©Disney WDWSALES-12-22964

New Fantasyland

Artist Rendering

©Disney/Pixar

Cars Land

WITH ENCHANTING AAA BENEFITS!

LET AAA BE YOUR GUIDE...

With a *AAA Vacations*® package, you can create the Disney vacation that fits your family, your taste and your budget. And not only will your AAA Travel professional help put everything (like accommodations, tickets and flights) together, you'll also get to enjoy great Disney benefits on top of the exclusive AAA benefits and savings once you get there! Then all you need to do is relax and have fun.

READY TO START MAKING MAGIC?
Then contact your **AAA Travel professional** today!

Disney PARKS

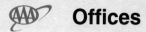

Offices

Cities with main offices are listed in **BOLD TYPE** and toll-free member service numbers in *ITALIC TYPE*.
All are closed Saturdays, Sundays and holidays unless otherwise indicated.
The addresses, phone numbers and hours for any AAA/CAA office are subject to change.
The type of service provided is designated below the name of the city where the office is located:

✚ Auto travel services, including books and maps, and on-demand TripTik® routings.
● Auto travel services, including selected books and maps, and on-demand TripTik® routings.
■ Books/maps only, no marked maps or on-demand TripTik® routings.
▲ Travel Agency Services, cruise, tour, air, car and rail reservations; domestic and international hotel reservations; passport photo services; international and domestic travel guides and maps; travel money products; and International Driving Permits. In addition, assistance with travel related insurance products including trip cancellation, travel accident, lost luggage, trip delay and assistance products.
❍ Insurance services provided. If only this icon appears, only insurance services are provided at that office.
🇨 Car Care Plus Facility provides car care services.
🔌 Electric vehicle charging station on premises.

AAA NATIONAL OFFICE: 1000 AAA DRIVE, HEATHROW, FLORIDA 32746-5063, (407) 444-7000

MAINE

AUBURN—AAA NORTHERN NEW ENGLAND, 600 CENTER ST SHAWS PLAZA, 04210. WEEKDAYS (M-F) 8:30-5:00, SAT 9:00-1:00. (207) 786-0664, *(800) 310-1222.* ✚ ▲ ❍

AUGUSTA—AAA NORTHERN NEW ENGLAND, 20 WHITTEN RD STE 11, 04330. WEEKDAYS (M-F) 8:30-5:00, SAT 9:00-1:00. (207) 622-2221, *(800) 640-5608.* ✚ ▲ ❍

BANGOR—AAA NORTHERN NEW ENGLAND, 339 GRIFFIN RD, 04401. WEEKDAYS (M-F) 8:30-5:00, SAT 9:00-1:00. (207) 942-8287, *(800) 223-3700.* ✚ ▲ ❍

BIDDEFORD—AAA NORTHERN NEW ENGLAND, 472 ALFRED ST STE 102, 04005. WEEKDAYS (M-F) 8:30-5:00, SAT 9:00-1:00. (207) 282-5212, *(866) 485-8812.* ✚ ▲ ❍

BRUNSWICK—AAA NORTHERN NEW ENGLAND, 147 BATH RD STE A130, 04011. WEEKDAYS (M-F) 8:30-5:00, SAT 9:00-1:00. (207) 729-3300, *(800) 499-3111.* ✚ ▲ ❍

ELLSWORTH—AAA NORTHERN NEW ENGLAND, 130 OAK ST STE 3, 04605. WEEKDAYS (M-F) 8:30-5:00, SAT 9:00-1:00. (207) 667-6260, *(800) 437-0281.* ■ ▲ ❍

PORTLAND—AAA NORTHERN NEW ENGLAND, 191 MARGINAL WAY, 04101. WEEKDAYS (M-F) 7:30-5:30, SAT 8:00-4:30. (207) 772-5477 🇨

PORTLAND—AAA NORTHERN NEW ENGLAND, 68 MARGINAL WAY, 04101. WEEKDAYS (M-F) 8:30-5:00, SAT 9:00-1:00. (207) 780-6800, *(800) 482-7497.* ✚ ▲ ❍

SOUTH PORTLAND—AAA NORTHERN NEW ENGLAND, 401 WESTERN AVE, 04106. WEEKDAYS (M-F) 8:30-5:00, SAT 9:00-1:00. (207) 775-6211, *(800) 336-6211.* ✚ ▲ ❍

WATERVILLE—AAA NORTHERN NEW ENGLAND, 13 WASHINGTON ST, 04901. WEEKDAYS (M-F) 8:30-5:00, SAT 9:00-1:00. (207) 873-0692, *(800) 359-2106.* ✚ ▲ ❍

NEW HAMPSHIRE

CONCORD—AAA NORTHERN NEW ENGLAND, 48 FT EDDY RD, 03301. WEEKDAYS (M-F) 8:30-5:00, SAT 9:00-1:00. (603) 228-0301, *(800) 222-3422.* ✚ ▲ ❍

KEENE—AAA NORTHERN NEW ENGLAND, 429 WEST ST, 03431. WEEKDAYS (M-F) 8:30-5:00, SAT 9:00-1:00. (603) 358-0460, *(800) 222-3407.* ✚ ▲ ❍

MANCHESTER—AAA NORTHERN NEW ENGLAND, 560 S WILLOW ST, 03103. WEEKDAYS (M-F) 8:30-5:00, SAT 9:00-1:00. (603) 669-0101, *(800) 222-3445.* ✚ ▲ ❍

NASHUA—AAA NORTHERN NEW ENGLAND, 379 AMHERST ST UNIT 6B, 03063. WEEKDAYS (M-F) 8:30-5:00, SAT 9:00-1:00. (603) 889-0165, *(800) 222-3750.* ✚ ▲ ❍

PORTSMOUTH—AAA NORTHERN NEW ENGLAND, 599 LAFAYETTE RD #15, 03801. WEEKDAYS (M-F) 8:30-5:00, SAT 9:00-1:00. (603) 436-8610, *(800) 222-3420.* ✚ ▲ ❍

SALEM—AAA SOUTHERN NEW ENGLAND, 489 S BROADWAY, 03079. WEEKDAYS (M-F) 9:00-5:00, SAT 9:00-1:00. (603) 898-9953 ✚ ▲ ❍

SOMERSWORTH—AAA NORTHERN NEW ENGLAND, 8 TRI-CITY PLZ, 03878. WEEKDAYS (M-F) 8:30-5:00, SAT 9:00-1:00. (603) 750-3080, *(866) 484-5681.* ✚ ▲ ❍

VERMONT

MONTPELIER—AAA NORTHERN NEW ENGLAND, 317 RIVER ST, 05602. WEEKDAYS (M-F) 8:30-5:00, SAT 9:00-1:00. (802) 229-0505, *(800) 717-0222.* ✚ ▲ ❍

RUTLAND—AAA NORTHERN NEW ENGLAND, 302 US RT 7 SOUTH, 05701. WEEKDAYS (M-F) 8:30-5:00, SAT 9:00-1:00. (802) 775-1558, *(800) 388-1558.* ✚ ▲ ❍

WILLISTON—AAA NORTHERN NEW ENGLAND, 28 WALNUT ST STE 160, 05495. WEEKDAYS (M-F) 8:30-5:00, SAT 9:00-1:00. (802) 878-8233, *(800) 477-1323.* ✚ ▲ ❍

Metric Equivalents Chart

TEMPERATURE

To convert Fahrenheit to Celsius, subtract 32 from the Fahrenheit temperature, multiply by 5 and divide by 9.
To convert Celsius to Fahrenheit, multiply by 9, divide by 5 and add 32.

ACRES

1 acre = 0.4 hectare (ha)   1 hectare = 2.47 acres

MILES AND KILOMETRES

Note: A kilometre is approximately 5/8 or 0.6 of a mile.
To convert kilometres to miles multiply by 0.6.

Miles/Kilometres		Kilometres/Miles	
15	24.1	30	18.6
20	32.2	35	21.7
25	40.2	40	24.8
30	48.3	45	27.9
35	56.3	50	31.0
40	64.4	55	34.1
45	72.4	60	37.2
50	80.5	65	40.3
55	88.5	70	43.4
60	96.6	75	46.6
65	104.6	80	49.7
70	112.7	85	52.8
75	120.7	90	55.9
80	128.7	95	59.0
85	136.8	100	62.1
90	144.8	105	65.2
95	152.9	110	68.3
100	160.9	115	71.4

Celsius ° / Fahrenheit °

Celsius °		Fahrenheit °
100	BOILING	212
37		100
35		95
32		90
29		85
27		80
24		75
21		70
18		65
16		60
13		55
10		50
7		45
4		40
2		35
0	FREEZING	32
-4		25
-7		20
-9		15
-12		10
-15		5
-18		0
-21		-5
-24		-10
-27		-15

LINEAR MEASURE

Customary	Metric
1 inch = 2.54 centimetres	1 centimetre = 0.4 inches
1 foot = 30 centimetres	1 metre = 3.3 feet
1 yard = 0.91 metres	1 metre = 1.09 yards
1 mile = 1.6 kilometres	1 kilometre = .62 miles

WEIGHT

If You Know:	Multiply By:	To Find:
Ounces	28	Grams
Pounds	0.45	Kilograms
Grams	0.035	Ounces
Kilograms	2.2	Pounds

LIQUID MEASURE

Customary	Metric
1 fluid ounce = 30 millilitres	1 millilitre = .03 fluid ounces
1 cup = .24 litres	1 litre = 2.1 pints
1 pint = .47 litres	1 litre = 1.06 quarts
1 quart = .95 litres	1 litre = .26 gallons
1 gallon = 3.8 litres	

PRESSURE

Air pressure in automobile tires is expressed in kilopascals. Multiply pound-force per square inch (psi) by 6.89 to find kilopascals (kPa).

24 psi = 165 kPa	28 psi = 193 kPa
26 psi = 179 kPa	30 psi = 207 kPa

GALLON AND LITRES

Gallons/Litres				Litres/Gallons			
5	19.0	12	45.6	10	2.6	40	10.4
6	22.8	14	53.2	15	3.9	50	13.0
7	26.6	16	60.8	20	5.2	60	15.6
8	30.4	18	68.4	25	6.5	70	18.2
9	34.2	20	76.0	30	7.8	80	20.8
10	38.0	25	95.0	35	9.1	90	23.4

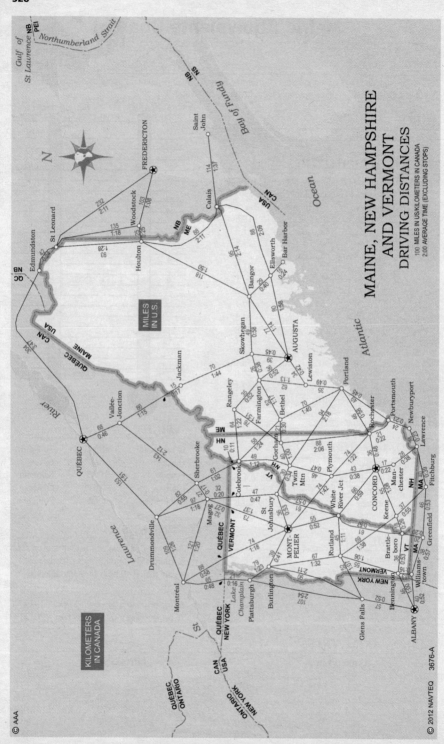

MAINE, NEW HAMPSHIRE
AND VERMONT
DRIVING DISTANCES

100 MILES IN US/KILOMETERS IN CANADA
2:00 AVERAGE TIME (EXCLUDING STOPS)

© 2012 NAVTEQ   3676-A

© AAA

Border Information

U.S. Residents Traveling to Canada

Border crossing requirements: Travelers are required to present proper travel documents in order to enter Canada and return to the U.S.

Air travel: A U.S. passport is required.

Land or sea travel: Proof of citizenship and proof of identity are required. Approved documents include a passport or passport card, Enhanced Driver's License or NEXUS trusted traveler program card. Visit the U.S. Department of State website travel.state.gov for the most current information on these requirements. Canadian citizens should refer to the Canada Border Services Agency website www.cbsa-asfc.gc.ca.

U.S. resident aliens: An Alien Registration Receipt Card (Green Card) as well as a passport from the country of citizenship is required.

Children: All children must provide their own travel documents. In lieu of a U.S. passport or passport card, children under 16 traveling to Canada by land or sea may present an original or copy of their birth certificate, a Report of Birth Abroad obtained from a U.S. consulate or a Naturalization Certificate. Minors must be accompanied by parents, or have a notarized letter of consent from one or both absent parents giving permission to go on the trip.

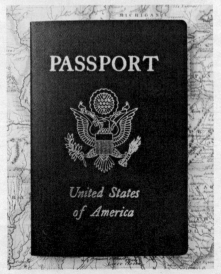

Legal Issues: Persons with felony convictions, DUI convictions or other offenses may be denied entry into Canada.

Firearms: Canada has strict laws regarding the importing, exporting, possession, use, storage, display and transportation of firearms. These are federal laws that apply across the country. Firearms are divided into classes: non-restricted (most ordinary rifles and shotguns); restricted (mainly handguns) and prohibited (full and converted automatics and certain handguns, among others).

To bring a non-restricted or restricted firearm into Canada you must:

- Be 18 years of age or older
- Declare firearm(s) at the first point of entry
- Obtain an Authorization to Transport (ATT) from a provincial or territorial Chief Firearms Officer prior to arrival at the point of entry; contact the Canadian Firearms Centre at (800) 731-4000 for additional details.

Hunters may bring in, duty-free, 200 rounds of ammunition; a valid license or declaration to purchase ammunition is required. Those planning to hunt in multiple provinces or territories must obtain a hunting license from each one.

Firearms are forbidden in many of Canada's national and provincial parks, game reserves and adjacent areas. For additional information regarding the temporary importation and use of firearms consult the Canada Border Services Agency website.

Personal items: Clothing, personal items, sports and recreational equipment, automobiles, snowmobiles, cameras, personal computers and food products appropriate for the purpose and duration of the visit may be brought into Canada duty and tax-free. Customs may require a refundable security deposit at the time of entry.

Tobacco products: Those meeting age requirements (18 years in Alberta, Manitoba, Northwest Territories, Nunavut, Saskatchewan, Quebec and Yukon; 19 years in other provinces) may bring in up to 50 cigars, 200 cigarettes, 200 grams of tobacco and 200 tobacco sticks.

Alcohol: Those meeting age requirements (18 years in Alberta, Manitoba and Quebec; 19 years in other provinces and territories) may bring in limited alcoholic beverages: 40 ounces of liquor, 1.6 quarts of wine or 9 quarts of beer or ale (equivalent to 24 12-ounce bottles or cans).

- Amounts exceeding the allowable quantities are subject to federal duty and taxes, and provincial/territorial liquor fees.
- Provincial fees are paid at customs at the time of entry in all provinces and Yukon.
- It is illegal to bring more than the allowable alcohol quantity into the Northwest Territories or Nunavut.

Purchases: Articles purchased at Canadian duty-free shops are subject to U.S. Customs exemptions and restrictions; those purchased at U.S. duty-free shops before entering Canada are subject to duty if brought back into the United States.

Prescription drugs: Persons requiring medication while visiting Canada are permitted to bring it for their own use. Medication should be in the original packaging with a label listing the drug and its intended use. Bring a copy of the prescription and the prescribing doctor's phone number.

Gifts: Items not exceeding $60 (CAN) in value (excluding tobacco, alcoholic beverages and advertising matter) taken into or mailed to Canada are allowed free entry. Gifts valued at more than $60 are subject to regular duty and taxes on the excess amount.

Pets: You must have a certificate for a dog or cat 3 months and older. It must clearly describe the animal, declare that the animal is currently vaccinated against rabies and include a licensed veterinarian signature.

- Collar tags are not sufficient proof of immunization.
- Be sure the vaccination does not expire while traveling in Canada.
- The certificate is also required to bring the animal back into the U.S.

Exemptions: Service animals; healthy puppies and kittens under 3 months old with a health certificate signed by a licensed veterinarian indicating that the animal is too young to vaccinate.

Vehicles
- Vehicles entering Canada for leisure travel, including trailers not exceeding 8 feet 6 inches (2.6 m) in width, are generally subject to quick and routine entry procedures.
- To temporarily leave or store a car, trailer or other goods in Canada if you must leave the country, you must pay an import duty and taxes or present a valid permit. Canadian Customs officials issue vehicle permits at the point of entry.
- You are required to carry your vehicle registration document when traveling in Canada.
- If driving a car other than your own, you must have written permission from the owner.
- If driving a rented car, you must provide a copy of the rental contract.
- A valid U.S. driver's license is valid in Canada.
- In all Canadian provinces and territories except Alberta, British Columbia and Saskatchewan, it is illegal to use radar detectors, even if unplugged.
- Seat belt use is required for the driver and all passengers.

Financial Responsibility Laws in Canada: When an accident involves death, injury or property damage, Canadian provinces and territories require evidence of financial responsibility.

U.S. motorists should check with their insurance company regarding whether they are required to obtain and carry a yellow Non-Resident Inter-Province Motor Vehicle Liability Insurance Card (accepted as evidence of financial responsibility throughout Canada). Those not carrying proper proof may be subject to a substantial fine. If renting a vehicle, check with the rental car company.

U.S. Residents Returning to the U.S.

U.S. citizens returning to the U.S. from Canada by air must have a valid passport. Those returning by land or sea are required to present the appropriate travel documents outlined above.

Every individual seeking entry into the United States—foreign visitors, U.S. citizens or lawful permanent residents—must be inspected at the point of entry. Random searches may be conducted by U.S. Customs and Border Protection agents.

U.S. Exemptions for a Stay in Canada of 48 Hours or More

- Each individual may bring back tax- and duty-free articles not exceeding $800 in retail value.
- Any amount over the $800 exemption is subject to duty.
- The exemption is allowed once every 30 days.
- A family (related persons living in the same household) may combine purchases to avoid exceeding individual exemption limits.
- Exemptions are based on fair retail value (keep receipts of all purchases as proof).
- Exemptions apply to articles acquired only for personal or household use or as gifts and not intended for sale.
- The exemption may include 100 cigars, 200 cigarettes and 1 liter of liquor per person over age 21 (state liquor laws are enforced).
- All articles must accompany you on your return.

U.S. Exemptions for a Stay in Canada Less Than 48 Hours

- Each individual may bring back tax- and duty-free articles not exceeding $200 in retail value.
- The exemption may include no more than 50 cigarettes, 10 cigars, 5 fluid ounces (150 milliliters) of alcoholic beverage or 150 milliliters of perfume containing alcohol.
- A family may not combine purchases.
- If purchases exceed the $200 exemption, you forfeit the exemption and all purchases become subject to duty.
- All articles must be declared and accompany you upon return.

Gifts

- Gifts up to $100 fair retail value may be sent to friends or relatives in the United States provided no recipient receives more than one gift per day (gifts do not have to be included in the $800 exemption).
- Gifts of tobacco products, alcoholic beverages or perfume containing alcohol valued at more than $5 retail are excluded from this provision.
- Mark the contents, retail value and "Unsolicited Gift" on the outside of the package.

Prohibited: Narcotics and dangerous drugs, drug paraphernalia, obscene articles and publications, seditious or treasonable matter, lottery tickets, hazardous items (fireworks, dangerous toys, toxic or poisonous substances) and switchblade knives. Also prohibited are any goods originating in embargoed countries.

Canadian Residents Traveling to the U.S.

Canadian citizens entering the U.S. by air must have a valid passport. Canadian citizens entering the U.S. by land or sea are required to present the appropriate travel documents; refer to the Canada Border Services Agency website www.cbsa-asfc.gc.ca for the most current information on these requirements.

If traveling to the United States with a minor, carry documentation proving your custodial rights. A person under age 18 traveling to the United States alone or with only one parent or another adult must carry certified documentation proving that the trip is permitted by both parents.

U.S. Customs permits Canadian residents to bring—duty-free for personal use and not intended for sale—the following: clothing, personal items and equipment appropriate to the trip, up to 200 cigarettes, 50 cigars or 2 kilograms of tobacco, and 1 liter of alcoholic beverage.

Canadian Residents Returning to Canada

Canadian residents may bring back, free of duty and taxes, goods valued up to $400

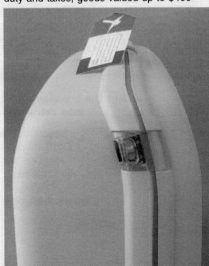

(CAN) any number of times a year, provided the visit to the United States is 48 hours or more and all goods accompany the purchaser (a written declaration may be required).

You may claim a $50 (CAN) exemption on goods, excluding alcoholic beverages and tobacco products, if returning after an absence of less than 48 hours and not using any other exemption. If bringing back more than $50 worth of goods, the regular duty and tax rate is levied on the entire value. This exemption may apply any number of times in a year. No tobacco or alcohol may be brought back if returning from a visit of less than 48 hours.

If returning after 7 days or more (not counting the departure day from Canada)

you may claim up to a $750 (CAN) exemption. Goods other than alcohol and tobacco products need not accompany you (a written declaration may be required).

Permitted within the $400 and $750 exemptions: up to 50 cigars, 200 cigarettes, 200 tobacco sticks and 6.4 ounces of tobacco, and up to 40 ounces of liquor or 1.6 quarts of wine or 9 quarts of beer or ale (the equivalent of 24 12-ounce bottles or cans). You must meet the minimum age requirement of the province or territory entered to claim alcohol or tobacco products.

While AAA makes every effort to provide accurate and complete information, AAA makes no warranty, express or implied, and assumes no legal liability or responsibility for the accuracy or completeness of any information contained herein.

Points of Interest Index

 Attractions appear at the top of each category
and offer a Great Experience for Members®.

ART & CULTURE

▽ THE CURRIER MUSEUM OF ART........MANCHESTER, NH 213
▽ OGUNQUIT MUSEUM OF AMERICAN
   ART..OGUNQUIT, ME 116
▽ PORTLAND MUSEUM OF ART.............PORTLAND, ME 129
▽ SHELBURNE MUSEUM......................SHELBURNE, VT 307
ACADIAN CROSS HISTORIC
   SHRINE...MADAWASKA, ME 112
ACADIAN VILLAGE.........................VAN BUREN, ME 153
AMPHITHEATRE AND HARBOR PARK.....CAMDEN, ME 75
AROOSTOOK COUNTY HISTORICAL AND ART
   MUSEUM..HOULTON, ME 94
ART GALLERY AT THE UNIVERSITY OF
   MAINE-FARMINGTON.................FARMINGTON, ME 86
BARN GALLERY..............................OGUNQUIT, ME 116
BARRE OPERA HOUSE............................BARRE, VT 271
BARRY FAULKNER.........................CONCORD, NH 183
BATES COLLEGE................................LEWISTON, ME 108
BATES COLLEGE MUSEUM OF ART.......LEWISTON, ME 109
THE BELFAST MASKERS......................BELFAST, ME 63
BELKNAP MILL...................................LACONIA, NH 206
BENNINGTON CENTER FOR THE
   ARTS...BENNINGTON, VT 273
BOWDOIN COLLEGE.......................BRUNSWICK, ME 71
BOWDOIN COLLEGE MUSEUM OF
   ART...BRUNSWICK, ME 71
BRATTLEBORO MUSEUM & ART
   CENTER.......................................BRATTLEBORO, VT 277
BRYAN MEMORIAL GALLERY.......JEFFERSONVILLE, VT 286
CAMDEN OPERA HOUSE....................CAMDEN, ME 75
CAPITOL CENTER FOR THE ARTS..........CONCORD, NH 182
CATHEDRAL OF THE PINES....................RINDGE, NH 245
CENTER FOR MAINE CONTEMPORARY
   ART...ROCKPORT, ME 144
CHAFFEE ART CENTER........................RUTLAND, VT 304
CHAMP ....LAKE CHAMPLAIN, VT 287
CHAMPLAIN COLLEGE....................BURLINGTON, VT 278
CITY THEATER...............................BIDDEFORD, ME 66
COLBY COLLEGE.........................WATERVILLE, ME 155
COLLINS CENTER FOR THE ARTS.............ORONO, ME 124
COLONIAL THEATRE..............................KEENE, NH 204
CONGREGATIONAL CHRISTIAN
   CHURCH..FRANKLIN, NH 193

CUMSTON HALL..........................MONMOUTH, ME 113
DARTMOUTH COLLEGE.....................HANOVER, NH 198
THE DOMES OF THE YOSEMITE.....ST. JOHNSBURY, VT 306
DYER LIBRARY AND SACO MUSEUM...........SACO, ME 145
ELECTRA HAVEMEYER WEBB
   MEMORIAL...................................SHELBURNE, VT 307
ELIZABETH DE C. WILSON
   MUSEUM......................................MANCHESTER, VT 290
FARNSWORTH ART MUSEUM AND THE WYETH
   CENTER..ROCKLAND, ME 142
FIRST PARISH CHURCH....................BRUNSWICK, ME 71
FIRST PARISH CHURCH....................KENNEBUNK, ME 95
FLETCHER FARM SCHOOL FOR THE ARTS AND
   CRAFTS..LUDLOW, VT 288
FRANCO-AMERICAN HERITAGE
   CENTER..LEWISTON, ME 109
FRANKLIN PIERCE UNIVERSITY...............RINDGE, NH 245
GOULD ACADEMY.............................BETHEL, ME 65
THE HELEN DAY ART CENTER.................STOWE, VT 310
H.O.M.E. ....ORLAND, ME 124
HOOD MUSEUM OF ART....................HANOVER, NH 198
HOPKINS CENTER............................HANOVER, NH 198
HUTCHINS CONCERT HALL.....................ORONO, ME 124
INSTITUTE OF CONTEMPORARY ART....PORTLAND, ME 127
JOSÉ CLEMENTE OROZCO..................HANOVER, NH 198
KEENE STATE COLLEGE REDFERN ARTS
   CENTER...KEENE, NH 204
KENNEBUNKPORT..................................ME 96
KING ARTHUR FLOUR BAKING EDUCATION CENTER,
   BAKERY AND THE BAKER'S STORE.......NORWICH, VT 300
LA SALETTE SHRINE AND CENTER...........ENFIELD, NH 190
LAKEWOOD THEATER...................SKOWHEGAN, ME 148
LOUISE ARKELL PAVILION..............MANCHESTER, VT 290
MAINE MARITIME ACADEMY.................CASTINE, ME 80
MAINE STATE BUILDING AND ALL SOULS
   CHAPEL..................................POLAND SPRING, ME 125
MAINE STATE MUSIC THEATER.........BRUNSWICK, ME 71
MARLBORO COLLEGE.....................MARLBORO, VT 294
MEMORIAL BELL TOWER.....................RINDGE, NH 245
MIDDLEBURY COLLEGE.................MIDDLEBURY, VT 294
MONMOUTH MUSEUM.................MONMOUTH, ME 113
MOUNT WASHINGTON VALLEY THEATRE
   COMPANY..........................NORTH CONWAY, NH 223

Index Legend

NB.............................national battlefield		NR.................................national river	
NBP.......................national battlefield park		NS..............................national seashore	
NC................................national cemetery		NWR.......................national wildlife refuge	
NF..................................national forest		PHP......................provincial historic(al) park	
NHM.................national historic(al) monument		PHS........................provincial historic(al) site	
NHP.....................national historic(al) park		PP...................................provincial park	
NHS......................national historic(al) site		SF.......................................state forest	
NL.................................national lakeshore		SHM.....................state historic(al) monument	
NME..............................national memorial		SHP.........................state historic(al) park	
NMO.............................national monument		SHS...........................state historic(al) site	
NMP..........................national military park		SME.................................state memorial	
NP....................................national park		SP..state park	
NRA.........................national recreation area		SRA............................state recreation area	

MUSEUM OF ART............................WATERVILLE, ME 155
NEW HAMPSHIRE INSTITUTE OF
ART...MANCHESTER, NH 214
THE NORMAN ROCKWELL EXHIBIT AND SUGAR
SHACK..ARLINGTON, VT 270
NORMAN ROCKWELL MUSEUM OF
VERMONT.......................................RUTLAND, VT 304
NORTH COUNTRY CENTER FOR THE
ARTS..LINCOLN, NH 208
NORWICH UNIVERSITY...................NORTHFIELD, VT 299
OGUNQUIT...ME 116
OGUNQUIT PLAYHOUSE...................OGUNQUIT, ME 116
OLD FIRST CHURCH........................BENNINGTON, VT 273
THE OLD ROCKINGHAM MEETING
HOUSE.......................................ROCKINGHAM, VT 303
PALACE THEATRE.........................MANCHESTER, NH 213
PAUL CREATIVE ARTS CENTER..............DURHAM, NH 189
PEMAQUID ART GALLERY........PEMAQUID POINT, ME 125
PENOBSCOT MARINE MUSEUM..........SEARSPORT, ME 148
PETERBOROUGH PLAYERS..........PETERBOROUGH, NH 235
PHILLIPS EXETER ACADEMY...................EXETER, NH 190
PORTLAND STAGE............................PORTLAND, ME 126
PORTLAND SYMPHONY ORCHESTRA...PORTLAND, ME 126
REED FINE ART GALLERY...............PRESQUE ISLE, ME 140
THE ROUND CHURCH NATIONAL HISTORIC
LANDMARK....................................RICHMOND, VT 303
ST. ANNE'S SHRINE......LAKE CHAMPLAIN ISLANDS, VT 288
ST. JOHN'S EPISCOPAL CHURCH......PORTSMOUTH, NH 238
ST. JOHNSBURY ATHENAEUM.......ST. JOHNSBURY, VT 306
ST. MARY'S STAR OF THE SEA
CHURCH..NEWPORT, VT 299
ST. PATRICK'S CHURCH...................NEWCASTLE, ME 114
SEACOAST REPERTORY THEATRE....PORTSMOUTH, NH 236
SHARON ARTS CENTER..............PETERBOROUGH, NH 235
SOUTHERN VERMONT ARTS
CENTER.......................................MANCHESTER, VT 290
T.W. WOOD GALLERY AND ART
CENTER.......................................MONTPELIER, VT 296
UNIVERSITY COLLEGE AT SACO.........BIDDEFORD, ME 66
UNIVERSITY OF MAINE..........................ORONO, ME 124
UNIVERSITY OF MAINE AT
FARMINGTON............................FARMINGTON, ME 86
UNIVERSITY OF NEW ENGLAND.........BIDDEFORD, ME 66
UNIVERSITY OF NEW HAMPSHIRE.........DURHAM, NH 189
UNIVERSITY OF VERMONT.............BURLINGTON, VT 278
VERGENNES OPERA HOUSE...............VERGENNES, VT 316
VESPER HILL CHILDREN'S CHAPEL.......ROCKPORT, ME 144
WALDO THEATRE........................WALDOBORO, ME 154
WATERVILLE OPERA HOUSE............WATERVILLE, ME 154
WEBB GALLERY OF AMERICAN ART....SHELBURNE, VT 307
WESTON PLAYHOUSE..........................WESTON, VT 319
THE WESTON PRIORY..........................WESTON, VT 319
"WHALING WALL"..........................PORTLAND, ME 126
YESTER HOUSE.............................MANCHESTER, VT 290

CHILDREN'S ACTIVITIES

AQUABOGGAN WATER PARK...................SACO, ME 145
BLACKBEARD'S FAMILY FUN PARK.........BANGOR, ME 43
CANOBIE LAKE PARK............................SALEM, NH 246
CHILDREN'S DISCOVERY MUSEUM........AUGUSTA, ME 42
CHILDREN'S MUSEUM & THEATRE OF
MAINE..PORTLAND, ME 126
CHILDREN'S MUSEUM OF NEW
HAMPSHIRE......................................DOVER, NH 188

CLARK'S TRADING POST........................LINCOLN, NH 208
ECHO LAKE AQUARIUM AND SCIENCE
CENTER.....................................BURLINGTON, VT 279
FUNTOWN SPLASHTOWN USA...................SACO, ME 145
MAINE STATE
AQUARIUM............WEST BOOTHBAY HARBOR, ME 157
PALACE PLAYLAND AMUSEMENT
PARK....................OLD ORCHARD BEACH, ME 122
SANTA'S VILLAGE............................JEFFERSON, NH 204
SIX GUN CITY & FORT SPLASH WATER
PARK...JEFFERSON, NH 204
SQUAM LAKES NATURAL SCIENCE
CENTER....................................HOLDERNESS, NH 201
STORY LAND...GLEN, NH 194
WATER COUNTRY.......................PORTSMOUTH, NH 238
THE WHALE'S TALE WATER PARK.........LINCOLN, NH 208
YORK'S WILD KINGDOM ZOO AND AMUSEMENT
PARK..YORK BEACH, ME 161

EVENTS & FESTIVALS

AMERICAN FOLK FESTIVAL...................BANGOR, ME 44
FIELDS OF LUPINE FESTIVAL.............FRANCONIA, NH 191
LEAGUE OF NEW HAMPSHIRE CRAFTSMEN'S
FAIR..NEWBURY, NH 221
MAINE LOBSTER FESTIVAL................ROCKLAND, ME 142
NEW HAMPSHIRE HIGHLAND GAMES &
FESTIVAL...LINCOLN, NH 208
NORTH AMERICAN WIFE CARRYING
CHAMPIONSHIP..................................NEWRY, ME 115
OKTOBERFEST ....STOWE, VT 310
WINDJAMMER DAYS..........BOOTHBAY HARBOR, ME 67
AMOS FORTUNE FORUM......................JAFFREY, NH 203
BENNINGTON BATTLE DAY
CELEBRATION.............................BENNINGTON, VT 272
BREAD LOAF WRITERS'
CONFERENCE.............................MIDDLEBURY, VT 294
FALL FOLIAGE FESTIVAL.......BOOTHBAY HARBOR, ME 67
KNEISEL HALL CHAMBER MUSIC
FESTIVAL.......................................BLUE HILL, ME 66
WASSAIL WEEKEND.....................WOODSTOCK, VT 322

HISTORIC SITES & EXHIBITS

BENNINGTON BATTLE
MONUMENT..............................BENNINGTON, VT 272
BENNINGTON MUSEUM.................BENNINGTON, VT 273
CANTERBURY SHAKER VILLAGE......CANTERBURY, NH 181
COLE LAND TRANSPORTATION
MUSEUM...BANGOR, ME 44
CRAWFORD NOTCH....................................NH 187
FRANCONIA NOTCH....................................NH 192
HILDENE, THE LINCOLN FAMILY
HOME.......................................MANCHESTER, VT 290
LONGFELLOW HOUSE......................PORTLAND, ME 127
MAINE MARITIME MUSEUM....................BATH, ME 63
MAINE STATE MUSEUM...................AUGUSTA, ME 42
MARSH-BILLINGS-ROCKEFELLER
MANSION....MARSH-BILLINGS-ROCKEFELLER NHP, VT 294
MONTSHIRE MUSEUM OF SCIENCE........NORWICH, VT 300
MUSICAL WONDER HOUSE...............WISCASSET, ME 158
PARK-McCULLOUGH HISTORIC
ESTATE.............................NORTH BENNINGTON, VT 299
PINKHAM NOTCH SCENIC AREA.......................NH 235
PRESIDENT CALVIN COOLIDGE SHS......PLYMOUTH, VT 301
VICTORIA MANSION........................PORTLAND, ME 130
WILSON CASTLE...............................PROCTOR, VT 302

19TH CENTURY WILLOWBROOK
VILLAGE......................................NEWFIELD, ME 114

ABBE MUSEUM AT SIEUR DE MONTS
SPRING......................................ACADIA NP, ME   40

ABBE MUSEUM DOWNTOWN.........BAR HARBOR, ME   46

ABENAKI INDIAN..........................SKOWHEGAN, ME 148

AMERICAN INDEPENDENCE MUSEUM.......EXETER, NH 190

AMERICAN MUSEUM OF FLY
FISHING..................................MANCHESTER, VT 289

AMERICAN PRECISION MUSEUM..........WINDSOR, VT 321

ANDRE THE SEAL............................ROCKPORT, ME 144

ANDROSCOGGIN HISTORICAL SOCIETY
MUSEUM......................................AUBURN, ME   41

BAGADUCE MUSIC LENDING LIBRARY...BLUE HILL, ME   66

BAKER-BERRY LIBRARY.....................HANOVER, NH 198

BALTIMORE COVERED BRIDGE..........SPRINGFIELD, VT 309

BANGOR MUSEUM AND CENTER FOR
HISTORY......................................BANGOR, ME   43

BAR HARBOR HISTORICAL SOCIETY
MUSEUM...................................BAR HARBOR, ME   46

BAR HARBOR WHALE MUSEUM......BAR HARBOR, ME   47

BASS HARBOR HEAD
LIGHT....................SOUTHWEST HARBOR, ME 151

BELKNAP MILL..................................LACONIA, NH 206

BETHEL HISTORICAL SOCIETY REGIONAL HISTORY
CENTER......................................BETHEL, ME   65

BIG INDIAN..................................FREEPORT, ME   86

BIRDS OF VERMONT MUSEUM........HUNTINGTON, VT 285

BIXBY MEMORIAL FREE LIBRARY........VERGENNES, VT 316

BLACK RIVER ACADEMY MUSEUM.........LUDLOW, VT 289

BOOTHBAY RAILWAY VILLAGE.........BOOTHBAY, ME   66

THE BOY WITH THE LEAKING BOOT.....HOULTON, ME   95

BREAD AND PUPPET MUSEUM.................GLOVER, VT 284

BRETTON WOODS.................................NH 179

THE BRICK STORE MUSEUM.............KENNEBUNK, ME   95

BROOKS MEMORIAL LIBRARY........BRATTLEBORO, VT 277

BURNHAM TAVERN MUSEUM..............MACHIAS, ME 111

BURNT ISLAND
LIGHT....................WEST BOOTHBAY HARBOR, ME 157

CAPE NEDDICK LIGHT................YORK HARBOR, ME 162

CARRIAGE AND SLEIGH MUSEUM........JEFFERSON, NH 204

CASTLE IN THE CLOUDS.......MOULTONBOROUGH, NH 219

CASTLE TUCKER HISTORIC HOUSE
MUSEUM....................................WISCASSET, ME 158

CASTLETON ....VT 281

CHARLOTTE ....VT 282

CHASE HOUSE............................PORTSMOUTH, NH 238

CHIMNEY POINT................................ADDISON, VT 270

CHIMNEY POINT SHS.........................ADDISON, VT 270

CINCINNATI HALL..................................EXETER, NH 190

CLARK HOUSE MUSEUM COMPLEX...WOLFEBORO, NH 253

COLD HOLLOW CIDER
MILL..............................WATERBURY CENTER, VT 318

COLONIAL PEMAQUID SHS AND FORT WILLIAM
HENRY..BRISTOL, ME   71

CONWAY HOMESTEAD-CRAMER
MUSEUM....................................ROCKPORT, ME 144

COOPER HOUSE........................MACHIASPORT, ME 112

CORNISH ....NH 187

CORNISH-WINDSOR COVERED BRIDGE...WINDSOR, VT 321

CRAIG BROOK ATLANTIC SALMON
MUSEUM..................................EAST ORLAND, ME   82

DANA HOUSE MUSEUM AT THE WOODSTOCK
HISTORICAL SOCIETY..................WOODSTOCK, VT 322

DANIEL WEBSTER............................FRANKLIN, NH 193

DANIEL WEBSTER BIRTHPLACE............FRANKLIN, NH 193

DELORME ....YARMOUTH, ME 159

DEXTER HISTORICAL SOCIETY'S GRIST MILL
CAMPUS..DEXTER, ME   81

DIXVILLE NOTCH...................................NH 188

DOROTHY THOMPSON.......................BARNARD, VT 270

DR. HOLMES COTTAGE MUSEUM.............CALAIS, ME   74

DRISCO HOUSE............................PORTSMOUTH, NH 238

EAGLE HOTEL...................................CONCORD, NH 182

EDNA ST. VINCENT MILLAY......................CAMDEN, ME   75

EDWARD MacDOWELL.............PETERBOROUGH, NH 235

ELISHA MARSTON HOUSE......CENTER SANDWICH, NH 181

ELIZABETH PERKINS HOUSE.......................YORK, ME 160

EMERSON-WILCOX HOUSE.......................YORK, ME 160

ENFIELD SHAKER MUSEUM....................ENFIELD, NH 190

ENOCH LINCOLN MONUMENT............AUGUSTA, ME   42

ETHAN ALLEN................................BURLINGTON, VT 278

ETHAN ALLEN................................MONTPELIER, VT 296

ETHAN ALLEN MONUMENT.............BURLINGTON, VT 278

EUREKA SCHOOLHOUSE.................SPRINGFIELD, VT 309

FAIRBANKS MUSEUM AND
PLANETARIUM.........................ST. JOHNSBURY, VT 305

FARNSWORTH HOMESTEAD.............ROCKLAND, ME 143

THE FELLS HISTORIC ESTATE AND
GARDENS.....................................NEWBURY, NH 221

FISHER BRIDGE..................................WOLCOTT, VT 321

FISHERMEN'S MUSEUM..........PEMAQUID POINT, ME 125

FITZWILLIAM ....NH 191

FOLSOM TAVERN.................................EXETER, NH 190

FORT AT NO. 4 LIVING HISTORY
MUSEUM...........................CHARLESTOWN, NH 182

FORT CONSTITUTION...................NEW CASTLE, NH 222

FORT EDGECOMB SHS.....................EDGECOMB, ME   83

FORT FOSTER.....................................KITTERY, ME 107

FORT GEORGE.....................................CASTINE, ME   80

FORT KENT SHS...............................FORT KENT, ME   86

FORT KNOX SHS.............................PROSPECT, ME 141

FORT McCLARY SHS............................KITTERY, ME 108

FORT O'BRIEN...........................MACHIASPORT, ME 112

FRANKLIN D. ROOSEVELT MEMORIAL
BRIDGE..LUBEC, ME 110

FRANKLIN PIERCE HOMESTEAD NATIONAL HISTORIC
LANDMARK...........................HILLSBOROUGH, NH 201

THE FROST PLACE.......................FRANCONIA, NH 191

GATES HOUSE.........................MACHIASPORT, ME 112

GEN. JOHN STARK.......................MANCHESTER, NH 213

THE GENERAL HENRY KNOX
MUSEUM/MONTPELIER...............THOMASTON, ME 153

GEORGE B. DORR MUSEUM OF NATURAL
HISTORY..................................BAR HARBOR, ME   47

GEORGE DEWEY...........................MONTPELIER, VT 296

GOODWIN MANSION..................PORTSMOUTH, NH 238

GOVERNOR JOHN LANGDON
HOUSE....................................PORTSMOUTH, NH 236

GRANDMA MOSES SCHOOLHOUSE...BENNINGTON, VT 273

THE GREAT HARBOR MARITIME
MUSEUM...................NORTHEAST HARBOR, ME 115

HAMILTON HOUSE.................SOUTH BERWICK, ME 149

HAMLIN MEMORIAL LIBRARY AND
MUSEUM...............................SOUTH PARIS, ME 149

HARRINGTON HOUSE.....................FREEPORT, ME   87

HARTMANN MODEL RAILROAD.........INTERVALE, NH 201

HASKELL FREE LIBRARY AND OPERA
HOUSE.......................................DERBY LINE, VT 283

HEMMINGS SUNOCO FILLING STATION AND
EXHIBITS.................................BENNINGTON, VT 272
HENDRICKS HILL MUSEUM..............SOUTHPORT, ME 149
HENRY BRIDGE.............................BENNINGTON, VT 272
HENRY SHELDON MUSEUM OF VERMONT
HISTORY....................................MIDDLEBURY, VT 294
HOPE CEMETERY....................................BARRE, VT 271
HORATIO COLONY HOUSE MUSEUM.........KEENE, NH 205
HUBBARDTON BATTLEFIELD SHS........CASTLETON, VT 282
HUDSON MUSEUM.....................................ORONO, ME 124
HYDE LOG CABIN.......LAKE CHAMPLAIN ISLANDS, VT 288
ISLESFORD HISTORICAL MUSEUM.......ACADIA NP, ME 40
JEFFERDS' TAVERN.....................................YORK, ME 160
JOHN COTTON DANA RESEARCH
LIBRARY...................................WOODSTOCK, VT 322
JOHN HANCOCK WAREHOUSE..................YORK, ME 160
JOHN PERKINS HOUSE..........................CASTINE, ME 80
JOHN WINGATE WEEKS HISTORIC
SITE...LANCASTER, NH 207
JOSEPH SMITH BIRTHPLACE MEMORIAL...SHARON, VT 306
JOSHUA LAWRENCE CHAMBERLAIN
MUSEUM......................................BRUNSWICK, ME 71
JUSTIN SMITH MORRILL SHS..............STRAFFORD, VT 315
KEENE ....NH 204
THE KENNEBUNKPORT HISTORICAL
SOCIETY............................KENNEBUNKPORT, ME 97
KENNETH E. STODDARD SHELL
MUSEUM.....................................BOOTHBAY, ME 67
KINGFIELD HISTORICAL HOUSE...........KINGFIELD, ME 107
KINSMAN NOTCH..NH 205
KITTERY HISTORICAL AND NAVAL
MUSEUM..KITTERY, ME 108
LAKE CHAMPLAIN MARITIME
MUSEUM....................................VERGENNES, VT 316
LAWRENCE L. LEE SCOUTING MUSEUM AND MAX I.
SILBER LIBRARY.........................MANCHESTER, NH 214
L.C. BATES MUSEUM.........................HINCKLEY, ME 94
LEONARD'S MILLS AND MAINE FOREST LOGGING
MUSEUM..BRADLEY, ME 70
LIBBY MUSEUM...........................WOLFEBORO, NH 254
LIGHTHOUSE HILL..............MONHEGAN ISLAND, ME 113
LILLIAN NORDICA.........................FARMINGTON, ME 86
LINCOLN BRIDGE.........................WOODSTOCK, VT 321
LINCOLN COUNTY MUSEUM AND OLD
JAIL..WISCASSET, ME 158
LITTLETON GRIST MILL......................LITTLETON, NH 212
MAINE DISCOVERY MUSEUM...............BANGOR, ME 44
MAINE GOLF HALL OF FAME.......POLAND SPRING, ME 125
MAINE HISTORICAL SOCIETY BROWN
LIBRARY.......................................PORTLAND, ME 128
MAINE HISTORICAL SOCIETY
MUSEUM.......................................PORTLAND, ME 128
MAINE LIGHTHOUSE MUSEUM..........ROCKLAND, ME 143
MAINE NARROW GAUGE RAILROAD CO. AND
MUSEUM.......................................PORTLAND, ME 128
MAINE STATE HOUSE.........................AUGUSTA, ME 42
MAINE VIETNAM VETERANS
MEMORIAL.....................................AUGUSTA, ME 42
MANCHESTER HISTORIC ASSOCIATION MILLYARD
MUSEUM....................................MANCHESTER, NH 214
MAPLE GROVE FARMS SUGAR HOUSE
MUSEUM..................................ST. JOHNSBURY, VT 306
MARGARET CHASE SMITH
LIBRARY....................................SKOWHEGAN, ME 148
MARSHALL POINT LIGHTHOUSE........PORT CLYDE, ME 126

MARSHALL POINT LIGHTHOUSE
MUSEUM....................................PORT CLYDE, ME 126
MARSH-BILLINGS-ROCKEFELLER NHP....................VT 294
MARY BAKER EDDY HISTORIC HOUSE.....RUMNEY, NH 246
MATTHEWS MUSEUM OF MAINE
HERITAGE...UNION, ME 153
McAULIFFE-SHEPARD DISCOVERY
CENTER...CONCORD, NH 183
THE McLELLAN HOUSE.....................PORTLAND, ME 129
MEETING HOUSE..............................JAFFREY, NH 203
MEETING HOUSE GREEN....................HAMPTON, NH 195
MEMORIAL ARCH................................CONCORD, NH 183
MIDDLE BRIDGE.........................WOODSTOCK, VT 321
MILLER LIBRARY.............................WATERVILLE, ME 155
MOFFATT-LADD HOUSE...............PORTSMOUTH, NH 237
MOORE STATION...............................LITTLETON, NH 212
MOUNT INDEPENDENCE SHS.................ORWELL, VT 300
MT. KEARSARGE INDIAN MUSEUM........WARNER, NH 251
THE MUSEUM OF AFRICAN CULTURE...PORTLAND, ME 128
MUSEUMS OF OLD YORK.........................YORK, ME 160
MV CARILLON.................................SHOREHAM, VT 307
NARRAMISSIC ....SOUTH BRIDGTON, ME 149
NEAL DOW MEMORIAL....................PORTLAND, ME 128
NEW ENGLAND MAPLE MUSEUM.........PITTSFORD, VT 301
NEW ENGLAND SKI MUSEUM...........FRANCONIA, NH 191
NEW HAMPSHIRE BOAT
MUSEUM................WOLFEBORO FALLS, NH 254
NEW HAMPSHIRE HISTORICAL SOCIETY
MUSEUM...CONCORD, NH 183
NEW HAMPSHIRE TELEPHONE
MUSEUM..WARNER, NH 251
NICKELS-SORTWELL HOUSE...............WISCASSET, ME 158
NORDICA HOMESTEAD MUSEUM....FARMINGTON, ME 86
NORTHEAST HISTORIC FILM..............BUCKSPORT, ME 74
NORTHFIELD ....VT 299
THE NOTT HOUSE.................KENNEBUNKPORT, ME 97
NOYES HOUSE MUSEUM...............MORRISVILLE, VT 298
THE NYLANDER MUSEUM OF NATURAL
HISTORY...CARIBOU, ME 79
OLD BURYING GROUND.................BENNINGTON, VT 273
OLD CONSTITUTION HOUSE.................WINDSOR, VT 321
OLD FORT WESTERN.........................AUGUSTA, ME 42
OLD GAOL..YORK, ME 160
OLD SCHOOLHOUSE...................................YORK, ME 160
OLD STONE HOUSE MUSEUM.......BROWNINGTON, VT 278
OLD TOWN MUSEUM.....................OLD TOWN, ME 123
OLSON HOUSE....................................CUSHING, ME 81
OWLS HEAD LIGHT...........................ROCKLAND, ME 142
OWLS HEAD TRANSPORTATION
MUSEUM....................................OWLS HEAD, ME 124
PAINTER HALL....................................MIDDLEBURY, VT 294
PAPER MILL VILLAGE BRIDGE..........BENNINGTON, VT 272
PASSACONAWAY HISTORIC
SITE......WHITE MOUNTAINS AND WHITE MOUNTAIN
NF, NH 253
PATTEN LUMBERMEN'S MUSEUM...........PATTEN, ME 125
PAUL BUNYAN...................................BANGOR, ME 43
PEARY-MacMILLAN ARCTIC
MUSEUM......................................BRUNSWICK, ME 71
PEJEPSCOT MUSEUM/SKOLFIELD-WHITTIER
HOUSE.......................................BRUNSWICK, ME 71
PEMAQUID POINT
LIGHTHOUSE.......................PEMAQUID POINT, ME 125

PENOBSCOT NARROWS BRIDGE &
  OBSERVATORY...............................PROSPECT, ME 141
PETERBOROUGH HISTORICAL SOCIETY
  MUSEUM.......................PETERBOROUGH, NH 235
PETTENGILL FARM & GARDENS............FREEPORT, ME 87
PIERCE MANSE..................................CONCORD, NH 183
PITTSFORD ....VT 301
POINT OF GRAVES.......................PORTSMOUTH, NH 236
PORTLAND HEAD LIGHT............CAPE ELIZABETH, ME 78
PORTSMOUTH HARBOUR TRAIL....PORTSMOUTH, NH 236
PORTSMOUTH HISTORICAL SOCIETY MUSEUM AT THE
  JOHN PAUL JONES HOUSE...........PORTSMOUTH, NH 237
POWNALBOROUGH COURTHOUSE........DRESDEN, ME 81
PRESIDENT CHESTER A. ARTHUR SHS.....FAIRFIELD, VT 284
QUECHEE ....VT 302
REDINGTON MUSEUM....................WATERVILLE, ME 155
REMICK COUNTRY DOCTOR MUSEUM AND
  FARM..TAMWORTH, NH 250
REV. TIMOTHY WALKER HOUSE..........CONCORD, NH 182
RIDER-WOOD HOUSE...................PORTSMOUTH, NH 238
ROBERT BURNS MONUMENT...................BARRE, VT 271
ROBERT E. PEARY SME......................FREEPORT, ME 87
ROBERT FROST.............................BENNINGTON, VT 273
ROBERT FROST STONE HOUSE
  MUSEUM.....................................BENNINGTON, VT 272
ROBERT HULL FLEMING MUSEUM.....BURLINGTON, VT 279
ROCKLAND BREAKWATER
  LIGHTHOUSE.............................ROCKLAND, ME 142
THE ROCKS ESTATE........................BETHLEHEM, NH 179
ROKEBY MUSEUM........................FERRISBURGH, VT 284
RUGGLES HOUSE...................COLUMBIA FALLS, ME 81
RUNDLET-MAY HOUSE.................PORTSMOUTH, NH 237
SABBATHDAY LAKE SHAKER
  VILLAGE.............................NEW GLOUCESTER, ME 114
SACO MUSEUM......................................SACO, ME 145
ST. ALBANS HISTORICAL MUSEUM......ST. ALBANS, VT 305
ST. CROIX ISLAND INTERNATIONAL HISTORIC
  SITE..CALAIS, ME 74
ST. JAMES CHURCH CEMETERY..........ARLINGTON, VT 270
SAMUEL DE
  CHAMPLAIN.............LAKE CHAMPLAIN ISLANDS, VT 288
SANDWICH HISTORICAL SOCIETY
  MUSEUM..........................CENTER SANDWICH, NH 181
SARAH ORNE JEWETT HOUSE.....SOUTH BERWICK, ME 149
SAYWARD-WHEELER HOUSE........YORK HARBOR, ME 162
SCOTT COVERED BRIDGE................TOWNSHEND, VT 316
SEAL COVE AUTO MUSEUM..............SEAL COVE, ME 147
SEASHORE TROLLEY
  MUSEUM..........................KENNEBUNKPORT, ME 97
SHAPIRO HOUSE.........................PORTSMOUTH, NH 238
SHEAFE WAREHOUSE..................PORTSMOUTH, NH 237
SHERMAN ADAMS SUMMIT
  BUILDING...................MOUNT WASHINGTON, NH 220
SIEUR DE MONTS SPRING.................ACADIA NP, ME 40
SILK ROAD BRIDGE......................BENNINGTON, VT 272
SKOWHEGAN HISTORY HOUSE MUSEUM & RESEARCH
  CENTER...................................SKOWHEGAN, ME 148
SONGO LOCK....................................SEBAGO, ME 148
SPRINGFIELD ....VT 309
THE STANLEY MUSEUM....................KINGFIELD, ME 107
STANWOOD HOMESTEAD MUSEUM AND WILDLIFE
  SANCTUARY (BIRDSACRE)..............ELLSWORTH, ME 83
STATE HOUSE................................CONCORD, NH 183
STATE OFFICE BUILDING.................MONTPELIER, VT 296

STRAWBERY BANKE MUSEUM.......PORTSMOUTH, NH 238
STRONG MANSION MUSEUM.................ADDISON, VT 270
SULLIVAN MUSEUM AND HISTORY
  CENTER......................................NORTHFIELD, VT 299
SULPHITE BRIDGE..........................FRANKLIN, NH 193
SUPREME COURT BUILDING.............MONTPELIER, VT 296
TAFTSVILLE BRIDGE......................WOODSTOCK, VT 321
TANTE BLANCHE MUSEUM...........MADAWASKA, ME 112
TATE HOUSE MUSEUM.....................PORTLAND, ME 130
TAYLOR UP-AND-DOWN SAWMILL..........DERRY, NH 187
THOMAS A. HILL HOUSE.....................BANGOR, ME 43
TICONDEROGA ....SHELBURNE, VT 307
TIP TOP HOUSE.............MOUNT WASHINGTON, NH 220
THE T.S. STATE OF MAINE....................CASTINE, ME 80
TUCK LIBRARY.................................CONCORD, NH 182
TUCK MUSEUM................................HAMPTON, NH 195
TWO LIGHTS...........................CAPE ELIZABETH, ME 78
USS ALBACORE.........................PORTSMOUTH, NH 238
VERMONT COVERED BRIDGE
  MUSEUM....................................BENNINGTON, VT 273
VERMONT HISTORY MUSEUM..........MONTPELIER, VT 296
VERMONT MARBLE MUSEUM...............PROCTOR, VT 302
VERMONT SKI & SNOWBOARD MUSEUM. . .STOWE, VT 310
VERMONT STATE HOUSE................MONTPELIER, VT 296
VILLAGE BRIDGE.............................WAITSFIELD, VT 316
VINALHAVEN HISTORICAL SOCIETY
  MUSEUM........................VINALHAVEN ISLAND, ME 154
VINEGAR BIBLE.........................PORTSMOUTH, NH 238
WAITSFIELD.......................................VT 316
WALDOBORO HISTORICAL SOCIETY
  MUSEUM....................................WALDOBORO, ME 154
WALSH HOUSE............................PORTSMOUTH, NH 238
WARNER HOUSE.........................PORTSMOUTH, NH 237
WENDELL GILLEY
  MUSEUM......................SOUTHWEST HARBOR, ME 151
WENTWORTH-COOLIDGE MANSION
  SHS......................................PORTSMOUTH, NH 238
WENTWORTH-GARDNER HOUSE....PORTSMOUTH, NH 237
WEST QUODDY HEAD LIGHT....................LUBEC, ME 110
WHEELWRIGHT HOUSE................PORTSMOUTH, NH 238
WIGGLEY BRIDGE......................YORK HARBOR, ME 162
THE WILHELM REICH MUSEUM...........RANGELEY, ME 141
WILLIAM PITT TAVERN.................PORTSMOUTH, NH 238
WILSON MUSEUM..............................CASTINE, ME 80
WINDHAM COUNTY HISTORICAL SOCIETY
  MUSEUM.......................................NEWFANE, VT 299
WINDSOR ....VT 321
WOODLAWN MUSEUM/BLACK
  HOUSE......................................ELLSWORTH, ME 83
WOODMAN INSTITUTE MUSEUM.............DOVER, NH 188
WOODSTOCK ....VT 321
WOOLWICH HISTORICAL SOCIETY RURAL
  MUSEUM...BATH, ME 63
THE WRIGHT MUSEUM OF WORLD WAR II
  HISTORY.................................WOLFEBORO, NH 254
WYMAN TAVERN.................................KEENE, NH 204
YARMOUTH HISTORY CENTER..........YARMOUTH, ME 159
ZERAH COLBURN....................................CABOT, VT 281
ZIMMERMAN HOUSE....................MANCHESTER, NH 214

OUTDOORS & SCIENCE

☙ ACADIA NP...ME 38
☙ BILLINGS FARM & MUSEUM............WOODSTOCK, VT 322

☞ COASTAL MAINE BOTANICAL
   GARDENS....................................BOOTHBAY, ME 67
☞ THE FLUME GORGE..............FRANCONIA NOTCH, NH 192
☞ LOST RIVER GORGE & BOULDER
   CAVES................................KINSMAN NOTCH, NH 206
☞ ROOSEVELT CAMPOBELLO INTERNATIONAL
   PARK..LUBEC, ME 110
☞ SAINT-GAUDENS NHS.......................CORNISH, NH 187
A.E. HOWELL WILDLIFE CONSERVATION CENTER AND
   SPRUCE ACRES REFUGE................NORTH AMITY, ME 115
AGAMENTICUS MOUNTAIN......................YORK, ME 160
AMERICA'S STONEHENGE.............NORTH SALEM, NH 234
APPALACHIAN
   TRAIL...WHITE MOUNTAINS AND WHITE MOUNTAIN
                                              NF, NH 253
ARETHUSA FALLS.................CRAWFORD NOTCH, NH 187
ARMBRUST HILL................VINALHAVEN ISLAND, ME 154
AROOSTOOK SP...........................PRESQUE ISLE, ME 140
THE BASIN...........................FRANCONIA NOTCH, NH 192
BATTERY PARK...............................BURLINGTON, VT 279
BAXTER SP...PATTEN, ME 124
BELGRADE LAKES..........................WATERVILLE, ME 154
BURNT ISLAND..........WEST BOOTHBAY HARBOR, ME 157
CADILLAC MOUNTAIN......................ACADIA NP, ME 39
CALENDAR ISLANDS.......................PORTLAND, ME 126
CAMDEN HILLS SP.............................CAMDEN, ME 75
CAMEL'S HUMP...............HUNTINGTON CENTER, VT 285
CAMEL'S HUMP SP.............HUNTINGTON CENTER, VT 285
CAMPOBELLO ISLAND............................LUBEC, ME 110
CAPE ARUNDEL....................KENNEBUNKPORT, ME 97
CAPITOL PARK..................................AUGUSTA, ME 41
CHAMPLAIN CANAL................LAKE CHAMPLAIN, VT 287
CHARMINGFARE FARM.........................CANDIA, NH 181
CLEARWATER LAKE....................FARMINGTON, ME 86
CONSERVATION CENTER....................CONCORD, NH 183
CRAIG BROOK NATIONAL FISH
   HATCHERY...................................EAST ORLAND, ME 82
CRAWFORD NOTCH SP..........CRAWFORD NOTCH, NH 187
CRESCENT BEACH SP................CAPE ELIZABETH, ME 78
CRYSTAL LAKE SP................................BARTON, VT 271
DESERT OF MAINE.............................FREEPORT, ME 87
DIXVILLE NOTCH SP..................DIXVILLE NOTCH, NH 188
DODGE POINT PUBLIC RESERVED
   LAND...NEWCASTLE, ME 114
DWIGHT D. EISENHOWER NATIONAL FISH
   HATCHERY.......................NORTH CHITTENDEN, VT 299
EAGLE ISLAND SP...............................FREEPORT, ME 87
EAST POINT SANCTUARY.........BIDDEFORD POOL, ME 66
ECHO LAKE...........................FRANCONIA NOTCH, NH 192
ECHO LAKE SP........................NORTH CONWAY, NH 223
ELLSWORTH MARINE WATERFRONT
   PARK..ELLSWORTH, ME 83
ENDICOTT ROCK........................WEIRS BEACH, NH 251
ETHAN ALLEN PARK....................BURLINGTON, VT 279
FERRY BEACH SP..SACO, ME 145
FIELDS POND AUDUBON CENTER...........HOLDEN, ME 94
FORE RIVER SANCTUARY...................PORTLAND, ME 127
FOUNDERS PARK:.............................HAMPTON, NH 195
FOX ISLANDS...................VINALHAVEN ISLAND, ME 154
FOX SF.....................................HILLSBOROUGH, NH 201
FRANCONIA NOTCH SP.........FRANCONIA NOTCH, NH 192
THE FRIENDLY FARM............................DUBLIN, NH 189
FULLER GARDENS..................NORTH HAMPTON, NH 234

GILSLAND FARM AUDUBON
   CENTER..FALMOUTH, ME 85
GRAFTON NOTCH SP............................BETHEL, ME 65
GRANVILLE GULF RESERVATION.............WARREN, VT 317
GREAT GULF
   WILDERNESS...........WHITE MOUNTAINS AND WHITE
                                      MOUNTAIN NF, NH 253
GREAT HEAD................................ACADIA NP, ME 40
GREAT MEADOW LOOP TRAIL........BAR HARBOR, ME 46
GREAT POND...................................WATERVILLE, ME 154
GREEN MOUNTAIN AUDUBON
   CENTER......................................HUNTINGTON, VT 285
GREEN MOUNTAINS AND GREEN MOUNTAIN NF.....VT 284
HAMILTON SANCTUARY..................WEST BATH, ME 157
HORATIO COLONY NATURE PRESERVE.......KEENE, NH 205
HUBBARD PARK............................MONTPELIER, VT 296
HUNTER COVE WILDLIFE
   SANCTUARY....................................RANGELEY, ME 141
IRON FURNACE INTERPRETIVE
   CENTER......................................FRANCONIA, NH 191
ISLE LA MOTTE...........LAKE CHAMPLAIN ISLANDS, VT 288
JACKSON LABORATORY................BAR HARBOR, ME 46
JASPER BEACH...........................MACHIASPORT, ME 112
JAY PEAK SF..JAY, VT 286
JOSEPHINE NEWMAN
   SANCTUARY..................................GEORGETOWN, ME 92
LAKE AUBURN..................................AUBURN, ME 41
LAKE CHAMPLAIN..VT 287
LAKE GLORIETTE...................DIXVILLE NOTCH, NH 188
LAKE MEMPHREMAGOG....................NEWPORT, VT 299
LAKE PARAN...............................BENNINGTON, VT 272
LAKE SHAFTSBURY SP..................BENNINGTON, VT 272
LAKE SUNAPEE...................................SUNAPEE, NH 249
LAKE WINNIPESAUKEE.....................LACONIA, NH 206
LAKE WINNIPESAUKEE..................WEIRS BEACH, NH 251
LAMOINE SP.................................ELLSWORTH, ME 83
LANE'S ISLAND.............VINALHAVEN ISLAND, ME 154
LIGHTHOUSE PARK.................PEMAQUID POINT, ME 125
LONG LAKE.....................................VAN BUREN, ME 153
LONG TRAIL.....................HUNTINGTON CENTER, VT 285
THE LOON CENTER............MOULTONBOROUGH, NH 219
LOON MOUNTAIN RESORT...................LINCOLN, NH 208
LOST RIVER NATURE GARDEN....KINSMAN NOTCH, NH 206
LT. GORDON MANUEL WILDLIFE MANAGEMENT
   AREA...HODGDON, ME 94
MACHIAS SEAL ISLAND..........................LUBEC, ME 110
MAINE WILDLIFE PARK............................GRAY, ME 92
MAST LANDING SANCTUARY..............FREEPORT, ME 87
MAYNARD F. JORDAN PLANETARIUM AND
   OBSERVATORY...................................ORONO, ME 124
McLANE CENTER & SILK FARM
   SANCTUARY....................................CONCORD, NH 183
MEMORIAL GARDEN...................PORTSMOUTH, NH 238
MERRILL PARK.................................CONCORD, NH 183
MERRYSPRING NATURE CENTER............CAMDEN, ME 75
MILLER SP.............................PETERBOROUGH, NH 235
MISSISQUOI NWR..............................SWANTON, VT 316
MONADNOCK MOUNTAIN....................JAFFREY, NH 203
MONADNOCK SP.............................DUBLIN, NH 189
MONADNOCK SP.............................JAFFREY, NH 203
MONHEGAN ISLAND...ME 113
MOOSALAMOO
   NRA.....GREEN MOUNTAINS AND GREEN MOUNTAIN
                                              NF, VT 285

MOOSE ....ST. JOHNSBURY, VT 305
MOOSE POINT SP............................SEARSPORT, ME 148
MOOSEHEAD MARINE MUSEUM.......GREENVILLE, ME 93
MOOSEHORN NWR.............................BARING, ME 62
MOSS GLEN FALLS.............................WARREN, VT 317
MOUNT BATTIE..................................CAMDEN, ME 75
MOUNT DAVID...............................LEWISTON, ME 108
MOUNT DESERT ISLAND...................ACADIA NP, ME 38
MOUNT DESERT MOUNTAINS............ACADIA NP, ME 38
MOUNT DESERT OCEANARIUM BAR
  HARBOR...................................BAR HARBOR, ME 48
MOUNT EQUINOX.......................MANCHESTER, VT 290
MOUNT KEARSARGE.........................WARNER, NH 251
MOUNT KINEO.............................GREENVILLE, ME 92
MOUNT MANSFIELD..VT 298
MOUNT MANSFIELD........................STOWE, VT 310
MOUNT MANSFIELD SF..........MOUNT MANSFIELD, VT 298
MOUNT MONADNOCK.........................DUBLIN, NH 189
MOUNT SUNAPEE SP.........................NEWBURY, NH 221
MOUNT
  TOM...........MARSH-BILLINGS-ROCKEFELLER NHP, VT 294
MOUNT WALDO...............................BUCKSPORT, ME 74
MOUNT WASHINGTON..............................NH 219
MOUNT WASHINGTON OBSERVATORY WEATHER
  DISCOVERY CENTER...............NORTH CONWAY, NH 223
NATURE CENTER..............................ACADIA NP, ME 40
NEW HAMPSHIRE FARM MUSEUM..........MILTON, NH 219
NEWFOUND AUDUBON CENTER............HEBRON, NH 200
NORTHERN FOREST HERITAGE PARK &
  MUSEUM...BERLIN, NH 178
ODIORNE POINT........................PORTSMOUTH, NH 236
OLD SOW......................................EASTPORT, ME 82
OTTER CLIFFS................................ACADIA NP, ME 40
OUTLET BEACH.......................POLAND SPRING, ME 125
OWL'S HEAD....................................NEWPORT, VT 299
PASSUMPSIC ....ST. JOHNSBURY, VT 305
PICKITY PLACE....................................MASON, NH 217
PIERCE PARK....................................HOULTON, ME 94
POLAR CAVES PARK.......................PLYMOUTH, NH 235
PORTLAND OBSERVATORY................PORTLAND, ME 129
PRESCOTT FARM ENVIRONMENTAL EDUCATION
  CENTER..LACONIA, NH 206
PRESCOTT PARK........................PORTSMOUTH, NH 237
PROJECT PUFFIN VISITOR CENTER.......ROCKLAND, ME 143
QUECHEE GORGE..............................QUECHEE, VT 302
QUODDY HEAD SP................................LUBEC, ME 110
RACHEL CARSON NWR...........................WELLS, ME 156
RHODODENDRON SP.................FITZWILLIAM, NH 191
ROBERT FROST FARM..........................DERRY, NH 188
ROBERT FROST INTERPRETIVE
  TRAIL. . GREEN MOUNTAINS AND GREEN MOUNTAIN
                                            NF, VT 285
ROCKPORT MARINE PARK.................ROCKPORT, ME 144
ROLLINS SP...WARNER, NH 251
ROQUE BLUFFS SP..............................MACHIAS, ME 111
ROYAL RIVER PARK.........................YARMOUTH, ME 159
RUGGLES MINE..................................GRAFTON, NH 195
SAND BEACH.................................ACADIA NP, ME 40
SCARBOROUGH MARSH AUDUBON
  CENTER..................................SCARBOROUGH, ME 146
SEACOAST SCIENCE CENTER.......................RYE, NH 246
SEBAGO LAKE...................................SEBAGO, ME 148
SEBAGO LAKE SP...............................SEBAGO, ME 148
SEE SCIENCE CENTER....................MANCHESTER, NH 214

SEGUIN ISLAND.................................FREEPORT, ME 87
SHELBURNE FARMS.........................SHELBURNE, VT 306
SILVER AND FLUME
  CASCADES.........................CRAWFORD NOTCH, NH 187
SLEEPER'S ....ST. JOHNSBURY, VT 305
SMUGGLERS NOTCH SP..........................STOWE, VT 309
SNOW FALLS GORGE.......................WEST PARIS, ME 158
SOUTHWORTH PLANETARIUM............PORTLAND, ME 130
STOWE RECREATION PATH.....................STOWE, VT 310
SUGARBUSH FARM.......................WOODSTOCK, VT 322
THE SUGARMILL FARM.........................BARTON, VT 271
TARBIN GARDENS.............................FRANKLIN, NH 193
THORNCRAG NATURE SANCTUARY......LEWISTON, ME 109
THUNDER HOLE...............................ACADIA NP, ME 40
THUYA GARDEN...............NORTHEAST HARBOR, ME 115
TWO LIGHTS SP.......................CAPE ELIZABETH, ME 78
UNIVERSITY OF MAINE.................PRESQUE ISLE, ME 140
URBAN FORESTRY CENTER............PORTSMOUTH, NH 238
VAUGHAN WOODS SP..............SOUTH BERWICK, ME 149
VERMONT INSTITUTE OF NATURAL
  SCIENCE......................................QUECHEE, VT 302
VERMONT WILDFLOWER FARM.........CHARLOTTE, VT 282
VINALHAVEN ISLAND..ME 154
WASHBURN-NORLANDS LIVING HISTORY
  CENTER.....................................LIVERMORE, ME 110
WELLS NATIONAL ESTUARINE RESEARCH RESERVE /
  WELLS RESERVE AT LAUDHOLM..............WELLS, ME 156
WHITE MOUNTAINS AND WHITE MOUNTAIN NF....NH 253
WHITE PARK.....................................CONCORD, NH 183
WHITE RIVER NATIONAL FISH
  HATCHERY.......................................BETHEL, VT 276
WHITE ROCKS
  NRA.....GREEN MOUNTAINS AND GREEN MOUNTAIN
                                            NF, VT 285
WOLFE'S NECK WOODS SP.................FREEPORT, ME 86
WOODFORD SP............................BENNINGTON, VT 272

SHOPPING

AROOSTOOK CENTRE MALL...........PRESQUE ISLE, ME 140
BATTENKILL & HIGHRIDGE OUTLET
  CENTERS....................................MANCHESTER, VT 289
BENNINGTON POTTERS YARD..........BENNINGTON, VT 272
BURLINGTON TOWN CENTER...........BURLINGTON, VT 279
CENTER AT KEENE......................................KEENE, NH 205
CHURCH STREET MARKETPLACE.......BURLINGTON, VT 279
COLONY MILL MARKETPLACE.....................KEENE, NH 204
DOCK SQUARE.....................KENNEBUNKPORT, ME 96
DUTY FREE AMERICAS............................CALAIS, ME 74
KITTERY OUTLETS..................................KITTERY, ME 107
L.L. BEAN..FREEPORT, ME 86
L.L. BEAN SHOPPING CENTER.....NORTH CONWAY, NH 223
MAIN STREET..................................ROCKLAND, ME 142
THE MALL OF NEW HAMPSHIRE......MANCHESTER, NH 213
MANCHESTER DESIGNER OUTLETS. . .MANCHESTER, VT 289
MANCHESTER MARKETPLACE.........MANCHESTER, VT 289
THE MILL...QUECHEE, VT 302
OLD HARBOR............................PORTSMOUTH, NH 236
OLD PORT EXCHANGE.....................PORTLAND, ME 126
PORTLAND FARMERS' MARKET..........PORTLAND, ME 126
QUECHEE GORGE VILLAGE..................QUECHEE, VT 302
RED BARN FACTORY STORES.....NORTH CONWAY, NH 223
SETTLER'S GREEN.................NORTH CONWAY, NH 223
STOWE FARMERS' MARKET...................STOWE, VT 309
TANGER OUTLET CENTER....................KITTERY, ME 108

TANGER OUTLET CENTER...................LACONIA, NH 206
UNIVERSITY MALL.........................BURLINGTON, VT 279
WHITE MOUNTAIN OUTLETS.....NORTH CONWAY, NH 223

SPORTS & RECREATION
APPALACHIAN/LONG
  TRAIL...GREEN MOUNTAINS AND GREEN MOUNTAIN
                                        NF, VT 285
ARBORTREK CANOPY
  ADVENTURES..........................JEFFERSONVILLE, VT 286
ATTITASH ALPINE SLIDE...................BARTLETT, NH 177
ATTITASH MOUNTAIN RESORT...........BARTLETT, NH 177
BARTLETT ....NH 177
BEECH RIDGE MOTOR
  SPEEDWAY...................OLD ORCHARD BEACH, ME 122
BLACK MOUNTAIN...........................JACKSON, NH 202
BOLTON VALLEY RESORT...........BOLTON VALLEY, VT 276
BRETTON WOODS.................BRETTON WOODS, NH 180
BROMLEY MOUNTAIN RESORT.............PERU, VT 301
BURKE MOUNTAIN SKI AREA...........EAST BURKE, VT 283
BURLINGTON BIKEPATH.................BURLINGTON, VT 278
CADILLAC MOUNTAIN SOUTH RIDGE
  TRAIL...ACADIA NP, ME 40
CAMDEN SNOW BOWL.......................CAMDEN, ME 75
CANNON MOUNTAIN..........FRANCONIA NOTCH, NH 192
COCHRAN'S SKI AREA....................RICHMOND, VT 303
CONTOOCOOK RIVER CANOE CO.........CONCORD, NH 183
GLEN ....NH 194
GREAT GLEN TRAILS........................GORHAM, NH 194
GREAT HEAD TRAIL.........................ACADIA NP, ME 40
GREAT POND MOUNTAIN
  WILDLANDS..............................EAST ORLAND, ME 82
GUNSTOCK MOUNTAIN RESORT...........GILFORD, NH 193
HOLLYWOOD CASINO HOTEL &
  RACEWAY...BANGOR, ME 43
HOLLYWOOD CASINO HOTEL &
  RACEWAY...BANGOR, ME 44
JACKSON SKI TOURING FOUNDATION....JACKSON, NH 202
JAY PEAK RESORT.....................................JAY, VT 286
JEFFERSON ....NH 204
KILLINGTON RESORT.....................KILLINGTON, VT 286
LEVERONE FIELD HOUSE....................HANOVER, NH 198
LINCOLN ....NH 208
LONG TRAIL.............MOUNT MANSFIELD, VT 298
LOST VALLEY SKI AREA.....................AUBURN, ME 41
MAD RIVER GLEN.......................WAITSFIELD, VT 316
MAGIC MOUNTAIN SKI AREA.......LONDONDERRY, VT 288
MOUNT SNOW...................................VT 298
MOUNT SNOW RESORT...............MOUNT SNOW, VT 298
MOUNT SUNAPEE...........................NEWBURY, NH 221
MT. ABRAM SKI RESORT...............GREENWOOD, ME 93
OKEMO MOUNTAIN RESORT................LUDLOW, VT 289
RINDGE ....NH 245
SADDLEBACK MAINE.......................RANGELEY, ME 142
SCARBOROUGH DOWNS....OLD ORCHARD BEACH, ME 122
SILVER RANCH & SILVER RANCH
  AIRPARK..JAFFREY, NH 203
SKI MUSEUM OF MAINE...................KINGFIELD, ME 107
SMUGGLERS' NOTCH.................JEFFERSONVILLE, VT 286
STOWE ....VT 309
STOWE ALPINE SLIDE.........................STOWE, VT 310
STOWE MOUNTAIN RESORT...................STOWE, VT 310
STRATTON MOUNTAIN
  RESORT.......................STRATTON MOUNTAIN, VT 315

SUGARBUSH RESORT..........................WARREN, VT 317
SUGARLOAF/USA SKI AND GOLF
  RESORT.......................CARRABASSETT VALLEY, ME 79
SUNAPEE ....NH 249
SUNDAY RIVER SKI RESORT...................NEWRY, ME 115
THOMPSON ARENA..........................HANOVER, NH 198
TUCKERMAN
  RAVINE.............PINKHAM NOTCH SCENIC AREA, NH 235
UVM MORGAN HORSE FARM..........MIDDLEBURY, VT 295
VIKING NORDIC CENTER.............LONDONDERRY, VT 288
WEIRS BEACH......................................NH 251
WILD WINGS SKI TOURING CENTER.............PERU, VT 301
WILDCAT MOUNTAIN........................JACKSON, NH 202

TOURS & SIGHTSEEING
⇔ CANNON MOUNTAIN AERIAL
  TRAMWAY.......................FRANCONIA NOTCH, NH 192
⇔ MOUNT WASHINGTON COG
  RAILWAY.............................BRETTON WOODS, NH 179
ACADIA NP TOURS......................BAR HARBOR, ME 47
ANHEUSER-BUSCH INC....................MERRIMACK, NH 218
AQUATERRA ADVENTURES............BAR HARBOR, ME 48
THE ATLANTIC BREWING
  COMPANY.................................BAR HARBOR, ME 47
ATLANTIC SEAL CRUISES....................FREEPORT, ME 87
AUBURN ....ME 41
AUGUSTA ....ME 41
BALMY DAYS II.................BOOTHBAY HARBOR, ME 67
BANGOR ....ME 43
BAR HARBOR.....................................ME 46
BAR HARBOR WHALE WATCH CO....BAR HARBOR, ME 47
BARE KNEE POINT KAYAK.......................SACO, ME 145
BARRE ....VT 271
BARTON ....VT 271
BATH ....ME 62
BELFAST ....ME 63
BELLOWS FALLS.....................................VT 272
BEN & JERRY'S ICE CREAM FACTORY
  TOURS....................................WATERBURY, VT 318
BENNINGTON ....VT 272
BETHEL ....ME 65
BIDDEFORD ....ME 66
BOOTHBAY HARBOR................................ME 67
BRAGG FARM SUGARHOUSE.....EAST MONTPELIER, VT 283
BRATTLEBORO ....VT 277
BRUNSWICK ....ME 71
BURLINGTON ....VT 278
CABOT CREAMERY..............................CABOT, VT 281
CALAIS ....ME 74
CAMDEN ....ME 75
CAPE ELIZABETH...................................ME 78
CAP'N FISH'S WHALE WATCH AND SCENIC NATURE
  CRUISES....................BOOTHBAY HARBOR, ME 67
CARIBOU ....ME 79
CARRIAGES OF ACADIA....................ACADIA NP, ME 40
CASCO BAY LINES..........................PORTLAND, ME 126
CHARLESTOWN ....NH 181
COASTAL KAYAKING TOURS..........BAR HARBOR, ME 48
CONCORD ....NH 182
CONNECTICUT RIVER BYWAY............LANCASTER, NH 207
CONNECTICUT RIVER BYWAY
  (US 5)...............................BELLOWS FALLS, VT 272
CONWAY SCENIC RAILROAD.....NORTH CONWAY, NH 223
DAMARISCOTTA ....ME 81

DERRY ....NH 187
DOVER ....NH 188
DOWNEAST DUCK ADVENTURES........PORTLAND, ME 126
DOWNEAST SCENIC RAILROAD.........ELLSWORTH, ME 83
EASTPORT ....ME 82
ELLSWORTH ....ME 83
EXETER ....NH 190
FALMOUTH ....ME 85
FARM BY THE RIVER BED AND BREAKFAST WITH
STABLES..............................NORTH CONWAY, NH 223
FARMINGTON ....ME 86
FINESTKIND SCENIC CRUISES..............OGUNQUIT, ME 116
FORT KENT ....ME 86
FRANKLIN ....NH 193
FREEPORT ....ME 86
GOODRICH'S MAPLE FARM.....................CABOT, VT 281
GRANITE STATE WHALE WATCH..................RYE, NH 246
GREENVILLE ....ME 92
HALLOWELL ....ME 94
HAMPTON ....NH 195
HANOVER ....NH 198
HARDY BOAT CRUISES.................NEW HARBOR, ME 114
THE HILL..............................PORTSMOUTH, NH 236
HILLSBOROUGH ....NH 200
HISTORIC SR 7A...............................ARLINGTON, VT 270
HOBO RAILROAD..............................LINCOLN, NH 208
HOULTON ....ME 94
HULLS COVE VISITOR CENTER............ACADIA NP, ME 40
I-89 ....BURLINGTON, VT 279
ISLAND EXPLORER........................BAR HARBOR, ME 46
ISLES OF SHOALS STEAMSHIP CO...PORTSMOUTH, NH 236
JACKSON ....NH 202
JAFFREY ....NH 203
JAY ....VT 285
KANCAMAGUS
HIGHWAY.............WHITE MOUNTAINS AND WHITE
MOUNTAIN NF, NH 253
KATAHDIN ....GREENVILLE, ME 92
KENNEBUNK ....ME 95
KENNEBUNKPORT HISTORICAL
SOCIETY...........................KENNEBUNKPORT, ME 97
KILLINGTON ....VT 286
LACONIA ....NH 206
LAKE CHAMPLAIN FERRIES.......LAKE CHAMPLAIN, VT 287
LAKE CHAMPLAIN ISLANDS.........................VT 288
LAKE SUNAPEE CRUISES.....................SUNAPEE, NH 249
LANCASTER ....NH 207
LEWISTON ....ME 108
LITTLETON ....NH 212
LUBEC ....ME 110
LUCKY CATCH CRUISES...................PORTLAND, ME 128
LUDLOW ....VT 288
MACHIAS ....ME 111
MADAWASKA ....ME 112
MAINE STATE FERRY
SERVICE..................VINALHAVEN ISLAND, ME 154
MAINE STATE SEA
KAYAK..........................SOUTHWEST HARBOR, ME 151
MANCHESTER ....NH 213
MANCHESTER ....VT 289
MARGARET TODD WINDJAMMER
CRUISES.............................BAR HARBOR, ME 48
MARGINAL WAY............................OGUNQUIT, ME 116
MIDDLEBURY ....VT 294

MONHEGAN ISLAND AND NEW
HARBOR...........................MONHEGAN ISLAND, ME 113
MONHEGAN ISLAND AND PORT
CLYDE............................MONHEGAN ISLAND, ME 113
MORRISVILLE ....VT 298
MORSE FARM MAPLE
SUGARWORKS.......................MONTPELIER, VT 296
MOUNT EQUINOX SKYLINE DRIVE....MANCHESTER, VT 290
MOUNT WASHINGTON AUTO
ROAD.......................MOUNT WASHINGTON, NH 219
MOUNT WASHINGTON CRUISES......WEIRS BEACH, NH 251
NAPLES ....ME 113
NATIONAL PARK SEA KAYAK
TOURS...............................BAR HARBOR, ME 48
NEW ENGLAND OUTDOOR
CENTER...............................MILLINOCKET, ME 112
NEWPORT ....VT 299
NORTH CONWAY...NH 223
NORTHERN LIGHTS CRUISES............BURLINGTON, VT 279
NORTHERN OUTDOORS...................THE FORKS, ME 152
ODYSSEY WHALE WATCH.................PORTLAND, ME 128
OLD ORCHARD BEACH.....................................ME 122
OLD TOWN CANOE CO...................OLD TOWN, ME 123
PARK LOOP ROAD..........................ACADIA NP, ME 40
PETERBOROUGH ....NH 235
PORT CLYDE..ME 125
PORTLAND ....ME 126
PORTLAND DISCOVERY LAND & SEA
TOURS.................................PORTLAND, ME 128
PORTLAND FREEDOM TRAIL.............PORTLAND, ME 126
PORTLAND SCHOONER CO...............PORTLAND, ME 130
PORTSMOUTH ....NH 236
PORTSMOUTH HARBOR CRUISES....PORTSMOUTH, NH 236
PRESQUE ISLE...ME 140
RICHMOND ....ME 142
ROCK OF AGES VISITORS CENTER....GRANITEVILLE, VT 284
ROCKLAND ....ME 142
ROCKPORT ....ME 144
RUTLAND ....VT 304
SACO ....ME 145
ST. ALBANS..VT 305
ST. JOHNSBURY...VT 305
SCHOODIC POINT.........................ACADIA NP, ME 40
THE SILVERLINING.........................OGUNQUIT, ME 116
SKOWHEGAN ....ME 148
SONGO RIVER QUEEN II..........................NAPLES, ME 113
SOUTHWEST HARBOR.....................................ME 151
SPIRIT OF ETHAN ALLEN III.............BURLINGTON, VT 279
SR 7...BURLINGTON, VT 279
SR 9...BENNINGTON, VT 272
SR 9...BRATTLEBORO, VT 277
SR 11...FORT KENT, ME 86
SR 16.................PINKHAM NOTCH SCENIC AREA, NH 235
SR 30..CASTLETON, VT 281
STATE HOUSE PLAZA.......................CONCORD, NH 183
STOWE AUTO TOLL ROAD....................STOWE, VT 310
TAPE TOURS...................................ACADIA NP, ME 39
THOMASTON ....ME 153
TICONDEROGA FERRY....................SHOREHAM, VT 307
TOURS OF LUBEC AND COBSCOOK...........LUBEC, ME 110
TWIN RIVERS PAPERS..................MADAWASKA, ME 112
UNION ....ME 153
US 1...CALAIS, ME 74
US 1...CAMDEN, ME 75

US 1..SEARSPORT, ME 148
US 4..WOODSTOCK, VT 321
US 7A...BENNINGTON, VT 272
U.S. RAFTING................................WEST FORKS, ME 157
VAN BUREN...ME 153
VERMONT TEDDY BEAR CO................SHELBURNE, VT 307
WALDOBORO ....ME 154
WATERBURY ....VT 318
WATERVILLE ....ME 154
WELLS ....ME 155
WEST PARIS...ME 157

WHITE MOUNTAIN CENTRAL
 RAILROAD...LINCOLN, NH 208
WHITE MOUNTAINS VISITOR
 CENTER..WHITE MOUNTAINS AND WHITE MOUNTAIN
                                                            NF, NH 253
WHITE RIVER FLYER.........WHITE RIVER JUNCTION, VT 320
WICKED WALKING TOURS.................PORTLAND, ME 130
WILDERNESS EXPEDITIONS................THE FORKS, ME 152
WINNIPESAUKEE SCENIC RAILROAD.....MEREDITH, NH 217
WOLFEBORO ....NH 253
YARMOUTH ....ME 159
YORK ....ME 159

Photo Credits

Page numbers are in bold type. Picture credit abbreviations are as follows:
- (i) numeric sequence from top to bottom, left to right ▪ (AAA) AAA Travel library.

- (Cover) Rockport, ME / © Jaynes Gallery / DanitaDelimont.com

- **2** (i) Courtesy of Maine Maritime Museum

- **2** (ii) Courtesy of The Currier Museum of Art

- **2** (iii) © AAA. Photo by AAA travel editor Suzanne Lemon for AAA

- **7** © Monashee Frantz / age fotostock

- **13** © Adivin / iStockphoto

- **18** (i) © SIME / eStock Photo

- **18** (ii) © Jerry Ginsberg / DanitaDelimont.com

- **19** © Jeff Greenberg / age fotostock

- **20** (i) © Plus One Pix / Alamy

- **20** (ii) Courtesy of Wikimedia Commons

- **23** (i) © Barbara Freeman / Coastal Maine Botanical Gardens

- **23** (ii) © dbimages / Alamy

- **23** (iii) © Blaine Harrington III / Alamy

- **23** (iv) © Mira / Alamy

- **23** (v) © Mira / Alamy

- **24** (i) Courtesy of Maine Maritime Museum

- **24** (ii) Courtesy of Portland Museum of Art

- **24** (iii) © Jeff Greenberg / Alamy

- **24** (iv) Courtesy of Ogunquit Museum of American Art

- **164** (i) © Paul Rocheleau / age fotostock

- **164** (ii) © Dan Bannister / awl-images

- **165** © Erin Paul Donovan / Alamy

- **166** (i) Courtesy of Wikimedia Commons

- **166** (ii) Courtesy of Wikimedia Commons

- **169** (i) Courtesy of The Currier Museum of Art

- **169** (ii) © Backyard Capture / Alamy

- **169** (iii) © Richard Cummins / SuperStock

- **169** (iv) © Henryk Kaiser / eStock Photo

- **169** (v) © Erin Paul Donovan / Alamy

- **170** (i) © Brad Mitchell / Alamy

- **170** (ii) © America / Alamy

- **170** (iii) © david a eastley / Alamy

- **170** (iv) © Washington Imaging / Alamy

- **256** (i) © SIME / eStock Photo

- **256** (ii) © Raymond Forbes / age fotostock

- **257** © Eric Carr / Alamy

- **258** (i) Courtesy of Wikimedia Commons

- **258** (ii) Courtesy of Wikimedia Commons

- **261** (i) © Don Landwehrle / SuperStock

344

AAA Travel Information

AAA delivers reliable travel
information just the way you want it.

In Print
Get printed TourBook® guides at
AAA and CAA offices.

Online
Access robust travel information and
planning tools like TripTik® Travel Planner
at AAA.com and CAA.ca.

On The Go
Download eTourBook® guides for ereaders
and smartphones at AAA.com/ebooks and
get the multi-featured AAA or CAA app
from the iTunes Store or Google Play.

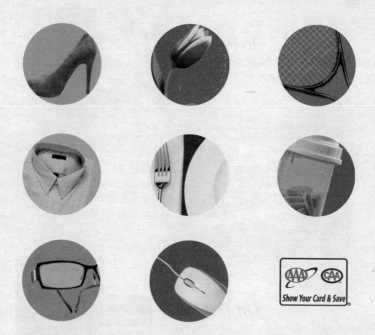

Vacation with Peace of Mind

Experience an incredible vacation with amazing value on select *AAA Vacations*® tour and cruise departures. Includes our **Best Price Guarantee** and **24/7 Member Care** for a worry-free vacation.

Contact your local AAA Travel Professional or visit **AAA.com/Travel** for full details on these exclusive *AAA Vacations*® benefits.

Terms and conditions apply